Investment Management

Investment Management

Edited by
Perry Stinson

Willford Press
www.willfordpress.com

Published by Willford Press,
118-35 Queens Blvd., Suite 400,
Forest Hills, NY 11375, USA

ISBN: 978-1-68285-351-1

Cataloging-in-Publication Data

Investment management / edited by Perry Stinson.
p. cm.
Includes bibliographical references and index.
ISBN 978-1-68285-351-1
1. Investments. 2. Portfolio management. 3. Investment analysis. 4. Stock exchanges. I. Stinson, Perry.
HG4515 .I58 2017
332.6--dc23

For information on all Willford Press publications
visit our website at www.willfordpress.com

Willford Press

Printed in China.

Contents

Preface

Investment management deals with the management of assets of a firm or business in the form of shares, bonds and real estate. This book on investment management discusses tangible and intangible assets and the systems that are employed for their monitoring and maintenance. This book is compiled in such a manner, that it will provide in-depth knowledge about the theory and practice of investment management. It aims to present this complex subject in the most comprehensible and easy to understand language. This book includes contributions of experts and scientists which will provide innovative insights into this field. From theories to research to practical applications, case studies related to all contemporary topics of relevance to this field have been included in this book. It will prove immensely beneficial to students and researchers in this field.

This book is a comprehensive compilation of works of different researchers from varied parts of the world. It includes valuable experiences of the researchers with the sole objective of providing the readers (learners) with a proper knowledge of the concerned field. This book will be beneficial in evoking inspiration and enhancing the knowledge of the interested readers.

In the end, I would like to extend my heartiest thanks to the authors who worked with great determination on their chapters. I also appreciate the publisher's support in the course of the book. I would also like to deeply acknowledge my family who stood by me as a source of inspiration during the project.

Editor

New Procedure for Assigning Drivers to Work Schedules at a Container Terminal

Khaled Mili[1], Ilhem Elghoul[2]

[1]Department of Economics and Quantitative Methods and Computer, Institute of Companies Administration of Gafsa, Gafsa, Tunisia
[2]Department of Computer Science, Mediterranean Institute of Nabeul, Nabeul, Tunisia

Email address:
Khaled.mili.1@ualaval.ca (K. Mili), ilhem.el.ghoul@gmail.com (I. Elghoul)

Abstract: One of the success factors of a terminal is related to the time in port for the retrieval and transport of containers. Straddle carriers (SCs) are the pivotal axis around which the terminal transportation system evolves and the success or failure of that process is an indicator of the reliability of the container terminal. Over the last years, the deficiency of efficient control and coordination mechanisms in practice produced a relaxation of transportation principles. The valorization of the academic environment represents nowadays one of the most important research challenges. In this paper, we present a collaborative filtering recommender system able to manage the work schedule's assignment to straddle carrier's drivers in a container terminal and provide preliminary results on customer's satisfaction.

Keywords: Recommendation System, Collaborative Filtering, Straddle Carrier's Assignment

1. Introduction

The RADES container terminal in Tunisia, which is the leading Tunisian port for the movement of containers (Africa infrastructure Country Diagnostic 2009) well equipped with necessary modern facilities and academic experience, has opted to provide a Straddle carrier's assignment recommendation system in order to reduce the malpractices that threaten the integrity of the transportation process and enter a new era in which growing number of e-transparency systems will be employed.

The goal of this work is to explore all aspects of the transportation problem and employ an intelligent system that can be more accurate and provide better recommendations to the straddle carrier's drivers. A work schedule for a straddle carrier driver is provided in the form of a sequence of container groups and a number of containers. The adopted strategy is based on a collaborative filtering mechanism by analyzing user's behaviors.

The remainder of this paper is arranged as follows: Section 2 gives the necessary background on collaborative filtering recommendation systems. Section 3 introduces the transportation management problem and the optimization model to solve it. In section 4, we give the details of the proposed implementation. Concluding remarks and future works are given in Section 5.

2. Background

Recommendation systems help users find and select items of interest based on their explicit and implicit preferences, the needs of other users and the item attributes (S. S. Anand , B. Mobasher, 2005).Three parallel categories have emerged in the context of recommender systems: Collaborative filtering, content-based filtering and hybrid methods (J. Herlocker et all, 2004). Collaborative filtering is usually addressed under the assumption that if users rate items similarly or have similar tastes, they will rate other items similarly (M. Khaled, 2013; D. Jannach et all, 2011). Content-based filtering makes recommendations based solely on a user's profile built up by analyzing the content of items that the user has previously evaluated and/or user's profile and preferences (G. Adomavicius, A. Tuzhilin, 2005). Hybrid approaches combine aspects of both content-based and collaborative filtering (N. Belkin , W. Croft, 1992).

From those categories, collaborative filtering is still considered as the most promising and efficient technologies in practice (Y. Blanco-Fernandez et all, 2011; G. Karypis, 2001)Collaborative filtering solutions usually employ user-item rating matrix to make predictions and recommendations, avoiding by this way the need of providing extensive information about users and items. The prediction function estimates the preference of a user for an item that he/she has not experienced before. So depending on its value, we can then compute the approximate "top-k" recommendation lists.

A basic collaborative filtering scheme can be divided into three main parts:

2.1. Neighborhood Formation

When adopting collaborative filtering strategy, the crucial task is to identify users that are similar or neighbors of an active user. The neighbors refer to a set of like-minded users who share similar interests for items and its formation needs to employ the appropriate similarity metric. Pearson's correlation coefficient is one of the most frequently used measures in recommender systems to estimate the similarity between users (G. Karypis, 2001). Generally, the Pearson's correlation coefficient reflects the linear dependence between two variables and provides a value between -1 (i.e. low similarity) and 1 (i.e. high similarity) inclusive. The Pearson coefficient also considers user's individual rating behavior by incorporating the user's average rating. Moreover, there are other correlation coefficients such as cosine similarity and adjusted cosine similarity (G. Adomavicius, A. Tuzhilin, 2005; D. Jannach, 2011; G. Karypis, 2001). The pure cosine similarity measure computes the similarity between two rating vectors $\vec{u}$ and $\vec{v}$ and returns values between 0 (i.e. orthogonal vectors) and 1 (i.e. parallel vectors), where elevated values mean a high similarity. Unlike the Pearson coefficient, the pure cosine similarity does not take the average rating behavior of the users into account. One solution to overcome this weak point is to use the adjusted cosine similarity metric which factors out the user's average rating behavior and converts the similarity to a value between -1 and 1 inclusive, similar to the Pearson coefficient.

2.2. Neighborhood Selection

Now we come to the question of how to choose the neighborhood size k without compromising the prediction quality of our collaborative filtering algorithm (M. Khaled, 2013). If k is set up too large, we risk amplifying noise in the data since not all considered neighbors are relevant predictors. Additionally, we may see an increase in the time required for generating recommendations. On the contrary, a too small k can affect the prediction quality. A detailed discussion of the relative value of this tradeoff can be found in (S. S. Anand, B. Mobasher, 2005; M. Khaled, 2013)

2.3. Aggregation of Ratings

Lastly, the nearest neighbors' ratings for the target item are aggregated to form the final rating prediction value. The standard prediction formula has been proposed by (P.N. Tan, 2006).

3. System Overview

In today's world, significant organizational reforms occur in the field of advanced maritime transportation like in most other fields. The idea that has inspired our research turns out to be completely different from the ones reported in the literature.

3.1. Context and Problem Description

Despite all scientific and technological advances in the transportation system, many container terminals continue to suffer from practical mismanagements. And the transportation process is not necessarily resistant from this phenomenon which has multiple negative impacts on terminal performance.

Usually, disappointment with the organizational process is commonly expressed by straddles carriers' drivers, who often complain of favoritism being shown in assigning work schedules. This is essentially due to the very high demand for work schedule with small number of containers and small number of reshuffling movements in order to avoid investing too much physical effort and be less exposed to conflicts with customers.

The customers equally complain about the drivers who tend to come late to be assigned as reinforcement and avoid recording availability and checking customer identification when starting the work. Such practices may indeed cause severe disturbances during transportation process since there are no preventive measures in place to penalize "bad" drivers and reward "effective" ones. In such context, recommender systems have proved to be the best option to automatically identify appropriate work schedule assignments from a large number of alternatives, on the basis of some specified constraints and preferences.

In collaboration with the RADES container terminal, we identified 7 priority areas to focus when designing our recommender system:

- Transparency: Further increase transparency when assigning work schedules to drivers and guaranty the highest level of confidence among the transportation process.
- Punctuality: drivers are expected to arrive punctually for the shifts indicated in their allocation advice; this requires attendance 20 minutes prior to the transport start time.
- Performance monitoring: Provide an interactive system to judge driver's performance during transportation plans. Drivers must be aware that the rules governing conduct in transportation are to be strictly applied.
- Training: Provide guidance and direction of trainee drivers.
- Quick access: Minimize the length of the queue in the transport office.
- Less conflicts: Prevention and resolution of conflicts that can arise between drivers and customers (resp. staff).
- More comfort: Improve the comfort and the welfare of customers by providing the best possible conditions to undertake their containers (this includes ensuring that no disruption or distraction to customers comes from

drivers themselves).

3.2. Proposed Approach

The recommender system we present in this paper is capable of intelligently assigning drivers to work schedules. A novel transportation management strategy will be discussed along with how the system is designed to support this. The general overview of the work schedule's recommendation system is given in Figure 1. As input, our system uses an e-exam database to load the driver's profiles (driver's ratings/scores, previously recorded conflicts) and all necessary details relative to work schedules and customers.

Given the drivers' previous ratings to some of their colleagues, similar drivers to the active driver are identified, and then, depending on the driver in charge, work schedules are recommended. This scenario will only happen if the total score associated to the active driver is greater than 10/20. Otherwise, he/she will be partnered with more experienced colleagues.

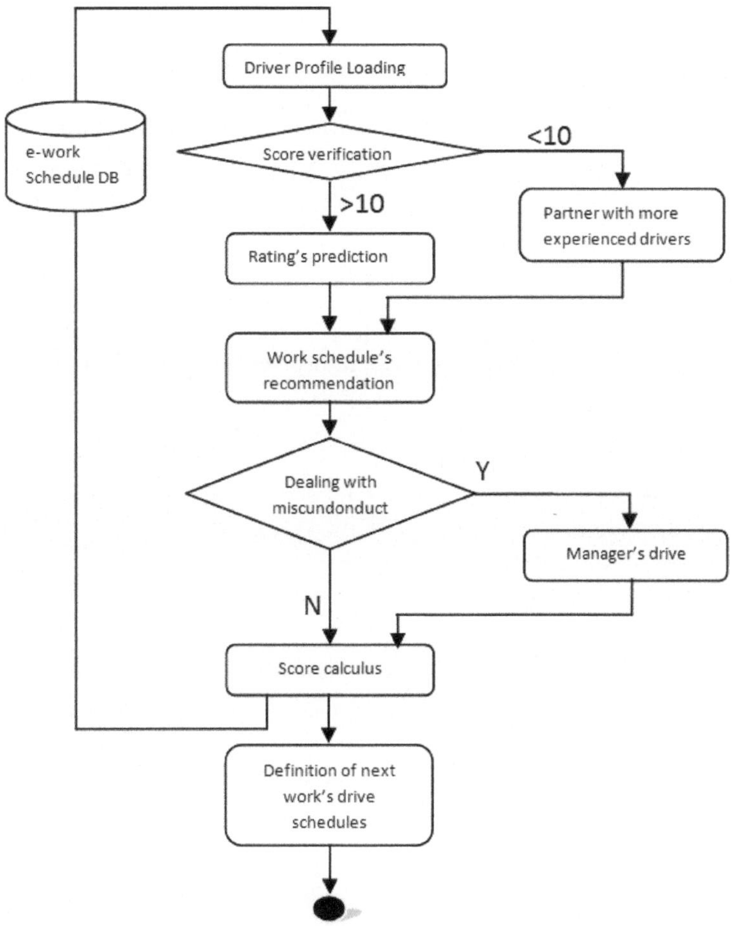

Figure 1. *Work schedules' recommendation system flow chart.*

This approach relies on neighbors' opinions, driver cumulative scores and eventual conflicts with customers. At the end of each transport plan, the drivers are asked to rate (in 1-5 rating scale) the work schedule suggested by the recommender system. More precisely, each driver's rate will be interpreted as a personal evaluation for the other drivers who are designated to accompany him/her during the transportation action plan. This is exactly the reason why the two dimensions of the rating matrix in table 1 involve only driver's identifiers.

Finally, for each driver, a total score will be computed based on various parameters (i.e. position, delays, absences, etc.). This score represents the most significant factor in the determination of the appropriate work schedules to suggest. Even, when all work schedules are provided, the system must be kept running until the end of the transportation action plan to ensure the recuperation of all manager's ratings. Our strategy follows an iterative scheme since it reprocesses those ratings to update the driver's scores, adapt the recommendations accordingly and define the future drive schedules.

Table 1. *Driver-Driver rating matrix.*

Driver ID	1	2	3	4	5	...
1		4	5	1	4	...
2	1		3	4	-	...
3	-	1		3	1	...
4	0	4	2		1	...
5	2	-	1	4		...
...	...	...	...	...	...	...

Table 2. *Driver-Driver seniority-based similarity matrix.*

Driver ID	1	2	3	4	5	...
1		-0.6	0.1	0.8	-1	...
2	-0.6		0.4	-0.3	0.5	...
3	0.1	0.4		-0.9	0.2	...
4	0.8	-0.3	-0.9		1	...
5	-1	0.5	0.2	1		...
...	...	...	...	...	...	...

3.2.1. Problem Formulation & Notations

Our recommendation system uses a processing system configured to determine driver's scores using a collaborative rating process. Before proceeding further in describing the proposed approach, it is essential to have an understanding of how the transportation plan office often works in practice in order to extract relevant information and provide the necessary controls for ensuring the competency and effectiveness of the employees.

Once all drivers have joined their work schedules, the transport's managers start their inspection. The primary task for transport's managers, in addition to detecting any misconduct, is to ensure optimum transportation conditions in the work. Examples of driver's illegal behavior include making and receiving phone calls during the transportation plan or leaving the yard area.

Accordingly, when dealing with suspected misconduct, the transport's managers notify the director and the transport office in order to take the necessary measures. This policy appears to be effective, but is also vulnerable because of the informal way of establishing communication. Usually, drivers who are suspected of misconduct are never notified. This deprives them of a real opportunity to be corrected.

When designing our recommender system, we found some useful to use rating-based scores in order to formalize the future action plan in such situations. Specifically, the score calculation will take into account various data that can be explicitly provided by users (manager's ratings) or implicitly inferred from the drive's plan (position, delays, absences, etc.). For notational convenience, we give the definitions of the sets, parameters and the variables in Tables 3-5, respectively.

Table 3. *The sets.*

Sets	Definition
T	Set of scheduled transportation's sessions
$N(t)$	Set of drivers for session t
$S(t)$	Set of work schedules for session t
$E(t)$	Set for not assigned work schedules for session t
$D(k)$	Set of drivers assigned to the work schedule k
$R(t)$	Set of the work schedules which need the assignment of drivers
$O(v)$	Set of drivers rated by driver v

Table 4. *The parameters.*

Parameters	Definition
$Conf(v,s)$	1 if a conflict is recorded betweendriver v and the customers who demand their containers in work schedule s, 0 otherwise
$Cap(k)$	The work schedule capacity

Table 5. *The variables.*

Variables	Definition
$r_{u,v}$	The rating attributed by driver u to driver v
$r^*_{i,v}$	The rating attributed by the manager i to driver v
$\hat{r}_{u,v}$	The rating attributed by driver u to driver v as predicted by the model
$\hat{R}_{u,k}$	The rating attributed by driver u to the work schedule k as predicted by the model
Sen_v	The driver's seniority
Del_v^t	The recorded delay to join the work schedule in session t
$Pres_v^t$	The driver's presence state in session t
$Score_v^t$	The driver's score in session t
$Score_v$	The accumulated driver's total score
$Work_v^t$	The work schedule assigned to driver v during session t

3.2.2. Recommendation Engine

Our collaborative filtering algorithm needs, as inputs, a first matrix representing the drivers' opinions on their colleagues (refer to table 1) and a second one for storing the seniority-based similarity between drivers (refer to table 2). Those similarities are calculated based on the attribute seniority when loading driver profiles and scattered into a [-1, 1] interval.

Table 6. *Driver's scores interpretation.*

Score	Interpretation
$0 \le Score_v < 5$	Recall the principle rules governing conduct in work schedules
$5 \le Score_v < 10$	Partner with more experienced drivers
$10 \le Score_v < 15$	Varying the drive-drive assignments
$15 \le Score_v < 20$	No drive problem

Given an active driver, the objective of the resolution recommendation is to find the similar colleagues when there is no available rate for the drivers in the considered work schedule.

A straightforward approach is to apply the K-Nearest Neighbors strategy (P. Resnick et all, 2010) and select the set of "neighbors" of user u, denoted by N_u, by choosing users who are sufficiently similar to u, i.e.

$$\overrightarrow{N_u} = \{v \mid Sim(u,v) \succ \gamma\} \tag{1}$$

Where Sim(u,v) is the similarity of u and v and is a threshold to select users who are qualified as "neighbors" of user u. The neighbor selection is a very important step before prediction because the prediction ratings of an active user on items will be inaccurate if the selected neighbors are not sufficiently similar to the active user. Instead of selecting the top-k neighbors, we set a threshold for selecting neighbors. If the similarity of a candidate user v and the active user u is greater than or equal to the threshold, v will be selected into $\overrightarrow{N_u}$ (i.e. the set of "neighbors" of u).The rating similarities between drivers are determined based on the Pearson correlation coefficient.

$$Sim_{Rat}(u,v) = \cos(u,v) = \frac{\vec{u}.\vec{v}}{\|\vec{u}\|.\|\vec{v}\|} = \frac{\sum_i (r_{u,i}-\bar{r}_u)\times(r_{v,i}-\bar{r}_v)}{\sqrt{\sum_i (r_{u,i}-\bar{r}_u)^2}\times\sqrt{\sum_i (r_{v,i}-\bar{r}_v)^2}} \quad (2)$$

And the total similarity will be computed as follows:

$$Sim(u,v) = \frac{\alpha.Sim_{Rat}(u,v)+\beta.Sim_{Sen}(u,v)}{2} \quad (3)$$

Where α and β are inversely proportional constants.

The prediction of an unknown rating $\hat{r}_{u,i}$ requires the search of users v that are similar to u, or the nearest neighbors of u according to cosine similarity measure

$$\hat{r}_{u,i} = \bar{r}_i + \frac{\sum_{j\in N(i)} Sim(i,j)\times(r_{u,j}-\bar{r}_j)}{\sum_{j\in N(i)} Sim(i,j)} \quad (4)$$

The final rating of user u to the work schedule k is given by:

$$\hat{R}_{u,k} = \sum_{u\in D(k)} \hat{r}_{u,v} \quad (5)$$

Finally, the score computed for each driver will be expressed as follows:

$$Score_u^t = \begin{cases} \dfrac{r_u^{*t}+Sen_u^t}{1-Del_u^t} & if\ \ Pres_u^t = 1 \\ 0 & otherwise \end{cases} \quad (6)$$

Where $t \in T$, $u \in N_t$.

The calculated scores can be then interpreted as shown in table 6 and reused when defining the future work schedule's driver. So the more the total score is low, the more driven plans will be attributed to the driver.

A more formal description of the proposed approach can be found in Algorithm 1.

4. Implementation of the Proposed Approach

The recommender system, which we named the Straddle carrier Assignment Model (SAM) software, is already finished and it has been successfully tested by the RADES transport's office. The preliminary results show a good performance in terms of recorded conflicts and drivers' (resp. transportation's staff) satisfaction. The success of our solution has also inspired other Tunisian container terminals to adopt and replicate its model for their own organizational needs.

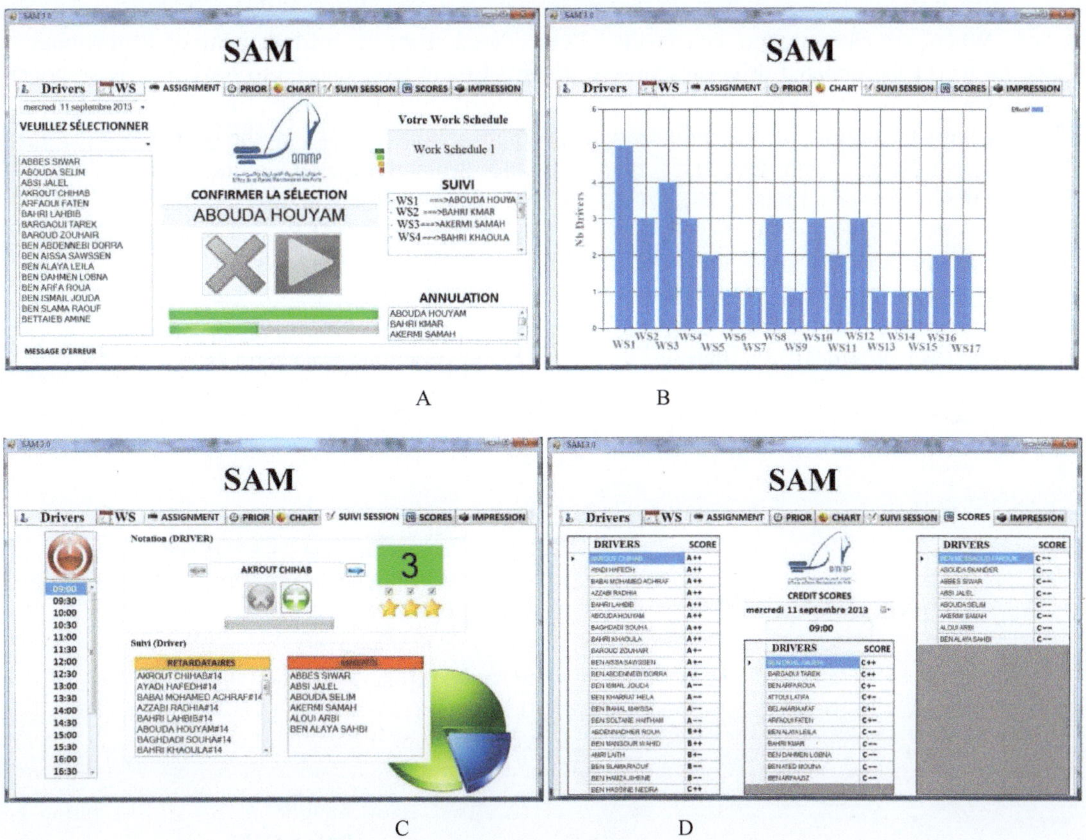

Figure 2. Sample screens from the SAM software.

To design our recommender system, modular three-tier architecture (client, server and back-end database) is employed. On the client side, SAM provides the users (transportation's office agents / managers and RADES director) with multi-task interfaces.

On the server side, intelligent module performs the calculation of all necessary scores and utilities. The back-end e-work schedule database stores preferences and information about more than 250 straddle carriers' drivers.

The system was implemented in a Microsoft Windows environment using Microsoft Visual Studio.Net for the development of our front-end system. The back-end database was managed using MySQL. The software implements the following main functions:

- Suggestive module: The interactive interface in Figure 2.A is projected on the wall providing visual feedback to all drivers who joined the queue in the transportation's office. The recommendation process must be undertaken with total transparency.
- Graphical tools: To facilitate verification, interpretation and validation of the system recommendations, graphical display tools (See Figure 2.B) are provided to the users. Although the procedure is totally automatic in normal use, the user can manually intervene in urgent circumstances. In such situations, the graphical representations can be of great use.
- Rating system: At the end of each transporter's plan, managers and supervisors return to the system to enter their observations in the form of ratings (See Figure 2.C).
- Score's generator: When all data are collected, the system generates the list of the updated driver's scores as shown in Figure 2.D.

The development and implementation of the proposed expert system is in direct congruence with several of the strategic goals of the RADES container terminal. The SAM software created a competitive advantage, increased job satisfaction and greatly reduced conflicts. Customers are also more satisfied because the system is in place. Time savings are significant, recorded delays when starting work schedules became quasi nonexistent and a social equilibrium is expected to take place in the short-term future.

5. Results

To evaluate the SAM project, we conduct a series of face-to-face interviews with the administration staff and posted a questionnaire on the RADES web site forum page. The results collected from the analysis concern all drive positions (replacement drivers, part-time drivers, contractual drivers...). According to the RADES transport's regulations, some volunteers can be engaged as managers.

We received a total of 24 valid responses. The questionnaire focused on the drivers' perceptions of how the SAM software influenced the conduct of transportations and were specifically designed to obtain feedbacks on four aspects: reasonableness, accuracy, equity and transparency of the work schedule's assignments.

The obtained results in Figure 2 revealed the paradoxical effects of applying our recommender system. The high experienced drivers are often favored ahead of their colleagues. The favoritism comes in the form of a monopoly of simple work schedules. Such situation gave rise to conflicts with the other drive profiles and indeed also to tensions between all the transportation's staff.

With its adoption in the year 2012, the SAM has completely changed the rules by treating all drivers the same without any discrimination. But we should realize that our system had not been welcomed by some drivers who considered it as an infringement of an acquired right and many of them have chosen to boycott it in response. Despite the remarkable decrease in the total number of recorded conflicts (about 30 %) in the year 2013,the mean scores obtained from the questionnaires in Figure 4 still reveal a significant difference in the responses of the two groups. Unfortunately, the SAM project is still struggling to persuade users to change their behaviors but we expect that this situation will not persist for long especially since we have introduced the scientific methodology that we have adopted for the construction of our models.

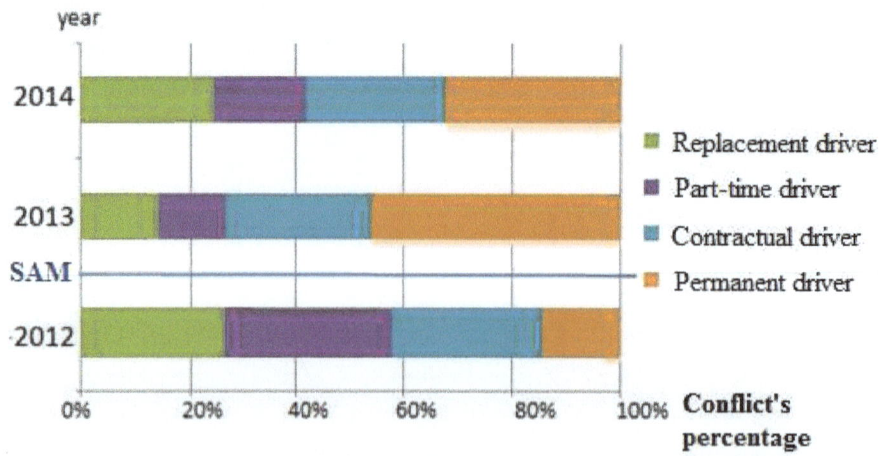

Figure 3. *Percentages of registered conflicts during work schedule assignments.*

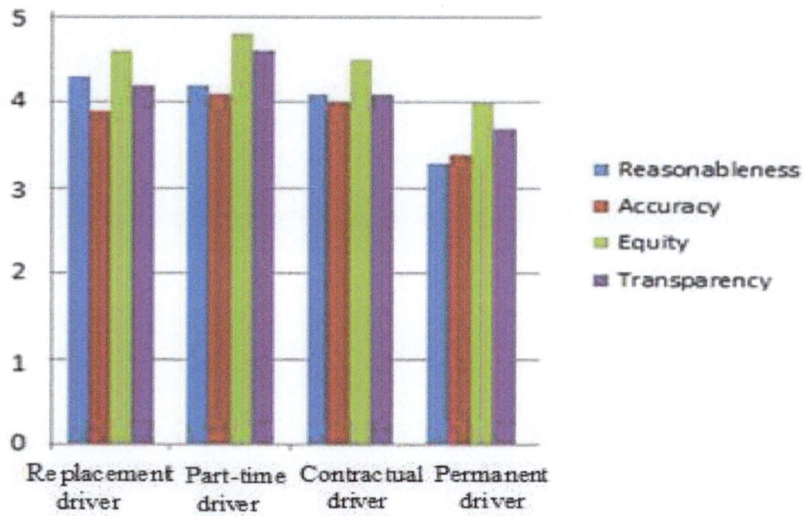

Figure 4. *Qualitative evaluations of the SAM recommendations.*

6. Conclusion

In this paper, we presented our design and implementation of a recommender system that can help straddle carrier's drivers select appropriate work schedule based on their preferences, scores and transport constraints. The proposed recommendation method is further strengthened by reusing all relevantly similar previous experiences to make the current suggestion more accurate. The SAM system is an initial attempt towards a more complete software package for automatically managing transportation of containers in container terminals.

Algorithm1 SAM collaborative filtering algorithm

Require: Driver-driver rating matrix, Driver-driver seniority-based similarity matrix, driver's profile information.

repeat

Random selection of a work schedule $k \in E(t)$

If Conflict (Driver u , Customer $s \in k = \varnothing$ then

Assign u to k

end if

until $E(t) = \varnothing$

foreach driver u do

Load the driver u 's profile

if $Score_u \succ 10$ then

for each work schedule k do

for each driver w in work schedule k do

Find the nearest drivers to u who have rated driver w

Predict the rating $\hat{r}_{u,w}$ for driver u on driver w

end for

Predict the rating $\hat{R}_{u,k}$ for driver u on work schedule k

if Conflict (Driver u , Customer $s \in k = \varnothing$ then

Recommend work schedule with maximum $\hat{R}_{u,k}$

end if

end for

else

Partner with more experienced colleagues

end if

end for

References

[1] G. Adomavicius , A. Tuzhilin."Toward the next generation of recommender systems: a survey of the state-of-the-art and possible extensions", IEEE Computer Society, volume 17, Issue 6. (2005).

[2] S. S. Anand, B. Mobasher., "Lecture Notes in Computer Science", Springer Berlin Heidelberg, volume 3169: 1–36,(2005).

[3] N. Belkin, W. Croft. "Information filtering and information retrieval: Two sides of the same coin?" Communications of the ACM, 35(12):29–38, (1992).

[4] Y. Blanco-Fernandez, M. L. Nores, J. J. P. Arias, and J. G. Duque. "An improvement for semantics-based recommender systems grounded on attaching temporal information to ontologies and user profiles". Eng. Appl. of AI, 24(8):1385–1397, (2011).

[5] J. Herlocker, J. Konstan, L. Terveen, and J. Riedl. "Evaluating collaborative filtering recommender systems". ACM Transactions on Information Systems, 22(1):5–53, (2004).

[6] D. Jannach, M. Zanker, A. Felfernig, and G. Friedrich. "Recommender Systems: An Introduction". Cambridge University Press, (2011).

[7] G. Karypis. "Evaluation of item-based top-n recommendation algorithms". In Proceedings of the tenth international conference on Information and knowledge management, pages 247–254, Atlanta, Georgia, USA, ACM Press, (2001).

[8] M. Khaled, "Six Sigma Approach for the Straddle Carrier Routing Problem", Journal of Maritime Research, vol. X. No.1 (2013), pp. 71-84, (2013).

[9] M. Khaled, T. Sadraoui "Optimizing the Operational Process at Container Terminal" International Journal of Econometrics and Financial Management, Vol. 3, No. 2, 91-98, (2015).

[10] M. Khaled, M. Faissal, "Genetic procedure for the Single Straddle Carrier Routing Problem" International Journal of Advanced Computer Science and Applications, Vol. 3, No. 11, (2012).

[11] P. Melville and V. Sindhwani. "Recommender Systems". Encyclopedia of Machine Learning, pages 829–838, (2010).

[12] P. Resnick, N. Iacovou, M. Suchak, P. Bergstrom, and J. Riedl. Grouplens,"An open architecture for collaborative filtering of net news", Proceedings of ACM 1994 Conference on Computer Supported Cooperative Work, pages 175–186. ACM Press, (1994).

[13] P.-N. Tan, M. Steinbach, and V. Kumar. "Introduction to Data Mining". Addison Wesley, (2006).

2

Impact of the Capital Structure Tools on the Performance Indicators in the Listed Companies in Tehran Stock Exchange

Mostafa Zangiabadi[1, *], Amin Rahimzade[2], Mahdie Taboli[3]

[1]Faculty of Management and Accounting, Allame Tabatabaei University of Tehran, Tehran, Iran
[2]Faculty of Management and Accounting, University of Qom, Qom, Iran
[3]Scientific Group of Accounting, Department of Payame Noor University, Zangiabad, Iran

Email address:
m.zangiabadi229@gmail.com (M. Zangiabadi), a.rahimzade2002@gmail.com (A. Rahimzade), mhd.taboli@gmail.com (M. Taboli)

Abstract: Today, one of the objectives of the financial managers is to maximize shareholder wealth, and in this context, determining the capital structure is a key factor. Due to tax benefits, the use of financial leverage is considered. On the other hand, due to higher interest costs associated with obtaining debt, bankruptcy may also exist. In conclusion, this study examines the impact of capital structure tools on the return on equity, return on assets and return on working capital. This paper examines the data from 2001 to 2011 companies listed in Tehran Stock Exchange. And the results after using the linear regression model, suggest that debt ratio is not affected on the return on equity, but is affected on the return on assets. while debt to net worth ratio and current and long-term debt to net worth ratio is affected on the return on equity. Also, the results show that debt to assets ratio and debt to net worth ratio and current and long-term debt to net worth ratio does not affect on the rate of return on working capital. And debt to net worth ratio and current and long-term debt to net worth ratio does not affect on the rate of return on assets. Overall, the results show that the capital structure affects on the performance of listed companies in Tehran stock exchange.

Keywords: Capital Structure, Debt Ratio, Debt to Net Worth Ratio, Debt to Assets Ratio, Return on Equity, Return on Assets, Return on Working Capital

1. Introduction

Capital structure, is the main topic at the finance of enterprises. There is not sufficient knowledge from the capital structure in the emerging markets and transition economies. Capital structure theories have tended to principles of evaluation and also play a developmental role in the stock markets[4]. Finance through an interest-bearing loan has benefits. First, interest on loan is an acceptable tax cost. And this will reduce the effective cost of loans and especially if the rate of return from the use of the loan is greater than the rate of financing costs shareholder, since the interest rate and principal on long-term loan is fixed, are not required to share the additional benefits with Lenders. and finally, because the lenders do not have the right to vote, shareholders can apply more control of the company with less money. On the other side, interest-bearing loans have some weak points as follows: First, on the one hand, the long-term interest-bearing debt make financial commitments and too much rely on it, increase the financial leverage and consequently, leads to increase the probability of bankruptcy and failure to pay the principal and interest on the loan. Especially in companies that do not live in good condition in view of the financial position, excessive use of long-term debt, outweigh the company's commitment and leads to increase the bankruptcy and financial risk and thereby damage to the shareholders. The second disadvantage of the use of the interest-bearing debt is by increasing the ratio of loans, creditors, to pay the loan, act with more cautious and also, due to the increasing of the loan payments risk, consider higher interest rates for loan payments that this issue will also affects on benefits from tax credits[3]. Therefore, this study investigates the effect of capital structure tools on the performance indicators at listed companies in Tehran Stock Exchange.

Capital structure represents a combination of debt and equity of the firms. Choosing the right combination of debt and equity, considered by many persons as company stakeholders, about the company's ability to continue and the potential impact of debt on the company's bankruptcy, and specifically is of interest to financial managers that their main mission is to maximize shareholder wealth. Thus, according to the methods of financing, the management to accomplish its goal, chooses one of the methods of financing or a combination of them with respect to advantages and disadvantages such the effect of stock returns on the firm's performance.

Thus, given the right combination of capital structure from the perspective of financial managers, identifying the effects that it has on firm performance has a particular importance.

In this study, we tried to examine the influences of the capital structure tools on performance indicators and the main research question is whether the capital structure tools (debt to asset ratio, debt to equity ratio, etc.) are effective on the performance indicators (ROE, ROA, ROWC) or not.

2. The Theoretical Basis and Background of Research

2.1. Capital Structure

There are different theories of capital structure and refer that the companies to finance and continue to operate consider three groups of resources: The first group resources that apparently does not have any costs include trade creditors and advances from Customers.

Second,are the internal financial resources that to finance through the second group requiered to the past profitability of the company that through the accumulation of past profits, the company provides a good source of financing that instead of dividing the earnings among the shareholders, use the earnings primarily in operational activities of company for higher yields.

And third, are the external financing such as bonds, loans and stocks. Of course the company may use these resources to short-term or long-term methods.

On the one hand, the existence of debt in the financial structure of firms because of the existence of the tax credits, thereby increasing earnings and consequently increase the return on equity and on the other hand, because of the existence of interest costs and the possibility of non-payment of debt at maturities, thereby increasing financial risk and reducing the market price per share, which consequently reduced the return on equity. The financial managers must choose the capital structure that has lower cost of capital that seek a better performance for companies. Therefore the financial managers must determine the weighted average cost of capital and the marginal cost of capital to determine the optimal capital structure. Managers should also determine the company's borrowing capacity by considering the incoming and outgoing cash flows, and then borrow by considering the other conditions. Optimal capital structure, is the following: determining the percentages of items that formed the capital that minimize the weighted average cost of capital of the company and thus to maximize the returns of company [19].

2.2. Theories of the Capital Structure

2.2.1. Modigliani and Miller Approach

These two scientists, in their theory with the assumption that the capital market is complete and the investors like the corporations can borrow and at a cost equal to companies studied the relationship between leverage and the firm value under the assumption of tax and no tax.

A) The Absence of Tax:

In the complete capital markets, the debt can not affect firm value, now that the debt does not increase the share value, investors instead of buying leveraged company shares, purchase the non-leveraged company shares that have less risk and personally borrow and invest in a combination of stocks and personal loans.

B) The Existence of Tax

Using the debt because of the debt interest cost is acceptable tax cost create a tax advantage for the company and increasing the tax advantage, reduced capital costs and thus increase the value of the company [15].

2.2.2. A New Approach

In the new approach, it is believed that there are many factors that the companies consider to determine the level of the debt and stocks. There are different theories that explain this issue includes:

A) The Preference Theory:

The enterprises initially prefer the internal financing. The company initially uses the retained earnings and cash from the company to finance. If they have more need, initially issue bonds and finally issue common shares.

B) The static trade-off theory:

According to this theory, the companies determine a debt ratio(optimal) and use various methods to keep the optimal debt ratio. The optimal debt ratio of a company is determined based on the balance between costs and benefits of borrowing. And the company will try to balance between the tax credits and bankruptcy costs of debt [15].

2.2.3. Signaling Theory

Due to the fact that managers often have more information to the outside investors of the company that this is a case of asymmetric information that has a major impact on the desirable capital structure. Thus, firms that have undesirable future ahead, tend to sell the shares to new investors to partner them at the cost. While companies that have a very good future do not provide capital needed through the sale of the new shares. Therefore declaration of shares offering usually see as a warning signal that the directors do not see the company's future very bright or shining [18].

2.3. Prior Related Literature

Shirzad (2001) in a study entitled The effect of capital structure on profitability of listed companies in Tehran Stock Exchange, found that there is not a strong and significant relationship between capital structure and profitability of listed companies in Tehran Stock Exchange[17].

Ebadi Dowlatabadi (2002) in a study entitled The effect of methods of financing on yields and price of shares of companies listed in Tehran Stock Exchange, found that the impact of issue of shares than the long-term debt, on the stock price is more. Also capital increases Compared with bank borrowings has a greater impact on stock returns[5].

Bahrami Kia(2003) in a study entitled The effect of capital structure on the capital cost and the market price of shares of companies listed in Tehran Stock Exchange for the food industry, found that the capital structure (debt ratio) does not affect on the cost of capital and the market price of shares and the total market value of the surveyed companies[2]

Izad Nia and Rahimi dastjerdi (2009), in a study entitled the impact of capital structure on the stock returns and earnings per share, concluded that there is meaningful relation between the debt-equity ratio and return on equity and earnings per share and also there is a significant relationship between the debt to asset ratio with earnings per share[7]

Khajavi and colleagues (2010),in a study pay to evaluate the effect of capital structure on the cumulative abnormal yields of companies listed in Tehran Stock Exchange. The results show that the capital structure does not meaningful influence on the cumulative abnormal yields. Also the systematic risk, P / E, BTM and firm size have positive and significant effect on the cumulative abnormal yields[10]

Izzie and Saidi (2012), in a study pay to evaluate the relationship between capital structure and performance of companies listed in Tehran Stock Exchange for the pharmaceutical companies during the years 2003-2010. And the results of their analysis shows that there is a significant relationship between the variables of capital structure, debt ratio, return on equity and corporate performance[8]

Antoniou et al (2002),in a research under the title the determinants of firms' capital structure, examined the impact of leverage Ratio on the capital structure and achieved to results that the companies configured the factors affecting on capital structure to achieve the optimal capital structure [1]

Another study by Mateus and Balla (2002) was performed in the selection of the optimal capital structure. They have used regression analysis of mixed data for 55 companies from 1995 to 1999 and concluded that the firm's size is directly related to leverage[11]

Richardson and Sloan (2003) in a study under the title the relationship between external financing with future stock returns, review all of the external financing and found there is a negative relationship between the changes in the net external financing and expected stock returns. They finally realized that predict future stock returns is largely dependent on the capital structure[16]

El-Sayed Ebaid (2009), in a study under the title The impact of capital-structure choice on firm performance: empirical evidence from Egypt Based on a sample of non-financial corporations during the years 1997-2005 And resulted that the capital structure decisions overall have low to the zero limit effect on firm performance[6]

Chakraborty (2010),in a study investigate the capital structure in an emerging stock market in India that his research results show that among the three theories of capital structure, seems that Hierarchical theory and the theory of information asymmetry vindicate the financing decisions of Hindi firms. However, little evidence supports the costs of agency theory [4]

Muradoglu and Sivaprasad (2012) in a study under the title Capital structure and abnormal returns examine the relationship between capital structure and abnormal stock returns and the results show that the average abnormal returns in the parts manufacturing industry increase risky and considered the characteristics of the industry in his research. This irregular behavior has seen in competitive and irregular industries and the low concentration. The classification of the risk of facilities increase abnormal efficiency in parts manufacturing companies that are similar to the findings of Miller and Modigliani (1958) [13].

Jin Xu (2012), in a study under the title profitability and capital structure showed that the results of information asymmetry approach (model) of capital structure, predicts a positive relationship between leverage and coming profitability. Their research evidence suggests that internal competitions affects on leverage through the change in the balance the tax benefits arising from debt and financing costs resulting from the sale of assets [9]

3. Research Hypotheses

The first hypothesis (original): There is an association between the capital structure and the performance of the firms listed in Tehran Stock Exchange.

The second hypothesis (sub-prime): There is an association between the debt to assets ratio and the return on equity.

The third hypothesis (sub-second): There is an association between the debt to net worth ratio and the return on equity.

The fourth hypothesis (sub-third): There is an association between the current debt to net worth ratio and the return on equity.

The fifth hypothesis (sub-fourth): There is an association between the Long-term debt to net worth ratio and the return on equity.

The sixth hypothesis (sub-fifth): There is an association between the debt to assets ratio and the return on assets.

The seventh hypothesis (sub-sixth): There is an association between the debt to net worth ratio and the return on assets.

The eighth hypothesis (sub-seventh): There is an association between the current debt to net worth ratio and the return on assets.

The ninth hypothesis (sub-eighth): There is an association between the Long-term debt to net worth ratio and the return on assets.

The tenth hypothesis (sub-ninth): There is an association between the debt to assets ratio and the return on working capital.

The eleventh hypothesis (sub-tenth): There is an association between the debt to net worth ratio and the return on working capital.

The twelfth hypothesis (sub-eleventh): There is an association between the current debt to net worth ratio and the return on working capital.

The thirteenth hypothesis (sub-twelfth): There is an association between the Long-term debt to net worth ratio and the return on working capital.

4. Methodology

This research regarding the type is analytic and regarding the target is applied. Library resources and literature on this subject are used to write the theoretical foundation and the main body of the research and data are collected by available software in the library of Tehran Stock Exchange and were collected the Information listed companies from 2001 to 2011. By calculating the research variables and logistic regression analysis between them, have tested the research hypotheses using SPSS software.

4.1. Data Collection Methods

There are several methods of data collection. In a study may be used of several methods to collect information. In this study are used of literature methods to literature review, in this method was studied literature and sources used in the research of their products. Into analysis obtained data are used of descriptive statistics and inferential statistics. Data analysis after collecting and organizing data and tests has been done with using, SPSS and Minitab software.

4.2. Research Community

Research population have been all listed companies in Tehran Stock Exchange for the years 2001-2011 that have been submitted the required financial information in particular its explanatory notes to the Stock Exchange.

4.3. Research Sample

Samples selected for analysis is all the companies that provide the data needed, and have the following conditions:

- They have been active In the 2001-2011 period in the stock exchange.
- They have provided the financial ratios fully.
- It is the fiscal year ending in March.
- They have not included holding companies and credit financial institutions and banks.

5. Research Findings

Table 1 shows the results of the descriptive statistics, such as mean and standard deviation of the variables.

Table 1. *The results of descriptive statistics.*

standard deviation	mean	Type of variable
620	15.65	return on assets
1163.36	68.66	return on equity
6578.92	-48.51	return on working capital
1.41	0.83	debt to assets ratio
70.25	0.51	debt to net worth ratio
16.63	-0.04	Long-term debt to net worth ratio
58.11	0.53	current debt to net worth ratio

According to Table 2, the significance level of the F statistic is 0.000, which indicates a regression model is significant at 99% confidence level. And the Adjusted R^2 equal to 1%, which suggests that about 1% of the variation in Performance of firms is due to the change in the capital structure. The significance level of the statistic t (probability of independent variable) is equal to 0.000, which indicates at confidence level of 95% capital structure affects on firm performance.

The results of the first hypothesis:

Table 2. *The results of the statistical test of the first hypothesis.*

sig.	t	beta	sig.	F	Adjusted R2	R2
0.000	-6.84	-6.882	0.000	46.793	0.01	0.01

According to Table 3, the significance level of the F statistic is 0.850, which indicates a regression model is not significant at 99% confidence level. And the Adjusted R2 equal to 0.000, which suggests that the variation in return on equity is not due to the change in the debt to assets ratio. The significance level of the statistic t (probability of independent variable) is equal to 0.850, which indicates at confidence level of 95% debt to assets ratio does not affect on return on equity.

The results of the second hypothesis:

Table 3. *The results of the statistical test of the second hypothesis.*

sig.	t	beta	sig.	F	Adjusted R^2	R^2
0.850	0.189	-2.296	0.85	0.036	0.000	0.000

According to Table 4, the significance level of the F statistic is 0.000, which indicates a regression model is significant at 99% confidence level. And the Adjusted R2 equal to 0.390, which suggests that about 39% of the variation in return on equity is due to the change in the debt to net worth ratio. The significance level of the statistic t (probability of independent variable) is equal to 0.000, which indicates at confidence level of 95% debt to net worth ratio affects on return on equity.

The results of the third hypothesis:

Table 4. *The results of the statistical test of the third hypothesis.*

sig.	t	beta	sig.	F	Adjusted R^2	R^2
0.0	-54.14	-10.36	0.000	2939	0.389	0.39

According to Table 5, the significance level of the F statistic is 0.000, which indicates a regression model is significant at 99% confidence level. And the Adjusted R2 equal to 0.380, which suggests that about 38% of the variation in return on equity is due to the change in the current debt to net worth ratio. The significance level of the statistic t (probability of independent variable) is equal to 0.000, which indicates at confidence level of 95% current debt to net worth ratio affects on return on equity.

The results of the fourth hypothesis:

Table 5. *The results of the statistical test of the fourth hypothesis.*

sig.	t	beta	sig.	F	Adjusted R^2	R^2
0.000	-53.146	-12.343	0.000	2824.5	0.380	0.380

According to Table 6, the significance level of the F statistic is 0.000, which indicates a regression model is significant at 99% confidence level. And the Adjusted R2 equal to 0.232, which suggests that about 23% of the variation in return on equity is due to the change in the long-term debt to net worth ratio. The significance level of the statistic t (probability of independent variable) is equal to 0.000, which indicates at confidence level of 95% long-term debt to net worth ratio affects on return on equity.

The results of the fifth hypothesis:

Table 6. *The results of the statistical test of the fifth hypothesis.*

sig.	t	beta	sig.	F	Adjusted R^2	R^2
0.000	-37.343	-33.727	0.000	1394.50	0.232	0.23

According to Table 7, the significance level of the F statistic is 0.035, which indicates a regression model is not significant at 99% confidence level. And the Adjusted R2 equal to 0.001, which suggests that about 0.1% of the variation in return on assets is due to the change in the debt to asset ratio. The significance level of the statistic t (probability of independent variable) is equal to 0.035, which indicates at confidence level of 95% debt to asset ratio affects on return on assets.

The results of the sixth hypothesis:

Table 7. *The results of the statistical test of the sixth hypothesis.*

sig.	t	bata	sig.	F	Adjusted R^2	R^2
0.035	-2.10	-13.607	0.035	4.426	0.001	0.001

According to Table 8, the significance level of the F statistic is 0.944, which indicates a regression model is not significant at 99% confidence level. And the Adjusted R2 equal to 0.000, which suggests that the variation in return on assets is not due to the change in the debt to net worth ratio. The significance level of the statistic t (probability of independent variable) is equal to 0.944, which indicates at confidence level of 95% debt to net worth ratio does not affect on return on assets.

The results of the seventh hypothesis:

Table 8. *The results of the statistical test of the seventh hypothesis.*

sig.	t	beta	sig.	F	Adjusted R^2	R^2
0.944	0.070	0.009	0.944	0.005	0.000	0.000

According to Table 9, the significance level of the F statistic is 0.945, which indicates a regression model is not significant at 99% confidence level. And the Adjusted R2 equal to 0.000, which suggests that the variation in return on assets is not due to the change in the current debt to net worth ratio. The significance level of the statistic t (probability of independent variable) is equal to 0.945, which indicates at confidence level of 95% current debt to net worth ratio does not affect on return on assets.

The results of the eighth hypothesis:

Table 9. *The results of the statistical test of the eighth hypothesis.*

sig.	t	beta	sig.	F	Adjusted R^2	R^2
0.945	0.068	0.011	0.945	0.005	0.000	0.000

According to Table 10, the significance level of the F statistic is 0.953, which indicates a regression model is not significant at 99% confidence level. And the Adjusted R2 equal to 0.000, which suggests that the variation in return on assets is not due to the change in the long-term debt to net worth ratio. The significance level of the statistic t (probability of independent variable) is equal to 0.953, which indicates at confidence level of 95% long-term debt to net worth ratio does not affect on return on assets.

The results of the ninth hypothesis:

Table 10. *The results of the statistical test of the ninth hypothesis.*

sig.	t	beta	sig.	F	Adjusted R^2	R^2
0.953	0.059	0.032	0.953	0.003	0.000	0.000

According to Table 11, the significance level of the F statistic is 0.808, which indicates a regression model is not significant at 99% confidence level. And the Adjusted R2 equal to 0.000, which suggests that the variation in return on working capital is not due to the change in the debt to asset ratio. The significance level of the statistic t (probability of independent variable) is equal to 0.808, which indicates at confidence level of 95% debt to asset ratio does not affect on return on working capital.

The results of the tenth hypothesis:

Table 11. *The results of the statistical test of the tenth hypothesis.*

sig.	t	beta	sig.	F	Adjusted R^2	R^2
0.808	0.244	16.722	0.808	0.059	0.000	0.000

According to Table 12, the significance level of the F statistic is 0.997, which indicates a regression model is not significant at 99% confidence level. And the Adjusted R2 equal to 0.000, which suggests that the variation in return on working capital is not due to the change in the debt to net worth ratio. The significance level of the statistic t (probability of independent variable) is equal to 0.997, which indicates at confidence level of 95% debt to net worth ratio does not affect on return on working capital.

The results of the eleventh hypothesis:

Table 12. *The results of the statistical test of the eleventh hypothesis.*

sig.	t	beta	sig.	F	Adjusted R^2	R^2
0.997	0.004	0.005	0.997	0.000	0.000	0.000

According to Table 13, the significance level of the F statistic is 0.998, which indicates a regression model is not significant at 99% confidence level. And the Adjusted R2 equal to 0.000, which suggests that the variation in return on working capital is not due to the change in the current debt to net worth ratio. The significance level of the statistic t (probability of independent variable) is equal to 0.998, which indicates at confidence level of 95% the current debt to net worth ratio does not affect on return on working capital.

The results of the twelfth hypothesis:

Table 13. *The results of the statistical test of the twelfth hypothesis.*

sig.	t	beta	sig.	F	Adjusted R^2	R^2
0.998	0.003	0.005	0.998	0.000	0.000	0.000

According to Table 14, the significance level of the F statistic is 0.995, which indicates a regression model is not significant at 99% confidence level. And the Adjusted R2 equal to 0.000, which suggests that the variation in return on working capital is not due to the change in the long-term debt to net worth ratio. The significance level of the statistic t (probability of independent variable) is equal to 0.995, which indicates at confidence level of 95% the long-term debt to net worth ratio does not affect on return on working capital.

The results of the thirteenth hypothesis:

Table 14. *The results of the statistical test of the thirteenth hypothesis.*

sig.	t	beta	sig.	F	Adjusted R^2	R^2
0.995	0.006	0.034	0.995	0.000	0.000	0.000

6. Discussion and Conclusions

The test results of hypotheses indicate that the debt to assets ratio does not affect the return on equity, but affect the return on assets. While the debt to net worth ratio and current and long-term debt to net worth ratio affect the return on equity. Also The results show that the debt to assets ratio and the debt to net worth ratio and current and long-term debt to net worth ratio does not affect the return on working capital. Also the debt to net worth ratio and current and long-term debt to net worth ratio does not affect the return on assets. Overall, the results suggest that capital structure affect the performance listed companies in Tehran stock exchange.

Suggestions

In this research from the financial statements data of listed companies in Tehran Stock Exchange has been used and suggested that in the future studies use the financial statements data of OTC. In this research were examined the information from the financial statements for the years 2001 to 2011. And suggested that in the future studies use from the another time interval. It is suggested that in the future studies use other factors than the rate of return on assets, return on equity and return on capital as the performance indicators.

References

[1] Antoniou; Antonio's, G.; Paudyal 2002. Determinants of Corporate Capital structure: Evidence From European Countries, social science research network. www.ssrn.com\abstract=285001

[2] Bahrami Kia, G. 2003. The effect of capital structure on cost of capital and the market price of shares of companies listed in Tehran Stock Exchange for the food industry, MS Thesis, University of Isfahan, IRAN

[3] Berry, G.; O-Jean F.; Gapnsky; dyvez 2003. The Intermediate Financial Management, Translated by Ali Parsayyan, Tehran, Terme

[4] Chakraborty, I. 2010. Capital structure in an emerging stock market: The case of India, Research in International Business and Finance 24: 295–314

[5] Ebadi Dowlatabadi, M. 2002. The effect of the methods of financing (external sources) on the yield and price of shares of companies listed in Tehran Stock Exchange, MS Thesis, University of Mazandaran, IRAN

[6] El-Sayed Ebaid, I. 2009. The impact of capital-structure choice on firm performance: empirical evidence from Egypt, Journal of Risk Finance, 10 (5): 477 – 487

[7] Izadi nia, N.; Dastjerdi Rahimi M. 2009. The effect of capital structure on the rate of return on equity and earnings per share, Accounting Research, 3: 136-161

[8] Izzie, R.; Saeedi, P. 2012. The relationship between capital structure and the performance of companies listed in Tehran Stock Exchange, The National Conference of modern management science, september 2012

[9] Jin Xu. 2012. Profitability and capital structure: Evidence from import penetration, Journal of Financial Economics 106: 427–446

[10] Khajavi, S.; Valipur, H.; Hakemi, B. 2010. The effect of capital structure on the cumulative abnormal returns of companies listed in Tehran Stock Exchange, Financial Studies, No. 5

[11] Mateus, D.; Balla 2002. Optimal capital structure, social science research network, www.ssrn.com\abstract=277019

[12] Miglo, A. 2010. Capital structure and earnings manipulation, Journal of Economics and Business 62: 367–382

[13] Muradoglu, Y. G. I.; Sivaprasad, SH. 2012. Capital structure and abnormal returns, International Business Review 21: 328–341

[14] Omran, M.; Pointon, J. 2009. Capital structure and firm characteristics: an empirical analysis from Egypt, Review of Accounting and Finance, 8(4) :454 – 474

[15] Qalibafe asl, H. 2010. The Financial Management (principles, concepts and applications), Eighth Edition, Tehran, Pooran Pajoohesh

[16] Richardson, S.; sloan2003. External financing and future stock returns, the rodeney1.white center for financial research, www.ssrn.com\abstract=285008

[17] Shirzad, J. 2001. The effect of capital structure on profitability of listed companies in Tehran Stock Exchange. MS Thesis, University of Shiraz, IRAN

[18] Yu Jin, F.; Brigham; Earhart, M.C. 1930. Financial Management in Theory and Practice, translated by Alireza Farahani, Tehran, Terme, 2012

[19] Zahmatkesh, J. 2005. The assessing the nature of the capital structure and its impact on stock returns of companies operating in the cement industry in the years 1998-2002, MA thesis, University of Science and Research, Tehran, IRAN.

3

Influence of Gender in the Saving Culture of Sacco Members in Nyandarua County, Kenya

Martin Muriithi[1], Dennis Muriithi[2]

[1]School of Business Studies, University of Nairobi, Nairobi, Kenya
[2]Department of Business Administration, Chuka University, Chuka, Kenya

Email address:
kamuriithi2011@gmail.com (Dennis M.), muriithi03@gmail.com (Martin M.)

Abstract: Saving is a key component in any development endeavor as it is believed to be the surest way of increasing income and boosting productivity in an attempt to break through the vicious cycle of poverty. A number of studies have demonstrated that the investment and retirement saving behaviors of women and men differ. However, inconsistencies in findings exist in the few studies conducted on the differences in general saving behaviors between men and women. The purpose of this study was to establish gender differences in saving culture with a special bias on SACCO members. Specifically, the study aimed at assessing the influence of income levels on saving culture; evaluate the effect of marital status on saving culture and establish the influence of age on saving culture of SACCO members in Nyandarua County. The research adopted a descriptive survey design and targeted all business and agricultural based SACCO members and officials in Nyandarua County. 18 SACCO officials and 375 SACCO members were sampled using purposive and stratified random sampling respectively. The researcher collected data using structured questionnaires. A descriptive analysis of the data after processing involved computing mean, mode and median with the help of Statistical Package of Social Sciences Software and Microsoft Excel and presented in frequency tables and charts. Marital status of the respondents was found to be statistically significant in terms of the annual saving. The result implies that a change in marital status will affect the annual savings negatively. The researcher is 99.952% confidence that the change in marital status will negatively have an impact on annual saving. The researcher recommends nurturing of marriage institution as a way of protecting saving culture among women and men members of the SACCO in Nyandarua County.

Keywords: Saving Culture, Gender, Income Levels, Financial Decisions

1. Introduction

1.1. Saving Culture

Saving is deferred spending, a preference to consume tomorrow rather than today (Strydom, 2007). Savings flow into the financial system and help provide funds for investment spending by firms. Tesar (1991) established that, there is a high correlation between savings and investment in the short run and long run. The study also found countries with high saving rates to have high investment rates too.

Saving is a key component in any development endeavor as it is believed to be the surest way of increasing income and boosting productivity in an attempt to break through the vicious cycle of poverty. Without saving people are likely to face severe problem of survival when they are no longer able to work (Wu, 2005). Schmidt and Sevak (2006) argue that when poor households' desire and need to save converge, a safe, easily accessible opportunity to do so, their capacity to save, commitment to saving, and the amounts they manage to save are remarkable. According to a poll conducted by Ipsos-Synovate (2011), only half of Kenyans put money aside regularly as savings. The highest proportion of those who saved came from Nairobi, Central and Rift valley.

Keynes (1936) came up with eight motives which determine the propensity to save and corresponding motives to consumption which turned around the shape of the consumption function. Browning and Lusardi (1996) in their paper reproduced Keynes (1936) eight motives of why people save with an additional ninth. The pre-cautionary motive; individuals save money to enable them deal with unexpected events. The life-cycle motive; households save at specific times in life so as to have sufficient funds available to spend on anticipated expenses, like, when starting a family or nearing retirement. The Inter-temporal substitution motive; individuals save to enjoy the returns on savings.

The improvement motive; individuals save with the aim of becoming better by having more to spend. The independence motive; households save with the aim of being self-reliant, not to depend on others for their needs. To enjoy a sense of independence and the power to do things on their own without being questioned. The enterprise motive; to have the capacity and readiness to engage in speculative or business projects. The be-quest motive; intergenerational transfer of wealth. Individuals save so that they can leave behind money when they die. People feel satisfied when they know that their descendants will enjoy their wealth after passing on. The avarice motive; a very strong desire to hold on to what is already yours.

Njung'e (2013) observes that Savings play a major role in economic development since an increase in savings leads to an increase in investment hence improve gross domestic product. If a country saves too little, it means that the households eventually struggle financially and for the broader economy it means that there will be insufficient funds available to finance investment in physical and social infrastructure. Low savings in an economy also means unfavorable growth of the economy, poor job creation and inferior overall living standards relative to nations with a better savings performance.

1.2. Gender

Mwangi (2009) defines gender as the socially accepted attributes of an individual related to his or her sex. It is differentiation in any context and treated as such. In the current study it refers to social relationship between men and women, allocation of roles, responsibilities, rights and women obligations in employment. According to Singh and Vinnicombe (2004) the notion of gender should be understood and be related race, class, age, ethnic group among others as cross-cutting variables. Different social-cultural contexts establish gender systems with specific contexts which determine what is valued, expected and allowed in a woman/man and girl/boy.

Through socialization processes, gender roles are learned as they are not fixed but are changeable. Traditions and culture, political, economic, legislation and educations systems institutionalize gender systems. The potential of decision making, control over resources, gender responsibilities/roles are focused on systems and not on individual men and women (Verloo, 2011).

1.3. Gender and Saving Culture

A number of studies have shown that the economic wellbeing and financial behaviors of men and women differ significantly. Women hold lower levels of wealth and have significantly lower earnings than men. In addition, women spend as many as five more years than men in retirement as a result of having longer life expectancies. Researchers and financial practitioners have reported that women invest their financial resources more conservatively and are, in general, more risk averse than men (Mulino & Chai, 2008).

Because the options and constraints that women face in developing economies differ from those of men, their saving behavior may also differ. One of the most important purposes of saving in developing economies is for consumption smoothing purposes (Deaton, 1990). There may be gender differences in responsiveness to this motive. Men who, by their position in the labor market, are more likely to be beneficiaries of social insurance policies may have less need to fall back on savings for consumption smoothing purposes. In his human capital theory, Becker (1975) stated that women rationally choose to invest less than men in human capital, including education, skills, and on-the-job training, affecting women's employment opportunities, incomes, and ability to accumulate wealth. Women make different choices than men due to greater family responsibilities with the gender division of labor within the family, resulting in women taking primary responsibility for household work and child care (Bajtelsmit & Bernasek, 1996).

1.4. SACCO Membership in Nyandarua County

A Savings and Credit Cooperative (SACCO) is a type of cooperative whose objective is to pool savings for the members and in turn provide them with credit facilities. Other objectives of SACCOS are to encourage thrift amongst the members and also to encourage them on the proper management of money and proper investments practices. The Cooperative movement in Kenya dates back to 1931 when the first ordinance to regularize the operations of the cooperatives in the country was enacted. The following decade witnessed increased intervention in the sector with the eventual enactment of the Co-operative Ordinance Act of 1945. However, in 1969 the government required that SACCOs be strictly based on a secure crop or employment relationship. In this "check off system" SACCOs received payments directly from employers, processors (cooperatives, parastatals or private companies) or marketing organizations. This system ensured that a member's income would have automatic deductions to repay loans and was a significant factor in the development of SACCO's. In the case of rural SACCO's, the exclusive right to trade for certain crops conferred on market cooperatives (monopsony) helped this arrangement. However, urban SACCO's proliferated at a much faster rate than rural SACCOs.

Nyandarua County is an administrative county in the former Central Province of Kenya. Its capital town is Ol-Kalou. Nyandarua county has a male population of 292,155, a female population of 304,113 and a total population of 596,268 (2009 Census). Nyandarua County is located on the northwestern part of the Central Province, west of the Aberdare Range. Nyandarua County has a reasonably stable rainfall pattern, which enables subsistence agriculture to be the main economic activity. However there are parts of the district that experience drier conditions. The dominant community in this county is Kikuyu, with other minority groups present especially in the towns. There are 6 SACCOs headquartered in

Nyandarua County with member base of 14,269 members.

1.5. Research Problem

Money saved or invested stands a greater chance of increasing to ensure the financial security of the family. Families' decision to or not to save, how much to save, the frequency of saving, where to save and the forms of saving they engage in are influenced by a multiplicity of factors. Knowledge about the available financial intermediation institutions, safety of the outlet, ease of accessibility, level of return among others are some of the factors that are likely to influence the saving and investment behaviour of families.

A number of studies have demonstrated that the investment and retirement saving behaviors of women and men differ. (Yuh & Hanna, 1997; Sunden & Surrette, 1998)Indeed the human capital theory postulates that women rationally choose to invest less than men in human capital, including education, skills, and on-the-job training, affecting women's employment opportunities, incomes, and ability to accumulate wealth Wu, (2005).

However, many economic researchers have focused on differences in income, poverty, and asset accumulation by gender. Inconsistencies in findings exist in the few studies conducted on the differences in general saving behaviors between men and women. For instance, (Sunden & Surrette, 1998) found that women are less likely to have a defined contribution retirement savings plan, while Agnew (2005) found the opposite. This creates a knowledge gap in literature on the saving culture behaviour across genders.

Women have lower incomes and wealth, on average, and are much more likely to be living in poverty during retirement, so it is important to better understand the factors related to saving among women and how these may differ from those of men. It is against this background that the researcher intends to carry out a study to establish gender differences in saving culture with a special bias on SACCO members.

1.6. General Objective

The main objective was to find out if there exists any significance gender difference in the saving culture among SACCO members in Nyandarua County.

2. Literature Review

2.1. Theoretical Framework

The study will review the life cycle theory, permanent income theory and relative income theory.

2.1.1. The Life Cycle Theory

The life cycle theory posits that the main motivation for saving is to accumulate resources for late expenditure and in particular to support consumption at habitual standard during retirement (Modigliani and Brumberg, 1954 and 1980). The basic idea in this theory is that individuals tend to distribute resources to smooth consumption over the life cycle. According to the model saving should be positive for household in their working span and negative for the retired ones and wealth therefore should be hump-shaped.

In the context of the current study, the life cycle theory is relevant in that it appreciates the importance of age in retirement planning. Age is one of the specific objectives in this study. The life cycle hypothesis has been utilized extensively to examine savings and retirement behaviour of older persons. This hypothesis begins with the observation that consumption needs and income are often unequal at various points in the life cycle. Younger people tend to have consumption needs that exceed their income. Their needs tend to be mainly for housing and education, and therefore they have little savings. In middle age, earnings generally rise, enabling debts accumulated earlier in life to be paid off and savings to be accumulated. Finally, in retirement, incomes decline and individuals consume out of previously accumulated savings.

2.1.2. The Permanent Income Theory

The permanent income theory states that people will spend money at a level consistent with their expected long term average income (Friedman, 1957). The level of expected long term income then becomes thought of as the level of "permanent" income that can safely be spent. A worker will only save if his or her current income is higher than the anticipated level of permanent income in order to guard against future declines in income. This theory is relevant to the current study because it considers a person's income as a determinant for their retirement planning. In Friedman's permanent income hypothesis model, the key determinant of consumption is an individual's real wealth, not his current real disposable income. Permanent income is determined by a consumer's assets; both physical (shares, bonds, property) and human (education and experience). These influence the consumer's ability to earn income. The consumer can then make an estimation of anticipated lifetime income.

2.1.3. Relative Income Hypothesis

Developed by James Duesenberry, the relative income hypothesis states that individual's attitude to consumption and saving is dictated more by his income in relation to others than by abstract standard of living. So an individual is less concerned with absolute level of consumption than by relative levels. The percentage of income consumed by an individual depends on his percentile position within the income distribution (Duesenberry, 1949).

Secondly it hypothesizes that the present consumption is not influenced merely by present levels of absolute and relative income, but also by levels of consumption attained in previous period. It is difficult for a family to reduce a level of consumption once attained (Blau & Kahn 2006). The aggregate ratio of consumption to income is assumed to depend on the level of present income relative to past peak income.

Relative income hypothesis has important economic implications. Perhaps the most obvious implication is that consumption creates negative externalities in the society, which are not taken into account in individual decision-making. According to Koçkesen et al., (2000) if individuals consume, and therefore work, to increase their status, then they will tend to work too much relative to the socially optimal level and hence income taxation could improve the social welfare. Men and women and varying consumption behaviour as such the relative income hypothesis is appropriate for this study

2.2. Importance of Saving

Salam and Kurlsam (2001) define savings as the difference between income and consumption. There is an inverse relationship between savings and consumption, other things being equal. Furthermore, the demographic characteristics of the population dictate the saving behaviour of a country (Schultz, 2004). Above all, income distribution is potentially an important factor that determines the capacity to save of the population. On the level of individual households, saving also plays a role as a protection mechanism against the vagaries of economic changes. According to Plessis (2008) such protection is of particular importance in developing economies, where governmental financial protection mechanisms are often lacking. Having cognizance of the importance of household saving as a contributor to a country's domestic saving (and therefore a factor in ensuring financial stability and growth) and as a shield for individual households, as well as the potential negative impact of consumerism on the inflation rate, the low African household saving rate is of significant concern.

Households' savings in financial institutions take the form of savings account, treasury bonds, corporate bonds, shares and stocks, mutual funds, cash value of life insurance, retirement plans and in non-financial assets such as land, houses, vehicles and other real property. Household savings in non-financial assets can be partly explained by the lower transaction costs of acquisition as compared to financial assets, and also households" perceptions that real assets have higher real rates of return as compared to bank deposits (Carpenter & Jensen, 2002). In addition, real assets can help households to hedge against domestic inflation (Kiiza & Pederson, 2002). Financial savings can be held in formal institutions such as banks, in semi-formal financial institutions such as Savings and Credit Cooperative Societies (SACCOs) and Micro Finance Institutions (MFIs), and in informal financial institutions such as rotating savings and credit institutions (ROSCAS). The place where savings are held has a great impact on their transformation into productive investments.

2.3. Influence of Gender on Personal Savings

A small but growing body of literature strongly suggests there are gender differences in saving decisions and in risk attitude, at least in some developed countries. Given their divergent social and economic circumstances within and outside the household, Floro and Seguino (2002) observe that women and men may have differing propensities to save at the household level. Since this constitutes the most significant component of gross domestic saves in many developing countries, changes in household saving critically influences aggregate saving rates. If so, shifts in women's relative bargaining power are likely to affect household saving rates, and by extension, domestic saving rates.

Women have experienced substantial labor market gains over the last half century. The gender gap in labor force participation and the gender gap in earnings have both declined. Several factors have been identified as contributing to these gains. First and foremost has been the reduction in the gender gap in education (Blau & Kahn 2006). Various technological innovations, such as the contraceptive pill, have favored women (Goldin & Katz 2002). Labor demand has shifted towards industries where female skills are overrepresented (Weinberg 2000, Black & Juhn 2000). According to (Black & Brainerd, 2004) better regulatory controls and greater competitiveness have reduced labor market discrimination against women

According to Fisher (2010), as single women live longer in retirement and may have lower earnings and fewer working years to accumulate retirement savings, it is critical to educate women on the importance of establishing a retirement plan. Financial advisors and employee retirement plan professionals need to advise single women with low risk tolerance on less risky investments that will allow them to save comfortably for retirement.

2.4. Empirical Review

Gender differences in personal saving behaviors among single person households were investigated using data from the 2007 Survey of Consumer Finances (SCF). Using logistic regression analysis, Fisher (2010) found that women were less likely to save in the short term if they were in poor health, but health made no difference for males. Women with low risk tolerance were less likely to save in the short term and to be regular savers. Education increased males' likelihood of saving in the short term and saving regularly. Mutyaba (2013) drew a comparison between the determinants of household discretionary savings in South Africa and China. The study as well investigated the effect of household savings on the stock market in South Africa and China. Empirical analysis was performed in order to determine the relationship between household savings and various variables, and the effect of household savings on the stock market. Money and quasi money (M2) is the only significant variable and having a negative relationship with household savings in South Africa yet in China, inertia is present the lagged household saving rate is significant. The regression results revealed significance of the explanatory variable household saving in South Africa and insignificance in China. Household savings have an effect on the level of stock market capitalization in South Africa but not in China.

Amu (2008) explored the savings and investment behaviour of rural families in the Ho Municipality of Ghana. The study found that the savings and investment among rural families in the municipality were low and rural households in the Municipality preferred informal forms of savings to the formal forms of savings. There was a negative correlation between age and savings as well investment. No significant relationship was found between family size and savings and investment; as well as knowledge in saving and investment as against actual savings and investment of the respondents. Inadequate income, over-reliance on natural conditions and other societal demands were found as constraints to respondents' investment, while inadequacy and fear of safety of income were constraints to their saving. The level of knowledge of respondents on savings and investment was also found to be low. The study concluded that rural households' low saving and investment is the result of economic, social and organizational factors.

Nieuwland (2013) sought to examine the role, if any, that the sex ratio plays as a determinant of the personal saving rate using a simple analysis of 33 countries. Results suggested that, when included in a model with other structural determinants, the sex ratio had a positive, statistically significant effect on the personal saving rate. Further, when examined by age cohort only the sex ratios of the older cohorts were found to be positively and significantly related to personal saving. According to the author, this result contradicts some of the current available theory on sex ratios and saving. Overall, it appears that the sex ratio does have a positive effect on the savings rate and should be included as a structural determinant in future saving rate analyses.

A Malawian study attempted to investigate factors that determine household savings in Malawi overtime. Lihiku (2006) found that the household savings function in Malawi has been unstable overtime and is influenced by factors like income, liabilities, dependence ratio, location and other demographic factors. Female and illiterate managed households are seen to save more on average than their counterparts. Amino et al (2003) they find that the rural Mozambican household saving decisions are responsive to income and amounts of assets owned by the households. They also found that the financial sector plays a crucial role by providing services that local people need. Aryeetey (2004) conducted a study in Ghana seeking to ascertain the assets kept by households and the relationship between choice of assets and the socio economic characteristics of rural households. The findings indicated that female headed households tended to concentrate more on non-farm enterprises while male headed households concentrated more on livestock. Women had more loans and fewer saving in their portfolio as compared to men, possibly due to more involvement in non-farm enterprises that required more capital.

In a study of household saving in Kenya, Njunge (2011) Results showed that savings is positively related to total income, gender and education but negatively to employment status, age and age squared of the household head. Being a male household head indicate that the household saving would increase by Kshs. 2,824.26 while being a female household head, the household saving would increase by Kshs. 13,047.4. Similarly Mukindia (2012) sought to determine the influence of social cultural factors on household savings among Maasai community in Transmara District, Narok County. According to the findings education plays a big role in influencing household savings. Gender also influences household savings; individual 'attitude also determines household savings and the household size determine the level of household savings. Mukhongo (2014) examined the rural household saving situation in Bungoma County with the ultimate goal of providing a tenable answer to the principal policy question of what are the determinants of rural household saving in Bungoma County. The study was organized around three. The framework for analysis involved the estimation of an extended saving model derived from the Permanent Income Hypothesis (Friedman, 1957). The study results indicated that permanent income, education level and wealth significantly contribute to rural household saving in Bungoma County. However, expenditure on children education and landholding significantly lead to negative rural household saving.

3. Research Methodology

3.1. Research Design

The research adopted a descriptive survey to gather data. Kombo and Tromp (2006) define a descriptive survey as a method of research which gathers data at a particular point in time with the intention of describing the nature of existing conditions of, or determining specific information. Kothari (2004) recommends descriptive design as it allows the researcher to describe, record, analyze and report conditions that exist or existed. The research questions were answered using a mixed method of study design. This involved collecting, analyzing and interpreting both qualitative and quantitative data in the same study or in a series of studies that investigate the same underlying phenomenon. It involved description of the data, in words and tables in order to demonstrate whether there is statistical relationship or merely descriptive in order to answer the research questions in the study.

3.2. Sampling Procedure and Sample Size

The choice of sample size is as important as is the choice of sampling scheme. This is because it determines the extent to which the researcher can make statistical or/ and analytical generalizations (Onwuegbuzie & Leech, 2004).

Krejcie (1970), in the table developed to determine the minimum return sample size for a given population size of 15,000 for a categorical data and a margin of error of 0.05 should yield a sample size of 375. To arrive at this sample, multi stage sampling procedure was used where sampling was done in stages.

(i) Stage I – Purposive Sampling

In the first stage Purposive Sampling was used. Purposive Sampling methods is based on some pre-determined characteristic where the researcher selects the sample subjectively based on this characteristic (Patton, 1990). Members of the six SACCOs were purposively selected for the study to form the sampling unit.

(ii) Stage II – Stratified Sampling

Stratified random sampling was used to sample SACCO members by gender to participate in the study. Stratified sampling technique is a method in which the researcher divides the entire target population into different sub-groups and then randomly selects the final subject proportionally from different sub-groups according to Kothari, (2006). The researcher chose this technique to give each gender equal chance of being selected and thus justifies generalizability of the findings. 39% and 61%

(iii) Stage III – Random Sampling

A random sampling technique was then used to select samples from each stratum to take in to considerations the differential gender representation among the SACCO members. Stratification by gender was done as shown in the Table 3.2; Of the 375 respondents, 146 were female and 229 male representing 39% and 61% respectively.

***Table 1.** Sampling Frame.*

SACCO	Target Population	Female	Male	Sample size
Nyala Vision SACCO	2,410	25	38	63
Muki SACCO	3,673	38	59	97
Olkalau SACCO	3,890	40	62	102
Jikaze SACCO	1,210	12	20	32
Taifa SACCO	1,765	18	28	46
Towers SACCO	1,321	14	21	35
Total	14,269	147	228	375

Source: County Co-operative officer, Nyandarua County, 2013

3.3. Data Collection Method

After the validity and reliability of the instruments were assessed, the researcher proceeded to the field. A permission letter to carry out the study in the area was sought from the National Council of Science and Technology. These letters helped the researcher to access the Organization, brief the head of operations on the purpose of the study and remove any important information by the managers. The researcher then sought to administer the questionnaires to the respondent and a drop and pick later method was used.

3.4. Data Analysis

Data collected from respondents was processed and analyzed. According to Kothari, (2004) this is essential for a scientific study and for ensuring that all relevant data for making contemplated comparisons and analysis are available. The process comprised of; editing which involved examination of raw data to detect errors and omissions in questionnaires and to make corrections where possible; coding which involved assigning numerals to answers so that responses can be classified into a limited number of categories appropriate to the research problem under consideration; classification which involved reducing the data into homogenous groups according to attributes or in class intervals; tabulation which is essentially displaying the data in compact form. A descriptive analysis of the data after processing involved computing mean, mode and median with the help of Statistical Package of Social Sciences Software (SPSS) and Microsoft Excel and presented in frequency tables and charts. Chi-square tests was used to identify relationships between age, income and marital status with saving culture while Mann-Whitney U test was employed in testing for gender differences in saving culture.

3.5. Analytical Model

Inferential statistics was used to analyse the collected data. Closed questions were analysed with the help of the Statistical Package for Social Science (SPSS) computer software by assigning numbers to responses. This is approved by Gliner and Morgan (2000) as they find it efficient and it gives straight formal analysis on practically all possible results. In this case, the following model was used to measure the relationship between the dependent variable and independent variable.

$$Y = f(X_1, X_2, X_3)$$

Where

Y= Saving Culture measure (Annual savings (KShs)

X_1 = Income levels

X_2= Marital status

X_3= Level of educations

The multiple regression equation assumes the form;

$Y = b_0 + b_1 X_1 + b_2 X_2 + b_3 X_3 + e : j = 1, 2, 3$

Where b_0= represent the y-intercept.

$b_j = j^{th}$ regression coefficient.

e = the random error

The magnitude of regression coefficient will help the researcher know the direction and magnitude of the relationship between the independent variables and the dependent variable.

4. Empirical Results and Discussion

4.1. Response Rate

A total of 375 questionnaires were distributed to the selected respondents in SACCO within Nyandarua County and the response rate was as shown in Table 2.

***Table 2.** Response Rate.*

SACCO	Targeted Sample size	Responses	Response rate (%)
Nyala Vision SACCO	63	63	100.0
Muki SACCO	97	76	78.4
Olkalau SACCO	102	100	98.0
Jikaze SACCO	32	30	93.8
Taifa SACCO	46	46	100.0
Towers SACCO	35	35	100.0
Total	375	350	93.3

A total of 350 questionnaires were duly filled and collected making a 93.3% response rate. This was an acceptable rate and could be attributed to the fact that the questionnaires were physically dropped to the respondents and collected at an agreed date.

4.2. Gender Versus Age Brackets

The study sought to find out the age bracket of respondents in terms of gender and the findings are shown in Table 3.

Table 3. *Gender versus Age Brackets.*

	Gender		
Age bracket	**Male**	**Female**	**Total**
21-30 years	22(10.4%)	26(18.8%)	48(13.7%)
31-40 years	60(28.3%)	58(42.0%)	118(33.7%)
41-50 years	58(27.4%)	30(21.7%)	88(25.1%)
Over 51 year	72(34.0%)	24(17.4%)	96(27.4%)
Total	212(60.6%)	138(39.4%)	350(100%)
Chi-square value=18.46	DF=3	P-value=0.001	

Table 3, shows that, 42% of the female respondents were aged 31-40 years while 28.3% were male in the same age brackets. About 60.6% of the respondents were male compared to 39.4% female. The findings found that there exist strong association between gender and age brackets. The Chi-square value is 18.46 with P-value of 0.001<0.05. This implies that the association is highly statistically significant with P-value less than 5% significant level. Gender factor influence age of respondents involved in saving in the SACCO.

4.3. Gender Versus Academic Qualification

The study sought to establish whether there is association between gender and education level and the findings are as shown in Table 4.

Table 4. *Gender versus Academic Qualification.*

	Gender		
Education level	**Male**	**Female**	**Total**
None	4(1.9%)	4(2.9%)	8(2.3%)
Primary	80(37.7%)	46(33.3%)	126(36.0%)
Secondary	98(46.2%)	64(46.4%)	48(46.3%)
College	26(12.3%)	22(15.9%)	48(13.7%)
Undergraduate	4(1.9%)	2(1.4%)	6(1.7%)
Total	212(60.6%)	138(39.4%)	350(100%)
Chi-square value=1.74	DF=4	P-value=0.783	

Table 4, shows that majority of the respondents (60.6%) were males compared to 39.4% of females. Indeed, 46.3% of the respondents had attained secondary school academic qualifications and less than 2% of the respondents had undergraduate qualifications. The study revealed that 2.9% of the female respondents had no formal qualifications. Also, the study found that there is no significant association between gender and education level. This is evident by the P-value of 0.783>0.05 significance level. In order the results to be statistically significant the significance level must be less that 5% allowable error, hence the results in this case are not statistically significant.

4.4. Gender Versus Marital Status

The study sought to establish any association between gender and marital status and the responses are as shown in Table 5.

Table 5. *Gender and Marital status.*

	Gender		
Marital status	**Male**	**Female**	**Total**
Single	16(7.6%)	34(24.6%)	50(14.4%)
Married	194(92.4%)	104(75.4%)	298(85.6%)
Total	210(60.3%)	138(39.7%)	348(100%)
Chi-square value=19.60	DF=1	P-value=0.001	

Table 5, indicates that majority of the respondents 85.6% were married compared to 14.4% who were single. The study found that there exist significant association between gender and marital status since the P-value is 0.001< 0.05 significance level. This implies that more married people come from one gender (male) and 24.6% of female's respondents were not married.

4.5. Gender Versus Monthly Income

The study sought to determine the average monthly income by the respondents and the findings are as shown in Table 6.

Table 6. *Gender and Monthly Income.*

	Gender		
Average Income	**Male**	**Female**	
Ksh 1,001-10,000	50(23.6%)	46(33.3%)	96(27.4%)
Ksh10,001-50,000	148(69.8%)	74(53.6%)	222(63.4%)
Ksh 50,001-100,000	8(3.8%)	18(13.0%)	26(7.4%)
Over Ksh 100,000	6(2.8%)	0(0%)	6(1.7%)
Total	210(60.6%)	138(39.4%)	348(100%)
Chi-square value=19.92	DF=3	P-value=0.001	

Table 6, indicate that majority of the respondents (63.4%) earn an average of 10,000-50,000 Kenya shillings. Only 1.7% of the respondents earn over Kshs 100,000. The study found that the average amount earn depends on the gender of the respondents. For instance, none of the female respondents earn more than Kshs 100,000. Also 33.3% of the respondents earn an average of 1,001- 10,000 Kenya shillings compare to 23.6% of the male respondents who earn the same amount. The results suggest that gender determine the amount earn by a person per month thus more males earn more than females working in the same institution. The P-value=0.001<0.05 suggest that there is association between gender and monthly income.

4.6. Gender Versus Duration of Saving

The study sought to find out the duration of savings by respondents in terms of gender and the finding are shown in Table 7.

As evident, there exist an association between gender and duration of saving. This implies that male respondents have saved many for a period more than 10 years compared to female respondents. This is supported by P-value=0.013<0.05 significance level. Also majority of the respondents (36%) have embraced saving having saved money for a period of

5-10 years. Most notably, only 1.4% of the female respondents have saved for a period of more than 10 years.

Table 7. *Gender and Duration of Saving.*

	Gender		
Duration of saving	**Male**	**Female**	**Total**
Less than a year	16(7.5%)	20(14.5%)	36(10.3%)
1-3 years	48(22.6%)	30(21.7%)	78(22.3%)
3-5 years	50(23.6%)	40(29.0%)	90(25.7%)
5-10 years	80(37.7%)	46(33.3%)	126(36.0%)
Over 10 years	18(8.5%)	2(1.4%)	20(5.7%)
Total	212(60.6%)	138(39.4%)	350(100%)
Chi-square value=12.60	DF=4	P-value=0.013	

4.7. Gender Versus Duration of Operating an Account

The study sought to establish whether there is association between gender and duration of operating an account and the findings are as shown in Table 8.

Table 8. *Gender and Duration of Operating an Account.*

	Gender		
Account operations durations	**Male**	**Female**	**Total**
Less than 1 year	12(6.8%)	20(18.5%)	32(11.3%)
1-3 years	56(31.8%)	20(18.5%)	75(26.8%)
3-5 years	52(29.5%)	32(29.6%)	84(29.6%)
5-10 years	50(28.4%)	34(31.5%)	84(29.6%)
Over 10 years	6(3.4%)	2(1.9%)	8(2.8%)
Total	176(62.0%)	108(38.0%)	284(100%)
Chi-square value=13.35	DF=4	P-value=0.001	

Table 8, indicates that majority of the respondents 59.2% have operated an account for a duration of 3-10 years. The study found that there exist significant association between gender and duration of operating an account since the P-value is 0.001< 0.05 significance level. This implies that duration of account operations depend more on the gender of the respondents.

4.8. Frequency of Saving

The study sought to establish the trend of saving by the respondents and the findings are as shown in the Figure 1.

This study found that majority of the respondents (over 50%) make monthly savings. However, only 1.9% of female respondents make daily savings. In general majority of the respondents have embraced the culture of saving with SACCO within the Nyandarua County.

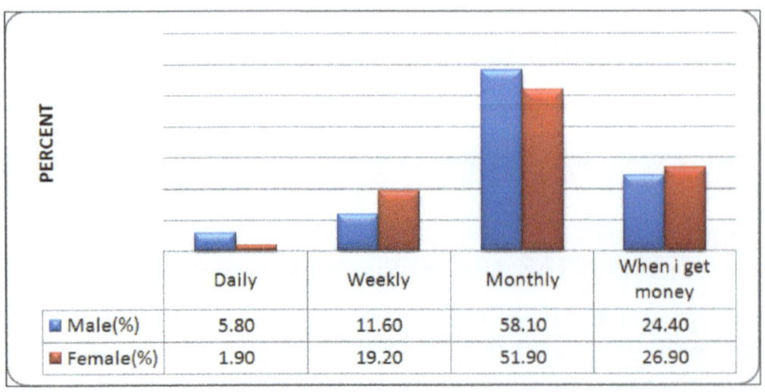

Figure 1. *How frequently saving is done by respondents.*

4.9. Average Annual Saving by the Respondents

This research further attempted to find out the average annual savings by the respondents (in terms of gender) annually and the findings are as shown in Table 9.

Table 9. *Average Annual Saving by the Respondents.*

	Gender		
Average annual saving	**Male**	**Female**	**Total**
Less Ksh1,000	0(.0%)	4(3.7%)	4(1.4%)
Ksh 1,000-10,000	40(23.3%)	20(18.5%)	60(21.4%)
Ksh10,001-50,000	68(39.5%)	34(31.5%)	102(36.4%)
Ksh 50,001-100,000	8(4.7%)	10(9.3%)	18(6.4%)
Over Ksh100,000	8(4.7%)	4(3.7%)	12(4.3%)
Depend on how much i have	48(27.9%)	36(33.3%)	84(30.0%)
Total	172(61.4%)	108(38.6%)	280(100%)
Chi-square value=11.23	DF=5	P-value=0.047	

In Table 9, it was found that, 36.4% of the respondents normally saved an average of 10,001-50,000 Kenya shillings annually with the SACCO in Nyandarua County. However, about 30% of the respondents said that the annual savings depends on how much their have. Furthermore, gender factor influence the average annual saving and results are statistically significant since the P-value = 0.047 <0.05 significance level. This implies that female respondents make more saving than male respondents and vice versus.

4.10. Financial Decisions

This research attempted to find out the maker of financial decisions by the respondents and the findings are as shown in Table 10.

Table 10. *Financial Decisions.*

	Gender		
Maker of financial decisions	**Male**	**Female**	**Total**
Myself	110(51.9%)	62(44.9%)	172(49.1%)
My spouse	2(0.9%)	22(15.9%)	24(6.9%)
Both	100(47.2%)	54(39.1%)	154(44.0%)
Total	212(60.6%)	138(39.4%)	350(100%)
Chi-square value=29.47	DF=2	P-value=0.001	

The study found that majority of the respondents (49.1%) makes their own financial decisions while 44% of the respondents' financial decisions are made by both parties. More importantly, gender factor influence financial decisions and the results are highly statistically significant since the P-value=0.001<0.05 significance level. The researcher is 99.999% confidence that financial decisions are based on the gender of the respondents.

4.11. Multiple Regression Model

The purpose of this study was to find out if there exists any significance gender difference in the saving culture among SACCO members in Nyandarua County. This was established by regressing income levels, marital status and education level. This section present the results of the analytical model with aim of establishing the predictive equation for this study and finding are shown in Table 11

Table 11. *Multiple Regression Model Results.*

Model	Unstandardized Coefficients		Standardized Coefficients	t	Sig.
	B	Std. Error	Beta		
(Constant)	3.642	.733		4.969	.000
Income levels	.355	.154	.139	2.299	.022
Marital status	-.543	.273	-.121	-1.990	.048
Education level	.052	.125	.025	.416	.678
R=0.844		R Squared=0.712		Adjusted R Square=0.701	

Table 11 shows that income levels influence average annual savings with a B value of 0.355 and a P-value of 0.022. This implies that an increase of income of the respondents led to an increase in annual saving. The results are statistically significant since P-value =0.022<0.05 significance level. In other word, the researcher is 99.978% confidence that any change in income level will affect annual savings. Marital status of the respondents was also found to be statistically significant in terms of the annual saving with a B value of -0.543 and a P-value of 0.048<0.05 significance level. This result implies that a change in marital status will affect the annual savings negatively. The researcher is 99.952% confidence that the change in marital status will negatively have an impact on annual saving by SACCO members in Nyandarua County. The study found that education level has no significant influence on average annual savings by SACCO members in Nyandarua County since the P-value=0.678>0.05 significance level. Therefore, education level variable will not be included in the predictive model. The predictive model is as follows;

$$\text{Annual savings} = 3.642 + 0.355\text{Income levels} - 0.543\text{Marital status}$$

The model as shown was modified to exclude the Education level variable. In general, the study found that 71.2% of the variation can be explained by predictors (Income levels and marital status) and the rest by the other factors beyond the control of the researcher. Further study can be commissioned to approve this finding.

5. Conclusions and Recommendations

5.1. Conclusions

The purpose of this study was to find out if there exists any significance gender difference in the saving culture among SACCO members in Nyandarua County. This was established by regressing income levels, marital status and education level.

The study found that majority of the respondents earns an average of 10,000-50,000 Kenya shillings. Most notably, 1.7% of the respondents earn over Kshs 100,000. Also, the study found that income levels influence average annual savings. This implies that an increase of income of the respondents led to an increase in annual saving. The results are statistically significant since P-value =0.022<0.05 significance level. In other word, the researcher is 99.978% confidence that any change in income level will affect annual savings.

Marital status of the respondents was also found to be statistically significant in terms of the annual saving. The result implies that a change in marital status will affect the annual savings negatively. The researcher is 99.952% confidence that the change in marital status will negatively have an impact on annual saving by SACCO members in Nyandarua County. The study found that majority of the respondents (49.1%) makes their own financial decisions while 44% of the respondents' financial decisions are made by both parties.

The study found that education level has no significant influence on average annual savings by SACCO members in Nyandarua County since the P-value=0.678>0.05 significance level. Therefore, education level has no significant impact on saving culture by the respondents.

In general, the study found that 71.2% of the variation can be explained by predictors (Income levels and marital status) and the rest by the other factors beyond the control of the researcher. Further study can be commissioned to approve this finding.

5.2. Recommendations

Based on the findings of this study the following recommendations were draw;

The study found that marital status influences the annual saving negatively. The study recommends nurturing of marriage institution as a way of protecting saving culture among women and men members of the SACCO in Nyandarua County.

The study found that education qualification has no significant influence on average annual savings by SACCO members in Nyandarua County. The researcher recommends sensitization of citizen to embrace saving culture. This can be done by the financial institution through public baraza's and educate citizen about important of saving for future use and emergencies cases.

Since the study found that some respondents normally saves money depending on how much they, the research recommend civic education to be conducted among the citizens and especially youth in order to embrace saving culture. Indeed, saving should be done by every account holder irrespective of how much they earn.

References

[1] Agnew, J., Szykman, L., Utkus, P., & Young, J. (2007). Literacy, Trust and 401 (K) Savings Behavior, Center for Retirement Research. Retrieved from https://institutional.vanguard.com/iip/pdfp.CCR Savings Behavior.pdf.

[2] Amino, A. et al, (2003). The Potential for Saving in the Rural Mozambican Households, Savings and Development, Quarterly Review, Issue No. 2

[3] Aryeetey, E. (2004). Household Asset Choice among the Rural Poor in Ghana. Paper presented at the 2004 author's workshop on "Understanding Poverty in Ghana", Institute of Statistical, Social and Economic Research, University of Ghana and Cornell University.

[4] Blau, Francine D. & Lawrence M. Kahn. (2006). The U.S. gender pay gap in the 1990s: Slowing convergence. Industrial and Labor Relations Review. 60(1): 45-66.

[5] Black, Sandra E. & Elizabeth Brainerd. (2004). The impact of globalization on gender discrimination. Industrial and Labor Relations Review. 57: 540(59).

[6] Browning, M. and Lusardi, A. (1996). Household Saving: Micro Theories and Micro facts, *Journal of Economic Literature,* 34(4), pp. 1797-1855.

[7] Carpenter, S., & Jensen, R. (2002). Household Participation in Formal and Informal Savings Mechanisms: Evidence from Pakistan, *Review of Development Economics*, 6(3), 314-328.bb.

[8] Duesenberry, J. S. (1949). Income, Saving and the Theory of Consumer Behaviour. Cambridge: Harvard University Press.

[9] Fisher, P. (2010). Gender differences in personal saving behaviors. *Journal of Financial Counseling and Planning Education*, 21'(1), pp. 14-24.

[10] Floro, M. S., & Seguino, S. (2002). Gender Effects on Aggregate Saving. *Gender and Development: Working Paper Series No. 23.*

[11] Goldin at el,. (2002). The power of the pill: Oral contraceptives and women's career and marriage decisions. Journal of Political Economy. 110(4): 730(770).

[12] Government of the Republic of Kenya. (1997). "Cooperatives in a Liberalized Economic Environment." Session Paper No.6. Nairobi, Kenya. June 1997.

[13] Keynes, J. M. (2006).the general theory of employment, interest and money, Atlantic Publishers & Distributors.

[14] Kiiza, B., & Pederson, G. (2002). Household Financial Savings Mobilization: Empirical Evidence from Uganda. *Journal of African Economies* 10(4), 390-409.

[15] Kombo, D.K., & Tromp, D.L. (2006). Proposal and Thesis Writing. Nairobi, Pauline.uwi.edu/pdf.

[16] Kothari, C. R. (2004). *Research Methodology.* New Delhi: Willy Eastern Limited.

[17] Koçkesen, Levent, Efe A. Ok, and Rajiv Sethi. 2000. The Strategic Advantage of Negatively Interdependent Preferences. *Journal of Economic Theory* 92 (2): 274-299.

[18] Lihiku, N. G. (2006). Determinants of savings in Malawi: a household level analysis. Lilongwe: University of Malawi.

[19] Lincoln,S et el(1985);Naturalistic Inquiry:Beverly Hills CA Sage Publications

[20] Mugenda, O. & Mugenda, A. (2003*).* Research methods: Quantitative and qualitative research. Nairobi: Nairobi acts press

[21] Mugenda, A. (2008). Social science research: Theory and principles. Nairobi: Kijabe Printing Press.

[22] Mugenda, A. & Mugenda, B. (2010) Research *Methods Quantitative and Qualitative Approaches.* Nairobi: ACTS Press.

[23] Mukhongo, W. (2014). *Determinants of Rural Household Savings in Bungoma County - Kenya.* Nairobi: Kenyatta University.

[24] Mukindia, S. M. (2012). Influence of socio-cultural factors on households savings among Maasai Community in Transmara District, *Narok County.* Nairobi: University of Nairobi.

[25] Mulino, F. R. D., & Chai, D. (2008). On the linkage between financial risk tolerance and risk aversion. Journal of Financial Research, 31(1), 1-23doi: 10.1111/j.1475-6803.2008.00229.x

[26] Nieuwland, J. (2013). Are Savings Sexy? The Role of the Sex Ratio as a Determinant of the Personal Saving Rate. Haverford: Haverford College.

[27] Njung'e, P. M. (2013). *Gender And Household Savings Behavior In.* Nairobi: University of Nairobi.

[28] Onwuegbuzie, A. J., & Collins, K. M. T. (2007). A typology of mixed methods samplingdesigns in social science research. The Qualitative Report, 12, 281-316. Retrievedfromhttp://www.nova.edu/ssss/QR/QR12-2/Onwuegbuzie2.pdf(35 Seiten)

[29] Orodho, A. & Kombo,D. (2005). *Research Methods.* Nairobi: Nairobi: Masola Publishers

[30] Patton, M. (1990). Qualitative evaluation and research methods (pp. 169-186). Beverly Hills, CA: Sage.

[31] Plessis, G. d. (2008). An exploration of the determinants of South Africa's personal savings rate: Why do South African households save so little? Pretoria: University of Pretoria.

[32] Schmidt, L., & Sevak, P. (2006).Gender, marriage, and asset accumulation in the United States. *Feminist Economics,12*(1), 139-166.

[33] Schultz, P. (2004), Demographic Determinants of Savings: Estimating and Interpreting the Aggregate Association in Asia, Centre Discussion Paper No. 901, Yale University.

[34] Strydom, P. (2007). Saving behaviour by South African households, *First National Bank,* 3.

[35] Sunden, A. E., &Surrette, B. J. (1998). Gender differences in the allocation of assets in retirement savings plans. American Economic Review, 88, 207-211.

[36] Tesar, L. L. (1991). Savings, investment and international capital flows, *Journal of International Economics,* 31(1–2), pp. 55-78.

[37] Weinberg, Bruce A. 2000. Computer use and the demand for female workers. Industrial and Labor Relations Review. 53: 290{308.

[38] Williams, M., Tutty, L.M., & Grinnell, R.M., Jr. (1995). Research in social work (2nd ed.). Itasca, IL: F.E. Peacock.

[39] Wu, K. (2005). *The material consequences of how socialsecurity keeps older persons out of poverty across developed countries*. Luxembourg Income Study Working Paper Series.

[40] Yuh, Y., & Hanna, S. (1997). The Demand for Risky Asset in Retirement Portfolios. Proceedings of the Academy of Financial Services.

4

Governance, Employee Engagement and Improved Productivity in the Public Sector: The Nigerian Experience

Nkogbu Godfrey Oshilim[1], Offia Patience Akpesiri[2]

[1]Human Resource/Administration Department, Odogun Nigeria Limited, Warri, Nigeria
[2]Library Department, College of Education, Warri, Delta State, Nigeria

Email address:
nkogbugodfrey@yahoo.com (N. G. Oshilim), offiap@yahoo.com (O. P. Akpesiri)

Abstract: This paper examines governance, employee engagement and productivity in the Nigerian public sector. Amidst the high expectations of the citizenry from the new administration of the 6th republic in the Nigerian civilian administration, the reality on ground at the commencement of the new administration in the 6th Republic calls for questions raised by governance in the past administration and consequently employee engagement in the Nigerian public sector as well as its impact on organizational productivity. Owing to the declining level of employee engagement and productivity in the Nigerian public sector, the paper concludes that for productivity to improve in the public sector and for employee engagement to occur, the three Hs (Head, Heart and Hand) of the employee must be effectively engaged in addition to the provision of good governance by government.

Keywords: Engagement, Employee Engagement, Governance, Productivity, Public Sector

1. Introduction

The clamour for massive *"CHANGE"* in governance greeted the Nigerian democratic atmosphere during the 2015 electioneering campaigns under the auspices of the All Progressive Congress (APC). This clamour became a reality when on March 28th, 2015 the APC's presidential candidate, Muhammadu Buhari emerged victorious at the polls with 15,424,921 votes (52.4%) to defeat Dr. Goodluck Ebele Jonathan of the Peoples Democratic Party (PDP) having 12,853,162 votes (43.7%). This change also saw the APC's candidates winning victories at the gubernatorial, national assembly and states houses of assembly elections. Thus APC became the dominant political party in Nigeria in the 6th republic displacing the Peoples Democratic Party which was the dominant political party in Nigeria during the second to fifth republics.

One might be prompted to ask, why the slogan for 'CHANGE' by the APC? What does the word "CHANGE" means to the uneducated citizens, Nigerians in general and to the party members of APC? Does it mean the entrance of new personalities into the arena of politics and governance? Does it connote the giving of opportunities to the youths to participate in governance? Does it mean the ending of the recycling of old politicians as well as former leaders in the political system of governance? Does it mean the cross carpeting of members from PDP to APC? Or could it be an innovative way towards the governance of the masses? As observers observed, "let's watch what they will do since most of the people in APC were former members of PDP.

In Nigeria, as in most other countries of the world, the attention from citizens has placed more demands on government than ever before (G.O. Nkogbu, 2015). Government's responsibilities as the largest employer of labour and also towards her citizenry is becoming more complex and demanding as a result of the high expectations of the citizenry for quality services amidst the global economic recession characterized by fall in the crude oil prices, and the mono-economy she is operating.

Issues in governance, employee engagement and public sector productivity in the public sector have attracted and is still attracting the attention of all organizational stakeholders in both the public and private sectors. This is as a result of the interaction of the forces of corruption, inappropriate behaviour of political office holders, globalization, advancement in knowledge and technology, the unpredictability of human behavior when given opportunities in the governance of a constitueny, insatiable needs of employees, coupled with the constant changes that accompany organizational operations. Within this premise, A. Ighoro (2014) posited that Human Resource (HR) practitioners as well as other relevant organizational stakeholders must position their organizations to stay alive and thus managing employees would require high level of knowledge, deft skills, strategic planning and concerted efforts.

Employee engagement has generated a great deal of interest in recent years as a widely used term in organizations, amongst HR practitioners/consulting firms and recently the academia (W. Macey and B. Scheider, 2008; S. Markos and M.S. Sridevi, 2010). Credible evidence points towards an engagement-profit linkage (C. Coffman, 2000; C. Coffman and G. Gonzalez-Molina, 2002; Hewitt Associates, 2004; R. Heintzman and B. Marson, 2005; M. Czarnowsky, 2008; Right Management, 2009; S. Markos and M.S. Sridevi, 2010; AonHewitt, 2013).

During and after economic disruptions, the way businesses react to economic cycles often predict how well they succeed or they will survive. At such turbulent times and uncertainty, many organizations have been less focused on how to manage their talents and engage their employees, rather they focus on how to reduce costs by cutting salaries, bonuses, rewards and other related employee development costs. Some shortsighted leaders may even think that employee engagement no longer matters because of their need for job security. In the Nigerian scenario, the maxim "a bird in the hand is worth two in the bush" best illustrates this position. However, smart leaders realize that while they need to find short-term solutions to cut costs, they must also identify longer-term talent management strategies to remain viable.

In the past years, Nigerians have been calling for improvement in public service delivery. Pressures for public organizational productivity have been further aggravated by limited resources, wide spread poverty, unemployment, failed infrastructures, high rate of corruption, and high cost of public services, etc. (G.O. Nkogbu, 2015). As noted by various scholars, "an organization cannot perform better than the quality of its workforce" and that "the employees cannot be productive more than the level of knowledge, skills, training, abilities they have".

The dwindling rate of performance in Nigerian public organizations demands some attention to the curious minded people. Of a concern are poor performance, declining productivity, low rate of employee engagement and the behavioural attitude of the bureaucratic system and public/civil servants. Could this be attributed to the maxim, "government's job is no man's job", and "you don't carry government's job on your head but on your shoulder'? This attitude is very obvious in Nigerian public sector organizations.

Despite various government interventions and efforts, the Nigerian public sector score-card has remained a subject of discuss among the academia of public administration and management as well as the curious minded citizens as a result of poor performance and inefficiency in the face of abundant natural and human resources. Reasons given for the massive purge or dismissal of an estimated 10,000 public officers in 1975 were alleged inefficiency, old age, declining productivity, and doubtful probity (A. Adebayo, 2004).

On a sad note, the 6th republic was greeted with obvious failure in governance by the previous administration as the gross financial mismanagement of the Nigerian economy became obvious. Across the federation and in various states, the new administration met little or no funds to commence the conduct of government businesses/functions. What a pitiable situation! Worse still, the previous administration have told the world and Nigerian that the Nigerian economy is booming. What a lie! Profile of Nigerian external debts skyrocketed to the tune of over $60 billion. Who is to account for this? Worst still, across the states of the federation, most public and civil servants were being owed several months of salaries. It is within this premise that the new president, Muhammadu Buhari, asserts that "if Nigeria does not kill corruption, corruption will kill Nigeria".

The above scenario calls for leadership accountability and an examination of governance in a democratic dispensation. Closely associated with this is the issue of employee engagement and productivity in the Nigerian public sector. How can one be meaningfully engaged when he/she has not been paid rewards for his/her labour for several months? How can one be productive seeing the gross mismanagement of funds? How can productivity be recorded when the organizational environment is not conducive? This scenario therefore lends credence to the saying by public/civil servants that "government job is no man's job", "don't carry government job on your shoulder", thus implying 'don't be too committed in government's job'.

The effect of governance on employee engagement and productivity in the public sector can be examined from the activities and actions of the political class over a country's public service. In developing countries, political corruption amongst other factors has resulted in declining level of employee engagement as well as decline in productivity in the public service. It is against this background that this paper seeks to examine governance, employee engagement and improved productivity in the public sector in Nigeria.

2. Operationalization of Concepts

a) Political Corruption: According to the Encyclopedia Americana (2004), political corruption takes place at the highest levels of political authority. It occurs when the politicians and the political decision-makers, who are entitled to formulate, establish and implement the laws in the name of the people are enriching themselves or further their cause and/or any other person at the expense of the public, in contravention of their oath of office and/or contrary to the laws that are in force. It also takes place when policy formulation and legislation are tailored to benefit politicians and legislators. Political corruption is sometimes similar to the corruption of greed as it affects the shoddy manner in which decisions are made, political institutions are manipulated, and rules of procedure are abandoned as well as the distortion and/or destruction of the institutions of government (O.O. Ogunbonna, 2009).

b) Public Sector: Public sector, as a concept, is used to describe the organizations, institutions, and departments of the State which are saddled with the responsibilities and functions of implementing the policies and programmes of government. It is an extension of the executive arm of government, whose personnel perform purely administrative and executive duties (N.P. Ibeme, 2013). In other words, public sector is an organization which is made up of Ministries, Departments and Agencies (MDAs) of government.

c) Public Service: Public service connotes the civil service of the federation and the state as well as the public services of the federation and of the states. It encompasses the federal and state civil services, local government, the Nigeria police, armed forces, judiciary, legislature, educational institutions established or financed mainly by federal and/or state governments, statutory corporations of the federal and state governments, companies or enterprises with full or majority ownership by either the federal or state government. Thus, the public service refers to all organizations that exist as part of government machinery for implementing policy decisions and delivering services that are of value to the citizenry.

The concept of public service as established by the Nigerian Constitution is provided for in sections 169,206, and 318 and in section 10 of the Third schedule of the 1999 constitution. T. Olaopa (2008) observed that though the constitutional provisions do not recognize the term "The Nigerian Public Service", the constitution only recognizes the Public Service of the Federation at the federal, state and local government levels.

d) Productivity: To Ulrich (1997), as cited in S. Bukar and A. B. Shehu and A. Idris (2012), productivity refers to a ratio of output to input. According to him, input may include labour hours or costs, production costs and equipment costs while output may consist of sales, earnings, and market shares. Productivity means the relationship between output and all factors of production required to achieve it (F. Ojo, 2006). J. Prokopenko (1996) defined productivity as the relationship between the output generated by a production or service system and the input provided to create this output.

According to D. A. Neugarten (1987), productivity is defined from three major perspectives that dominate the field: the economic, the industrial engineering, and the administrative. To the economists, productivity means more yield to the society which must be obtained from present resources and that efficient resource use is therefore paramount. Industrial engineers, on defining productivity, focus on work measurement and performance standards and tend to focus their efforts on those factors which are operational and quantifiable. As per productivity to the administrator, they are more concerned with organizational effectiveness than with the society.

To Menon (1956) as cited in C. Obisi (2005), productivity means an organized mass attack on waste of every type and in every sphere. Thus, it implies development of an attitude of mind and a constant urge to find better, cheaper, quicker, easier and safer ways of doing a job, providing service, and manufacturing an article. It aims at the optimum utilization of the available resources to yielding as many goods and services as possible at the lowest possible cost.

The above views on productivity implies that productivity ranges from efficiency, to effectiveness, to rates of turnover and absenteeism, to output measures, to measures of client or customer satisfaction, to intangibles such as disruption in the workflow and to further intangibles such as morale, loyalty and job satisfaction.

e) Engagement: To D. Zinger (2014), engagement boils down to an employee's passion and commitment to the organization and their job and the drive to deliver the organization's objectives, going the extra mile. According to him, engagement is about emotion, behavior and relationships and that engaged employees have pride in their job and the organization.

Right Management (2009) defined engagement using four definitive factors: commitment to the job and organization; pride in the job and in the organization; willingness to advocate the benefits and advantages of the job and organization; and satisfaction with the job and organization. They concluded that engagement can be described as the degree of employee-organization alignment.

N.P. Rothbard in 2001 described engagement as a psychological presence with two key mechanisms, attention and absorption. Attention is "cognitive ability and the amount of time one spends thinking about a role" and absorption is "being engrossed in a role and refers to the intensity of one's focus on a role" (A.M. Saks, 2006). An engaged employee is a person who is fully involved in, and enthusiastic about, his or her work (G.H. Seijts and D. Crim, 2006). Tim Rutledge in his book "*Getting Engaged: The New Workplace Loyalty*" explained that truly engaged employees are attracted to, and inspired by, their work ("I want to do this"), committed ("I am dedicated to the success of what I am doing"), and fascinated ("I love what I am doing"). Engaged employees, to him, care about the future of the company and are willing to invest discretionary effort-exceeding duty's call- to see that the organization succeed.

The Royal Bank of Scotland (2005) defined engagement as the state of emotional and intellectual commitment to the group and lists the components as satisfaction (how much I like working here), commitment (how much I want to be here) and performance (how much I want to actually do in achieving results).

D. Robinson (2004) defined engagement as a positive attitude held by the employee towards the organization and its values. An engaged employee is aware of business context, and works with colleagues to improve performance within the job for the benefit of the organization. Similarly, W. Kahn (1990) defined engagement as, "the harnessing of organization members' selves to their work roles. In engagement, people employ and express themselves physically, cognitively, and emotionally during role performances."

f) Employee Engagement: Dell Inc. defines employee engagement by stating, "to compete today, companies need to win over the minds (rational commitment) and the hearts (emotional commitment) of employees in ways that lead to extraordinary effort" (R.J. Vance, 2006). The Corporate Leadership Council (2004) defined employee engagement as the extent to which employees commit-both rationally and emotionally- to something or someone in their organization, how they work, and how long they stay as a result of that commitment.

Gallup organization defines employee engagement as the involvement with and enthusiasm for work. They posited that engaged employees are those who "work with a passion and feel a profound connection to their company" and "drive innovation and move the company forward" (GMJ, 2006). Gallup as cited in D. Dernovsek (2008) likens employee engagement to a positive employees' emotional attachment and employee's commitment.

Employee engagement refers to the individual's involvement and satisfaction with as well as enthusiasm for work (J. K. Harter, F.L. Schimdt, and T.L. Hayes, 2002). Employee engagement is a persistent, positive affective-motivational state of fulfillment in employees characterized by high levels of activation and pleasure (C. Maslach, W.B. Schaufeli and M.P. Leiter, 2001). In the same vein, A.M. Saks (2006) conceptualized employee engagement as "a distinct and unique construct that consists of cognitive, emotional and behavioural components that are associated with individual role performance". Commenting on employee engagement, M. Czarnowsky (2008) posited that (engaged) employees are mentally and emotionally invested in their work and in contributing to their employer's success.

K. Shaw (2005) defined employee engagement as "translating employee potential into employee performance and business success and thus "changing the way employees perform by utilizing the tools in the armory of internal communication professionals". According to Shaw, the International Survey research (ISR) refers to engagement as being "a combination of an employee's cognitive (think), affective (feel) and behaviour (act) commitment to a company" and they refer to these constructs-affective, cognitive and behaviour- as making up engagement and not as antecedents or precursors to engagement.

Employee engagement can be considered as cognitive, emotional and behavioural (A.M. Konrad, 2006). Cognitive engagement refers to employees' belief about the company, its leaders and the workplace culture. The emotional aspect of engagement is how employees feel about the company, the leaders and their colleagues. The behavioural aspect of engagement is the value-added component reflected in the amount of effort employees put into their work-e.g. brainpower, extra time and energy.

g) Governance: The concept of governance connotes the process of managing the affairs of a state. According to the International Encyclopedia of the Social Sciences, governance is the art of exercising of legitimate authority, and protecting and adapting the community by making and carrying out decisions.

h) Government: It is the instrument of the state by which its existence is maintained, its functions carried out and its policies and objectives are realized.

3. Indicators of Lack of Employee Engagement

According to G.O. Nkogbu (2015), some indicators of lack or low level of employee engagement include:

1. Lack of interest in work.
2. Carelessness.
3. Wastage of resources and materials.
4. Employees not accepting any responsibility for their work.
5. Decline productivity and profitability.
6. Loss of man-hour/time.
7. High rate of absenteeism.
8. High rate of employee turnover.
9. Employees show up for work, did what they were told to do, and, at the end of their shift, went home, the same routine would be repeated the next day.
10. Missed commitments met with excuses, explanations, rationalizations, and finger-pointing rather than a rigorous and energetic desire to ownership for what went wrong.
11. Employees don't speak up even when they know things are not being dealt with honestly and directly because of fear of cynicism.
12. Problems discussed and debated endlessly, with little lasting improvement from repeated attempts at solution.
13. Initiatives to improve organizational performance progressively slowly or stalling altogether, despite sizeable investments in resources and technology.
14. When people complain about how busy they are

rather than doing what needs to be done, or complain about the unreasonableness of a leader's expectations. Avoiding rather than taking responsibility.

4. An Overview of Productivity in the Nigerian Public Sector

R.R. Nordstrom, T. Lewinson and R.V. Hall (1987) contends that there is a public perception that public employees tend to be complacent and lazy. The questions agitating the minds of most Nigerian scholars, industrialists, leaders in public and private sector organizations as well as the general public about the productivity question include: What is happening? What can we do? How could it be done? Who has to do it? When will it be done?

Nwachukwu (2004) as cited in P.V.C Okoye and R.A. Ezejiofor (2013), identified four major factors of low productivity in the Nigerian public sector. They include:

1. Economic factor: This deals with the reward system of employees in the Nigerian public sector. There is no correlation between efforts spent by an employee and the rewards that he received in the organization. To encourage higher productivity, it is essential that a system of rewards must be designed that attempts to equate hard work and rewards.
2. Sociological factor: This deals with a situation where employees have a sense of belonging in an organization and resist any efforts on the part of management to perceive and treat them only as cost of production.
3. Management factor: He opined that the success or failure of an organization depends solely on the management. An unproductive and undisciplined supervisor can hardly motivate employees. The study conducted shows that in public sector low productivity arises due to managers' unwillingness to manage effectively.
4. Technological factor: This involves the use of new ideas, techniques, innovation, methods and materials to achieve organizational objectives. The lack of proper information to help entrepreneurs select the appropriate technology is one of the major causes of low productivity.

G.O Nkogbu (2015) identified some symptoms of low productivity in the Nigerian public sector to include tardiness, poor quality of service, absenteeism, loss of man-hours during strikes, lots of grievances among public/civil servants, etc.

To deal with problems of low productivity within the country's labour force, there was the establishment of the National Productivity Centre (NPC) in 1987. The aim of setting up this establishment was to tackle the problem of low productivity in the Nigerian economy. It was observed that the NPC established Productivity Improvement Schemes (PIS) in six organizations, comprising the Kaduna Water Board, NIPOST, NITEL, Star Mills, Inlets and West African Portland Cement. The PIS is a mechanism for identifying productivity related problems and developing techniques for solving them, especially for increasing the contributions of human and other resources to productivity.

4.1. Factors Impeding Productivity in the Nigerian Public Sector

Under the factors impeding productivity in the Nigerian public sector, G.O. Nkogbu (2015) used the *PESTLE* model in classifying the factors. PESTLE is a mnemonic where each of the letters stand for different factors affecting organizational productivity in the Nigerian Public Sector.

1. Political factors: This covers the attitudes and actions of legislators, political executives and government officials which affect productivity. It also includes the pressure exerted on the public service by political actors. It is no doubt that public service organizations are very much influenced by politics at the federal, state and local levels. Examples of political factors include retrenchment phenomenon, recruitment methods, and problem of corruption or graft.
2. Economic factors: This factor entails looking out into the organization in terms of the resources which it consumes and the economy outlook. For instance, the fluctuations of the price of crude oil in the international oil market do affect the public service in terms of financial constraints on the government. Economic factors include failure or financial constraints and/or inability to procure needed working materials; tax policy effect, which reduces the take-home pay of workers; high cost of personnel; and none or irregular payment of wages and salaries.
3. Social factors: The social factors is made up of the attitude, desires, expectations, degrees of intelligence and education, beliefs, and customs of people in a given group or society. Social factors also include lack of regard for client convenience; poor attitude of attention to clients/service consumers; attitude of public/service workers towards "tips", "kickbacks", "bribe" for the performance of their legitimate function(s); lack of respect for time; and poverty.
4. Technological factors: It refers to the sum total of knowledge we have of ways to do things. It includes inventions, techniques, etc. Its main influence is on ways of doing things, on how to design, produce, distribute and render services at a greater effectiveness and efficiency. Technological factors further include lack of equipment and working tools; poor maintenance culture of plants, equipment and technical machines; resistance to adoption of innovative ways of doing things, i.e., preference for the status quo.
5. Legal factors: It refers to the laws and regulations of government and the work environment. Example of legal factor includes excessively detailed regulations and procedural routines-bureaucracy.
6. Environmental or ecological factors: It refers to the work environment of organizations and the behaviour of the workers as well as the organization's system.

Examples of environmental or ecological factors include ineffective management system and method of supervision; poor communication; lack of respect for time; lateness to work; and absenteeism.

4.2. Improving Productivity in the Public Sector

According to G.O Nkogbu (2015), improving productivity implies making a commitment to capital investments that might not have immediate payoffs. It also means to increase the ratio of the quality and quantity of services provided to the resources consumed.

Productivity improvement-the production of more and/or better services for each tax naira and man-hour invested- has been an especially attractive strategy for many governments facing tight or shrinking resources (J.M. Greiner, 1992).The fundamental challenge for contemporary public managers is no mystery: how to do more (or almost as much) with less. Productivity is a concern that knows no boundaries. The private sector has productivity problems of its own, too. As B. Bozeman (1992) observed, productivity problems can't be solved by alchemy, wizardry or the quick fix. The key to doing more with less lies in how it is done. More effective management can do much to enhance productivity in government and business. Herein lies the impact of human capital as well as its development.

According to D.F. Kettl (1992), public managers are concerned with the development of strategies for efficiently and effectively overseeing their MDAs; build political support, both inside and outside the MDAs; and maintaining of the MDAs health-its organizational capacity and credibility- and obtain needed resources especially funding, personnel, legislation and favourable constituencies.

In furtherance of improving productivity, D.A. Neugarten (2008) and C. Obisi (2005) recommended that the under listed measures should be pursued.

1. Continued research in at least three distinct areas: one is research devoted to developing better indicators of performance-for people, for programmes and for organizations. This implies further development of performance standards and norms, including qualitative measures of performance outcomes. Second is research devoted to examining the implications of increased productivity on the budgetary process. Third is research devoted to the application of behavioural science knowledge to worker productivity.
2. Encouraging and supporting different kinds of demonstration projects and experiments.
3. Heavier capital investments in technology.
4. Establishment of a central information and referral bank.
5. Labour must participate in management.
6. There should be mutual trust and cooperation between employer and employee.
7. Workers should be assured that automation and technology would not displace them.
8. Maintenance of proper communication channel.
9. Proper training and development of workers.
10. Proper equipment be provided and plant maintenance be carried out.
11. Good working conditions and adequate safety measures in the work environment.

Improving productivity in public sector organizations is a shared responsibility among the employees (staff), the general public, elected representatives of the people, and line managers and supervisors (S. Aina, 2005). Thus the stakeholders of productivity in the Nigerian public sector include the public/civil servants (employees/staff of government organizations), political system (elected representatives of the people), organizational management (Chief Executives, Line Managers, Departmental/Divisional Heads, Supervisors), clients/service customers or consumers, and the general public(Civil societies, mass media).

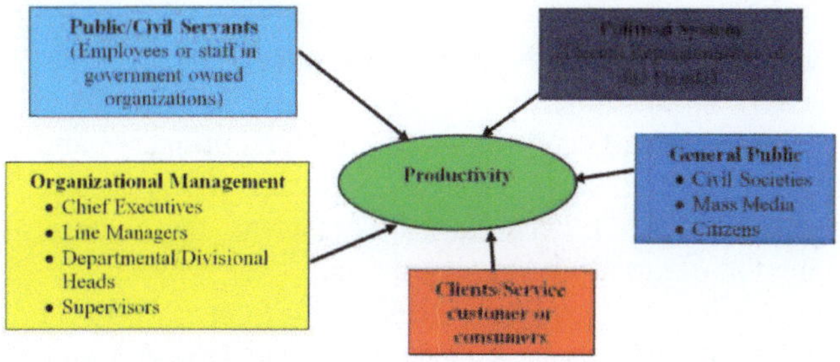

Source: G.O. Nkogbu (2015).

Figure 4.1. *Conceptualized Model of Stakeholders of Productivity in the Nigerian Public Sector.*

4.3. Methods of Productivity Improvement Adopted in the Nigerian Public Sector

In the Nigerian public sector, the under listed methods have been adopted towards improving productivity in different administrations.

1. Downsizing: It entails reductions in size of activity by an organization to boost Return on Investment (ROI) and reduce cost. It may increase the organization's value by reducing the number of employees to increase labour productivity, by closing down or selling off excess of obsolete production establishments.
2. Rightsizing: It entails the process of reducing the number of levels between the least employee and the chief executive in the organization. Its objective is to reduce time lag in decision making, encourage and empower prompt communication and action within the business. Critical path and prompt analysis of each action required to produce the desired result is laid out and the number of people required to do the job is clearly identified and the surplus eliminated.
3. Outsourcing: It is an approach whereby previously internally-produced components are contracted out to external organization/suppliers to allow the firm concentrate its resources, time, and personnel on its core activities. This enables the organization to obtain expert services as and when required without having

those rendering those skilled services on the payroll of the organization as full time employees.

4. Total Quality Management (TQM): It is a process whereby all employees are made to understand how their roles contribute to the process of production of goods and services.
5. Re-Engineering: It is the radical redesign of a company's business process. It seeks breakthrough not by enhancing existing processes but by discarding them and replacing them with new ones.
6. Technology Improvement.

5. Governance and Accountability in Nigeria

There is a general opinion that most of the public enterprises have failed to deliver on the purposes for which they were established. Political corruption, management ineffectiveness and inefficiency, low level of employee engagement have been advanced by practitioners and researchers as the bane of the Nigerian public sector (G.O.Nkogbu, 2015). The former president of Nigeria, Olusegun Obasanjo (2003) observed that:

> Nigerians have too long been feeling short-changed by the quality of public service. Our public offices have too long been showcases for combined evils of inefficiency and corruption, whilst being impediments for effective implementation of government policies. Nigerians deserve better and we will ensure they get what is better.

In a similar vein, Agagu (2008) asserts that:

> The public service which was seen as the custodian of rules and regulations and the engine of development had lost its prestige and confidence. The aftermath of this is the invention of series of reforms which, have led to privatization, downsizing and right-sizing of the public service and even minimizing the role of the public sector in the national life.

Nigeria, the 6th largest oil producing nation of the world, with a population of over 170 million is richly endowed with all kinds of natural and human resources. Yet, the standard of living of most Nigerians has left much to be desired of governance. This show that there is a missing link between governance, the government and the governed. The Human Development report of 2013 does not tell well of Nigeria as a nation. In this report, Nigeria is ranked 153rd out of 186 countries and is categorized under low development countries; 17.8% of Nigerian population is vulnerable to poverty; 33.9% of her population is in severe poverty; 54.7% of Nigerians live below the national poverty line; and 68% of Nigerians live below $1.25 a day under the multidimensional poverty index (HDR, 2013).

The need for accountability in governance and the increasing government involvement in various economic ventures in the economy makes accountability by political and public office holders necessary if one is to avoid a repeat of Mobutu, Ferdinand or General Sani Abacha type of government of plundering the treasury and impoverishing the poor.

Accountability for actions by public office holders was made insistent in the political and economic history of developed countries. According to O.O. Ogunbona (2009), only a few African heads of government like Leopold Senghor of Senegal, Kwame Nkrumah of Ghana, Julius Nyerere of Tanzania and Chief Obafemi Awolowo of Nigeria were up to the responsibility of being accountable to the public both in the use of power and government funds.

Kinds of Accountability

Mandatory Accountability: This is a type of accountability where constitutional, conventional or legal provisions and measures are put in place to ensure that those exercising authority over the use of public resources are made to answer to the people's wishes, failing, which the people, if they so desire can remove them from office.

Discretionary Accountability: This type of accountability also known as voluntary accountability exist where those who exercise political as well as administrative power take action based on the people's wishes in accordance with political ideological commitments or on grounds of morality rather than on grounds of law or constitutionalism or as a result of scale of preference determined by the people in a democratic manner. A. Sen (2004) referred to "the commitment to ideology which extracts a minimum standard of behaviour and performance from the government" as "political commitment of the system". According to him, a typical example is the response of the Chinese and Indian governments toward the issues of hunger and famine.

In Nigeria, the depth and severity of non-accountability and non-transparency in governance was heightened during the 5th republic. It was more evident as it was experienced across the local, states and federal governments. This situation makes it very uneasy for the new administration in the 6th republic to take-off effectively as the previous administration according to reports emptied the treasury of federal and state governments thus making little or no funds for the new administration to commence business successfully. Furthermore, the issues of federal and state governments owing several months of salaries of public and civil servants makes it very challenging. Worse still, this scenario have an impact on employee engagement.

Below is a table showing the debt profile of states of Nigeria as at April, 2015.

Table 5.1. *Table showing debt profile of states in Nigeria.*

South-East Geo-Political Zone			
S/N	**STATES**	**DEBT ($Million)**	**DEBT (in ₦Billion)**
1	Abia	33,791	6,758
2	Anambra	45,155	9,031
3	Ebonyi	45,411	9,082
4	Enugu	68,929	13,786
5	Imo	52,950	10,590
	TOTAL	246,235	49,247

South-South Geo-Political Zone			
S/N	STATES	DEBT ($Million)	DEBT (in ₦Billion)
1	Akwa Ibom	58,887	11,777
2	Bayelsa	34,832	6,966
3	Cross River	141,470	28,294
4	Delta	24,234	4,847
5	Edo	123,128	24,626
6	Rivers	44,725	8,945
	TOTAL	427,276	85,455
South-West Geo-Political Zone			
S/N	STATES	DEBT ($Million)	DEBT (in ₦Billion)
1	Ekiti	46,453	9,291
2	Lagos	1,169,713	233,943
3	Ogun	109,155	21,831
4	Ondo	52,689	10,538
5	Osun	74,053	14,811
	Oyo	72,351	14,470
	TOTAL	1,524,413	304,883
North-Central Geo-Political Zone			
S/N	STATES	DEBT ($Million)	DEBT (in ₦Billion)
1	Benue	33,074	6,615
2	FCT	36,636	7,327
3	Kogi	35,788	7,158
4	Kwara	52,722	10,544
5	Nassarawa	49,943	9,989
6	Niger	44,750	8,950
7	Plateau	30,948	6,190
	TOTAL	283,861	56,772
North-East Geo-Political Zone			
S/N	STATES	DEBT ($Million)	DEBT (in ₦Billion)
1	Adamawa	46,775	9,355
2	Bauchi	87,572	17,514
3	Borno	23,068	4,614
4	Gombe	39,546	7,909
5	Taraba	22,780	4,556
6	Yobe	31,238	6,248
	TOTAL	250,978	50,196
North-West Geo-Political Zone			
S/N	STATES	DEBT ($Million)	DEBT (in ₦Billion)
	Jigawa	35,718	7,144
2	Kaduna	234,416	46,883
3	Kano	59,797	11,959
4	Katsina	78,925	15,785
5	Kebbi	43,786	8,757
6	Sokoto	44,865	8,973
7	Zamfara	35,548	7,110
	TOTAL	533,054	106,611

Source: C. Ndujihe (April 18, 2015).

As at December, 2014 according to the Debt Management Office, Nigeria's total public debt stock was $67.73billion and ₦11.24 trillion (C. Ndujihe, 2015). The implication of the above information is that all is not well with governance in Nigeria from the financial management perspective. This effect transcended into public sector organizations resulting in the salary arrears being owed public/civil servants across the country. This is an abnormality given the resources coming into the nation's treasury. At this juncture, the curious minded stakeholder in Nigerian governance might be prompted to ask certain questions: what is happening to the management of the nation's financial resources? Can this high debt profile be justified given the high level of unemployment, inequality, poverty, low level of standard of living of the average Nigerian? What should the new administration do about this situation? Shouldn't the political office holders in the 5th republic be arraigned before the nation and the various states to give justifiable account for these debts? What is the impact of the acclaimed reasons for these debts in the various states that these monies were alleged to have been spent on? The irony of the situation is that these political office holders has amassed wealth at the expense of Nigerians. Will they (ex-political and public office holders in the 5th republic) go free? Will it be business as usual in this 6th republic? Only time will tell.

Often times, these "class of political holders" are regarded as sacred cows and in most time go free as if nothing had happened as it used to in time past. What an impunity in governance! In Delta State for instance, it was observed that the state is financially broke as the state's treasury was in red (empty) hence the new administration have to source for funds to get government running in the midst of huge debt left behind for the incoming administration in the 6th Republic.

6. Employee Engagement and Organizational Performance

Questions that often arise in the minds of practitioners, scholars, and other organizational stakeholders is, why should organizations should be concerned with employee engagement? The answer is that organizational stakeholders should be concerned because employee engagement impacts organization's performance as well as organizational outcomes. Studies have found positive relationship between employee engagement and organizational performance outcomes: employee retention, productivity, profitability, customer loyalty and safety. Researches also indicate that the more engaged employees are, the more likely their employer is to exceed the industry average in its revenue growth. Employee engagement is found to be higher in double-digit growth companies. Research also indicates that engagement is positively related to customer satisfaction (C. Coffman, 2000; C. Coffman and G. Gonzalez-Molina, 2002; Towers Perrin Talent Report, 2003; Hewitt Associates, 2004; R. Heintzman and B. Marson, 2005; C.M. Ellis and A. Sorensen, 2007).

Research has consistently shown that employee engagement is powerfully linked to a range of business success factors such as employee performance/efficiency (J.K. Harter, F.L. Schmidt and T.L. Hayes, 2002; L. Holbeche and N. Springett, 2003;), productivity (C. Maslach, W.B. Schaufeli and M.P. Leiter, 2001), safety (W. Kahn, 1990; D. R. May, R.L. Gilson and L.M. Harter, 2004; Vance, 2006), attendance and retention (L. Holbeche and N. Springett, 2003; W.B. Schaufeli, A. Bakker and M. Salanova, 2006), customer service and satisfaction (D.R. Roberts and T.O. Davenport, 2002), profitability (G.H Seiijts and D. Crim, 2006; R.J. Vance, 2006), health (S.

Crabtree, 2005).

For example, at the beverage company of Molson Coors, it was found that engaged employees were five times less likely than nonengaged employees to have a safety incident and seven times less likely to have a lost-time safety incident. In fact, the average cost of a safety incident for an engaged employee was $63, compared with an average of $392 for a nonengaged employee. Consequently, through strengthening employee engagement, the company saved $1,721,760 in safety costs in 2002. In addition, savings were found in sales performance teams through engagement. In 2005, for example, low-engagement teams were seen falling behind engaged teams, with a difference in performance-related costs of low- versus high-engagement teams totaling $2,104,823.9 (R.J. Vance, 2006).

Right Management (2009) posited that employee engagement is, arguably, the most critical metric for organizations in the twenty-first century. Most, if not all, other key measures that reflect and drive organizational performance (customer satisfaction, innovation, profitability, productivity, loyalty and quality) are products of engaged, committed employees. Their findings revealed that there is a strong relationship between the level of employee engagement and organizational performance as employee engagement is powerfully linked to a range of business success factors. Their survey of engagement of 28,810 employees from a broad range of industry sector from 15 countries in America, Europe, and Asia-Pacific confirmed that engagement leads to higher financial performance, higher customer satisfaction and higher employee retention, increased productivity, and profitability.

According to the Gallup research, organizations with high levels of engagement routinely outperform their competitors; they are 27% more profitable, they have 38% above average productivity, and have 50% higher customer loyalty. In a similar vein, the CLC (2004) in their survey of more than 50,000 employees of 59 global organizations found out that those employees who are most committed perform 20% better and are 87% less likely to leave the organization-indicating the significance of engagement to organizational performance.

Similarly, Stephen Young, the Executive Director of Towers Perrin, contended that only engagement (not satisfaction) is the strongest predictor of organizational performance (Human Resources, 2007).

Arising from the above, what will happen to an organization if its employees are disengaged? Employees who are not engaged are likely to be spinning (wasting their effort and talent on tasks that may not matter much), settling (certainly do not show full commitment, not dissatisfied enough to make a break) and splitting (they are not sticking around for things to change in their organization), have far more misgivings about their organization in terms of performance measures such as customer satisfaction (Blessing White, 2006; Perrin Report, 2003). M. Meere (2005) based on the survey conducted by ISR on 360,000 employees from 41 companies in the world's 10 economically strong countries found out that both operating margin and net profit margins reduced over a three year period in companies with low engagement, while these measures increased over the specified period in companies with high levels of engagement. Financial News, March 2001, as cited by Accord Management Systems (2004), reveals that disengaged employees are more likely to cost their organization. According to the report, employees who are disengaged miss an average of 3.5 more days per year; are less productive and cost the US economy $292 to $355 billion per year.

7. Conclusion

Productivity in the Nigerian public sector is dependent on employee engagement and governance. Put differently, without employee engagement and good governance there cannot be improved productivity. The system of governance in any given country provides the framework for organizational practices which to a great extent contributes to the level of employee engagement *inter alia* the determination of productivity level. Without a workplace environment for employee engagement, employee turnover will increase and efficiency will decline, thus leading to decline in organizational performance.

Having a holistic knowledge of employee engagement can be helpful in determining what is working and what is not. This will offer organizational leaders and HR practitioners a way to better understand what practices and policies in their organization effectively promote employee motivation, productivity and retention.

This paper therefore concludes that for productivity to improve in the public sector and for employee engagement to occur, the three Hs (Head, Heart and Hand) of the employee must be effectively engaged in addition to the provision of good governance by government.

Recommendation

Due to the strategic importance of public sector organizations in delivering the dividends of democracy and good governance, the following recommendations are made with a view to improving productivity in public sector organizations.

1. Employee engagement should be the concern of all stakeholders of productivity.
2. Engagement of employees should be complemented by the provision of opportunities and creation of a conducive environment for the employees to express their talents, creativity, initiatives and newly acquired skills, knowledge, experience, exposure and abilities.
3. Provision of resources for performance of job functions, training, learning and development opportunities, and establishment of a good and fair reward system is very vital in the improvement of productivity in public sector organizations.
4. Those saddled with the opportunity and responsibility

of governance should justify the people's trust on them and must be held accountable.

References

[1] G.O. Nkogbu. "Impact of Human Capital Development on Organizational Productivity in the Nigerian Public Sector: A Case Study of Nigerian Ports Authority (Delta Ports, Warri)". Unpublished M.Sc Dissertation. Lagos: National Open University of Nigeria, 2015.

[2] A. Ighoro. "Expanding the Frontiers of Human Resource Practice". HR Newsletter of Chartered Institute of Personnel Management of Nigeria, Delta State Branch, Vol., No. 3, pp. 2, 2014.

[3] W. Macey and B. Schenider. "The Meaning of Employee Engagement". Industrial and Organizational Psychology, Vol.1, pp. 3-30, 2008.

[4] S. Markos and M.S. Sridevi. "Employee Engagement: The Key to Improving Performance". International Journal of Business and Management, Vol. 5, No.12, pp. 89-96, 2010.

[5] C. Coffman. "Is Your Company Bleeding Talent? How to become a true "employer of choice". The Gallup Management Journal, 2000.

[6] C. Coffman and G. Gonzalez-Molina. "Follow this Path: How the World's Greatest Organizations Drive Growth by Unleashing Human Potential". New York: Warner Books, Inc., 2002.

[7] Hewitt Associates. "Employee Engagement Higher at Double Digit Growth Companies". Research Brief, Hewitt associates LLC, 2004.

[8] R. Heintzman and B. Marson, "People, Service and Trust: Links in a Public Sector Service Value Chain". International Review of Administrative Studies, Vol.7, No.4, pp. 549-575. December, 2005.

[9] M. Czarnowsky. "Learning's Role in Employee Engagement: An ASTD Research Study". Alexandria, VA: ASTD, 2008.

[10] Right Management. Employee Engagement: Maximizing Organizational Performance, 2009

[11] S. Markos and M.S. Sridevi. "Employee Engagement: The Key to Improving Performance". International Journal of Business and Management, Vol. 5, No. 12, pp. 89-96, 2010.

[12] Aon Hewitt. "Trends in Global Employee Engagement" In www.aonhewitt.com {Online: Accessed January 5, 2015}.

[13] A. Adebayo. "Principles and Practice of Public Administration in Nigeria". Ibadan: Spectrum Books Limited, 2004.

[14] N.P. Ibeme. "Ecology of Public Administration". Lagos: National Open University of Nigeria, 2013.

[15] T. Olaopa. "Theory and Practice of Public and Civil Service Reforms in Nigeria". Ibadan: Spectrum Books Limited, 2008.

[16] S. Bukar, A.B. Shehu, and A. Idris. "The Effect of Human Resource Management on Productivity of Workers in Nigeria", Journal of Business and Organizational Development, Vol. 4, pp.59, 2012.

[17] F. Ojo. "Personnel Management: Theories and Issues". Lagos: Allied Emant Company, 2006.

[18] J. Prokepenko. "Productivity Management: A Practical Handbook". Quarterly Journal of Economics, Vol. 45, No.57, pp. 407-443, 1996.

[19] D.A. Neugarten. "Themes and Issues in Public Sector Productivity". Public Personnel Management Journal, pp. 229-235, 1987.

[20] C. Obisi, C. "Substance of Employee, Industrial and Labour Relations". Lagos: Megavons (West Africa) Limited, 2005.

[21] D. Zinger. "The History of Employee Engagement". In www.davidzinger.com {online: Accessed December 20, 2014}

[22] A.M. Saks. "Antecedents and Consequences of Employee Engagement". Journal of Managerial Psychology, Vol. 21, pp.600-619, 2006.

[23] G.H. Seijts and D.Crim. "What Engages Employees the Most, or the Ten C's of Employee Engagement". Ivey Business Journal, March/April, 1-5, 2006.

[24] W. Kahn. "Psychological Conditions of Personal Engagement and Disengagement at Work". Academy of Management Journal, Vol. 33, No. 4, pp. 692-724, 1990.

[25] R.J. Vance. "Effective Practice Guidelines: Employee Engagement and Commitment". Alexandria, VA: SHRM Foundation, 2006.

[26] Corporate Leadership Council. "Driving Performance and Retention through Employee Engagement". Washington, DC: Corporate Executive Board, 2004.

[27] D. Dernovsek. "Creating Highly Engaged and Committed Employee Starts at the Top and Ends at the Bottom Line". Credit Union Magazine, May 2008. Credit Union National Association, Inc.

[28] J.K. Harter, F.L. Schmidt and T.L. Hayes. "Business-Unit-Level Relationship between Employee Satisfaction, Employee Engagement, and Business Outcomes: A Meta-Analysis". Journal of Applied Psychology, Vol.8, pp. 268-279, 2009.

[29] C. Maslach, W.B. Schaufeli and M.P. Leiter. "Job Burnout". Annual Review of Psychology, Vol.52, pp. 397-422, 2001.

[30] K. Shaw. "Employee Engagement, How to Build a High-Performance Workforce". Melcrum Publishing Limited, 2005.

[31] A.M. Konrad. "Engaging Employees through High Involvement Work Practices". Ivey business Journal Online: www.iveybusinessjournals.com {Online: Accessed January 5, 2015}.

[32] R.R. Nordstrom, T. Lewinsohn, and R.V. Hall. "Productivity in the Public Sector: A Discussion of the Issues". Public Personnel Management Journal, Vol. 16, No. 1, pp. 1-8., 1987.

[33] P.V.C. Okoye, and R.A. Ezejiofor, R.A. "The Effect of Human Resources Development on Organizational Productivity". International Journal of Applied Research in Business and Social Sciences, Vol. 3, No. 10, pp. 250-268 ,2013.

[34] J.M. Greiner. "Motivational Programs and Productivity Improvement in Times of Limited Resources". In R.B. Denhardt and B.R. Hammond "Public Administration in Action: Readings, Profiles and Cases". California: Brooks/Cole Publishing Company, 1992.

[35] B. Bozeman. "Strategic Public Management and Productivity: A "Firehouse Theory". In R.B. Denhardt and B.R. Hammond "Public Administration in Action: Readings, Profiles and Cases". California: Brooks/Cole Publishing Company, pp. 332, 1992.

[36] D. F. Kettl. "The Perils and Prospects of Public Administration". In R.B. Denhardt and B.R. Hammond "Public Administration in Action: Readings, Profiles and Cases". California: Brooks/Cole Publishing Company, pp. 15, 1992.

[37] S. Aina. "Managing the Human Capital in Nigeria". Lagos: Fountain Training Consult, pp.30, 2005.

[38] Human Development Report. "The Rise of the South: Human Progress in a Diverse World". Basingstoke, Hampshire: Palgrave Macmillan Houndmills, 2013.

[39] O.O. Ogunbonna. "Analysis of Non-Accountability in Nigeria". Human Resource Management Journal, Vol.1, No.2, pp. 26-38, 2009

[40] A. Sen, A. "Development: Which Way Now?" The Economic Journal, pp.757. December, 2004.

[41] C. Ndujihe. "Huge Debts Await Buhari, In-Coming Governors",2015 In www.vanguardngr.com {Online: Accessed 24th June, 2015}

[42] Towers Perrin. "Winning Wtrategies for a Global Workforce". Retrieved October 25, 2006, from www.towersperrin.com.

[43] C.M. Ellis and A. Sorensen. "Assessing Employee Engagement: The Key to Improving Productivity". Perspectives, Vol.1, No. 15, 2007. The Segal Group, Inc.

[44] L. Holbeche and N. Springett. "In Search of Meaning in the Workplace". Horsham: Roffey Park, 2003.

[45] D.R. May, R.L. Gilson and L.M. Harter. "The Psychological Conditions of Meaningfulness, Safety and Availability and the Engagement of the Human Spirit at Work". Journal of Occupational and Organizational Psychology, Vol.77, pp.11-37, 2004.

[46] W.B. Schaufeli, A. Bakker and M. Salanova. "The Measurement of Work Engagement with a Short Questionnaire: A Cross-National Study". Educational and Psychological Measurement, Vol. 66, pp. 701-716, 2006.

[47] D.R. Roberts and T.O. Davenport. "Job Engagement: Why It's Important and How to Improve It". Wiley Periodicals, Inc, pp. 21-29, 2002.

[48] S. Crabtree. "Engagement Keeps the Doctor Away". Gallup Management Journal, 2005 in http:gmj.gallup.com

[49] M. Meere. "High Cost of Disengaged Employees", 2005. Victoria: Swinburne University of Technology. [Online] Available: http://www.swinburne.edu.au/corporate/industrysolutions/ee/reports/Employee%20Engagement%20industry%20Breifing%20Paper%20Dec%202005%20.pdf (October 30, 2008).

5

Savings, Inflation and Economic Growth Linkages: A Re-Examination with Nigeria Data

Richardson Kojo Edeme, Innocent Ifelunini

Department of Economics, Faculty of Social Science, University of Nigeria, Nsukka, Enugu State-Nigeria

Email address:
richard.edeme@unn.edu.ng (R. K. Edeme), kojodynamics@yahoo.com (R. K. Edeme), innocent.ifelunini@unn.edu.ng (I. Ifelunini)

Abstract: The inter-relationship among savings, inflation and economic growth is an important conjuncture in the linkage evaluation of economic performance. Towards making them sustainable, the Nigeria government has initiated reforms, some of which in the last seven years. Despite these reforms, no study has been undertaken on the linkages among these variables with existing studies having confided themselves to looking only at the relationship between inflation and investment and the impact of inflation and economic growth. Using annual time series data from 1980-2013, this study examined the linkages among savings, inflation and economic growth in Nigeria using the 2-stage least squares (2SLS) method. The study found inflation and real interest to be negatively related with economic growth while exchange rate has positive effect on economic growth. Also economic growth, unemployment and real interest rate negatively affected inflation rate, while indirect taxes had positive impact on inflation. The result further shows that economic growth; exchange rate and foreign direct investment engender savings while depreciation rate endangers savings. The study also established threshold level of 8 percent of inflationary level was found to be consistent with Nigeria growth; beyond this point inflation will endanger growth.

Keywords: Savings, Inflation, Economic Growth, Investment, Interest Rate, 2-Stage Least Squares

1. Introduction

The Nigeria growth experience in the last decade has generated keen interest among economists and policy makers. This is because while variables such as inflation and foreign exchange rate has been on the rise, others such as savings, external reserve, real growth and total investment have been on the decline and in some cases increased marginally. For instance, in 2002 real gross domestic product (GDP) growth was 21.2 percent which declined to 10.3 percent in 2003, 5.4 percent in 2005. In 2011 and 2012, it was 7.2 percent and 7.1 percent respectively. Despite various monetary policies introduced by Central Bank over the years, Nigeria's inflation experience since 1980 has been mixed. A review of inflationary data shows that in the period from early 1980s to the second quarter of the 1990s, annual inflation has averaged around 20 percent. Subsequently, average annual inflation came down to one-digit rate. However, since 2001, inflation is back in the two-digit rate territory with an average of about 10 percent over 2000-2002. It has also been observed that the savings rate was high from 1999-2004 (17.61 percent of total GDP) while it remained low in the period of 2005-2011, representing 5.81 percent of GDP (NBS 2012).

An examination of the inter-relationship among savings, inflation and economic growth is imperative because it is an important conjuncture in the linkage evaluation of economic performance of a country. In Nigeria, towards making them sustainable, government has initiated series of reforms, some of which in the last seven years. Despite these reforms, no study has been undertaken on the linkages among these variables with existing studies having confided themselves to looking only at the relationship between inflation and investment and the impact of inflation and economic growth. This gap will be filled by this study by taking a linkage view of savings, inflation and economic growth. This will make it possible to analyze the interactions, links and coordination among these variables. Adopting a linkage approach reinforces the fact that savings, inflation and economic growth should not be seen and considered in isolation. They work simultaneously to determine the pace of development. This means, for instance, that government cannot lose sight of the need to encourage savings and reduce inflation as it exerts improvement in investment and growth. Indeed, a linkage approach highlights that complementary policy are needed to promote savings and investment. International experience shows that combining domestic investment and savings can generate employment and dependency ratio (1PAR 2014). However, the concern is to provide a suite of complementary role to saving and investment as it is the synergy between enabled economic growth to improve domestic investment and exchange rate.

This analysis adopted in this study builds upon previous studies but provides both a broader perspective and deepens analysis of specific means of implementation. Moreover, be estimating a threshold level of inflation that is consistent with Nigeria's growth, this study provides a further insight on the inflation level that is effective to stimulate and enhance savings and investment. Following the introduction above, the remainder of the paper is organized as follows: Section 2 is literature review, section 3 methodology, section 4 is presentation and discussion of empirical results while section 5 is conclusion and recommendations.

2. Literature Review

Along with economic growth savings is considered as a major macroeconomic factor which has a strong relation with inflation. In a general equilibrium framework by Sidrauski (1967) it was found that money remained neutral in the time of steady state, implying that inflation has no impact on savings in the long run. There are however another argument that a negative relationship exist between inflation and savings. This conflicting view has thrown up further debate on inflation-saving interaction in the growth process. On the average GDP is an important indicator for the economy of a country. If GDP of a country increases with the faster rate than the population then it shows that GDP per capita of that country is increasing and standard of living of peoples is also improving. In recent years, discourse has been on among the economist and policy makers about the relationship between inflation and economic growth with some with the opinion that there is positive relationship between inflation and economic growth while others like World Bank (2012) posited that a negative relationship exist between inflation and economic growth. In the famous Philip's curve, it has been demonstrated that there exist a positive relationship between inflation and economic growth. This relationship was shown through the channel of aggregate demand and aggregate supply. In an economy, saving is considered very important factor for the improvement of an economy of a country. The conventional perception is that savings contribute to higher investment and hence higher GDP growth in the short run. Beside, it also plays an important role in the individual's life. It has been demonstrated that individuals who has more savings are more satisfied to face the adverse shocks. According to Modigliani, the rational people earn in the one part of their life such as in the working age and save money in this era for the older age. There are however other economists such as Keynes who believe that when the income of individual increase then the proportion of savings will also increase. The association between economic growth and the savings is not only most important but has also received considerable attention among researchers and analyzed this dilemma as cause and outcome relationship. Although Earbaykal and Okuyan (2008) have confirmed the positive relationship between savings and growth, a different category favors the capital fundamentalist point of view that savings cause growth while others are in favors of Keynesian theory that growth is necessary for savings.

Various strands of literature exist on the nexus among inflation, savings and economic growth. A famous study by Davidson and Mackinnon (1982) investigated the relationship between inflation and savings rate for the economy of America and Canada. Employing the chow test the study found that high inflation leads to high savings and unanticipated inflation leads to involuntary savings. In another study, Sahoo (2001) found that higher economic growth is necessary for increasing the savings of a country, thus supporting the traditional thesis that savings had been the engine of the economic growth. On the contrary Sheggu (2004), in a study conducted for Ethiopia economy, a bi-directional causality was exhibited between savings and economic growth. In another study to determine the impact of high inflation on economic growth both in the short-run and long-run, Faria and Carneiro (2001) employed VAR model and found that inflation had negative impact on economic growth in the short run while no relationship was found between inflation and economic growth in the long run. The study showed that although a negative relationship exist between inflation and economic growth, a 9 percent rate of inflation is tolerable for Pakistan economy beyond which the economy may experience harmful and detrimental growth. In a panel analysis of South east and South Asian countries, Chaturvedi, Kumar and Dholakia (2009) examined the inter-relationship among economic growth, savings and inflation and found that saving promotes economic growth. Also inflation was positively related to saving but negatively related to economic growth. However, in a specific country study for Pakistan, Muhammad, Hazoor, Shehzad and Naeem (2012) aptly repudiated that inflation and real interest rate negatively affect economic growth, whereas depreciation rate positively affect the economic growth. The result further shows that economic growth and foreign direct investment are beneficial for enhancing the savings of a country while depreciation rate is harmful for savings. Ramesh (2011) examined the direction of the relationship between saving, investment and economic growth in India at both aggregate level and sectoral level for the period 1950/51 to 2007/08 using Granger causality test through VAR/VECM framework. Besides, cointegration test based on Johansen-Juselius (1990) method was used to test the long-run relationship among the variables. The cointegration test result suggests that there exist co-integration relationship among all series with GDP except private corporate saving. The study also found that the direction of causality runs from saving and investment to economic growth collectively as well as individually and there is no causality from economic growth to saving and (or) investment. Although, a reciprocal causality exists from saving and investment of the private sector to economic growth, this causality comes from the household sector where saving and investment led growth and growth driven saving and investment were observed. In the examination the effect of inflation in the growth process of an economy, Dewan and Hussein (1990), Barro (1995), Mishkin (2000), Ahmed and Murtatza (2005), Akerlof, Dickson and George (2006), Hussain and Malik (2011), Bruno and William (2012) was able to demonstrate that high level of inflation is harmful to savings and capital accumulation and economic, most especially for import-dependent economies. Another strand of literature, studies also examined foreign direct investment and economic growth linkage. One of such was conducted by Verma and Wilson (2005) for Indian economy using annual time series from 1950-2001. The finding showed little evidence that savings and investment affect GDP in the long run while GDP has significant but small effects on household savings and investment in the short run. The feedbacks to GDP are absent in the long run and only small and not precise in the short run. While savings influences investment, the links from investment to output are weak. Other studies in this area include Chung, Chung and Zhang (1995) for Chima, Egbor and Onwumere (2011) for Nigeria. A major conclusion arrived by these studies is that a positive link exist between investment and economic growth, although they have not been able to reinforce each other significantly due to unfavorable investment climate.

3. Methodology

Data employed by this study are annual time series covering 1980-2013 and they are generated from Central Bank of Nigeria Statistical Bulletin. For robustness of analysis, variables under consideration are economic growth (proxied by gross domestic product), savings rate, inflation rate, interest rate, exchange rate, unemployment rate, domestic investment and foreign domestic investment. Building on previous studies such as Chaturvedi, et al (2009) and Muhammad, et al (2012), this paper develops and adopts a simultaneous equation model and the formal structure of the model can be expressed as:

$$GDPt = f(SVt, IFt, IRt, DRt, UPt, DIt, FDt) \quad (1)$$

$$SVt = f(GDPT, IFt, IRt, DRt, DIt, FDt) \quad (2)$$

$$IFt = f(GDPt, SVt, UPt, IRt) \quad (3)$$

In linear form, equations (1) – (3) can be written as:

$$GDPt = \alpha_1SVt + \alpha_2IFt + \alpha_3IRt + \alpha_4ERt + \alpha_5UPt + \alpha_6DIt + \alpha_7FDt) \quad (4)$$

$$SVt = \varphi_1GDPT+\varphi_2IFt+\varphi_3IRt+\varphi_4ERt+\varphi_5DIt+\varphi_6FDt) \quad (5)$$

$$IFt = \chi_1GDPt + \chi_2SVt + \chi_3UPt + \chi_4IRt \quad (6)$$

where α_1-$\alpha_;$ φ_1-φ_7; χ_1-χ_4 are parameters, economic growth (proxied by GDP), SV= savings rate, IF = inflationary rate, ER = exchange rate, UP = unemployment rate, DI = domestic investment, FD = foreign direct investment, unemployment rate, domestic investment and foreign direct investments are included in the model as control variables.

A further extension of this study is the estimation of the threshold level of inflation consistent with Nigeria's growth. The essence of this is to determine the point of inflexion or non-linear relationship between economic growth and inflation. Using a threshold model, Ahmad (2005) and Khan and Senhadji (2011) estimated the threshold level of inflation for Bangladesh. Relying heavily on the model, the subsequent equation for the estimation of the threshold level of inflation for Nigeria can be estimated as

$$Ln\ GDP_t = \beta_0 + \beta_1IF_t + \beta_2DIF_t - K + \varepsilon \quad (7)$$

In that above equation, economic growth and inflation ware computed as: $LnGDP_t$ = economic growth, IF_t = inflation rate (percentage annually) respectively. D is the dummy variable defined as follows: $D = 1$ *if* $IF > K$; *and* $= 0$ *if* $IF \leq K$. K depicts the threshold level of the inflation at which structural break occurs and ε is random error term. The threshold level of inflation would be ascertained at that point where the value of R^2 is maximum. This implies that the value of threshold level which minimizes the residual sum of squares (RSS) would be selected. To do this, the method of ordinary least square (OLS) is employed.

4. Presentation and Discussion of Results

The empirical result entails the presentation of the descriptive statistics, 2-stage least square and inflation threshold. The descriptive statistics of the variables under consideration is presented in Table 1 below.

Table 1. *Descriptive Statistics.*

Variable	Mean	Standard Deviation
Gross domestic product	1701.67	221.9
Savings rate	154.24	58.9
Inflation rate	9.92	1.2
Exchange rate	29.07	4.5
Interest rate	42.16	9.8
Unemployment rate	56.85	3.8
Domestic investment	50.00	5.5
Foreign direct investment	62.87	18.9

Table 2. *The result of structural parameters of GDP growth rate.*

Variables	Coefficients	Standard error	t-statistics
C	0.1209	0.00121	0.0001
SV	0.1213	0.0621	1.5500
IF	-0.5231	0.0145	-.2.0190
IR	-0.6201	0.1089	-2.2348

$R^2 = 0.7624$

Table 3. Parameter estimates of Savings rate.

Variables	Coefficients	Standard error	t-statistics	Probability
C	0.1245	0.0231	0.1012	0.0012
GDP	5.1082	0.5472	2.3401	0.0331
IR	-0.0130	0.3122	-0.8721	0.0235
DR	0.2311	0.1121	2.3400	0.2109
FI	5.1230	0.7612	5.6012	0.0514
ER	-4.3412	1.7613	2.5632	0.0233

$R^2 = 0.6702$

Table 4. Parameter estimates of Inflation rate.

Variables	Coefficients	Standard error	t-statistics	Probability
C	0.1245	0.0134	-2.1012	0.1290
GDP	0.3452	0.3241	0.4531	0.0213
SV	-0.8231	0.4452	0.3452	-0.5020
UR	-0.9912	0.4512	-2.1239	0.0089
IR	-0.7823	0.0671	-9.1232	0.0202

$R^2 = 0.8723$

Table 5. Threshold level of inflation consistent with Growth.

K	Variables	Coefficient	Standard error	t-statistics	R^2
	Constant	20.2130	0.2009	23.1098	
5 percent	*IF*	-.0.0234	0.0021	-0.1209	0.1230
	Δ(Dummy)	0.0341	0.1412	0.15612	
	Constant	18.2123	0.1801	102.02	
6 percent	*IF*	0.0023	0.0023	-1.2310	0.1094
	Δ(Dummy)	0.2543	0.1012	0.1240	
	Constant	17.6701	0.0345	99.012	
7 percent	*IF*	-0.0342	0.1209	-1.3421	0.2310
	Δ(Dummy)	0.2390	0.0023	0.8901	
	Constant	17.1230	0.0982	100.19	
8 percent	*IF*	-0.0124	0.0912	-1.4543	0.5612
	Δ(Dummy)	0.1210	0.9801	0.9231	
	Constant	18.1098	0.0231	102.123	
9 percent	*IF*	-0.0234	0.1901	-2.2435	0.1089
	Δ(Dummy)	0.2331	0.3210	1.2310	
	Constant	18.2109	0.3012	102.09	
10 percent	*IF*	-0.0234	0.0023	-1.3248	0.0981
	Δ(Dummy)	0.2390		1.4323	
	Constant	18.2109	0.3012	102.09	
11 percent	*IF*	-0.0254	0.0023	-1.3248	0.0129
	Δ(Dummy)	0.2390		1.4323	
	Constant	18.0989	0.3011	100.00	
12 percent	*IF*	-0.0034	0.0011	-1.098	0.1902
	Δ(Dummy)	0.2221		1.2100	

From the descriptive statistics, economic growth, savings rate, inflation rate, exchange rate, interest rate, unemployment, domestic investment and foreign direct investment exhibited respective average value of 170, 154, 9, 29, 42, 57, 53, 50 and 63. The standard deviation shows that the observed variables vary so much from the average figure. The coefficient of inflation in Table 2 indicates that 1 percent increase in the prices leads to a 52 percentage reduction in economic growth. The result further shows that there is positive relationship between savings and economic growth. The coefficient of interest rate is an indication that higher interest rate endangers economic growth. This can be explained by the fact that during increase in real interest rate people prefer to deposit their money in the banks rather than investment which will ultimately retard economic growth. The result has also shown that a positive relationship exist between exchange rate and economic growth. The implication of this is that depreciation of currency has the ability of enhancing the exports of that country because now exports become cheaper. With increased demand of exports, domestic investors will increase the production of goods, given all other things. This will result in increase in economic growth. As indicated in Table 3, about 67 percent variation in savings in Nigeria is ascribed to inflation, economic growth and foreign direct investment. The calculated coefficient for economic growth depicts that it has significant impact of economic growth. This is a justification of the positive relationship between output and savings. With increased economic growth, incomes will be enhanced and ultimately savings will improve. The result is in tandem with the Keynesian theory which postulates that savings depend on the level of output. Similar conclusion was also reached by Modigliani (1970) and Jappelli and Pagano (1994). However, the negative sign of inflation is an indication that an inverse relationship exist between savings and inflation. The result further shows that there is a positive relationship between foreign direct investment and saving rate. This can be explained by the fact that that foreign capital inflow increased the supply of funds for investment thus enhancing the capital accumulation in host country. Increased investment stimulates economic growth and consequently saving rate would increase. In Table 4 above, the result shows that economic growth has significant impact on inflation. Specifically, a 1 percentage increase in economic growth led to 62 percentage reduction in the rate of inflation. This result supports the findings of Barro (1995). When savings rate was regressed on the inflation rate, it is found that savings rate has no significant impact on prices. However, a positive relationship exists between the variables analyzed. The negative relationship found between unemployment and the prices can be explained by the fact that with increased unemployment it means that people have less money so the demand of goods and services decreased and as a result inflation also decreases. The coefficient of real interest rate also shows the significant impact of real interest rate on the price level. The negative sign of the coefficient shows that there exist negative relationship between inflation and interest rate. The justification of negative relationship is that in general it has been seemed that when interest rate is low then people can borrow more money. As a result the purchasing power of the consumers will increase and may result to a situation where too much money is chasing too few goods in the economy.

For the threshold level of inflation that is consistent with Nigeria's growth, the OLS procedure was repeated severally in order to arrive at an acceptable R^2. The estimated R^2 and residual sum of square were taken into account and the assumed values of K covering from 1 to 27. However, taking into consideration the value of residual sum of square and the value of R^2 the anticipated results have been presented given tables for the K values ranging from 5 percent to 12 percent and the result is presented in Table 5. The result shows that 8 percent rate of inflation is tolerate able for Nigeria's economic growth. This is point where the value of R^2 is maximum and residual sum of square is minimum. This implies that the model is best fit at 8 percent level. The value of probability also shows that the two variables significantly affected each other in the long run. However, the sign of the coefficient remained negative at all the K levels. This outcome confirmed the theoretical postulation that a double digit inflation rate is harmful and detrimental to economic growth.

5. Conclusion

In this study, it has been established that the key gamut to ensuring growth sustainability is to improve domestic savings and reduce inflation. Based on the simultaneous equation model developed, the study found that there exist bi-directional causality between inflation and economic growth, although they negatively affect each other in the long run. The analysis also found that indirect taxes have positive relation with prices whereas unemployment and real interest rate are negatively correlated with inflation. The results of the study further show that GDP growth and foreign direct investment has positive effect on savings whereas exchange rate decreases savings. The threshold level of inflation for economic growth was also estimated using OLS method and the result showed that at 8 percent rate of inflation, growth would be sustainable in Nigeria. There is need therefore for coordination among savings and economic growth policies as this will form the basis to improve investment in both public and private sectors of the Nigerian economy.

References

[1] Ahmad, S and M. G Murtatza (2005), "Inflation and Economic Growth in Banggledesh: 1981-2005", *Working Paper Series: WP 0604,* Policy Analysis Unit

[2] Akerlof, G. W, T. Dickson and I. P George (2006), "The Macroeconomics of Low Inflation", *Brookings Paperon Economic Acivities,* Vol. 1

[3] Barro, R. J (1995), "Inflation ane Economic Growth", *Working Paper, 5326,* Nation Bereau of Economic Research

[4] Bruno and William (2012), "Inflation and Long-run Growth", NBER Working Paper No: 5209 (Cambridge, Massachusetts, National Bureau of Economic Reearch)

[5] Chung, C, L. Chung and Y. Zhang (1995), "The Role of Foreign Direct Investment in China's Post 1978 Development" , *World Development,* 23 (4)

[6] Chaturvedi, V. K and R. Dholakia (2009), "Inter-relationship between Economic Growth, Savings and Inflation in Asia", *Indian Institute of Management Ahmadadad Working Paper* No. 01

[7] Davison, D and J. Mackinnon (1982), "Inflation and Savings Rate", *Queen's Economics Department Working Paper,* No. 493

[8] Dan Haan, W. J (1990), "The Optimal inflation Path in a Sidrauski-Type Model with Uncertaintity", *Journal of Monetary Economics,* Vol. 28

[9] Dewan, E and S. Hussein (2001), "Detreminants of Economic Growth", *Working Paper,* Reserve Bank of Fiji

[10] Eabaykai, E and H. Okuyan (2008), "Does Inflatiin depress Economic Growth? Evidence from Turkey", *International Research Journal of Finane and Economics*

[11] Egbo, O and J. Onwumere (2011), "Analysing the impact of Foreign direct investment on Nigeria's Economic Growth: A Cointegration approach", *International Journal of Research and Management,* Vol. 3: 78-97

[12] Faria, J and F. Carneiro (2001), "Does High Inlation affect Economic Growth in the Long and Snort run?", *Journal of Applied Economics,* 4 (1): 89-105

[13] Gbosh, A and P. Steven (1998), "Inflation, Disinflation and Growth" *International Monetary Fund,*Working Paper, WP/98/68

[14] Hussain, S and S. Malik (2011), "Inflation and Economic Growth: Evidence from Pakistan", *International Journal of Economics and Finance,* 3 (5): 32-54

[15] Institute of Policy Analysis and Research (IPAR) (2014), Policy Brief. Vol 11, Issue 2

[16] Jappeli, T and M. Pagano (1994), "Saving, Growth and Liquidity Constraints", *The Quaterly Journal of Economics,* Vol. 109 (1): 83-109

[17] Khan, M and D. Sinhadji (2001), "Threshold Effects in the Relationship between Inflation and Economic Growth", *International Monetary Fund Staff Paper,*Vol.48(1)

[18] Malik, G and A. Chowdhury (2001), "Inflation and Economic Growth: Evidence from four South Asian Countries", *Asia-Percific Development Journal,* Vol. 8 (1): 121-135

[19] Mishkin, F.S (2000), "Inflation Targeting in Emerging Market Countries", NBER Working Paper No: 7618 (Cambridge, Massachusetts, National Bureau of Economic Reearch)

[20] Modigliani, F (1970), The life cycle hypothesis of savings and inter-country difference in the saving ration, In: Eltis, W.A, M.F Scott and J.N Wolfe (eds*), Introduction to Trade and Growth essay in honor of Sir Roy Harrod*, London, Clarendon Press

[21] Muhammad, Hazoor, Shehzad and Naeem (2012), "The inter-relationship among Inflation, Savings and Economic growth in Pakistan"

[22] National Bureau of Statistics (2012), Nigeria Economic Outlook, Federal Ministry of Finance, Abuja

[23] Verma, R and E. Wilson (2005), "Savings, Investment, Foreign Inflows and Economic of the Indian Economy, 1950-200 *Economic Working Paper Series, University of Wollongong*

[24] Rosegrant, V and S. Evenson (1992), "Agriculture Investment and Productivity in Developing Countries", *American Journal of Economics,* Vol. 74 (3): 757-761

[25] Sheggu, D (2004), “Causal Relationship between Growth and Gross Domestic Savings: Case of Ethiopia”, *Second International Conference on the Ethiopian Economy organized by Ethiopian Economic Association*

[26] World Bank. (2012), *World Development Report 1995:Workers in an Integrating World.* Washington, D. C.: Oxford University Press for the World Bank.

6

Uncertainty Handling in Ship Assessment: A Case Study of Bangladesh

Muhammed Jamshed Alam Patwary[1], Mohammad Osiur Rahman[2,*], Mohammad Shahadat Hossain[2]

[1]Department of Computer Science and Engineering, International Islamic University Chittagong, Chittagong, Bangladesh
[2]Department of Computer Science and Engineering, University of Chittagong, Chittagong, Bangladesh

Email address:
jap_cse@iiuc.ac.bd (M. J. A. Patwary), osiur.ukm@gmail.com (M. O. Rahman), hossain_ms@cu.ac.bd (M. S. Hossain)

Abstract: Shipping is the oldest and internationally recognized industry. It helps many national and international businesses by transporting vast amount of goods from one place to another. Most of the businesses in Bangladesh are depended on sea ports. For this reason, shipping services are very important in Bangladesh. To maximize the profit from a ship oriented business, it is essential to select the right ship for intended purpose. However, ship selection is a very critical process, because it requires handling of both qualitative and quantitative information under uncertainty. While evaluating the quality of a ship in Bangladesh, particularly in Chittagong and Mongla sea port, only quantitative parameters are considered. Qualitative and uncertain data are ignored. Sometimes it causes not to select the right ship, as a result, serious losses in businesses. The goal of this study is to overcome the existing limitations of ship selection through handling of both qualitative and quantitative data under uncertainty. In this article, evidential reasoning (ER) approach is used for aggregating both qualitative and quantitative data under uncertainly for ranking among the alternatives and finally selecting the best ship out of many alternatives. The proposed method is applied on five alternative ships of Western Fishers Shipyard Ltd (WFSL). Using the method it has been possible to rank among alternatives successfully and both qualitative and quantitative data have been collated to handle uncertainty in ship selection. It is recommended to use the ER method in ship selection, because it can handle uncertainty and helps businessmen to get maximum benefit from their businesses through selecting the best ship.

Keywords: Evidential Reasoning (ER), Uncertainty, Ship Assessment, Qualitative and Quantitative Data

1. Introduction

International shipping industry helps over 90 percent of world trade. It helps export and import of goods from one place to another. Seaborne trade continues to expand day by day as its demand is increasing. There are around 50,000 merchant ships trading internationally, and they transport every kind of cargo. For this reason, shipping services are very important for maritime world. It is a common and frequent event in the maritime industry to familiarize new trends and capacities of a ship, as the industry and the demand for new ship is increasing day by day. Now, choosing or deciding the best ship out of many alternatives is a big challenge faced by the decision makers. The assessment of the quality of ships is cruial since it requires many complex decisions to make as well as linear and nonliear information to be considered. Consequently, a large number of criteria of both qualitative and quantitative types are to be simultaneously measured and evaluated. From a shipbuilder's perspective the detailed design process [1] of a ship consists of the following steps:

- Market analysis is required to determining the transport demand.
- In the concept design stage, logical model of ship is designed.
- With the help of computer modeling different alternative ships are designed technically.
- Some economic criteria such as first cost, operating cost and income of different alternative ships are estimated and assessed.
- Using computer program or comparing economic criteria of alternatives optimal option is selected.

Once the design process of different alternatives is completed, they need to be compared to determine the best one among them. To determine the best one, the entire ship need not be compared rather some of the criteria are compared, for example, designs with higher net present value (NPV) is better than that of lower one and in the same way, lower required freight rate (RFR) is better than that of higher one. Taking risk factor into account different alternatives can be compared [2]. The total ship readiness assessment (TSRA) is used to assess the material condition of any operating ship. Comparison among alternatives is possible using TSRA.

To assess the economic and technical performance of alternative ships, ship designer requires adequate information. Economic performance evaluation is easier than technical performance evaluation because in economic performance evaluation criteria are linearly related. The success of comparing alternative ship designs depends on huge number of practical data and the use of appropriate economic analysis method. Sometimes it is difficult to have sufficient data.

The shipbuilding industry of Bangladesh has a long history. The industry is based on building simple boats and sea vessels. Many countries around the world bought ships from Bangladesh. Bangladesh has become the most prominent shipbuilding country because it has more than 200 rivers from small sizes to big sizes with a total length of around 22155 km. Once the design and building of different ships is completed, they are required to compare to determine the best ship and rank [3], [4] among them, so that decision makers can take their decision to buy their intended ship. To compare among different alternative ships, both qualitative and quantitative criteria need to be considered [5].

The main limitation of evaluating a ship in Bangladesh is that, decision makers usually consider only quantitative criteria, in addition, they take a very few criteria into account. However, the evaluation methods do not consider any qualitative parameters and hence, the existing methods are insufficient to handle uncertainty [6] which is considered as a challenge by many researchers [7] - [16].

The proposed evidential reasoning (ER) approach [3], [17] is very different from most conventional multi-attribute decision making modeling methods. The ER approach employs a belief structure to represent a measurement as a distribution [6], [17]-[19] and aggregates nonlinear information. It aggregates distributed assessment results from lower level to higher level attributes. The ER approach uses evidential reasoning algorithm, developed on the basis of decision theory and the evidence combination rule [20] of Dempster-Shafer theory [21] to aggregate belief degrees. In the ER system both quantitative and qualitative criteria are considered and aggregated simultaneously [3], [4], [18], [19]. As a result, the uncertainty [6], [14], [18], [22]-[24] issues are resolved. The decision-makers will be able to take appropriate decision during purchasing of a ship in a short span of time because most of the significant criteria, both qualitative and quantitative are considered.

In the rest of the article, section 2 introduces the life cycle of a ship; section 3 describes the ER based ship assessment algorithm; section 4 discusses on the experimental results; and finally, describes the concluding remarks in section 5.

2. Life Cycle of a Ship

The life time of a modern ship is about 25-30 years. Figure 1 illustrates the different steps of life cycle of a modern ship. The life cycle consists of initial planning, ordering, ship building, ship operation, ship assessment and ship recycling. The article especially emphasized on the ship assessment under uncertainty.

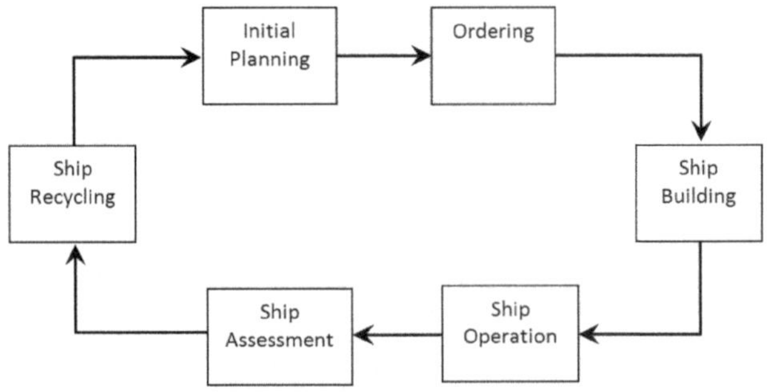

Figure 1. *Life cycle of a ship.*

2.1. Initial Planning

During this step, ship owner will contact with naval architects for planning a new ship design. To design a new ship, typically earlier designs are considered as well as the state-of-the-art technology is also included.

2.2. Ordering

Ordering of a ship needs to communicate among ship owner, ship yard and ship broker. Once they have agreed on their conditions then ordering is occurred.

2.3. Ship Building

All actions such as signing of contract, production design, material and equipment purchase, production plan, steel cutting, assembly and mounting of ship sections, launching, finishing of the ship, sea trial, delivery and warranty, are done at ship building stage.

2.4. Ship Operation

After building the ship now it is prepared for operation.

2.5. Ship Assessment

The quality of the ship is evaluated at this stage, which helps to rank among various alternative ships.

2.6. Ship Recycling

During recycling stage of the life cycle of a ship, ship owners sell the ship for recycling to ship-breaking yard.

3. Proposed ER Based Ship Assessment System

The ER based ship assessment approach considered both quantitative and qualitative parameters for ship assessment and ranking. The overall assessment of ships evaluated based on performance, equipment, appearance, automation and economy. The evaluation hierarchy [4], [6], [19] for ship assessment is shown in Figure 2 and the block diagram of the ER based ship assessment algorithm is shown in Figure 3.

In the evaluation hierarchy, the overall ship assessment is obtained from the fusion of performance, equipment, appearance, automation and economy. The performance is evaluated based on safety, fire protection, and seaworthiness; the equipment consists of living facilities, cargo systems, anchor facilities, and communication; the appearance quality is evaluated based on waterline and internal arrangement; the parameters for automation are engine room, navigation and cargo monitor; and the net present value and required fright rate are considered to calculate the economy condition.

The main objective of this ER based ship assessment algorithm is ranking among alternative ships and it involves the following steps which are also illustrated in Figure 3.

Step 1. Representation of definition of multi-attribute decision problem

Step 2. Basic probability assignments for each basic attribute

Step 3. Combined probability assignments for a general attribute

Step 4. Combined degrees of belief for a general attribute

Step 5. Expected utility is measured

Step 6. Utility interval

Step 7. Ranking of the options

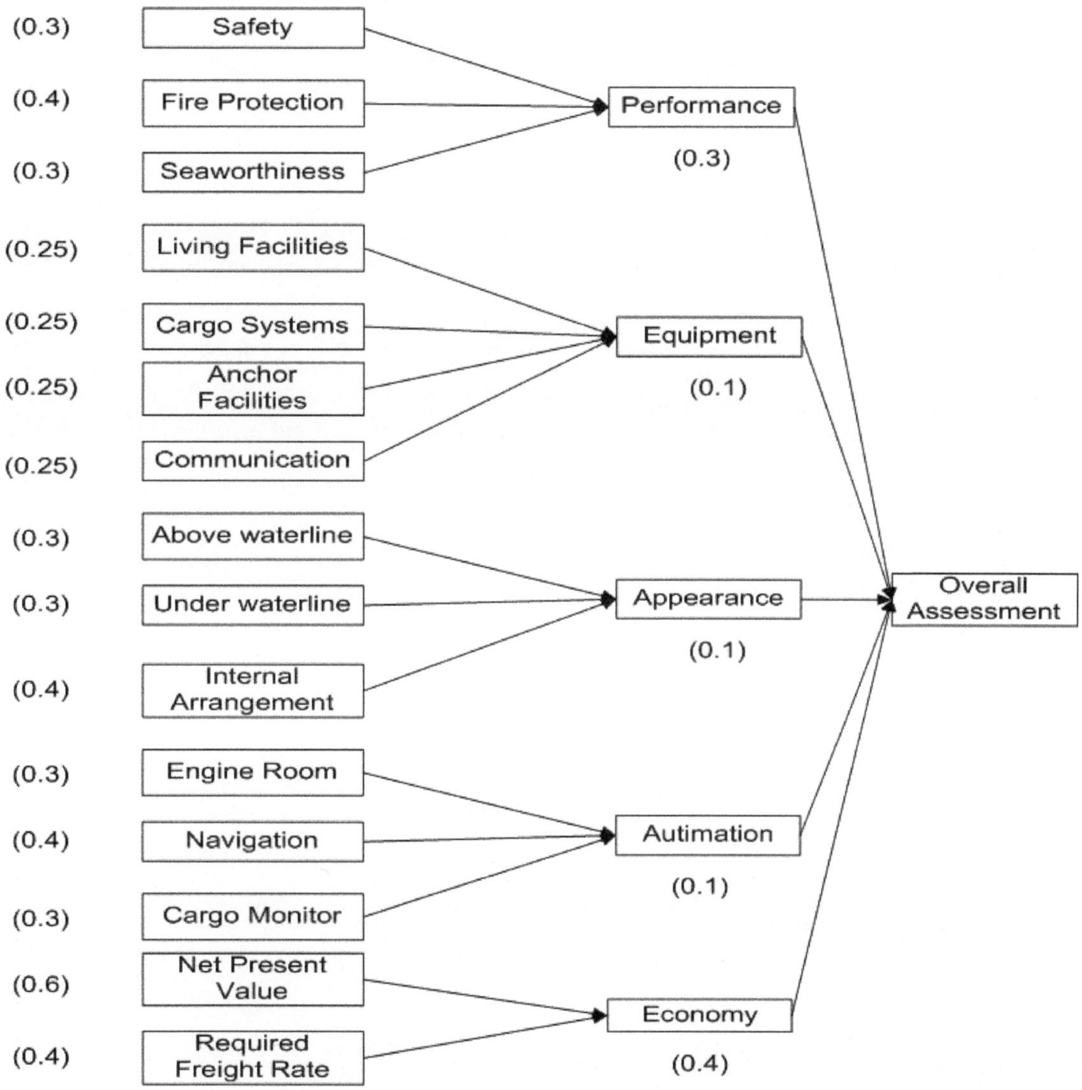

Figure 2. *Evaluation Hierarchy for Ship Assessment.*

3.1. The Detailed Description of ER Based Ship Assessment Algorithm

Suppose an aggregated attribute x is calculated, taking some basic attributes into account, in a two level evaluation hierarchy [3], [5], [25]. Assume there are P basic attributes. $a_i (i = 1, ..., P)$. Here are computational steps of ER approach that are used to aggregate nonlinear information.

Step 1. Representation of definition of multi-attribute decision problem: A multi-attribute decision problem [26], [27], [28], [25].

a) Definition of a set of P basic attributes a_i according to the following equation:

$$A = \{a_1, a_2, a_3, ...a_i, ...a_P\} \quad (1)$$

b) Estimation of the relative weights of the P basic attributes $w = \{w_1, w_2, w_3, ...w_i, ...w_P\}$ where w_i is the relative weight for basic attribute i and satisfied the following equations:

$0 \leq w_i \leq 1$ and

$$\sum_{i=1}^{P} w_i = 1 \quad (2)$$

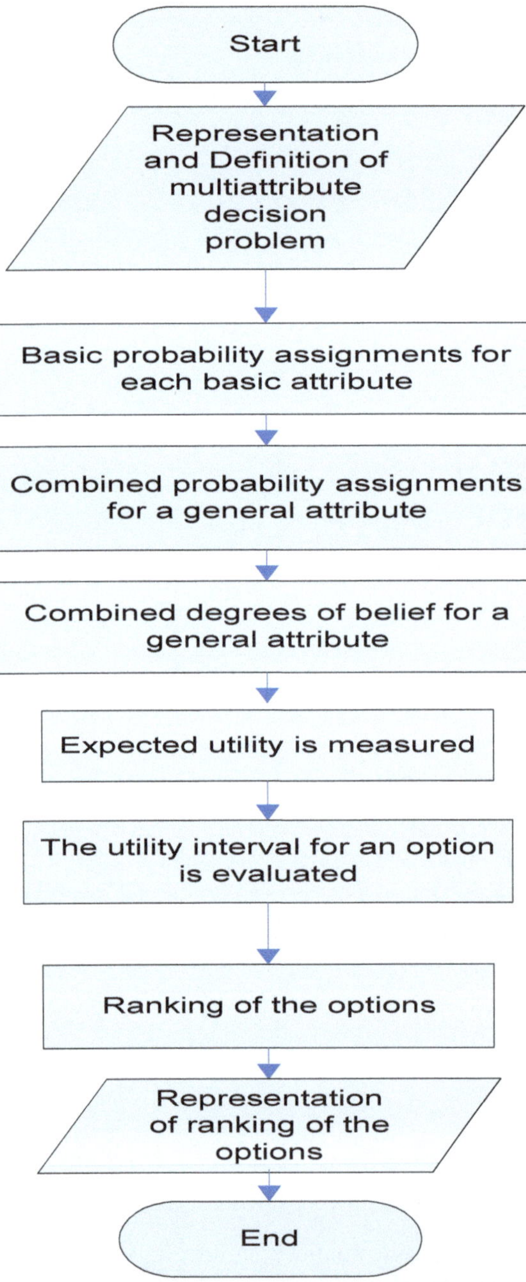

Figure 3. *ER based ship assessment algorithm.*

c) Definition of Q different evaluation grades $H_n(n = 1,...,Q)$. as a complete set of standards for assessing each alternative option on all attributes,

$$H = \{H_1, H_2, H_3 ..., .H_n ....H_Q\} \quad (3)$$

d) Now, a multi-attribute decision problem can be represented using the following distributions for an option $option_l (l = 1,..., R)$ on an attribute $a_i (i = 1,..., P)$:

$$S(a_i(option_l)) = \{(H_n, \beta_{n,i}(option_l)), n = 1,..., Q\} i = 1,...P, l = 1,..., R \quad (4)$$

Where, $\beta_{n,i}(option_l)$ indicates a degree of belief and $\beta_{n,i}(option_l) \geq 0$ with $\sum_{n=1}^{Q} \beta_{n,i}(option_l) \leq 1$. A distribution, as shown in equation (4), reads that an attribute a_i at an option $option_l$ is assessed to a grade H_n with a degree of belief $\beta_{n,i}(option_l)(n = 1,..., Q)$.

Step 2. Basic probability assignments for each basic attribute: Calculation of basic probability assignments for each basic attribute at an option, $option_l$ Suppose $m_{n,i}$ be a basic probability mass representing the degree to which the i th basic attribute a_i supports a hypothesis that the aggregated attribute x at $option_l$ is assessed to the nth evaluation grade H_n . Suppose $m_{H,i}$ be a remaining probability mass unassigned to any individual grade after a_i has been assessed. $m_{n,i}$ and $m_{H,i}$ are calculated as follows:

FOR i := 1 to P do
FOR n := 1 to Q do

$$m_{n,i} = w_i \beta_{n,i}(option_l) \quad (5)$$

ENDFOR
ENDFOR
FOR i := 1 to P do
FOR n := 1 to Q do

$$m_{H,i} = 1 - m_{n,i} = 1 - w_i \beta_{n,i}(option_l) \quad (6)$$

ENDFOR
ENDFOR

Decomposition of $m_{H,i}$ into $\bar{m}_{H,i}$ and $\tilde{m}_{H,i}$

FOR i := 1 to P do
FOR n := 1 to Q do

$$\bar{m}_{H,i} = 1 - w_i \text{ and } \tilde{m}_{H,i} = w_i(1 - \beta_{n,i}) \quad (7)$$

ENDFOR
ENDFOR

With $m_{H,i} = \bar{m}_{H,i} + \tilde{m}_{H,i}$.

Step 3. Combined probability assignments for a general attribute: Calculation of combined probability assignments for a general attribute x at an option $option_l$.

Suppose, $m_{n,I(1)} = m_{n,1}(n = 1,..., Q)$, $\bar{m}_{H,I(1)} = \bar{m}_{H,1}$,

$\tilde{m}_{H,I(1)} = \tilde{m}_{H,1}$ and $m_{H,I(1)} = m_{H,1}$. The combined probability assignments $m_{n,I(P)}(n=1,...,Q)$, $\overline{m}_{H,I(P)}$, $\tilde{m}_{H,I(P)}$ and $m_{H,I(1)}$ can be calculated by aggregating all the basic probability assignments using the following recursive ER algorithm:

FOR i := 1 to P do
FOR n := 1 to Q do

$$\{H_n\}: \quad m_{n,I(i+1)} = Z_{I(i+1)}\left[m_{n,I(i)}m_{n,i+1} + m_{n,I(i)}m_{H,i+1} + m_{H,I(i)}m_{n,i+1}\right] \tag{8}$$

$$m_{H,I(i)} = \overline{m_{H,I(i)}} + \tilde{m}_{H,I(i)},\ n = 1,............,Q,$$

$$\{H\}: \quad m_{H,I(i)} = \overline{m_{H,I(i)}} + \tilde{m}_{H,I(i)}, n = 1..............,Q \tag{9}$$

$$\tilde{m}_{H,I(i+1)} = Z_{I(i+1)}\left[\tilde{m}_{H,I(i)}\tilde{m}_{H,i+1} + \tilde{m}_{H,I(i)}\overline{m}_{H,i+1} + \overline{m}_{H,I(i)}\tilde{m}_{H,i+1}\right] \tag{10}$$

$$\overline{m}_{H,I(i+1)} = Z_{I(i+1)}\left[\overline{m}_{H,I(i)}\overline{m}_{H,i+1}\right] \tag{11}$$

ENDFOR
ENDFOR

Where $Z_{I,I(i+1)}$ is a normalization factor, used to resolve the conflict and this can be calculated as follows

$if(j \neq t)$
FOR i := 1 to P-1 do
FOR j := 1 to Q do
FOR t := 1 to Q do

$$Z_{I(i+1)} = \left[1 - m_{t,I(i)}m_{j,i+1}\right]^{-1} \tag{12}$$

ENDFOR
ENDFOR
ENDFOR

Step 4. Combined degrees of belief for a general attribute: Combined degrees of belief for an aggregated attribute x at an option $option_l$ are calculated with the help of following equations:

$$\{H_n\}: \beta_n = \frac{m_{n,I(P)}}{1 - m_{H,I(P)}}, n = 1,.........,Q \tag{13}$$

$$\{H\}: \beta_H = \frac{\tilde{m}_{H,I(P)}}{1 - m_{H,I(P)}}, \text{ Where } m_{n,I(1)} = m_{n,1}(n=1,....Q) \tag{14}$$

Where β_n and β_H represent the belief degrees of the aggregated assessment, to which the general factor (such as "facilities") is assessed to the grade H_n and H, respectively.

Step 5. Expected utility is measured: The distributed overall assessment of the option a_l is given by the following equation:

$$S(x(option_l)) = \{(H_n, \beta_n(option_l)), n = 1,......,Q\} \tag{15}$$

Where the utility of a grade H_n, is denoted by $u(H_n)$.

If the overall assessment is complete, the expected utility of $option_l$ on x is then calculated by the following equation:

$$u(option_l) = \sum_{n=1}^{Q} \beta_n(option_l)u(H_n) \tag{16}$$

Step 6. Utility interval: Utility interval for an option is calculated in this step. The maximum, minimum and average utilities of a_l can be calculated by:

$$u_{\max}(option_l) = \sum_{n=1}^{Q-1} \beta_n(option_l)u(H_n) + (\beta_N(option_l) + \beta_H(option_l))u(H_Q)) \tag{17}$$

$$u_{\min}(option_l) = (\beta_1(option_l) + \beta_H(option_l))u(H_1) + \sum_{n=2}^{Q} \beta_n(option_l)u(H_n) \tag{18}$$

$$u_{average}(option_l) = \frac{u_{\max}(option_l) + u_{\min}(option_l)}{2} \tag{19}$$

Step 7. Ranking of the options: The ranking of two alternatives $option_l$ and $option_k$ is based on their utility intervals, $option_l$ is said to be preferred to $option_k$ if and only if $u_{\min}(option_l) > u_{\max}(option_k)$; $option_l$ is said to be indifferent to $option_k$ if and only if $u_{\min}(option_l) = u_{\max}(option_k)$; and $u_{\max}(option_l) = u_{\max}(option_k)$. Otherwise, the average utility may be used to generate the ranking.

3.2. Transformation from Quantitative Attribute to Qualitative Assessment

To assess the overall performance of a ship we need to consider both qualitative data and quantitative data. These quantitative data must be converted to its equivalent qualitative assessment [4] so that, we can aggregate all data together with the help of ER algorithm. In order to transform a quantitative attribute [19], [29], [30] to a qualitative attribute the following equations are used.

$$S(a_i(v)) = \{(v_{n,i}, \beta_{n,i}), n = 1,...,Q\} \tag{20}$$

If $v_{Q,i}$ and $v_{1,i}$ are the highest and lowest quantitative values respectively of any criteria or sub-criteria, then the value $v_{n,i}$ can be evaluated to an evaluation grade $H_n, n = 1,...,Q$. Now the value v is associated on the attribute a_i to the degrees of belief $\beta_{n,i}$ can be calculated with the help of above equation. Again $\beta_{n,i}$ and $\beta_{n+1,i}$ can be calculated as follows:

$$\beta_{n,i} = \frac{v_{n+1,i} - v}{v_{n+1,i} - v_{n,i}}, \beta_{n+1,i} = 1 - \beta_{n,i} \quad if \quad v_{n,i} \le v \le v_{n+1,i} \quad (21)$$

and n=1,..., Q-1

$$\beta_{k,i} = 0 \text{, Where k=1,…,Q and } k \neq n, n+1 \quad (22)$$

3.3. Evaluation of Economic or Quantitative Criteria

The most important economic criteria can be summarized as follows:

i. Net Present Value (NPV):

$$\text{NPV}=\sum_{1}^{N}[PW(annualcargoquality * freightrate) - PW(ammualoperating costs) - PW(shipacquisition costs)] \quad (23)$$

Where, Present Worth Factor (PW) $= \frac{P}{F}$; P = Principal (investment), or a present sum of money and F = Future sum of money.

If the cash flows are uniform over the ship's life cycle, and the ship is paid for in a single installment, Series Present Worth (SPW) factors may be used:

Where, SPW $= \frac{P}{A}$; P = Principal (investment), or a present sum of money and A = Annual return (i.e. income minus expenditure).

NPV = SPW (annual cargo quality * freight rate – operating costs) – ship first cost

The design with the highest NPVs is good.

ii. Required Freight Rate (RFR)

If the ship's attainment cost, the required rate of return, all the in service costs, and the yearly transported freight quantities are known, the Required Freight Rate (RFR) [1].

] is calculated using the following equation:

$$\text{RFR} = \sum_{1}^{N} \frac{PW(annualoperaing costs) + (PW(shipacquisition cost))}{annualcargoquality} \quad (24)$$

For uniform cash flows a useful simplification is possible:

$$\text{RFR} = \frac{annualoperating costs + CR(shipfirst cost)}{annualcargotonnage} \quad (25)$$

Where, Capital Recovery Factor (CR) $= \frac{1}{SPW}$.

The design with the lowest RFR is best.

iii. Yield or DCF Rate of Return.

If the freight income in known, the yield also called Discounted Cash Flow Rate of Return can be calculated [1].Yield we can compare among widely different alternatives, particularly when funds available for investment are comparatively clear.

3.4. Performance Evaluation

The distributed overall assessment of the option $option_l$ is given by the following equation:

The present worth of each item of income and expenditure is determined if the ship's attainment cost, the required rate of return on the capital invested, the operating costs of ship each year, the transported cargo amount each year and the corresponding freight rate of a ship are known. Then these items can be summed up to find the Net Present Value (NPV) [1].

The general formula for calculating NPV is:

$$S(x(option_l)) = \{(H_n, \beta_n(option_l)), n = 1, \ldots\ldots, Q\}.$$

If the overall assessment is complete, the expected utility of $option_l$ on x is then calculated by

$$u(option_l) = \sum_{n=1}^{Q} \beta_n(option_l) u(H_n) \quad (26)$$

Where the utility of a grade H_n, is denoted by $u(H_n)$.

The maximum, minimum and average utilities of $option_l$ can be calculated by:

$$u_{\max}(option_l) = \sum_{n=1}^{Q-1} \beta_n(option_l) u(H_n) + (\beta_Q(option_l) + \beta_H(option_l)) u(H_Q) \quad (27)$$

$$u_{\min}(option_l) = (\beta_1(option_l) + \beta_H(option_l)) u(H_1) + \sum_{n=2}^{Q} \beta_n(option_l) u(H_n) \quad (28)$$

$$u_{average}(option_l) = \frac{u_{\max}(option_l) + u_{\min}(option_l)}{2} \quad (29)$$

3.5. Implementation of ER Algorithm in Ship Assessment

The proposed system represented in this paper uses ER algorithm in the assessment and ranking of ships with some common criteria. Different steps of ER algorithm are implemented by the equations, stated in the earlier section of this paper. The architectural design of the system is presented to expose the overall implementation of the computer based system in figure-4.

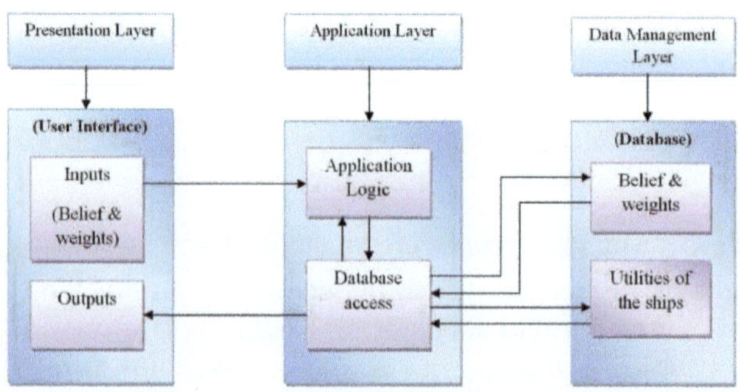

Figure 4. *Architectural Design of the System.*

The Architecture of the system consists of three layers-presentation layer, application processing layer and data management layer [31]. The presentation layer consisting of two basic parts of the system (inputs and outputs) provides the interface for the users while the application layer conceivers all application logics. An adequate environment to access database is also assured in this layer. The data management layer maintains the database of the system.

4. Experimental Results

The ER based ship assessment algorithm is implemented using Turbo C version 3.0 and the graphical block diagrams are drawn using Microsoft Office Visio 2003. The real raw data are collected from Western Fishers Shipyard Ltd, a renowned company of Bangladesh. The raw data are based on five fishing trawlers, namely FT Agro Food 1, FT Agro Food 2 and FT Agro Food 3 FT JK 1 and FT JK 2. Each attribute is measured in one of the four evaluation grades: Poor, Average, Good and Excellent. The belief degrees of attributes for different ships are shown in Table 1.

Table 1. *Assessment of basic attributes of different ships.*

Criteria	FT Agro Food 1	FT Agro Food 2	FT Agro Food 3	FT JK 1	FT JK 2
Safety	P(0.0),A(0.9),G(0.1),E(0.0)	P(0.0),A(0.8),G(0.2),E(0.0)	P(0.0),A(0.0),G(0.2),E(0.8)	P(0.0),A(0.8),G(0.0),E(0.2)	P(0.0),A(0.0),G(0.1),E(0.9)
Fire protection	P(0.3),A(0.5),G(0.2),E(0.0)	P(0.2),A(0.3),G(0.5),E(0.0)	P(0.2),A(0.4),G(0.4),E(0.0)	P(0.0),A(0.0),G(1.0),E(0.0)	P(0.0),A(1.0),G(0.0),E(0.0)
Seaworthiness	P(0.0),A(0.0),G(0.8),E(0.2)	P(0.1),A(0.9),G(0.0),E(0.0)	P(0.0),A(0.0),G(1.0),E(0.0)	P(0.2),A(0.8),G(0.0),E(0.0)	P(0.0),A(0.0),G(1.0),E(0.0)
Living facilities	P(0.0),A(0.2),G(0.7),E(0.1)	P(0.0),A(0.0),G(0.8),E(0.2)	P(0.0),A(0.0),G(1.0),E(0.0)	P(0.0),A(0.5),G(0.5),E(0.0)	P(0.0),A(0.0),G(8.0),E(0.2)
Cargo systems	P(0.0),A(0.3),G(0.5),E(0.2)	P(0.0),A(0.3),G(0.2),E(0.5)	P(0.0),A(0.3),G(0.6),E(0.1)	P(0.0),A(0.4),G(0.6),E(0.0)	P(0.0),A(0.5),G(0.5),E(0.0)
Anchor facilities	P(0.0),A(0.0),G(0.2),E(0.8)	P(0.0),A(0.0),G(0.1),E(0.9)	P(0.0),A(0.0),G(0.5),E(0.5)	P(0.0),A(0.0),G(0.3),E(0.7)	P(0.0),A(0.0),G(0.1),E(0.9)
Communication	P(0.0),A(0.0),G(1.0),E(0.0)	P(0.0),A(0.0),G(0.0),E(1.0)	P(0.2),A(0.8),G(0.0),E(0.0)	P(0.0),A(1.0),G(0.0),E(0.0)	P(0.0),A(0.0),G(1.0),E(0.0)
Above waterline	P(0.2),A(0.8),G(0.0),E(0.0)	P(0.3),A(0.7),G(0.0),E(0.0)	P(0.2),A(0.8),G(0.0),E(0.0)	P(0.6),A(0.4),G(0.0),E(0.0)	P(0.2),A(0.8),G(0.0),E(0.0)
Under waterline	P(0.0),A(0.0),G(0.2),E(0.8)	P(0.0),A(0.7),G(0.3),E(0.0)	P(0.0),A(0.1),G(0.9),E(0.0)	P(0.0),A(0.0),G(0.0),E(1.0)	P(0.0),A(0.1),G(0.9),E(0.0)
Internal arrangement	P(0.0),A(0.0),G(0.9),E(0.1)	P(0.0),A(0.0),G(1.0),E(0.0)	P(0.0),A(0.0),G(0.1),E(0.9)	P(0.0),A(0.5),G(0.5),E(0.0)	P(0.0),A(0.0),G(0.1),E(0.9)
Engine room	P(0.3),A(0.7),G(0.0),E(0.0)	P(0.2),A(0.8),G(0.0),E(0.0)	P(0.1),A(0.9),G(0.0),E(0.0)	P(1.0),A(0.0),G(0.0),E(0.0)	P(0.2),A(0.8),G(0.0),E(0.0)
Navigation	P(0.1),A(0.9),G(0.0),E(0.0)	P(0.0),A(1.0),G(0.0),E(0.0)	P(0.0),A(0.0),G(1.0),E(0.0)	P(0.0),A(0.0),G(0.0),E(1.0)	P(0.0),A(0.0),G(1.0),E(0.0)
Cargo monitor	P(0.0),A(0.0),G(0.2),E(0.8)	P(0.0),A(0.0),G(0.0),E(1.0)	P(0.0),A(0.0),G(0.1),E(0.9)	P(0.0),A(0.0),G(1.0),E(0.0)	P(0.0),A(0.0),G(0.1),E(0.9)
Net Present Value	1620	4635	6810	4250	6805
Required Freight Rate	14.7	13.8	13.8	12.5	12.6

Here, P=Poor, A=Average, G=Good and E=Excellent.

4.1. Transformation of the Quantitative Attributes

In the ER approach, the quantitative attributes are converted into its equivalent qualitative attributes using a common set of evaluation grades in the format of belief structures [4].After then, all qualitative attributes are aggregated for assessment. For doing this, a set of best and worst values for each quantitative attribute needs to be identified, then the best value is considered as highest evaluation grade and the lowest value is considered as the lowest evaluation grade. For example, in Table 1, the value of NPV, 1000 is equivalent to Poor and 7000 is equivalent to Excellent. The values equivalent to Average and Good are calculated based on the two equal intervals in between Poor and Excellent. For example, the values equivalent to Average and Good are 3000 and 5000, respectively. Quantitative attributes are converted to their equivalent qualitative attributes using equation-21. For example, Net Present Value and Required Freight Rate are found for the ship FT Agro Food 1 are (Poor(0.8), Average(0.2)) and (Good(0.3), Excellent(0.7)), respectively. All the quantitative values of each alternative are converted in the same way. Using the above belief degrees for attributes of all alternative ships is shown in Table 2.

Table 2. Assessment of Bottom Level Attributes at each option.

Level 3	FT Agro Food 1	FT Agro Food 2	FT Agro Food 3	FT JK 1	FT JK 2
Safety	P(0.0),A(0.9),G(0.1),E(0.0)	P(0.0),A(0.8),G(0.2),E(0.0)	P(0.0),A(0.0),G(0.2),E(0.8)	P(0.0),A(0.8),G(0.0),E(0.2)	P(0.0),A(0.0),G(0.1),E(0.9)
Fire protection	P(0.3),A(0.5),G(0.2),E(0.0)	P(0.2),A(0.3),G(0.5),E(0.0)	P(0.2),A(0.4),G(0.4),E(0.0)	P(0.0),A(0.0),G(1.0),E(0.0)	P(0.0),A(1.0),G(0.0),E(0.0)
Seaworthiness	P(0.0),A(0.0),G(0.8),E(0.2)	P(0.1),A(0.9),G(0.0),E(0.0)	P(0.0),A(0.0),G(1.0),E(0.0)	P(0.2),A(0.8),G(0.0),E(0.0)	P(0.0),A(0.0),G(1.0),E(0.0)
Living facilities	P(0.0),A(0.2),G(0.7),E(0.1)	P(0.0),A(0.0),G(0.8),E(0.2)	P(0.0),A(0.0),G(1.0),E(0.0)	P(0.0),A(0.5),G(0.5),E(0.0)	P(0.0),A(0.0),G(8.0),E(0.2)
Cargo systems	P(0.0),A(0.3),G(0.5),E(0.2)	P(0.0),A(0.3),G(0.2),E(0.5)	P(0.0),A(0.3),G(0.6),E(0.1)	P(0.0),A(0.4),G(0.6),E(0.0)	P(0.0),A(0.5),G(0.5),E(0.0)
Anchor facilities	P(0.0),A(0.0),G(0.2),E(0.8)	P(0.0),A(0.0),G(0.1),E(0.9)	P(0.0),A(0.0),G(0.5),E(0.5)	P(0.0),A(0.0),G(0.3),E(0.7)	P(0.0),A(0.0),G(0.1),E(0.9)
Communication	P(0.0),A(0.0),G(1.0),E(0.0)	P(0.0),A(0.0),G(0.0),E(1.0)	P(0.2),A(0.8),G(0.0),E(0.0)	P(0.0),A(1.0),G(0.0),E(0.0)	P(0.0),A(0.0),G(1.0),E(0.0)
Above waterline	P(0.2),A(0.8),G(0.0),E(0.0)	P(0.3),A(0.7),G(0.0),E(0.0)	P(0.2),A(0.8),G(0.0),E(0.0)	P(0.6),A(0.4),G(0.0),E(0.0)	P(0.2),A(0.8),G(0.0),E(0.0)
Under waterline	P(0.0),A(0.0),G(0.2),E(0.8)	P(0.0),A(0.7),G(0.3),E(0.0)	P(0.0),A(0.1),G(0.9),E(0.0)	P(0.0),A(0.0),G(0.0),E(1.0)	P(0.0),A(0.1),G(0.9),E(0.0)
Internal arrangement	P(0.0),A(0.0),G(0.9),E(0.1)	P(0.0),A(0.0),G(1.0),E(0.0)	P(0.0),A(0.0),G(0.1),E(0.9)	P(0.0),A(0.5),G(0.5),E(0.0)	P(0.0),A(0.0),G(0.1),E(0.9)
Engine room	P(0.3),A(0.7),G(0.0),E(0.0)	P(0.2),A(0.8),G(0.0),E(0.0)	P(0.1),A(0.9),G(0.0),E(0.0)	P(1.0),A(0.0),G(0.0),E(0.0)	P(0.2),A(0.8),G(0.0),E(0.0)
Navigation	P(0.1),A(0.9),G(0.0),E(0.0)	P(0.0),A(1.0),G(0.0),E(0.0)	P(0.0),A(0.0),G(1.0),E(0.0)	P(0.0),A(0.0),G(0.0),E(1.0)	P(0.0),A(0.0),G(1.0),E(0.0)
Cargo monitor	P(0.0),A(0.0),G(0.2),E(0.8)	P(0.0),A(0.0),G(0.0),E(1.0)	P(0.0),A(0.0),G(0.1),E(0.9)	P(0.0),A(0.0),G(1.0),E(0.0)	P(0.0),A(0.0),G(0.1),E(0.9)
Net Present Value	P(0.8),A(0.2),G(0.0),E(0.0)	P(0.0),A(0.2),G(0.8),E(0.0)	P(0.0),A(0.0),G(0.9),E(0.1)	P(0.0),A(0.6),G(0.4),E(0.0)	P(0.0),A(0.0),G(0.9),E(0.1)
Required Freight Rate	P(0.0),A(0.0),G(0.3),E(0.7)	P(0.0),A(0.8),G(0.2),E(0.0)	P(0.0),A(0.8),G(0.2),E(0.0)	P(0.5),A(0.5),G(0.0),E(0.0)	P(0.6),A(0.4),G(0.0),E(0.0)

Table 3. Obtained assessments for evaluation of level 2 attributes.

Level 2	FT Agro Food 1	FT Agro Food 2	FT Agro Food 3	FT JK 1	FT JK 2
Performance	P(0.1162),A(0.4927),G(0.3413),E(0.0498)	P(0.0977),A(0.6620),G(0.2403),E(0.0000)	P(0.0781),A(0.1562),G(0.5649),E(0.2008)	P(0.0522),A(0.4894),G(0.4062),E(0.0522)	P(0.0000),A(0.4323),G(0.3176),E(0.2501)
Equipment	P(0.0000),A(0.1073),G(0.6476),E(0.2452)	P(0.0000),A(0.0605),G(0.2396),E(0.6999)	P(0.0435),A(0.2567),G(0.5656),E(0.1342)	P(0.000),A(0.4966),G(0.3515),E(0.1519)	P(0.0000),A(0.1049),G(0.6519),E(0.2433)
Appearance	P(0.0536),A(0.2145),G(0.4613),E(0.2706)	P(0.0757),A(0.4060),G(0.5184),E(0.0000)	P(0.0548),A(0.2560),G(0.3056),E(0.3836)	P(0.1627),A(0.3554),G(0.2108),E(0.2711)	P(0.0548),A(0.2560),G(0.3056),E(0.3836)
Automation	P(0.1190),A(0.6307),G(0.0501),E(0.2002)	P(0.0490),A(0.7065),G(0.0000),E(0.2446)	P(0.0276),A(0.2485),G(0.4755),E(0.2485)	P(0.2813),A(0.0000),G(0.2813),E(0.4375)	P(0.0552),A(0.2209),G(0.4755),E(0.2485)
Economy	P(0.5538),A(0.1385),G(0.0923),E(0.2154)	P(0.0000),A(0.3995),G(0.6005),E(0.0000)	P(0.0000),A(0.2273),G(0.7088),E(0.0639)	P(0.1351),A(0.6216),G(0.2432),E(0.0000)	P(0.1846),A(0.1231),G(0.6231),E(0.0692)

Table 4. Overall evaluation of alternative ships.

Alternatives	FT Agro Food 1	FT Agro Food 2	FT Agro Food 3	FT JK 1	FT JK 2
Evaluation	P(0.2955),A(0.2965),G(0.2407),E(0.1673)	P(0.0334),A(0.5013),G(0.4018),E(0.0635)	P(0.0277),A(0.1938),G(0.6448),E(0.1336)	P(0.1021),A(0.5262),G(0.2979),E(0.0738)	P(0.0826),A(0.2217),G(0.5298),E(0.1658)

4.2. Expected Average Utility of Alternatives

After getting the overall assessment of five different alternative ships, the average utilities [29] of all alternatives are calculated for ranking among them. The evaluation grade's utilities are considered to be as follows:

U (Poor) =0.2, U (Average) = 0.4, U (Good) = 0.8, U (Excellent) =1.0

The total expected utilities of five ships as follow:

U (FT Agro Food 1) =
0.2*0.2955+0.4*0.2965+0.8*0.2407+1.0*0.1673 = 0.5376

U (FT Agro Food 2) =
0.2*0.0334+0.4*0.5013+0.8*0.4018+1.0*0.0635 = 0.5922

U (FT Agro Food 3) =
0.2*0.0277+0.4*0.1938+0.8*0.6448+1.0*0.1336 = 0.7325

U (FT JK 1) =
0.2*0.1021+0.4*0.5262+0.8*0.2979+1.0*0.0738 = 0.5430

U (FT JK 2) =
0.2*0.0826+0.4*0.2217+0.8*0.5298+1.0*0.1658 = 0.6948

4.3. Final Results

Final results and ranking among the five alternative ships are shown in Table 5.

Table 5. *Final results.*

Alternatives	FT Agro Food 1	FT Agro Food 2	FT Agro Food 3	FT JK 1	FT JK 2
Expected Utilities	0.5376	0.5921	0.7325	0.5430	0.6948
Ranking	5	3	1	4	2

5. Conclusion

Ship assessment is a very important problem around the world. In ship assessment, the traditional methods mainly uses economic data that are linear in nature, hence, the methods are not sufficient to deal uncertainties and non-linear information. So, ER approach is the most appropriate technique that can handle uncertainty and nonlinear information.

ER approach based algorithm is implemented and evaluated in this research. Five fishing trawlers, namely, FT Agro Food 1, FT Agro Food 2 and FT Agro Food 3 FT JK 1 and FT JK 2 from Western Fishers Shipyard Ltd has been considered in experiment. The five main factors such as Performance, Equipment, Appearance, Automation and Economy are focused in the assessment of ships. In this research, it is concluded that the performance of FT Agro Food 3 is the highest among all other ships and have the highest ranking. In the case of particular ship assessment process the relative gravity of each feature is also measured by identifying the strengths and weaknesses of its own on every single ship. This research presents the result of an individual ship in the form of interval from minimum utility to maximum utility in a systematic and effective way. Only 15 attributes are considered in this experiment, further works could be carried out with considering a large number of uncertain and risky attributes to generate a robust and efficient result. It is strongly recommended to use ER approach based algorithm in ship industry because it can handle both qualitative and quantitative attributes and provide robust and accurate result to minimize risk and uncertainty.

References

[1] I. L. Buxton, Engineering Economics and Ship Design, 2nd edition, pp 57, 58.

[2] Hans Liwang, "Risk-based ship security analysis – an approach based on civilian and military methods," ISSN 1652-9189 Report No 12:141, 2012.

[3] Jian-Bo Yang and Dong-Ling Xu, "Nonlinear Information Aggregation via Evidential Reasoning in Multi-attribute Decision Analysis Under Uncertainty," IEEE Transactions on systems, Man, Cybernetics- Part A: system and humans, vol. 32, no. 3, May 2002.,

[4] Xinlian Xie, Dong-Ling Xu, Jian-Bo Yang, Jin Wang, Jun Ren, Shijun Yu, " Ship selection using a multiple-criteria synthesis approach," J Mar Sci Technol (2008) 13:50-62.

[5] I. Bogardi and A. Baedossy, "Application of MADM to geological exploration," in Essays and Surveys on Multiple Criteria Decision Making, P. Hansen, Ed. New York: Springer-Verlag, 1983.

[6] J. B. Yang and M. G. Singh, "An evidential reasoning approach for multiple attribute decision making with uncertainty," IEEE Trans, Syst.,Man, Cypern., vol. 24, no. 1, pp, 1-18, 1994.

[7] G. Balestra and A. Tsoukias, "Multicriteria analysis represented by artificial intelligence techniques," *J. Oper. Res. Soc.*, vol. 41, no. 5, pp.419–430, 1990.

[8] B. G. Buchanan and E. H. Shortliffe, *Rule-Based Expert Systems*. Reading, MA: Addison Wesley, 1984.

[9] A. Bufardi, "On the construction of fuzzy preference structures," *J. Multi-Criteria Decision Analysis*, vol. 7, no. 3, pp. 57–88, 1998

[10] C. H. Cheng and D. L. Mon, "Evaluating weapon systems by analytical hierarchy process based on fuzzy scales," *Fuzzy Sets Syst.*, vol. 63, no.1, pp. 1–10, 1994.

[11] R. L. Keeney and H. Raiffa, *Decisions With Multiple Objectives*, 2nded. Cambridge, U.K.: Cambridge Univ. Press, 1993

[12] C. C. White, "A survey on the integration of decision analysis and expert systems for decision support," *IEEE Trans. Syst., Man, Cybern.*, vol. 20, no. 2, pp. 358–364, 1990.

[13] R. R. Yager, "On the Dempster–Shafer framework and new combination rules," *Inf. Sci.*, vol. 41, no. 2, pp. 93–137, 1987.

[14] R. R. Yager, "Decision-making under various types of uncertainties," *J. Intell. Fuzzy Syst.*, vol. 3, no. 4, pp. 317–323, 1995.

[15] J. Yen, "Generalizing the Dempster–Shafer theory to fuzzy Sets," *IEEE Trans. Syst., Man, Cybern.*, vol. 20, no. 3, pp. 559–570, 1990.

[16] H. J. Zimmermann, "Problems and tools to model uncertainty in expert and decision support systems," *Math. Comput. Model.*, vol. 14, pp. 8–20,1990.

[17] J. B. Yang and D. L. Xu, "On the evidential reasoning algorithm for multiattribute decision analysis with uncertainty," *IEEE Trans. Syst., Man, Cybern. A*, vol. 32, pp. 289–304, May 2002.

[18] J. B. Yang and P. Sen, "A general multilevel evaluation process for hybrid MADM with uncertainty," *IEEE Trans. Syst., Man, Cybern.*, vol.24, pp. 1458–1473, 1994.

[19] J. B. Yang, "Rule and utility-based evidential reasoning approach for complex decision analysis," *Eur. J. Oper. Res.*, vol. 131, no. 1, pp. 31–61, 2001.

[20] Lotfi A. Zadeh, A Simple View of the Dempster-Shafer Theory of Evidence and its Implication for the Rule of Combination, AI Magazine Volume 7 Number 2 (1986) (© AAAI).

[21] R. Lopez de Mantaras, *Approximate Reasoning Models*. Chichester, U.K.: Ellis Horwood Ltd., 1990.

[22] J. L. Corner and C. W. Kirkwood, "The magnitude of errors in proximal multiattribute decision analysis with probabilistically dependent attributes," *Manage. Sci.*, vol. 42, no. 7, pp. 1033–1042, 1996.

[23] C. W. Kirkwood, "Estimating the impact of uncertainty on a deterministic multiattribute evaluation," *Manage. Sci.*, vol. 38, no. 6, p. 819, 1992.

[24] "An algebraic approach to formulating and solving large models for sequential decisions under uncertainty," *Manage. Sci.*, vol. 39, no. 7, p. 900, 1993.

[25] T. L. Saaty, *The Analytic Hierarchy Process*. Pittsburgh, PA: Univ. Pittsburgh, 1988.

[26] J. Barzilai, "Deriving weights from pairwise comparison matrices," *J. Oper. Res. Soc.*, vol. 48, pp. 1226–1232, 1997.

[27] G. Islei and A. G. Lockett, "Judgmental modeling based on geometric least square," *Eur. J. Oper. Res.*, vol. 36, pp. 27–35, 1988.

[28] N. C. Proudlove, "The support of group decision making using judgmental modeling: An exploration of the contribution of behavioral factors," Ph.D. dissertation, Manchester Business School, Manchester, U.K., 1999.

[29] E. Jacquet-Lagreze and J. Siskos, "Assessing a set of additive utility functions for multicriteria decision making, the UTA method," Eur, J. Oper, Res., vol. 10, pp. 151-164, 1982.

[30] J. B. Yang and P. Sen, "Preference modeling by estimating local utility functions for multiobjective optimization," *Eur. J. Oper. Res.*, vol. 95, pp. 115–138, 1996.

[31] Roger S. Pressman.(2005) Software engineering: a practitioners approach.— 6th ed. p. cm.— (McGraw-Hill series in computer science) Includes index. ISBN 0 -07-365578-3, p373- 374.

7

The Impact of Firm's Level Corporate Governance on Market Capitalization

Md Shamimul Hasan, Normah Omar

Accounting Research Institute, Universiti Teknologi MARA, Shah Alam, Malaysia

Email address:
dr.mdshamimulhasan@rocketmail.com (M. S. Hasan), normah645@salam.uitm.edu.my (N. Omar)

Abstract: The examination of the influence of firm's level CG on market capitalization is potentially important for managers to improve CG system in context of Bangladesh. The linear relationship between CG and market capitalization is recognized at one percent level of significance. A positive and significant relationship between board independence and market capitalization is identified. On the other hand, a negative and significant relationship between public ownership and market capitalization is detected by the model. The present practice of CG does not capable to bring back the eroded confidence of external shareholders. The study recommend some steps for improve the situation such as at least two independent directors or one-third whichever is higher, mandatory training for directors to improve their mindset, introduce audit review system, introduce VFM review mechanism, establishing a high powered financial reporting council (FRC) and so on.

Keywords: Corporate Governance, Market Capitalization, Board Independence, Family Ownership, Capital Market

---

1. Introduction

The central bank of Bangladesh categorizes the financial system into three sectors on the basis of degree of regulation. They are formal sector, semi-formal sector and informal sector. The formal sector includes all regulated institutions like banks, non-bank financial institutions, insurance companies, capital market intermediaries (like brokerage houses, merchant banks etc.) and micro-finance institutions. The semi formal sector includes those institutions which are regulated otherwise but do not fall under the jurisdiction of central bank, insurance authority, Securities and Exchange Commission (SEC) or any other enacted financial regulator. This sector is mainly represented by specialized financial institutions like house building finance corporation (HBFC), palli karma sahayak foundation (PKSF), samabay bank, grameen bank etc. non government organization (NGOs) and discrete government programs. The informal sector includes private intermediaries which are completely unregulated. Financial market could be segregated primarily into short-term (Money market) and long-term (Capital market); long-term market is segregated into security segment (share, debenture, preference share, bond etc.) and non-security segment (long-term bank loan); and security segment is segregated into primary (IPO) and secondary market (Stock market). The market mechanism for the buying and selling of new issues of securities is known as primary market. In this process, the company issues their share to the people directly by following necessary formalities with the regulator. The secondary market, also called stock exchange, on the other hand, deals with securities that have already been issued for trading. In this case, transactions of shares are made between old investors (seller) and new investors (purchaser) in the stock exchange through stockbrokers where beneficiary owners (BO) accounts are maintained. The companies need two type of financing based on time reference such as short-term and long-term financing to operate the business. Money market is used for short-term financing (working capital) and primary market is used for long-term financing (long-term investment such as machinery purchase, extension of building etc.). When we talk about the capital market we usually mean secondary market or stock exchange where a lot of shares of different companies are traded every working day. The flow of money in the stock exchange does not flow to the company but it provides liquidity support for the shareholders of the company. Formation of capital through savings and investments is necessary precondition for development of an economy and capital market has an important role in this process. The various indicators of stock market are used to guess the status of a country economy. Market capitalization is one of the important stock market indicators. The up-down of market capitalization depends on the movement of investors. Generally, the movement of investors towards a particular company depends on the positive information of that company and vice-versa. Corporate governance (CG) mechanism provides assurance to investors and the degree of assurance depends upon the level of practices of CG in the firm.

The high number and high value of corporate scandals during the first years of the 21st century have had a dramatic effect on CG (Marlene and John, 2011). It refers to the structures and processes for the direction and control of companies. Good CG has a contribution to sustainable economic development through enhancing the performance of corporate entities and increasing their access to outside capital. Sound CG enhances the level of investors' of confidence in the firm's future cash-flows and growth prospects (Haque et al., 2013). The present scenario of CG is far below the expected level in Bangladesh (Hasan et al., 2014c). CG practices are gradually being introduced in most companies and organizations. 66.7 percent companies have adopted CG and 43 percent have compliance policy with national or international benchmarks. A considerable percentage of the top management does not fully understand the concept of CG (Du, 2006). Bangladesh has lagged behind its neighbors and the global economy in CG (Gillibrand, 2004). Greater independence and professionalism is required in the boardrooms of both listed companies and state-owned enterprises (World Bank, 2009). Moreover, there is hardly any pressure group for enforcing CG principles.

In addition, the corporate sector depends on bank loan as their major source of financing. Capital market is in the embryonic stage as market capitalization amounting to only 6.5 percent of GDP with low investor confidence on CG and financial disclosure practices in many publicly traded companies (Du, 2006). Awareness of the importance of CG is growing very slowly. As such the largest financial market repeatedly faces challenges with great fall down of share price and a large portion of liquid money just go missing from the market in a single moment. Up and down is the common feature of capital market but there must have certain consistency and level of protection which is missing in Bangladesh (Hoque and Nasrin, 2013). The overall performance of stock market shows low trading volume, intermittent bumps, not many new offerings, unsteady valuations more on the declining side than otherwise (Hossain, 2005). In 2009-2010 the number of participants dramatically increased in the stock market and hence market capitalization. The market capitalization to GDP ratio is over 20 percent (The Daily Star, July 19, 2009). But the stock market crash in 2011, which is the largest crash in the corporate history of Bangladesh, has seriously eroded investors' confidence. The overall framework for investors' protection and CG has a number of important weaknesses that have delayed the capital market development (Khan, 2007).

CG practices matter because it allows firms to have greater access to financing, reduces the cost of capital, ensures higher valuation of the firm and allows for better operational performance (Claessens and Yurtoglu, 2012). According to Capiro and Levine (2002), CG influences the efficiency of a firm's production at the firm level so that the effectiveness of a nation's CG system shapes economic performance at the country level. A best-practice approach encompasses other stakeholders not merely the shareholders and the directors (Marlene and John, 2011). With better investor protection and lower expropriation by controlling shareholders, outsider investors intend to invest more or pay higher share prices in the hope that more of the firm's profits would come back to them as interest or dividends (La Porta et al., 2002). Claessens (2003) identifies several channels, through which CG frameworks influence the growth and development of economies, financial markets and firms. These include, greater access to financing, lower cost of capital, better firm performance, reducing risks of financial distress and financial crisis, and more favorable treatment of all stakeholders. When firms stick to sound CG practices, they are able to balance multiple stakeholders' interests, meet both legal obligations and general societal expectations. Since good CG practices enhance transparency and accountability in companies, investors are better placed to make informed investment decisions. Shleifier and Vishny (1997) observe that a firm is likely to get external finance due to assurances provided by the CG system.

Therefore, we argue that firms' level CG practices might have an impact on market capitalization. As of today, the previous researchers focus on the relationship between CG and firm's performance and they measure firm's performance in various ways such as return on equity, return on capital employed, Tobin-q equation etc. However, the past researchers did not focus on the impact of CG over market capitalization. Market capitalization is a dynamic measure of market value of the company. All sort of information either positive or negative of the company is adjusted in the share price immediately after release the information. A research gap exists and we strive to fill this research gap. The objective of this study is to examine the influence of firm's level CG on market capitalization. This study contributes a new insight of firm's level CG if we find a linear relationship with market capitalization. Management might be motivated to improve their level of CG practices to enhance their reputation in the capital market.

The next section presents literature review and this is followed by a description of the research method, the discussion of the findings, and the conclusion.

2. Literature Review

The previous researchers on CG focused on many issues like firm's performance, capital market development, compliance, regulations, financial reporting, etc. based on CG index, regulations, Tobin's q formula, overall disclosure index, voluntary disclosure etc. We carefully review the existing CG literature to identify the research gap. Sarkar (2007) examines the impact of shareholder protection on stock market developments as well as the impact of stock market developments on private fixed capital formation. In both cases, he finds non-existent of long-term relationship.

He observes that law does not matter for stock market development. He used CBR index based on the book law–not the actual implementation. There is a view that the rule of law is at a very miserable stage in many LDCs including India because of corruption and other imperfections. Haque et al., (2008) outline a conceptual framework of the relationship between CG and two important elements of capital market development namely, a firm's access to finance, and its financial performance. The framework assumes that a firm's CG is concurrently determined by a group of connected governance components and other firm characteristics. Whereas the capital markets play a crucial role in augmenting CG standards, the effectiveness and genuineness of such effort might be embarrassed by poor firm-level CG. Moreover, the cause and effect relationship can work in the reverse direction for instance firm-level CG quality can augment both the firm's ability to gain access to finance and its financial performance, which ultimately lead to capital market development. Santner and Villalonga (2010) exploit an exogenous shock to corporate ownership structures created by a recent tax reform in Germany to explore the link between CG and internal capital markets. They find that firms with more concentrated ownership are less diversified and have more efficient internal capital markets. Their findings provide direct evidence in support of Scharfstein and Stein's (2000) model, which recommends that internal capital misallocations are partially an outcome of poor CG. Ariadna (2010) analyzes the affects of CG on the performance of financial markets. He models the interaction between a firm's manager and its shareholders, and highlights the role played by the dividend report in information disclosure and information communication. The researcher uses three channels such as the dividend willingly paid; the profits held by shareholders in case of interference; and the price set by the market maker. The result shows that CG affects market liquidity: higher monitoring costs, lower ownership concentration, effective disclosure regulation and effective shareholder protection, all lead to higher market liquidity. Balasubramanian et al. (2010) contribute to the literature on CG indices and the connection between governance and firm value. They form a broad Indian CG Index (*ICGI*) and examine the association between ICGI and firm market value. ICGI Index consists of five groups namely, board structure, disclosure, related party transactions, shareholders' rights and board procedure. They rely on the survey and firm annual reports to create an India CG Index (ICGI). They use "Tobin's *q"* as principal measure of market value. They find a positive and statistically significant association between ICGI and firm market value in India but sub-indices for board structure, disclosure, board procedure, and related party transactions are not significant. The non-results for board structure contrast to other recent studies, and suggest that India's legal requirements are sufficiently rigid so that over compliance does not produce valuation gains. Anglin and Gao (2011) examine how changes in CG regulations, especially those related to disclosure, affect the market process. With many sources of information, a policy designed to improve information quality should combine the obvious direct effect with indirect effects, some of which are not usually considered. They display that the effects on total information quality depend on the relations between public reports and the information obtained by private investor. Therefore, governance reforms can touch the level of private information by affecting the behavior of private investors and, indirectly, the market maker. Kowalewski (2012) investigates the association between CG, measured by CG Index (CGI), and firm's performance and dividend payouts during the financial crisis in Poland. The results show a positive association between CG and performance measured by "Tobin's q". Moreover, he finds evidence that higher CG leads to an increase in cash dividends. Finally, the results presents that during the recent financial crisis CG is definitely associated with return on assets. However, in the period of the financial crisis better governed companies pay dividends less generously than do firms with lower CG standards. Claessens and Yurtoglu (2012) study current research on CG, with an exceptional focus on developing markets. They find that improved corporate outlines help firms through greater access to financing, lower cost of capital, better performance, and more favorable treatment of all stakeholders. The paper concludes by identifying issues requiring further study, including the special CG issues of banks, and family-owned and state-owned firms, and the nature and elements of public and private enforcement.

We also review the past researchers works on CG in Bangladesh. Rashid et al. (2007) explore an overview of CG in Bangladesh. They identify six specific CG characteristics in relation to current CG practices in Bangladesh namely legal and regulatory frame work, weak institutional control, predominance of individual investors, limited transparency & weak disclosure practices etc. Andres and Vallelado (2008) examine the role of the board of directors while applying CG in banking business. They point out that board composition and size are related to directors' ability to monitor and advice management and that larger and not excessively independent board might prove more efficient in monitoring and advising functions, and create more value. Kha et al. (2009) critically review the legal systems and CG guidelines issued by SEC. To reduce conflict of interest between shareholders (Principal) and management (Agent), it is necessary to have strong CG practices which can be monitored by capital market regulators. This study is a descritive one. Karim et al. (2010) investigate the extent to which listed companies comply with the CG guidelines of SEC. They survey annual report for the period of 2007 of 51 companies. The mean disclosure is 85.5 percent compliance. However, the practical CG compliance test is much more important as most of the companies tick the comply column under 'comply or explain' format of CG reporting whereas the financial reporting of companies suffers the lack of qualitative characteristics. Rashid et al. (2010) examine board composition and firm performance from Bangladesh perspective. The study also tests the influence of corporate board composition in the form of representation of outside independent directors on firms' economic performance. The finding of the study provides an insight to the regulators in this pursuit for harmonization of internal CG practices. Kutubi (2011) examine the impact of board size and the independent directors on the performance of the local private commercial banks. The study reveals that statistically significance positive relationship existed between the proportions of the independent directors and the performance of the banks. Hossain (2011) underlines the CG practices pointing out that good CG has implication for company behavior towards employees, shareholders, customers & bankers. He suggests that improved CG can provide noteworthy rewards to both individual companies and countries. Huq and Bhuiyan (2012) examine 10 specific problems through survey of an open ended questionnaire by selecting 24 repondents out of 66 personnels from 6 selected banks. They survey annual report to examine the organogram of both Islamic and Conventional banks. One of the ten specific problems is the weak role of the cpaital market. Bangladesh does not have depth in its equity market. All respondents point out that the Bangladesh capital market is still weak in its journey towards strengthening CG. Meah (2013) examine some definitions, principles, concepts and legal framework of CG. The study also investigate the extent to which the capital market comply with the CG guidelines of Bangladesh Securities and Exchange Commission (BSEC) and he also indicates that only sound CG practices are the foundation upon which the confidence of investors is originated. However, the CG guidelines issued by BSEC is only applicable for the listed companies of capital market and not applicable for capital market. Hasan et al. (2013b) examine the relationship between corporate governance and disclosures. They find a linear relationship between corporate governance and disclosures. External auditor, a corporate governance variable, can significantly influence the level of corporate financial disclosures. Hasan et al. (2014c) study family performance and corporate governance structures. They find weak practices of corporate governance comparing with CG guidelines. Hasan et al. (2014b) examine the linear relationship between corporate governance and corporate accruals (discretionary accruals). They find that corporate accrual does not depend upon the corporate governance rather it comes from the mindset of management.

Although there is an extensive body of research on CG and capital market development, less attention has been paid on the issue of impact of degree of assurance (firm level CG) on market capitalization. This paper attempts to bridge this gap testing empirically five research hypotheses relating to firm's level CG and market capitalization. The findings of this study would motivate corporate managers to introduce best practice of standard in the firm for sustainable development e.g., corporate responsibility and corporate citizenship.

3. The Variables and Hypotheses

We select some variables in order to test the linear relationship between CG and market capitalization (*MC*). The market values of equity of sampled companies (*MC*) is used as a dependent variable while Board Independence (*BI*), Dominant Personality (*DP*), Board Size (*BS*), Public Ownership (*PO*), and Family Ownership (*FO*), are used as independent variables and Institutional Ownership (*IO*) and AGM Expenses (*AE*), are used as control variable in this study.

The definition and measurement of the variables included in the model and the range of their values are presented in Table 1. We will now briefly review the CG literature about independent variables to see what it states about their role in governance practices.

Table 1. *The definition, measurement and range of values of variables.*

Variables	Definition	Measurement	Range of Values
Dependent Variable			
Market Capitalization (*MC*)	Market value of equity of the sampled companies.	Closing share price multiplied by outstanding number of ordinary shares.	Any positive value
Independent Variables			
Board Independence (*BI*)	Board independence is defined as the proportion of independent directors in the board.	Number of independent non-executive directors divided by total number of directors on the board	0 - 1
Family ownership (*FO*)	Sponsor shareholders i.e., Family ownership	Code "1" for majority of share held by family members and "0" otherwise.	0, 1
Public Ownership (*PO*)	Public ownership is defined as the ratio of shares held by general people in the ownership structure of sample companies.	Total number of shares held by general people divided by total number of issued shares	0 - 1
Dominant Personality (*DP*)	Dominant personality is defined as the position of Chairman and CEO of sample companies are the same person.	Code "1" if Chairman also holds the position of CEO and "0" otherwise	0, 1
Board Size (*BS*)	Board size is defined as total number of directors in the board of sample companies.	Number of the board of directors.	≤ 20
Control Variables			
Institutional Ownership (*IO*)	Institutional ownership is defined as the ratio of institutional holdings in the ownership structure of sample companies.	Total number of shares held by institutions divided by total number of issued shares or "0" otherwise	0 - 1
AGM Expenses (*AE*)	Annual general meeting expenses of the sampled companies.	Actual expenses of annual general meeting expenses that are shown in the annual reports of sampled companies.	Any positive value

3.1. Board Independence

The first step of good CG system is board independence. Following the Anglo-American model, Bangladeshi companies conform to the unitary board structure (one-tier system), where the board is the highest governing body in the company. As the board is at the apex of internal control system, the role of outside independent directors becomes crucial in monitoring the performance of management. The board which comprises a number of independent directors has a greater monitoring and controlling ability over management (Fama and Jensen, 1983). The Cadbury report (1992) define 'independent' as being free from any business or financial connection with the company other than their fees or shareholdings. According to CG guidelines for listed companies in Bangladesh, "one-fifth of the total number of the company's board of directors, subject to a minimum of one, should be independent directors". While according to the listing requirement (Chapter 15 Section 02 Subsection1) of Malaysia, "A listed issuer must ensure that at least 2 directors or 1/3 of the board of directors of a listed issuer, whichever is the higher, are independent directors." As per this condition, if a company has only three board members, two of them are required to be independent (Malaysia, 2006). Board independence seeks fairness in the strategic decisions taken by the Board and effective monitoring of the decisions and activities of managers, thus ensuring transparency of information and proper image on the outside of organizations (Chen and Jaggi, 2000; Patelli and Prencipe, 2007). The agency theory supports the idea that to increase the board's independence from management, boards should be dominated by outside directors (Abdul Rahman and Salim, 2010). The following hypothesis is taken to examine the linear relationship between board independence and market capitalization.

H_1: There is a significant association between board independence and market capitalization.

3.2. Board Size

The number of directors in the boardroom may affect the monitoring ability of the board. A larger board size may bring a greater number of directors with experience (Xie et al., 2001) that may represent a multitude of values (Halme and Huse, 1997) on the board. Larger boards are often believed to be more capable of monitoring the actions of top management, because it is more difficult for CEOs to dominate larger boards (Zahra and Pearce, 1989). Similarly, Singh and Harianto (1989) suggest that larger boards can make it more difficult for the CEO to obtain consensus for taking actions that will harm shareholders' interests. In contrast, smaller boards may be more effective because they might be able to make timely strategic decisions (Goodstein et al., 1994). Fiegner and Brown (2000) find that smaller board size along with outsider representation is conducive to an active board with high level of involvement in strategic formulation. A reduced number of directors imply a high degree of coordination and communication between them and managers (Jensen, 1993). Chaganti et al. (1985) claim that smaller boards are manageable and more often play a role as a controlling function whereas larger boards may not be able to function effectively as the board leaves the management relatively free. CG guidelines of Bangladesh provide that the number of the board members of the company should not be less than 5 (five) and more than 20 (twenty). The following hypothesis is taken to examine the linear relationship between board size and market capitalization.

H_2: There is a significant association between board size and market capitalization.

3.3. The CEO-Chairman (Dominant Personality)

The board exists to keep management accountable for the vast discretionary power it wields. Thus, when the chairman of the board is also the CEO, it makes management accountable to a body led by management. It can mean that the CEO is put in the position of evaluating his own performance. A 1992 survey of company directors by Korn/Ferry find that just below than 20 percent believe that separating the CEO and chairman positions will have a "very negative impact" on boardroom performance. A little more than 20 percent think it will have a "very positive impact" and not quite 60 percent think the impact of separating the roles will be neutral. Those who are in favour of separating the roles believe it will lead to more objective evaluation of the CEO and create an environment of greater accountability. When the CEO is also the chairman there is "too great temptation to 'tilt' things toward protecting CEO career interests" commented by one outsides director in the survey (Monks and Minow, 2010). Rechner and Dalton (1991) find that companies with separate CEOs and chairman consistently outperform those companies that combine the roles. The CG literature has emphasized the need to separate the position of CEO (chief executive officer) and board chairman to guarantee the board independence and improve transparency (Jensen, 1993). Dechow et al. (1996) reveal that the duality CEO-chairman increases the likelihood of violating the accounting principles in American firms. Byard and Weintrop (2006) indicate that the presence of a CEO who serves also as the board chairman is associated with poor quality of financial information. Similarly, Beekes et al. (2004) and Firth et al. (2007) report that the financial reporting is more relevant in the case of separating the positions of CEO and board chairman for British and Chinese firms. Nevertheless, other authors do not detect a significant association between CEO duality and financial reporting (Ahmed et al., 2006; Bradbury et al., 2006; Petra, 2007). The following hypothesis is taken to examine the linear relationship between dominant personality and market capitalization.

H_3: There is a significant association between dominant personality and market capitalization.

3.4. Family Ownership

Family – owned business are found to be common in continental Europe, Latin America and Asia. It is estimated that over two-thirds of worldwide firms are owned and managed by families (Gersick et al., 1997). Schulze et al. (2003) find that family firms make up 80 percent of organizations in the U.S. In Chile, it is estimated that 75 percent of all firms and 65 percent of medium to large firms are families (Martinez, 1994) and in Germany, family companies comprise 80 percent of German Organizations (Reidel,1994). A survey by the Bank of Italy illustrates that almost 80 percent family members are employees in the family companies (Corbetta, 1995). Likewise, average 85 percent of listed companies are family firms in Bangladesh, a family dominant country (Hasan et al., 2014c). Family firms are very much governed by family traits (Mishra et al., 2001). Families can combat the potential conflicts between families and firm, therefore, family firms may outperform their competitors, at least economically (Lee, 2004). Families are able to maintain the continuity of the family firms by transferring company assets over time. Thus, the market value of the firm can increase (James, 1999). Castilo and Wakefield (2006) find that family firms are uniquely suited to succeed over other publicly traded firms due to strong family ties. In addition, the extensive knowledge about a firm by the family members encourages quick and flexible decisions (James, 1999). In contrast, Barclay and Holderness (1989) note that large ownership stakes reduce the probability of bidding by other agents, thereby reducing the value of the firm. The family's role in selecting managers and directors creates an impediment to outsiders in capturing control of the firm, suggesting greater managerial entrenchment and lower firm values relative to non-family firms. Lauterbach and Vaninsky (1999) evidence that family firms run by their owners perform worse than the non-family firms. In Italy, Cuculelli and Micucci (2008) find that the negative impact of family companies' performance is exacerbated when company control is passed to the next family generation. The following hypothesis is taken to examine the linear relationship between family ownership and market capitalization.

H_4: There is an association between family ownership and market capitalization.

3.5. Public Ownership

Public ownership reflects the dispersion of ownership, which has a relationship with disclosure and transparency (Legenzova, 2008). Differences in the proportion of a firm that is owned by outsiders may account for some of the observed differences - in the comprehensiveness of mandatory disclosure, because the greater number of people who need to know about the affairs of a firm, the greater will be the details required of an item of information and the more comprehensive the disclosure of a firm will be (Apostolou et al., 2009). Leftwich et al. (1981) suggest that issuing financial reports can solve monitoring problems associated with increases in the proportion of the firm owned by outsiders. It is expected that if a company has a large proportion of public ownership, the political cost will be bigger and the company will decide to disclose more information to satisfy them. Thomsen and Pedersen (2003) examine the relationship between owner identity and market valuation among the largest European companies. They differentiate owner identity into four types: family, financial institutions, government and companies. They find that the firm's largest owner of financial institutions and company have positive significant effect on firm value. The following hypothesis is taken to examine the linear relationship between public ownership and market capitalization.

H_5: There is a significant association between public ownership and market capitalization.

4. Research Framework

The research idea could be visualized by drawing a diagram to give a graphical view of diagnostic pattern of the problem under study. Figure 1 shows that board independence, board size, dominant personality, family ownership, and public ownership are used as firm's level corporate governances. Then, degree of influence of every step of firm's level corporate governances is estimated. The influence of board impendence on market capitalization is estimated by testing the hypothesis 1 (H_1), the linear relationship between board size and market capitalization is estimated testing the hypothesis 2 (H_2), the association between dominant personality and market capitalization is estimated by testing of hypothesis 3 (H_3), the impact of family ownership on market capitalization is estimated by testing the hypothesis 4 (H_4), and the relationship between public ownership and market capitalization is examined testing the hypothesis 5 (H_5).

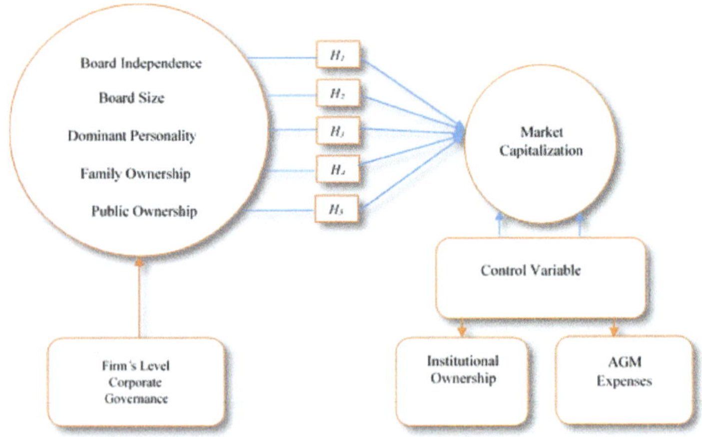

Figure 1. *Research framework.*

5. Data and Methods

5.1. Data

Of the 155 non-financial companies listed on the premier bourse, Dhaka Stock Exchange (DSE) in Bangladesh, 68 are taken as a sample data set for the current study, based on access to their corporate annual reports for 2010-2011(Table 5, Appendix 1). The sample size equates to 44 percent of the population so allows us to generalize the findings of this study. Market capitalization data are collected from DSE and the remaining data for all other variables are extracted from a survey of annual reports of sampled companies.

5.2. Methods

Descriptive statistics technique is used to form a central idea or overall situation of stock market and corporate governance as there is diversity in the level of market capitalization and CG practices across companies. Correlation matrix is used to analyze the multicollinearity between independent variables. It is essential to examine the multicollinearity between independent variables before going to use these variables in the multiple regression analysis. Because, if we find multicollinearity between two variables then one variable is needed to drop from the model as these two variables measure the same thing. If we do not want to drop the variable then we can go for second tier relationship by using second generation method - AMOS but it is not possible to build second tier relationship in SPSS. In SPSS, we must drop one variable if we find multicollinearity between two variables. A linear regression model is developed for in-depth analysis of the effect of assurance provider (firm level CG) on market capitalization. In other words, the model is used to estimate the effect of the relationship between *MC* and *BI*, *DP*, *BS*, *FO* and *PO*. We run the model in SPSS to see the adjusted R^2, ANOVA and coefficients. The adjusted R^2 tells us the about the fitness of the model, the p-value of ANOVA gives us an overall direction regarding accepting or rejecting the hypothesis and the p-values of coefficients tell us the significance level of the impact of the CG variables on market capitalization individually. The p-values of coefficients are used either accepting or rejecting the hypotheses. The acceptances criterion of hypothesis is at 1 percent or 5 percent level of significance. The model could be presented in the following form:

$$MC = \alpha + \beta_1 BI + \beta_2 BS + \beta_3 DP + \beta_4 FO + \beta_5 PO + \beta_6 IO + \beta_7 AE + \varepsilon$$

6. Results and Discussion

If we look at the results from the descriptive statistics, Table 2 shows that the average rate of board independence is 15 percent but as per CG guidelines the minimum rate of board independence is 20 percent meaning that the relationship of independent directors to board size is 1 (one) divided 5 (five) i.e., 20 percent (= 1/5 x 100). Board independence is the primary element of CG. As per CG guidelines, one independent director is required against four board members for board independence. The ratio between board size and number of independent directors are not duly followed by many companies. Even some companies have not yet appointed independent directors and some companies have ten board members but they have appointed only one independent director. But in Malaysia, if a company has only three board members, two of them are required to be independent (Malaysia, 2006). The average number, minimum number and maximum number of directors of the board are 8, 3 and 17 respectively. According to the CG guidelines, the minimum number of directors is 5 and maximum number is 20 members in the board. So, the condition of minimum number of directors in the board room does not fulfill the requirement by CG guidelines. Although, the board size is not enough for ensuring good governance but it is essential to create an environment where everybody will respect and follow the rules of CG guidelines. Besides, the academic qualification, professional experience, corporate integrity, ethical behavior, caring for others, and the like qualities of directors is utmost important to ensure good governance meaning that better companies means better society. Usually, members with these qualities in the board room are unexpected under family based CG. CEO-chairman (or CEO duality or dominant personality) is not allowed in the CG guidelines. The result shows that 26 percent of sampled companies are being operated by dominant personality. The CG guidelines stated that chairman and CEO position should be filled up by separate individual. The condition is not being fulfilled by some sampled companies. The rate is lower because these two positions have been fulfilled by separate individuals but our observation is to focus the relationship between two individual of these two positions for ensuring transparency, accountability and integrity. We see that sometimes wife is chairman and husband is CEO, sometime father is chairman and son is CEO, sometime elder brother is chairman and younger brother is CEO. So, the separation of control is not happening here in true sense. It is almost impossible to ensure good governance without separation of control. The concerned authority should look into the matter in such a positive way so that directors may come forward enthusiastically for their own sake. We also observe that some companies produce an excuse of financial burden and this is not acceptable at all for public limited companies. Therefore, the regulator as well as operators of stock market should take initiative to improve the CG scenario in the corporate sector in Bangladesh. Family ownership is the most influential component of ownership structure in Bangladesh. Table 1 reveals that 85 percent of the sampled companies have family ownership and hence most of the listed companies are one-man show. There is both side of argument on family ownership in the literature. For example, Fama & Jensen (1983 p.306) claims that "family ownership is particularly efficient to minimize agency problems because shares are in the hands of agents who have special relations with other decision agents that allow agency problems to be controlled without separation of the management and control decisions". However, family-companies can make sub-optimal decisions since the interests of the family are not necessarily consistent with those of other shareholders (Fama and Jensen, 1985). Restricted ownership also reduces external governance and potential problems may arise when a firm is headed by a powerful owner / manager or family relationships tend to make agency problems more difficult to resolve (Schulze et al., 2001). The internal control system is usually poor in family firms and all sort of decisions are taken from personal perspective and power of authority is highly centralized. These organizations cannot offer good working environment for professionals as the chain of command is not maintained here and only toadies enjoy the job by flattering their boss. Moreover, the business entity concept of accounting does not allow the mixing between family and business. According to this concept, the entity is completely separate from the owner otherwise we cannot measure the accurate performance of the business. The average percentage of public ownership of in the ownership structure of the sampled companies is 41 percent. The result shows that a good number of individual participates in the capital market. This is spread ownership and they are considered as minority shareholders also called external shareholders. The companies publish annual report especially for them as they do not have access to the company accounts. Therefore, it is essential to provide reliable information in the annual report so that they can measure the performance of the company and take decisions accordingly. In the history of capital market in Bangladesh, two crashes had been occurred - one in 1996 and the other in 2010-2011. In 1996, the cause of crash was speculative bubble and in 2010-2011 the cause was asset pricing bubble. According to the inquiry report of 2011, accounting manipulation such as earnings manipulation, over valuation of assets in the name of revaluation, false reporting, payment of dividends from unrealized gain, non-compliance of accounting standards, non recognition of deferred tax implications on revaluation, poor quality of work of some audit firms etc., had been done to artificially increase share price. Besides, a section of directors of listed companies' especially family firms were involved in the manipulation of capital market. Therefore, shareholders do not have confident on the information published in the annual report. The users' perception about the qualitative characteristics of corporate financial reporting is far below the acceptable level and as such users' have a negative attitude towards disclosures of financial reporting (Hasan et al., 2014a).

Table 2. *Descriptive Statistics.*

Variables	N	Minimum	Maximum	Mean	Std. Deviation	CV
MC	68	71.45	267224.38	10067.54	33909.14	3.37
BI	68	0.00	1.00	0.15	0.14	0.96
BS	68	3.00	17.00	7.40	2.29	0.31
DP	68	0.00	1.00	0.26	0.44	1.71
FO	68	0.00	1.00	0.85	0.36	0.42
PO	68	0.05	0.94	0.41	0.22	0.53
IO	68	0.00	0.86	0.20	0.21	1.07
AE	53	36960	62161349	2975631	8742362	2.94

Table 3. *Correlations Matrix.*

Variables	BI	DP	BS	IO	PO	AE	FO
BI	1						
DP	-0.133	1					
BS	0.03	-0.061	1				
IO	0.153	-0.17	0.092	1			
PO	-0.127	0.083	-0.104	-.410**	1		
AE	-0.027	-0.138	0.221	0.209	-.237*	1	
FO	-.380**	.249*	-.403**	-.358**	.403**	-.548**	1

Table 4. *Results of regression test of the Model.*

Predictors	Coefficients	T - Value	P – Value
BI	0.189	3.852	0.000**
BS	0.03	0.611	0.544
DP	-0.013	-0.293	0.771
FO	0.094	1.465	0.15
PO	-0.105	-2.156	0.036*
IO	-0.077	-1.57	0.124
AE	0.976	18.07	0.000**

R	0.958
R^2	0.918
Adjusted R^2	0.906
F Value	72.372
P Value	0.000*
DF Model	7
DF Error	45

Legend :	
BI	Board independence
BS	Board size
DP	Dominant personality
FO	Family ownership
PO	Public ownership
IO	Institutional ownership
AE	Annual general meeting expenses
R^2	The explanatory power of regression equation

If we look at the results from the correlation matrix, Table 3 shows that there is no multicollinearity issue between independent variables. The examination of multicollinearity between independent variables is necessary because if multicollinearity exists between two variables then one variable should be dropped from the model as these two variables measure the same thing. Judge et al. (1985) and Bryman and Cramer (1997) suggest that simple correlation is not harmful unless they exceed 0.80 or 0.90. The observed correlation between variables does not exceed 0.80 and therefore, the variables are not considered harmful in the interpretation of the results of the linear regression analysis.

Finally, if we look at the outcome from the regression model, Table 4 shows that the model is capable to explain 90 percent variation in market capitalization by the variation of CG variables and we also find a significant relationship between CG and market capitalization at one percent level of significance. So our research hypothesis is accepted. The table also shows that the board independence has a significant influence on market value of equity at one percent level of significance and public ownership has a linear correlation at five percent level of significance. Board size, family ownership and dominant personality do not have significant influence on market value of equity or market capitalization. Therefore, hypothesis one and hypothesis five are accepted as they are supported by the results. Likewise, hypothesis two, three and four are rejected as they are not supported by the results of this study.

We find two important variables such as board independence and public ownership that have a significant association with market capitalization. Board independence is a necessary prerequisite for one of the board's most fundamental responsibilities – unbiased oversight of management (Abdul Rahman and Haniffa, 2005). There is a need of a board that is capable of taking strong independent action (and this means that a majority of directors should be truly independent) and also able to understand the company and its business. In other words, the board would be in a better position to achieve a better balance between independence and understanding of the business (Abdul Rahman and Salim, 2010). The composition of the board is a critical factor in establishing the effectiveness of the board as an objective monitor of management. The word "independent" has no universal definition and different countries have adopted different definitions of the word in their respective CG code. "Independent" is generally taken to mean that there is no relationship or circumstances which could affect the director's judgment. In order to be independent, a director must have no connection to the company other than sit on the board. Political motivation of independent director is also an important factor in context of Bangladesh. If chairman, CEO and independent director have the same political motivation then there is a possibility of using this network in the board room. If business leader have a motivation for independency of the board then it will have a positive image in the society which is very much useful for extending their business. The market value of the company will be higher and more business opportunity will come because an effective board can build trust in the society. It is disastrous for the marginal shareholders when directors themselves exercise opportunism (Hasan et al., 2014b).

Public ownership is also called spread ownership or external shareholders meaning that they do not have right to access to the company accounts. They are to rely on published annual reports for both information i.e., financial or non-information. According to the Companies Act 1994, the company will send their annual report to the address of shareholders before 14 days of annual general meeting (AGM). Shareholders can interact with the chairman of the board in the AGM if they need more explanation for the items in the annual report. It is alleged that most of the companies do not send their annual reports within the stipulated time. This misbehavior creates a negative impression about the corporate financial reporting among external users of annual reports. In a recent study we observe that 30 percent respondents opine that the financial statements is not prepared in an understandable manner, 81.05 percent respondents believe that corporate management is conservative while disclosing information, 44.21 percent respondents think that auditors do not perform their duties with adequate competency, 54.74 percent respondents opine that existing financial reporting is not effective enough to protect the interest of shareholders, 58.42 percent of respondents believe that there is no possibility of good governance under family based culture and 91.58 percent respondents feel that establishing a monitoring cell is utmost important to oversee the reporting as well as auditing activities of the companies that can bring the trust on the annual reports (Hasan, 2013a). Moreover, earnings manipulation, improper revaluation of assets, non-recognition of deferred tax, non-compliance of accounting standards, inadequate disclosure, improper valuation of share price at the time of IPO etc. are mentioned in the probe committee report (2011). In addition to that, the committee also reports the name of some directors who are involved in manipulating of capital market and very influential in terms of money, industry, and political connections. This environment creates a negative attitude towards directors as well as auditors of the companies. The probe committee also recommends establishing a financial reporting council (FRC) to oversee the reporting and auditing activities of the companies.

7. Conclusion

This study concludes that firm's level CG has a linear relationship with market capitalization. We find a positive and significant linear relationship between board independence and market capitalization meaning that the more independency of the board, the more of the market capitalization i.e., market reputation in the stock market. This is positive result for ensuring good governance. On the other hand, we find a negative and significant relationship between public ownership and market capitalization meaning that public ownership is neither satisfied with the behavior of the reporting entity nor have trust of corporate reporting. This environment is not positive for good CG. We see the results of descriptive statistics and find the current practice of CG is in a very poor shape that needs to be addressed immediately for reinforcing confidence of the stakeholders in the capital market as well as in the society.

We recommend some mechanism that may help concerned stakeholders to find out a solution of the present problem such as introduction of audit review system, introduction of value for money review mechanism, establishing of high powered financial reporting council, ensure uniform corporate reporting of the companies in an industry, stopping the use of revaluation methods as if U.S. GAAP does not permit revaluation, opening awareness program of CG, mandatory for directors to participate in the training of CG, increase the number of independent directors at least 2 (two) or 1/3 (one-third) whichever is higher to ensure freedom in the board room, discourage unethical behavior of directors and auditors, introducing continuous professional education (CPD) for corporate executive and directors to change their negative attitude and develop their mindset for corporate good governance, the background of directors must be supported by his / her education, professional experience, and personal traits, introduce an attractive as well as informative code of CG, introduce a group for inspecting physically the compliance of CG and stop the breathing space for them and the like. The limitation is small sample size although it is 44 percent but it would have been better if we took whole population as it is a small number i.e., 155 companies.

Acknowledgement

The researchers gratefully acknowledge the financial support and generosity of Accounting Research Institute (ARI) and the Ministry of Education, Government of Malaysia without which the present study could not have been completed.

Appendix -1

Table 5. *List of Sampled Companies*

SN	Company Name	SN	Company Name
1	Rahim Textile	35	Ambee Pharma
2	Samorita Hospitals	36	Pama Oil Company
3	Savar Refractories ltd	37	Salvo Chemical Industry Limited
4	Beach Hatechery ltd	38	British American Tobacco
5	Tallu Spinning Mills	39	Eastern Housing Limited
6	Imam Button	40	Bata Shoe Company
7	Safko Spinning	41	National Tea Company Limited
8	Anlima Yarn Dyeing ltd	42	Aziz Pipe
9	Bangladesh Auto Cars Limited	43	Jamuna Oil Company Limited
10	Eastern Cables	44	National Polymer Industries Limited
11	Atlas Bangladesh Limited	45	Quasem Drycells Ltd
12	Meghna Petrolium Limited	46	CMC Kamal Textile Mills Limited
13	Apex Adelchi Footwear Limited	47	Bangladesh Lamps Ltd.
14	Deshbandhu Polymer Limited	48	Metro Spinning Mills Limited
15	Fine Foods Limited	49	MJL Bangladesh Limited
16	Khulna Power Company Limited	50	Aftab automobiles limited
17	GBB Power Limited	51	Square Textiles Limited
18	Libra Infusion Limited	52	Singer Bangladesh Limited
19	The Dacca Dyieng &b Manufacturing	53	ACI Formulations Limited
20	R. N. Spinning Limited	54	Prime Textile Spinning Mills Limited
21	BSRM Steels Limited	55	Saiham Textile Mills Limited
22	Bangladesh Thai Aluminium Ltd.	56	H. R. Textile Mills Limited
23	Keya cosmetics ltd	57	Agricultural Marketing Co Ltd
24	M I Cement Factory Ltd.	58	Apex Spinning & Knitting Mills Limited
25	Fuwang Foods Ltd.	59	Makson Spinning Mills Limited
26	Pharma Aids Limited	60	Malek Spinning Mills Ltd.
27	Kohinoor Chemical Company	61	Jute Spinners Limited
28	Samata Leather Complex Ltd	62	BD COM Limited
29	Sonali Aansh Industries Limited	63	Daffodil Computers Limited
30	Navana CNG Limited	64	United Airways Limited
31	Grameen Phone	65	Standard Ceramic Industries Limited
32	Dhaka Electric Supply Company Limited	66	Beacon Pharma
33	Titas Gas Transmission and Distribution	67	Orion Infusion Ltd.
34	Square Phrmaceuticals	68	Active Fine Chemicals Ltd

References

[1] Abdul Rahman, R., & Haniffa, R. (2005). The effect of rolle duality on corporate performance in Malaysia. International Scientific Journal of Corporate Ownership and Control, 2 (2), 40 - 47.

[2] Abdul Rahman, R., & Salim, M. R. (2010). Corporate Governance in Malaysia. Petaling Jaya, Selangor, Malaysia: Sweet & Maxwell Asia.

[3] Ahmed, K., Hossain, M and Adams, M. (2006). The effects of board composition and board size on the informativeness of annual accounting earnings. Corporate Governance: An International Review, 14 (5), 418 - 431.

[4] Andres, P. D., & Vallelado, E. (2008). Corporate governance in banking: The role of the boardof directors. Journal of Banking and Finance (32), 2570 - 2580.

[5] Anglin, P. M., & Gao, Y. (2011). Corporate governance and information quality in capital markets. Research Paper.

[6] Apostolou, A. K., & Nanopoulos, K. A. (2009). Voluntary accounting disclosure and corporate governance: evidence from Greek listed firms. International Journal of Accounting and Finance, 1 (4), 395 - 414.

[7] Ariadna, D. (2010). Corporate governance and market liquidity. www.suef.org.

[8] Balasubramanian, N., Bernard, S. B., & Khanna, V. (2010). The relation between firm-level corporate governance and market Value: A study of India. Emerging Market Review, 11, 319 - 340.

[9] Barclay, M., & Holderness, C. (1989). Private benefits from control of public corporations. Journal of Financial Economics, 25 (2), 371 - 396.

[10] Beekes, W., Pope, P., & Young, S. (2004). The link between earnings and timeliness, earnings conservatism and board composition: Evidence from the UK. Corporate Governance: An International Review (12), 14 - 59.

[11] Bradbury, M., Mak, Y., & Tan S. (2006). Board characteristics, audit committee characteristics and abnormal accruals. Pacific Accounting Review (18), 47 - 68.

[12] Bryman, A. E., & Cramer, D. (1997). Quantitative data analysis with SPSS for Windows: A guide for social scientists. New York and London: Routledge.

[13] Byard, D., Li, Y., & Weintrop, J. (2006). Corporate governance and the quality of financial analyst's information. Journal of Accounting and Public Policy (25), 609 - 625.

[14] Cadbury, S. A. (1992). Report of the Committee on the Financial Aspects of Corporate Governance: The Code of Best Practice. London: Gee Professional Publishing.

[15] Capiro, G. Jr., & Levine, R. (2002). Corporate governance in finance: Concepts and international observations. Global Governance Forum Research Network Meeting (pp. 17 - 50). Washington D.C: The Brookings Institution.

[16] Castilo, J., & Wakefield, M. W. (2006). An exploration of firm performance factors in family businesses: Do families value only the bottom line. Journal of Small Business Strategy, 17 (2), 37 - 51.

[17] Chaganti, R. S., Mahajan, V., & Sharma, S. (1985). Corporate board size, composition and corporate failures in retailing industry. Journal of Management Studies, 22 (4), 400 - 417.

[18] Chen, C.J. P., & Jaggi, B. (2000). Association between independent non-executive directors, family control and financial disclosures in Hong Kong. Journal of Accounting and Public Policy (19), 285 - 310.

[19] Claessens, S., & Yurtoglu, B. (2012). Corporate governance in emerging markets: A survey. http://ssrn.com/abstract=1988880.

[20] Corbetta, G. (1995). Patterns of development of family businesses in Italy. Family Business Review, 8 (4), 255 - 265.

[21] Cuculelli, M., & Micucci, G. (2008). Family succession and firm performance: Evidence from Italian family firms. Journal of Corporate Finance, 14 (1), 17 - 31.

[22] Dechow, P. M., Solan, R. G, & Sweeney, A. P. (1996). Causes and consequences of earnings manipulation: An analysis of firms subject to enforcement actions by the SEC. Contemporary Accounting Research, 13 (1), 1 - 36.

[23] Du, H. (2006). Round table discussion on corporate governance guidelines of SEC and its implementation practices in Bangladesh. Dhaka: Asian Development Bank.

[24] Fama, E., & Jensen, M. (1983). Separation of ownership and control. Journal of Law and Economics, 26 (2), 301 - 325.

[25] Fama, E., & Jensen, M. (1985). Organizational forms and investment decisions. Journal of Financial Economics, 14 (1), 101 - 119.

[26] Fiegner, M., & Brown, B. (2000). CEO stakes and board composition in small private firms. Entrepreneurship Theory and Practice (24), 5 - 24.

[27] Firth, M., Fung, P., & Rui, O. (2007). Ownership, two-tier board structure, and the informativeness of earnings: Evidence from China. Journal of Accounting and Public Policy, 26 (4), 463 - 496.

[28] Gersick, K. E., Davis, J. A., Hampton, M. M., & Landsberg, I. (1997). Generation to Generation - Life Cycles of the Family Business. Boston: Harvard Business School Press.

[29] Gillibrand, M. (2004). Corporate management essential for industrialization. Dhaka: The Bangladesh Observer.

[30] Goodstein, J., Gautam, K., & Boeker, W. (1994). The effects of baord size and diversity on strategic change. Strategic Management Journal (15), 241 - 250.

[31] Halme, M., & Huse, M. (1997). The influence of corporate governance, industry and country factors on environmental reporting. Scandinavian Journal of Management, 13 (2), 137-157.

[32] Haque, F., Arun, T., & Kirkpatrick, C. (2008). Corporate governance and capital markets: A conceptual framework. Corporate Ownership & Control, 5 (2), 264 - 276.

[33] Haque, F., Arun, T., & Kirkpatrick, C. (2013). Corporate governance and capital markets: A conceptual framework. Retrieved November 12, 2013, from http://virtusinterpress.org: http://virtusinterpress.org/additional_files/journ_coc/full-text-papers-open-access/Paper012.pdf&sa=U&ei=kjuKUs28CIXtrQfLmYCQAw&ved=0CBgQFjAA&usg=AFQjCNFZU7Z0wPcZWo9h9V5R1HIT8GbAUA

[34] Hasan, M. S. (2013a). Corporate Financial Reporting in Developing Countries. Saarbrucken: OmniScriptum GmbH & Co. KG.

[35] Hasan, M. S., Abdullah, S. N., & Hossain, S. Z. (2014a). Qualitative characteristics of financial reporting - an evaluation of users' perception in Bangladesh. The Pakistan Accountant, 50 (1), 23 - 31.

[36] Hasan, M. S., Hossain, S. Z., & Abdul Rahman, R. (2014b). Corporate governance and corporate accruals : the situation in Bangladesh. The IEB International Journal of Finance, 9, 90 - 111.

[37] Hasan, M. S., Abdul Rahman, R., & Hossain, S. Z. (2014c). Monitoring family performance: family ownership and corporate governance structure in Bangladesh. Procedia-Social and Behavioral Sciences, 145, 103 - 109.

[38] Hasan, M. S., Hossain, S. Z., & Swieringa, R. J. (2013b). Corporate Governance and Financial Disclosures: Bangladesh Perspective. Research Journal of Finance and Accounting, 4 (1), 109 - 119.

[39] Hoque, S. M and Nasrin, S. (2013, June 27). Corporate governance in stock market. Dhaka, Dhaka, Bangladesh: academia.edu. Retrieved October 2, 2014, from https://independent.academia.edu/NasrinSyeda/posts

[40] Hossain. (2011). Corporate governance practices in Bangladesh. Retrieved 11 12, 2013, from http://papers.ssrn.com/ssl3/papers,cfm?abstract_id=1971852

[41] Hossain, M. (2005). Why shareholders' activitism is still an illusion in Bangladesh? Dhaka: The Financial Express.

[42] Huq, B. I. A., & Bhuiyan, M. Z. H. (2012). Corporate governance- Its problems & prospects in banking industry in Bangladesh. World Review of Business Research, 2 (2), 16 - 31.

[43] James, H. S. (1999). Owner as manager, extended horizons and the family business. International Journal of Economics of Business, 6 (1), 41 - 55.

[44] Jensen, M. (1993). The modern industrial revolution, exit, and the failure of internal control systems. Journal of Finance, 25 (3), 831 - 873.

[45] Judge, G., Griffiths, W. E., Hill, R. C., Lutkepohl, H., & Lee, T. C. (1985). The theory and practice and econometrics. NewYork: John Wiley.

[46] Karim, R., Sarkar, J. B., & Fowzia, R. (2010). Corporate governance pracices in Bangladesh with reference to SEC corporate governance guidelines. ASA University Review, 4 (2), 223 - 231.

[47] Kha, M., Hossain, G. S., Islam, A.K.M. Zahirul, Rashid, H. A., & Sufian, M. A. A. (2009). Current status of the corporate governance guidelines in Bangladesh: A critical evaluation with legal aspect. Bangladesh Research Publications, 3 (2), 971 - 981.

[48] Khalid, I. (2011). Stock market investigation report. Ministry of Finance. Dhaka: Government of Bangladesh.

[49] Khan, S. (2007). Economic policy paper on institutionalization of corporate governance in Bangladesh. Dhaka: The Dhaka Chamber of Commerce and Industry (DCCI).

[50] Kowalewski, O. (2012). Does corporate governance determine corporate performance and dividends during financial crisis: Evidence from Poland.

[51] Kutubi, S. (2011). Board of director's size, independent and performance: An analysis of private commercial banks in Bangladesh. World Journal of Social Science, 1 (4), 159 - 178.

[52] La Porta, L., Lopez-de-Silanes, F., Shleifer, A., & Vishny, R. (2002). Investor protection and corporate valuation. Journal of Finance, 57, 1147 - 1170.

[53] Lauterbach, B., & Vaninsky, A. (1999). Ownership structure and firm performance: Evidence from Israel. Journal of Management and Governance, 3 (2), 189 - 201.

[54] Lee, J. (2004). The effect of family ownership and management on firm performance. S.A.M. Advanced Management Journal, 69 (4), 46 - 53.

[55] Leftwich, R., Watts, R., & Zimmerman, J. (1981). Voluntary corporate disclosure: Tthe case of interim reporting. Journal of Accounting Research (19), 50 - 77.

[56] Legenzova, R. (2008). An assessment of interaction between ownership structure and voluntary financial disclosure of Lithuanian corporation. Economics and Management, 48 - 55.

[57] Malaysia, B. (2006). Listing requirements of Bushra Malaysia Securities Berhad. Retrieved 2013, from http://www.bursamalaysia.com/website/bm/rules and regulations/listing requirements/downloads/LR_MBSB.pdf

[58] Marlene, D., & John, A. (2011). Auditing fundamentals. England: Pearson Education Limited.

[59] Martinez, J. I. (1994). Family Business in Chile. FBN Newsletter (9), p. 5.

[60] Meah, M. S. (2013). Corporate governance of capital market of Bangladesh. IOSR Journal of Business Management, 12 (5), 1 - 4.

[61] Mishra, C. S., Randoy, T., & Jenssen, J. I. (2001). The effect of family influence on firm value and corporate governance. Journal of International Financial Management and Accounting, 12 (3), 235 - 259.

[62] Monks, R. A. G., & Minow, N. (2010). Corporate Governance (Fourth Edition ed.). Sahibabad, India: John Wiley & Sons, Inc.

[63] Patelli, L., & Prencipe, A. (2007). The relationship between voluntary disclosure and independent directors in the presence of a dominant shareholders. European Accounting Review, 16 (1), 5 - 33.

[64] Petra, S. (2007). The effect of corporate governance on the informativeness of earnings. Economics of Governance (8), 129 - 152.

[65] Rashid, A., De Zoysa, A., Lodth, S., & Rudkin, K. (2010). Board composition and firm performance: Evidence from Bangladesh. Australasian Accoiunting Business and Finance Journal, 4 (1), 76 - 95.

[66] Rashid, A., De Zoysa, A., & Rudkin K. (2007). Corporate governance in Bangladesh: An overview. 19th Asian-Pacific Conference on International Accounting Issues. Kuala Lumpur, Malaysia: http://eprints.usq.edu.au/id/eprint/9120.

[67] Rechner, P. L., & Dalton, D. R. (1991). CEO duality and organizational performance: A longitudinal analysis. Strategic Management Journal (12), 155 - 160.

[68] Reidel, H. (1994). Family Business in Germany. FBN Newsletter (9), p. 6.

[69] Santner, Z., & Villalonga, B. (2010). Corporate governance and internal capital markets. Working Paper, 10 (100).

[70] Sarkar, P. (2007). Does better corporate governance lead to stock market development and capital accumulation? A case of India. Political Economy Seminar Series. Queens College, University of Cambridge.

[71] Scharfstein, D., & Stein, J. (2000). The dark side of internal capital markets: divisional rent-seeking and inefficient investment. Journal of Finance,55, 2537 - 2564.

[72] Schulze, W. S., Lubatkin, M. H., & Dino, R. N. (2003). Toward a theory of agency and altruism in family firms. Journal of Business Venturing, 18 (4), 473 - 490.

[73] Schulze, W.S., Lubatkin, M. H., Dino, R.N., & Buchholtz, A. K. (2001). Agency relationships in family firms: theory and evidence. Organization Science, 12 (2), 99 - 116.

[74] Shleifier, A., & Vishny, R.W. (1997). A survey of corporate governance. Journal of Finance,52 (2), 737 - 783.

[75] Singh, H., & Harianto, F. (1989). Management-Board Relationship, Takeover Risk and the Adoption of Golden Parachutes. Academy of Management Journal (32), 7 - 24.

[76] Thomsen, S., & Pedersen, T. (2003). Ownership structure and value of the largest European firms: the importance of owner identity. Journal of Management and Governance, 7, 27 - 55.

[77] World Bank. (2009). Report on the observance of standards and codes. Dhaka: World Bank.

[78] Xie, B., Davidson, W.N., & Dalt, P.J. (2001). Earnings management and corporate governance: The roles of the board and the audit committee. Retrieved from www.ssrn.com: http://SSRN.com/ Abstract=304195.

8

The Role of Intellectual Capital in the Development of the Competitive Capacities in the Cement Company of "Ain Touta" Algeria

Yahiaoui Naima[1], Megri Zakia[1], Yousfat Ali[2]

[1]Faculty of Economic, Commercial and Management Sciences, Batna University, Batna, Algeria
[2]Faculty of Economic, Commercial and Management Sciences, Ahmed Draia University, Adrar, Algeria

Email address:
yahiaoui966@gmail.com (Y. Naima), megrizakia@yahoo.fr (M. Zakia), yousfatali@gmail.com (Y. Ali)

Abstract: This study aimed to analyze and testing the relationship between intellectual capital and the development of competitive capacities by adopting a virtual model and a research questionnaire and by testing the validity of hypotheses based on the statistical methods used in the study. The results showed the existence of a relationship between the independent variable which is only the relations capital and the development of the competitive capacities of the direction, and that there is a strong impact between intellectual capital and the development of competitive capacities in the direction. The study showed also that there is no relationship between the independent variables which are human capital and structural capital and the dependent variable which is competitive capacities.

Keywords: Intellectual Capital, Competitive Capacities, Cement Company

1. Introduction

The data of the past millennium nineties demonstrated the progression of concern with the knowledge and concepts associated with cognitive capital and Information Society. This coincided with the increasing of cognitive, intellectual and mental contents as a logical consequence of the technological development associated with the increase in the proportion and number of intellectual human resources on the one hand, and of business and intensive-knowledge jobs on the other hand.

The competition faced by the organizations became a reality by many changes in their environments; the organizations began to be aware of this competition and has touched the increase of its intensity, as well as the emergence of many new competitors encouraging them to look for strategies and multiple policies through which they can achieve competitive advantage and to reserve it. So, the organizations, in various forms, sought to achieve competitive advantage in the quality of services, the methods of providing them, the means of satisfying the needs of their clients, and the search for best practices that they can apply.

There is no doubt that all organizations have not come to an accurate understanding of the importance of intellectual capital and how to exploit its three dimensions (human capital, structural capital, relations capital). We find that the concern with the individual as competitive advantage has not appeared only in a relatively late times. Today, in the context of knowledge world, the domain is no longer opened to all organizations to enter to the competition and to stay actively involved in the market. So, it has become imperative for organizations to determine their intellectual capital and learn how to turn it into profits or to a strategic situation and competitive advantage, then they must look for intellectual wealth, unexploited creative and innovative skills, abilities and ideas contained in their human resources so that they can invest their higher value through developing and turning them into profits or to better strategic center, or to achieve competitive advantage in these difficult economic conditions.

2. Study's Problem

What is the role of intellectual capital in the development of competitive capacities in the cement direction of "Ain Touta"?

3. Study's Hypotheses

3.1. Principle Hypothesis

There is a relationship of statistical significance between the availability range of intellectual capital requirements and the development of competitive capacities at the level of significance α = 0.05.

3.2. Secondary Hypotheses

- There is a relationship of statistical significance between the availability range of human capital requirements and the development of competitive capacities at the level of significance α = 0.05.
- There is a relationship with statistical significance between the availability range of structural capital requirements and the development of competitive capacities at the level of significance α = 0.05.
- There is a relationship with statistical significance between the availability range of relations capital requirements and the development of competitive capacities at the level of significance α = 0.05.

4. Study's Importance

The importance of this study is related to the importance of intellectual capital as an important source of corporates profitability and the basic support of competitiveness; Interesting in it by organizations and companies is imposed by the nature of scientific and economic challenges, fast technological developments and pressures.

5. Study's Objectives

Since scientific research seeks to achieve general and personal objectives with scientific value and significance, this research aims to the following:

- Shedding light on the nature of intellectual capital and its relationship with competitive advantage.
- Identifying the availability of intellectual capital components in the cement direction.

6. Study's Methodology

In order to reach the objective of the research and answer the questions asked in the problem, the inductive method will be adopted: case study method.

Study's Structure

To treat this issue and take its aspects, it is divided into two chapters, one is theoretical and the other is practical:

- Chapter one: the theoretical framework of the relationship between intellectual capital and competitive capacities.
- Chapter two: the study of intellectual capital and its role in raising competitive capacities in the general direction of cement "Ain Touta".

7. First: Theoretical Framework of the Relationship Between Intellectual Capital and Competitive Capacities

In the light of the knowledge economy, intangible assets have become the basic support and strategic resource to the organization wealth and prosperity. The success of organizations in the fierce competition environment has become dependent on the value of these assets and their management strategies, due to their active role in the exploitation of staff capacities and skills in reinforcing competitive advantage of the company and creating the value. Researchers have named this: "intellectual capital" term (Stewart & Thomas, 1997).

7.1. What is Intellectual Capital?

The concept of capital has been expanded to cover the entire material, financial, moral, intellectual and cultural potentials of the establishment; this term was borrowed to be used in the field of social sciences and management as what is known by human capital which refers to the overall skills, experiences, education and knowledge accumulated in the human element. After, the continuous development of this term, it has been focused on intellectual capital as one of the most important intangible assets affecting competitive advantage of the establishment.

7.1.1. The Concept of Intellectual Capital

Ralph Stayer, manager of Johnsonville company for foods, was the first person that launched the term of "intellectual capital" in 1990 when he said: "In the past, natural resources were the most important national wealth components and the most significant assets of the companies, then capital represented by money and fixed assets became the most important components of companies and society. But now, natural resources, money and fixed assets are replaced by intellectual capital which is the most important component of the national wealth and the most expensive asset of corporates."

Edvinsson (1999) defines intellectual capital as the "intangible assets characterized by the absence of a physical entity, in addition to the uncertainty of future benefits expected of them because of the difficulty in predicting their productive age, which makes it difficult to be measured and evaluated, these assets are among the determinants of competitive capacities of the organization.

Guthrie (2001) points out that intellectual capital is "distinct capabilities enjoyed by a limited number of personnel in the organization, which will enable them to provide intellectual contributions to enable the organization to increase its productivity, and to achieve higher levels of performance compared to similar organizations".

From the above, a general definition of intellectual capital can be drawn as "distinct intellectual capacities and contributions owned by the individuals of the organization which in turn helps them to employ them through its programs and regulations to be embodied in excellence services and products for clients."

Curado, Henriques and Bontis (2011) present quite a new attitude to intellectual capital and its nature. Scientists emphasize that nowadays the most important element of intellectual capital is Knowledge Based-View of the firm (KBV). Knowledge is considered to be the main factor for growth of intellectual capital. They also presented a new methodology called MMRIC – Measure, Manage and Report of Intellectual Capital – which encouraged companies to measure, manage, and control their intellectual capital. The methodology allows managers to increase a company's value added with little costs.

Bontis, Richards and Serenko (2011) emphasized the importance of Knowledge Management (KM). Knowledge Management is defined as accumulation, concentration, maintenance, and sustention of intellectual capital. This also depends on the type of the company and on the area the company is working in. Nevertheless, Knowledge Management depends also on the mission and vision of the company and its anticipated goals and tasks.

7.1.2. The Importance of Intellectual Capital

The following criteria show the importance of intellectual capital for society and business organizations:

1. The importance of intellectual capital is highlighted as the most important source of profitability and competitive pillar of the establishment; normal intellectual capacities have become one of the most important factors of competitive success and distinction in the knowledge-based world economy; all creations begin with creative ideas, and intellectual base construction process represents a significant commitment for higher direction, the reorganization and the new engineering for various activities and operations.
2. In the light of the knowledge-based economy, intellectual capital has become a strategic resource, a competitive weapon with a powerful force for this economy and the main source of wealth and prosperity.
3. Intellectual capital is an important basis in building smart organizations, through the availability of clever minds that are able to invest the rest of the resources and exploit it for expanding the excellence space for their organizations, because those minds are able to adapt to changing circumstances, and this is the intellectual capital.
4. The importance of intellectual capital is derived from being the most valuable asset in the XXI century in an economy called (knowledge economy) because it represents scientific forces able to introduce essential amendments to everything in their organization business as well as their successive innovations.

7.2. Elements and Components of Intellectual Capital

There is no doubt that the determination of elements and components of intellectual capital is one of the fundamental things that helps in its measurement and evaluation, and thus in determining the true value of the business organizations in the modern era. The following is a review of the most important of these categories:

7.2.1. Brookings Institute Classification

Brooking Institute (1996) classified intellectual capital into four categories or components:

- Market Assets: include all intangible market-related aspects such as clients, brands and distribution outlets.
- Human Assets: include accumulated experiences, capabilities of innovation and indicators related to the extent of the ability of individuals to perform in certain situations.
- Individual Property Assets: include relations, trade secrets, patents and design rights.
- Infrastructure Assets: include all the elements that determine how the establishment works, such as: the establishment's culture, methods of risk assessment, management methods of the labor force, customer databases and communication systems.

7.2.2. Stewart, 1997 & Mayo, 2000 Classification and McElroy 2002 Classification

According to the above classification, intellectual capital consists of the following elements:

- Structural Capital: it is regulatory capacities of the organization that regulate and satisfy the requirements of clients and contribute to the knowledge transfer and reinforcement through intellectual structural assets represented by information systems, patents, copyrights, and the extent of trademark protection which represents the personality and identity of the organization, gives a benefit to the client and increases his satisfaction, as well as a benefit of the organization to increase its efficiency and effectiveness.

  Human capital refers to the value of knowledge, skills and experience held by individual employees in a firm. (Ngah. R&Abdul Razak. I, 2009).
- Human Capital: it is the basic source to train and individualize people who have mental ability and necessary skills and experiences to find appropriate practical solutions to the requirements and desires of clients because they are the source of innovation and renewal in the organization.
- Relations capital: it refers to relations between the organization and its clients, suppliers and strategic alliances (McElroy, 2002).

It also can be contain Social capital that defines as the network of relationships that individuals have throughout the organization ;such relationships are critical in sharing and leveraging knowledge and in acquiring resources.Social capital also can extend beyond the organizational boundaries to include relationships between the firm and its suppliers,customers,and alliance partners (Lumpkin Eisner.D,2008).

8. Bases About Competitive Advantage

The study of competitive advantage in the organization focuses on the internal factors that make the organization strong or weak; the analysis at the sector level focuses on the interest of the ruling policy on the specific economic domain, the consideration of organizations as independent entities and making comparisons between them. The analysis at the macroeconomic performance level focuses on the study of the factors that lie behind the strength or weakness of the economic performance.

8.1. Concepts of Competitive Advantage

Michael Porter (1993) is the most important researcher in the field of strategic management and competitive advantage analysis for organizations. He sees that competitive advantage is not concerned with the state, but with the organization (Porter, 1993). Competitive advantage arises mainly from the value that an organization was able to create for its clients so it can take the form of lower prices than the competitors ones with equal benefits, and proving single benefits in a product to consciously compensate the imposed price increase.

Competitive advantage indicates the areas in which the organization can compete with others in a more effective manner. Thus, it represents a point of strength characterizing the organization from its competitors in one of its production, marketing or financing activities, or with respect to human resources and competencies. Competitive advantage depends on the results of the examination and analysis of all of the internal points of strength and weakness as well as the opportunities and risks surrounding and prevailing in the organization environment compared to its competitors.

Competitive advantage is that strategic concept which reflects the relative and constant competitive position of an organization over its competitors, so that manifests in the form of presenting products or services of single characteristics to which the client is prepared to pay more, or providing products or services which are not less valuable than competitors' products and at lower prices.

The realization of competitive advantage depends on the availability of many elements and on the nature of the interaction and integration between them; the most prominent elements of competitive advantage are the availability of natural resources, capital, technology and human resources.

Evans and Collier (2007) noted that competitive advantage is the ability of company to superiority in the areas of marketing, finance, above all priority which in turn requires an understanding of the general framework of the company through: The senior management must determine the needs and desires of the customer and how to deliver it to the customer through processing chain in order to meet the customer plugged in and handed over the goods or services in a timely manner, as well as to take into account the operational capacity rate.

8.2. The Degree of Competitive Advantage Durability

To become a durable advantage, two principle properties are necessary in the distinctive capacities of the establishment; the first one is the "durability" and the other is the "imitability". The durability indicates the rate of depreciation or depletion of the establishment resources or its distinctive capacities; the developed technology may lead to finish the distinctive capacity of an establishment. The imitability refers to the possibility of simulating distinctive capacities or competitive resources of an establishment by competitors.

Many companies resort to reverse engineering which is based on analyzing the contender product to identify its components, attracting the workers of the competitor companies or laying hands on patents. It is easy to imitate essential capacities if they are transparent, transferable and reliable (McGee & Love, 1999).

- Transparency: It refers to the speed of understanding the relations between the resources and capacities supporting the strategy of a successful establishment. For example, the Company *Gillette* for shaving kits excels through adopting researches and development in the design of blades and shavers; this technique is difficult to be imitated by competitors.
- Transferability: It refers to the ability of competitors to gather the resources and capacities needed to support the competitive challenge. For example, it is difficult to simulate necessary environmental and climatic conditions for the cultivation of tea in India and Ceylon.
- Reliability: It is the ability of competitors to use counterfeit resources and capacities to emulate the success of competitors. We must admit that the success reflects a certain combination of tangible and intangible resources and abilities that cannot be often imitated and emulated by competitors.

The resources and capacities of the establishment can be expressed through the perspective of durability which is shown in Figure (01).

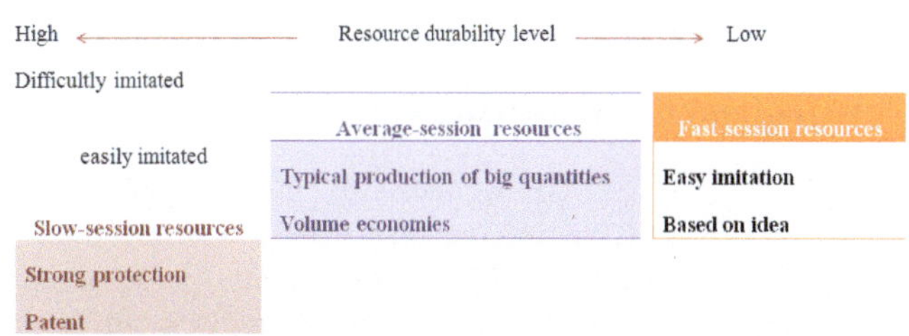

Figure 01. *Resource durability perspective (Williams, 1992).*

This figure shows that the durability of resources ranges between "low" and "high"; resources with slow-session are durable resources due to their protection through "patents", the geographical area, strong brand or knowledge emanating from the experiences and culture of the establishment's workers. On the other side, there are fast-session resources that are easily imitated.

It is known that organizations seek to achieve the greatest possible productivity of high level of quality and durable renovation of its products, services and all of its divisions due to the ongoing changes in the tastes and needs of customers and all of these interactions to achieve excellence.

1. Excellent Competence: The organization is a system for converting inputs to outputs, so we find that the simplest measure of competence is the amount of inputs required to produce given outputs; if the competence rate of the organization's operations increases, the inputs required to produce given outputs decrease, so the cost of the production structure of the organization goes down.
2. Excellent Quality: The achievement of high levels of quality in the products and services by the organization will increase the value of these products and services for their clients, and will enable it to impose a higher price for its products, which leads to realize competitive advantage for the organization and enable it to survive and continue.
3. Excellent Creativity: It refers to all the progress that occurs to the products or services of the organization, its administrative structures, methods and strategies, in the sense that it is achieved through the provision of a new product or the work in a new way which is different from competitors.
4. Renovation is one of the building foundations of competitive advantage that allows to the organization to be distinctive, and thus to impose higher prices or reduce its production costs.
5. Excellent responsiveness to the needs of clients: The organization can achieve competitive advantage through its ability to provide and produce goods and services saturating the needs of its clients better than its competitors. Therefore, there will be harmonization between these goods and services with individual or collective demands. The quality and renovation can be considered complementary aspects of the responsiveness to the needs of the client.

9. The Relationship Between Intellectual Capital and the Achievement of Competitive Advantage

As a result of the difficulties faced by organizations in their analysis of these distinctive resources, some people tried to find some theories and analyzes. At this point, we will try to clarify some of them and how to apply them to achieve competitive advantage.

9.1. Resources-Based Theory

It is also known as resources-based vision in the strategic management field. Competitive advantage is determined, according to this theory, through the following: distinctive resources, organizational capacities and competencies, technological capabilities, invisible assets represented by knowledge, skills, experiences and human resources, and the axial capacities associated with skills, knowledge, technology management, attitudes and values. This theory gives great attention to the resources and capacities which are available to the organization as a basis to achieve competitive advantage (Carmeli &Cohen). It believes that the achievement of competitive advantage by organization depends on the acquisition of strategic resources enjoyed by a set of characteristics and conditions, as well as the capacities of the organization to use these resources.

9.2. VRIO Framework for Resources Analysis

Barney (2003) provided a framework (VRIO) for the analysis of each resource of the principle resources of the establishment in terms of its contribution in achieving competitive advantage through having the following characteristics:

- Value: does it add value to clients and provide competitive advantage?
- Scarcity: do competitors have something like it?
- Imitability: is the cost of its imitation high?
- Regulation: Does the regulation of the establishment allow exploiting this resource? Are there available alternatives to this resource?

In case of the answer with "yes" to those questions within VRIO framework for a particular resource, that resource will reflect a point of strength and distinctive ability for the establishment. The evaluation of the importance of these resources contributes to make sure they represent strategic internal factors – that is to say strength and weakness elements that will help to determine the future of the establishment. This can be done by comparing the standards of these resources with the standards of: (1) past performance of the establishment, (2) major competitors of the establishment, (3) industry average as a whole. The resource is a strategic element that must be taken into account when making strategic decisions if it is significantly different from the past, competitors or the industry average.

10. Chapter two: the Role of Intellectual Capital in the Development of Competitive Capacities of the Cement Company of Ain Touta

After we determined in the first chapter the theoretical framework of the study's variables which are intellectual capital, the development of competitive capacities and also the nature of the relationship between the two variables, this chapter is an attempt to project what has been theoretically studied on one of the production companies which is the cement company of "Ain Touta".

11. Designation of the Cement Company "Ain Touta"

11.1. Origination of the Cement Company "Ain Touta"

It is a subsidiary company of the cement complex GICA. It seeks through its activities to satisfy the various needs of the construction sector in terms of the cement. It appeared by concluding a contract between *the Enterprise of Cement and its Derivatives of the East*, in 1983, with the Danish company *F.L.S* to realize the cement unit "Ain Touta" with collaboration, according to the competence, as the Belgian company competent in the affairs of civil engineering and a company of electricity and mechanical installation works.

The first experience of production was in September 3rd, 1986 with production capacity of 1 million tons per year, equivalent to 84,000 tons per month.

11.2. The Company's Objectives

The ultimate objective of the company is the financial profit, but there are sub-objectives relating to achieve the required levels of service and quality to win the satisfaction of clients. The company's objectives can be illustrated as follows:

- The work to fill the needs of the market;
- The promotion of the national and international production and providing products with high quality and favorable prices;
- The use of the latest technology.

The company tends, through these objectives, to increase its market share, to flood the market and to raise the company's reputation by satisfying clients and ensuring adequate levels of required quality.

11.3. Obtained Certificates

The cement company "Ain Touta" obtained many certificates which are summarized in the following table:

Table (01). *Obtained Certificates.*

Systems	Certificate	Year
Environment functioning system	ISO 14001	2004
Health and safety at work functioning system	OHSAS 18001	2007
Quality functioning system	ISO 9001	2008
Health and safety at work functioning system	OHSAS 18001	2013

12. Field Study

This part will be about how to test the study's tool to make sure of the extent of its sincerity and constancy. After, we move to highlight the statistical treatment methods used in the study and we conclude with displaying the results and testing the hypotheses.

12.1. Research Methodology and Used Tools

In this part, we will explain the method taken in the study with mention of the study's population, the time, space and human boundaries, and the tools used in the study.

1. The Study's Method
   The method in the field study is the intended way to reach the underlined objectives, and it is the approach that the researcher can route to access to the declared objective; the nature of the research which highlights the relationship between the dimensions of intellectual capital and competitive capacities requires us to use the descriptor-analytical method to concrete the reality of the relationship between the study's variables and their indicators. The method is based on the data collection process and their analysis, explaining and obtaining generalizations. So, the function of the method is understanding and explaining, as well as description and analysis.
2. The study's Limits: the limits of the study are:
   - Time framework: in fact, this study began in the second semester of 2014 with the distribution of questionnaires, unloading, tabulation and analysis of data.
   - Space framework: This field research was conducted from the province of Batna.
3. The study's population: the study's population is composed from the total mass of workers at the General Direction of the Cement "Ain Touta". Considering that the General Direction is a part of the original cement company "Ain Touta" and because of the large number of workers that requires a lot of effort and time, the questionnaire was distributed to a sample of 35 workers at the direction representing the whole number of the direction. 35 questionnaires were distributed and only 20 were retired (recovery rate: 57%).
4. Used Tools:
   Questionnaire: the questionnaire is an important tool of data collection; it is a series of questions written in the form of a series of questions that must be easy and clear. Considering that the research population is workers, the form has been delivered by hand to most of them and we came back later to receive them. Before this, this questionnaire has been designed out of 24 questions according to Likert's scale (NOT COMPLETELY OK, COMPLETELY OK).

Questions were divided as follows:

- First class: concerns the personal data of the research community.
- Second class: intellectual capital dimensions.
- Third class: competitive capacities.

12.2. Analysis of the Questionnaire's Results

We will deal with how to test the study's tool to ensure its sincerity and constancy, then we will move to highlight the statistical treatment methods used in the study, and finally we conclude with displaying the results and testing hypotheses.

1. Study's Tool Testing (Questionnaire):

We will try to study the seeming and structural sincerity and constancy of the study's tool:

a. Study's tool sincerity: it means that the form should involve all of the elements that must be included in the analysis on one hand. On the other hand, its paragraphs and vocabulary must be clear so that they can be understood by the users. The study's tool sincerity has been confirmed by:
   - The seeming sincerity of the tool: to see the extent of the tool seeming sincerity, it was presented to a group of expert and specialist professors;

according to their opinions and suggestions, this questionnaire was drafted in its final form which was distributed to the researched sample.

- The constancy of the questionnaire: the constancy of the questionnaire is defined as "the extent of the ability of the tool to give similar results if applied under the same conditions and on the same subjects", we used in the study Cronbach's alpha way to calculate the constancy of standards using the statistical software package SPSS; the value of the correlation coefficient alpha ranges between (0-1). In order that the scale will be constant, the minimum value of the coefficient in this test should not be less than (0,6). Alpha results, in our study, are shown in the following table:

Table (02). *Results of the Study's tool Constancy Using Cronbach's Alpha.*

Number of phrases	Degree of Cronbach's alpha coefficient
24	0,858

Source: prepared by the researchers using the results of the questionnaire analysis and SPSS software outputs.

It is clear from the previous table that the value of Cronbach's alpha coefficient was 85.8%, thus the analysis results based on this form are acceptable.

b. Description of the Study's Sample Characteristics: The following is a display of the obtained results relating to the study's sample characteristics according to the personal variables using the descriptive analysis presented by frequencies and percentages.

It is noted from table (03) what follows:

1. The distribution of the study's sample by sex: it is seen in the table (03) that the highest percentage in the category of sex is (65%) recorded in males, while the percentage of females is (35%).
2. The distribution of the study's sample by age: it is noted in the table (03) the high percentage of the two categories of age "30-40 years" and "40-50 years" (30%), as we note that the lowest percentage is recorded at the category of "21-30 years," (15%), while the ages category "50 years and more" recorded (25%) of the total of the study's sample.
3. The distribution of the study's sample by marital status: it is seen in the table (03) that the highest percentage in terms of marital status is (80%) to the category of married subjects, while the lowest percentage is in the category of divorced (5%).
4. The distribution of the study's sample by academic qualification: it is seen in the table (03) that the university level achieves the highest percentage (70%) which indicates that a large proportion of the sample holds academic qualifications- one of the positive indicators, then followed the higher studies level (15%), the secondary one (10%) and the middle level (5%).
5. The distribution of the study's sample by experience in current job: we can note in the table (03) a high percentage of "10 years and more" of experience (50%) which means that the organization has competences. We see also that the lowest percentage is recorded at "6-10 years" (10%), while for the "less than 3 years" the percentage is (25%), and at "3-6 years" (15%).

Table (03). *Distribution of the Sample's Subjects According to Personal Variables.*

Variable		Frequencies	Percentages %
Sex	Male	13	65
	Female	7	35
Age	From 21-30 Y.O	3	15
	From 30-40 Y.O	6	30
	From 40-50 Y.O	6	30
	50 Y.O and more	5	25
Marital status	Single	3	15
	Married	16	80
	Divorced	1	5
	Widower	0	0
Academic qualification	Middle	1	5
	Secondary	2	10
	University	14	70
	Higher studies	3	15
Experience in current job	Less than 3 years	5	25
	From 3-6 years	3	15
	From 6-10 years	2	10
	10 years and more	10	50

Source: prepared by the researchers using the results of the questionnaire analysis and SPSS software outputs.

2. Descriptive Scales of the study's variables:

Likert dual scale was used, then the extent (2-1=1) was calculated and divided by the number of the scale's cells to get the correct length of the cell (2/1 = 0.50). After, the value was added to the lowest value in the scale (the whole one) in order to determine the upper limit of this cell. Thus the length of the cells became as follows:

From (1 to 1.50) represents very weak toward every phrase of the form.

From (1.51 to 2) represents very high toward every phrase of the form.

- Descriptive standards of the independent variable: the following table represents the arithmetic averages and standard deviations of the independent variable:

Table (04). *Arithmetic Averages and Standard Deviations of the First Chapter Phrases.*

Phrases	Arithmetic average	Standard deviation	Classification	Degree
Workers have constantly full knowledge about all new related to the services provided by the company	1,70	0,470	3	Very high
The company's workers have high experience in the domain of their works	1,85	0,366	1	Very high
The direction's workers have the capacity to generate ideas and give quick solutions to face work problems	1,70	0,470	4	Very high
Workers have creative and distinctive capacities in dealing with emergency situations at work.	1,60	0,503	5	Very high
Spirit of cooperation between managers and workers in the direction is available.	1,80	0,410	2	Very high
Total	1,73	0,313	Very high	

Source: prepared by the researchers using the results of the questionnaire analysis and SPSS software outputs.

Table (04) shows that the general arithmetic average of all of the paragraphs of (human capital), which is located within the area of evaluation, is very high (1.73) and it is an acceptable value indicating a very high acceptance by the sample's subjects.

- Descriptive scales of the dependent variable: The following table represents the arithmetic averages and standard deviations of the dependent variable:

Table (05). *Arithmetic Averages and Standard Deviations of the Second Chapter phrases.*

Phrases	Arithmetic average	Standard deviation	Classification	Degree
Information systems used in the direction provide to the decision-makers the necessary information efficiently and quickly.	1,80	0,410	2	Very high
There is a continuous development of administrative processes in the direction in a way that realizes distinctive performance in doing works.	1,70	0,470	5	Very high
Work policies and procedures ensure, at the company, the creation of new and continuous knowledge.	1,70	0,470	4	Very high
The direction encourages scientific development of workers through education and training programs offered to them.	1,90	0,308	1	Very high
The organizational structure of the direction provides high degree of clarity in the nature of relationships between superiors and subordinates.	1,75	0,444	3	Very high
Total	1,77	0,299	Very high	

Source: prepared by the researchers using the results of the questionnaire analysis and SPSS software outputs.

Table (05) shows that the general arithmetic average of all of the paragraphs of (structural capital), which is located within the area of evaluation, is very high (1.77) and it is an acceptable value indicating a very high acceptance by the sample's subjects.

- Descriptive scales of the third chapter: the following table represents the arithmetic averages and standard deviations of the third chapter:

Table (06). *Arithmetic averages and standard deviations of the third chapter phrases.*

Phrases	Arithmetic average	Standard deviation	Classification	Degree
The direction devotes adequate balance to provide distinctive after-sale services to clients.	1,30	0,470	3	Very weak
The direction devotes considerable time to choose suppliers.	1,65	0,489	2	Very high
The direction makes a range of strategic alliances with other establishments to realize its works.	1,70	0,470	1	Very high
Total	1,55	0,363	Very high	

Source: prepared by the researchers using the results of the questionnaire analysis and SPSS software outputs.Table (06) shows that the general arithmetic average of all of the paragraphs of the independent variable (relations capital), which is located within the area of evaluation, is very high (1.55) and it is an acceptable value indicating a very high acceptance by the sample's subjects due to the importance of the relations capital at the direction. We note that the arithmetic average of the first paragraph is (1,30) and the standard deviation is (0,470) and it is very weak within the second category of Likert's scale; it means that the direction does not devote adequate balance to provide distinctive after-sale services to clients.

Table (07). Arithmetic averages and standard deviations of the second section phrases.

Phrases	Arithmetic average	Standard deviation	Classification	Degree
The centers providing services are attractive and comfortable for clients.	1,65	0,489	8	Very high
The direction's workers perform services to clients quickly, on time and as required.	1,75	0,444	7	Very high
The direction reviews its various activities and operations and works to cancel unnecessary and duplicated activities and operations.	1,80	0,410	4	Very high
The direction seeks to adopt all ways, methods and strategies to develop the efficiency of its processes.	1,90	0,308	2	Very high
Information systems used at the direction contribute to reduce the costs of operations and services.	1,80	0,410	5	Very high
The internal control range at the direction includes the examination and evaluation of the efficiency and effectiveness of operations.	1,90	0,308	3	Very high
Information technology used in the direction helps the quick development and the diversification of services provided to clients.	1,80	0,410	6	Very high
The direction adopts introducing and experimenting innovative ideas generated by workers to face work problems	1,40	0,503	11	Very weak
The direction interests in developing the services provided to clients according to what competitors offer.	1,65	0,489	9	Very high
The direction interests in opinions, suggestions and preferences of clients to provide new services and make ameliorations to the provided services.	1,55	0,510	10	Very high
The direction seriously seeks to apply domestic and international quality.	2	0,000	1	Very high
Total	1,75	0,210	Very high	

Source: prepared by the researchers using the results of the questionnaire analysis and SPSS software outputs.

Table (07) shows that the general arithmetic average of all of the paragraphs of the independent variable (competitive capacities), which is located within the area of evaluation, is very high (1.75) and it is an acceptable value indicating a very high acceptance by the sample's subject due to the importance of competitive capacities at the direction. We note that the arithmetic average of the eighth paragraph is (1,40) and the standard deviation is (0,503) and it is very weak within the second category of Likert's scale; it means that the general direction does not adopt the introduction and experimentation of innovative ideas generated by workers to face work problems.

First: Testing the Principle Hypothesis

In order to test the principle hypothesis, we need to put two hypotheses: nothingness hypothesis and alternative hypothesis, considering that nothingness hypothesis is subject to test, that is to say it can be incorrect, which requires to put alternative hypothesis.

- Nothingness hypothesis H0: there is no relationship of statistical significance between the availability range of intellectual capital requirements and the development of competitive capacities the level of significance $\alpha = 0.05$.
- Alternative hypothesis H1: there is a relationship of statistical significance between the availability range of intellectual capital requirements and the development of competitive capacities at the level of significance $\alpha = 0.05$.

1. Analysis of Impact Relationship:
   - To identify the existence range of an impact relationship of intellectual capital requirements on developing competitive capacities, and in order to test the model's ability to explanation, correlation coefficient (R), determination coefficient (R^2) and modified determination coefficient ($\bar{R}^2$), which provides more accurate and correct explanation due to the presence of more than one independent variable, have been used. This is shown in the following table:

Table (08). Summary of the declination model of intellectual capital requirements impact on the development of competitive capacities.

correlation coefficient (R)	Determination coefficient square (R^2)	Determination Coefficient ($\bar{R}^2$)	Standard error
0,610	0,373	0,338	0,171

Source: prepared by the researchers using SPSS software results.

Table (09). Analysis of declination variance ANOVA.

	Total of variance Square	Degrees of freedom	Variance average square	Value of the calculated (F)	level of significance
Declination	0.373	3	0.124	4.297	0.21
Remainders	0.463	16			
Total	0.836	19	/	/	/

Source: prepared by the researchers using the results SPSS software SPSS.

Table (08) shows that:

- Correlation coefficient (R) equals to (0,610) and this means the existence of a medium-power direct relationship between intellectual capital requirements and the development of competitive capacities.
- Determination coefficient (R2) equals to (0,373) and this means that intellectual capital requirements explain only (37%) of the change in competitive capacities development, while the remainder percentage is attributed to other factors which are not studied.

Table (09) shows that: The value of the test (F) equals to (2,75) and the calculated corresponding level of significance is (0.06), and it is not significant at the level (5%) which means that the variable of intellectual capital requirements affects the competitive capacities development.

Based on the previous results of the statistical analysis

Alternative hypothesis H1, which states that there is a relationship of statistical significance between the availability range of intellectual capital requirements and the development of competitive capacities at the level of significance α = 0.05, is accepted.

Second: Testing Partial Hypotheses

To test the first and second partial hypotheses, multiple declination and (T) test have been adopted to test separately the significance of each parameter of the model, at the level of significance α=5%. This is shown in the following table:

Table (10). *Test of declination coefficients significance according to the statistical (T).*

Variables	Declination coefficient (B)	Standard error	Standard declination	Test (T)	Level of significance	Statistical significance
Constant	0,847	0,274		3,093	0,007	Significant
Human capital	0,118	0,179	0,177	0,660	0,518	Insignificant
Structural capital	0,150	0,174	0,214	0,861	0,402	Insignificant
Relations capital	0,276	0,118	0,487	2,330	0,033	Significant

Source: prepared by the researchers using SPSS software results.

In order to explain the results of the above table, it is necessary to give a precise detail about partial hypotheses to be tested, which will be displayed as follows:

2. The first partial hypothesis HA
   - Nothingness hypothesis HA0: there is no relationship of statistical significance between human capital and the development of competitive capacities at the level of significance α = 0.05.
   - Alternative hypothesis HA1: there is a relationship of statistical significance between human capital and the development of competitive capacities at the level of significance α = 0.05.
   - It is shown in the table (10) that declination coefficient (B) equals to (0,118) which means that the relationship between human capital and the development of competitive capacities is direct; it is an insignificant at the level (5%). The value of the test (T) equals to (0.660) and the corresponding significance level is (0.518), and it is insignificant at the level (5%), which means that there is no impact relationship between human capital and the development of competitive capacities. Thus, we accept the nothingness hypothesis (HB0) which states that there is no impact relationship of statistical significance between human capital and the development of competitive capacities at the level of significance α = 0.05.
3. The second partial hypothesis HB
   - Nothingness hypothesis HB0: there is no relationship of statistical significance between structural capital and the development of competitive capacities at the level of significance α = 0.05.
   - Alternative hypothesis HB1: there is a relationship of statistical significance between structural capital and the development of competitive capacities at the level of significance α = 0.05.
   - It is shown in the table (10) that declination coefficient (B) equals to (0,150) which means that the relationship between structural capital and the development of competitive capacities is direct; it is insignificant at the level (5%). The value of the (T) test equals to (0.861) and the corresponding significance level is (0.402); it is insignificant at the level (5%), which means that there is no impact relationship between structural capital and the development of competitive capacities. Thus, we accept the nothingness hypothesis (HB0) which states that there is no impact relationship of statistical significance between structural capital and the development of competitive capacities at the level of significance α = 0.05.
4. The third partial hypothesis HC
   - Nothingness hypothesis HC0: there is no relationship of statistical significance between relations capital and the development of competitive capacities at the level of significance α = 0.05.
5. Alternative hypothesis HC1: there is a relationship of statistical significance between relations capital and the development of competitive capacities at the level of significance α = 0.05.
   - It is shown in the table (10) that declination coefficient (B) equals to (0,270) which means that the relationship between relations capital and the development of competitive capacities is direct; it is significant at the level (5%). The value of the(T) test equals to (2.330) and the corresponding significance level is (0.033); it is significant at the level (5%), which means that there is an impact relationship

between relations capital and the development of competitive capacities. Thus, we accept the alternative hypothesis (HC1) which states that there is an impact relationship of statistical significance between relations capital and the development of competitive capacities at the level of significance α = 0.05.

Third: Study's Results

1. Principle hypothesis: there is a relationship of statistical significance between the availability range of intellectual capital requirements and the development of competitive capacities at the level of significance α = 0.05, is a correct hypothesis.
2. The first secondary hypothesis: there is a relationship of statistical significance between the availability range of human capital requirements and the development of competitive capacities at the level of significance α = 0.05, is an incorrect hypothesis.
3. The second secondary hypothesis: there is a relationship of statistical significance between the availability range of structural capital requirements and the development of competitive capacities at the level of significance α = 0.05, is an incorrect hypothesis.
4. The third secondary hypothesis: there is a relationship of statistical significance between the availability range of relations capital requirements and the development of competitive capacities at the level of significance α = 0.05, is a correct hypothesis.

13. Conclusion

By projecting theoretical ideas and concepts on the practice, a set of results and suggestions have been reached:

First: Study's Results:

Through this study, we conclude to the following results:

1. There is a strong relationship between the availability of intellectual capital requirements and the development of competitive capacities at the direction.
2. There is no relationship between human capital and the development of competitive capacities.
3. There is no relationship between structural capital and the development of competitive capacities.
4. There is a relationship between relations capital and the development of competitive capacities.

Second: Recommendations

1. The direction should give great importance to human capital, in its various aspects of knowledge, exploit the available experiences and capacities and encourage the work by teams.
2. The organization should give more attention to structural capital to help workers to know the policies, programs and operations carried out by the organization.
3. Also, it should exploit its good relation with suppliers and clients and particularly develop it with clients by providing after-sale services.
4. The direction should adopt the introduction and experimentation of innovative ideas generated by workers to face sale problems.

References

[1] Barney, J. (2003), Gaining & Sustaining Competitive Advantage, 2nd edition, Upper Saddle River, NJ: Prentice Hall.

[2] Bontis, N., Richards, D. & Sernko, A. (2011), "Improving Service Delivery. Investigating The Role Of Information Sharing, Job Characteristics, And Employee Satisfaction", The learning organization, Vol.18, No. 3, pp. 239-250.

[3] Brooking, A. (1996), Intellectual Capital: Core Asset for the Third Millennium Enterprise, London, International Thomas business Press.

[4] Carmeli, A. & A.Cohen, (1999), "Organizational Reputation as a Source of Sustainable Competitive Advantage and Above- Normal Performance", Available on line at http://www.pamij.com.

[5] Curado, C., Henriques, L. & Bontis, N. (2011), "Intellectual capital disclosure payback", Management decision, Vol. 49, No.7, pp.1080-1098.

[6] Edvinsson, L. (1999), "Intellectual Capital of Nations for Future Wealth Creation", Journal of Human Resource Costing and Accounting, Vol. 4 Iss: 1, pp.22-30. http://dx.doi.org/10.1108/eb029051.

[7] Evans, and Collier, (2007), Operation Management an Integrated Goods and services, Approach, Thomson, South western, U.S.A international, studentedition,www.swlearing.com.

[8] Guthrie, J. (2001), "the Management, Measurement and Reporting of Intellectual Capital", Journal of Intellectual Capital, Vol. 2 Iss: 1, pp.27 - 41. http://dx.doi.org/10.1108/14691930110380473

[9] Hill, Charles & Johns Jarret (2001), Strategy Management: Integrated Introduction.

[10] McElroy, M. W. (2002), "Social Innovation Capital", Journal of International Capital, Vol. 3 Iss: 1, pp.30 - 39, http://dx.doi.org/10.1108/14691930210412827.

[11] Lumpkin Eisner, D. (2008), Strategic Management: Text and Cases, McGraw-Hill International Edition.

[12] McGee, J. E. & Love, L. G. (1999), "Sources of Competitive Advantage for small independent retailers: Lessons from the neighborhood drugstores", association for small business & entrepreneurship, Houston.

[13] Ngah, R. & Abdul Razak, I. (2009), "The relationship of Intellectual Capital, Innovation and Organizational Performance: a Preliminary Study in Malaysian SMEs", International Journal of Management Innovation Systems.Vol. 1, N 1.

[14] Porter, M. (1993), "Competitive Advantage of Nations", Harvard Business Review, Inter-edition.

[15] Stewart, A. Thomas (1997), Intellectual Capital: the New Wealth of Organization, Doubleday, New York.

[16] Williams, J.R. (1992), "How Sustainable Is Your Competitive Advantage?", California Management Review, Spring, Vol. 34, Issue. 3.

9

Efficiency of Macedonian Insurance Companies: A DEA Approach

Vesna Micajkova

Integrated Business Faculty, Skopje, Macedonia

Email address:
vmicajkova@yahoo.com

Abstract: The purpose of this paper is to estimate the efficiency of the insurance sector of Republic of Macedonia for the period 2009-2013. Technical, pure technical and scale efficiency of 11 Macedonian insurance companies have been measured using Data Envelopment Analysis (DEA), both CCR and BCC output-oriented model. The results from the analysis indicate an increase of the average efficiency during the almost whole observed period. The scale efficiency follows the same trend. When estimating the BCC model, the number of efficient insurance companies and the average efficiency for the sector is higher than in the CCR case, implying that the main source of inefficiency is due to scale inefficiencies. The average technical efficiency score of Republic of Macedonia in 2013 of 0.84387 indicates relatively high efficiency of the insurance sector. The efficiency problem of each insurance company has been specified particularly.

Keywords: Data Envelopment Analysis, Macedonia, Insurance Sector Efficiency, Scale Efficiency, Technical Efficiency, Pure Technical Efficiency

1. Introduction

Insurance companies are financial institutions that play an important role in the economy of a country through saving mobilization, risk transfer and financial intermediation. In addition, insurance companies provide economic and social benefits in the society by prevention of losses, reduction in anxiousness, fear and increasing employment. Resent research shows that the efficiency of financial intermediation and transfer of risk can affect economic growth while at the same time institutional insolvencies can result in system crises which have unfavorable consequences for the economy as a whole (Ayele, 2012). Therefore, the efficiency of the insurance companies is an important subject of scientific interest. Measurement of insurance companies' efficiency increases the quality of their activities and also assists them to identify and solve their problems (Shahroudi at all, 2012).

The purpose of this paper is to estimate the efficiency of the insurance sector of the Republic of Macedonia using Data Envelopment Analysis (DEA). Using both CCR and BCC output-oriented models, the relative efficiency of the Macedonian insurancesector has been measured for the period 2009-2013 (separately for each year and each insurance company). According to our knowledge this is the first efficiency study of the insurance sector of Republic of Macedonia.

2. Data Envelopment Analysis (DEA)

Data envelopment analysis (DEA) is a nonparametric method, most popular in operations research and economics for the estimation of production frontier. It is used to empirically measure productive efficiency of Decision Making Units (or DMUs). The efficiency of a DMU is measured relative to all other DMUs with the simple restriction that all DMUs lay on or below the extreme frontier. Unlike statistical procedures that are based on central tendencies, DEA is a process of extremes directed at the frontier rather than at central tendencies. DEA analysis each DMU separately and calculates a maximum performance measure for each unit.

DEA was introduced in 1978 by Charnels, Cooper and Rhodes. Their model, known as the CCR model, was named after its founders. The CCR model is a basic DEA model that presupposes that there is no significant relationship between the scale of operation and efficiency by assuming constant return to scale (CRS) and it delivers the overall technical efficiency. The CRS assumption is only justifiable when all

DMUs are operating at an optimal scale. Because in practice DMUs face economies or diseconomies to scale, in 1984 the CCR model was extended by relaxing the CRS assumption. The BCC model was introduced in order of assessing the efficiency of DMUs characterized by variable return to scale (VRS). (Stavarek&Repkova, 2012)

Vincova (2005) defines DEA models as models that evaluate n productive units, DMUs, where each DMU takes m different inputs to produce s different outputs. The essence of DEA models in measuring the efficiency of productive unit DMUq lies in maximising its efficiency rate. However, subject to the condition that the efficiency rate of any other units in the population must not be greater than 1. The models must include all characteristics considered, i.e. the weights of all inputs and outputs must be greater than zero. The CCR model can be defined as a linear divisive programming model:
maximize

$$\frac{\sum_i u_i y_{iq}}{\sum_j v_j x_{jq}} \qquad (1)$$

subject to

$$\frac{\sum_i u_i y_{ik}}{\sum_j v_j x_{jk}} \leq 1 \; k = 1, 2, ..., n,$$

$$u_i \geq \in i = 1, 2, ..., s \; v_j \leq \in j = 1, 2, ..., m$$

This model can be transformed into a matrix:
Maximize

$$z = u^T Yq \qquad (2)$$

subject to $v^T Xq = 1$

$$u^T Y - v^T X \leq 0$$

$$u \geq \in$$

$$v \leq \in$$

The dual model to this can be stated as follows:
Minimize

$$f = \theta - \in (e^T s^+ + e^T s^-) \qquad (3)$$

subject to $Y\lambda - s^+ = Y_q$

$$X\lambda + s^+ = \theta X_q$$

$$\lambda, s^+, s^- \geq 0$$

where $\lambda = (\lambda_1, \lambda_2, ..., \lambda_n)$, $\lambda \geq 0$ is a vector assigned to individual productive units, s+ and s are vectors of addition input and output variables, $e^T = (1, 1, ..., 1)$ and $\in$ is a constant greater than zero, which is normally pitched at 10^{-6} or 10^{-8}. In evaluating the efficiency of unit DMU_q, model (3) seeks a virtual unit characterised by inputs $X\lambda$ and outputs $Y\lambda$, which are a linear combination of inputs and outputs of other units of the population and which are better that the inputs and outputs of unit DMU_q which is being evaluated. Unit DMU_q is considered to be CCR efficient if the optimum value of the model (3) objective function equals one. In the inefficient units the objective function of the model is lower than one.

Models (2) and (3) are input-oriented – they try to find out how to improve the input characteristics of the unit in order of efficiency increase. There are output-oriented models as well. Such a model could be written as follows:
Maximize

$$g = \Phi + \in (e^T s^+ + e^T s^-) \qquad (4)$$

subject to $Y\lambda - s^+ = \Phi Y_q$

$$X\lambda + s^- = X_q$$

$$\lambda, s^+, s^- \geq 0$$

In the output-oriented models as well as in the input-oriented, a DMU is considered to be efficient if the objective function of the model is one.

Models (2), (3) and (4) are CCR models i.e. they assume constant returns to scale. These models can be converted to a BCC models with a variable return to scale by inclusion of a condition of convexity $e^T\lambda = 1$. The results of the CCR model are considered as technical efficiency scores, the results of a BCC model are considered as pure technical efficiency scores, and the ratio of the CCR scores to BCC scores gives the scale efficiency score.

Kumar and Gulati (2008) give a very concise elaboration of the concept of technical, pure technical and scale efficiency which we consider to be very important in understanding the DEA method and reading its results. Technical efficiency (TE) relates to productivity of inputs. A technical efficiency of a firm is comparative measure of how well it is actually processes inputs to achieve its outputs, as compared to its maximum potential for doing so, as represented by its production possibility frontier. The TE is measured under the assumption of constant return to scale. The pure technical efficiency (PTE) measure is obtained by estimating the efficient frontier under the assumption of a variable return to scale. It reflects the managerial performance to organize the inputs in the production process. On the other site, the measure of scale efficiency provides the management to choose the scale of production that will attain the expected production level. Inappropriate size of an insurance company (too large or too small) may sometimes be a cause of technical inefficiency. This is referred as scale inefficiency and takes two forms: decreasing returns to scale (DRS) and increasing returns to scale (IRS). DRS (also known as diseconomies of scale)imply that aninsurance company is too large to take full advantage of scale and has supra-optimum scale size. In contrast, an insurance experiencing IRS (also known as economies of scale) is too small for its scale of operations and, thus, operates at sub-optimum scale size. An insurance company is scale efficient if it operates at constant returns to scale (CRS).

3. Model and Input and Output Selection

An important decision when employing frontier efficiency models involves the choice of inputs and outputs, since the definition of these factors can significantly impact the results of a study (Eling and Luhnen). The selection of appropriate variables representing inputs and outputs is particularly difficult for insurance companies compared to manufacturing firm where attributing inputs and outputs is less challenging (Diboky and Ubl, 2007). In follows we will present some theoretical discussion on this subject.

3.1. Output Specification

In existing studies of insurance companies' efficiency we find three principal approaches to define outputs: the asset (intermediation) approach, the user-cost approach and value-added approach.

The assets (intermediation) approach treats financial service firms as pure financial intermediaries which borrow funds from their customers which are invested and than transformed into assets. Interest payments are paid out to cover the time value of the funds used (Sinha and Chatterjee). The main objective of this approach is to maximize simultaneously the value of claims' ownership and capital return adjusted to risk (Jarraya and Bouri, 2012). Taking into consideration only the intermediation service of the insurance company is considered as the main disadvantage of this approach. Insurance companies offer other services in addition to financial intermediation. Ignoring these other services, such as risk-pooling and risk-bearing services, allocated to the insurance company leads to erroneous results in efficiency studies.

The user-cost approach was developed by Hancock (1985). It determines whether a financial product is an input or an output by analyzing if its net contribution to the revenues of an insurance firm is positive or negative. According to that, a product is considered an output, if its financial return exceeds the opportunity costs of funds or if the financial costs of a liability are lower than the opportunity costs. Otherwise, the financial product would be classified as an input (Sinha and Chatterjee).Jarraya and Bouri (2012) consider this approach, at the theoretical level, as the most ideal, but at a practical level it is almost impossible to find the necessary data.Eling and Luhnen confirm that there is no practical applicability of this approach, since they haven't found any study on efficiency measurement in the insurance industry, out of 83 analyzed, that employs the user-cost approach.

The value-added approach differs from the asset approach and the user-cost approach as it considers all asset and liability categories to have some output characteristics. Those categories which have substantial value added are than used as the important outputs. The remaining categories are treated as rather unimportant outputs, intermediate products, or inputs. Sinha and Chatterjee emphasize that an important advantage of this approach compared to the user-cost approach consists in the fact thatthe value added approach uses operating cost data rather than determining the costs implicitly or using opportunity costs. Many authors (Jarraya and Bouri (2012), Sinha and Chatterjee, Eling and Huang (2011), Eling and Luhnen) consider the value-added approach as the most appropriate method for measuring output of financial firms. This approach is widely used in insurance companies' efficiency studies.

In the value-added approach, insurer's outputs consist primarily of intangible financial services, therefore, it is necessary to define suitable proxies that are highly correlated with the quantity of financial services provided (Laverty and Grace, 2008).The most common proxies used in the literature for value-added are either premiums or the present value of real losses incurred. Eling and Huang (2011) emphasizes that out of 69 studies using value-added approach for efficiency measurement in the insurance industry, 35 studies use insurance premium as output and 32 specify claims/present value of claims (property-liability) or benefit/net incurred benefits (life) as output in the efficiency analysis. Two of 69 studies use neither of the two main proxies.

We have decided to adopt the value-added approach when investigating the efficiency of the insurance sector of Republic of Macedonia. Regarding the data availability we will consider gross written premium and gross claims settledas outputs in our efficiency study.

3.2. Input Specification

There are three main insurance inputs: labor, business service and materials, and capital. Labor can be further divided into agent and home-office labor. The category of business service and materials is usually not further subdivided, but includes items like travel, communications, and advertising. At least three categories of capital can be distinguished: physical, debt and equity.

Qui and Chen (2006) consider labor as the most important input in the financial service industry. In insurance companies, no raw materials are required, and cost of labor is the major component of costs. Since data on numbers of employees or hours worked in many countries are not publicly available some authors define the quantity of labor as administration or management cost divided by a publicly available wage variables or price index (see Diboky and Ubl (2007), and Eling and Huang, (2011)).Most studies use the operating expenses as a proxy for labor, since the authors consider that the majority of operating expenses in the insurance industry are due to commissions and employees salaries (see Jarraya and Bouri (2012), Sihna and Chatterjee,Shahroudi at all (2012)).Physical capital is often included in the business service and material category (Diboky and Ubl, 2007), but many authors consider equity capital as an imperative input (Borges at all, 2008, Qui and Chen, 2006). There are authors that think that equity and debt capitalhave the same importanceand use both of them in the insurance companies' efficiency studies (see Eling and Huang, (2011), Barros and Obijiaku, (2007)), andsome studies do not include any category of capital as an input(Shahroudi and all, 2012, Sihna and Chatterjee).

Eling and Luhnen have reviewed 83 studies on frontier efficiency measurement in the insurance industry and made the following conclusions regarding the choice of input factors: 55 out of 83 studies use at least labor and capital as inputs and most of them also add a third category (miscellaneous, mostly business services). Out of those 55 studies, 15 differentiate between agent and non agent labor. Also, the number of studies differentiating between equity and debt capital is quite low; only ten papers do so. There are a further nine studies that do not cover capital explicitly, i.e., they consider labor only or labor and an additional composite category.

Regarding the data availability as inputs in the study investigating the efficiency of Macedonian insurance sector we will consider the following: administrative expenses, commission expenses and total capital. The administrative expenses will be consider as a proxy for a home-office labor, assuming that staff costs have the largest part in the administrative expenses of the Macedonian insurance companies. The commission expenses represent theagents' costs and the total capital consists of equity and debt capital.

3.3. Model Specification

When choosing the inputs and outputs of the model few suggestions from Sarkis (2002) have been taken into consideration. First suggestion is about the number of inputs and output compared to number of DMUs. Second suggestion is to reduce the correlated data sets for input/output factors. And the third suggestion is to fix the imbalance in data magnitudes by mean normalize of the data.

Sarkis (2002) emphasizes that the choice and the number of inputs and outputs, and the DMUs determine how good of a discrimination exists between efficient and inefficient units. He gives a review of different authors' opinion about the number of inputs and outputs compared to a number of DMUs in a DEA model. According to Boussofiane at al. (1991) the minimal number of DMUs should be the multiple of the number of inputs and number of outputs. Golany and Roll (1989) establish a rule of thumb that the number of units should be at least twice the number of inputs and outputs considered, while Bowlin (1998) thinks that the number of DMUs should be at least three times of the number of the inputs and the outputs. Dyson at al (2001) recommend a total of two times the product of the number of input and output variables. For example in a 3 input and 4 output model Boussofiane at all recommend using 12DMUs, Golany and Roll recommend using 14 DMUs, while Bowlin recommends 21 DMUs, and Dyson et al. recommend 24. The number of DMUs in the model applied in this study is predefined by the number of insurance companies operating on the financial marketof Republic of Macedonia in the observed period from 2009 to 2013. The number of DMUs is 11. According to the literature recommendation the maximum total of the number of inputs and outputs should vary between 3 and 6.

The first step in choosing the inputs and the outputs that will be applied in this study is examining the correlation between the inputs and outputs that we consider using. The results of the correlation analysis are presented in the following tables.

***Table 1.** Selected inputs correlation analysis.*

	Administrative Expenses	Commission Expenses	Total Capital
Administrative Expenses	1		
Commission Expenses	0.566566305	1	
Total Capital	0.555206291	0.259196177	1

Source: Author[1]

Table 1 presentsrelatively weak correlation between the analyzed inputs.Sarkis (2002) recommends that eliminating the highly correlated inputs will have an insignificant effect on the efficiency scores. But in this case we can not eliminate any of the inputs due to high correlation, so our model will include all three above mentioned inputs.

Regarding the output selection, the results from the output correlation analysis (presented in table 2) suggest very strong correlation between the gross written premium and gross claims settled.Using two highly correlated outputs will have insignificant effect on the efficiency score, so we have decided to eliminate the gross claims settled, and to use gross written premium as a single output in our efficiency model.

***Table 2.** Selected outputs correlation analysis.*

	Gross Written Premium	Gross Claims Settled
Gross Written Premium	1	
Gross Claims Settled	0.956966273	1

Source: Author[2]

The model that we have chosen has three inputs, two outputs and 11 DMUs and as such is suitable for efficiency measurement according to every above mentioned literature recommendation, except of Bowlin's[3]. After the inputs and the outputs are selected Sarkis (2002) recommends mean normalizing of the data in order of reducing their imbalance. The first step of that process is to find the mean of the data set for each input and output. The second step is to divide each input or output by the mean for that specific factor. Before efficiency scores calculation we have followed Sarkis recommendation and mean normalized the data on inputs and outputs applied in our model.

Regarding the input-output orientation of the model, according to Borges at all (2008) the choice should be based on the market conditions of the DMU's. As a general rule of thumb, in competitive markets, DMU's are output-oriented, since we assume that inputs are under control of the DMU, which aims to maximize its output subject to market demand. Therefore we choose output orientation for our DEA model.

4. Efficiency and Empirical Results

Using both CCR and BCC output-oriented models, the relative efficiency of the Macedonian insurance sector has

1 The analysis is made upon data for every particular insurance company included in the analysis for period from 2009 to 2013.

2 The analysis is made upon data for every particular insurance company included in the analysis for period from 2009 to 2013.

3 According to Bowlin our model should have 12 DMUs.

been measured for the period 2009-2013 (separately for each year and each insurance company). As a statistical basis for input and output data, ISA (The Insurance Supervision Agency) insurance industry reports have been used.Table 3 presents descriptive statistics for inputs and outputs applied.

The results from the CCR model (table 4) indicate a growth in the efficiency score of the Macedonian insurance sector in almost whole observed period from 2009 to 2013. A decrease of the efficiency has been detected only in 2010.The average efficiency in 2013 was 0.84387 that implies that there is room for the mean insurance company's efficiency to be upgraded by 15.6%. The most efficient insurance companies are Eurolink, Sava and Triglav with average efficiency score higher than 0.9. The most inefficient insurance company is Insigwith average score of 0.46966. The number of efficient units per year varies from two to four.[4]

When estimating the BCC model (Table 5), the number of efficient insurance companies and the average efficiency for the sector is higher than in the CCR case, implying that the main source of inefficiency is due to scale inefficiencies. The number of efficient units per year varies from 5 to 8.[5]Five insurance companies (Viner, Eurolink, Kroacija, Sava and Triglav) are efficient unitsduring the whole observed period. In general the picture remains the same i.e. the average efficiency of the Macedonian insurance sector rises during the whole observed period.

Table 3. *Descriptive statistics for inputs and outputs.*

		2009	2010	2011	2012	2013
Inputs						
Administrative Expenses	Mean	145,914	131,616	120,681	111,857	114,503
	Med	139,318	114,977	98,841	108,773	120,177
	StDev	85,721	62,550	69,646	50,908	43,536
Commission Expenses	Mean	38,145	31,960	36,330	37,036	39,533
	Med	30,629	30,249	34,580	37,198	29,223
	StDev	27,460	15,299	20,153	16,542	19,446
Total Capital	Mean	380,401	331,647	329,468	323,907	341,718
	Med	209,955	204,773	241,645	221,934	233,092
	StDev	368,002	326,295	306,236	254,536	314,876
Outputs						
Gross Written Premium	Mean	557,640	556,942	573,752	583,226	587,640
	Med	461,019	437,141	530,588	576,847	638,138
	StDev	383,092	357,651	300,382	283,465	247,562

Source: Author

Table 4. *CCR model-efficiency scores.*

DMU	2009	2010	2011	2012	2013	Mean
Albsig	0.42849	0.50109	0.70874	0.75304	0.88089	0.65445
Viner	0.68191	0.74668	1.00000	1.00000	1.00000	0.88572
Evroins	0.51966	0.63767	0.74361	0.89800	0.81266	0.72232
Eurolink	1.00000	0.97253	1.00000	1.00000	1.00000	0.99451
Insig	0.33009	0.40532	0.55968	0.49945	0.55377	0.46966
Kjubi	0.86513	0.46304	0.43388	0.48078	0.56247	0.56106
Kroacija	0.63578	0.44792	0.66086	0.72089	1.00000	0.69309
OsiguritelnaPolisa	0.84016	0.71727	0.85724	0.78546	0.84446	0.80892
Sava	1.00000	1.00000	1.00000	1.00000	0.97779	0.99556
Triglav	1.00000	1.00000	1.00000	0.98749	0.90514	0.97853
Unika	0.55314	0.56539	0.66700	0.66242	0.74539	0.63867
Mean	0.71403	0.67790	0.78464	0.79887	0.84387	0.76386

Source: Author

Table 5. *BCC model-efficiency scores.*

DMU	2009	2010	2011	2012	2013	Mean
Albsig	0.61734	0.62859	1	1	1	0.84919
Viner	1	1	1	1	1	1
Evroins	0.59625	0.71753	0.74388	1	0.83129	0.77779
Eurolink	1	1	1	1	1	1
Insig	0.67936	1	1	1	1	0.93587
Kjubi	0.87513	0.60812	0.61899	0.55863	0.65218	0.66261
Kroacija	1	1	1	1	1	1
OsiguritelnaPolisa	0.97228	0.79954	0.88079	0.79969	0.84509	0.85948
Sava	1	1	1	1	1	1
Triglav	1	1	1	1	1	1

DMU	2009	2010	2011	2012	2013	Mean
Unika	0.60592	0.64398	0.6842	0.66401	0.84668	0.68896
Mean	0.84966	0.85434	0.90253	0.91112	0.92502	0.88854

Source: Author

Table 6. *Scale efficiency scores (CCR/BCC) and returns to scale specification.*

DMU	2009		2010		2011		2012		2013	
Albsig	0.694	IRS	0.797	IRS	0.709	IRS	0.753	IRS	0.881	IRS
Viner	0.682	IRS	0.747	IRS	1.000	CRS	1.000	CRS	1.000	CRS
Evroins	0.872	IRS	0.889	IRS	1.000	DRS	0.898	IRS	0.978	IRS
Eurolink	1.000	CRS	0.973	IRS	1.000	CRS	1.000	CRS	1.000	CRS
Insig	0.486	IRS	0.405	IRS	0.560	IRS	0.499	IRS	0.554	IRS
Kjubi	0.989		0.761	DRS	0.701	DRS	0.861	DRS	0.862	DRS
Kroacija	0.636	IRS	0.448	IRS	0.661	IRS	0.721	IRS	1.000	CRS
OsiguritelnaPolisa	0.864	IRS	0.897	IRS	0.973	IRS	0.982	DRS	0.999	DRS
Sava	1.000	CRS	1.000	CRS	1.000	CRS	1.000	CRS	0.978	DRS
Triglav	1.000	CRS	1.000	CRS	1.000	CRS	0.987	DRS	0.905	DRS
Unika	0.913	IRS	0.878	IRS	0.975	IRS	0.998	DRS	0.880	DRS
Mean	0.830		0.800		0.871		0.882		0.912	
DMU's operating at CRS (%)	27%		18%		36%		27%		27%	
DMU's operating at DRS (%)	9%		9%		18%		36%		45%	
DMU's operating at IRS (%)	64%		73%		45%		36%		27%	

Source: Author

The scale efficiency of the Macedonian insurance sector follows the same trend as the technical efficiency i.e. permanent growth during the whole observed period with exception of the year 2010. From 2009 till 2011 the insurance companies in Republic of Macedonia are dominantly operating at increasing return to scale meaning that their small size was an efficiency problem. This situation changes from 2012, since when the largest portion of insurance companies are operating at decreasing return of scale i.e. most of the Macedonian insurance companies need downsizing in order of efficiency increase.

5. Conclusion

This paper endeavors to evaluate the extent of technical, pure technical and scale efficiency of the Macedonian insurance sector for the period 2009-2013. The efficiency has been measured using both CCR and BCC output-oriented DEA models. The results from the analysis indicate an increase of the average efficiency during the almost whole observed period. The scale efficiency follows the same trend.When estimating the BCC model, the number of efficient insurance companies and the average efficiency for the sector is higher than in the CCR case, implying that the main source of inefficiency is due to scale inefficiencies. The average technical efficiency score of Republic of Macedonia in 2013 of 0.84387 indicates relatively high efficiency of the insurance sector.

The results of the analysis show that three insurance companies (Eurolink, Sava and Triglav) are the most efficient on Macedonian insurance market, both technically and scale, during the whole observed period. Those companies show a great input productivity and highly successful managerial performance in organization of that inputs in the production process. During the almost whole observed period they are operating at constant return of scale i.e. the companies' size is optimal.

Viner is an insurance company that has experienced scale inefficiency in 2009 and 2010 due to operating at sub-optimum scale size. The problem has been exceeded in 2011, and since then Viner has the highest both technical and scale efficiency scores. Kroacija has been in the same situation as Viner, operating at increasing return to scale, but in 2013 its technical and pure technical efficiency scored the maximum score of 1.

Albsig and Insig have the highest pure technical efficiency scores since 2010. The main source of their inefficiency is due to the scope of production. Since these companies are operating at sub-optimum scale size it is expected that their enlarging will lead to an efficiency increase.

The rest of the Macedonian insurance companies have both technical and scale efficiency problems. While the main source of scale inefficiency in the insurance sector of Republic of Macedonia is in the sub-optimum scale size, Kjubi is the only company that is operating at decreasing return of scale during the whole observed period. Downsizing of its operations should lead to an efficiency increase.

References

[1] Ayele, A. G. (2012): Factors Affecting Profitability of Insurance Companies in Ethiopia: Panel Evidence, Addis Ababa University, Addis Ababa, Ethiopia,available at: http://etd.aau.edu.et/dspace/bitstream/123456789/4326/1/Factors%20Affecting%20Profitability%20of%20Insurance%20Companies%20in%20Ethiopia.pdf, assessed on 12.05.2014.

[2] Barros, C., P. and Obijiaki, E., L. (2007), Technical Efficiency of Nigerian Insurance Companies, Working Paper 018/2007/DE/UECE, School of economics and management, Technical university of Lisbon, available at: http://www.iseg.utl.pt/departamentos/economia/wp/wp0182007deuece.pdf, assessed on 01.07.14.

[3] Borges, M. R., Nektarios, M. and Barros, C., P. (2008), Analyzing the Efficiency of the Greek Life Insurance Industry, European Research Studies, Volume XI, Issue (3) 2008.

[4] Diboky, F., and Ubl, E. (2007), Ownership and Efficiency in the German Life Insurance market: A DEA Bootstrap Approach, available at: http://www.aria.org/meetings/2007papers/VIB%20-%202%20-%20Diboky.pdf, assessed on 08.07.14.

[5] Eling, M. and Huang, W., (2011), An Efficiency Comparison of the Non-life Insurance Industry in the BRIC Countries, Working Papers on Risk Management and Insurance, No. 94 – November 2011, available at: http://www.ivw.unisg.ch/~/media/internet/content/dateien/instituteundcenters/ivw/wps/wp94.pdf.

[6] Eling, M. and Luhnen, M., Frontier Efficiency Methologies to Measure Performace in the Insurance Industry: Overview and New Empirical Evidence, available at: http://www3.imperial.ac.uk/pls/portallive/docs/1/48187710.PDF, assessed on 01.07.14.

[7] Insurance Supervision Agency: Insurance Industry Reports – Various editions, available at: http://www.aso.mk/index.php?option=com_sectionex&view=category&id=6&Itemid=72&lang=en.

[8] Jarraya, B. and Bouri, A. (2012), Efficiency concept and investigations in insurance industry: A survey, MPRA Paper No. 53544, Management Science Letters, Vol. 3, No. 1 (2013): pp. 39-54.

[9] Kumar, S., Gulati, R., (2008), An Examination of Technical, Pure Technical, and Scale Efficiencies in Indian Public SectorBanks Using Data Envelopment Analysis, Eurasian Journal of Business and Economics 2008, 1 (2), 33-69.

[10] Leverty, J., T. and Grace, M., F. (2008), Issues in measuring the efficiency of property-liability insurers, available at: http://www3.imperial.ac.uk/pls/portallive/docs/1/48217697.PDF, assessed on 08.07.14.

[11] Sarkis, J., (2002), Preparing Your Data for DEA, Productivity Analysis in the Service Sector with Data Envelopment Analysis, 2nd Edition, available at: www.clarku.edu/~jsarkis/SarkisChapter.doc, assessed on 22.07.13

[12] Shahroudi, K., Teleghani, M., Mohammadi, G. (2012), Application of Two-Stage DEA Technique for Measuring of Private Insurance Companies in Iran, International Journal of Applied Operational Research, Vol. 1, No. 3, pp. 91-104, Winter 2012.

[13] Sihna, R. P.,Chatterjee, B., Are Indian Life Insurance Companies Cost Efficient?,available at: http://www.igidr.ac.in/money/mfc-11/Sinha_Rampratap.pdf assessed on 11.07.14.

[14] Stavarek, D., Repkova, I., (2012), Efficiency in the Czech Banking Industry: a Non-parametric Approach, Actauniversitatisagriculturaeetsilviculturaemendelianaebrunensis, Volume LX, Number 2, 2012.

[15] Qui, S., and Chen, B. (2006), Efficiencies of Life Insurers in China – An Application of Data Envelopment Analysis, available at: http://www.ccfr.org.cn/cicf2006/cicf2006paper/20060130033345.pdf,assessed on 08.07.14.

[16] Vinkova, Kristina (2005), Using DEA Models to Measure Efficiency, BIATEC, Volume XIII, 8/2005, National Bank of Slovakia.

---

[4] Efficient banks are those with efficiency score of 1.

[5] Ibid.

10

Performance Assessment of Industrial Real Estate Contribution to Nigerian Economy

Nurudeen Akinsola Bello[1], Ismail Kolawole Bello[2], Olufola Toyosi Elegbede[3]

[1]Department of Estate Management, Faculty of Environmental Sciences, University of Ilorin, Kwara State, Nigeria
[2]Department of Estate Management, School of Environmental Studies, Moshood Abiola Polytechnic, Abeokuta, Ogun State, Nigeria
[3]Department of Estate Management, Faculty of Environmental Studies, The Polytechnic, Ibadan, Oyo State, Nigeria

Email address:
bello4all007@yahoo.com (N. A. Bello), ismailbello@yahoo.com (I. K. Bello), foldot@yahoo.com (O. T. Elegbede)

Abstract: This work is set to measure the contribution of real estate to the production output of manufacturing industries in Nigeria and relate it to the gross domestic product of Nigeria with a view to providing guidance for the industrial investors, measuring past achievements and providing the basis for planning and control decisions. 44 of the 108 industries in industrial town of Ota in Nigeria were randomly sampled to elicit data between 2008 and 2012 from heads of administration of each industry and data collected were analyzed using descriptive statistics. The findings indicated that at aggregate level, industrial properties in Ota, Nigeria contributed 19% performance to the manufacturing success of industrial establishments. Furthermore, while both contributions of manufacturing sector to the national economy and the industrial real estate to manufacturing output are not steady or specific in trend, the average of the contribution of manufacturing/industrial sector to Nigerian economy from 2008-2012 as gathered from various sources indicated 3.41%, the implication of this is that the industrial real estate's actual contribution to Nigerian economy is 0.65%. This work did not measure the value (capital or rental) to determine performance of industrial properties; rather it rated the performance of each standard economic factors of production (land, labour, capital and entrepreneur) base on their contribution to the production activities of the industries by conversion of qualitative perception of the respondents to quantitative measurement. Further endeavor is desired to have pure quantitative measurement as improvement on this qualitative perception. The field of real estate of manufacturing industry lacks empirical measurement to quantify the value that it adds to the firm's performance and this has made the contribution of real estate to the firm not properly considered or recognized. This work is therefore non-economic parameter used to quantify the contribution. The benchmarks developed in this work were found to be measurable and appropriate for owner occupied industrial buildings and makes collection of data simple. The work advanced the benchmarks required for the performance evaluation of industrial buildings without resorting to determination of actual value. This will be useful for government to fix industrial real estate in the national economic importance as against the usual real estate investment contribution to the national economy.

Keywords: Industrial Real Estate, Industrial Sector, Performance, Production Output, National Economy, Gross Domestic Product

1. Introduction/Background to the Study

Land and real estate proved not only to be central to man need and activities but also as the most crucial factor of production. In view of today's globally difficult economic situations, more and more groups of companies realize that their real estate property does not belong among the core business anymore.

The value of industrial real estate is primarily examined in relation to local economic conditions, property location and physical characteristics. The objectives of having industrial property according to [1] include; fulfilling workplace need of business growth, meeting the individual need of business operating divisions and maximizing the investment and capital value of portfolio. The management of industrial property may be in-house affair or hands-off affair depending on the policy of the industrial establishment. Industrial property has always been the poor relation in any sectoral assessment of real estate markets [1].

These assets in most cases have therefore been assessed on the ability of the occupier to pay for the space, resulting in an expression of the financial return from the investment. This concept is being expanded today by astute investors who are taking account of longer-term considerations, and, in particular, the sustained optimal utility of the space.

Maximizing the contribution of property to the wealth maximization of the firm's shareholders will require development of an organizational strategic plan that drives a supporting real estate strategy. Successful implementation of the selected real estate strategies will require the development of a comprehensive performance management system to provide a feedback loop to assess progress and make adjustments as needed.

The Real Estate Sector's contribution to Gross Domestic Product (GDP) of Nigeria has been previously established at 7% region between 2010 and 2012 as it went from 7.56% in 2010, down by 0.28% points in 2011 and showing a slight increase in 2012 up to 7.73% [2], none of such was noted as regards the contribution of the industrial real estate, this work is an attempt to measure the performance of property held for industrial usage but not industrial investment or investment in industrial property.

In measuring performance of industrial investment generally, economic and non-economic parameters may therefore be used. Property performance evaluation has traditionally been accepted as referring to the performance of an investment asset, this is different from performance as a corporate asset (where property is used as operational asset).

This is basically to measure the contribution of industrial property as a factor or contributor to the overall industrial investment performance and at ultimate end determines its actual contribution to the gross national product of Nigeria.

To achieve this aim, the reminder of the paper has been structured into 7 sections. The next section states the research problem. The third section is on conceptual framework, the fourth section review the related literature, followed by study area and methodology in the fifth section. The sixth section is on the findings and discussion of the findings before the work is eventually concluded.

2. The Research Problem

Corporate occupiers have begun to understand the importance of real estate to the business function-to know if they are reaping the benefit or not. The data for evaluation performance include estimated rental value, rent passing, capital value, physical characteristics, management costs, tenure and yield which in most cases may not be easily gotten because of absence of a decent time-series of market data in most industrial markets across the channel caution of taxation taken by most establishments.

The question to answer while evaluating the performance of industrial property includes; is the property use to maximize revenue- investment return or business profit?, are their identifiable ways of improving the performance of the property? and is the property appropriate within the overall portfolio? Performance measurement can be made even more effective if there is opportunity to compare the performance of the organization's real estate as a cost base and as an operating base with other occupiers in similar business. As businesses strive to improve their competitive position in an ever more crowded marketplace, strategic use of all their resources, including real estate is necessary to succeed.

The number of studies devoted to examining the performance of commercial or industrial real estate as an investment category is very small compared with studies for other asset markets, and yet real estate represents an important component of invested funds [3]. The roles of property in business transaction are in asset base, cost base and trading base [1]. Performance measurement studies on investment in Nigeria show that performance indicators used are based on ease of measurement or access to information [4].

The basic principles of a successful real estate policy are a customer-oriented organizational structure as well as the creation of efficient business processes. The classification of real estate will have a stronger focus on the features of efficiency and usability than in the past where the emphasis was rather on operational necessities. Whereas in the real sense of it, current situation of companies requires a group-wide adoption of responsibility for the real estate management and the actual contribution of each of the partakers in the production process.

Measuring performance has an important role in measuring past achievements and providing the basis for planning and control decisions. Measurement of service delivery/performance is aimed at establishing the satisfaction of clients or users of a product and services. This is done by comparing the actual perception of the service/product against the expectation of the users. The degree of discrepancy between consumer's perceptions and expectations dictates the service quality and level of satisfaction of consumers/users of the products/services.

In the view of [5] performance of real estate depends on a number of factors and statistical analysis provides a useful tool in analyzing the importance of industrial property characteristics in performance.

The field of real estate of manufacturing industry lacks empirical measurement to quantify the value that it adds to the firm's performance. This indicate that the contribution of real estate to the firm and the possibilities that exist for adding value are often not recognized nor properly considered. Realization that both tangible and intangible assets are important to the successful support of the core business calls for a broader view of real estate's contribution to the firm and ultimately to the overall national economy.

Current methods of investment performance measurement have been derived from stock market and fixed interest data and the theory of investment performance measurement of fixed interest and stock market investments has been addressed in detail in recent years, but very little attention has been paid to the measure of performance of property investments in the works of [6,7,8,9,10,11,12,13,14, 15,16] etc.

These methods cannot be applied to property performance

measurement without substantial adjustment because of its different characteristics, in particular the difficulties of placing a value on properties, their indivisibility and duration of the property cycle[17]

The contribution of industrial/manufacturing sector to the national economy has been previously done using performance indicators such as index of manufacturing production, manufacturing capacity, inflation rate and sector growth rate, and these has indicated that the contribution of manufacturing sector to the gross domestic product of developing country like Malaysia is 45% (more than the one obtained from developed nations 35%-45%).

[18] has however put the contribution of industrial/manufacturing sector to the gross domestic product of Nigeria as less than 5% and this was also corroborated by Manufacturing Association of Nigeria (MAN) as it also documented that the average contribution of industrial/manufacturing from period of 2007-2013 is less than 5%, but no noted work has actually documented the contribution of industrial property to the gross domestic product of Nigeria.

In addition, while a lot have been written on property performance generally and industrial property performance of investment asset specifically, little was actually written on industrial property performance of operational asset and this is a noted gap in literature that this work is set to fill. This work is therefore set to measure the contribution of real estate to the production output of manufacturing industries in Ota, Ogun State, Nigeria and relate it to the gross domestic product of Nigeria with a view to providing guidance for the industrial investors, measuring past achievements and providing the basis for planning and control decisions.

3. Conceptual Framework

Production is the basic process of transforming naturally occurring materials that provide little satisfaction in their natural state to goods and services that provide more satisfaction. Generally, the production of any good or service inevitably requires four types of inputs; Labor, capital, land, and entrepreneurship used by society to produce consumer satisfying goods and services. Economists have used these four general categories since the days of Adam Smith and the lines between these four resource categories are frequently blurred in the modern complex economy and society.

Labor is the mental and physical efforts of humans excluding entrepreneurial organization used for the production of goods and services. Entrepreneurship is the special sort of human effort that takes on the risk of bringing labor, capital, and land together to produce goods. Capital is the manufactured, artificial, or synthetic goods used in the production of other goods, including machinery, equipment, tools and vehicles while Land is the naturally and artificial occurring materials of the planet that are used for the production of goods and services, including the land itself and buildings build on it to accommodate production processes.

Industry can be said to be "a particular way of organizing production and assumes there is a constant process of technical and social change which continually increases society's capacity to produce a wide range of goods" [19]. The manufacturing sector is particularly important in the process of industrialization because of its multi-dimensional benefits to the development process. Indeed, some authors define industrialization in terms of increase in the share of the gross domestic product contributed by the manufacturing sector [20].

According to [21], the manufacturing sector of any economy worldwide is reputed to be the engine of growth and a catalyst for sustainable transformation and national development. This is because of its enormous potentials as a tool for creating wealth, generating employment, contributing to the country's Gross Domestic Product as well as alleviating poverty among the citizenry, hence, [22] described industry and in particular the manufacturing sub-sector, as the heart of the economy, but there cannot be manufacturing activities without the industrial properties in form of land and real asset.

Industrial properties are land, structural improvement and equipment connected with a particular property which is being used for the conversion of materials into finished manufactured produces. It is expected that industrial property is highly correlated with property characteristics.

In developing its Competitive Industrial Development Index, the United Nations Industrial Development Organization (UNIDO) defined the components of the index in terms of the attributes of a country's manufacturing sector [23]. Accordingly, industrial development report identified Manufacturing Value Added (MVA) as one of the measurement of industrial performance in which industrial properties are prominent.

Most of industrial real estate are used as whole usage rather than share usage, for instance, in US one half of industrial space is owner occupied and majority of rental structures have a single tenant, therefore most industrial property are built by or for its occupancy directly making the issue of rent passing difficult to come by in industrial performance measurement [24] and collection of industrial property data hamper by market data problem, this is also noted in Nigeria.

In the view of [5] performance of real estate depends on a number of factors and statistical analysis provides a useful tool in analyzing the importance of industrial property characteristics in performance. The metrics used to determine the contribution of real estate are primarily focused on cost reduction or capital minimization. What is often not recognized is that property can also help to improve revenues. Both avoiding costs and enabling others in the organization to improve their services and consequently increasing revenues contributes to profitability and add value to the firm.

One way of looking at how real estate can add value to the firm is using the framework shown in [25] Balanced Scorecard (BSC). In their model, organizations can increase economic value through revenue growth and/or productivity.

Revenue growth comes from new markets, new products, new customers, and expand sales to existing customers. Productivity results from reducing expenses and using assets more efficiently.[26] translates the BSC view to show how corporate real estate can add value through growth and profitability.

From an organization and management perspectives, performance is measured by the realization of the organization's goals. From performance measurement perspective, performance is seen as an object's ability to achieve desired results but from corporate real estate management point of view, performance can be seen as the ability of the real estate to support the organizational objectives, strategies and at the end, business success [27] Applying the disciplines of performance evaluation helps property managers and operators to determine important issues that are crucial to the overall success of an organization and also to determine those issues that are critical to the successful delivery of the specific function or operation concerned. According to [28] performance evaluation categories for a property can be graphically represented as shown in Figure I

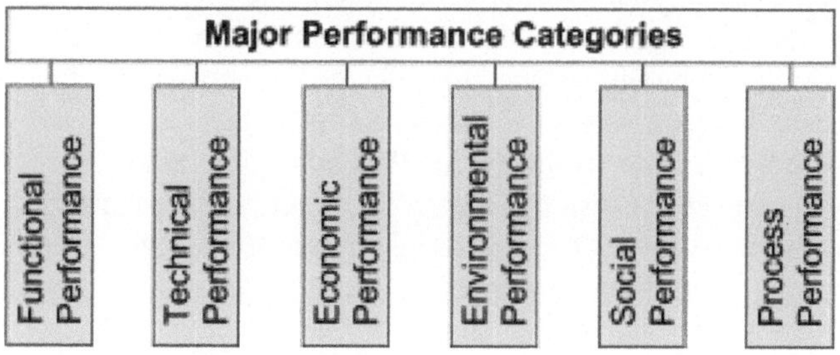

Figure I. *Major performance categories Source: Adapted by Durodola et al 2014 from Lutzkendorf et al. (2005).*

Most firms only consider how property decisions can improve profitability through space efficiency, cost reduction and capital minimization. Performance measures at times focus on cost per square metre and space per employee. However, real estate decisions contribute to increased revenues as well. Measuring the value of corporate real estate decisions is much more difficult than calculating the financial return on traditional "investment" real estate. Corporate real estate outputs are usually internal outputs to another part of an overall process.

In addition, differently structured and focused firms want different results from their real estate assets, so there is no one indicator of "good" performance by real estate. Rather, the firm should develop a performance measurement system of valid and reliable measures that match their objectives and are reasonable considering available data and resources. Corporate real estate industries believe property and facilities decisions can create value for the core business in several ways; by providing a pleasant and productive physical workplace and provision of responsive and high quality property services to the internal customers. However, there can be a link between the real estate and overall business strategy or no link at all.

4. Literature Review

The survey of literature on property performance generally interchanges the use of the following; Improved working environment, Reduced building operating costs, Reduced facilities maintenance costs, Greater capital cost, Lower operating expenditure, Greater demand for space, Lower operating and/or capital expenditure, lower initial return on capital, higher rents, less vacancies, Increases net income or decreases capital, positive impact on value/negative impact on value. All these and others are the major characteristics of an operational nature with particular reference to the utility of the building adopted for measurement of performance of industrial property.

[21]examines the performance of the Nigerian manufacturing sector since independence in 1960 to 1983, using such performance indices as percentage contribution to the Gross Domestic Product, index of manufactured products, percentage growth rate, manufacturing value added, employment growth rate and percentage of capacity utilization within this period. Secondary sources like the Central Bank of Nigeria Statistical Bulletin, Annual Reports and Statements of Accounts as well as the Statistical Facts sheets of the National Bureau of Statistics and other publications were used in collecting the data. The findings indicate that the Nigerian manufacturing sector has average growth rate of 8.4% between 2001-2005 while average contribution to the gross domestic product for the period is 5.5%, but the contribution of industrial real estate was not included in the findings.

[29] used panel data analysis on secondary data that was extracted from CBN Statistical Bulletin from 1980-2008 to examine the growth rate and contribution of manufacturing to GDP and found out that positive relationship exist in manufacturing performance for sustainable economic development in Nigeria, between manufacturing and each of capacity utilization and import as 1 percent change in capacity utilization and import lead to 43081 and 3.8 percent change in manufacturing respectively.

[19] examined the relationship between foreign direct investment and the value added to the manufacturing industry in Nigeria between 1970 and 2009. In view of the development and industrializing desires of Nigeria, as well as the foreign aid received in form of private investments, it is pertinent to examine the effect the presence of multinationals has had in shaping the Nigerian manufacturing industry. Using the autoregressive lag distribution technique to determine the relationship between foreign direct investment and manufacturing value added, it was discovered that in the long-run, foreign direct investments have had a negative effect on the manufacturing sub-sector in Nigeria, again the work does not extend to know what is the actual contribution of the real estate to manufacturing production and national economy.

In the foreign countries, [30] contributes to a deeper understanding of the organizational variables "responsibility" and "performance" of real estate functions by identifying different organizational models concerning both the functions and responsibilities assigned to corporate real estate (CRE) professionals in European and North American companies and the determination of factors influencing the occurrence of these different management models. 74 major European and 38 North American companies from the banking, energy, telecommunication, and transportation and logistics industries were sampled. The research revealed 5 typical models describing the allocation of responsibility of real estate functions within a company and the performance of those identified responsibilities and infers that no "best practice" CRE management model exist in a specific situation as often stated, but instead, various promising organizational models seem to exist. Although this work is empirical, but it is limited to the organization management of industry but not on industrial contribution measurement

[31] found out that activity-based office concept of the modern office is set to increase productivity through the stimulation of interaction and communication while retaining employee satisfaction and reducing the accommodation costs in the Netherlands. This study shows that the office concept is not always used as intended, what could result in a loss in productivity, illness and dissatisfaction. People's personal preferences seem to have a bigger effect on the use of certain types of workplaces than some workstation facilities, although ergonomics and IT equipment and systems are expected to be satisfactory everywhere. There is however, a need for sound data on the relationship between office design, its intentions and the actual use after implementation.

[32] identified corporate occupiers among the important interest groups in the real estate business. The whole value network in the real estate sector, consisting of, developers, investors, and service providers depend on the occupier organizations and meeting their needs and preferences. The work further investigate the methods applied by the parties in the real estate sector in identifying and evaluating office occupiers' needs and preferences regarding the physical, virtual, social as well as financial elements of the workplace. The findings present an efficient and relevant evaluation of the applied methods in matrix form and recommendations for the development of the methods are suggested with practical implication of analyzing the occupiers' needs and preferences related to physical, virtual, social, and financial elements of offices which require applicable methods.

[33] provided a comparative analysis of industrial corporations in Ireland and those in the non-industrial sector with respect to their corporate real estate management objectives using a behavioural questionnaire targeted at the top 150 companies operating in Ireland and classified on the basis of number of employees. The findings indicate that significant differences are apparent between companies in the industrial sector and companies not in the industrial sector in the use of real estate assets. In particular companies in the industrial/manufacturing sectors have weakly developed corporate real estate strategies. The main limitation of this study is its relatively small sample size, a function of targeting the survey at senior executives. Under-utilization of real estate assets was noted by the work which calls for further investigation on the effects of this on corporate balance-sheets. The work highlights that companies in Ireland, notably those in the industrial sector, have some significant way to go in utilizing their corporate real estate assets more effectively.

26 corporate real estate executives in several countries were interviewed by [34] to present how real estate strategies can add value to the core business, providing real estate managers a tool to illustrate how real estate functions and add value to the corporations. This is with the view to examine the approaches for developing real estate strategies, to measure performance and inquire how real estate adds value to the company and how to measure the value. The work was only able to indicate the contribution of corporate real estate to the core business and that wealth maximization can be modeled to illustrate the effects of real estate to financial performance. Like other previous works, the industrial real estate actual contribution to national economy was however not captured by this work.

5. The Study Area and Methodology

Ogun State in South-western Nigeria borders Lagos State to the South, Oyo and Osun states to the North, Ondo State to the east and the republic of Benin to the west. Abeokuta is the capital and largest city in the state. Other notable cities and towns in Ogun State are Ijebu Ode, Sagamu, Ijebu Igbo, Ilaro, Ayetoro and Ota. This study is specifically set in Ota Township, Ogun State, Nigeria. Ota is a peripheral settlement adjoining the Lagos metropolis, located on latitude 6o 42' N and longitude 6o 13' E. In area distance, Ota is about 53km to Abeokuta - the Ogun State capital, and 22km to Ikeja-the Lagos State capital. Ota is a fast growing medium size industrial town whose physical growth is mainly driven by proximity to two major highways: the Lagos - Abeokuta Expressway and Idiroko Road. These two roads intersect at Sango, the commercial node [35]. Ota is undoubtedly bulkily dominated by manufacturing and industrial establishments.

This work did not measure the value (capital or rental) to determine performance of industrial properties; rather it rated the performance of each standard economic factors of production (land, labour, capital and entrepreneur) base on their contribution to the production activities of the industries. It is an attempt to convert the qualitative perception of the respondents to quantitative measurement. The work adopted the use of questionnaire to elicit the required data for the study. Survey research design was adopted by administering questionnaire through the cross sectional survey.

The questionnaire was semi-structured questions to test the view of the respondents. The study population was the identified head of administration of each industries sampled. Out of 108 industries located in Ota (Ogun State Ministry of Commerce and industries, 2013) 40% representing 44 industries were randomly sampled to elicit data such as: name of the industries, location, production classification, ownership structure, stock of built assets, average age of assets, usage structure, nature of usage, measurement of utility between

2008 and 2012, derived in relation to the goal of the establishment among others. To eliminate bias and allow the respondents to have equal chance of being selected random sampling technique was adopted with the use of table of random numbers to select the sample size.

The instrument used for data collection was content validated and Cronbach Alpha Technique index was used for reliability test which gave a value of 0.90. This technique was pre-tested on a sample of the head of administration of those industries. After collection of data however, appropriate statistical tools were used to analyse the data which meet the scope and nature of data and still were able to answer the research questions.

The data were however collected on the randomly selected industries to represent the whole industries in the study area. Information gathered from the administration of the questionnaires in the study areas were analyzed using both descriptive and inferential statistics. Also, survey of literature on the subject matter was fully explored through journals, textbooks and internet.

6. Findings and Its Discussion

This work as earlier indicated does not measure the value (capital or rental) to determine performance of industrial properties; rather it rates the performance of each standard economic factors of production (land, labour, capital and entrepreneur) base on their contribution to the production activities of the industries as perceived by the respondents. The survey findings in table I indicates that 26 of the industries representing (59%) were owned by Nigerians, 12 representing (27%) were owned by foreigners while 6 representing (14%) were jointly owned by Nigerians and Foreigners.

Table I. *Ownership structure of industrial property.*

Ownership Structure	Frequency	Percentage (%)
Nigerians Only	26	59
Foreigners Only	12	27
Combination of Nigerians And Foreigners	06	14

Source; Authors' Field work (2013)

Only 4 representing (9%) of the industries have staff housing in addition to administrative, manufacturing and storage housing, 8 representing 18% use the property for administrative block and storage while 24 representing 55% use the property for manufacturing purpose as indicated in table II

Table II. *Use of industrial property.*

Use of industrial Real Estate	Frequency	Percentage (%)
Administrative block	08	18
Manufacturing	24	55
Storage	08	18
Staff Housing	04	09

Source; Authors' Field work (2013)

Also table III shows that 38 representing (87%) of the industrial properties were built more than 6 years ago, only 6 representing (13%) were built 1-10 years ago indicating decline in construction of industry during the period of study.

Table III. *Age of industrial property.*

Age Range	Frequency	Percentage (%)
1-5 years	02	04
6-10 years	04	09
11-15 years	14	32
16-20 years	18	41
21 years above	06	14

Source; Authors' Field work (2013)

Generally, the state of the properties was good as indicated by 55% responses from the respondents, 14% of the respondents are of the view that the state of their industrial property was fair, 4% of the respondents were of the view that the state of repair is poor as indicated in table IV.

Table IV. *Condition of industrial property.*

Condition of industrial property	Frequency	Percentage (%)
Very poor	00	00
Poor	02	04
Fair	06	14
Good	24	55
Very Good	12	27

Source; Authors' Field work (2013)

The responses from the nature of usage of industrial property indicated in table V that 42 representing (96%) was owner's occupied, hence no evidence of rent passing on them, while 2 (4%) respondent was of the view that the property was shared in usage with other occupier as tenant. Tables I-V display the attributes of Nigerian manufacturing/industrial industry and graphically presented in figure II

Table V. *Use nature of industrial property.*

Nature of Use	Frequency	Percentage (%)
Whole usage	42	96
Share Usage	02	04

Source; Authors' Field work (2013)

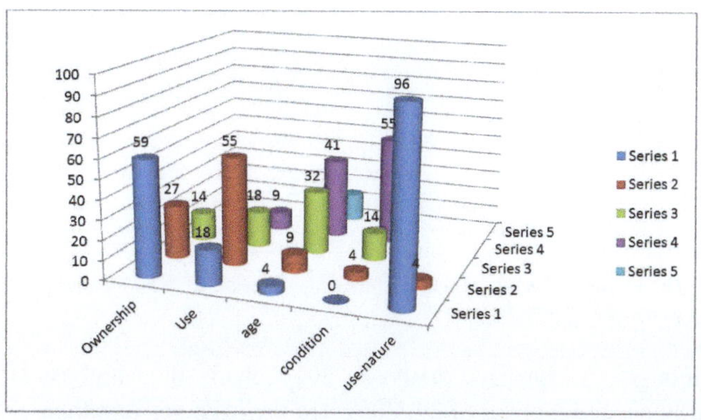

Figure II. *Attributes of Manufacturing industry in Nigeria.*

Table VI indicated that land contribution to industrial process is 20%, labour 45%, capital 15% and entrepreneur 20%

in 2008; in 2009, 15%, 47%, 12% and 26% are the contributions of land, labour, capital and entrepreneur respectively; 24%, 43%,17% and 16% was responded as contribution of land, labour, capital and entrepreneur in 2010. In 2011, 17%, 38.5%, 16.5% and 28% are for land, labour capital and entrepreneur respectively while land contribution in 2012 is 19%, labour 31%, capital 19% and 31% for entrepreneur. This is represented in figure III. Furthermore, industrial property average contribution for the years 2008-2012 shows that labour has the highest performance rate of 40.9% followed by entrepreneur which has 24.2%, then land which has 19% while capital has the least 15.9% of the overall participation measurement of industrial performance in Ota, Nigeria. This is presented in figure IV.

Table VI. *Distribution of Industrial Income Base on Factors Participation.*

The Factors	2008	2009	2010	2011	2012	Average Contribution
Land	20	15	24	17	19	19
Labour	45	47	43	38.5	31	40.9
Capital	15	12	17	16.5	19	15.9
Entrepreneur	20	26	16	28	31	24.2

Source: Authors' Field Work (2013)

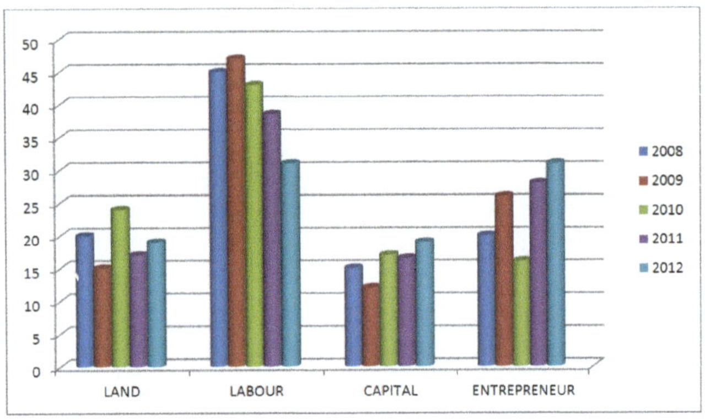

Figure III. *Yearly Contribution of factors in production to manufacturing process in Nigeria (2008-2012).*

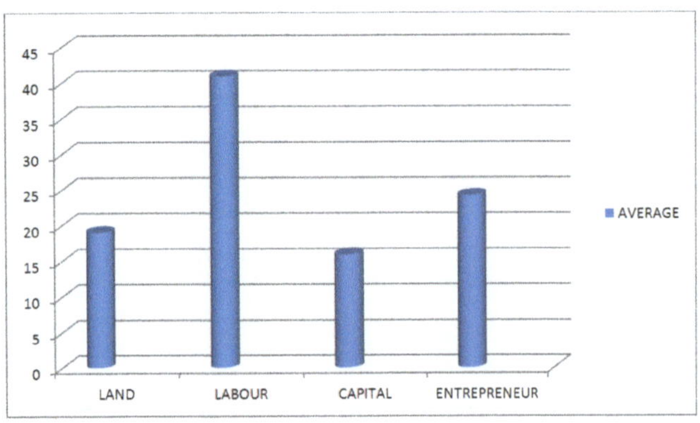

Figure IV. *Average Contribution of factors in production to manufacturing process in Nigeria (2008-2012).*

Although in yearly analysis 2010 had the highest performance percentage of 24, 2009 had the least performance percentage of 15. Year 2008, 2011 and 2012 have 20% 17% and 19% respectively. In terms of meeting the objectives of having industrial properties, the survey established that the industrial properties have strong responses in term of ability to fulfill the workplace need of business growth and meeting the industrial needs, but the responses was weak as regards ability of the industrial properties to maximize the investment/capital value of the portfolio. It is broadly agreed that rating systems are a powerful driver of sustainable built asset performance. There is very useful research emerging detailing the costs and financial benefits of improving the sustainability of buildings. In fact the standard economic factors of production were used as benchmark of measurement, and data collected were not made to seem implicative as regard possible taxation or other government financial policies. The findings of this survey indicated that industrial properties in Ota contributed 19% performance to the manufacturing success of industrial establishments, though this contribution is lower than that of labour (40.9%) and entrepreneur (24.2%), but it is higher than that of capital (15.9%). This indicates that between year 2008 and 2012, at aggregate performance, the industrial properties is relevant to the overall industrial activities in Ota. However, this performance does not have a specific trend (upward or downward), rather it fluctuates during the years of consideration. However, the average of the contribution of manufacturing/industrial sector to Nigerian economy from 2008-2012 as gathered from Central Bank of Nigeria, National Bureau of Statistics, [36] and [37] indicated 3.41% as presented in table VII and figure V. Also the contribution of manufacturing sector to the national economy just like that of the contribution of industrial real estate to manufacturing output is not steady or specific in trend as shown in figure VI. The implication of this is that while the average contribution of manufacturing sector to national economy during period of study is put at 3.41%, the industrial real estate's actual contribution to Nigerian economy is 0.65% (19% of 3.41)

Table VII. *Manufacturing/Industrial sector share in the Nigerian Gross Domestic Products (2008-2012).*

Year of Consideration	Percentage Contribution of Manufacturing sector to GDP
2008	2.70
2009	4.13
2010	4.14
2011	3.00
2012	3.10
Average	3.41

Source: Central Bank of Nigeria (2013); National Bureau of Statistics (2013), [38] Manufacturing Association of Nigeria (2014) and [39] Nigerian Society of Chemical Engineers (2013).

Table VIII. *Combined Contribution of Industrial Real Estate and Industrial sector (2008-2012).*

Year of Consideration	Industrial Real Estate	Industrial Sector
2008	20	2.70
2009	15	4.13
2010	24	4.14
2011	17	3.00
2012	19	3.10
Average	19	3.41

Source: Authors Field Work and Combined Secondary sources (2013)

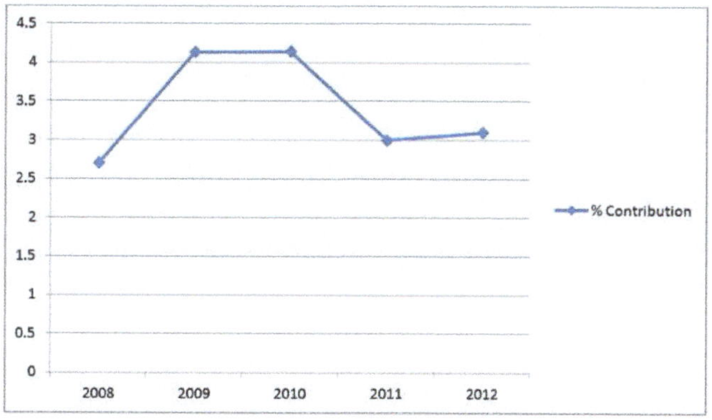

Figure V. Contribution of Industrial/Manufacturing sector to Nigerian GDP (2008-2012).

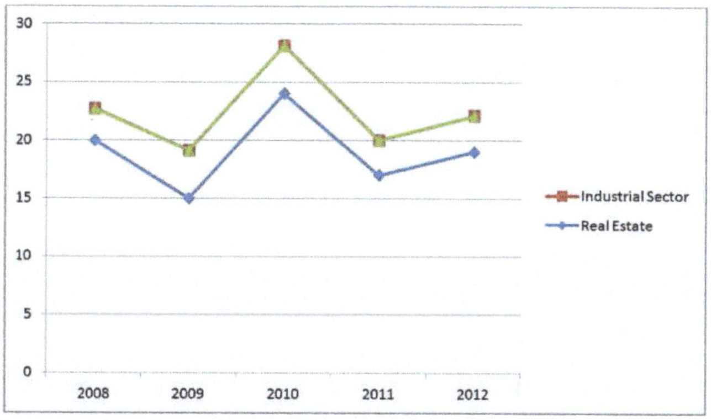

Figure VI. Combined Contributions of Real Estate and Industrial Sector (2008-2012).

However, much more research needs to be undertaken to help determine the market implications of these innovations, and particularly the economic implications of efforts to satisfy the benchmarks like those advanced in this paper. It is only when it can be emphatically and empirically demonstrated to property investors and managers that such efforts are not just affordable but have significant performance benefits and actually contribute to higher returns performance and premium values that the utility measurement of industrial properties will have meaning and become an integral part of the evaluation approach for industrial investment buildings and be connected to the national economy.

7. Conclusions

The significant part of assessing functionality performance of built assets at general term involved determining the measure of achievable sustainability relative to the market. Technological advancement has the potential to produce high sustainability outcomes for buildings, but the cost of much of this innovation is difficult to justify to 'rational economic' investors.

In the case of industrial buildings, stakeholders not only include owners, managers and occupants, but the wider public and government also have a stake in their operation. By this it is meant that management decisions need to be informed by society norms, habits and values, as well as by economic and utility objectives of the parties which this work has attempted to address. In particular there has been keen interest from property investors and managers on the benchmarks for industrial property evaluation.

This work has attempted to advance the benchmarks required for the performance evaluation of industrial buildings without resorting to determination of actual value. Moreover, the benchmarks developed in this work were found to be measurable and appropriate for owner occupied industrial buildings and to make researchers collection of data simple.

The finding of this work supports the claim that the sooner the owner of industrial built asset are able to measure the contribution of their built asset to the overall aim of the establishment and the national economy as a whole, the best will be for them in the sectional appraisal of the contributors to the achievement of the establishment goals and a need to improve and update appropriately. This outcome is also going to be useful for government to fix industrial real estate in the national economic importance as against the usual real estate investment contribution to the national economy.

References

[1] S.Tsolacos, T. Mcgough & B. Thompson "Affordability and performance in industrial property market" *Journal of property investment & finance* vol. 23 No 4 p 311-328 (2005)

[2] National Bureau of Statistics NBS 'Nigerian Real Estate Sector, Summary Report 2010- 2012' 2015 Real Estate outlook in Nigeria February 2015.

[3] A. Krystalogianni, G. Matysiak, & S. Tsolacos, "Forecasting UK Commercial Real Estate Cycle Phases With Leading Indicators: A Probit Approach" in Applied Economics (2004)

[4] Y.A. Adewunmi, & M.M. Ominrin, "Locational choice and business performance in Nigeria" *The Estate Surveyor and Valuer* Journal of NIESV vol. 32 No. 1 January. (2009)

[5] Y. Zhao 'Industrial property performance and building functionality' an M Sc. In real estate development thesis submitted to the department of architecture, Massachusetts Institute of Technology (2003)

[6] A. Olaleye, 'A study of property portfolio management practice in Nigeria', an unpublished M.sc. Thesis of the department of estate management, Obafemi Awolowo University, Ile-Ife, Nigeria (2000)

[7] Olaleye, A, Adegoke, O.J. and Oyewole, M.O. (2010) 'A Comparative Analysis of the Investment Features of Real Estate and Stocks in Nigeria' *Readers Journal* 2 (1): 47-65

[8] O.M. Bello, 'Comparative Analysis of the Performance of Residential Property Investment and Investment in Securities in Lagos Nigeria' *Journal of Nigerian Institution of Estate Surveyors and Valuers* 26 (4):7-14. (2003).

[9] O.M. Bello, 'The Inflation Hedging Characteristics of Nigerian Residential Property Investment' *Journal of Property Research and Construction.1* (1):40-55. (2004).

[10] O.B.A. Idowu, 'Analysis of Residential Property returns in Lagos metropolis (1991- 2004) *Environlink – Journal of Physical and Environmental Development* 1 (1):166-176 (2006)

[11] M.O. Oyewole, 'A Comparative Study of the Performance of Direct and Indirect Property Investment in Lagos', an unpublished M.Sc. thesis of the Department of Estate Management, Obafemi Awolowo University, Ile-Ife. (2006).

[12] A. Amidu, & B.T. Aluko, 'Performance analysis of listed construction and real Estate Companies in Nigeria' *Journal of Real Estate Portfolio Management* 12 (2):177- 185 (2006)

[13] D.I. Dabara, 'Inflation hedging potential of commercial real estate investments in selected state capitals of South-western Nigeria' being an M Sc thesis submitted to Department of Estate Management, Faculty of Environmental Design and Management, Obafemi Awolowo University, Ile-Ife, Nigeria. (2014)

[14] M.O. Ajibola, S.A. Oloyede, & A.O.E. Oni'Real Estate Investment Trust: An Attractive Investment Vehicle for Real Estate Development in Nigeria' *Journal of The Nigerian Institution of Estate Surveyors and Valuers 32 (1):60-66* (2009)

[15] B. Tijjani, S.M.G.Fifield & D.M. Power The appraisal of equity investments by Nigerian investors. *Journal of Qualitative research in financial markets.* 1 (1):6-26 (2009).

[16] N.A. Bello 'Comparative Analysis of Commercial Property and Stock-market Investments in Nigeria' *World Academy of Science, Engineering and Technology* WASET Issue 70 Lucerne October. www.waset.org & *International Journal of Social, Management Economics and Business Engineering* vol;6 No 10 (2012)

[17] M.A.Green, "A standard method of property performance measurement; investment analysts" *Journal –Spring* (1991)

[18] The National Bureau of Statistics (2013)

[19] A.V. Adejumo, "Foreign Direct Investments and Manufacturing Sector Performance In Nigeria, (1970-2009)" *Australian Journal of Business and Management Research* Vol.3 No.04 [39-56] | July-2013

[20] C. Rajnesh "Industrialization and Development in the third world". *Routledge, London.* (1992).

[21] S.A. Banjoko, I.I.Iwuji,& K. Bagshaw, "The Performance of the Nigerian manufacturing Sector: A 52-Year Analysis of Growth and Retrogression (1960-2012)" *Journal of Asian Business Strategy*, Vol. 2, No. 8, pp. 177 -191. (2012)

[22] M.O. Kayode, "Nigeria since independence: The first 25 years". Ibadan, Nigeria: Heinemann Books Ltd. (1989)

[23] UNIDO "Changing patterns industrial performance: A UNIDO competitive industrial performance perspective implications for industrial development" *Working Paper 05/ 2009, UNIDO, Research and Statistics Branch.* (2009)

[24] Torto Wheaton Research modeling the industrial market in United State of America, (2002)

[25] R.S. Kaplan, & D.P. Norton "Using the Balanced Scorecard as a Strategic Management System", *Harvard Business Review,* January-February, 75-85. (1996)

[26] R.S. Kaplan, & D.P. Norton, "Having Trouble with Your Strategy? Then Map It", *Harvard Business Review,* September-October, 167-76. (2000)

[27] R.S. Kaplan, & D.P. Norton, "Strategy Maps: Converting Intangible Assets into Tangible Outcomes", Boston: Harvard Business School Publishing Corporation. (2004)

[28] C.M. Burns, "Analysing the Contribution of Corporate Real Estate to the Strategic Competitive Advantage of Organizations" *Occupier.org*, working papers, available at: http://www.occupier.org/papers/working_paper10.pdf (2002)

[29] A. Lindholm & S. Nenonem, "A conceptual framework of CREM performance Measurement tools". *Journal of Corporate Real Estate.* 8 (3):108 – 119. (2006)

[30] T. Lützkendorf, T. Speer, F. Szigeti,G. Davis, P. Le Roux, A. Kato,& K. Tsunekawa, "A comparison of international classifications for performance requirements and building performance categories used in evaluation methods". Technical Research Centre of Finland (VTT) / Association of Finnish Civil Engineers (RIL). Assessed from http://www.irbnet.de/daten/iconda/CIB6731.pdf (2005)

[31] Olorunfemi, S., Tomola, M. O., Felix, O. A. and Ogunleye E.O. (2013) "Manufacturing Performance In Nigeria: Implication For Sustainable Development" *'Asian Economic and Financial Review*, 2013, 3(9):1195-1213

[32] S. Hartmann, P. Linneman, A. Pfnür, D. Moy & B. Siperstein, "Responsibility for and performance of corporate real estate functions", Journal of Corporate Real Estate, Vol. 12 Iss: 1, pp.7 – 25 (2010)

[33] R. Appel-Meulenbroek, P. Groenen, & I. Janssen, "An end-user's Perspective on activity-base office concepts", *Journal of Corporate Real Estate,*Vol. 13 Iss: 2, pp.122 – 135 (2011)

[34] J. Niemi, & A. Lindholm, "Methods for evaluating office occupiers' needs and preferences" *Journal of Corporate Real Estate*, Vol. 12 Iss: 1, pp.33 – 46 (2010)

[35] S. Roulac, A. Adair, S. McGreal, J. Berry, L. Brown & George Heaney, "Corporate strategic decision making: A comparative analysis of companies in the industrial and non- industrial sectors", Journal of Property Investment & Finance Vol. 23 Iss: 4, pp.364 – 378 (2005)

[36] A. Lindholm, K.M. Gibler, & K.I. Levainen "Modelling the value adding attributes of real estate to the wealth maximization of the firm", *Journal of Real Estate Research,* Forthcoming (2006)

[37] T. Salau, T. Lawanson & O. Yadua 'Amoebic urbanization: the Lagos-Ota nexus in: Laryea, S. and Agyepong, S. (Eds) *Procs 5th West Africa Built Environment Research (WABER) Conference,* 12-14 August 2013, Accra, Ghana, 99-110. (2013)

[38] Manufacturing Association of Nigeria (MAN) 2014

[39] Nigerian Society of Chemical Engineers (2013) 'Assessment of the manufacturing sector performance in relation to power infrastructure in Nigeria' available at www.nsche.org.ng/cms/publicatios_cms/uploads/assessment/pdf.

11

Identifying Stakeholders in Land Use Management Process and Its Critical Factors in ASEAN[1]

Tulus Tahi Hamonangan Tambunan

Center for Industry, SME and Business Competition Studies, University of Trisakti, Jakarta, Indonesia

Email address:
ttambunan56@yahoo.com

Abstract: The main aim of this qualitative-based research is two folds: to identify the main stakeholders who are directly and indirectly impacted by land and who have actually or potentially influence on land use management (LUM) and the critical factors which determine the smooth coordination and cooperation among stakeholders in member countries of the Association of Southeast Asian Nations (ASEAN). Through reviewing available key literature in individual ASEAN member states (AMSs), it shows that at the macro (aggregate)-level, there are three key stakeholders in LUM, i.e. government, companies, and community. Whereas, at the micro (disaggregate)-level, there can be a large number of stakeholders. With respect to government, many department or agencies may involve in LUM. One important finding of this study is that individual villagers or farmers are not always easy to be integrated in the land use planning and LUM; while farmer groups should be the engine of this integration.

Keywords: LUM, ASEAN, Indonesia, Thailand, Philippines, Cambodia, Lao PDR, Malaysia, Vietnam

1. Introduction

Total population in ASEAN is growing every year, and so demand for food is also growing. This means that every year farmers in ASEAN member states (AMS) (except Singapore) will need to produce more and more food from land which continues to decline because of population growth, rapid industrialization and urbanisation. As a result, land conflicts, which are disagreements and disputes over access to, and control and use of land often emerge because people have different uses for land, or want to manage them in different ways. In Indonesia, for instance, land conflicts between basic food (especially rice) farmers and plantation owners who are mainly big export-oriented companies on one hand, and between rice farmers and real estate and highway developers have been intensified in the past one decade. The fact is that farmers as the key stakeholder in land use management (LUM) are always the victim of the conflict. But, this is not only happened in Indonesia. Land conflicts are often occurred in other AMS as well especially in countries where military influence is still strong, such as Cambodia, Lao PDR, and Viet Nam, and where law enforcement is weak and corruption is in all levels of government administration such as the Philippines (Albano, 2003; Brits, et al, 2002; Davuth, et al.,2008; Dealca, 20091 Ducourtieux, at al., 2005; and Natalie and Pred, 2009).

Based on the above current situation, this qualitative-based research aims to answer the following two research questions. First, how many stakeholders that have influence on LUM? Second, what are the critical factors which determine the smooth process of coordination and cooperation between stakeholders? The importance of the first question is due to the fact that there are either too many stakeholders (i.e. those who are directly as well as indirectly affected and those whose "interests" determine them as stakeholders), or not clear who have the right to use or manage land (e.g. FAO, 2000; IFC, 2007). Most conflicts are characterized by the presence of too many or multiple stakeholders who themselves may have subgroups with varying interests. Disagreements also arise when these interests and needs are incompatible, or when the priorities of some user groups are not considered in policies, programs and projects (FAO, 2000). Certainly, if these conflicts are not well addressed can escalate into violence, cause environmental degradation, disrupt projects and undermine livelihoods.

The importance of the second question is due to the fact

[1] This study could not have been undertaken without the generous support of the 2013-14 Senior Scholar Fellowship Programme under the 2012-2015 ASEAN-Canada Research Partnership.

that LUM issue is inherently complex as it involves not only many stakeholders with different needs for land, different interests on land use, different behaviours, different knowledges related to LUM, and differences in other backgrounds, but it also involves many physical factors such as the ecological cycles, hydrological cycles, climate, animals, plants and geography etc., and non-physical factors including land title security, laws, political system, and socio-economic as well as institutional factors, which vary by individual AMS. In other words, a good LUM based on coordination and cooperation of stakeholders will not happen if all these factors are not in favour of it. All these factors are dynamic and many of them are inter-related. A change in one of them may have far reaching and/or long term impacts which may even be irreversible. So, having good knowledge on critical factors in determining a good coordination and cooperation among all parties involved or impacted by land use is crucial.

2. Analytical Approach and Conceptual Framework

To answer these questions, this study adopts stakeholder analysis approach, as it is suggested generally in the literature as an appropriate (if not the best) approach for natural resources management (NRM) including LUM. According to many, e.g. Allen and Kilvington (2001) (quoted from Abdulharis, et al, 2008), and Billgrena and Holme (2008), stakeholder analysis is the identification of stakeholders that may have influence directly as well as indirectly on LUM, an assessment of their interests, and the ways in which those interests affect project riskiness and viability

In its published Stakeholder Engagement: A Good Practice Handbook for Companies Doing Business in Emerging Markets, IFC (2007) gives the main reason why the stakeholder is more suitable than other approaches for a good risk management, including in natural resources management (NRM), namely as a means of describing a broader, more inclusive, and continuous process between land or natural resources (NR) using company and those potentially impacted that encompasses a range of activities and approaches, and spans the entire life of a project. Especially when there are many stakeholders, in which the company is not necessary to engage with all stakeholders with the same level of intensity all of the time, the company needs to be strategic and clear as to whom it is engaging with and why it is crucial. In this practical handbook it is stated clearly that the land or NR-using companies should prioritize their stakeholders and, depending on who the stakeholders are and what interests they might have, figure out the most appropriate ways to engage. Stakeholder analysis therefore assists in this prioritization by assessing the significance of the project to each stakeholder group from their perspective, and vice versa.

With respect to land use, this concept provides a basis on designing a sustainable LUM system by identifying different affected groups, well known as stakeholders (e.g. local communities including farmers, local government authorities, non-governmental and other civil society organizations, local institutions and other interested or affected parties), and their the goals and roles, and by helping to formulate appropriate forms of engagement with these groups. The stakeholders approach gives better insight about the degree of complexity of NRM or LUM. The more number of persons or groups engaged, who are directly or indirectly affected by land use or a project, as well as those who may have interests in a project and/or the ability to influence its outcome, either positively or negatively, the higher is the expected degree of complexity. But, on the other hand, if their goals and roles can be identified, and ranges of activities and interactions among them can be established, the risk of NRM or LUM can be minimized. The risk is not only in the form of production failure, actual revenues are less than expected or should be, total costs higher than revenues, or soil degradation, but also in the form of conflicts. Conflicts can occur because planners and managers identify stakeholders inadequately, or they refuse to acknowledge a group's interest in a resource. When planners and managers fail to identify and consult with the full spectrum of stakeholders, they limit their understanding of these groups' diverse needs and priorities and their indigenous knowledge of the situation. This increases the likelihood of conflicts emerging (FAO, 2000).

With so many stakeholder, it is of course not practical, and usually not necessary, to engage with all stakeholders with the same level of intensity all of the time. Therefore, being strategic and clear as to whom the land-using company is engaging with and why is crucial, as this strategy, can help the company to save both time and money. IFC (2007) in its practical handbook for companies to engage effectively and efficiently with their projects-related stakeholders, state clearly that the land or natural resource-using companies should prioritize their stakeholders and, depending on who the stakeholders are and what interests they might have, figure out the most appropriate ways to engage. For example, some stakeholders will be more affected by a particular phase of a project, such as construction activities, while others will be impacted by the implementation of the project, e.g. production processes.

According to the handbook, when prioritizing or selecting stakeholders by degree of importance or level of engagement, the following questions are important:

1) What type of stakeholder engagement is mandated by law or other requirements?
2) Who are the most vulnerable among the potentially impacted parties, and are special engagement efforts necessary?
3) At which stage of project development will stakeholders be most affected (e.g. procurement, construction, operations, decommissioning)?
4) What are the various interests of project stakeholders and what influence might this have on the project?

5) Which stakeholders might help to enhance the project design or reduce project costs?
6) Which stakeholders can best assist with the early scoping of issues and impacts?
7) Who strongly supports or opposes the changes that the project will bring and why?
8) Whose opposition could be detrimental to the success of the project?
9) Who is critical to engage with first, and why?
10) What is the optimal sequence of engagement?

In stakeholder theory literature, the question of who is, and who is not, a stakeholder has long been a point of debate. The critical question here is: should stakeholder status be reserved for constituencies that have a very close relationship with the company? Or, should stakeholder status be broadly interpreted and take into account all of people or parties that can affect, and be affected by, the company? According to the literature, at the minimum, stakeholders are those groups or people or parties from whom the company has voluntary accepted benefits and to whom the company has therefore incurred obligations of fairness. Typically, this includes groups such as financiers, employees, customer, suppliers, and local communities. Stakeholder theory maintains that normative or legitimate stakeholders are owned an obligation by the company, while derivative stakeholders hold power over the company and may exert either a beneficial or harmful influence on it (e.g. Phillips, 2004).

Thus, according to this theory, in the case of LUM, the legitimate stakeholders are including farmers, local communities, direct related government department/agency, suppliers, financiers. While, other groups such as environment activists or local NGO providing trainings or technical assistances to local farmers are not normative or legitimate stakeholders, but the land-using company may choose to care for the environment and welfare of local farmers because its legitimate stakeholders (e.g. customer) may care deeply about it.

However, given time and financial limitations, this study is fully based on a literature review consisting key case studies in ASEAN member states (except Singapore). There is a number of good case studies which adopt stakeholder analytical approaches based on field investigations. They include case studies ever done more than one decade ago (and no new studies after their period can be found) by Grimble and Wellard (1997), and Grimble (1998) on some Asian countries e.g. Nepal, Indonesia and Koreas' community forestry. Those case studies show successful examples of how stakeholder analysis can be incorporated into the NRM. This allowed the stakeholders to identify their needs and level of involvement with the forests.

3. The Study

3.1. Land Use Management

LUM is the process of managing the use and development of land, covering the debate about norms and visions driving the policy-making and sector-based planning both in the strategic and operative time spans, as well as the spatial integration of sectoral issues, decision-making, budgeting, participation, implementation of plans and decisions and the monitoring of results and evaluation impacts. LUM is driven by various decisions taken at different levels (local, regional, national) and in different sectors (public, private, civil society). It is a continuing process which improves the coordination of regional development policy as well as public investments and public-private investments and the involvement of inhabitants and local stakeholders in common visions. Sustainable LUM acts in a multi-level governance structure between an operational project level and a strategic level of region (urban and/or rural) management. Therefore, land use planning as an instrument of LUM or rather a tool to reach the broader aim of sustainable land development is concerned with the formulation of policies and plans on the use and development of land (Engelke and Biehl, 2010).

LUM in general is not an easy task as it is challenged by a diversity of issues including demography, politic, cultural, ethnic and religious diversity, economics, environment, climate and geography. There are also structural factors that play a role in the process of LUM, e.g. location, the physical infrastructure, different levels of government agencies namely central government (e.g. Ministry of Forestry, Ministry of Agriculture, Ministry of Industry, Ministry of Trade, Ministry of Environment, Ministry of Finance) versus regional or local government agencies, competition between agencies in authority. Also are functional factors which include political issues inherent in the special interests of the different stakeholders that influence understanding of those diverse issues and factors that impact the process.

At the macro (aggregate)-level, there are three key stakeholders in LUM, i.e. government, companies, and community. Government has a role in i) develop and establish law, regulation, guideline and socialization, ii) guidance and surveillance, and iii) administration and law enforcement. Corporate/company/operator has a role in: i) preventing and controlling pollution to environment, ii) monitoring and reporting, iii) provide information/report that correct, accurate, and right, and iv) manage, recover and rehabilitate pollution of environment. Community has a role in: i) giving a recommendation/idea, ii) social control, iii) giving report and complain on the occasion pollution on environment that harmful for community.

At the micro (disaggregate)-level, there can be a large number of stakeholders. With respect to government, many department or agencies may involve in LUM. With respect to companies, there can be more than one company holding/using the same land. Whereas, with respect to community, it comprises of many individuals or households, not only individual farmers or herders or growers but also other villagers with different natural needs of land. Unfortunately, these individual villagers or farmers are not always easy to be integrated in the land use planning and LUM; while farmer groups should be the engine of this integration.

With such many stakeholders who may have conflicting views about the best land management practices to achieve sustainable land management, conflicts sometimes cannot be prevented. Therefore, knowing behavior of stakeholders regarding land use on a case by case basis is important which leads to a sector view on land use by the different stakeholders and their requirements and needs. It is indeed important to open up the stakeholders view to an integrative view on land use and coordinate and combine different sector requirements and needs on land use (Engelke and Biehl, 2010).

3.2. Brief Overview of Land Policy and Administration in AMS

a) Indonesia

The importance of the colonial influence on the development of land tenure systems in Asia cannot be overemphasized: in Cambodia and Lao PDR to the French, Indonesia to the Dutch and Japanese and the Philippines to the Spanish and Americans, Malaysia and Myanmar to the British.. In Indonesia the strong colonial influence resulted in land laws becoming a dualism between western systems and customary systems, with elements of the latter being incorporated into the former. Today the customary elements incorporated into the new systems continue to feature strongly (Brits *et al*., 2002). In Indonesia, the Basic Agrarian Law No. 5 of 1960 is based on *adat* or customary law; it provides the basis for land administration. An important change in regulations (the first amendment in 30 years) provided for a right to title after 20 years of occupancy 'in good faith', and a recognition of occupancy by the surrounding community (Brits *et al*., 2002)..

In other words, the Law should be seen as a key step in the implementation of the Constitution and providing a stronger basis for customary right protection. It confirmed the constitutional right of the State to control all unclaimed land and resources while recognizing customary rights under certain conditions (Articles 3 and 5). In fact, customary rights are applicable to lands not owned by the State, as long as they do not interfere with national interests or the common good. The validity of *ulayat* rights is strongly restricted by Article 5. The Law is compounded by land policies that have favoured land consolidation to facilitate investment, especially foreign direct investment, without resolving underlying conflicts over ownership and use rights. However, the Law has in many cases been ignored by related sectoral laws and policies governing forestry, environment, water, and mining, severely limiting management opportunities for small farmers and fishermen (Kayoi *et al*, 2006).

As in many other AMS (e.g. Thailand, Lao PDR, the Philippines), the land administration or registration in Indonesia is undertaken in all Municipality/Regency land offices. Regarding land tenure, Indonesian National Land Agency (BPN) to hold full control on delivering land tenureship and permits related to land use. Considering its wide-spread coverage, BPN is capable on performing this task. Considering full authority of Provincial and Municipal Government due to Regional Governance Act, Provincial and Municipal Government could consult further arrangement in relation to permit granting on land use management to BPN (Abdulharis, *at al*., 2008).

b) Cambodia

There are 3 pillars of the land policy in Cambodia: (1) land administration: focusing on an effective land titling programs in systematic and sporadic, dispute resolution, land market orientation; (2) land management: focusing on sustainable development by e.g. developing of zoning, and land use planning; and (3) land distribution: designing to provide residential and farming land to the poor landless and land poor households (Davuth, et al., 2008). As the Ministry of Land Management, Urban Planning and Construction is the lead institution for land-related questions, it is therefore the main important stakeholder in land use management in the country.

However, despite the Cambodian government's efforts to have a good land management system, as in Indonesia, land conflicts are becoming a serious problem in Cambodia. Sokha, et.al. (2008) who studies land transaction in rural areas in Cambodia have found that the main type of land dispute has changed from disputes over boundaries to ownership rights. The land market has expanded and this has led to many cases of land disputes due to various reasons, which include unclear land rights before land transfers or sales; absence of demarcation between the state forest land and private, or community land; ignoring traditional rights of fallow land in shifting agriculture areas; illegal encroachment on forested land for selling; and overlapping of administrative boundaries.

Even, a report from the Cambodian Forestry Administration (FA, 2010) concludes that currently, insecure title over forested land and unclear rights to use de facto open access forest resources mitigate efforts to maintain the forest cover, to secure livelihoods or to contribute to rural economic growth in the country. According to the report, this situation reflects a lack of coherence in rural land management policies, weak capacities of sub-national sector line agency departments, poor service delivery mechanisms and the limited involvement of rural land and resource users in formalized NRM procedures.

c) Lao PDR

The Lao People's Democratic Republic (PDR) is a mountainous land-locked country with relatively low population density. Some 87 percent of its territory is upland, where there are high incidences of poverty and little infrastructure. Lao PDR is rich in wetland biodiversity and the least damaged ecosystems in Southeast Asia. Wetlands play a very important role in the lives of Lao people since the majority of the people live in the wetland-rich Mekong basin and rely on wetlands for their dairy subsistence and income generation. Besides, wetlands provide a diverse range of valuable services to society. But unsustainable NRM is beginning to reverse this situation caused by such as government policies, socio-economic change and population pressure (Sopha and Sharp, 2013).

All land and forestland in Lao PDR is owned by the State, based on Forestry Law 2008. In Article 4 it is stated that natural forest and forest is the property of the national community. Customary rights are not acknowledged in this Law but only in minor Ministerial recommendations. But, it is able to grant certain rights of management, use and exploitation to different entities, with the form of rights dependent on the classification of land. The Law also dictates that a registered land title is the highest form of property right; analogous to ownership. A land title is the only legal document demonstrating permanent land use rights and grants the holder a variety of rights, such as to use the land as collateral, to transfer the land, and to give the land as inheritance. Such land titles can be granted to individuals or families on up to three hectares (Sipaseuth and Hunt, 2009).

Recently, Lao PDR has developed a new policy aiming for the sustainable land/forest management including through targets for increased national forest cover, namely the Forestry Strategy to the Year 2020. Two ministries are directly responsible for the success of this strategy, i.e. the Ministry of Agriculture and Forestry (MAF) and the Ministry of Natural Resources and Environment (MoNRE). Concurrently, management of the forestry sector more broadly was transferred from MAF to the Department of Forest Resource Management (DFRM) within MoNRE. (REDD, 2012).

d) Malaysia

The Federation of Malaysia comprises Peninsular Malaysia in the East and the states of Sabah and Sarawak on the island of Borneo (or Kalimantan) at the West side. In land administration contexts, the right of the individual to own land is safeguarded under the Federal Constitution, in which land is administered by the State Authority, although the Federal Government plays a very important role in legislating land matters (Samsudin, 2011).

These three parts of Malaysia are different in land administration. In peninsular Malaysia, which is a federation of states, each state is responsible for its own land issues. But, all states operate the Torrens system of registration, administered by the State District Office and coordinated by Director General of Lands and Mines of the State Department of Land and Mines (Samsudin, 2011). Land administration in Peninsular Malaysia is governed by the National Land Code 1965 (Act 56) which was created to provide a consolidated legislation in all aspects of land tenure and registration, land transfer, leases, charges, easement and other rights of alienation and development of land. In Sarawak, land is administrated by Land and Survey Department, headed by the Director of Lands and Surveys, under the State Ministry of Planning and Resource Management. Sarawak also operates the Torrens system of registration and its current land law is governed by the National Land Code Chapter 81, 1958. Land administration organizational structure in Sabah share almost the same structure as Sarawak, i.e. administrated by Lands and Surveys Department under the portfolio of the Chief Minister's Department through the office of the Secretary of Natural Resources, and its current framework for land policy is provided by the Sabah Land Ordinance Chapter 68, 1930 (Samsudin, 2011).

e) Myanmar

The majority of its population lives in rural areas and depends on land as a primary means of livelihood. But, because all land in Myanmar ultimately belongs to the state, citizens and organizations do not own land; they depend upon use-rights, and tenure rights vary depending on the type of land involved. The country's laws grant women equal rights in some respects and also recognize certain customary laws that provide women equal rights in relation to land. In practice, however, the rights of many women are governed by customs that do not afford them equal access to or control over land (USAID, 2013).

Differently than in other AMS, Myanmar does not have a written policy on land use and land tenure. But, the country does have Farmland Law issued in March 2012, which defines rights and responsibilities relating to tenure and establishes a hierarchy of management over farmlands. The Farmland Law affirms that the state is the ultimate owner of all land and creates a private-use right that includes the right to sell, exchange, inherit, donate, lease and "pawn" farmland. It also establishes a system of registered land-use certificates. The law effectively replaces the 1963 Tenant Farming Law and the 1963 Protection of Peasants' Rights Law, and repeals the 1953 Land Nationalization Act, the Disposal of Tenancies Law and the Agriculturalist's Rights Projection Law. It also covers: conditions under which farmers can retain farmland use-rights; the state's power to rescind such rights; the process for settling certain land-related disputes; and basic requirements for compensation in the case the government acquires the land for public purposes (USAID, 2013).

f) The Philippines

Before 2003, Philippines had used almost 100-year old land administration system from the West that has been institutionalized across, and implemented by, different government agencies. As it is a very old system, not suitable anymore for the current condition of the country, especially with respect to the use of land, the system was found to have the following structural defects: (i) conflict among laws regulating the system and its administration; (ii) two processes for titling land (administrative and judicial processes); (iii) multiplicity in forms of ownership rights in land; (iv) multiplicity of property taxes and related disincentives to formalization of land transactions; (v) multiplicity in land valuation methods; and (vi) duplication and overlap in the roles, functions and activities of land administration agencies (Albano, 2003). In response to this problem, the government has undertaken an initiative undertaken to improve its land administration system, through the Land Administration and Management Project (LAMP). LAMP was conceptualized to respond to the weak and inefficient land administration system in the country which has eroded confidence and trust in the titling and registration system as a whole (Dealca, 2009). Then, in 2003, the government issued The Land Administration Reform Act of 2003, which is the new law on land administration in the Philippines (Albano, 2003).

g) Thailand

Thailand, although not colonized, borrowed extensively from the west in establishing its legal and administrative system. A titling system for private rights in land was introduced in 1901, based on the Australian system. As in other AMS like Indonesia, Lao PDR and the Philippines, title registration systems also operate in Thailand, but titles are not guaranteed by the state, not like for instance, in the Philippines.

The following five major pieces of legislation constitute the core of Thailand‘s land regulation and governance framework (USAID, 2013). First, Thailand's Constitution which provides that the state shall adopt land policies, including policies relating to land use, land distribution, town and country planning, and the sustainable protection of land and other natural resources. Second, the Land Code (LC) 1954, which is, as amended, Thailand‘s primary land legislation. The LC recognizes a range of land documents with the main ones are pre-emptive claims, which are non-transferable, and certificates of utilisation and titles, both or which are transferable and accepted as collateral (Brits *et al.*, 2002). Third, the Agricultural Land Reform Act of 1975 that was enacted in an effort to address the high rate of tenancy in certain regions of the country, the large number of landless households, and the encroachment of public lands for cultivation. Fourth, the Land Development Act of 1983 which established a national Land Development Committee to help improve the utilization and productivity of the country‘s agricultural land. Fifth, the Land Readjustment Act of 2004, which governs processes for land re-plotting and development in order to improve land utilization.

As in many other AMS (e.g.. Indonesia, Lao PDR and the Philippines), the land administration systems in Thailand, are all decentralized. In Thailand the title register is maintained in the 16 Bangkok Metropolitan, 76 provincial and 272 branch land offices. Registers for the lesser documents in Thailand are maintained in the 758 district land offices (Brits *et al.*, 2002).

Thai government has implemented a 20 year project 1984-2004, named the Land Titling Project (LTP) in four five year phases. The project is considered as one of the largest land titling programs implemented throughout the world, and it is recognized as having been very successful and has served as a model for other countries in the region (e.g. Indonesia, Lao PDR and the Philippines) and throughout the world (Brits *et al.*, 2002).

Within ASEAN, Thailand has very efficient systematic land titling (first registration) procedures and has issued over 8.5 million titles since 1984 under the LTP). The procedures in Thailand have largely served as a model for systematic land titling in the region. Land titling is being undertaken in Indonesia and Lao PDR, with pilot land titling being undertaken in the Philippines and Cambodia (Brits *et al.*, 2002).

h) Vietnam

Following the introduction of *đổi mới* reforms, a new Land Law was enacted in 1987, which ratified the ongoing de-collectivization of agriculture and began to allocate agricultural land holdings of cooperatives to individual households based on family size. The second Land Law in 1993 granted five rights to land users, i.e. transfer, exchange, lease, inherit and mortgage, and extended lease terms to 20 years for annual crops and 50 years for perennial crops and forest land through the issuing of Land Use Rights Certificates (Wells-Dang, 2013). Further, in 1994 the government issued Decree 02/CP on allocation of forest land, followed in 1995 by Decree 01/CP on contracting of land for agriculture, forestry, and aquaculture purposes, and in 1999 Decree 163 on leasing of land for forestry purposes (Tan, 2011).

The political economy of land shifted once again after 2000 as Vietnam embarked on a new policy emphasizing "industrialization and modernization". The 2003 revision of the Land Law allowed the State to appropriate land for economic development purposes, also serving to legitimize previous practices of land appropriation (Wells-Dang, 2013). The new Land Law in 2003 is recognizing the legal status of village communities in land tenure, and in 2004 the government issued Forest Protection and Development Law which is recognizing legal status of village communities in forest management (Tan, 2011).

In recent years, land rights have become highly contested in Vietnam in recent years, as the economy has grown rapidly from a system of collectivized agriculture after 1975 to a mixed model of state and private management described as a "socialist-oriented market economy". Vietnam's land endowment is one of the lowest in the world: each agricultural household holds, on average, less than 0.5 hectare. The national priority on "industrialization and modernization" has placed new demands on agricultural and forest land for urban-industrial expansion. The high level of public concern over land tenure and its links to political and social stability have led to widespread calls for revision of the 2003 Land Law (Wells-Dang, 2013).

3.3. Some Evidence on Main Stakeholders in LUM Processes and Their Critical Factors in ASEAN

Based on limited case studies from selected AMS, the next table in a matrix form showing evidence on efforts to improve LUM through community-based/stakeholder approach. The fourth column shows key stakeholders that were currently involved in LUM, and the last column presents the critical factors that need to be solved (i.e. lacked supporting factors) for sustainable land management identified by the particular authors.

As can be seen in this table, in each cases many people or parties are considered as stakeholders. Although the authors do not make a distinction between legitimate and non-legitimate stakeholders, in this table the stakeholders are grouped into these two categories. As can be seen from the all cases presented in the table, there are four key legitimate stakeholders in a LUM, namely farmers or land owners, companies or land users, local community, and government (central and regional/local). Whereas, the most important non-legitimate stakeholder reveals to be non-government organizations/NGOs, and in some cases donor organizations also involved as non-legitimate stakeholders, at least according to the definition adopted in the stakeholder theory literature.

Those stakeholders can also be distinguished into the followings: direct, indirect, and no impacted stakeholders. Direct impacted stakeholders are not only those whose revenues or income or welfare change (decline or increase) directly because of the land use: i.e. the land-using company, farmers and other local community/villagers (e.g. local transport owners, local suppliers, local traders, etc), but also those whose daily way of life will be disturbed because of production activities of the land-using company (i.e. local surrounding villagers). In other words, direct impacted stakeholders are the most vulnerable among the potentially impacted, and therefore special engagement efforts are necessary.

Indirect impacted stakeholders are those whose revenues will change (e.g. increase) because of activities of the land-using company, e.g. income or value added taxes payments to local and/or central government. But local business owners whose activities will be disturbed indirectly can also be considered as indirect impacted stakeholders. For instance, many agricultural laborers have lost their job because the land where they used to work in has been sold or rented to a company. Because of this, unemployment has increased which has a negative impact on local businesses such as shops, transport, services, food stalls, etc. Direct as well as indirect impacted stakeholders are included as legitimate stakeholders.

For those who are not impacted at all are considered as no impacted stakeholders. But they may have various interests of and therefore influences on activities of the company. This type of stakeholders includes activist groups, press people/media, NGOs, donor organizations, universities, etc. According to the stakeholder theory, they are considered as non-legitimate stakeholders from the company's perspective. Although, depending on type of project and hence type of its potential impacts and the degree of significance of the impacts, these groups are too important to be ignored at all by the company.

The table also shows that although the types of critical (lacked supporting) factors for having a good LUM vary by case, there are some common critical factors, and the most important ones that revealed from many cases are issues related to ownership (i.e. lack of customary or land owner's rights and system, security of land ownership, land tenure system), followed by lack of fully involvement of local communities in all aspects of LUM, and lack of coordination, either among government agencies or between government and other stakeholders or among other stakeholders, especially between farmers/land owners and land-using companies. While in some other cases, lack of data or information especially on potential stakeholders and their need, the real owners of land revealed as the most crucial factors.

With respect to the issues related to the land ownership or land tenure security, it seems that despite the efforts given by the governments in these countries to improve their land administration system by issuing laws and regulations, as discussed before, they have not yet managed to solve these problems. Two main factors may explain this, namely lack of law enforcement and corruption especially at the lower level of government administration (regional or local government).

Table 1. *Efforts to improve LUM through community-based/stakeholder approach in individual AMSs.*

Member state	Region/area	Case	Identified Main Legitimate and Non-legitimate Stakeholders	Source	Critical factors which need to be solved for sustainable LUM
Indonesia	Papua	Tropical forest management	Legitimate (i) local communities/villagers (including farmers, forest or land resources dependent communities, land owners) (ii) land-using companies (iii) central government (related ministries and agencies) (iv) provincial, and local (district) government Non-legitimate (v) NGOs/local civil society groups	Kayoi *et al* (2006)	-Legal recognition to customary rights (ongoing struggle between the provincial and central governments over powers to regulate customary rights) -Availability of data on customary land -Clear standards or procedures in place that take adequate account of community land-use systems -Institutional mechanisms to guarantee the transparent, fair, and equitable distribution of funds and development support under company-community agreements. -Allocation of forest resources between communities and large-scale commercial concessionaires, including the allocation of areas for direct community management, based on participatory mapping of customary lands; -Clearl definition of rights and responsibilities with respect to compensation and community development in areas assigned to external investors; -Local community and government institutional support,

Member state	Region/area	Case	Identified Main Legitimate and Non-legitimate Stakeholders	Source	Critical factors which need to be solved for sustainable LUM
	Around the country	marine cadastre	Legitimate (i) central government (related ministries and agencies) (ii) provincial, and local government (iii) local community (e.g. fishermen, fish farmers, tourism, and other eligible subject of exploitation and cultivation of fishery resources within 12-nautical-mile territory); Non-legitimate (iv) overseas legal persons, (v) navy, army, and police; (vi) higher learning institution, including university	Abdulharis, *et al.* (2008)	-Coordination among government agencies (e.g. overlapping of jurisdiction of the Ministry of Marine and Fisheries with other public institutions, in particular on marine issues). -Special organisation focused on management of marine resources, or, alternatively, authority on marine relegated to specific ministries and agencies that have been performing tasks related to management of marine resources, in particular on marine cadastre. - Separation on management land and marine resources in ministry and agency in question. -National coordinator on marine cadastre issues.
	Kapuas Hulu, West Kalimantan	Oil palm plantation	Legitimate (i) villagers (ii) using companies, (iii) central government (related ministries and agencies) (iv) provincial and local (district) government, Non-legitimate (v) local customary authorities (village head, sub-village head, and *patih*), (vi) NGOs.	Clerc (2012)	- Local communities involvement in all aspects of LUM. - Acknowledged and accommodation of customary system -Trust between the company and the villagers.. -The role of NGOsto strengthen the bargaining position/power of the local community. -Recognition of the landowner's right to decide whether or not to hand over the land -Security of ownership of the used land after the leasing period which is critical in assessing the long-term tenure security of local communities.
	Kampong Pring Village in Kandal province; Kampong Thnoat Village in Kampot Province, Baboang Village in Prey Veng Province, and some others.	e.g. rice field	Legitimate (i) central government (related ministries and agencies) (ii) local government (iii) local communities (e.g. farmers0 Non-legitimate (iv) NGO	Sovannarith, et al. (2001)	-Weak implementation of decentralized land governance -Weak implementation of law on land right (land title) -Availability of data.
Cambodia	Siem Reap	Rice field	Legitimate (i) central government (related ministries and agencies) (ii) local government (iii) land using company (iv) villagers Non-legitimate (v) brokerage and intermediary actors (e.g. village chiefs, commune chiefs, commune counsellors, policemen, military, local leaders)	Sokha, *et.al.* (2008).	-Land title security -The rights of farmers on former deep water and floating rice land should not be ignored.
	Sre Ambel and Botumsakor Districts (Koh Kong province)	Sugar plantation	Legitimate (i) central government (related ministries and agencies) (ii) local government (iii) local communities Non-legitimate (iv) local civil society organization/NGOs	Haakansson, (ed.) (2011),	-Land title security (land certificate) -Bargaining power of farmers -Coordination and dialogue between farmers and government
Lao PDR	Some parts in the country	Forest	Legitimate (i) Central government (related ministries and agencies) (ii) private companies	Manivong, and Sophathilath (2007)	-Supports from government with respect to budget, human capacity, legal instruments, legal enforcement (legal and institutional support), technical instructions, etc.

Member state	Region/area	Case	Identified Main Legitimate and Non-legitimate Stakeholders	Source	Critical factors which need to be solved for sustainable LUM
			(iii) local communities Non-legitimate (iv) NGOs (v) Donor countries/organizations (ADB, GTZ, JICA)		-Level of participation local community -Management of the process -Roles and responsibilities among stakeholders
	Central Lao	Coconut plantation	Legitimate (i) Central government (related ministries and agencies) (ii) using companies (iii) local communities Non-legitimate (iv) NGOs (v) Donor countries/organizations (ADB, GTZ, JICA)	Sipaseuth and Hunt (2009),	-Cooperation among stakeholders -Coordination and cooperation among various ethnic groups within the local communities -Awareness/knowledge of local communities on laws and their rights surrounding concession agreements; -Legal forest land tenure system, -Independency of government oversight -Village level forest management systems
	Xe Champhone	wetland	Legitimate (i) central government (related ministries and agencies) (ii) local government (iii) local communities Non-legitimate (iv) NGOs	Sopha and Sharp (2013)	-Participation of stakeholders and good cooperation among them -Knowledge of stakeholders about related issues -Bottom-up management practice
	Northern Thailand	Wetland	Legitimate (i) Central government (related ministries and agencies) (ii) local government (iii) local communities (iv) usng company and other user groups	Trisurat (2006)	-Consensus-based decision-making approach to prevent or to reduce potential conflict; -Participation of local stakeholders and their full commitment ((resources and effort) to manage the land in a sustainable manner -involvement of local communities in all stages, i.e. from the start in the planning process, implementation and monitoring
Thailand	Northeastern Part of Thailand	Saline Soil	Legitimate (i) Central government (related ministries and agencies) (ii) local government (iii) local communities (iv) usng company and other user groups	Pongwichian, et al. (2008)	-Participation of local community -Community participatory network -Information
	Pak Phanang River Basin	River basin	Legitimate (i) Central government (related ministries & agencies) (ii) regional/local government (iii) farmers and agricultural laborers (iv) using company (oil palm/rubber plantations) Non-legitimate (v) NGOs, academics (vi)local media	Mumtas, Meraman and Chatupote (2013),	-Identification of most disadvantageous/vulnerable stakeholders who depended on land or the natural resources for their livelihood and their capacity -Classification of stakeholders according to their importance and influence on decision making processes
Vietnam	In all forest areas	Forest land	Legitimate (i) Central government (related ministries and agencies) (ii) local government (iii) local community/villagers (iv) using companies Non-legitimate (v) military	Tan (2011)	-Participation of all stakeholders in a good sustainable co-operations -Legal access to forestland -Allocation of forest rights to individual households which is appropriate to customary practice of collective forest management in the upland -Capacity of local authorities (in the upland area) to provide support after forest land allocation -Supports for forestry (including local forest governance) and its community -Recognition of multiple management traditions to expand forest land allocation to villages

3.4. The Overall Analysis: Common Trends, Differences and Challenges from the Country Cases

From the above limited country studies, it reveals at least four common trends:

1) The colonial influences on the development of land tenure systems is still strong in all individual AMS;

2) All AMS have national laws or policies on land administration and land customary rights, and the land administration systems are all decentralized, undertaken in all Municipality/Regency land offices. But these national laws on land always in conflicts with other laws (e.g. sectoral laws). Indeed, a good national coordination among government agencies/department in dealing with various issues, including land, is still lacking in most of the member states;
3) Land conflicts occur in all AMS (excluding Singapore), and the main type of land dispute has changed from disputes over boundaries to ownership rights. However, the degree (the seriousness) of the problem varies by country, depending on many factors including culture and social factors, population pressure, urbanisation process, level of economic development especially industrialization, coordination among government agencies, the strength of military influences, political system, degree of regional autonomy or centralization, degree of law enforcement, degree of violations of human rights; and4) although governments have realized the importance of the involvement of all stakeholder, in reality, the implementation with great success has been found to have occured rarely. The main constraints or the lacked supporting factors (i.e. critical factors) vary however by individual countries. For instance, in Cambodia, Lao PDR and Viet Nam, influences of local government or military officials are too strong. In the Philippines and Indonesia, law enforcement is weak and corruption is in all level of government administration is obvious.

But there are also some differences. For instance, in Myanmar, as land ultimately belongs to the state, citizens and organizations/companies do not own land; they depend upon use-rights, and tenure rights vary depending on the type of land involved. Myanmar also does not have a written policy on land use and land tenure. But, the country does have Farmland Law issued in March 2012, which defines rights and responsibilities relating to tenure and establishes a hierarchy of management over farmlands.

With respect to challenges, there are at least five challenges for having a good coordination and cooperation among all stakeholder to implement a good LUM, and the seriousness of these challenges may vary among AMS, because they are different in many issues, including demography, politic, cultural, ethnic and religious, economics, environment, climate and geography. The first challenge is related to structural factors that play a role in the process of LUM, e.g. location, the physical infrastructure, different levels of government agencies namely central government versus regional or local government agencies, competition between agencies in authority. The second challenge is linked to functional factors which include political issues inherent in the special interests of the different stakeholders that influence understanding of those diverse issues and factors that impact the process. The third challenge is about local culture, namely to have all stakeholders to sit and work together in a cooperative and fair way, especially to fully integrate individual villagers or farmers in the land use planning and LUM. Fourth, to identify the appropriate way that different stakeholders with different background influence the LUM. Fifth, to protect local community which is generally considered as the least powerful stakeholders for 'overpowered; by more powerful stakeholders (e..g big companies).

3.5. Looking for the Best Way to Manage Land

A good LUM consists of the following key elements. First, there should be good co-operations or interactions among stakeholders with zero conflicts. The stakeholders should be engaged from the start to enable a proactive cultivation of relationships among them. Second full integration of local community or farmers in the land use planning and LUM; they should be the engine of this integration. Third, the land should not only secure food but also generate high and sustainable production or revenues, and benefits exceed the costs of conservation, without harming the environment. Finally, the welfare or quality of life of local community or farmers should be better off.

To have a good LUM, there are a number of key preconditions. Among them is land right (or tenure) security. Land tenure security is defined as the assurance that the right holders (including the vulnerable users such as the poor and women) can exercise their right now and in the future, and be able to reap the benefits of the labor and capital invested in the resource (Nyamu-Musembi 2008; Clere, 2012). It is included in property rights security which is a critical incentive for investment in land because it guarantees the right holder will reap the benefits of their investment. Land tenure security also gives the right holder access to credit because the land can be used as collateral (Clerc, 2012). Not only crucial for securing access to food, land tenure security is related to social equity, as land tenure insecurity and land access may link to rural poverty and social position. In addition, by reducing the likelihood of competitive claims, it can decrease land-based conflicts, thus contributing to social order and peace (Clerc, 2012). Land rights security corresponds to the certainty that a right holder will not be arbitrarily deprived of his or her rights in the present or future. It depends upon a range of rights, their assurance and duration (Fuys *et al.* 2008).

However, land rights security alone cannot guarantee sustainable LUM, as the latter acts in a multi-level governance structure between an operational project level and a strategic level of rural/regional/national economic development management, dissolving the often occurring conflict between short-term and long-term orientation within the planning process. Here, sustainable LUM improves the coordination of economic and agricultural development policies as well as public investments and public-private investments and the involvement of inhabitants and local stakeholders in common visions. This way, LUM can be a strategic asset to allow sustainable economic growth and meet growing food demand. Therefore, land use planning as an instrument of LUM or rather a tool to reach the broader aim of sustainable development is concerned with the formulation of policies and plans on the use and development of land (Engelke and Biehl, 2010).

4. Conclusion

The above country cases have demonstrated that sustainable LUM acts in a multi-level decision processes between the lowest or micro level, i.e. an operational project level, the medium level, i.e. rural or regional economic development management, and the highest or macro level, i.e. a national economic development management. This means dissolving the often occurring conflict between short-term and long-term orientation within the planning process. Here, sustainable land use management improves the coordination of economic and agricultural development policies as well as public investments and public-private investments and the involvement of inhabitants and local stakeholders in common visions. This way, LUM can be a strategic asset to allow sustainable economic growth and meet growing food demand. Therefore, land use planning as an instrument of LUM or rather a tool to reach the broader aim of sustainable development is concerned with the formulation of policies and plans on the use and development of land.

Since LUM in general involves many stakeholders and therefore there is a need of good cooperation, there should be a body acting as the coordinator. Since the land is used for agricultural production, then the Ministry of Agriculture should focus on agricultural issues, while at the same time, acting as coordinator of stakeholders. While other stakeholders should perform their tasks in a cooperation way.

Indeed, given many stakeholders, the main challenge of LUM is to sit together and to have a smooth consultative and cooperation process, given the differences in stakeholders' interests, needs and goals to be reached, in their understandings of governance and their varying access to information. Actors from different backgrounds, such as government, civil society, academia, business, farmers and local communities rarely sit together to discuss, let alone propose solutions, governance associated challenges, although they are all affected by them.

To sum up, there are at least three most important challenges in implementing stakeholder involvement-based LUM in Indonesia and other AMS (except Singapore): (i) to have all stakeholders to sit and work together in a cooperative and fair way (ii) to identify the way and its significance that different stakeholders with different background influence the LUM; and (iii) to protect local community which is generally considered as the least powerful stakeholders for 'overpowered; by more powerful stakeholders (eg. big companies). But, in order to meet these three main challenges, some pre-conditions should be met first, and they are the critical (lacked) supporting factors as discussed before, especially, landownership or land tenure system, availability of data, law enforcement, no-corruption, and, of course, a strong political will. In many AMS, lack of these factors impedes the smooth process of LUM. Thus, to be able to meet these pre-conditions is another big challenge the countries are currently facing.

References

[1] Abdulharis, Eka Djunarsjah, and Andri Hernandi, 'Stakeholder Analysis on Implementation on Marine Cadastre in Indonesia. Integrating Generations', paper presented at the FIG Working Week 2008, 14-19 June 2008, Stockholm (Sweden).

[2] Albano, Mylene G, 'The Land Administration Reform Agenda', paper presented the International Conference on Reform in Land Administration Systems (Lessons & Challenges), 24-26 November 2003, Makati City, Manila (Philippines).

[3] Andrianto, A., Obidzinski, K., Wajdi, F., Tetuka, B., 'Deforestation and Forest Degradation in Papua Post-New Order Regime', mimeo, Center for International Forestry Research (CIFOR) (2008), Bogor (Indonesia).

[4] Billgrena, C. and Holme, H., 'Approaching reality: Comparing stakeholder analysis and cultural theory in the context of natural resource management', Land Use Policy, 25 (2008): 550–562.

[5] Brits, Anne-Marie, Chris Grant and Tony Burns, 'Comparative Study of Land Administration Systems. With special reference to Thailand, Indonesia and Karnataka (India)', paper presented at the Regional Workshops on Land Policy Issues, Asia Program, 4-6 June 2002, Phnom Penh (Cambodia) (Land Equity International Pty Ltd – www.landequity.com.au).

[6] Clerc, Johanna, 'Unpacking tenure security', Working Paper No.102 (2012), Center for International Forestry Research, Bogor (Indonesia).

[7] Contreras-Hermosilla, A. and C. Fay, *Strengthening Forest Management in Indonesia through Land Tenure Reform, Forest Trends*, CIFOR (2005): Bogor (Indonesia).

[8] Dandy, N, Mark S. Reed, C. H. Quinn, H. Posthumus, C. Prell, J. Morris, K. Hubacek, A. Graves and L. C. Stringer,'Who's in and why? A typology of stakeholder analysis methods for natural resource management,' Journal of Environmental Management, 90 (2009): 1933–1949

[9] Davuth, Lor; Suon Sopha; and Seng Thany, 'Land Administration in Cambodia', power point presentation in International Seminar on Land Administration Trends & Issues in the Asia Pacific Region, 19-20 August 2008, Kuala Lumpur (Malaysia).

[10] Dealca, Rhea Lyn M., 'Initiatives to Improve Land Administration System in the Philippines', paper presented at the 7th FIG Regional Conference on Spatial Data Serving People: Land Governance and the Environment – Building the Capacity, 19-22 October 2009, Hanoi (Viet Nam).

[11] Ducourtieux, O., Laffort, J. R. and Sacklokham, S., 'Land policy and farming practices in Laos', *Development and Change*, 36(3) (2005):499–526

[12] Engelke E. D, and Dorothea Biehl, 'Land Use Management as Key Part of Metropolitan Governance for for Sustainable Urbanisation', paper presented at the 46th ISOCARP Congress 2010, Nairobi (Kenya).

[13] FA, 'Cambodia Forestry Outlook Study', Working Paper No. APFSOS II/ WP/ 2010/ 32, Asia-Pacific Forestry Sector Outlook Study II, the Forestry Administration, Phnom Penh (Cambodia).

[14] FAO, 'Conflict and Natural Resource Management', Community Forestry, 2000, June, Roma.

[15] Fujita, Y., Vongvisouk, T., Chantavong, H. and Chanthaleunnavong, S., 'Decentralized forest management in production forest in Central Laos Forest, Dong Phousi Production Forest and Dong Sithuoane Production Forest', in P. Durst, C. Brown, H. D. Tacio and M. Ishikawa (eds.), *In Search of Excellence: Exemplary Forest Management in Asia and the Pacific* (2005), Food and Agriculture Organization of the United Nations, Regional Office for Asia and the Pacific, and the Regional Community Forestry Training Center for Asia and the Pacific (RECOFTC), Bangkok (Thailand).

[16] Fuys, A., Mwangi, E. and Dohrn, S., 'Securing common property regimes in a globalizing world. Synthesis of 41 case studies on common property regimes from Asia, Africa, Europe and Latin America', CGIAR System wide Program on Collective Action and Property Rights (2008), Rome (Italy): International Land Coalition (http://dlc.dlib.indiana.edu/dlc/bitstream/handle/10535/5363/ILC_ Securing_Common_ Property_ Regimes_E.pdf?sequence=1).

[17] Grimble, R., 'Stakeholder methodologies in natural resource management, Socioeconomic Methodologies', Research Report (1998), Chatham (England): Natural Resources Institute.

[18] Grimble, R. and Wellard, K., 'Stakeholder methodologies in natural resource management: a review of principles, contexts, experiences and opportunities', Agricultural Systems, 55(2) (1997): 173–193

[19] Guiang, Ernesto S. and Gem Castillo, 'Trends in Forest Ownership, Forest Resources Tenure and Institutional Arrangements in the Philippines: Are They Contributing to Better Forest Management and Poverty Reduction?', paper prepared for FAO as one of a series of country-specific case studies from Asia, Manila: Philippine Environmental Governance Project Phase 2 (EcoGov 2), the United States Agency for International Development (USAID), Development Alternatives Inc. (DAI), and the Philippines Department of Environment and Natural Resources (DENR) (2006), Manila (the Philippines).

[20] Haakansson, Malene (ed.), 'Stolen Land Stolen Future. A Report on Land Grabbing in Cambodia', Association of World Council of Churches related Development Organisations in Europe (APRODEV), December 2011, Brussel (Belgium).

[21] IFC, 'Stakeholder Engagement: A Good Practice Handbook for Companies Doing Business in Emerging Markets', May 2007, Washington, D. C. (the United States): International Finance Corporation

[22] Kayoi, Martin, Adrian Wells, and Gill Shepherd, 'Poverty and Natural Resource Conflict in Indonesian Papua: Reconciling Growth and Social Justice', research paper, September 2006, http://www.profor.info/Documents/pdf/livelihoods/IndonesianPapuaCaseStudy.pdf, Jakarta (Indonesia).

[23] Larsen, Rasmus Klocker, Jo Marie Acebes, and Alejandro Belen, ' Philippines Integrated Coastal Management: diverging Stakeholder Agendas and Elite Co-option in the Babuyan Islands', Working Paper, October 2010, Stockholm (Sweden): Stockholm Environment Institute

[24] Manivong, Khamphay and Phouthone Sophathilath, 'Status of Community Based Forest Management in Lao PDR', January 2007, Bangkok (Thailand) and Vientiane (Lao PDR): The Regional Community Forestry Training Center for Asia and the Pacific (RECOFTC) and National Agriculture and Forestry Institute (NAFRI), Ministry of Agriculture and Forestry.

[25] MK16 Project Team,'Fostering Evidence-Based IWRM in the Stung Pursat Catchment (Tonle Sap Great Lake) Cambodia CPWF-Mekong Basin Development Challenge. Stakeholder Analysis Report', prepared for Mekong Basin Leader CGIAR Challenge Program on Water and Food, March 2013, North Vancouver, British Columbia, Canada,.

[26] Mumtas, Meraman and Chatupote, 'Stakeholder Analysis for Sustainable Land Management of Pak Phanang River Basin, Thailand', Procedia-Social and Behavioral Sciences, 91 (2013): 349-356.

[27] Natalie Bugalski and David Pred (eds.), 'Untitled. Tenure Insecurity and Inequality in the Cambodian Land Sector', (2009) Bridges Across Borders Southeast Asia, Centre on Housing Rights and Evictions, Jesuit Refugee Service, Phnom Penh (Cambodia)

[28] Nyamu-Musembi, C., Breathing life into dead theories about property rights in rural Africa, lessons from Kenya', in B. Englert and E. Daley (eds.), *Women's land rights and privatization in Eastern Africa*, (2008) Oxford (UK): James Currey.

[29] Phillips, Robert, 'Some Key Questions About Stakeholder Theory', Ivey Business Journal, March/April 2004 (http:.//iveybusinessjournal.com/topics/the-workplace)

[30] Pongwichian, Pirach, Chaiyanam Dissataporn and Kulras Ananpongsuk, 'Community Participatory Network on Sustainable Land Management: A Case Study on Saline Soil in Northeastern Part of Thailand', (2008) Office of Research and Development for Land Management, LDD, Bangkok (Thailand) (http://www.ldd.go.th/web_LDDAPEC/PDF/30/30nov_10%20Pirach%20Community%20Participatory%20Network.pdf).

[31] Prell, C., K. Hubacek, M. S. Reed, T. P. Burt, J. Holden, N. Jin, 'Stakeholder Analysis and Social Network Analysis in Natural Resource Management', (2007) Leeds (United Kingdom), Sustainability Research Institute, University of Leeds.

[32] REDD, 'Laos', REDD Countries, the REDD Desk, 04/07/2012, Vientiane (Laos), (http://theredddesk.org/sites/default/files/resources/countries/readiness_overview/laos_ro_en.pdf).

[33] Sawathvong, Silavanh, *Participatory Land Management Planning in Biodiversity Conservation Areas of Lao PDR*, Doctoral thesis (2003), Department of Forest Resource Management and Geomatics, Swedish University of Agricultural Sciences, Uppsala, Sweden.

[34] Sawathvong, Silivanh, 'Experiences from developing an integrated landuse planning approach for protected areas in the Lao PDR', Forest Policy and Economics 6 (2004): 553-566, Vientiane (Lao PDR) (http://www.elseveier. com/ locate/ forpol).

[35] Sipaseuth, Phetdavan and Glenn Hunt, 'Customary Land Rights in Laos – an overview', power point presentation (2009), JVC Laos, Vientiane (Lao PDR).

[36] Sirait, M. T., 'Indigenous peoples and oil palm plantation expansion in West Kalimantan, Indonesia', research paper (2009), Amsterdam University Law Faculty and Cordaid, Amsterdam & The Hague (the Netherlands).

[37] Sokha, Pel, Pierre-Yves Le Meur, Sam Vitou, Laing Lan, Pel Setha, Hay Leakhena and Im Sothy, 'Land Transactions in Rural Cambodia. A Synthesis of Findings from Research on Appropriation and Derived Rights to Land', Gret - Collection Études et Travaux - Série en ligne n° 18, May 2008, Phnom Penh (Cambodia): GRET Organisation (www.gret.org).

[38] Samsudin, Salfarina, 'A Review of Organizational Arrangements in Malaysia Land Administration System towards Good Governance: Issues and Challenges', paper presented at the FIG Working Week 2011, 18-22 May 2011, Bridging the Gap between Cultures, Marrakech (Morocco).

[39] Sar, Sovann, 'Land Reform in Cambodia', paper presented at the FIG Congress 2010 'Facing the Challenges – Building the Capacity', 11-16 April 2010, Sydney (Australia),

[40] Sopha, Thienthong and Alice Sharp, ' Sustainable Wetland Management in Lao PDR: A Case Study of Xe Champhone Wetlands', paper presented at the 3rd International Conference on Ecological, Environmental and Biological Sciences (ICEEBS'2013), 29-30 April 2013, Singapore.

[41] Sovannarith, So, Real Sopheap, Uch Utey, Sy Rathmony Brett Ballard and Sarthi Acharya, 'Social Assessment of Land in Cambodia. A Field Study', Working Paper No. 20, November 2001, Cambodia Development Resource Institute, Phnom Penh (Cambodia).

[42] UNDP, 'Participatory Governance Assessment: The 2012 Indonesia Forest, Land, and REDD+ Governance Index', UN-REDD Programme (2013), Jakarta (Indonesia).

[43] USAID, 'Thailand', USAID Country Profile 2013, Property Rights and Resource Governance, Washington, DC (the USA) (http://usaidlandtenure.net/Burma).

[44] USAID, 'Burma', USAID Country Profile 2013, Property Rights and Resource Governance, Washington, DC (the USA) (http://usaidlandtenure.net/Burma).

[45] Tan, Nguyen Quang, 'Forest Land Allocation and Community Forest Management in Vietnam', Session J, 13 July 2011, RECOFTC – The Center for People and Forests, Lombok (Indonesia).

[46] Thongmanivong, S. and Fujita, Y., 'Recent land use and livelihood transition in Northern Laos', Mountain Research and Development, 26(3) (2006):237–244

[47] Thongmanivong, S., Fujita, Y. and Fox, J., 'Resource use dynamics and land-cover change in Ang Nhai Village and Phou Phanang National Reserve Forest, Lao PDR', Environmental Management, 36(3): (2005) 382–393

[48] Trisurat, Yongyut,'Community-based Wetland Management in Northern Thailand', International Journal of Environmental, Cultural, Economic and Social Sustainability, 2(1) (2006):49-62.

[49] Wells-Dang, Andrew, 'Promoting Land Rights in Vietnam: A Multi-Sector Advocacy Coalition Approach', Annual World Bank Conference on Land and Poverty, 8-11 April 2013, The World Bank, Washington DC (the USA).

12

Ranking Multi Criteria Decision Making Methods for a Problem by Area Under Receiver Operating Characteristic

Seyed Behnam Khakbaz[1, *], **Maryam Karimi Davijani**[2]

[1]Faculty of Management, University of Tehran, Tehran, Iran
[2]College of Farabi, University of Tehran, Qom, Iran

Email address:
Khakbazbehnam@yahoo.com (S. B. Khakbaz), mk.karimi.d@gmail.com (M. K. Davijani)

Abstract: One of the major challenges in decision making is selection among MCDM (multi criteria decision making) methods. These methods do not provide same answer to decision maker. Therefore selecting the best answer is an important dilemma. To solve this problem, methods like Borda and Copeland compilation have been proposed. However, applying these methods leads to a hybrid solution which is not necessarily the best answer. In this paper a new approach is proposed to rank different MCDM methods. This approach is AUROC (area under receiver operating characteristic) which is a data mining tool for ranking classification models. The results would show great potential of applying AUROC for ranking MCDM methods in an immense selection problem with historical outcome.

Keywords: Receiver Operating Characteristic, Multi Criteria Decision Making, Area Under ROC, Ranking MADM Methods

1. Introduction

There are many multi criteria problems in decision making which have been solved by multi criteria decision making (MCDM) methods. The main goal of MCDM methods is to find the best alternative described by quantitative and qualitative criteria. For this purpose decision makers (DMs) need to determine criteria preference and then MCDM methods that weight the criteria and evaluate the alternatives. MCDM methods are applied for both decision making and technology foresight [1].

Because of MCDM methods variety, decision makers (DMs) face with a dilemma in many cases, so they need a solution to choose one of these methods.

Up to now, a few researches have studied to compare and choose among MCDM methods. One of these researches is done to develop a conceptual framework to articulate tentative guidelines and choose an appropriate MCDM method for a problem that a DM face to it. In this article, by use of proposed situation tables, DM can compare the situation of his/her problem by them and then choose the appropriate MCDM method [2]. Another solution for this purpose is statistical solutions. In this solution, after ranking the alternatives by MCDM methods, DM can use statistical coefficients (for example Spearman's rank correlation coefficient or Kendall's coefficient of concordance), and choose the best MCDM method for that problem [3]. However, some of problems which use MCDM methods, have a little statistical significant, that DM can't choose the best MCDM method for the problem [4]. Moreover, E. Triantaphyllue et al. proposed a systematic solution to choose the best MCDM method for a problem [5]. In 2007 [6] compared SAW, TOPSIS and VIKOR methods for their problem conditions, and ranked them. In another research, Opricovic and Tzeng compared the TOPSIS and VIKOR methods with their principles [7]. Antucheviciene compared three MCDM methods (TOPSIS, COPRAS and VIKOR) by statistical approach [8]. However, as we can see, these approaches have deficiencies in a general compartment.

As we know, a similar problem is in classification which is selecting best classifier for a problem. In data mining, this problem has been solved by methods like Receiver Operating Characteristic (ROC) curves [9]. Therefore, this approach has been proposed for applying in MCDM problems in this article.

This method (ROC) apply for four different MCDM

methods (SAW, ELECTRE, TOPSIS and VIKOR) for a marketing decision making problem by historical data. Then AUROC is used to rank these methods. In the next section, literature of ROC and then four MCDM methods would describe. Afterward research methodology and then findings of this article would explain in the latter section.

2. Literature Review

In the beginning of this section, literature of ROC and its analyzing method would be explained. Afterwards, a brief description of four different MCDM methods (SAW, ELECTRE, TOPSIS and VIKOR) which have been applied for the problem, is expressed.

2.1. ROC

The ROC (Receiver Operating Characteristic) curves was first used for signal detection in the World War II, in the war a noisy channel should be refined, and because of this purpose, ROC curves were used for signal detection to characterize the tradeoff between true and false alarms. Also ROC curves have widely been used in data mining. By this tool, data miners can compare the performance of different models (classifier models) [9], [10]. ROC curves depict the performance of a classifier regardless to class distribution or error costs [9]. Using ROC curves, TPR (True Positive Rate) versus FPR (False Positive Rate) are plotted and the best classifier model by comparing shape of the curve and AUROC is chosen. [9], [10].

ROC curves demonstrate the performance of models and compare them by drawing a graph in a two dimensional space. This space consists of TPR and FPR. TPR is the percentage of TP (True Positive) over the positives (Equation 1), and FPR is the percentage of FP (False Positive) over the negatives (Equation 2).

$$TPR = \frac{TP}{P} \quad \text{(Equation 1)}$$

$$FPR = \frac{FP}{N} \quad \text{(Equation 2)}$$

Positives are the alternatives or tuples (like an alternative, a tuple is a row in a dataset that have attributes or criterion that should be classify by a classifier) that are actuall target, and negatives are the alternatives or tuples that in the reality are non-target.

TP is the alternatives or tuples which is predicted target (for example those customers who are determined to accept the marketing plan), and actually is the target. FP is also the alternatives or tuples which is predicted in targeting, but they are not actually target. In the table 1, TP and FP are shown.

Table 1. *TPR and FPR.*

		Predicted
		Target
Actual	Target	TP
	Non Target	FP

The area under ROC (AUROC) is a critical issue to select the best model. AUROC is a value between 0.5 and 1, the method that has the closest AUROC to 1, is the best method. For example the graph in the left side of Figure 1 has better efficiency than the graph in the right side [9], [10], [11]i.

Classifier can be binary (for example: for a marketing problem, the customers who accept the marketing plan and they, who do not) or multi classes (for example for a marketing plan that the company proposed three different marketing plans to its customers). Binary classifications are very similar to decision making problems. In decision making, DMs have to accept or reject the alternatives. Correspondingly, this paper propose the use of ROC curve for MCDM problems to choose the best MCDM method for a historical marketing plan problem.

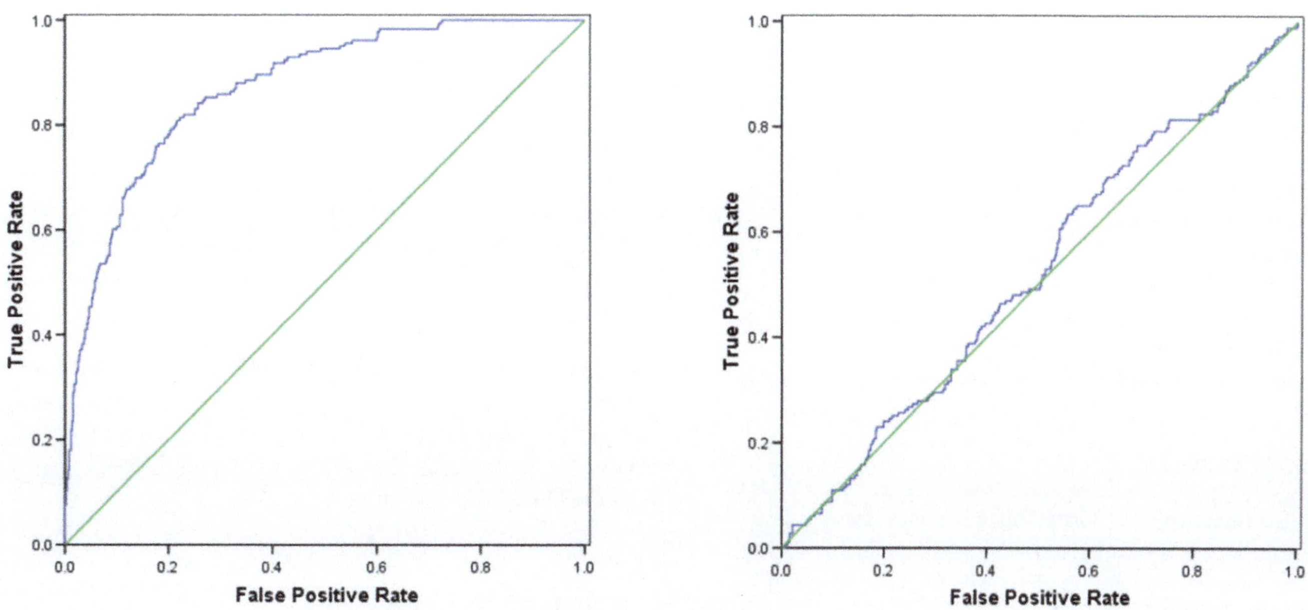

Figure 1. *Sample ROC curve.*

The numerical example of this paper is to choose among customers of a bank, to distinguish those who accept the marketing plan.

2.2. SAW Method

The SAW (Simple Additive Weighted) method was first introduced by Harsanyi in 1955. Because of simple procedure, SAW method has gotten popular, and widely been used in MCDM problems [12].

Step by step: SAW method:

1. Normalizing decision matrix.
2. Multiplying weight of criteria by normal value of each criteria of every alternatives.
3. Sum up the values created in the last step, and make the point of each alternatives.
4. Choose the alternative that has the maximum point.

2.3. ELECTRE Method

The ELECTRE method (in English: elimination and choice translating reality) was first introduced by Benayoun, et al. in 1966. This method is related to paired comparison of different alternatives. In the end, ELECTRE rank the alternatives by their priorities over others and choose the best of them. ELECTRE's alternatives comparison is based on comparing each criterion for every paired alternative [13]. DMs can use ELECTRE for the problems that have a large number of alternatives and eliminate less favorable ones of them, then because of limited alternatives, DMs can choose the best of them [14].

Step by step: ELECTRE method:

1. Normalizing decision matrix.
2. Multiplying weight of criteria by normal value of each criterion of every alternative.
3. Determining concordance or discordance of each criterion for every paired comparison of different alternatives.
4. Calculating concordance matrix by summing up the weight of each concordance in paired comparison.
5. Calculating discordance matrix by dividing maximum weight of each discordance in paired comparison by maximum weight of every paired comparison.
6. Determining effective coordinated matrix by concordance matrix.
7. Determining effective uncoordinated matrix by discordance matrix.
8. Calculating effective matrix by multiplying each array of effective coordinated and uncoordinated matrixes.
9. Choose the alternative that has the maximum point in the effective matrix.

2.4. TOPSIS Method

TOPSIS (Technique for Order of Preference by Similarity to Ideal Solution) is a multi criteria decision analysis method, which was originally developed by Hwang and Yoon [15], [16] and [17]. TOPSIS is based on closest Euclidean distance to ideal point and longest distance to nadir point. DMs should specify cost and profit criterions when using TOPSIS for the MCDM problems. TOPSIS is a compensatory method that make trade-offs between poor and good resulted criterions.

Step by step: TOPSIS method:

1. Normalizing decision matrix.
2. Multiplying weight of criteria by normal value of each criterion of every alternative.
3. Determining the ideal and nadir point for every criterion.
4. Calculate the Euclidean distance from ideal and nadir alternative for each alternative.
5. Calculate the relative closeness to ideal alternative.
6. Elect the alternative with the highest relative closeness.

2.5. VIKOR Method

The VIKOR (Vise Kriterijumska Optimizacija I Kompromisno Resenje) method focuses on ranking some alternatives based on some criterions. This method was established by Yu and Zeleny. This method determines a ranking list and a solution by introducing the multi-criteria ranking index based on the particular measure of closeness to the ideal solution [18].

Steps of this method are:

1. Determine the best and worst values of all criterion functions. If the criterion is a benefit type then the best is max and the worst is min of the function.
2. Compute S_i (the maximum group utility) and R_i (the minimum individual regret of the opponent) values.
3. Compute the value Q_i by the relation between S_i and R_i.
4. Sort the alternatives by the S, R and Q in a decreasing order and rank them.
5. An alternative is ranked the best by the minimum of Q under two below conditions:
   - Acceptable advantage
   - Acceptable stability in decision making

3. Methodology

To draw a ROC curve for a MCDM historical problem, this research amends the original ROC method. In the beginning all alternatives are ranked in a decreasing list by one of the MCDM method. then, next the value of positives and negatives in the historical data must be calculated (for example for a marketing problem, it must be a dataset that have historical data about the previous marketing plan with the response of customers to it, and the criterions that described each of them). By determining the positives, negatives and also ranking list of alternatives, from the first alternative in the ranking, this procedure would follow:

1. If the alternative is a target:

$$TPR = TPR + (1/P)$$

2. If the alternative is not a target:

FPR= FPR + (1/N)

3. Specify the point (FPR, TPR) in the two dimensional graph.
4. If the list is not empty return to 1.
5. Draw the curve that passes through the specified points (drawing ROC curve).

After following these procedures, the ROC curve is ready. Then the area under curve is calculated, so as to calculating AUROC. ROC curve can develop good criterion to compare MCDM methods. For example the method that goes up faster is better, in the case that the cost of surveying is high; however AUROC of this method is lower than other methods, the method preceding the vertical up border is the best method.

In this paper to show the potential of using ROC and AUROC in comparing MCDM methods, a marketing campaign has been applied. The dataset which is used for this purpose is a bank dataset that have about 1000 customers' data. Each customer is an alternative that it must decide on investing on that customer or not. Therefore, MCDM methods have been used to decide on customers. Fortunately the response of customers to the marketing plan is available; therefore ROC and AUROC can be used to compare MCDM methods and choose the best of them for the future marketing campaign. Each customer is described by nominal, ordinal and numerical criterions, which ordinal criterions are converted to numeric scale by their importance, and each nominal criterion is converted to binary criterions (for example a nominal criterion by three different class convert to three binary criterions). Furthermore, MATLAB 2012 has been used as an analyzing tool.

4. Findings

In this section the analyzing results of applying different MCDM methods for this problem is demonstrated.

4.1. VIKOR Method

For the marketing plan problem, VIKOR is the weakest method, the AUROC for this method is only 0.6046, slightly over 0.5 (Random Predictor that accidentally predicts the target and has the equivalent probability for TPR and FPR). Because of the AUROC's weak result, it can be concluded that VOKOR is a weak method for this problem.

As it can be seen in the (Figure 2), the ROC curve of VIKOR method (the green curve) is very close to the blue straight line (Random Predictor), and it shows the weak result of this method (As it can be seen that in the (FPR= 0.2, TPR= 0.4) point the VIKOR has the best result). Furthermore, VIKOR has more computational complexity cost than SAW and TOPSIS methods. Therefore, this method is an inappropriate method for this problem.

4.2. SAW Method

For this marketing campaign problem, SAW is the second method. The AUROC for this method is 0.6891. This method has better result compare with VIKOR; as a result, SAW is a better method. In addition the AUROC of this method is very close to TOPSIS method which would discuss in the next subsection.

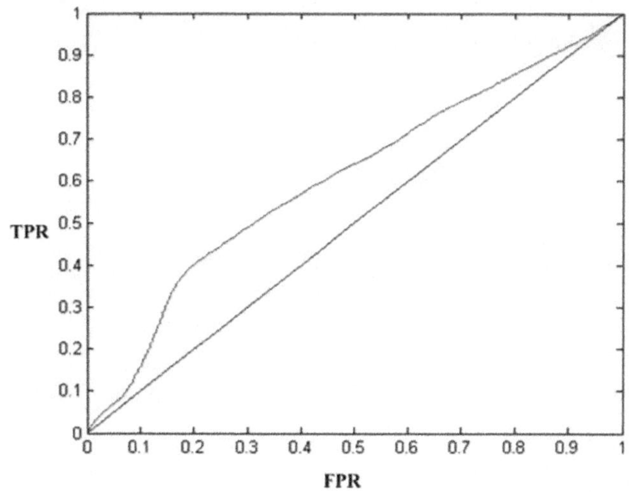

Figure 2. *ROC curve for the VIKOR method for this problem (green curve).*

As it can be seen in the (Figure 3), the ROC curve of SAW method (the green curve), has better shape compare with ROC curve of VIKOR method. Moreover, in the (FPR= 0.2, TPR= 0.4) point (best point of SAW), the gradient of SAW and VIKOR ROC are different (they both have equivalent best point). SAW has a very moderate decreasing gradient, compare with VIKOR. Furthermore, the low computational complexity cost of SAW method is a positive point to select it for this problem; it can be the first choice, if the dataset is very huge.

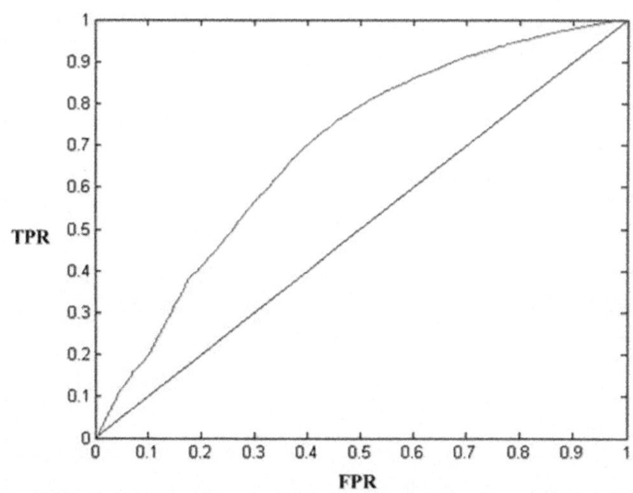

Figure 3. *ROC curve for the SAW method for this problem (green curve).*

4.3. TOPSIS Method

AUROC of TOPSIS method for this marketing campaign problem is 0.7011. This is the best AUROC of MCDM methods which have been applied for this problem. Therefore,

TOPSIS is the best choice for this problem.

As it can be seen in Figure 4, ROC curve for TOPSIS method has a good result in the middle of the curve, which has long distance from Random Predictor (the blue straight line). The best point of ROC curve for TOPSIS method is (FPR=0.4, TPR= 0.8); however the overall AUROC for this method is higher than the SAW method. Choosing between them depends on situation, because the SAW method reaches to the best point sooner, but TOPSIS's best point covers 80% of customers who might accept the marketing plan. Moreover, TOPSIS's computational complexity cost is appropriate for large database.

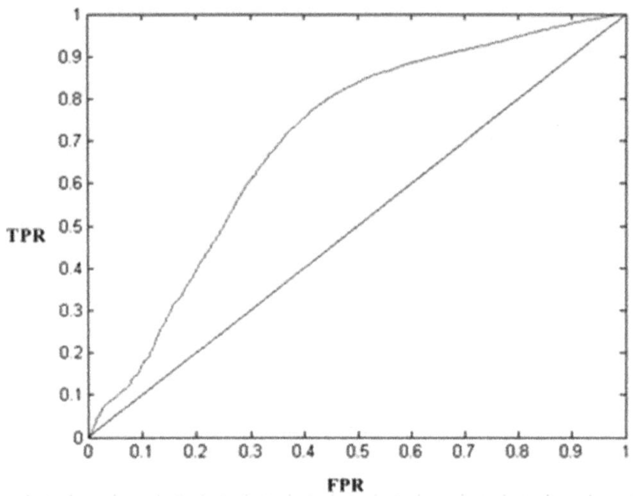

Figure 4. ROC curve for the TOPSIS method for this problem (green curve).

4.4. Comparing MCDM Methods

To conclude the comparing of MCDM methods in this article, the methods have been compared in one smaller dataset, in six different conditions. The dataset that is used in this section are sampled from original dataset and have information of 100 customers. The six conditions are:

1. Limited criterions- numerical only: in this condition, dataset has only numerical criterions to compare MCDM methods.
2. Limited criterions- nominal only: in this condition, dataset has only the nominal criterions that have selected by feature selection method.
3. Limited criterions- ordinal only: in this condition, dataset has only ordinal criterions to compare MCDM methods.
4. Limited criterions- blend: in this condition, dataset has all the criterions that are selected by feature selection method.
5. Only nominal: in this condition, dataset has all of the nominal criterions to compare the MCDM methods.
6. Complete criterions: in this condition, dataset has all of the criterions of the original dataset.

The result of analyzing is as below:

SAW: This method's AUROC and thus efficiency has dropped as the number of alternatives increase; however remains a good method. Furthermore SAW method has a good result in facing with dataset which consist of numerical or selecting criterions. Totally SAW is a very good method for these problems (marketing campaign).

TOPSIS: TOPSIS is the best MCDM method for the marketing campaign; however the result of TOPSIS has fallen when the number of alternatives increases or when facing with nominal and ordinal criterions.

ELECTRE: ELECTRE method has a good performance; however, because of high computational complexity cost, it can be used for the dataset that has a limited number of alternatives,. In addition ELECTRE has limitations for facing with similar alternatives (for example alternatives which have only nominal or ordinal criterions). Therefore this method is good for the marketing campaign problems, which have limited number of alternatives with blend criterions.

VIKOR: According to analysis, VIKOR is a good method for the problems that have limited alternatives. Also VIKOR is weak to face with nominal and ordinal criterions, thus this method is proposed only for marketing campaign problems which have a small dataset.

The analyzing results have been summarized in the (Table 2).

Table 2. *AUROC results for MCDM methods in marketing campaign problem (each cell multiply by 10^4).*

		Limited criterions				Non limited criterions	
# alternatives	Method	Numerical	Nominal	Ordinal	Blend	Nominal	Blend
100	SAW	7358	5339	4173	7954	6084	7337
	TOPSIS	7459	5352	4234	8150	6111	7453
	ELECTRE	7927	-	-	7175	-	7852
	VIKOR	7527	4946	4031	7534	3970	7175
1000	SAW	7026	5873	5707	7137	6628	6891
	TOPSIS	7084	5878	5911	7226	6649	7011
	ELECTRE	7151	-	-	6901	-	6913
	VIKOR	7336	5471	5503	7385	6160	6046

5. Conclusion

With regards to the contents of previous sections, ROC curves and AUROC are appropriate tools for evaluating MCDM methods. Furthermore, the numerical example of this article has shown that the best MCDM method (between SAW, TOPSIS, ELECTRE and VIKOR) for a marketing campaign problem is TOPSIS; however the SAW method has shown better results when only a section of whole dataset is considered in the problem, because of sooner best point of this method. SAW and VIKOR have the equivalent best point, but because of better AUROC of SAW from beginning point to the best point, SAW is better and has the preference to select. This shows another use of ROC curves to evaluate MCDM methods.

This paper shows AUROC is a good tool for overall evaluating of different methods, and the shape of ROC curve can result in better comparison of them. Applying this tool can be consequences to the conditions of different problems and preferences. For example despite.

TOPSIS has the best result for this article's marketing plan, when the goal is to select only limited customers in the conditions of problem, with regards to ROC curves of MCDM methods, it can be concluded that the SAW method maybe is the best method for the conditions of this particular problem.

At the end of this article, Table 3 has shown the summery of comparing five MCDM methods (SAW, TOPSIS, ELECTRE, PROMETHEE and VIKOR) that are used for analyzing this paper's numerical example, and compared by their ROC curves and AUROC values.

Table 3. *Summary of comparing MCDM methods by AUROC.*

Method	Numerous alternatives	Few alternatives	Nominal- ordinal criterions	Complete criterions	Selected criterions by feature selection
SAW			-		
TOPSIS	Best		-		Best
ELECTRE		Best	Weakest	Best	Weakest
VIKOR			-		

References

[1] A. Salo, T. Gutafsson and R. Ramanathan, "Multicriteria methods for technology foresight," Jurnal of Forcasting, pp. 235-255, 2003.

[2] A. Guitouni and J.-M. Martel, "Tentative guidelines to help choosing an appropriate MCDA method," European Journal of Operational Research, pp. 501-521, 1998.

[3] S. H. Zanakis, A. Solomon, N. Wishart and S. Dublish, "Multi-attribute decision making: A simulation comparison of select methods," European Journal of Operational Research, pp. 507-529, 1998.

[4] V. M. Athawale and S. Chakraborty, "A comparative study on the ranking performance of some multi-criteria decision-making methods for industrial robot selection," International Journal of Industrial Engineering Computations, pp. 831-850, 2011.

[5] E. Triantaphyllou, B. Shu, S. Nieto Sanchez and T. Ray, "Multi-Criteria Decision Making: An Operations Research Approach," Encyclopedia of Electrical and Electronics Engineering, pp. 176-186, 1998.

[6] M.-. T. Chu, J. Shyu, G.-. H. Tzeng and R. Khosla, "Comparison among three analytical methods for knowledge communities group-decision analysis," Expert Systems with Applications, pp. 1011-1024, 2007.

[7] S. Opricovic and G.-. H. Tzeng, "Compromise solution by MCDM methods: A comparative analysis of VIKOR and TOPSIS," European Journal of Operational Research, pp. 445-455, 2004.

[8] J. Antucheviciene, A. Zakarevicius and E. K. Zavadskas, "Measuring Congruence of Ranking Results Applying Particular MCDM Methods," INFORMATICA, pp. 319-338, 2011.

[9] I. H. Witten and E. Frank, Data Mining Practical Macine Learning Tools and Techniques, San Francisco: Morgan Kaufmann, 2005.

[10] H. Jiawei, M. Kamber and J. Pei, Data Mining Concepts and Techniques, Waltham: Morgan Kaufmann, 2012.

[11] Clementine® 12.0 Algorithms Guide, Chicago: Integral Solutions Limited, 2007.

[12] J. C. Harsanyi, "Cardinal welfare, individualistic ethics, and interpersonal comparisons of utility," Journal of Political Economy, pp. 309-321, 1955.

[13] R. B. R. a. N. S. Benayoun, "Manual de reference du programme electre, Note de Synthese et Formation," Direction Scientifique SEMA, 1966.

[14] F. T. M. a. F. V. Lootsma, "Multi-criteria analysis and budget reallocation in long-term research planning," European Journal of Operational Research, pp. 293-305, 1990.

[15] C. L. Hwang and K. Yoon, Multiple Attribute Decision Making: Methods and application, New York: Springer-Verlag, 1981.

[16] K. Yoon, "A reconcilation among discrete compromise situation," Journal of Operational Research Society, pp. 277-286, 1987.

[17] C. L. Hwang, Y. J. Lai and T. Y. Liu, "A new approach for multiple objective decision making," Computers and Operational Research, pp. 889-899, 1993.

[18] M. F. El-Santawy, "A VIKOR Method for Solving Personnel Training Selection Problem," INTERNATIONAL JOURNAL OF COMPUTING SCIENCE, pp. 9-12, 2012.

13

An Experimental Research of Small Hydropower Plant Investments Selection in Turkey by Carrot^2, DEXi, DEXiTree

Burak Omer Saracoglu

Orhantepe Mahallesi, Tekel Caddesi, Geziyolu Sokak, Dragos, Kartal, Istanbul, Turkey

Email address:
burakomersaracoglu@hotmail.com

Abstract: Nowadays, human daily lives depend very much to electricity. Hence, electricity generation plays a key role not only in countries' economies, but also in people's welfare and comfort in any region. This situation isn't also different for Turkey. Turkish electricity generation policy gives the opportunity for foreign and domestic private investments plans and schemes. Private investors have many private power plant investment options to invest in Turkey. One of the main groups is hydropower plants. Small hydropower plant investments are grouped under the hydropower plant investments. Their characteristics are very different from other types of hydropower plants. This experimental research study investigates the possibility of using a qualitative Multi Attribute Decision Making (MADM) model based on DEXi (Decision EXpert for Education) and DEXiTree software. Attributes in the current experimental research model are analyzed by help of a text mining tool Carrot^2. In the experimental case study, the most appropriate small hydropower plant investments amongst five alternative ones at the predevelopment investment stages (an assumption) in Turkey are evaluated, and prioritized by help of seventeen basic factors (catchment area, project runoff, net head, discharge, firm energy, secondary energy, investment cost, river basin, conveyance structure, community attitude, transportation, topography, geology, security conditions, terrorism conditions, protected areas, substation conditions) based on the experimental DEXi decision model. There are some interesting findings such as Option 5 gets the highest priority in the overall experimental decision model. Similarly, Option 5 has the very good preference in the objective attributes evaluation. Option 3 comes afterwards with the good preference. But, both Option 4 and Option 5 get the good preference in the subjective attributes evaluation. The DEXi model file (*.dxi) is also presented to readers for giving opportunity to readers for preparing their models based on this experimental research model. This experimental research study is seen as another very small research step to deeply understand the nature of the small hydropower plants investments decisions in the way of developing an autonomous computer based intelligent decision support system for the real world cases.

Keywords: Carrot^2, DEXi, DEXiTree, Investment, Multi Attribute Decision Making, Private, Small Hydropower, Turkey

1. Introduction

Today, electricity is a must for our world. It is consumed at homes, on streets, at factories, and almost anywhere. Researchers work to understand deeply the relations between the electricity demand and the causes and the reasons of this electricity demand. Some researchers indicate that one of the main important factors of the electricity demand is the population growth [1, 2, 3]. The historical data of the annual population in Turkey is given by "Tab. 1".

The annual population growth in this study is calculated by the equations "(1)" and "(2)". The annual population growth in Turkey is presented in "Fig. 1".

Table 1. *Annual total population in Turkey (data:[4], generated by the Microsoft Office 2007 Word http://www.microsoft.com/en-us/).*

Year	Population (total)
2003	65.938.265
2004	66.845.635
2005	67.743.052
2006	68.626.337
2007	69.496.513
2008	70.363.511
2009	71.241.080
2010	72.137.546
2011	73.058.638
2012	73.997.128

$$\text{POY } i{+}1 - \text{POY } i = \text{POD} \quad (1)$$

$$\text{POD} / \text{POY } i = \text{POG} \quad (2)$$

PO is the annual population, Y is the year and i stands for 2003, 2004, 2005, 2006 until 2012. D is the difference. G stands for the growth. For example; the annual population difference in Turkey between 2003 and 2004 (907.370) is calculated as the annual population in Turkey in 2004 (66.845.635) subtracted from the annual population in Turkey in 2003 (65.938.265). The annual population growth in Turkey between 2003 and 2004 (1,38%) is calculated as the division of the annual population difference in Turkey between 2003 and 2004 (907.370) by the annual population in Turkey in 2003 (65.938.265).

The total annual population growth in the current study is calculated by the equation "(3)" and the arithmetic mean of the annual population growth in this study is calculated by the equation "(4)".

$$\sum \text{POG } j = \text{TPOG} \quad (3)$$

$$\text{TPOG} / \sum j = \text{AMAPOG} \quad (4)$$

TPO_G is the total annual population growth in Turkey. j stands for the instances of years, and $AMAPO_G$ is the arithmetic mean of the annual population growth. The TPO_G between 2003 and 2012 in Turkey is found 11,60%, $\sum j$ is counted as 9 and finally $AMAPO_G$ in this period is calculated as 1,29%.

As a result, it is believed that the electricity consumption in Turkey will increase in the mid to long term under these conditions (if conditions will be the same or similar). Hence, this subject takes the attention and the interest of this study.

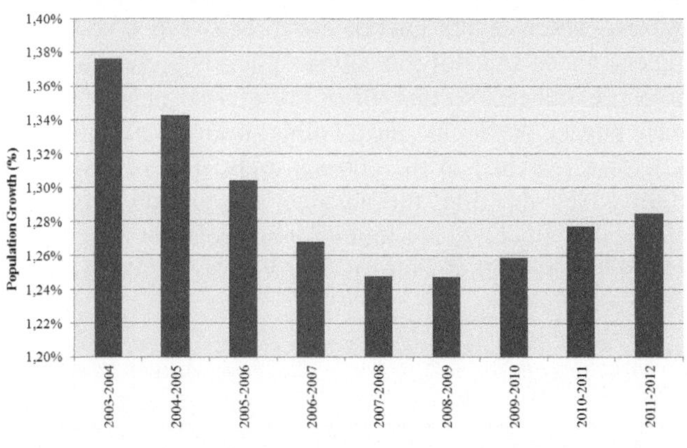

Figure 1. *Total population growth in Turkey (generated by the Apache OpenOffice 4.1.1 Calc http://www.openoffice.org/ & the Paint.NET http://www.getpaint.net/index.html).*

When the private electricity generation market in Turkey is investigated in detail, it is observed that there are several types of power plants investments alternatives. For instance, coal power plants, natural gas power plants, hydropower plants and wind power plants.

Foreign and domestic private investors may invest in several different ways, whichever the power plant type they want to, according to the Electricity Market Legislations in Turkey (visit [5]). Hydropower plant investments are one of the attractive ones due to their relatively low levelized cost of electricity (LCOE) (visit [6]).

The LCOE is simply calculated as in the equation "(5)" to "(12)" (visit [7]).

$$(\text{OCC}\times\text{CRF}+\text{FOMC}) = \text{EP1N} \quad (5)$$

$$i\times(1+i)^{\wedge}n=\text{CRFN} \quad (6)$$

$$[(1+i)^{\wedge}n]-1=\text{CRFD} \quad (7)$$

$$\text{CRFN}/\text{CRFD} = \text{CRF} \quad (8)$$

$$(8760\times\text{CF}) = \text{EP1D} \quad (9)$$

$$\text{EP1N}/\text{EP1D} = \text{EP1} \quad (10)$$

$$(\text{FC}\times\text{HR}) = \text{EP2} \quad (11)$$

$$(\text{EP1}+\text{EP2}+\text{VOMC}) = \text{LCOE} \quad (12)$$

OCC represents the overnight capital cost ($/kW: United States Dollar per kilowatt), CRF represents the capital recovery factor, FOMC is for the fixed O&M cost ($/kW-yr: United States Dollar per kilowatt per year), and EP1N represents the numerator in the equation "(5)" and "(10)". CRF is calculated by the equation "(6)", "(7)", and "(8)" (visit [8]). i represents the interest rate, n represents the number of annuities received in the equations "(6)" and "(7)". CRFN stands for the numerator of the capital recovery factor in the equation "(6)" and "(8)". CRFD stands for the denominator of the capital recovery factor in the equation "(7)" and "(8)". 8760 is the number of hours in a year, CF is for the capacity factor (between 0 and 1) and EP1D is for the denominator in the equation "(9)" and "(10)". EP1 stands for the equation part 1 (the first part of the equation) in the equation "(10)" and "(12)". FC stands for the fuel cost ($/MMBtu: dollars per million british thermal units) and HR stands for the heat rate (Btu/kWh: british thermal units per kilowatt-hour) in the equation "(11)". These two terms are only for the non-renewable power plants. Renewable power plants such as hydro, solar and wind don't consume any fuel. EP2 is for the equation part 2 (the second part of the equation) in the equation "(11)" and "(12)". VOMC stands for the variable O&M cost ($/kWh) in the equation "(12)". Thus, LCOE is a good cost evaluation criteria for the power plant types. It can be calculated by some practical tools such as the Simple Levelized Cost of Energy Calculator (visit [9]).

According to the practical industry experience and information, it can be underlined very well that private investors should always look for some private hydropower investment alternatives for their real world mid to long term investment portfolio. Thus, this study pays attention in this subject.

Hydropower plants are usually classified based on their installed power or capacity (kW: kilowatt) as large, medium, small, mini, micro and pico [10, 11]. In this study, small hydro power plants are accepted as the hydropower plants, which have the installed capacity between 1 megawatt and

10 megawatts (1 MW < P ≤ 10 MW).

Small hydropower plant investments segment is an appropriate choice for small to midsize private investors in the world, because they need relatively small initial capital and they have relatively small LCOE values.

In Turkey, they have some additional advantages such as a great number of private small hydropower plant projects have been granted their licenses from EMRA and then some of them are already connected to the national electric grid after their preconstruction and construction periods and also these small hydropower plants are decentralized considering their locations (visit [12], [13]).

Foreign and domestic private investors can own them as one or buy their shares and become shareholders of them (see acquisition, joint venture, merger, portfolio, and share terms on [14] to understand the ways to become real world investors).

Hence, small hydropower plant investments should be studied in a detailed manner. This study is one of the studies that investigates the small hydropower plant investments.

There are many small hydropower plant investment problems to be researched such as the investment policy research area, the small hydropower design field, the small hydropower investment analysis research area, the investment forecasting and modeling field, and the real world investment selection research topics.

This study focuses clearly in the private small hydropower plants investments selection research field (only private and only small hydropower).

There are also many approaches and methodologies under this field. This paper only investigates the Multi Attribute Decision Making (MADM), or the Multi criteria Decision Making (MCDM).

There are a lot of methods under the MADM, or the MCDM. A few of them are the Analytic Hierarchy Process (AHP) [15], the Analytic Network Process (ANP) [16], The DEX (Decision EXpert) or the DEXi (Decision EXpert for Education) [17], the Elimination and Choice Translating Reality (Elimination Et Choix Tradusiant la Realite) (ELECTRE) [18], and the Preference Ranking Organization METHod for Enrichment Evaluations (PROMETHEE) [19]. In this paper, the private small hydropower plant investment selection problem in Turkey by the DEX (Decision EXpert) or the DEXi (Decision EXpert for Education) is studied and presented in a detailed, but simplified manner.

An experimental research DEXi decision model is built and an experimental research case study with seventeen criteria and five alternative or options (private small hydropower plant investments) is conducted in this study.

This paper has four sections. The literature review is the next section. The experimental research model and its case study are explained in the third section. Finally, the conclusions and future research are discussed and presented in last section.

2. Literature Review

The previous research studies in this specific field (private small hydropower plant investments selection by a multi attribute decision making method DEXi) are tried to be reviewed by help of some scientific online database and journal websites (fifteen scientific websites). These websites are presented in “Tab. 2”.

Table 2. *Scientific websites reviewed in this study (review until 17/07/2015) (generated by the Microsoft Office 2007 Word).*

Title	Website Address
ACM Digital Library	http://dl.acm.org/
ASCE Online Research Library	http://ascelibrary.org/
American Society of Mechanical Engineers	http://asmedigitalcollection.asme.org
Cambridge Journals Online	http://journals.cambridge.org
Directory of Open Access Journals	http://doaj.org
Emerald Insight	www.emeraldinsight.com
Google Scholar	http://scholar.google.com.tr
Hindawi Publishing Corporation	www.hindawi.com
Inderscience Publishers	www.inderscience.com
Science Direct	www.sciencedirect.com
Science Publishing Group	www.sciencepublishinggroup.com
Springer	www.springer.com/gp
Taylor & Francis Online/Journals	www.tandfonline.com
Wiley-Blackwell/Wiley Online Library	http://onlinelibrary.wiley.com
World Scientific Publishing	www.worldscientific.com

The search queries on these scientific websites are defined based on author's experiences during author's previous research studies. These search queries are given by “Tab. 3”. There are ten queries, which hopefully cover the whole publications in this field (general point of method and its applications). These search queries are directly typed on the search query boxes and full truncation option is preferred on the search preferences, so that all of the journal papers, the conference papers, the books, and all other means and types of documents are searched in the current study. The review is then followed by the title, the abstract and the key words investigations. If any clues are found for any relation with the current subject, then full documents are tried to be found for detail review purposes.

Table 3. *Search queries in this study (review until 17/07/2015) (generated by the Microsoft Office 2007 Word).*

No (#)	Search Queries
#1	"small hydropower" AND "DEXi"
#2	"small hydropower" AND "Decision EXpert"
#3	"power" AND "DEXi"
#4	"power" AND "Decision EXpert"
#5	"project" AND "DEXi"
#6	"project" AND "Decision EXpert"
#7	"investment" AND "DEXi"
#8	"investment" AND "Decision EXpert"
#9	"electric" AND " DEXi"
#10	"electric" AND "Decision EXpert"

There are 16, 13, 33, 26, 13, 13, 3, 9 search results (hit rate of 2.402.988 documents) respectively for queries #3, #4, #5, #6, #7, #8, #9, #10 on the ACM Digital Library. There are only few studies (3 documents) in the agricultural and information and communication technology (ICT) research fields according to the title abstract and keywords review.

There are 1, 2, 1 search results respectively for queries #4, #6, #8 on the ASCE Online Research Library. None of these publications are related with the method and its applications.

There isn't any search results found for any of the queries on the American Society of Mechanical Engineers.

There are 62, 62, 62, 62, 62, 2, 6, 1 search results respectively for queries #3, #4, #5, #6, #7, #8, #9, #10 on the Cambridge Journals Online. None of these publications are related with the method and its applications.

There is only 1 search result (hit rate of 1.887.399 documents) for query #5 on the Directory of Open Access Journals. This study is in the agricultural research field.

There are 10, 2, 8, 5, 3 search results respectively for queries #4, #5, #6, #8, #10 on the Emerald Insight. None of these publications are related with the method and its applications.

There are 1, 1.650 (visit [20]), 527, 1.160, 562, 222, 230, 984, 147 search results respectively for queries #1, #3, #4, #5, #6, #7, #8, #9, #10 on the Google Scholar. There are some studies (45 documents) in the agriculture (business as usual agriculture and energy crops for biogas), decision support, education, environment, finance, health, human resources/career development, media, and military research fields according to the title abstract keywords review and full text document review.

There isn't any search results found for any of the queries on the Hindawi Publishing Corporation.

There isn't any search results found for any of the queries on the Inderscience Publishers.

There are 137, 118, 114, 134, 14, 73, 57, 19 search results (hit rate of 13.397.561 documents) respectively for queries #3, #4, #5, #6, #7, #8, #9, #10 on the Science Direct. There are only few studies (11 documents) in the agricultural, education, health and ICT research fields according to the title, abstract and keywords review.

There isn't any search results found for any of the queries on the Science Publishing Group.

There are 45, 206, 81, 385, 15, 135, 14, 115 search results respectively for queries #3, #4, #5, #6, #7, #8, #9, #10 on the Springer. There are only few studies (10 documents) in the agricultural, health and ICT research fields according to the title, abstract and keywords review.

There are 2, 9, 21, 2, 11, 3, 2 search results respectively for queries #4, #5, #6, #7, #8, #9, #10 on the Taylor & Francis Online/Journals. There are only few studies (6 documents) in the agricultural, health, transportation and ICT research fields according to the title, abstract and keywords review.

There are 62, 76, 66, 73, 12, 43, 22, 11 search results respectively for queries #3, #4, #5, #6, #7, #8, #9, #10 on the Wiley-Blackwell/Wiley Online Library. There are only few studies (2 documents) in the agriculture, human resources, and research fields according to the title, abstract and keywords review.

There are 7, 2, 2, 6, 2, 1, 1 search results respectively for queries #3, #4, #5, #6, #7, #9, #10 on the World Scientific Publishing. None of these publications are related with the method and its applications.

This literature review shows that this study is most probably the first study in its research field (in general point of view with the tags of power plant, investment, DEXi).

The DEXi is first presented in 2000s [17]. It is developed based on the DEX and the DECMAK [21]. The DECMAK, proposed in 1980's, is developed in the United Kingdom by Efstathiou and Rajkovic and in Slovenia by Rajkovic and Bohanec [21, 22]. The DEX (Decision EXpert) is developed to be an expert system shell in 1987 and the DEXi is first introduced to research community in 2000's by Jereb, Bohanec, and Rajkovic [23, 24]. The DEX is a DOS tool and deals with the probabilistic and fuzzy distribution of values [17]. The DEXi is the most powerful one amongst these three tools. The detailed information about these methods can be gathered from Dr. Marko Bohanec's website (Jožef Stefan Institute, Department of Knowledge Technologies, Ljubljana, Slovenia: http://kt.ijs.si/MarkoBohanec/)

3. Experimental Research Model, Case, Results, and Discussion

The experimental research model and the experimental case study in this study is based on author's previous studies by different methods such as the one with the ELECTRE III, the ELECTRE IV, Shannon's Entropy objective criteria weighting and Saaty's subjective criteria weighting (ELECTRE: Elimination and Choice Translating Reality: Elimination Et Choix Tradusiant la Realite) (see [25]) and the one with the AHP (Analytic Hierarchy Process) (see [26]). In that base models, there are 17 criteria as presented in given by "Tab. 4". These factors (attributes) aren't revised and changed in this study. These attributes are organized by the approach of clustering to developed the current DEXi structure according to the DEXi's main structural guidelines and recommendations. One of the recommendations is as below:

A well organized DEXi model has two to four descendants for each of its aggregate nodes.

According to this recommendation, these 17 attributes are accepted as the basic attributes of the current experimental research model. The basic attributes and possible aggregation nodes are at first investigated by help of Carrot^2.

"Carrot^2 is an open source software project that includes several text clustering algorithms. Among these are bisecting K-means, Suffix Tree Clustering and Lingo algorithm" [41, 42, 43]. Each basic attribute is searched on the Carrot^2 desktop and the related documents with this attribute and their words or phrases are found on the visualization tools as shown in "Fig. 2", "Fig. 3", and "Fig. 4". Generally speaking, this activity should be performed for improving the perception of experts and decision makers on the attributes.

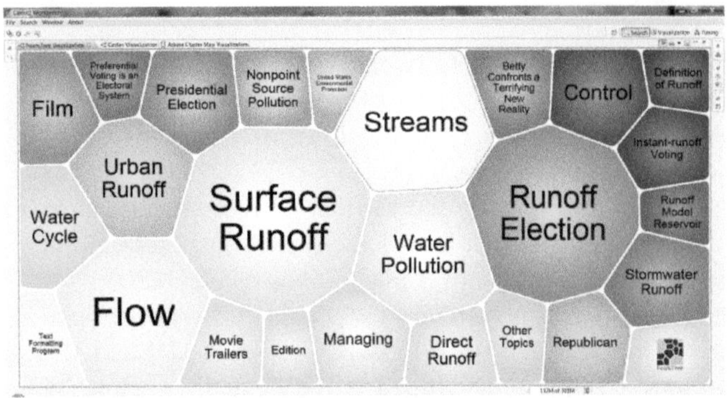

Figure 2. Carrot2-workbench "runoff" FoamTree visualization (generated by the Carrot2 http://carrot2.org & the Paint.NET).

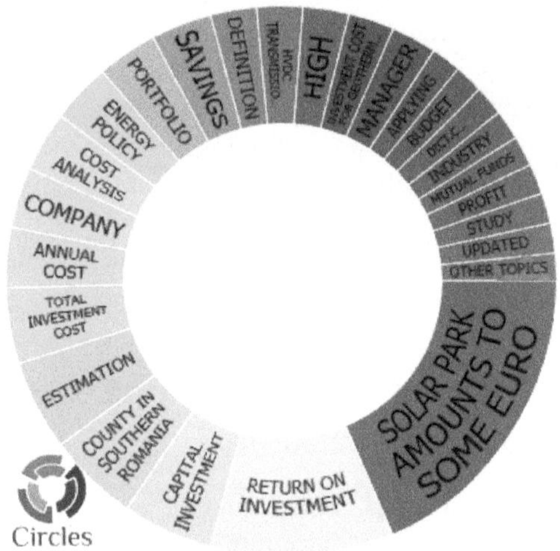

Figure 3. Carrot2-workbench "investment cost" Circles visualization (generated by the Carrot2 & the Paint.NET).

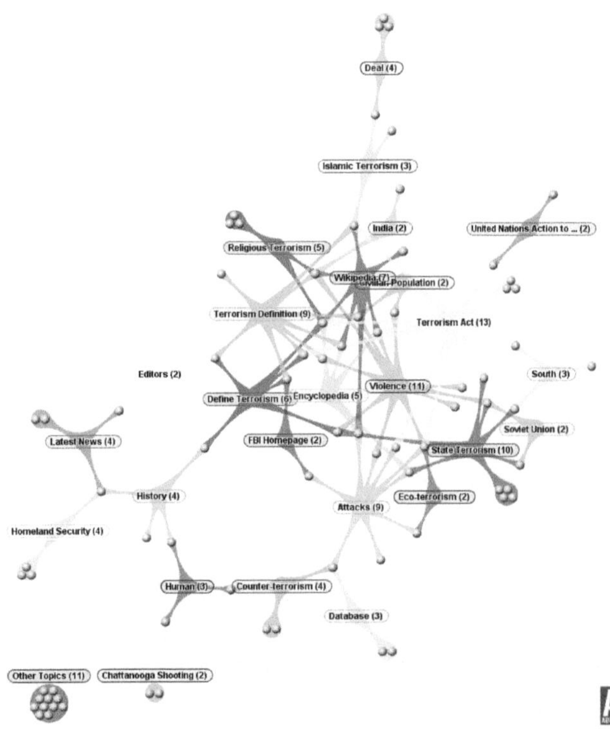

Figure 4. Carrot2-workbench "terrorism" Aduna Cluster Map visualization (generated by the Carrot2 & the Paint.NET).

The first clustering approach for these attributes depends on their objectivity and subjectivity. Catchment area (km^2), project runoff (hm^3), net head (m), discharge (rate of flow) (m^3/s), firm energy (GWh), secondary energy (GWh), and investment cost (million USD) attributes are objective attributes. Other attributes are subjective attributes. Hence, the current experimental research DEXi structure should consider this discrimination.

The second clustering approach depends social features and none social features. Community attitude, security conditions and terrorism conditions attributes are grouped under social features. Other ones are none social features.

The third clustering approach is about the essential items of the private small hydropower plants and complementary features of the private small hydropower plants. River basin, catchment area (km^2), project runoff (hm^3), net head (m) and discharge (rate of flow) (m^3/s) attributes are at first investigated in the small hydropower plant development studies. Conveyance structures are designed and often revised several times during the design process. Investment cost (million USD) is calculated based on the designs and the costs (daily to annual changes during the whole process). These two attributes can be grouped under complementary features.

The fourth clustering approach is related with the electricity generation features. Firm energy (GWh) and secondary energy (GWh) are the electricity generation features of the small hydropower plants. Others don't present the electricity generation.

The fifth clustering approach is related with the site or location essential items. Topography, geology, protected areas (conservation areas), substation conditions can be grouped under essential features of the private small hydropower plant sites.

As a consequence, the experimental research DEXi decision model starts with the "Private Small Hydropower Plant Preference" and it is modeled as in this paragraph.

It has two main aggregate nodes "Objective Attributes Evaluation" and "Subjective Attributes Evaluation" (according to two to four descendants).

The "Objective Attributes Evaluation" main aggregate node is divided into three sub aggregate node "Electricity Generation Features of Private Small Hydropower Plant Investment", that includes "Firm Energy (GWh)", and "Secondary Energy (GWh)" attributes, "River Basin Objective Features", that has "Catchment Area (km^2)", and "Project Runoff (hm^3)" attributes, and finally "Private Small Hydropower Plant Main Objective Features", that includes "Net Head (m)", "Discharge (rate of flow) (m^3/s)", and "Investment Cost (million USD)" attributes.

The second main aggregate node "Subjective Attributes Evaluation" are divided into four sub aggregate node "Social Features of Private Small Hydropower Plant Site", that has three attributes as "Community Attitude", "Security Conditions", and "Terrorism Conditions", "Technical Evaluation Features of Private Small Hydropower Plant Site", that has three attributes "River Basin", "Topography", and "Geology", "Technical Evaluation Features of Private Small Hydropower Plant", which has two attributes "Conveyance

Structure", and "Substation Conditions", and finally "General Evaluation Features of Private Small Hydropower Plant Site", that has two attributes as "Transportation" and "Protected Areas (conservation areas)".

The current experimental DEXi decision model is drawn by the DEXiTree Software (http://kt.ijs.si/MarkoBohanec/dexitree.html) and shown in "Fig. 5".

Table 4. *Attributes of the current experimental model (also details in [25, 26]) (generated by the Microsoft Office 2007 Word).*

Attributes	Terminological Description
Catchment Area (km2)	"area drained by a river and all its tributaries" [27]. The practical usage in small hydropower applications is considered for the attribute.
Project Runoff (hm3)	"Surface runoff is precipitation runoff over the landscape.", "Only about a third of the precipitation that falls over land runs off into streams and rivers and is returned to the oceans. The other two-thirds is evaporated, transpired, or soaks (infiltrates) into groundwater. Surface runoff can also be diverted by humans for their own uses." [28]. The practical usage in small hydropower applications is considered for the attribute.
Net Head (m)	"gross head minus all hydraulic losses except those chargeable to the turbine." [29]
Discharge (rate of flow) (m3/s)	"Discharge is the volume of water moving down a stream or river per unit of time, commonly expressed in cubic feet per second or gallons per day. In general, river discharge is computed by multiplying the area of water in a channel cross section by the average velocity of the water in that cross section" [30]. The practical usage in small hydropower applications is considered for the attribute.
Firm Energy (GWh)	"power delivered during a certain period of time with at least 90–95% certainty" [31]
Secondary Energy (GWh)	difference between total energy generation (GWh) and firm energy generation (GWh)
Investment Cost (million USD)	initial capital cost
River Basin	characteristics of the river basin (see [22])
Conveyance Structure	weir, canal, tunnel, conduits, culverts, syphons, settling tanks, etc. (see [31, 32])
Community Attitude	"attitudes held by groups of people that live in communities" [33]
Transportation	" the act or process of moving people or things from one place to another", "a way of traveling from one place to another place", "a system for moving passengers or goods from one place to another" [34]
Topography	"the configuration of a surface and the relations among its man-made and natural features", "precise detailed study of the surface features of a region" [35]
Geology	"In general, geology is the scientific study of the earth- the material of which it is made, the processes that act on these materials, the products formed, and the history of the planet and its life forms since origin. Geology now includes the study of other planets as well" [36]
Security Conditions	"The state of being free from danger or threat", "The safety of a state or organization against criminal activity such as terrorism, theft, or espionage", "Procedures followed or measures taken to ensure the security of a state or organization", "The state of feeling safe, stable, and free from fear or anxiety" [37]
Terrorism Conditions	"Terrorism has been described variously as both a tactic and strategy; a crime and a holy duty; a justified reaction to oppression and an inexcusable abomination. Obviously, a lot depends on whose point of view is being represented. Terrorism has often been an effective tactic for the weaker side in a conflict. As an asymmetric form of conflict, it confers coercive power with many of the advantages of military force at a fraction of the cost. Due to the secretive nature and small size of terrorist organizations, they often offer opponents no clear organization to defend against or to deter.", "....there are three key elements—violence, fear, and intimidation—and each element produces terror in its victims.", " Terrorism is a criminal act that influences an audience beyond the immediate victim.", "Those billion people watching were to be introduced to fear - which is terrorism's ultimate goal." [38]
Protected Areas (conservation areas)	"A protected area is a clearly defined geographical space, recognised, dedicated and managed, through legal or other effective means, to achieve the long term conservation of nature with associated ecosystem services and cultural values" [39]
Substation Conditions	"Substations are essential parts of the electrical distribution system. The link between high-voltage transmission lines and low-voltage power systems is the substation." [40]. The practical usage in small hydropower applications is considered for the attribute.

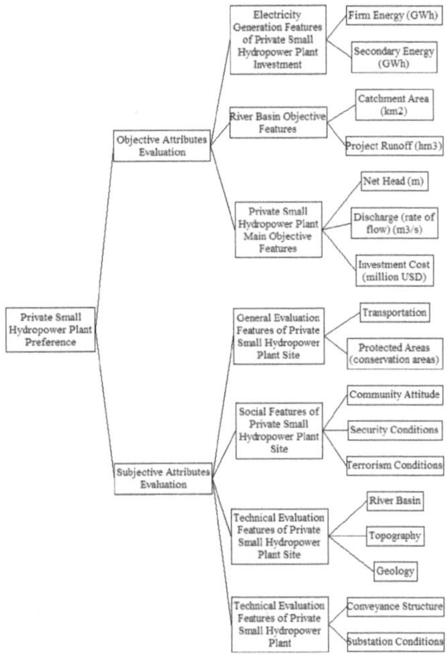

Figure 5. *Experimental DEXi research decision model on DEXiTree (generated by the DEXi http://kt.ijs.si/MarkoBohanec/dexi.html & the DEXiTree http://kt.ijs.si/MarkoBohanec/dexitree.html & the Paint.NET).*

The scales of attributes are very important in DEXi decision models like the other MADM models. The human's cognitive capability and limitations (human multitasking and working memory) are taken into account during modeling of the current scales. The increasing scales are preferred considering the human cognition limitations.

In addition, the current model by itself (structure of basic and aggregate attributes) and its scales are designed according to human cognitive capacity for processing information (short term memory capacity). The magical number 7, 7±2 rule is followed and obeyed in this study (see [44, 45, 46, 47].

The scale size of the basic attributes is limited with the least number of distinguishable values. The scale size of the sub aggregate nodes and aggregate nodes are increased gradually. The target attribute or objective or main aggregate node "Private Small Hydropower Plant Preference" is scaled as the lowest priority, the low priority, the normal priority, the high priority, and the highest priority. It is believed that these hedges and set of words for discrimination of the scales can represent the preferences very well for experts, decision makers and readers. The structure and the scales of attributes are presented by "Tab. 5".

Table 5. *Attributes, main aggregate nodes, sub aggregate nodes and their scales (generated by the Microsoft Office 2007 Word).*

Aggregate Nodes/Attributes	Scale
█ Private Small Hydropower Plant Preference	+lowest priority(-); low priority; normal priority; high priority; highest priority(+)
► Objective Attributes Evaluation	+very poor(-); poor; good; very good(+)
◙ Electricity Generation Features of Private Small Hydropower Plant Investment	+low(-);medium; high(+)
Firm Energy (GWh)	+low(-); high(+)
Secondary Energy (GWh)	+low(-); high(+)
◙ River Basin Objective Features	+low(-);medium; high(+)
Catchment Area (km^2)	+small(-);large(+)
Project Runoff (hm^3)	+low(-); high(+)
◙ Private Small Hydropower Plant Main Objective Features	+low(-);medium; high(+)
Net Head (m)	+low(-); high(+)
Discharge (rate of flow) (m^3/s)	+low(-); high(+)
Investment Cost (million USD)	+ high(-); low(+)
► Subjective Attributes Evaluation	+very poor(-); poor; good; very good(+)
◙ General Evaluation Features of Private Small Hydropower Plant Site	+unsuitable(-);probably suitable; suitable(+)
Transportation	+poor(-); good(+)
Protected Areas (conservation areas)	+many(-); few(+)
◙ Social Features of Private Small Hydropower Plant Site	+unsuitable(-);probably suitable; suitable(+)
Community Attitude	+negative(-); positive(+)
Security Conditions	+poor(-); good(+)
Terrorism Conditions	+poor(-); good(+)
◙ Technical Features of Private Small Hydropower Plant Site	+unsuitable(-);probably suitable; suitable(+)
River Basin	+poor(-); good(+)
Topography	+poor(-); good(+)
Geology	+poor(-); good(+)
◙ Technical Evaluation Features of Private Small Hydropower Plant	+poor(-); fair; good(+)
Conveyance Structure	+poor(-); good(+)
Substation Conditions	+unsuitable(-); suitable(+)

After all of the scale of attributes are defined in this model, the utility functions are determined for the current DEXi decision model. The utility functions in DEXi is explained as "components of multi-attribute models that define the aggregation aspect of option evaluation. For each aggregate attribute Y, whose descendants in the tree of attributes are X_1, X_2,..., X_n, the corresponding utility function f defines the mapping: $f: X_1 \times X_2 \times ... \times X_n \rightarrow Y$" and "a utility function maps all the combinations of the lower-level attribute values into the values of Y" [48]. The utility functions of this experimental model is presented in "Tab. 6".

By finalizing defining the aggregate nodes and attributes, deciding the scales of these aggregate nodes and attributes, and defining the utility functions, the current experimental DEXi decision model for private small hydropower plants investment selection can be used for the evaluation of the options in an experimental case.

There are five private small hydropower plant investment options in this experimental case study (Option 1 to Option 5). These private small hydropower plant investments are assumed that they are in their pre-development investment stages and free for sale by any means such as acquisitions, joint ventures, and mergers. Their data and information are gathered from several sources and presented by "Fig. 6" to "Fig. 12" (only objective attributes).

These objective attributes are directly evaluated based on these values, so that there isn't any additional efforts to be spent for the evaluation. The experts, decision makers and expert decision makers also don't need to evaluate these attributes.

The subjective attributes need to be evaluated in this experimental model. The evaluations are made one by one and presented by "Tab. 7" to "Tab. 16".

These evaluations are entered into the related cells on the DEXi Version 4.00 to get the results.

Table 6. *Utility functions of the current experimental DEXi decision model (generated by the Microsoft Office 2007 Word)*

Aggregate Nodes	Utility functions	
Private Small Hydropower Plant Preference	1	111+
	2	121+
	3	132+
	4	142+
	5	212+
	6	222+
	7	233+
	8	243+
	9	313+
	10	323+
	11	334+
	12	345+
	13	413+
	14	424+
	15	435+
	16	445+
Objective Attributes Evaluation	1	1111+
	2	1121+
	3	1131+
	4	1211+
	5	1221+
	6	1231+
	7	1311+
	8	1321+
	9	1331+
	10	2112+
	11	2122+
	12	2132+
	13	2212-
	14	2223+
	15	2233+
	16	2312+
	17	2323+
	18	2333+
	19	3112+
	20	3122+
	21	3133+
	22	3213+
	23	3223+
	24	3233+
	25	3313+
	26	3324+
	27	3334+
Electricity Generation Features of Private Small Hydropower Plant Investment	1	111+
	2	122+
	3	213+
	4	223-
River Basin Objective Features	1	111+
	2	122+
	3	212+
	4	223+
Private Small Hydropower Plant Main Objective Features	1	1111+
	2	1122+
	3	1212+
	4	1223+
	5	2112+
	6	2122+
	7	2212+
	8	2223+
Subjective Attributes Evaluation	1	11111+
	2	11121+
	3	11131+
	4	11211+
	5	11221+
	6	11231+
	7	11312+
	8	11322+
	9	11332+
	10	12111+
	11	12121+
	12	12132+
	13	12211+
	14	12222+
	15	12232+
	16	12312+
	17	12322+
	18	12332+
	19	13112+
	20	13122+
	21	13132+
	22	13212+
	23	13222+
	24	13232+
	25	13312+
	26	13322+
	27	13332+
	28	21112+
	29	21122+
	30	21132+

Aggregate Nodes	Utility functions	
	31	21212+
	32	21222+
	33	21232+
	34	21312+
	35	21322+
	36	21332+
	37	22112+
	38	22122+
	39	22132+
	40	22212+
	41	22223+
	42	22233+
	43	22312+
	44	22323+
	45	22333+
	46	23112+
	47	23123+
	48	23133+
	49	23212+
	50	23223+
	51	23233+
	52	23312+
	53	23323+
	54	23334+
	55	31112+
	56	31122+
	57	31132+
	58	31212+
	59	31222+
	60	31232+
	61	31312+
	62	31322+
	63	31332+
	64	32112+
	65	32122+
	66	32132+
	67	32212+
	68	32223+
	69	32233+
	70	32312+
	71	32323+
	72	32333+
	73	33112+
	74	33123+
	75	33133+
	76	33212+
	77	33223+
	78	33234+
	79	33313+
	80	33324+
	81	33334+
General Evaluation Features of Private Small Hydropower Plant Site	1	111+
	2	122+
	3	212+
	4	223+
Social Features of Private Small Hydropower Plant Site	1	1111+
	2	1122+
	3	1211+
	4	1222+
	5	2111+
	6	2122+
	7	2211+
	8	2223+
Technical Features of Private Small Hydropower Plant Site	1	1111+
	2	1121+
	3	1211+
	4	1222+
	5	2111+
	6	2122+
	7	2212+
	8	2223+
Technical Evaluation Features of Private Small Hydropower Plant	1	111+
	2	122+
	3	211+
	4	223+

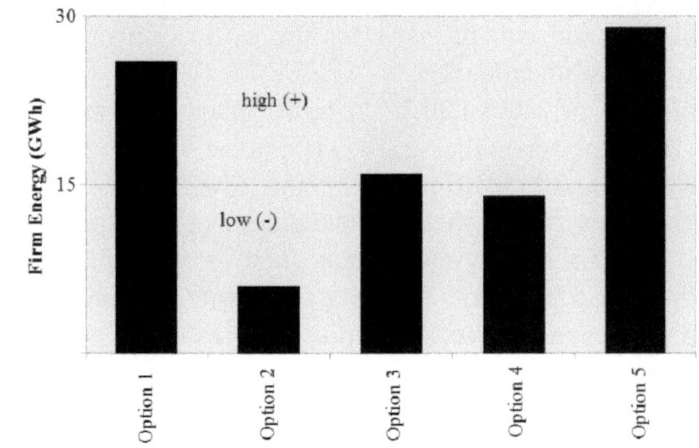

Figure 6. *Firm energy (GWh) evaluation of options (generated by the Apache OpenOffice 4.1.1 Calc & the Paint.NET).*

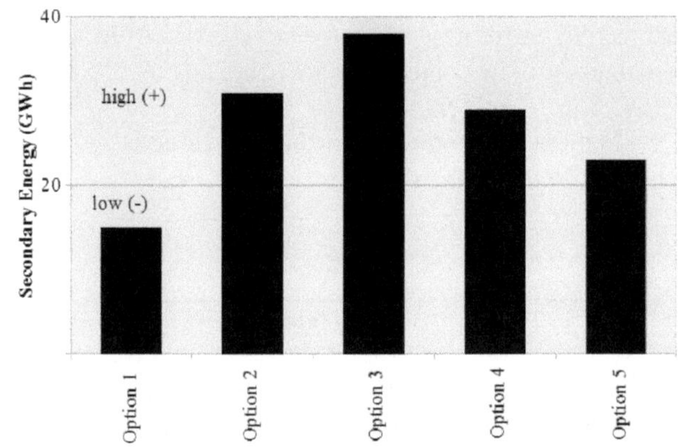

Figure 7. *Secondary energy (GWh) evaluation of options (generated by the Apache OpenOffice 4.1.1 Calc & the Paint.NET).*

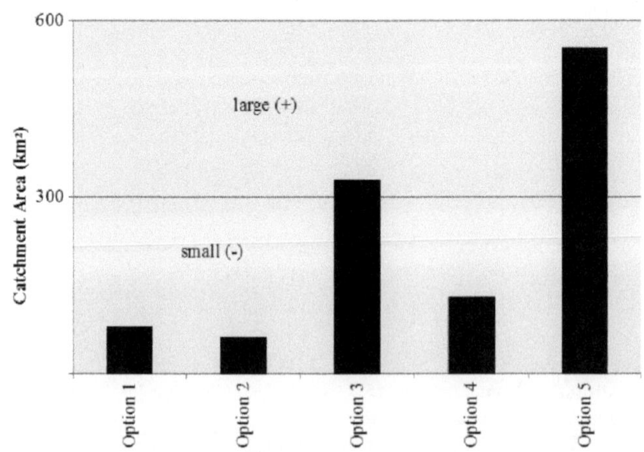

Figure 8. *Catchment area (km^2) evaluation of options (generated by the Apache OpenOffice 4.1.1 Calc & the Paint.NET).*

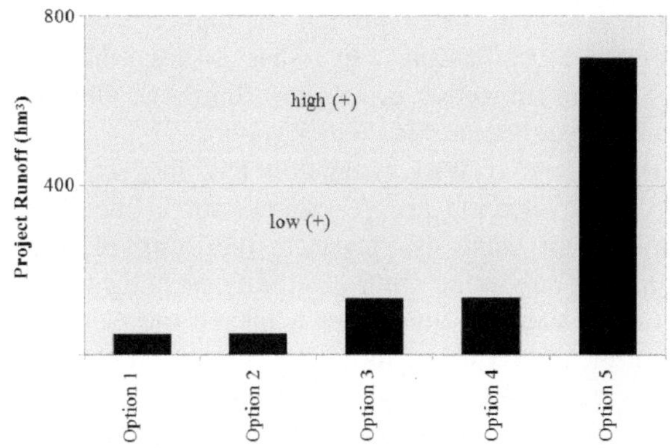

Figure 9. *Project runoff (hm^3) evaluation of options (generated by the Apache OpenOffice 4.1.1 Calc & the Paint.NET).*

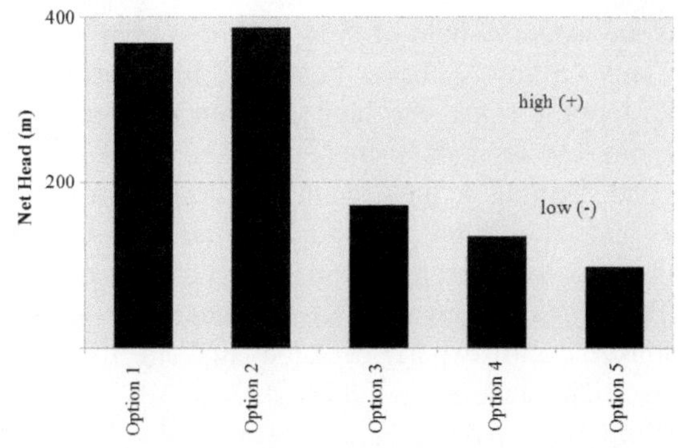

Figure 10. *Net head (m) evaluation of options (generated by the Apache OpenOffice 4.1.1 Calc & the Paint.NET).*

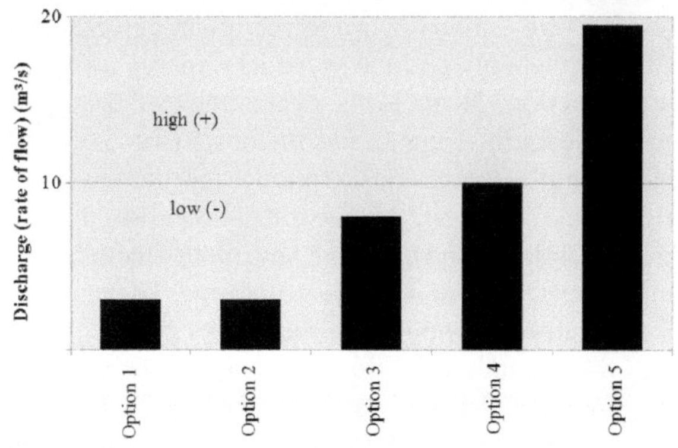

Figure 11. *Discharge (rate of flow) (m^3/s) evaluation of options (generated by the Apache OpenOffice 4.1.1 Calc & the Paint.NET).*

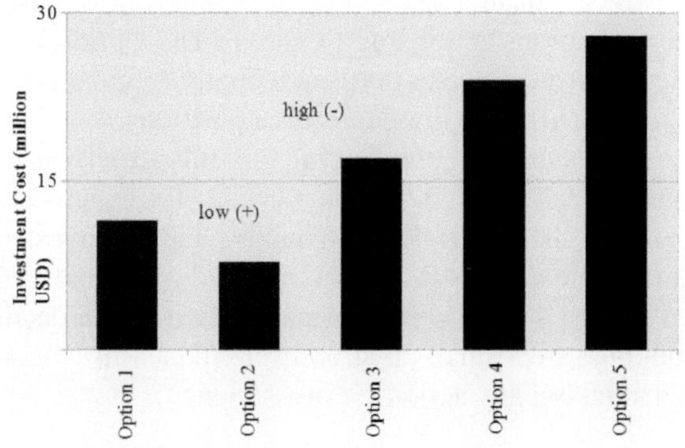

Figure 12. *Investment cost (million USD) evaluation of options (generated by the Apache OpenOffice 4.1.1 Calc & the Paint.NET).*

Table 7. *Subjective attributes evaluation of transportation (generated by the Microsoft Office 2007 Word).*

Options	Evaluation
Option 1	good(+)
Option 2	poor(-)
Option 3	poor(-)
Option 4	good(+)
Option 5	good(+)

Table 8. *Subjective attributes evaluation of protected areas (conservation areas) (generated by the Microsoft Office 2007 Word).*

Options	Evaluation
Option 1	many(-)
Option 2	many(-)
Option 3	few(+)
Option 4	few(+)
Option 5	few(+)

Table 9. *Subjective attributes evaluation of community attitude (generated by the Microsoft Office 2007 Word).*

Options	Evaluation
Option 1	positive(+)
Option 2	negative(-)
Option 3	positive(+)
Option 4	negative(-)
Option 5	negative(-)

Table 10. *Subjective attributes evaluation of security conditions (generated by the Microsoft Office 2007 Word).*

Options	Evaluation
Option 1	good(+)
Option 2	good(+)
Option 3	poor(-)
Option 4	good(+)
Option 5	poor(-)

Table 11. *Subjective attributes evaluation of terrorism conditions (generated by the Microsoft Office 2007 Word).*

Options	Evaluation
Option 1	good(+)
Option 2	poor(-)
Option 3	poor(-)
Option 4	good(+)
Option 5	good(+)

Table 12. *Subjective attributes evaluation of river basin (generated by the Microsoft Office 2007 Word).*

Options	Evaluation
Option 1	poor(-)
Option 2	good(+)
Option 3	poor(-)
Option 4	good(+)
Option 5	good(+)

Table 13. Subjective attributes evaluation of topography (generated by the Microsoft Office 2007 Word).

Options	Evaluation
Option 1	good(+)
Option 2	poor(-)
Option 3	poor(-)
Option 4	good(+)
Option 5	good(+)

Table 14. Subjective attributes evaluation of geology (generated by the Microsoft Office 2007 Word).

Options	Evaluation
Option 1	good(+)
Option 2	poor(-)
Option 3	poor(-)
Option 4	good(+)
Option 5	good(+)

Table 15. Subjective attributes evaluation of conveyance structure (generated by the Microsoft Office 2007 Word).

Options	Evaluation
Option 1	good(+)
Option 2	good(+)
Option 3	poor(-)
Option 4	poor(-)
Option 5	poor(-)

Table 16. Subjective attributes evaluation of substation conditions (generated by the Microsoft Office 2007 Word).

Options	Evaluation
Option 1	unsuitable(-)
Option 2	suitable(+)
Option 3	suitable(+)
Option 4	suitable(+)
Option 5	suitable(+)

When only objective attributes evaluations are investigated as shown in "Fig. 14", Option 5 has the very good evaluation or preference. Option 3 comes after Option 5 with the good evaluation. Option 1, Option 2 and Option 4 have same evaluations as the poor preference. This approach shows that when only one objective attribute is evaluated the optimal solutions can't be reached in these kinds of problems, because one alternative may be good for one of the attribute or one group of attributes, but it may be bad for other ones or other groups. Hence, multi attribute decision making approaches should be studied in detail to reach the optimal solutions as much as possible in these kind of problems.

When only subjective attributes evaluations are investigated as in "Fig. 15", Option 4 and Option 5 have the good preference evaluations. In other words, they are indifferent in the subjective evaluation. Similarly, Option 1 and Option 3 have the same evaluation (poor).

The firm energy (GWh) evaluation and the secondary energy (GWh) evaluation are very important in the power plants investment analysis, because the aim of these investments are only generating electricity, nothing else. If there isn't any electricity generation achieved (no electricity generation), then all types of resources such as money, time and manpower are wasted (waste, loose). Generally speaking, firm energy is more important than secondary energy in practical daily life. Total energy generation is the most important one amongst three of these attributes. When the firm energy attribute and the secondary energy attribute evaluations are made by help of "Fig. 16", it is observed that Option 5 and Option 3 have both the high preference evaluations. Option 1 has the high firm energy preference evaluation, but low secondary energy preference evaluation. Option 2 and Option 4 have both the low firm energy preference and the high secondary energy preference evaluations. This total energy, firm energy, and secondary energy (GWh) evaluations are very crucial for experts, decision makers and expert decision makers in energy industry (electricity generation industry).

Another important investigation is between the investment cost (million USD) and the electricity generation features of private small hydropower plant investments. As explained in above paragraphs and sections, the electricity generation features of private small hydropower plant investments considers the firm energy and the secondary energy attributes in its utility function. Henceforth, evaluations of these two items show the benefits (gains) and the costs (looses) at the same time. In simple expressions, Option 1 has the low costs, but the high gains. Option 2 has also the low costs, but the medium gains. Option 3 and Option 5 have both the high costs and the high gains. Option 4 is the worst one, because it is located in the high costs and the medium gains point.

The final investigation in this study is made on three aggregate nodes "Private Small Hydropower Plant Preference", "Objective Attributes Evaluation" and "Subjective Attributes Evaluation" at the same time as shown in "Fig. 18". Option 5 has almost reach to the corners of the pyramid, which means that Option 5 has the highest preference evaluations in this study. Option 3 and Option 4 get the middle preference evaluations and finally Option 1 and Option 2 get placed in the low preference positions.

In very short summary, the findings of this experimental research DEXi decision model recommends to the experts, the decision makers, the expert decision makers and the investors that Option 5 should first be investigated in detail and afterwards Option 4 and Option 3 should be studied in detail, before making any small hydropower plant investment decisions and taking any action for investments.

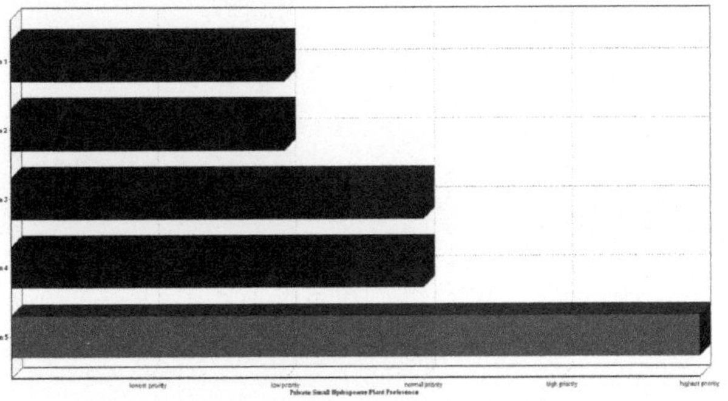

Figure 13. *Private Small Hydropower Plant Preference on the DEXi (generated by the DEXi & the Paint.NET).*

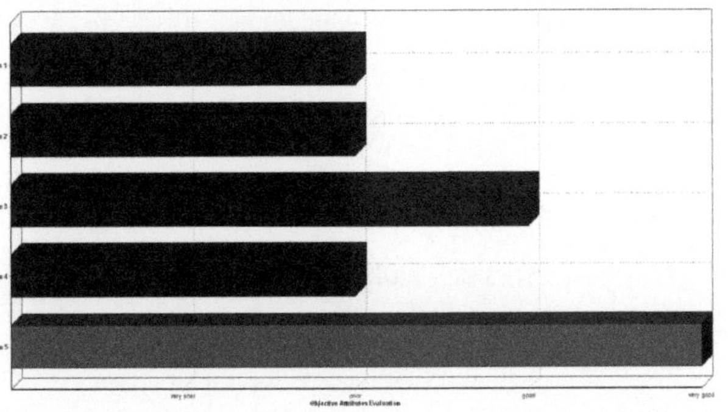

Figure 14. *Objective Attributes Evaluation on the DEXi (generated by the DEXi & the Paint.NET).*

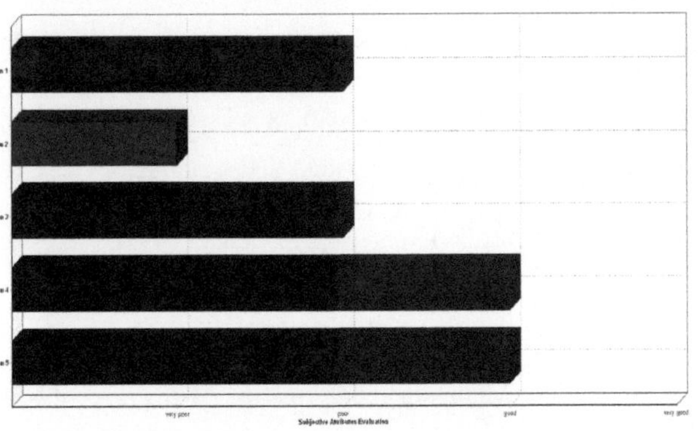

Figure 15. *Subjective Attributes Evaluation on the DEXi (generated by the DEXi & the Paint.NET).*

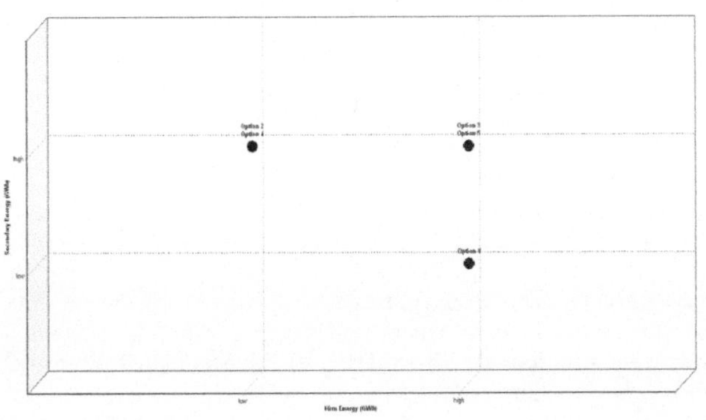

Figure 16. *Firm Energy (GWh) & Secondary Energy (GWh) Evaluation on the DEXi (generated by the DEXi & the Paint.NET).*

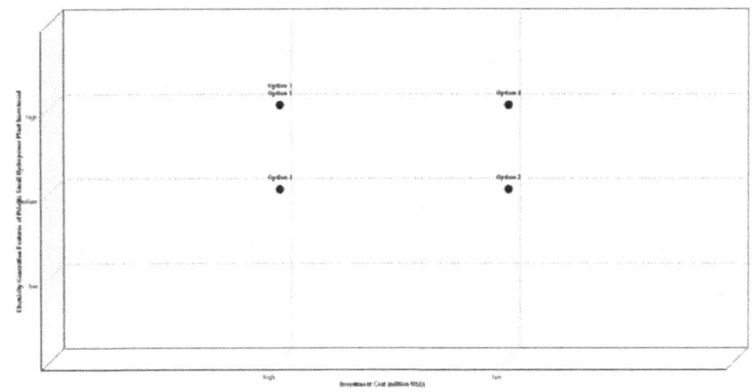

Figure 17. *Investment Cost (million USD) & Electricity Generation Features of Private Small Hydropower Plant Investment Evaluation on the DEXi (generated by the DEXi & the Paint.NET).*

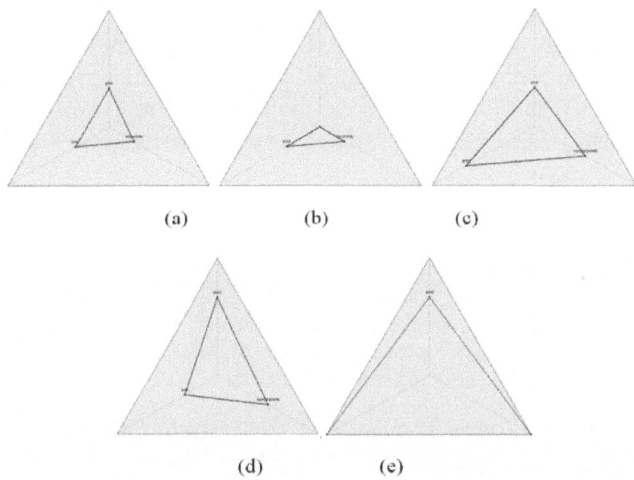

Figure 18. *Private Small Hydropower Plant Preference (right corner) & Objective Attributes Evaluation (left corner) & Subjective Attributes Evaluation (top corner) Option 1 (a), Option 2 (b), Option 3 (c), Option 4 (d), Option 5 (e) on the DEXi (generated by the DEXi & the Paint.NET).*

4. Conclusions, Future Applications and Research

In this paper, the DEXi decision making approach is applied to determine the best solution of a private small hydropower plant investment selection problem in the energy industry in the Turkish private small hydropower electricity generation market. It is observed that DEXi method has some advantages for gathering the expert's opinion, because it uses the words (daily words) for the evaluations. The disadvantages of the DEXi method are also experienced during this study, such as the modeling difficulty with increasing the attributes, and the utility function definition complication with increasing the attributes. It is very well experienced and understood during this experimental research study, that the number of alternatives and the number of attributes are two important issues to be considered in these kinds of studies. When the number of attributes are increased in these kind of studies, the total effort required for the modeling, the evaluation and the analysis increases very much.

It is hoped that the decision making process in the private small hydropower industry will deeply be studied and understood with these kinds of studies. An autonomous computer based intelligent decision support system or executive support system for the private small hydropower plant investments can only be imagined, designed, planned, developed, demonstrated and deployed after deeply studying and understanding all of the items of the small hydropower plant investments. A few of these items are humans, small hydropower plants, real world investments, and decision making models.

During taking these small steps for developing an autonomous computer based intelligent decision support system or executive support system, the real world applications will hopefully help experts, decision makers, expert decision makers, and investors. Their happiness and satisfaction with their investments is very important for the economic growth and the wealth of our world. It is believed that humankind can only fight against hunger and malnutrition by help of sufficient scientific tools in the real world investments. One of them is tried to be investigated and presented in this study.

References

[1] Chandran, V.G.R., Sharma, S., and Madhavan, K.. "Electricity consumption-growth nexus: The case of Malaysia". Energy Policy, Vol. 38, No. 1, pp.606–612 (2010).

[2] Cook, P. "Infrastructure, rural electrification and development. Energy for Sustainable Development", Vol. 15, No. 3, pp.304–313 (2011).

[3] Dalgaard, C.J. and Strulik, H. "Energy distribution and economic growth". Resource and Energy Economics, Vol.33, No.4, pp.782–797 (2011).

[4] World Bank. http://data.worldbank.org accessed in 05/09/2013 (2013).

[5] Republic of Turkey Energy Market Regulatory Authority, http://www.emra.gov.tr/index.php/electricity-market/legislation accessed in 17/07/2015 (2015).

[6] Open Energy Information. "Transparent Cost Database Levelized Cost Of Electricity", http://en.openei.org/apps/TCDB/ accessed in 17/07/2015 (2015).

[7] National Laboratory of the U.S. Department of Energy Simple. "Levelized Cost of Energy (LCOE) Calculator Documentation", http://www.nrel.gov/analysis/tech_lcoe_documentation.html accessed in 17/07/2015 (2015).

[8] Khatib, H. Economic Evaluation of Projects in the Electricity Supply Industry, London: The Institution of Engineering and Technology, (2003).

[9] National Laboratory of the U.S. Department of Energy Simple Levelized. "Cost of Energy Calculator" http://www.nrel.gov/analysis/tech_lcoe.html accessed in 17/07/2015 (2015).

[10] European Renewable Energy Council. "REN21 Renewables 2012 Global Status Report". European Focus, Paris, France (2012).

[11] Dragu, C., Sels, T., and Belmans, R. "Small hydro power-state of the art and applications". ESAT-ELEN, Energy Institute, Leuven, Belgium (2010).

[12] Republic of Turkey Energy Market Regulatory Authority. "Hydropower Plant Licenses" http://lisans.epdk.org.tr/epvys-web/faces/pages/lisans/elektrikUretim/elektrikUretimOzetSorgula.xhtml accessed in 17/07/2015 (2015).

[13] State Hydraulic Works. "Hydropower Plant Licenses" http://www.dsi.gov.tr/faaliyetler/hessu-kullanim-anlasmalari accessed in 17/07/2015 (2015).

[14] Investopedia (2015). http://www.investopedia.com/ accessed in 17/07/2015.

[15] Saaty, T.L. "How to make a decision: The Analytic Hierarchy Process". European Journal of Operational Research, Vol.48, pp.9–26, (1990).

[16] Saaty, T.L. "Relative Measurement and Its Generalization in Decision Making Why Pairwise Comparisons are Central in Mathematics for the Measurement of Intangible Factors The Analytic Hierarchy/Network Process". RACSAM (Revista Serie A Matemáticas: Rev. R. Acad. Cien. Serie A. Mat.), Vol. 102, No. 2, pp.251–318, (2008).

[17] Bohanec, M. DEXi: Program for multi-attribute decision making user's manual version 4.00. Ljubljana: Jožef Stefan Institute, (2013).

[18] Roy, B. "The outranking approach and the foundations of ELECTRE methods". Theory and Decision, Vol.31, pp.49–73 (1991).

[19] Brans, J.P., and Vincke, P.H.. "A preference ranking organisition method: The PROMETHEE method for MCDM". Management Science, Vol.31, No.6, pp.647–656 (1985).

[20] Google Scholar. ""power" AND "DEXi" search results" http://scholar.google.com.tr/scholar?start=990&q=%22power%22+%22DEXi%22&hl=en&as_sdt=1,5&as_vis=1 accessed in 17/07/2015 (2015).

[21] Bohanec, M., Znidarsic, M., Rajkovic, V., Bratko, I., and Zupan, B.. "DEX Methodology: Three Decades of Qualitative Multi-Attribute Modeling". Informatica, Vol.37, pp.49-54, (2013).

[22] Efstathiou, J., and Rajkovič, V.. "Multiattribute decisionmaking using a fuzzy heuristic approach". IEEE Trans. on Systems, Man, and Cybernetics, SMC-9, pp.326-333, (1979).

[23] Bohanec, M., Bratko, I., and Rajkovic, V. "An expert system for decision making". Processes and Tools for Decision Making (ed. H.G. Sol), North-Holland, pp.235–248, (1983).

[24] Bohanec, M., Rajkovic, V. "DEX: An expert system shell for decision support". Sistemica, Vol.1, No.1, pp.145-157, (1990).

[25] Saracoglu, B.O. "An Experimental Research Study on the Solution of a Private Small Hydropower Plant Investments Selection Problem by ELECTRE III/IV, Shannon's Entropy, and Saaty's Subjective Criteria Weighting", Advances in Decision Sciences, Vol. 2015, Article ID.548460, 20 pages (2015). doi:10.1155/2015/548460

[26] Saracoglu, B.O. "An AHP application in the investment selection problem of small hydropower plants in turkey", International Journal of the Analytic Hierarchy Process, in press.

[27] Dictionary.com. "drainage basin" http://dictionary.reference.com/browse/drainage%20basin accessed in 18/07/2015 (2015).

[28] U.S. Department of the Interior, U.S. Geological Survey, The Water Cycle - USGS Water Science School, "Surface Runoff - The Water Cycle" http://water.usgs.gov/edu/watercyclerunoff.html accessed in 21/07/2015 (2015).

[29] US Energy Information Administration. "net head" http://www.eia.gov/tools/glossary/index.cfm accessed in 18/07/2015 (2015).

[30] U.S. Department of the Interior, U.S. Geological Survey, "How Streamflow is Measured Part 2: The discharge measurement" http://water.usgs.gov/edu/streamflow2.html accessed in 21/07/2015 (2015).

[31] ESHA (European Small Hydropower Association). "Guide on How to Develop a Small Hydropower Plant", Brussels, Belgium, (2004).

[32] NPTEL (National Programme on Technology Enhanced Learning) "Water Resources Engineering Dr. Dhrubajyoti Sen" http://nptel.ac.in/downloads/105105110/ accessed in 18/07/2015 (2015).

[33] Wikia. "community attitudes" http://psychology.wikia.com/wiki/Community_attitudes accessed in 18/07/2015 (2015).

[34] Merriam-Webster. "transportation" http://www.merriam-webster.com/dictionary/transportation accessed in 21/07/2015 (2015).

[35] Vocabulary.com "topography" http://www.vocabulary.com/dictionary/topography accessed in 21/07/2015 (2015).

[36] University of Minnesota, Department of Earth Sciences, Newton Horace Winchell School of Earth Sciences. "What is Earth Science" https://www.esci.umn.edu/whatis accessed in 21/07/2015 (2015).

[37] Oxford University Press. "security" http://www.oxforddictionaries.com/definition/english/security accessed in 21/07/2015 (2015).

[38] Terrorism-Research.com. "terrorism" http://www.terrorism-research.com/ accessed in 21/07/2015 (2015).

[39] IUCN, International Union for Conservation of Nature. "What is a protected area?" https://www.iucn.org/about/work/programmes/gpap_home/pas_gpap/ accessed in 21/07/2015 (2015).

[40] Patrick, D.R., Fardo, S.W. Electrical distribution systems, 2nd ed. Lilburn: The Fairmont Press, (2009).

[41] Carrot2. http://search.carrot2.org/stable/search accessed in 18/07/2015 (2015).

[42] Zamir, O., and Etzioni, O. "Grouper: a dynamic clustering interface to Web search results". Computer Networks, Vol.31, No.11, pp.1361–1374, (1999).

[43] Osinski, S., and Weiss, D. "A concept-driven algorithm for clustering search results". Intelligent Systems, IEEE, Vol.20, No.3, pp.48–54, (2005).. DOI:10.1109/MIS.2005.38

[44] Miller, G.A. "The magical number seven, plus or minus two: some limits on our capacity for processing information". The Psychological Review, Vol.63, pp.81–97 (1956).

[45] Shiffrin, R.M., and Nosofsky, R.M. "Seven plus or minus two: a commentary on capacity limitations". Psychological Review, Vol.101, No.2, pp.357–361 (1994).

[46] Kintsch, W., and Cacioppo, J.T. "Introduction to the 100th anniversary issue of the psycological review". Psychological Review, Vol.101, No.2, pp.195-199, (1994).

[47] Schweickert, R., and Boruff, B. "Short-term memory capacity: Magic number or magic spell?". Journal of Experimental Psychology: Learning, Memory, and Cognition, Vol.12, No.3, pp.419-425 (1986).

[48] DEXi Version 4.00 Help Manual

14

Does Earnings Management Reflect Real Condition of Listed Companies or It Does Whitewashing

Bai Yinghui[1,*], Xiong Yuanyuan[2], Wang Binru[3]

[1]Xinglin School, Nantong University, Nantong, China
[2]Bank of Jiangnan, Changzhou, China
[3]School of Business, Nantong University, Nantong, China

Email address:
baiyinghui@ntu.edu.cn (Bai Yinghui)

Abstract: This paper investigates the action、the motivation and the character of earnings management in the process of IPO using a sample of 281 IPO firms in the Growing Enterprise Market(GEM) of A-share market of Shenzhen Stock Exchange during 2009~2011. First, the evidence result shows that these listed companies revise earnings upwards in the year of issuance, while revise earnings downwards in the first year of post-IPO. Second, there is a significant correlation between these listed companies' initial offering prices and the level of earnings management which illustrate one of the motivations of earnings management is the high initial offering price, even though this correlation between them is weak. Third, the level of earnings management of those listed companies who belong to manufacturing industry is less than that of those listed companies who don't belong to manufacturing industry in the year of issuance.

Keywords: Earnings Management, GEM, IPO, Initial Offering Price

1. Introduction

This paper investigates Chinese IPO (Initial Public Offering) firms' over-propaganda action of earnings management in the process of IPO in the GEM (Growing enterprise Market).Over-propaganda during the issuance of new shares is one of the biggest threatening in Chinese market, this phenomenon actually exists in publisher's business performance. This paper analyzes the changes and character of DA (discretionary accruals) of IPO firms in the GEM, explains the loopholes of GEM distribution, and gives the conclusions and solutions of this case.

Compare to the condition of A-shares appear on the market, the profit standard and net profit set by GEM are lower than main board requirement, medium and small businesses with creativity have opportunities to IPO in the GEM successfully, on the other hand, the publishing standard of GEM motivate that publishers might reflect achievement growth through smooth performance.

China launched GEM in 2009, compare to main board of A-shares and SMB (small and medium business) board, GEM exerts unique impact on enhancing capacity for independent innovation of SMB, promoting high-growth ability and providing more investment opportunities for investors. In these three years, more than 300 enterprises have succeeded in IPO at GEM, encouraging that they focus on development. Meanwhile, 'Three High' (High Price of Publishing, High Price Earnings Ratio and High Over-Raised Fund) phenomena, declining performance of GEM after businesses went to public and big drop of GEM index make study group have reasons to suspect that if they conduct profit management around IPO. During issuance period, there is badly information asymmetry between publishers and investors. Therefore, investors can only saw business financial condition from publisher's transaction, then, they made their own investment decision. The high earnings might cause high publishing price directly. Because the most listed companies are private enterprises before they went to public, also, high share price can help that shareholders earn profit rapidly after on the market, that's the reason of requestor of companies' management layer making decisions on earnings management for high price of publishing.

The empirical analysis of study group adopted the model that based on Modified Cross Section Jones Model. This model used discretionary part of total accrued profits to measure the levels of earnings management. The model controlled accrued profits that influenced by economic condition preferably. The errors are smaller according to other scholars' researches.

This paper might make contributions below: (1) Break the limits that the lack of samples of earnings management because of companies appeared on market in batches at GEM. This paper used regression equation during absolute years, it is able to make sure that samples be the same throughout macro-economic environment, and measure publisher's earnings management level around IPO. Compared to previous studies, this paper has much amount of samples, and the time is more accurate. (2)Investigate character of GEM issuance and actions of earnings management by empirical study, combining issuance character in the GEM. Investigate correlation between high offering price and the level of earnings management by empirical study, aiming at the 'Three High'; followed by businesses guide during the publishing, studying the differences between manufacture and non-manufacture. (3) The result of the study can be guidance for investors and regulator.

In the view of the structure of this paper, the second part are study basis and system background, the third part build samples hypothesis and model, the forth part does empirical design, the fifth part includes empirical study and result analysis, the last part makes conclusion and provides suggestion.

2. The Basis of Study and System Background

2.1. The Basis of Study

Earnings management is one of most important direction in accounting since the early nineteen eighties. Earnings, also the profit of companies, as the significant details of accounting information, earnings is the reflection of financial status and business results, especially it becomes a signal of earnings information from initial business, therefore it will get greatest concern from the most of investors, similarly, securities regulators ask for high quality information of initial market could be a reasonable requirement. As the reflection of financial status, profit affects vital interests of stakeholders. Every escrow is opportunism, they followed the business earnings to modify their business relationship, make profit maximum. As the decision maker and discloser of accounting information, senior managers keep doing information disclosure for their own profit.

Earnings management is meaningful because people have many different point of views, majority of business men are unable to decide which meaning is right. Binghong Zhang(2011) pointed out that Chinese earnings management has three categories, the "Earnings Management of Institutional View", the "Earnings Management of Economic consequences view" and the "Earnings Management of Information View". From the institutional view of earnings management the companies managers controlled the earnings by using the disadvantages of accrual basis and accounting standard, and picking accounting solution, changing the earnings differences during the different accounting period; from the view of information, profit on data (report benefit) would increase or decrease by changing earnings management, it affected beneficiaries' decisions; from the economic consequences view, cashing flow of business profit would not changed by earnings management, but earnings management would change data during the profit changing.

XiaoBing Hui and FangZheng Chen (1999) came out eight earnings management motives of initial companies, they include reward contract motive, IPO, rationed shares motive, the motive of keeping the honor, bank loan motive, motive of senior staff placement, market motive and taxes motive.

Currently, the models of studying earnings management are three categories, "Total Accrued Profit model", "Specific Accrued Profit model" and "Earnings Frequency Distribution model", "Total Accrued Profit model" is the most extensive in study of earnings management, the Jones(1991) model has the more impact. The main study is about discussing the measurement of earnings management model and analyzing, this can reduce errors, and conclusion of essay is more persuasive. Dechow (1995) is the first person who assessed the effects of earnings management model, and she had a conclusion, Jones model after modified is the most convincing, and his model also laid a good foundation on earnings management. LiJun Xia(2003) found out that modified Jones model could be better on estimating excess accrual based on cross section of industry classification.

Nowadays, there are three ways of studying Chinese earnings management in GEM, (1) Does distribution system of GEM induce the actions of earnings management in listing companies? As the issue term with second sets of standards, distribution system reflects the growth requirement of businesses. (2) Does every character of listing companies affect standard of earnings management on GEM? Including ownership structure, risk capital rate, internal governance structure, etc. (3)The relationship between the character and earnings management during the listing companies on GEM, such as "Three High" (High Price of Publishing, High Price Earnings Ratio and High Over Raised Fund).

Overall, worldwide scholars have studied concept, character, motive, model and the affection of earnings management. Some of Chinese scholars studied the relationship between the action of earnings management and GEM, then they dedicate a lot great suggestion provided market with conclusion and decision.

2.2. System Background

During the national twelfth five-year plan period, Chinese economic development is changing. China sticks to the implementation of independent innovation and becomes innovative country. China published GEM in 2009. Compared to A-shares and SMB (small and middle business) board, GEM enforced the creativity of medium and small business, promoted their growth and provided more opportunities for investors. In these three years, more than 300 enterprises have succeeded in IPO at GEM encouraging that they focus on development.

'Interim Measures on Administration of Initial Public Offering and Listing on Growth Enterprise Board' (May 1st, 2009) set that publishers are eligible when they IPO on GEM. One of condition is earnings requirement. The second rule of accounting condition is that making profit in the recent two consecutive years, with accumulative net profit of not less than RMB10 million in the recent two years and with a continuous growth; or, making profit in the most recent year, with the net profit of not less than RMB 5 million, the business income of not less than RMB 50 million in the most recent year and the growth rate of business income of not lower than 30% in the recent two years. Net profit shall be calculated on the basis of the amount before or after deducting the excluding extraordinary profit and loss, whichever is smaller.

Compared to A-shares main board, the requirement of 'the net profit not less than RMB 30 million within 3 years' is higher than earnings requirement in Chinese growing enterprise market, however, Chinese GEM earnings requirement is still higher than GEM from other countries and areas. The one requirement of NASDAQ initial listing, "The gross profit include 100 million U.S dollar in a fiscal year or two years of most recent three years. Other requirements have no rules about financial profit, gross profit and net profit; Hong Kong GEM has no requirement about earnings. As we see, the requirement of earnings is too high.

This high requirement setting might cause many adverse effects. Such as: (1) Current earnings standard hard to adapt innovative companies' requirement. Those companies put too much concerns on market extension, research and development, but earnings ability is hard to see. Innovative companies are still "hungry for money". There are 277 Chinese companies established oversea after two years of GEM published, such as IT corporate champion; (2) There are some over-propaganda behaviors during IPO. Publishers chose wrong way for IPO successfully, and made a perfect achievement through earnings management. (For example, early recognition of revenue, deferred revenue) From the result, during the examining period, there are 9 out of 69 listed enterprises had failed in 2009, and 13 out of 156 listed enterprises had failed in 2010, and there are 15 out of 127 listed enterprises had failed. The accounting result from those failed companies showed that their earnings per share, net profit per share, net assets income are higher than other companies, examination committee paid too much attention on profit index, they need found out prettified data, and this would cause that they might neglecting one or the other, the information disclosed are not effective monitored, risk capital of investors. Similarly, "Three High" (High Price of Publishing, High Price Earnings Ratio and High Over-Raised Fund) could also make investors that they suspect securities regulatory commission of making decision, even distrust.

The price of share not only estimating and writing the study report, also include specific communication, negotiating inquiry, bidding and other activities. According to the Securities Law, Article 34, if shares are issued at a premium, the issuing price shall be determined through consultations between the issuer and the securities company who is handling the distribution. The " Measures for the Administration of Securities Issuance and Underwriting" written by China Securities Regulatory Commission (2006), in article 37, "When a listed company makes non-public issuance of securities, it shall comply with the relevant provisions of the CSRC on securities issuance by listed companies in choosing issuing objects and determining the quantities." Pricing stock is a multi-aspect process, it has complexity. During listed companies are growing, "Three High" affects the development of those companies. There are other threats such as "give present" to participate in quotation, "get profit" to participate in subscription, "gambling lottery" to participate in speculation. From the point of earnings management, the history of listing companies could be over-propaganda, therefore, the estimate price is not reasonable based on history business, another side, estimate earning of listed might be higher than it should be, it also caused higher stock price.

Regard to character of listed companies at GEM. There are 90% well-paid enterprises, half of which are IT, new energy and other strategic emerging industries, because China supports those industries for developing capital market. Recently, China Securities Regulatory Commission is considering further plan about character requirements of industries at GEM. The standard followed 9 major industries in "Guidelines for Further Work on the Recommendation of the GEM", 10 major industries, 137 high technological industries in "The Current Priority Areas for The Development of High - Tech Industrialization", it means that GEM has an obvious industrial guide. Other regions and countries have no restrict industry of listing companies, such as IT industries dominant American NASDAQ after long time competition, so, the different industries would have affection on earnings management in China.

From all above, Chinese distribution system is not reasonable at GEM. Some of systems might induce earnings management, stock market and transaction of secondary market. They all go against most investors.

3. Study Hypothesis and Model Construction

3.1. Study Hypothesis

The process of IPO makes people suspect on earnings management, because it provides motives and chances for issuers to implement earnings management.

Hypothesis One: Listed companies made earnings management after IPO at GEM.

Chinese GEM examination includes publishing condition of financial situation. In the process of approval at GEM, CSRC estimated the abilities of listing companies by according to the requirements of "Interim Measures on Administration of Initial Public Offering and Listening Growth Enterprise Board". Issue conditions explicit that listing companies use net profit and operating income and others earnings requirement, it makes that listing companies make earnings management for IPO successfully. Therefore, study group came out with Hypothesis one, listed companies made earnings management after IPO in GEM.

Hypothesis Two: IPO enterprises made earnings management because of higher issue price.

During the publishing, there are much misfit information between investors and publishers. Publisher were usually unknown to public before companies listed, social media didn't spend a lot of time on them, investors can only make decisions by following publishers' information, the most important are asset size, growth of performance and others financial situation. As hypothesis, the method of earnings management are growth and hidden, publishers could made earnings management through the profit, but this makes that investors don't understand the standard of earnings management. The high stock price has bought by more earnings management information. On the other hand, most of publishers were from private enterprises, and higher stock price might earn much money for shareholders. That's the reason why shareholders made earnings management. For hypothesis two: IPO enterprises made earnings management for higher issue price, and for earning much money.

Hypothesis Three: The level of non-manufacturing companies' earnings management is higher than manufacturing companies' earnings management in GEM.

Currently, the majority of listed companies are manufacturing companies in GEM. It reflects the character of Chinese industrialization. Compared to manufacturing companies, other non-manufacturing companies such as IT, they have greater risks because their financial instability, but they need followed the same rules to come to the market, so this made that non-manufacturing companies have more probability to make earnings management. For hypothesis three, the level of non-manufacturing companies' earnings management is higher than manufacturing companies'.

Also, the top managers have chances to control earnings management. In China, listed companies are allowed to make restatement about their balance sheets. Because there are many new listed companies at Chinese GEM, finance is not perfect, therefore it caused that most of businesses have restatement of balance sheets. Restatement provides managers with free space to manage business earnings. However, accounting policy are selective, financial staff are able to consider and decide, including choice of accounting, application of accounting and asset purchase, time management, etc.

During the publishing period, some reasons restricted the space of earnings management. Certified public accountants (CPA) should audit balance sheet, sponsors should oversee publishers, and time of supervision should be longer (longer than one accounting year at GEM), some of these intermediaries could help prevent earnings management.

3.2. Model Construction

3.2.1. Measurement of Earnings Management Level

To test hypothesis one, we estimate the earnings management level of sample companies at first. Empirical accounting think, earnings has two parts, one is the real flowing cash (Cash Flow of operations), another part is unreal flowing cash, this part followed accrual basis principle, but there is no flowing cash, so it's called Total Accruals. The formulation of Total Accruals is below:

$$\textit{Total Accruals} \equiv \textit{Net Income} - \textit{Cash Flows of Operations} \quad (3\text{-}1)$$

Jones used the model to calculate accruals, it is Jones model. In this model, total accruals can be discretionary accruals and non-discretionary accruals, discretionary accruals can be used in measurement of earnings management. The formulation of discretionary accruals is below:

$$\textit{Discretionary Accruals} \equiv \textit{Total Accruals} - \textit{Nondiscretionary Accruals} \quad (3\text{-}2)$$

Jones model adopts time series data, and it has restriction. So, continuously, many scholars modified the model. Defond (1994) modified it, which based on cross section data model. One of IPO firms in this paper has total accruals that based on the same year. Therefore, one enterprise IPO used least square method to calculated cross section data at t year:

$$\frac{TA_{i,t}}{A_{i,t-1}} = \alpha_0\left(\frac{1}{A_{i,t-1}}\right) + \alpha_1\left(\frac{\Delta REV_{i,t}}{A_{i,t-1}}\right) + \alpha_2\left(\frac{PPE_{i,t}}{A_{i,t-1}}\right) + \varepsilon_{i,t} \quad (3\text{-}3)$$

From the formulation above, ΔREV means sales variables, PPE means fixed assets, A means total assets, ΔREV means receivable accounts variables. Because managers could control credit policy, receivable accounts variables should be removed from sales variables, thus formulation of total non-discretionary accruals should be below:

$$NDA_{i,t} = \hat{\alpha}_0\left(\frac{1}{A_{i,t-1}}\right) + \hat{\alpha}_1\left(\frac{\Delta REV_{i,t}-\Delta REC_{i,t}}{A_{i,t-1}}\right) + \hat{\alpha}_2\left(\frac{PPE_{i,t}}{A_{i,t-1}}\right) \quad (3\text{-}4)$$

$\hat{\alpha}_0$ means intercept estimated values, $\hat{\alpha}_1$ and $\hat{\alpha}_2$ are both estimated slope coefficient of IPO enterprises. Discretionary accruals is residual of formulation 3-3, it is showing below:

$$DA_{i,t} = \frac{TA_{i,t}}{A_{i,t-1}} - NDA_{i,t} \quad (3\text{-}5)$$

3.2.2. Stock Pricing Model

Estimated model of stock has many types, including traditional valuation method, relative valuation method and option valuation method. Frequently-used method in new listing stock is the P/E ratio multiplier method of relative valuation method. The majority of new listing companies use this kind of method, the formulation is below:

$$PE = \frac{Price}{EPS} \quad (3\text{-}6)$$

$$\textit{Issue Price} = \textit{Issue PE} \times \textit{Issue EPS} \quad (3\text{-}7)$$

$$EPS = \frac{Earnings}{Quantity} \quad (3\text{-}8)$$

During the testing of hypothesis two, the theoretical basis of this article is the model that widely used in the main board, SMB board and GEM — Earnings Ratio model.

3.2.3. Modified Jones Model in Industrial Classification

The paper based on the cross section Jones model of

industrial classification during testing the hypothesis three. According to industrial classification information of Resset Database and Shenzhen stock exchange, this context divided samples to manufacturing companies and non-manufacturing companies. And the discretionary accruals in hypothesis three was calculated by regression results in different industries, this is the difference between 3-3 (other formulation earnings management are the same). One IPO enterprise's total accrual was estimated in same industry in fixed year, the calculation is below:

$$\frac{TA_{j,t}}{A_{j,t-1}} = \alpha_0\left(\frac{1}{A_{j,t-1}}\right) + \alpha_1\left(\frac{\Delta REV_{j,t}}{A_{j,t-1}}\right) + \alpha_2\left(\frac{PPE_{j,t}}{A_{j,t-1}}\right) + \varepsilon_{j,t} \quad (3\text{-}9)$$

$$j \in estimation\ sample$$

4. Empirical Study and Design

4.1. Empirical Analysis Period

According to regulatory requirements, GEM apply to China Securities Regulatory Commission for listing by using reporting form in 3 years or 1 period of three years (reporting period). Meanwhile, the disclosure principle of the annual report cannot be later than next year April 30th. Therefore, some information have included in this context, financial data during 2006 to 2011 while company listing on 2009, financial data during 2007 to 2011 while company listing on 2010, and financial data during 2008 to 2011 while company listing on 2011.

As current situation of listing and information of listing companies, the empirical period includes two years before sample companies IPO, one year before and after IPO. For the convenience of research, the text assumes that IPO period is at the beginning, and figure out the years after listing. According to study purpose and hypothesis, the empirical study of context focus on year-2, -1, 0 and 1, as the result, the context verified that listing company IPO and had earnings management listing or not.

4.2. Sample Descriptive Data

Chart 4-1. *The number of listed companies IPO in the GEM in different years.*

Year	Listing Particulars Time		Raised funds reflected in balance sheet	
	Amount	Proportion(%)	Amount	Proportion(%)
2009	50	17.54	42	14.95
2010	113	39.65	116	41.28
2011	122	42.81	123	43.77
Total	285	100	281	100

PS: Samples in this paper use raised funds reflected in balance sheet in the end of term to divide listing year.

The study samples of this text were picked from listing companies of Shenzhen stock exchange. Until the end of 2011, there are 285 listing companies on GEM (Listing time accord to announcements)

Chart 4-1 reported the number of listed companies IPO in the GEM in different years. From the stock code 300283, they didn't report raised fund on balance sheet, if study group didn't count information of balance sheet, the sample of listing companies should be 281.

Chart 4-2 demonstrated the size and distribution of sample firms' assets. Because the listing companies IPO in the different time, it is not accurate to compare end of period assets in the same year, and this context calculated total assets of listing companies before IPO at GEM. In 281 samples, 0.2~0.3 billion companies are the most, there are 82 companies and 29.18% about total samples; there are 82 companies about 0.1~0.2 billion assets, about 25.98% in total; 82.56% companies are under 0.5 billion assets, there are only a few companies above 1 billion, only 2.14%; and 1.42% companies have assets under 0.1 billion. The conclusions are: 1. Listing companies didn't have many assets before came to market at GEM. 2. The size of assets is comparatively centralized.

Chart 4-2. *The size and distribution of sample firms' assets.*

Asset Size(¥)	Amount of firms	Proportion (%)	Frequency number	Frequency rate(%)
0~0.1 billion	4	1.42	4	1.42
0.1~0.2 billion	73	25.98	77	27.40
0.2~0.3 billion	82	29.18	159	56.58
0.3~0.4 billion	44	15.66	203	72.24
0.4~0.5 billion	29	10.32	232	82.56
0.5~0.6 billion	19	6.76	251	89.32
0.6~0.7 billion	12	4.27	263	93.59
0.7~0.8 billion	4	1.42	267	95.02
0.8~0.9 billion	5	1.78	272	96.80
0.9~1 billion	3	1.07	275	97.86
>1 billion	6	2.14	281	100.00
Total	281	100.00		

Graph 4-1 reported the number of the first earning ratio in different assessment districts. Because of "Three High", according to statistic, the main board's earning ratio are 53 times, 59 times and 47 times in recent three years, but the earning ratio of GEM are 64 times, 71 times and 51 times, compare to each other, GEM is higher obviously. At the same time, context compared price earnings ratio with bank ratio. Currently, Chinese deposit rate is 3.50%, according to price earning ratio formulation: 100/3.50=28.57 times. Therefore, the text has three assessment districts, they are ideal assessment district (lower than 28.57 times), main board's assessment district (28.57~59 times), overestimate assessment district (higher than 59 times). There are more than 141 listing companies at GEM that they are overestimate assessment district, and 132 listing companies at main board district, overall, GEM had a very high starting price earning ratio. Study group think that listing companies made earning management because listing companies need high stock price.

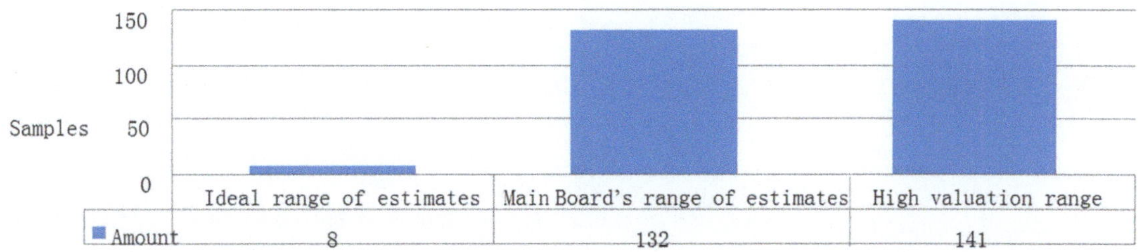

Graph 4-1. *The number of the first earning ratio in different assessment districts.*

Chart 4-3 showed the different industrial distribution. China Securities Regulatory Commission gave explicit directions to listing companies IPO in GEM, support strategic emerging industries development, so industrial distribution of listing companies became meaningful in GEM. The character can be below from the graph: (1) industrial distribution is not widely, there are 281 companies in 9 industries. But real estate, financial insurance, electric power companies and public services have no sample enterprises, the result is about the growth and innovation of industrial distribution in GEM, and also it can be the explicit direction during listing companies IPO in GEM. (2) Manufacture are the most, there are 189 manufactures, about 67.26% in total sample companies, compare to American NASDAQ, Chinese GEM represents the character of China—manufacturing industry. Inside, SITC7, C5 electricity, C4 plastic petrochemical industries are in the front, they are 29.18%, 12.46%, 11.03%, they reflected the strategic emerging industries development. (3) IT also has many sample companies, it's about 18.86% of total samples, and this is much higher than main board. Compare to manufacturing industries, these companies have more probabilities to make earnings management.

Chart 4-3. *The different industrial distribution.*

Industry	Amount	Proportion (%)
A Animal husbandry and fishery	6	2.14
B Mining	4	1.42
C0 Food and beverage	3	1.07
C3 Paper printing	2	0.71
C4 Petrochemical and plastics	31	11.03
C5 Electronic	35	12.46
C6 Metal and non-metal	10	3.56
C7 Mechanical equipment	82	29.18
C8 Medical biological	23	8.19
C9 Other manufacturing	3	1.07
E Building	2	0.71
F Transportation and storage	2	0.71
G Information technology	53	18.86
H Wholesale and retail	2	0.71
K Social service	14	4.98
L Media	9	3.20
Total	281	100.00

5. Empirical Test and Result Analysis

5.1. Empirical Test and Analysis Earnings Management Before and After Ipo

The text estimate regression equation of the total and coefficient (3-3) by using SPSS 17.0 regression equation software, to get total and factorial estimates. As chart 5-1 showing, from significance, sig. (most of the sig. is smaller than 0.005), totality of model with an obvious significant standard. During the testing of coefficient, average estimating coefficient of $\frac{\Delta REV_{i,t}}{A_{i,t-1}}$ is greater than 0, total accrued profit has positive correlation with gross profit; estimating coefficient average of $\frac{PPE_{i,t}}{A_{i,t-1}}$ is less than 0, it told that total accrued profit has negative correlation with fixed assets, it is about the truth. However, another truth is that regression coefficient is too lower and it means that other factors might affect total accrued profit of listing companies at GEM.

Chart 5-1. *The regression equation of the total and factorial test.*

Time	2008	2009	2010	2011
Sample size	221	281	281	281
R^2	0.22	0.081	0.065	0.215
F (sig)	20.349 (0.000)	8.168 (0.000)	6.430 (0.000)	25.337 (0.000)
ΔREVi,t/Ai,t-1	0.091	0.037	0.093	0.26
T (sig)	6.793 (0.000)	1.438 (0.151)	3.556 (0.000)	7.126 (0.000)
PPEi,t/Ai,t-1	-0.223	-0.18	-0.135	-0.047
T (sig)	-3.599 (0.000)	-4.205 (0.000)	-2.942 (0.004)	-0.982 (0.327)

PS: The lack of 2008's sample because it's not necessary to disclose 2007's information.

According to samples of regression result in 2008, 2009, 2010 and 2011, the text calculated that the DA (discretionary accruals) of listing companies in GEM in different years, it is to figure out standard of earning management. The context also used relative years to judge earnings management around listing companies IPO in GEM, therefore DA data were divided by following relatively years, the method can be seen in part 4.

Chart 5-2 reported earnings management in relative year -2, -1, 0 and 1. The average number of (DA) should be 0.0152 and 0.0033 in relative year -2 and -1, the trend of this report could be a big earnings management, but it had no difference with 0, this means that earnings management is not obvious before listed two years. Similarly, the averages of listing companies DA earnings management are 0.0643 and -0.0202 in relative year 0 and 1, and it is obvious different from 0, this means that listing companies IPO had earnings management at that time, after one year, listing companies decrease adjusted earnings management. The hypothesis one reflected the truth of earnings management after listing companies IPO.

Chart 5-2. The level of listed companies' earnings management in the GEM.

Relative year	Sample size	Average value	T-test	P-value
-2	281	0.0152	1.521	0.129
-1	281	0.0033	0.394	0.694
0	281	0.0643**	6.728	0.000
1	159	-0.0202**	-3.348	0.001

PS: **represents correlation is significant at 0.01 level (two-tailed test).

5.2. Testing and Analysis of Offering Price and Earnings Management Level

The assumption No.2 of this paper put forward that the motivation of earnings management in the process of IPO is to gain high offering price, which needs to analyze the relevance between initial offering prices and the level of earnings management.

According to current offering PE ratio (price earning ratio) confirm process, the sponsor proposes feasible range of PE on the basis of publishers' materials and trade PE in the market, then the CSRC issued IEC makes consideration in different situation and provides guidance. This leads to publishers hard to decide offering PE, as change offering PE is too high a price to pay.

Chart 5-3. Correlation between basis EPS (earnings per share) and IPO price in the year of IPO.

		Basis EPS	Offering Price
Basis EPS	Pearson correlation coefficient	1	.688**
	Significance (two-tailed test)		.000
	N	281	281
Offering Price	Pearson correlation coefficient	.688**	1
	Significance (two-tailed test)	.000	
	N	281	281

PS: **represents correlation is significant at 0.01 level (two-tailed test).

The chart 5-3 represents correlation between basis EPS (earnings per share) and IPO price in the year of issuance. Pearson's correlation coefficient of basis EPS and IPO price is 0.688, and the correlation is significant at 0.01 level (two-tailed test). It illustrates the scientificity of our theoretical deduction, which is that IPO price of listed companies in the GEM is greatly influenced by the EPS in the year of issue. It's necessary to note that predicted EPS in the year of issue used in the issuance pricing, while management layer of firms in the GEM try hard to maintain reputation and sponsors accomplish the duty of marketing supervising, so predicted EPS is in accordance with actual EPS in the year of issue.

Stockholders' meeting of publishers made decisions about types and amount of offering stocks, so, if enterprises want to raise offering price, they might gloss over reports by earning management to improve profit, as to increase numerator in formula 3-8.This paper estimates assumption No.2 by verifying the correlation between listed companies' levels of earnings management in the GEM in current year and IPO price.

Chart 5-4 reports the correlation between samples' levels of earnings management in the GEM in current year and IPO price. Correlation coefficient of earnings management level and IPO price is 0.141, and a correlation is significant at 0.05 level (two-tailed test).This proves assumption No.2, which illustrates one of the motivations of earnings management is the high initial offering price.

Chart 5-4. Correlation between samples' earnings management level and IPO price in the year of issuance

		The level of earnings management (DA)	Offering Price
The level of earnings management (DA)	Pearson correlation coefficient	1	.141*
	Significance (two-tailed test)		.000
	N	281	281
Offering Price	Pearson correlation coefficient	.141*	1
	Significance (two-tailed test)	.000	
	N	281	281

PS: ** represents correlation is significant at 0.05 level (two-tailed test)

5.3. Testing and Analysis of the Level of Earnings Management in Different Industries

In this paper, samples of listed companies who belong to manufacturing industry and those who don't, substituted into equation 3-9, and then calculate discretionary accruals (DA) of manufacturing industry and non-manufacturing industry's earnings management level. This paper judges if earnings management level is different in different industries.

Chart 5-5 descriptively analyzes samples in relative annual. In relative year -2, -1, and 1, there is little difference between average DA values and median, this represents that there is no significant difference between the levels of earnings management in those different industries during these years. In relative year 0, the average and median of DA of manufacturing industries are 5% and 4%, while which of non-manufacturing industries are 8% and 9%. This represents the level of earnings management of manufacturing industries is higher than that of non-manufacturing industries in the year of issuance. As we can see from standard deviation, in each relative year, values of which in manufacturing industries is lower than that in non-manufacturing industries, this represents the level of earnings management in manufacturing industries is more centralized than that in non-manufacturing industries. Observe from kurtosis values, they are exceed 3 in relative year -2, -1, non-manufacturing industries distribute in high kurtosis, while manufacturing industries distribute in low kurtosis. Observe from skewness, most values are greater than 0 (distribute in right-skewed), which means listed companies have the tendency to manipulate profits higher than actual profits. In relative year 0, non-manufacturing industries distribute in left-skewed, which means they have the tendency to manipulate profits lower than actual profits.

The DA values of non-manufacturing industries are higher than manufacturing industries in the year of issuance, which approves the Hypothesis Three, the level of non-manufacturing companies' earnings management is higher than manufacturing companies' earnings management in GEM. Apparently, the level of manufacturing and non-manufacturing industries earnings management is close. The reason is that the method to separate manufacturing and non-manufacturing industries is affected by outlier.

Chart 5-5. *Descriptive analysis about samples in relative annual.*

	Relative year -2		Relative year -1		Relative year 0		Relative year 1	
	Manu-facturing industries	Non-manufacturing industries	Manu-facturing industries	Non-manufacturing industries	Manu-facturing industries	Non-manufacturing industries	Manu-facturing industries	Non-manu-facturing industries
Sample size	188	93	188	93	188	93	106	52
Average	0.00	(0.00)	(0.01)	(0.00)	0.05	0.08	(0.02)	(0.02)
Median	(0.01)	(0.02)	(0.01)	(0.01)	0.04	0.09	(0.04)	(0.03)
Standard deviation	0.15	0.18	0.12	0.17	0.14	0.18	0.07	0.09
Kurtosis	2.88	3.36	2.47	11.67	2.57	1.13	3.07	(0.32)
Skewness	0.83	(0.10)	0.49	1.78	1.08	0.14	1.16	0.22

PS: Numbers in brackets are minus.

6. Conclusions and Suggestions

Chinese GEM includes business achievement, publishing requirement of industrial guide and restrict examination. The restriction of policy induced that IPO companies made earnings management with legality and hidden. Meanwhile, companies made earnings management also for IPO successfully and high stock price.

This context used cross section data that based on Jones model, from the point of discretionary to measure the standard of earnings management, and confirmed three hypothesis:

1. View from the result of empirical study, companies made earnings management by increasing profits in the year of IPO, after one year, companies made earnings management again by decreasing profits. Enterprises which would like to be listed are inspected strictly by issuance examination regulators during issuance examination will. So they whitewash their profits by earnings management, and gloss over their predicted profits. Regulation stipulates that if publisher has given predicted profits but actual profits couldn't live up to 80% of it, legal representative will be punished. But those enterprises which would like to be listed escape supervision punishment by manipulating 6.43% of the beginning assets, and after one year, manipulating profits 2.02% lower than actual profits is just so 'clever'.

2. Another motivation of earnings management is the high initial offering price. During the price enquiry, prettified performance attracts more investors, and sponsors' reports can be more convinced. The weak correlation between them is realistic on account of stock pricing's complex process. It's affected by many factors, including the time, etc. Except that, listed companies' financial reports will be inspected by accounting firms and the issuance examination commission, so, the space of listed companies' conducting earnings management is limited.

3. This paper discusses the difference of earnings management between different industries, which is the level of earnings management of those listed companies who belong to manufacturing industry is less than that of those listed companies who don't belong to manufacturing industry in the year of issuance. This year, China carried out PE ratio (price earning ratio) on pricing mechanism. The alternative are not only the companies choosed by sponsors, but also companies which would like to be listed. This is a big progress. However, these companies in different industries have different extent of whitewash, they might do over-propaganda, too, which is also need to pay attention.

According to the conclusion in this paper, there are some policies and suggestions:

First, modify issue terms on the GEM, cancel the requirement of enterprises' profits, especially innovative enterprises' profits requirement. This is beneficial to issue system's construction which focused on information disclosure, and can weaken regulators' judgment about listed companies' profitability. The issuance examination commission should focus on temporal financial data, and response to publishers' predicted profits in the long run. Once find changes in certain listed company's future performance, the commission ought to investigate relative material during the process of issuance, control whitewashing behavior and aggravate punishment. Nowadays, China lack investigation standards, it could use discretionary accruals as a kind of standard.

Second, establish responding mechanism combining issue price and performance in secondary stock market to control "Three High" phenomenon in the process of issuance, urge new issued stock to reflect companies' real value, and coordinate primary market and secondary market in solid development. If certain company's PE ratio higher than the average, supervision agencies need to follow it's performance in secondary market, examine issue materials when perform bad, and remind investors of relative risks. In the meantime, regulators should improve price enquiry mechanism, avoid over-high price occupying other resources in the GEM. Super raise funds will leads to capitals wash away or even waste, which is bad for improvements in capital market.

Last but not the least, enlarge the coverage of GEM, put GEM delist mechanism into practice. Listing is market oriented behavior of demand side of fund and supply side of fund. So, providing diverse listed companies is respecting the market. Over- stressed in certification will increase earnings management behaviors and is harmful to the reality of information and investments. China should put delist mechanism into practice and protect natural competition in the GEM, thus can form Chinese GEM style.

References

[1] Siew Hong Teoh, Ivo Welch, T. J. Wong. Earnings Management and the Long-Run Market Performance of Initial Public Offerings [J]. The Journal of Finance, 1998, vol. 53, No. 6: 1935-1974

[2] Jennifer J. Jones. Earnings Management during import relief investigations [J]. Journal of Accounting Recearch, 1991, vol. 29, No. 2: 192-228

[3] Paul Kalyta. Accounting Discretion, Horizon Problem, and CEO Retirement Management [J]. The Accounting Review, 2009, vol. 84, No. 5: 1553-1573

[4] Christian Laux, Volker Laux. Board Committees, CEO Compensation, and Earrings Management [J]. The Accounting Review, 2009, vol. 84, No. 3: 869-891

[5] Douglas F. Prawitt, Jason L. Smith, David A. Wood. Internal Audit Quality and Earnings Management [J]. The Accounting Review, 2009, vol. 84, No. 4: 1255-1280

[6] Victor S. Maas, Michal Matejka. Balancing the Dual Responsibilities of Business Unit Controllers: Field and Survey Evidence [J]. The Accounting Review, 2009, vol. 84, No. 4: 1233-1253

[7] Kiridaran Kanagaretnam, Gopal V. Krishnan, Gerald J. Lobo. Balancing the Dual Responsibilities of Business Unit Controllers: Field and Survey Evidence [J]. The Accounting Review, 2009, vol. 84, No. 4: 1233-1253

[8] Patricia M. Dechow, Richard G. Sloan, Amy P. Sweeney. Detecting earnings management [J]. The Accounting Review, 1995, vol. 70, No. 2: 193-225

[9] Stephen R. Stubben. Discretionary Revenues as a Measure of Earnings Management [J]. The Accounting Review, 2010, vol. 85, No. 2: 637-717

[10] Sharon P. Katz. Earnings Quality and Ownership Structure: The Role of Private Equity Sponsors [J]. The Accounting Review, 2009, vol. 84, No. 3: 623-658

[11] De Fond, M., and J. Jiambalvo. 1994. Debt covenant violation and manipulation of accruals [J]. Journal of Accounting and Economics 17: 145–176.

[12] Bernard, V., and D. Skinner. 1996. What motivates managers' choice of discretionary accruals [J]? Journal of Accounting and Economics 22: 313–325.

15

The Relationship Between Organizations' Acquired Knowledge, Skills, Abilities (SKAs) and Shareholders Wealth Maximization: The Mediating Role of Training Investment

Gabriel Dwomoh[1], Williams Kwasi Boachie[2], Kofi Kwarteng[3]

[1]Institute of Entrepreneurship and Enterprise Development, Kumasi Polytechnic, Kumasi, Ghana
[2]Department of Accounting Education Studies Education, University of Education, Kumasi, Ghana
[3]School of Business, Takoradi Polytechnic, Takoradi, Ghana

Email address:
gabdwumoo@yahoo.com (G. Dwomoh)

Abstract: The study examined the relationship between organizations' acquired knowledge, skills, abilities and shareholders wealth with training playing the mediating role. The sample of the study consisted of organizations that spent 10% or more of its annual budget on training and those whose training budget is less than 10% of the organization's annual budget. A total of 620 questionnaires were distributed to employees working in various organizations out of which 580 representing 93.5% were retrieved. The sample was drawn using convenience sampling. The data collection instrument was mainly questionnaires supported by the use of Regression models for analysis to be made. Analyzing multiple models, it was discovered that organizations training investment plays a considerable indirect and direct effect with partial mediation between organizations acquired skills, knowledge, abilities and shareholders wealth. Shareholders should allow their agents to invest part of their holdings to develop the human capital of the organization but this should be done with caution since shareholders returns do not depend much on how much organizations spend in developing its human resource capital.

Keywords: Skills, Knowledge, Abilities, Shareholders Wealth, Training Investment

1. Introduction

All organizations no matter its size cannot operate on smoothly without training. This means that training investment is crucial for organizations. If organizations want to use employees to maximize shareholders wealth, they cannot rely solely on the skills and knowledge that public or private educational institutions had helped employees to acquire. These skills and knowledge do not fit into the culture as well as the core values that drive the organization forward. It is on the basis of this that many human resource practitioners are of the view that despite the employee receiving formal education, for an organization to improve its performance, tailored made training that focus on strategic directions of the organization should be provided. Nickel et al (2002) in support of training investment commented that investors are now recognizing the importance of organization's acquired skills and knowledge and its relevance to managers who manage their investments. To them, an organizational training investment data is one of the criteria investors consider which organizations they need to invest. This is based on the assumption that, the higher the training investment data of an organization, the more skilful and knowledgeable their managers are and as such it is believed that they have all the abilities to manage shareholders funds effectively.

Despite the support that many writers throw on training investment, there are others who also belief that most training programmes of organizations are routine and they are not tailored towards improving employees skills and knowledge, hence has no correlation with shareholders wealth. Just like any other investments engaged by Finance Managers, if organizations training investment does not improve the needed skills, knowledge and abilities of employees, the associated cost of such investment will not be accounted for and hence has the tendency of diluting shareholders wealth in the long run. Organizations that spend huge amount of money training their employees may not recognize any benefit from the training especially if the employees do not stay long after the training and if this happens managers will find it very difficult to account for shareholders money which they spend on the training. Again, many people also believe that training investment does not improve the needed skills and knowledge and hence dilutes shareholders wealth simply because proper needs assessment which is one of the phases of any training may not be done by managers. If managers select the wrong employees for training, then transfer of knowledge as well as application of newly acquired skills becomes difficult since it is possible that such employees may not apply what they had learned from the training. If transfer of knowledge and application of skills acquired from the training is not forthcoming, then shareholders money can be said to have been thrown away and this affects the profitability of the firm.

Looking from these two scenarios with regard to the mediating role training investment play between organization's acquired knowledge, skills, abilities and shareholders wealth maximization, one is tempted to investigate the relationship between these two variables with training investment serving as the mediator. It is believed that if an organization's training investment brings the needed knowledge, skills and abilities that employees need, then all things been equal, high profitability is expected and hence shareholders wealth maximized. If opposite is the case, then it is expected that shareholders wealth will be affected since training cost cannot be accounted for.

Research Questions and Hypothesis

The research questions and hypothesis of the study are as follows:

Research Questions

i. Does organization's acquired knowledge, skills and abilities have any relationship with shareholders wealth?
ii. Does training play mediation role between shareholders wealth and organization's acquired knowledge, skills and abilities?

Hypothesis

H1: There is significant relationship between organization's acquired skills and productivity.

H2: There is significant relationship between organization's acquired knowledge and productivity.

H3: There is significant relationship between organization's acquired abilities and productivity.

H4: There is significant relationship between organization's acquired skills and profitability.

H5: There is significant relationship between organization's acquired knowledge and profitability.

H6: There is significant relationship between organization's acquired abilities and profitability.

H7: There is significant relationship between organization's acquired skills and dividends.

H8: There is significant relationship between organization's acquired abilities and dividends.

H9: There is significant relationship between organization's acquired knowledge and dividends.

H10: There is significant relationship between organization's acquired skills and shareholders wealth.

H11: There is significant relationship between organization's acquired knowledge and shareholders wealth.

H12: There is significant relationship between organization's acquired abilities and shareholders wealth.

H13: There is mediation between productivity and organizations' training investment.

H14: There is mediation between profitability and organization's training investment.

H15: There is mediation between dividends and organization's training investment.

H16: There is mediation between shareholder's wealth and training investment.

2. Literature Review

Many writers have commented that training should not be seen as cost but rather an investment provided it facilitates the acquisition of knowledge, skills and abilities needed by employees to perform their job satisfactorily. According to the American Society for Training and Development (ASTD), (2010) quoted by Heathfield (2012), though many businesses are not favoured by economic conditions, business leaders still continue to commit huge sums of money in training because they need to improve the knowledge and skills of their employees. The ASTD estimates that about US$125.88 billion were invested in employees by means of training in 2009. Out of this total figure, according to them about two-thirds of the amount which is US$78.61 billion were spent on internal learning function whilst US$47.27 billion were allocated to external services. Looking at such huge sums of money spent on training, there is no doubt that organizations are reaping benefits from such investments through the improvement of employees' skills and knowledge. Again this can also be evident from a comment made by them that the best award winning organizations are those that have all the needed skills and knowledge needed to achieve both short term and long term objectives.

From the words of Grobler et al (2006), employee training investment is a big business in many countries such as South Africa. According to them, training costs is estimated to be R5 billion per year. The writers see employee training as investment since it is a key factor in meeting the employer's strategic, business and operational goals. The writers also emphasized that technological advances as well as social, political and economic pressures mean that an organization cannot do away with training. This is one of the main reasons why training is seen as vital in the mining and manufacturing industries in Ghana. In the mining industry of Ghana, training is one of the tools used to avoid non compliance of both domestic and environmental laws as well as health and safety laws which help the mining industry to avoid financial penalties associated with mistakes and unorthodox practices by its employees. It is believed that if these investments in training are not done, the financial penalties associated with it as a result of mistakes and unorthodox practices by employees can add to the cost of these companies and this has implications on shareholders wealth in terms of dilution.

Looking at the words of Huselid (1995), training is considered as very important to organizations such that the main problem facing organizations is not whether there should be training or not but rather the problem is which employees should be trained and what methods should be used to train them. From this statement, one can point out that if organizations face the problem of who should be trained, then those who are not in favour of an organization's training investment playing a mediating role between employees' knowledge, skills, abilities and shareholders wealth maximization can argued that it is proper for shareholders who want returns on their investment to kick against training investment since proper training needs assessment is one of the ingredients needed for training benefits to be realized. Again, if organizations cannot identify the right people to be trained, then transfer of knowledge acquired from the training becomes difficult and this has serious implications on shareholders wealth since it will add to cost of the organization which will intend affect productivity and profit.

Training is not considered as important only to organizations owned by private individuals but to nations and various governments who are considered as the major employer in many countries. For instance according to Grobler et al (2006), the passage of various Acts in relation to enhancing workers skills and knowledge by the South African government indicates the seriousness nations place on training investment. Some of these Acts according to the writers include the South African Qualifications Authority Act, No. 58 of 1995, the Skills Development Act, No. 97 of 1998 and the Skills Development Levies Act, No. 9 of 1999. In Ghana, majority of the government institutions such as the Ghana Police Service, Bank of Ghana, Prisons Service, Ghana Broadcasting Corporation and others have their own training centres and huge amount of money is allocated to these training centres with the belief that the returns derive from sharpening employees' skills and knowledge will far outweigh the cost associated with it.

From the words of Barney (2005), one of the reasons why companies spent huge sums of money investing in training is that it serves as a means of achieving competitive advantage as a result of the acquisition of certain unique skills and knowledge which are not available to competitors. According to the writer, one of the companies that have used training to achieve this advantage is the Southwest Airlines. The writer sees this airline as one of the major airlines that have remained profitable after the September 11 tragedy. To him, the ability of the company to retain its customers is based on the excellent and quality services provided by its workers, thanks to the company's training playing a mediating role.

Apart from Southwest Airlines which is benefiting a lot from training investment, there are companies which cannot be left out as pointed out by Bateman and Snell (2000). According to the writers, companies such as Motorola, General Motors and International Business Machines (IBM) have invested over billions of dollars in training. The returns on the training enjoyed by these companies far exceed the amount that was invested. In support of this assertion, they emphasized that Motorola has been gaining US$30 on every US$1 invested in training. Going by this comment, it means that training investment is seen as a big business which has positive correlation with shareholders wealth. Alan (2009) adding his voice to the relationship between organization's acquired knowledge, skills, and shareholders wealth maximization with training serving as a mediating role, training yields dividends but it is not easy to measure them in monetary terms. The dividends provided by training can be noticed in terms of increased in productivity, improved communication and participation, reduced labour turnover as employees now have the skills and knowledge to fit into their positions, waste reductions as less errors are committed by employees and reduction in accidents.

From the words of Devanna et al (2005), Guest (2009) as well as Wright and Taylor (2004), training mediates acquisition of knowledge and skills and firms' performance. Whilst Devanna et al (2005) see training as increasing individual performance which is believed to lead to higher firm performance, Wright and Taylor (2004) believes that human capital is considered as very important and if an organization does not have the right skills and knowledge, it will be very difficult for that organization to achieve its goals which is mostly geared towards profit maximization. Other writers who have also contributed to acquisition of knowledge, skills and shareholders wealth maximization with training playing a mediating role are Bottomley (2000), Cole (1996), Beach (2004), Pratt and Bennet (2001), Crane (2002) and Graham and Bennet (2001). According to Bottomley (2000), the fundamental purpose of training is to provide for the organization's manpower needs. This writer in support of Beach (2004) is of the view that organizations spend huge sums of money advertising and recruiting from external but at the end, these cost associated with the recruitment and selection process cannot be recovered if the newly recruited employee does not stay in the organization for long.

As a means of reducing recruitment and selection cost which also adds to the cost of the organization and hence dilution of shareholders wealth, it is important for organizations to first consider investing in their existing employees by means of training so that they can occupy vacant positions. Their arguments also points to the fact that, getting skilled and knowledgeable employees to fill vacant positions serve as a means of intrinsic motivation for employees to put up their best so that in future they can be considered. Second, such employees are already familiar with the culture and customs of the organization and as such the propensity that they will stay in their new positions is higher than those recruited externally since their expectations may not be what they find on the job.

Looking at a comment by the American Bankers Association on the role of training investment on firm's performance, they emphasized that Chief Learning Officers have a significant leadership responsibility to see that workplace learning and development dollars are spent in ways that support business goals and yield the greatest return to the organization. They concluded that training investment is becoming something which organizations cannot do without in the banking industry since it is seen as one of the greatest investment which an organization can make. From their point of view, training investment lead to improved performance of banks through gains in quality, customer satisfaction, productivity, profitability, and dividends for limited liability companies. Many of the Banks in Ghana such as Standard Chartered, Barclays, Ghana Commercial, Ecobank have all established training centres which aimed at training their employees. The establishment of these training centres aimed at equipping the skills and knowledge of employees proves that, the responsibility of ensuring increase in companies sales, profit and dividends are not left to the Finance Manager or Operations Manager but Training Managers who should ensure that training offered to employees equipped them with the necessarily skills, knowledge and abilities for those variables to be realized.

Though many writers have argued in favour of training investment playing mediating role of organization's acquired skills, knowledge, abilities correlating positively to shareholders wealth maximization, according to Gall et al (2002), an organization's training investment does not necessarily bring the acquisition of knowledge and skills which will correlate positively to shareholders wealth. Their arguments point to the fact that, there are many hidden motives why organizations invest in training rather than training the employee to acquire the needed skills and knowledge. Secondly, much depends on the employee's preparedness and willingness to acquire the knowledge and skills which the training is meant. This means that training itself does not automatically lead to the acquisition of skills and knowledge but other factors need to come into play before the organization's needed skills and knowledge can be realized. The literature by Howe (2004) supports the argument given by Gall et al (2002) that training itself does not necessarily bring acquisition of skills and knowledge since organizations have different reasons why they invest in training and not necessarily to improve employees' skills and knowledge. To the writer, if the training is meant to enable employees release stress by taking time off the job to go for external training programme which is not tailored to the employees need, then the argument that an organization's training investment plays a mediating role of organization's acquired skills, knowledge and abilities needs to be questioned.

Looking at the literature review and the hypotheses set, a conceptual model for the dependent variables, independent variables and the moderator variable was set as follows:

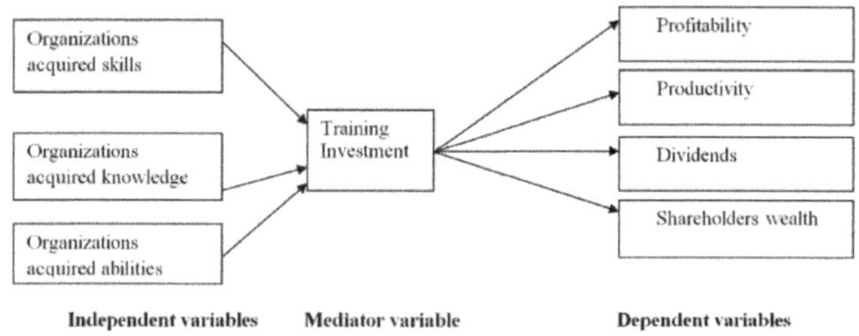

Figure 1. *Proposed Conceptual Model of Dependent, Independent and Moderator variable.*

The above conceptual model means that organizations acquired skills, knowledge and abilities comes into existence through the organization's investment in training and this will in turn maximizes shareholders wealth as a result of increase in productivity, profit and high declaration of dividends.

3. Methodology

Though the researchers could not cover all the companies that are owned by shareholders in Ghana, a multiple case study approach which covers a significant number of companies were adopted by the researchers. These companies were drawn from mining, beverage; breweries and filtered water industries. The population of the study covers a wide range of professionals and this includes account officers, personal secretaries, managers, computer operators, complaint officers, customer relation officers, production workers, heads of department, human resource managers, internees, information technology engineers, information technology officers, corporate lawyers, mechanics, corporate medical doctors, marketing officers and public relation officers. The purpose of targeting these categories of employees was to make generalization of the research findings easier.

3.1. Sampling Techniques

The researchers adopted a multi-stage sampling technique for the study. First different organizations were conveniently selected. At the second stage, the population of these organizations amounting to 3,285 was divided into two strata namely organizations (Study 1) that spent 10% or more of their total annual budget on staff training and those (Study 2) that spent less than 10% of their total annual budget training their staff. The researchers decided to choose 10% because from the literature of Taylor and Bogdan (1984) any serious organization that want to develop its human capital should not spend less than 10% of its annual budget on employee training. In the third stage, the researchers selected a total of 620 employees out of 3,285 drawn from these organizations using convenience sampling. The data collection instrument used was questionnaires which were distributed to the selected number of employees from study 1 and 2 but 580 questionnaires representing 93.5% response rate was recorded. The distribution of respondents for both Study 1 and 2 can be seen from table 1:

Table 1. *Distribution of respondents (Study 1 and 2).*

	Study 1	Study 2
Respondent type	≥10% annual budget on training	<10% annual budget on training
Total questionnaire distributed	290	330
No of responses (response rate)	280	300

For both study 1 and 2, the researchers used the same questions with the same scale to solicit responses from the respondents. Responses were coded as 5=strongly agree to 1=strongly disagree. Data from the questionnaires were analyzed using SPSS 16.0 version.

Regression analysis was also used to test if there is mediation among the independent and the dependent variables.

3.2. Definition of Variables as Used in the Study

In order for us to be clear about the definitions of different terms which will also be used throughout the study, the researchers looking at various literature defined the terms or variables used for the study. Organizations acquired knowledge refers to the theoretical or practical understanding of a subject. For example, an employee might have knowledge of ADDIE model used in instructional design. This does not mean the employee have skills in the application of the model when it comes to designing training programmes at the workplace. Organizations acquired Skills are the proficiencies developed through training or experience. For example using the ADDIE example, the employee must demonstrate skills in applying the ADDIE model when designing training programmes. Organizations acquired abilities are the competence to perform an observable behavior or a behavior that results in an observable product. Productivity is the average measure of the efficiency of production. Profitability is the ability of a business to earn profit or revenue exceeding total cost. Dividends refer to the payment made by organizations to its shareholders, usually as a distribution of profits. Shareholders wealth maximization is the process that increases the current net value of business or shareholder capital gains, with the objective of bringing in the highest possible return.

4. Results and Discussion

The main objective underlying the study is to assess the relationship between organizations' acquired knowledge, skills, abilities (SKAs) and shareholders wealth maximization with training investment serving as the mediating role. The researchers conducted normality test to check if the data is normally distributed with no extreme values and outliers in data set. The value of Skewness was 0.85 which is within -1 to +1. Talking about the value of Kurtosis test conducted, the study recorded 7.65, which shows normality in the data set.

The mean and standard deviation for each of the variables used for the study, revealed the following:

Table 2. *Descriptive statistics.*

Variables	Study 1: ≥10% annual budget Mean	Std. deviation	Study 2:<10% annual budget Mean	Std. Deviation
Organization acquired skills	3.5	0.82	3.5	0.82
Organization acquired knowledge	3.2	0.89	3.2	0.89
Organization acquired abilities	3.6	0.86	3.6	0.86
Productivity	3.6	0.77	3.6	0.77
Profitability	2.9	0.74	2.9	0.74
Dividends	2.8	0.84	2.8	0.84
Shareholders wealth	2.7	0.92	2.7	0.92

The above table shows the mean and standard deviation for each item for both studies. The mean values, as seen from table 2 indicates that profitability, dividends and shareholders wealth are lower than the average 3.0 for both studies. Looking at organization's acquired skills, knowledge and abilities as well as productivity, they are above the average of 3.0.

Correlation analysis was conducted based on the data retrieved from the questionnaires distributed to the respondents. Table 3 shows the kind of relationship that exists between the variables in both studies.

Table 3. *Correlation coefficient of study 1 (≥ 10% annual budget on training).*

	OAK	OAS	OAA	OTI	PDT	PRO	DVD	SHW
Organization acquired knowledge (OAK)	1	.488**	.197**	.186*	.115**	.030**	.135**	.124**
Organization acquire skills (OAS)	.488**	1	.126*	.057*	.184*	.039*	.348**	.166*
Organization acquired abilities (OAA)	.197**	.126*	1	.547**	.316**	-024**	.195**	.018*
Training investment (OTI)	.186**	.057*	.542**	1	.430**	.462**	.167*	.016*
Productivity (PDT)	.115**	.184*	.316**	.430**	1	.298**	.141*	.038*
Profitability (PRO)	.038**	.039*	-.024**	.462**	.298**	1	.334**	.112*
Dividends (DVD)	.135**	.348**	.195**	.167*	.141*	.334**	1	.176**
Shareholders wealth (SHW)	.124**	.166*	.018*	.016*	.038*	.112*	.176**	1

**. Correlation is Significant at 0.01 level (2 tailed)

*. Correlation is Significant at 0.05 level (2 tailed)

***Table 4.** Correlation coefficient of study 2 (< 10% annual budget on training).*

	OAK	OAS	OAA	O TI	PDT	PRO	DVD	SHW
Organization acquired knowledge (OAK)	1	.486**	.193**	.188*	.219**	.055**	.138**	.129**
Organization acquire skills (OAS)	.486**	1	.122*	.052*	.382*	.020*	.342**	.163*
Organization acquired abilities (OAA)	.193**	.122*	1	.542**	.391**	.410**	.193**	.010*
Training investment (OTI)	.188**	.052*	.542**	1	.410**	.455**	.153*	.010*
Productivity (PDT)	.219**	.382*	.391**	.410**	1	.291**	.132*	.133*
Profitability (PRO)	.133**	.020*	.410**	.455**	.291**	1	.324**	.110*
Dividends (DVD)	.138**	.342**	.193**	.153*	.132*	.324**	1	.171**
Shareholders wealth (SHW)	.129**	.163*	.010*	.010*	.133*	.110*	.171**	1

**. Correlation is Significant at 0.01 level (2 tailed)
*. Correlation is Significant at 0.05 level (2 tailed)

The Tables above (3 & 4) show the correlation analysis results for both study 1 and 2. Correlation analysis gives the relationship that exists among variables. If there is strong relationship among variables, one can interpret it as high correlation existing among those variables. Organization acquired knowledge, skills and abilities are positively correlated with organization's productivity ($r= .115^{**}$, $p<0.01$), ($r= .184^{*}$, $p<0.05$), ($r= .316^{**}$, $p<0.01$) respectively for study 1 and ($r= .219^{**}$, $p<0.01$), ($r= .382^{*}$, $p<0.05$), ($r= .391^{**}$, $p<0.01$) respectively for study 2. Hence, hypothesis1, 2 and 3: There is positive relationship between organizations acquired knowledge, skills, abilities and productivity had been proved. Literature also supports there is positive relation between those independent variables and productivity as can be witnessed in the literature provided by Cho et al (2006), Huang (2000) and Pine and Judith (1993)

Though there is positive relationship between the independent variables and productivity, both studies recorded a weak relationship existing among the variables. This means that taking the co-efficient of determination (r^2) into consideration; organizations acquired knowledge, skills and abilities only contribute 1.32%, 3.39%, 9.99% respectively to organizations productivity when it comes to study 1 whilst for study 2, it was 4.80%, 14.60%, 15.29% respectively. The above presentation shows that there are other variables that play significant role in determining the productivity of organizations. Employees may have all the required knowledge, skills and abilities but both intrinsic other than organizations training and extrinsic motivation is necessary for the application of these independent variables by employees. Organizations also need to provide all the necessary logistics as well as conducive environment for employees to apply these independent variables. If these are missing, application becomes difficult and hardly will it have significant contribution in terms of improvement in work of the employee.

The relationship between organizations acquired knowledge, skills, abilities and profitability, shows a positive correlation between the independent variables and the dependent variable except the relationship between organizations acquired abilities and profitability which recorded negative relationship for study 1 as can be witnessed in Table 3 ($r= .030^{**}$, $p<0.01$), ($r= .039^{*}$, $p<0.05$), ($r= -.024^{**}$, $p<0.01$) respectively. For Table 4, the relationship between all the independent variables and the dependent variable recorded positive relationship ($r= .055^{**}$, $p<0.01$), ($r= .020^{*}$, $p<0.05$), ($r= .410^{**}$, $p<0.01$) respectively for study 2. From this, one can say that hypothesis 4 and 5: There is positive relationship between organizations acquired knowledge and skills had been proven. For hypothesis 6, whilst it holds in study 2, it was not proven in study 1. The above presentation tells us that though organizations in study 1 spend 10% or more of its annual budget on employees training, the relationship between organizations acquired abilities and profitability is negative as opposed to study 2. Literature from Chapman (1993) and Gelade and Ivery (2003) support the assertion that it is not the quantum of money that organizations spend on its training programme that will increase its profit but several factors such as the ability to control or minimize cost in all areas of the organization will go a long way to determine the profitability of an organization. From this literature, it means that though organizations in study 1 might spend more on training as compared to organizations in study 2, the ability of organizations in study 2 to develop a cost conscious culture in their organization will help boost their profits rather than relying mainly on training as a means to increase profits.

The relationship between the independent variables, organizations acquired knowledge, skills, abilities and the dependent variable (dividends) recorded positive relationships as can be witnessed in table 3 for study 1 ($r= .135^{**}$, $p<0.01$), ($r= .348^{**}$, $p<0.01$), ($r= .195^{**}$, $p<0.01$) and table 4 for study 2 ($r= .138^{**}$, $p<0.01$), ($r= .342^{**}$, $p<0.01$), ($r= .193^{**}$, $p<0.01$). The same situation applies to the relationship between the independent variables and shareholders wealth for both studies as can be witnessed in tables 3 and 4. The above presentation proves the hypotheses 7, 8 and 9 that there are positive relationships between organizations acquired knowledge, skills and abilities respectively and dividends declared to shareholders. Hypotheses 10, 11 and 12 was also proven that there is positive relationship between organizations acquired knowledge, skills, abilities respectively and shareholders wealth maximization. The literature from Ahmad & Schroeder (2003); Fey, Bjórkman and Pavlovskaya (2000); Garcia (2005) and Khatri (2000) support hypotheses 7, 8, 9, 10, 11 and 12 that there is positive relationship between the independent variables (organizations acquired knowledge, skills and abilities) and the dependent variables (dividends; shareholders wealth). Though these authors' support that such relationship exists among the variables, Ahmad & Schroeder (2003) and Garcia (2005) were of the view that an organization cannot claim strong relationship among those variables and as such dividends attributed to equity shareholders does not depend significantly on how much the organization spend on its training. Their argument is based on the fact that an organization can spend huge sums of money to train their employees but the dividends that the organization will declare does not depend on how much was invested in employees by means of training. To them training can be used to improve the skills and knowledge of employees for profitability of the organization to be improved but the dividends declared attributable to equity shareholders will depend on a number of factors such as the organization's dividend policy and availability of cash. For instance, an organization's training can be successful for profitability to be improved but if majority of the organization's sales are on credit basis, it may lack cash for dividends to be declared and paid to equity shareholders for their wealth to be maximized. It therefore sounds good idea for companies to regulate how much they spend on their training investment since it is not a significant contributor to declaring huge dividends to equity shareholders for their wealth to be maximized.

Testing for Mediation using Regression

Mediation is a hypothesized causal chain in which one variable affects a second variable that, in turn, affects a third variable. The intervening variable, assuming 'M', is the mediator. It "mediates" the relationship between a predictor, X, and an outcome as can be represented in figure 2 below:

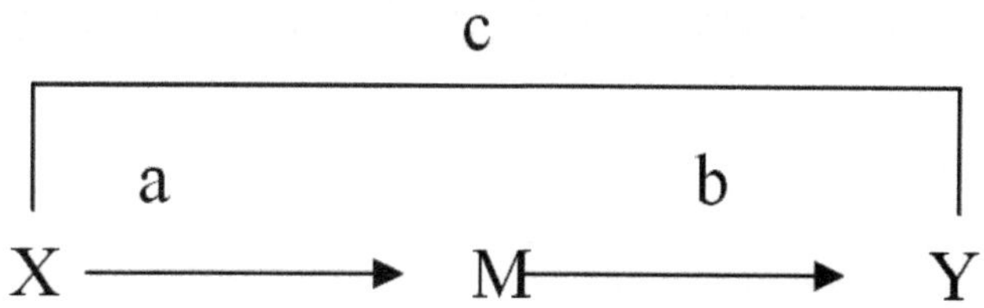

Figure 2. *Proposed Conceptual Model of three chain affecting variables.*

In figure 2, path 'a' and 'b' are direct effect. A meditational effect in which 'X', the independent variable leads to Y, the dependent variable through 'M' the mediator variable is called indirect effect. It is obvious that without identification of an indirect effect, mediation is incomplete.

According to Baron and Kenny (1986), a four step approach where several regressions have to be run and significance of regression co-efficient determined at each step is required for mediation testing to be complete. The mediation test conducted for the study using the approach of Baron and Kenney (1986) produced the following results as can be seen in Table 5:

Table 5. *Regression Models.*

	Study	R Square	Adjusted R Square	F
Simple Regression, I.V predicting D.V for path c only				
PDT=$\alpha + \beta_1\,OAK + \beta_2\,OAS + \beta_3\,OAA +$	1	.178	.166	13.31
	2	.175	.180	13.32
PRO=$\alpha + \beta_1\,OAK + \beta_2\,OAS + \beta_3\,OAA +$	1	.129	.116	9.25
	2	.128	.117	10.24
DVD=$\alpha + \beta_1\,OAK + \beta_2\,OAS + \beta_3\,OAA +$	1	.032	.015	2.06
	2	.033	.014	3.12
SHW=$\alpha + \beta_1\,OAK + \beta_2\,OAS + \beta_3\,OAA +$	1	.052	.036	3.37
	2	.054	.037	4.46
Simple regression analysis with all I.V predicting mediator variable for identification of path a:				
OTI= $\alpha + \beta_1\,OAK +$	1	.020	.017	5.21
	2	.021	.018	6.20
OTI= $\alpha + \beta_1\,OAS +$	1	.003	.001	.656
	2	.005	.002	.660
OTI= $\alpha + \beta_1\,OAA +$	1	.505	.214	69.12
	2	.503	.215	70.14
Simple Regression Analyses with mediator variable predicting D.V for identification the significance of path b:				
PDT= $\alpha + \beta_1\,OTI +$	1	.535	.160	47.80
	2	.544	.162	48.90
PRO= $\alpha + \beta_1\,OTI +$	1	.026	.023	6.95
	2	.027	.024	6.96
DVD= $\alpha + \beta_1\,OTI +$	1	.012	.041	.001
	2	.021	.042	.002
SHW= $\alpha + \beta_1\,OTI +$	1	.006	.001	1.34
	2	.004	.001	1.33
Multiple Regression Analyses with I.V and mediator, predicting D.V in order to identify significance of path c`:				
PDT=$\alpha + \beta_1\,OAK + \beta_2\,OAS + \beta_3\,OAA + \beta_4\,OTI +$	1	.240	.223	15.46
	2	.242	.224	15.45
PRO=$\alpha + \beta_1\,OAK + \beta_2\,OAS + \beta_3\,OAA + \beta_4\,OTI +$	1	.142	.125	8.09
	2	.144	.123	8.11
DVD=$\alpha + \beta_1\,OAK + \beta_2\,OAS + \beta_3\,OAA + \beta_4\,OTI +$	1	.023	.011	1.67
	2	.013	.011	1.68
SHW=$\alpha + \beta_1\,OAK + \beta_2\,OAS + \beta_3\,OAA + \beta_4\,OTI +$	1	.054	.035	2.79
	2	.055	.036	2.80

A summary of mediation test from table 5 indicates that all independent variables (organizations acquired knowledge, skills, and abilities) have significant indirect effect with dependent variables (productivity, profitability, dividends, shareholders wealth) at path 'a'. Looking at path 'b', one can see that all the dependent variables have indirect effect with the mediator variable. Lastly, all the independent and moderator variable significantly predict dependent variable at path c.

The above presentation from that table indicates that in effect, there is full direct and partial indirect mediation existing among the study variables.

5. Theoretical and Empirical Contributions

The study has looked into the relationship between organizations acquired knowledge, skills, abilities and productivity, profitability, dividends and shareholders wealth. Theoretical contributions claim that if organizations are to improve on productivity, they need to invest in their human capital as that is the only way by which employees knowledge can be enhanced to render better service or produce quality products (Krueger & Rouse, 1998), Katou & Budhwar (2007), Ghebregiorgis & Karsten (2007). When employees acquire the necessary knowledge, it also helps them to develop the needed skills which bring the ability to perform. To the writers especially Ghebregiorgis & Karsten (2007), 'ability to perform' results in increase in productivity which is strongly correlated with increase in profit and hence high dividends and shareholders wealth maximized. The current study does not agree entirely with the literature as increasing productivity cannot be claimed to have strong correlation with profit, dividends and shareholders wealth. These variables are determined by several factors which an organization's ability to develop a conscious culture and a low cost structure play a key role rather than organizations investment in training to enhance employees' knowledge, skills and abilities.

6. Conclusions

On the whole, the study provides a new theoretical direction towards understanding that, if an organization's training investment achieves it desired objective of improving employees' knowledge, skills and abilities, it should correlate positively with shareholders wealth. It also revealed experiential backing of positive outcomes of a well planned and executed organization's training investment as a mediator and this is supported by hypotheses 13, 14, 15 and 16.

7. Limitation and Recommendations for Future Research

Convenience sampling technique which is a non probability sampling type was used and based on that the results of the study cannot be generalized to the whole population since not all members in the population had equal chance to be selected for the study. Secondly, data was collected with the use of only the questionnaire technique. Combining other techniques such as focus group or interview might have enriched the results.

Again, the study only looked at three independent variables (knowledge, skills, abilities) and its relationship with shareholders wealth. This means that there are other variables that play key role in the determination of shareholders wealth based on the weak positive correlation results and as such future research should looked into these other variables and its role in determining shareholders wealth.

Lastly, the researchers could not do higher statistical analysis for the mediation test and it is believed that future research should consider higher statistical analysis such as the use of structural equation modeling to look at the mediation role training investment play between the independent and the dependent variables.

Competing Interest

The authors declare that they have no competing interests.

Authors' Contribution

Dr. Gabriel Dwomoh identified the problem and consulted the two other authors for a paper to be written on that. He assisted in the design of questionnaires as well as the general write up of the paper. Mr. Kofi Kwarteng and Mr. Williams Kwasi Boachie did the data entry and helped in the analysis of the data with the use of SPSS 16.0.

References

[1] Ahmad, S., & Schroeder, R. G. (2003). The impact of human resource management practices on operational performance, Journal of Operational Management, 21(1)

[2] Alan, Gillies (2009). '5 Reasons to start training your staff', Ezine Articles

[3] ASTD (2010). 'Training: Your investment in people development and retention', Quoted by: Heathfield (2012)

[4] Barney, J. (2005). 'Firm resources and sustained competitive advantage', *Journal of Management,* vol. 17(1)

[5] Baron, R. M and Kenny, D. A (1986). The moderator-mediator variable distinction in social psychological research: Conceptual, strategic and statistical considerations, *Journal of Personality and Social Psychology,* 51(6)

[6] Bateman, Thomas S. and Snell, Scott (2000). Management: Building Competitive Advantage, 3rd ed., New York, McGraw-Hill

[7] Beach, Dales S. (2004). Management of People at Work, 5th ed., New York, Macmillan Publishing Company

[8] Bottomley, Michael H. (2000). Personnel Management, London, Pitman Publishing

[9] Chapman, P.G. (1993). The economics of training, Exeter, UK: BPCC Whearons Ltd

[10] Cho et al (2006). Measuring the impact of human resource management practices on hospitality firms' performances, International Journal of Hospitality Management, 25(2)

[11] Cole, G.A (1996). Management: Theory and Practice, 5th ed., London, DP Publishing

[12] Crane, Donald P (2002). The Management of Human Resources, 3rd ed., Massachusetts, Kent Publishing

[13] Devanna et al (2005). Human Resource Management, 2nd ed., London, Pitman Publishing

[14] Gall et al (2002). Human Resource Management, 4th ed., London, Thompson Learning

[15] García, M. (2005). Training and business performance: The Spanish case. International Journal of Human Resource Management, 16(9)

[16] Gelade, G.A., & Ivery, M. (2003). The impact of human resource management and work climate on organizational performance, Personnel Psychology, 56(3)

[17] Ghebregiorgis, F., & Karsten, L. (2007). Human resource management and performance in a developing country, International Journal of Human Resource Management, 18(2)

[18] Grobler et al (2006). Human Resource Management in South Africa, 3rd ed., London, Thompson Learning

[19] Guest, D E (2009). Current Trends in Human Resource Management in Europe, London, Kogan Page

[20] Howe, Sally (2004). Essential Elements of Human Resource Management, London, DP Publishing

[21] Huang, T. (2000). Are HR practices of effective firms distinctly different from those of poorly performing ones. International Journal of Human Resource Management, 11(2),

[22] Huselid Mark A. (1995). 'The impact of human resource management practices on turnover, productivity, and corporate financial performance', *Academy of Management Journal,* Vol.3 (1)

[23] Katou, A., & Budhwar, P. (2007). The effect of HRM policies on organizational performance in Greek manufacturing firms, Thunderbird International Business Review, 49(1)

[24] Khatri, N. (2000). Managing human resources for competitive advantage, International Journal of Human Resource Management, 11(2)

[25] Krueger, A., & C, Rouse. (1998). The impact of workplace education on earnings, turnover and job performance. Journal of Labor Economics, 16(11)

[26] Nickel et al (2002). Introduction to Human Resource Management, USA, Granta

[27] Pine, J., & Judith, C.T. (1993), ROI of soft-skills training. Training

[28] Pratt, K.J and Bennet, S.E (2001). Elements of Personnel Management, 2nd ed., London, Chapman and Hall

[29] Taylor, S.J. and Bogdan R (1984). Introduction to qualitative research methods: The search for meanings, John Wiley, New York

[30] Werner, Jon M and DeSimone, Randy L (2009). Human Resource Development, Mason, South-Western Cengage Learning

[31] Wright, V and Taylor A (2004). The Handbook of Performance Management, London, Institute of Personnel Management

[32] World Bank (1991). 'Vocational and Technical Education and Training', Discussion Paper, Population and Human Resource Development, Washington D.C.

16

Prospect of Private-Public Partnership in Tourism of Bangladesh

Nymatul Jannat Nipa[1,*], Jakia Sultana[1], Md.Habibur Rahman[2]

[1]Department of Management Information Systems, Faculty of Business Administration, University of Dhaka, Dhaka, Bangladesh
[2]Department of Management Studies, Faculty of Business Administration, University of Dhaka, Dhaka, Bangladesh

Email addresses:
nipa@du.ac.bd (N. Jannat Nipa), jakia@du.ac.bd (J. Sultana)

Abstract: Tourism sector is a potential sector for the economic growth of Bangladesh. This paper is prepared to find out the prospect of Private-public-partnership (PPP) for economic growth in tourism sector in Bangladesh. The relationship between tourism industry of Bangladesh and its contribution to economic growth are analyzed to strengthen the probability of this private-public partnership. The market for tourism industry is identified through SCP (Structure, conduct, performance) framework and prospect of creating such market though PPP for greater revenue of the private sector which are showed in this article. Tourism is playing very diverse role in many developing countries and prospect of this industry in Bangladesh is very high. The objective of the paper is to present the recent trends of earning from tourism, tourist arrivals and identifications of barriers of tourism industry in Bangladesh. Further, government's different projects regarding tourism sector development are considered to see the greater prospect of profit from private sector which will contribute to economic growth of Bangladesh.

Keywords: Tourism, Economic Growth, Private Public Partnership (PPP), Tourism Market, SCP Framework, Bangladesh

1. Introduction

People move one place to another on their vacation. They search for natural beauty which can keep their mind calm and make their time wonderful. Tourism industry blooms on the people's necessity of moving across inside and outside of the country. Now days, Tourism industry is expanding and playing contribution to GDP growth as well as economic development of the country. Globalization accelerates this rapid expansion of tourism industry across the world. Recently, it has become one the promising sectors for revenue generation of a nation. European Commission communication on PPPs highlights "public sector infrastructure investment is an important means of maintaining economic activity". Greater investments in infrastructural development can ensure improved standard of living of the population of a nation and generation of higher revenue from this sector. (UNWTO, 2010) Worldwide tourism contribution to GDP is about 5% and 6% to 7% contribution to employment generation. Tourism is going to be the key economic sector for the developing countries like Bangladesh. Coastal areas, natural beauty and cultural diversity are the main attractions of tourists. Tourism creates employment opportunities through direct employment, indirect placement and induced retirement. Tourism provides great opportunity of competitive labor cost advantage for developing countries (Bangladesh) than those of technology-oriented industries which demand knowledgeable workers. Abraham Maslow's hierarchy theory of motivation was one the most applied in the tourism literature. Maslow's model base consists of Psychological needs followed by higher level of psychological and self-actualization needs. Despite that tourism industry in Bangladesh is not so dominating to contribute economic growth of the country. Tourism has been known as potential contributor in economic sector based on long experience of many countries that sustain and improve the national economy through tourism industry (Winckler, 2008). Bangladesh is place of natural beauty. Bangladesh is listed as the "best value destination" by lonely planet in 2011. Government of Bangladesh should play significant role in infrastructural development to boast up tourism sector through public-private-partnership (P3). P3 is a contractual agreement between private and public (govt.) entity for sharing skills and assets for delivering services and facilities to general public. This strategy will provide the opportunity to pay clear attention to tourism sector development. Ultimately, this will have positive impact to gross domestic production through improving variables of macroeconomic factors of the country.

PPPs can be used in financial, developmental, efficiency, ideological and political reasons (IOB, 2013).

Financial reasons (risk diversification): P3 can be implemented as the government doesn't have enough resources to execute a project alone. Through PPP government and public sector can diversify Risk involve infrastructure development and implementation.

Development reasons: Environmental sustainability is one of the millennium development goal. P3 can generate a friendly business environment.

Efficiency reasons: With the participation of both public and private entity higher efficiency can be ensured in all aspects of tourism industry.

Ideological/political reasons: The changes in political environment means changes in policy and projects in Bangladesh. But, when it is in P3, the smooth performance and development will be ensued. For political reasons, government of Bangladesh may patronize economic liberalization and less state interventions. There are different types of PPP model: (Ayodele, 2011)

Build, Operate, Transfer (BOT): The private investor's challenge of construction risk, operating risk and social risk create obstacles to make profit. Under this model, the private entity plays role as a developer and financier who will build and own the property with the agreement that the client will possess the property in the future.

Design, Build, Finance, and Own (DFBO): It is a Public Finance Initiative (PFI) in which a private sector firm conceived a development idea, design, construct it, operate it and own in perpetuity.

Design, Build, finance, Operate and Transfer (DBFOT): in P3 model, the private investor is charged with the responsibility to design a project, build it, finance it and operate within an agreed period of time, after specific period transfer ownership title and operations to the government. The Gulisthan- Jatrabari fly over is built under this contract.

Rehabilitate, Operate and Transfer (ROT): P3 is an agreement to rehabilitate public infrastructure, operate it for an agreed period of time and transfer ownership to government at the expiration of the contract.

Joint Development Agreement (JDA): P3 encourages the private and public sector to come together and sponsor the development of a project from scratch. At completion, both parties maintain the stakes in the management and running of the venture.

Operation and Maintenance (OM): In P3, the operation and maintenance function of the project remain at private hand but ownership and management remains with the government.

Management/Lease Contract: Management contract and lease contracts involve a private firm taking over the management and control of a public enterprise for a given period of time but the facility to be owned by the public sector. The public sector may retain the responsibility of financing the investments in fixed assets. In the case of management contracts, the public sector also finances working capital. In this plan, it is 100% Public sector owned.

Outsourcing: In P3 government outsources some supporting services to the private sector such as billing, postage, stationary supplies, metering, transport, or cleaning.

Greenfield projects: Under Greenfield project a private organization or a public-private joint venture develops and executes a new facility for project contract period. The facility may return to the government at the end of the contract period or may remain under private ownership.

Divestiture: Under P3 model, Private entity may take over Government entity and operate profitably. Bangladesh Biman has taken over by private entity and it is operating well now.

Concession: The private entity needs not to be financer in concession. Government will provide funds and private entity will execute construction and maintenance activities for the project.

1.1. Objective of the Study

The main objective of the paper is to identify the contribution of tourism industry in the economic growth of Bangladesh after independent and then assess the possibility of PPP in tourism for infrastructural development of tourism industry to generate substantial revenue for the economy. Others objectives of this study are as follows-

- To find out the relationship between employment generation and revenue growth of tourism, and then create opportunities of employment for the huge unemployed people of Bangladesh.
- To create tourism facilities in international standard and ensure proper maintenance in Bangladesh through public-private-partnership has got priority in the paper, which identify the role of public-private partnership in different infrastructural development of the country and prospect of such public-private-partnership to tourism industry's development will be anticipated on the basis of the success rate PPP in Bangladesh.
- To anticipate the possibility of creating oligopolistic market for tourism industry through PPP and ensure maximum outcome from tourism industry.

1.2. Potential Contributions to Knowledge

This paper is papered to contribute to the field of "Macroeconomics" specially the contribution of "service sector (Tourism) of developing countries to GDP growth by:

- Developing a framework about the relationship of tourism and Creation of employment opportunities through PPP and then GDP Growth of the countries.
- To validate the assumptions of Tourism and GDP growth through PPP by using cause and effect relationship approach which may not be used previously.

1.3. Limitation of the Study

There are so many limitations of the study conducted. The study is totally based on projection. As Bangladesh did not implement any PPP project to provide support and develop infrastructure of tourism industry. So, we don't have any empirical data to anticipate that it will be successful if implemented. The interest of private sector under PPP proposal is not considered to conduct the study. Though the initiatives from both government and private sectors are taken into consideration but how those initiatives would be implemented remain unearth. Different natural and social constraints are not considered in the PPP implementation process in case of tourism sector development. Projection on the arrival of tourist is based on historical analysis but reliability of receipts from that tourist is uncertain. The natural calamity of Bangladesh is not considered which is relevant in both south and north region of the country. The political turmoil of the country is not considered which is uncertain in Bangladesh.

2. Literature Review

Tourism is an important and dynamic sector for the world economy and for developing country like Bangladesh (Chowdhury, Fahim, & Dooty, 2013). For many developing and under developed country in the world tourism has emerged as a major income driving industry. As a promising alternative tourism sector along with the export sector has a positive effect on economy like employment generation, impacts on the expansion of linked industries, and poverty alleviation (Khondker & Ahsan, 2015). Any initiative by government and tourism authority has a positive impact on tourism and the arrivals o the tourist (Karambakuwa, et al., 2011).

There is a relationship between tourism and economic growth. The research findings on tourism and economic growth may be from tourism-led economic Growth, Economic-driven tourism growth, two-way casual relationship or uncommon no relationship between tourism and economic growth. By research it is identified that tourism led-economic growth in Spain (Balaguer & Cantavella-Jorda, 2002). The casual relationship is found between GDP growth and tourist arrivals in Taiwan (Kim, Chen, & S.Jang, 2006). In Turkey there is also found a relationship between tourism and economic development (Katircioglu, 2009). A total amount receipt is the factor in determining tourism and GDP growth. Huge amount is not factor in tourism. Generally, it is assumed that export growth led to economic growth of the country. Export-led growth hypothesis affirmed the contribution of export on economic development. Some researchers focused on non-trade goods tourism and economic growth tourism and trade, like (Balaguer & Cantavella-Jorda, 2002), (Dritsakis & Nikolas, 2004), (R.Durbarry, 2004), (Belloumi, 2010), (Katircioglu, 2009). Tourism industry of Bangladesh can contribute to achieve the vision of Bangladesh for 2021, by investing short, mid and long term projects with sufficient budgetary allocation (Parveen, 2013).

Tourism development is a win-win strategy as it provides the opportunity of jobs creation, infrastructural development and sustainability of the country (Baisakalova, 2009). Improving business environment, eliminating bottlenecks like visa obtaining procedures, incentives for innovations and knowledge for development can lead to the growth of inbound and domestic tourism. Investments in physical and human resources receipts from the tourism sector contribute to both current level of GDP and Economic Growth of Sub-Arabian African Countries (Fayissa, Nsiah, & Tadasse, 2007). This finding indicates that PPP can lead to economic development through tourism sectors development. Public properties and continuity in governance can be ensured by providing proper training to the stakeholder in the area of PPP and domesticating established law (Oluwasanmi, 2014). By giving priority to PPP Eco-Tourism can also be benefited (Uddin, 2013).

Locations and price of services in tourism have positive influence on Tourism industry for Bangladesh (ali & mohsin, 2008). Authors mentioned that synergy between tourism marketing plan and its implementation process can lead to tourism sector as important constituents of economic development. Tourism is one the fastest growing economic industries in the world include so many SME which shows potentiality to be successful in the ever changing and competitive business environment (Yilmaz, 2008). Public private partnership can introduce a strategy to get competitive advantage in this environment. Tourism promotes well being of tourists as healthcare tourism that relates to travel and tourism (Leea & Changb, 2008). There is a strong relation between tourists' succors to employment generation and economic development (Deegan, Moloney, & Tourism, 2005). Appropriate policy and regulations with public private partnership can show the path of economic development in the coming years. Development of tourism industry results in the benefit of poor people. So acceleration of economic growth, employment generation and poverty reduction come from tourism industry development (as tourism is labor intensive) (ProPoorTourism). ECM approach discovered two way relationships between receipts from tourism and GDP. Tourism is a macroeconomic variable which will raise the Goss Domestic Product (Ali & Parvin, 2010). There is a potential impact of tourism in generating employment, accelerating growth and adding revenue to government (Sinclair & Stabler, 1997). International tourism is a potential strategic agent of economic development (Stabler, 2002). So investment in tourism, can be considered as an alternative to exports, provides foreign remittance facilities to a nation. (Cohen & McKinnon, 1964) Both government and private sectors conduct investment in capital goods to provide services to tourists, to make tourism attractive that ultimately ensures countries growth. International tourism generates extra earning facilities to the nation by increasing competition among service providers and different tourist locations (Krueger, 1980). By proper collaboration and cooperation between government and private units the success of PPP project can be ensured (Khan & Ojha, 2015). Market structure and perfect competition in economy brings economics of scale among local companies (HELPMAN & KRUGMAN, 1986) .Tourist can be attracted by making the information about the tourism sector available to the tourist (Nabi & Zaman, 2014).

3. Research Methodology

The study is primarily based on secondary data. The data is collected from different journals, magazines, newspapers, report of Bangladesh Parjaton Corporation. The trends of tourist's arrival and receipts from them are considered and analyzed to forecast about the contribution from tourism industry in the future in Bangladesh. The world most attractive tourist spots facilities are considered to provide such facilities in different tourist spots in Bangladesh through PPP. Trend analysis on different aspects regarding direct contribution to GDP, Total contribution to GDP, Investment and Employment etc is done using Statistical Tools of Microsoft Excel. Moreover, Standard Deviation, Skewnss, Correlation, F-Ratio, ZTEST, SRQ, TTEST, Intercept, ANOVA were done by using standard statistical technique. Different project, to facilitate tourists in terms of accommodation, has been undertaken under PPP is also considered to conduct study. Granger casualty test is done between direct contribution of tourism to GDP and Total contribution of Tourism to GDP and between Total contribution of Tourism to GDP and Purchase by tourism providers. This test is performed by using Box-cox transformation parameter 1, 1 seasonal period, "0" degree of seasonal and non-seasonal differencing and number of non-seasonal time lags in test 1. The vice-versa test is performed to provide greater strength of the test. Market structure for the growth of tourism industry is indentified in the study through SCP framework. Purpose of tourism of the people across the world is identified and prospect of Bangladesh to fulfill such purpose can be very high considering natural beauty and culture.

4. Scenario of Tourism in Bangladesh

4.1. Necessity of Public Private Partnership

Financing a project is one of the most important aspects of any infrastructural development. PPP has become one of powerful way of creating all the facilities in a project both service and manufacturing sector. Participation of government and private entity make a project strong in different way. Moreover under PPP risk can be effectively transferred to private sector and private sector can share some risk and transfer some to government.

Table 4.1. *Risk scenario in different entity*

Criteria	Risk Scenario			
	Public	Private	PPP	Transferred?
Development Risks				
Performance	Public	Private	Private	X
Interface	Public	Private	Private	X
Design Risks				
Scope	Public	Private	Shared	X
Errors and Omissions	Public	Private	Private	X
Interference/Coordination	Public	Private	Private	X
Life Cycle	Public	Private	Private	X
Construction Risks				
Performance	Private	Private	Private	
Schedule	Public	Private	Private	X
Cost Overruns	Public	Private	Private	X
Changes in Scope	Public	Private	Public	
Force Majeure	Shared	Private	Shared	
Financing Risks				
Schedule Slippage Additions	Public	Private	Private	X
Interest Rate Risk	Public	Private	Private	X
Interest Rate Risk	Public	Private	Private	
Supply Risk	Private	Private	Private	
Financing Risks	Public	Private	Private	X
Defects	Private	Private	Private	
Maintenance and Life Cycle Risks				
Maintenance Level	Public	Private	Private	X
Maintenance/Repair	Public	Private	Shared	X
Defective Components	Private	Private	Private	
Residual Value	Public	Private	Shared	X
Operations Risks				
Revenue	Public	Private	Shared	X
Service Level and Quality	Public	Private	Shared	X

P3's can provide necessary capital to finance different projects through maximizing innovations and efficiencies in private entity. In a survey in 2007 expressed two primary causes for PPP; cost reduction 86.7% and external financial pressures including 50.3% tax restrictions.P3 can deliver project faster than any other way within the budget limit. Due to pre-construction fundraising delays reduction the design and construction process is expedited. Tourism is a high value and large scale infrastructural project and for such projects using private funds for capital expenditure means P3 based project will ensure quick delivery just after completion of negotiations. PPP is seen as joint venture or collaborative enterprises occupying high level control and care from public sector avoiding negative perception involved in privatization or selling public property.

P3 can ensure total cost reduction and ensure maximum revenue for both private and public sector.P3 provides 7-10% cost saving for a project over the life of the project. One study found 24% cost reduction. Under P3 some costs are high but most of the costs are minimized than those of in public entity. Comparative picture of different cost structure in public and PPP run projects are depicted in figure below.

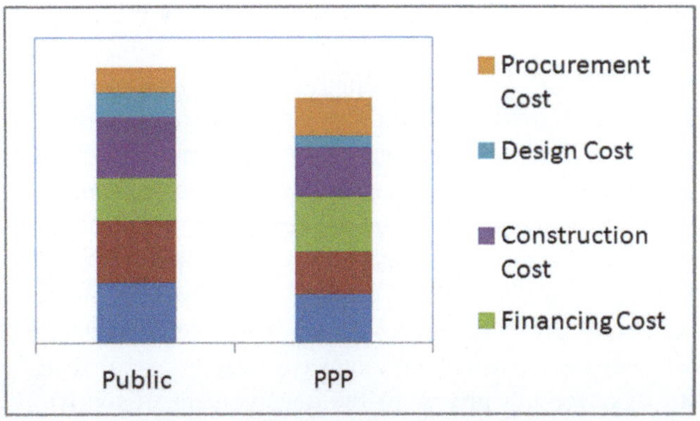

Figure 4.1. *Cost structures in Public and PPP.*

As revenue is shared by both Private and public entity so both private and public entity try to optimize benefits. In long term perspective PPP can provide benefits for both sectors.

When the Private entity will look for long term perspective, private sector will design project in the way to generate benefit in long term perspectives. Because, repair, maintenance and replacement cost will be considered by private sector for additional savings.

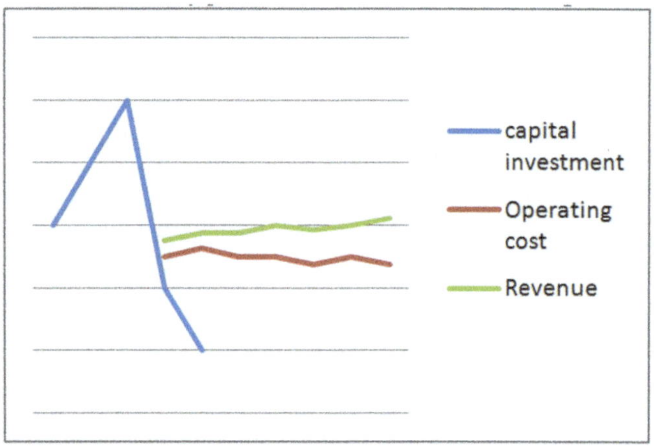

Figure 4.2. *Overview of Tourism Industry and Its Role to Economic Development*

Geographical locations and topography make Bangladesh one of the most promising nations in the world with immense tourism development prospects. The natural based and culture oriented tourism all over the beautiful Bangladesh provides Bangladesh the opportunity to be one the attractive tourist spots for both national and international tourists. Bangladesh Parjatan Corporation under the Ministry of Civil Aviation and Tourism was formed in September, 1972 to promote tourism sector development and attract tourists. Ever increasing number of tourist destinations across the world and increasing investments to this sector convert tourism as one of the key drivers of economic Growth by generating export revenue and creating employment opportunities. Over the past six decades tourism experienced continuous expansion and diversification to be one of the largest and ever-growing economic sectors with many emerging destinations of tourists despite economic melt-down in different parts of world. International tourist arrivals show uninterrupted growth from 25 million in 1950 to 278 million in 1980,528 million in 1995 and 1087 million in 2013.International Tourism Receipts increased from 1078 billion in 2012 to US$ 1159 billion 2013 worldwide which represents 7.51% increase. But this trend is not so satisfactory in Bangladesh though increasing. Economic benefits derived from tourism are often considered as one of the major sources to reduce dependency on foreign earnings and natural resources. Bangladesh tourist Industry is Referenced as one of the potential stakeholder to provide extensive economic benefits from preserved forests. In Bangladesh in-depth research and development is conduct in public and private level to discover the proper to the development of tourism industry. Bangladesh Parjaton corporation was formed in 1972 with some sound policy but implementation far way. Strategic partnership from both private and government level can open the door of infrastructural development of tourism industry. (Morshed, 2004)

Resource allocation for tourism industry is the most important issue. In Bangladesh most of the high quality hotels are located in Dhaka. But these hotels are used by tourists come for business or sports purpose. The rest part of the country is much neglected like Kuakata at potuakhali, shundharban at bagerhat etc. Not only accommodation facilities and other facilities are also absence in those areas. Due to lack of tourism facilities in September 2014 7, 32,105 Bangladeshis visited in India which is 14.79 % of total tourists' arrival in India in September 2014. But this 7, 32, 105 Bangladeshis should find their destinations in any part of the country, if facilities were so sound. Government of Bangladesh alone cannot provide all the facilities to tourism sector development. PPP can be the tool to clean obstacles involved in tourism industry of Bangladesh.

Tourism is one of the easiest ways to reduce the inequality of rich and poor in terms of earrings. Tourism is mainly a labor based industry. The people both male and female from root level involve in these sector that generate extra income through creating additional source of income for those people. Through tourism different economic units start operation. The regional development policies objectives can be achieved by sufficient capital investment from both public and private initiatives. Tourism is an eco-friendly industry which does not hamper environment but relates other components of the local economy. Tourism and development (Britton, 1982) and life-cycle model (Butler, 1980) are two approaches dominated tourism in dependency perspective in the period of tourism research. According to demand theory, Income of the consumer and price related to tourist's products service are the prime factors shaping tourists budget line. Income of origin country, price of destinations and price of alternatives destinations are the determinants of tourist arrivals (Song, Witt, & Li, 2009). Considering those factors, Bangladesh can be the most attractive location for tourist to visit. Comparative prices of tourist destinations and goods/services are low compared to the level income of tourists. Tourism is contributing to the economy of Bangladesh and it is increasing which is shown in research of (WTTC, 2014). This contribution is related with GDP growth and Employment generation. Though, historical data regarding employment generation from tourism sector shows negative trend. Bangladesh parjaton Corporation has made a positive projection of employment generation in future. Bangladesh is getting benefitted from direct, indirect and induced economic impact. Tourism is a composite product which involves different goods and services including transportation, accommodation, tour operators, travel attractions and retailing. Tourism is a worldwide market. It is not a single industry or single market. The maturity of tourism economics as a field of study comprises comprehensive bodies of knowledge and theoretical foundations in the context of tourism (Stabler, Papatheodorou, & Sinclair, 2010). So, Bangladesh can expand it tourism market across the world. As it has exclusive natural beauty that attracts people from all walks of life across the world. According to WTTC, in 2013 direct contribution tourism to Bangladesh GDP is Tk. 222.6 billion (2.1% of total

GDP). It is forecasted that GDP growth in 2014 would be 7.7% in 2014 and total contribution would be Tk. 239.8 billion which is 6.1% of total GDP. Between 2014 and 2024 the contribution would rise by 6.1%. In 2013, total contribution of travel and tourism to GDP was TK. 460.3 which is 4.4 % of total GDP. The forecasted growth of tourism to GDP in 2014 is 7.9%. The growth rate will continue at 6.5% per annum till 2024. In 2013 travel & tourism directly supported 1328500 jobs (1.8% of total employment). It is forecasted that in 2024 total contribution would be 180900 which is 1.9% of total employment. Indirectly travel and tourism contributed 2846000 jobs in 2013. It is predicted to grow by 4.2% in 2014 to 2014 to 2,965,000. Travel and tourism will contribute to 3,974,000 jobs in 2024, 4.2% of total employment.

From visitors export Bangladesh generated TK. 8.3 billion in 2013. It is expected to grow by 7.1% this year. By 2024, Bangladesh is expected to attract 611000 tourists contributing TK. 15.5 billion. Tourism of Bangladesh is mainly domestic based. Because in 2013, the contribution from domestic tourists was 97.8% of total spending and only 2.2% from foreign tourists. But this 2.2% spending did not come for the purpose of Recreation, holidays and leisure etc. but mostly from those tourists who came for business, professional purpose. The total contribution of travel and tourism is twice as its direct contribution. As tourism is labor intensive industry. Accommodation, transportations and many other services are related with tourism which increase employment opportunities and earning for those people involve with those professions.

"Internal" spending on tourism is the direct contribution of tourism to GDP as well as government spending on tourism services. Hotels, travel agencies, leisure and recreation services are directly related with tourism services. Direct contribution of tourism is consistent with output. It is calculated from total internal spending "netting out" expenditure made in purchase by different tourist sectors.

The indirect contribution tourism to GDP growth is very high. It includes government spending in infrastructural development, construction of hotels etc. For tourism marketing, promotion, administration, security and sanitation services, government made spending. The induced contribution of tourism of to GDP growth and job creation is related with such spending.

4.3. Major Attractions and Tourist Destinations in Bangladesh

Bangladesh is a place of natural beauty. World renowned tourist Ibne Botuta has termed Bangladesh as "Hell with full of wealth and prosperity". Culture and nature based tourism of Bangladesh has always been the attraction of tourists. But, it could not become the destinations of those tourists due to lack of facilities. The tourist destinations of Bangladesh are limited with Dhaka, Chittagong and Sylhet Divisions.

Table 4.2. *Tourist's destinations in Bangladesh.*

Destinations in Dhaka	Destinations in Chittagong	Destinations in Sylhet
Sonargaon: cultural capital	Port city Chittagong	Madhobkundo
Chota & bora Katra	Sitakunda	Tamabil, Jaflong
Mukti juddho Museum & Bangabandhu Memorial Meseum	Himchori, Moheshkhali & Inani Beach of Cox'Bazar	Hakaluki Haor, Tangoe Haor, lawachara, Madhabpur Lake
The Dhaka Zoo	Cox'bazar and Saint Martin	Gour Gobinda Fort
Lalbagh Forth	Chimbuk, Bandharban	
Bahadur Shah Park	Khagrachori	
Central Shahid Minar	Kaptai Lake	

There are so many tourists spots in Bangladesh basically Kuakatha Sea Beach at Patuakhali, World Largest Mangrove forest which is renowned all over the world, Shatgambuj Mosque in Bagerhat, In Rajshahi Division some attractive tourists spots are Paharpur at Noagoan, Mohasthangarh at Bogra, Rajbari, kantaji's temple, Ramsagor, swapnapuri at Dinajpu etc. These spots are world renowned but absence of tourism facilities create drawback to reach tourists in those places.

4.4. Tourism by Purpose

People travel for different reason from one country to another country. But the reason behind it is different. As most of facilities of life are available in most of the countries of the world so people travel basically for leisure, recreation and holidays. According World Tourism Organization (UNWTO) More than 50% people travel for leisure. These activities basically involve seeing natural beauty and knowing cultural diversity at the same time heritage also. Bangladesh is place of Beauty in world map, so tourism industries prospect is very sound in Bangladesh. Every year huge number of people comes to Bangladesh as religious tourists and gathers in Tongi. Those people can be attracting through infrastructural development all over the country. World heritage Sundhaban and "Daughter of Sea" Patuakhali can be the desired destinations. This is also a potential source to make them as actual tourist. People also come to Bangladesh for visiting Friends and Relatives (VFR) is a source to attract tourist. Bangladesh is a developing country; businessmen across the world come to Bangladesh to analyze the potentiality of business in Bangladesh. The share of different purpose of tourism depicts that 52% tourist travel for recreation and leisure purpose.

4.5. Market for Tourism Development

Every firm operates in different market that ultimately determines its output decisions, pricing behavior, creativity and innovation. Profitability, efficiency and growth of the firm dependent on that market structure. This market may be monopolistic, monopolistically competitive or oligopolistic etc. the SCP paradigm provides a framework to study tourism form a different market position. Market structure directly influences the performance of a firm (Davies, 1999) and (Pan, 2005). Franchising Strategy contributes to increase market concentration by hotel chains (Cunill & Forteza, 2010). Private sector or private organization can take this advantage to generate profit and expand business. Tourist usually expend in transportation, accommodation, food, recreation and treatment etc. that turn into the income of tourist industry. Those services can be provided most effectively by private industry with the strong regulations of government. PPP can help in this respect. According to SCP framework, oligopolistic market structure provides the highest opportunity for tourism to be successful. Though, Bangladesh is practicing open market policy, but very few private organizations are operating in this sector. Private-public partnership can motivate public sectors to join in PPP project. As, government intervention will be there so it will a lucrative opportunity to expand business in future. Because, PPP will create oligopolistic market for private sector due to have government involvement in this sector. Second component "C" conduct means pricing behavior. Under private-public- partnership, two projects are in preparation stage that will prove low hotel facilities. Some other projects are in development stage and some projects under approval stage by cabinet committee of Economic Affairs. Pricing effects on hotel industry is examined on the basis of hedonic pricing approach by (Abrate, Capriello, & Fraquelli, 2011). Innovative Investment and diversification can be helpful in tourism. Public-Private-Partnership can promote such environment in better way."P" of SCP framework means performance is measured by productivity and efficiency are important issue in tourism supply experiments. Inter-firm strategic interaction is important in tourism supply chains. In tourism, transportation, accommodation, treatment, recreation works together to generate revenue. One unit extra revenue of one industry turns into another extra revenue of other related industries. The game theoretical approach has examined the interaction among tourism supply members and their strategic options. Through private-public-partnership partnership such industry cluster can be formed.

Cost of production, supply of labor and competition-related policy concern are prevalent in tourism industry. Hotels, transpirations, accommodation and security etc. have got more attention than tourist in tourism industry. Knowledge based and resources based have got attention to create and utilize competitive advantage in tourism industry.

4.6. Different Project under PPP to Develop Tourism in Bangladesh

Bangladesh Parjatan Corporation under Ministry of Civil Aviation and Tourism has undertaken a project to construct a 5 star hotel in Cox's Bazar in the name of Development of Tourism resort and Entertainment village at Parjatan Holiday Complex under PPP basis. This project will provide multiple facilities and services. This project is in preparation stage with estimated cost $80 -200m. Bangladesh Parjatan Corporation will establish this hotel with participation of private sector due to lack of Fund. Bangladesh Railway under Ministry of Railway has undertaken a project to establish a 5 star hotel in the unused land of Bangladesh Railway at Zakir Hossen road, Chittagong. Total estimated capital requirement is $80-200m. Due to fund limitations, Bangladesh railway has decided to construct the hotel with PPP basis. This project is in development stage. Moreover, cabinet committee of Economic Affairs has already two projects for tourism sector development in the name of "Establishment of Sabrang Exclusive Tourism Zone" and "Establishment of Intl. Standard Tourism Complex at Existing Motel Upal Compound of BPC at Cox's Bazar". (Public, 2015)

5. Statistical Analysis and Discussion

To validate the assumption that investment in tourism will expedite economic growth of the country different statistical analysis are done. Granger casualty test shows relationship between spending in tourism and GDP growth. The direct, indirect and induced contribution of tourism to GDP growth is considered to calculate Total GDP. Dickey-Fuller Unit root test with stationary, explosive, intercept, without intercept, trend with intercept showed the relationship between investment and GDP growth. KPSS test with trend and level for Investment and GDP shows hypothetical relation. To strengthen the investment and GDP Growth relationship Von Neumann's test, Standard normal homogeneity test (SNHT), Buishand's test, Mann-Kendall trend test provides dependable findings. The analysis is conducted using 5% significance level. It indicates that there is a long-run relationship between tourism development and GDP. So, the prospect of PPP in tourism sector is high in this respect.

Granger causality test between spending in tourism and contribution to GDP:

Table 5.1. *Granger Causality Test.*

Granger Causality Test: Y = f(X)				
Model	**Res.DF**	**Diff. DF**	**F**	**p-value**
Complete model	1			
Reduced model	2	-1	0.0143934705877519	0.923986260234152
Granger Causality Test: X = f(Y)				
Model	Res.DF	Diff. DF	F	p-value

Granger Causality Test: Y = f(X)				
Model	**Res.DF**	**Diff. DF**	**F**	**p-value**
Complete model	1			
Reduced model	2	-1	289.821441298657	0.0373521939229046

Interpretation:

Ho: There is a Granger Causality between spending and GDP.

Ha: There is no Granger Causality between spending and GDP. As the computed p-value is greater than the significance level alpha=0.05, one cannot reject the null hypothesis H0. If the relation is built in revered way, the computed p-value is lower than the significance level alpha=0.05., so we can not reject the Null hypothesis Ho.

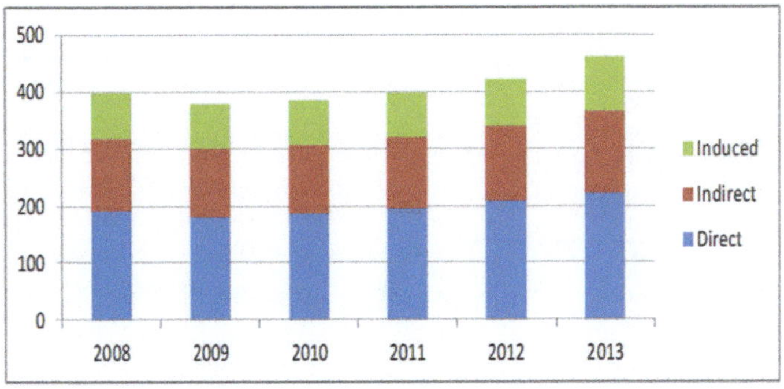

Figure 5.1. *Trend of total and direct contribution of tourism to GDP.*

Table 5.2. *Dickey-Fuller test (DF-investment).*

	Stationary	Explosive	Intercept	No intercept	Intercept with trend
Observed value	0.000	0.000	-0.452	3.999	-1.795
Critical Value	0.000	0.000	0.389	1.441	-0.120
P-value (one-tailed)	<0.0001	1.000	0.179	0.002	0.435
Alpha	0.05	0.05	0.05	0.05	0.05

Test Interpretation:

H0: There is a unit root for the series

Ha: There is no unit root for the series.

When the series is stationary, As the computed p-value is lower than the significance level alpha=0.05, one should reject the null hypothesis H0, and accept the alternative hypothesis Ha. The risk to reject the null hypothesis H0 while it is true is lower than 0.01%.

The series is explosive. As the computed p-value is greater than the significance level alpha=0.05, one cannot reject the null hypothesis H0. The risk to reject the null hypothesis H0 while it is true is 100.00%

In case of intercept, as the computed p-value is greater than the significance level alpha=0.05, one cannot reject the null hypothesis H0. The risk to reject the null hypothesis H0 while it is true is 17.95%.

In case of no intercept, as the computed p-value is lower than the significance level alpha=0.05, one should reject the null hypothesis H0, and accept the alternative hypothesis Ha. The risk to reject the null hypothesis H0 while it is true is lower than 0.25%.

In case of no intercept, as the computed p-value is greater than the significance level alpha=0.05, one cannot reject the null hypothesis H0. The risk to reject the null hypothesis H0 while it is true is 43.46%.

Table 5.3. *Dickey-Fuller test (DF-GDP).*

	Stationary	Explosive	Intercept	No intercept	Intercept with trend
Observed value	0.000	1.163	0.995	1.163	-1.623
Critical Value	0.000	0.000	0.389	1.441	-0.120
P-value (one-tailed)	<0.0001	1.000	0.019	0.076	0.370
Alpha	0.05	0.05	0.05	0.05	0.05

Test Interpretation:

H0: There is a unit root for the series

Ha: There is no unit root for the series.

When the series is stationary, as the computed p-value is lower than the significance level alpha=0.05, one should reject the null hypothesis H0, and accept the alternative hypothesis Ha. The risk to reject the null hypothesis H0 while it is true is lower than 0.01%.

The series is explosive. As the computed p-value is greater than the significance level alpha=0.05, one cannot reject the null hypothesis H0. The risk to reject the null hypothesis H0 while it is true is 100.00%

In case of intercept, as the computed p-value is greater than the significance level alpha=0.05, one cannot reject the null hypothesis H0. The risk to reject the null hypothesis H0 while it is true is 1.9%.

In case of without intercept, as the computed p-value is lower than the significance level alpha=0.05, one should reject the null hypothesis H0, and accept the alternative hypothesis Ha. The risk to reject the null hypothesis H0 while it is true is lower than 7.6%.

As the computed p-value is greater than the significance level alpha=0.05, one cannot reject the null hypothesis H0. The risk to reject the null hypothesis H0 while it is true is 37.04%.

Table5.4. *KPSS test ((Trend/level) / Lag: Short / Investment).*

	Trend	Level
Observed value	0.138	0.621
Critical Value	0.143	0.442
P-value (one-tailed)	0.070	< 0.0001
Alpha	0.05	0.05

Test Interpretation:

H0: The series is stationary.

Von Neumann's test:

Ha: The series is not stationary.

As the computed p-value is greater than the significance level alpha=0.05, one cannot reject the null hypothesis H0. The risk to reject the null hypothesis H0 while it is true is 7.01% Trend and 0.01% for level.

Table 5.5. *KPSS test ((Trend/level) / Lag: Short / GDP).*

	Trend	Level
Observed value	0.138	0.463
Critical Value	0.143	0.463
P-value (one-tailed)	0.016	0.038
Alpha	0.05	0.05

Test Interpretation:

H0: The series is stationary.

Ha: The series is not stationary.

As the computed p-value is greater than the significance level alpha=0.05, one cannot reject the null hypothesis H0. The risk to reject the null hypothesis H0 while it is true is 1.58% for Trend and 3.79% for Level.

Table 5.6. *Standard normal homogeneity test (SNHT).*

	GDP	Investment		GDP	Investment
	0.581		T0	3.850	4.209
N	0.012	0.272 0.0001	t	4	3
P-value(one-tailed)	0.05	0.05	p-value (Two-tailed)	< 0.0001	0.047
Alpha			alpha	0.05	0.05

For VON Neumann's Test the p-value has been computed using 10000 Monte Carlo simulations. 99% confidence interval on the p-value:

Test interpretation: GDP and Investment.

H0: Data are homogeneous

Ha: There is a date at which there is a change in the data.

As the computed p-value is lower than the significance level alpha=0.05, one should reject the null hypothesis H0, and accept the alternative hypothesis Ha. The risk to reject the null hypothesis H0 while it is true is lower than 1.12% for GDP and 0.01% for Investment.

For Standard normal homogeneity test (SNHT), the p-value has been computed using 10000 Monte Carlo simulations. 99% confidence interval on the p-value:

Buishand's test:

Test interpretation: GDP and Investment.

H0: Data are homogeneous

Ha: There is a date at which there is a change in the data.

For GDP, as the computed p-value is lower than the significance level alpha=0.05, one should reject the null hypothesis H0, and accept the alternative hypothesis Ha. The risk to reject the null hypothesis H0 while it is true is lower than 0.01%.

For Investment, as the computed p-value is lower than the significance level alpha=0.05, one should reject the null hypothesis H0, and accept the alternative hypothesis Ha. The null hypothesis H0 while it is true is lower than 4.67%.

Table 5.7. *Mann-Kendall trend test / Two-tailed test.*

	GDP	Investment		GDP	Investment
Q	2.482	2.753	Kendall's tau	0.733	1.000
T	3	3	S	11.000	3
P-value(two-tailed)	< 0.0001	0.061	p-value (Two-tailed)	0.201	0.003
Alpha	0.05	0.05	alpha	0.05	0.05

The p-value has been computed using 10000 Monte Carlo simulations. 99% confidence interval on the P-value:

Test interpretation: GDP and Investment

H0: Data are homogeneous,

Ha: There is a date at which there is a change in the data. As the computed p-value is lower than the significance level alpha=0.05, one should reject the null hypothesis H0, and accept the alternative hypothesis Ha. The risk to reject the null hypothesis H0 while it is true is lower than 0.01% for GDP and 6.1% for Investment.

Mann-Kendall trend test / Two-tailed test:

An approximation has been used to compute the p-value.

Test interpretation:

H0: There is no trend in the series.

Ha: There is a trend in the series. As the computed p-value is greater than the significance level alpha=0.05, one cannot reject the null hypothesis H0. The risk to reject the null hypothesis H0 while it is true is 20.12% for GDP and 0.3% For Investment.

6. Conclusion

This paper investigates the relationship of tourism and investment in Bangladesh by using historical data. The paper tries to find out the prospect of PPP in tourism sector of Bangladesh and Find different tourist spots which are still latent in real terms. PPP can open the door to develop those spots and contribute to the economy and strength the industry through cost reduction, maintenances, supporting facilities etc. A great deal of importance is given in the national budget of FY2014-2014 on Private-Public initiatives. Deficit Budget is the most alarming problem for infrastructural development of Bangladesh. The involvement of Private funds through PPP initiatives can open the door to overcome the constraint of sufficient fund. The total cost and revenue shared advantages in PPP can provide the opportunity to develop world largest mangrove forest Sundharban, Daughter of Sea patuakhali and convert them into the desired tourist destinations boat for inbound and outbound tourists. In 2013 tourism contributed 2.1% to total GDP of Bangladesh which is 5% higher than GDP of 2012. This initiative will harness both private and public sector "Know-How" and identify key policy to make PPP successful.

Appendix

Table 7.1. *Tourism In the world: Key Figures.*

GDP	Employment	Exports	% of Export
9% of direct, indirect and Induce impact	1 out of 11	US$1.4 trillion	6% of world export

Sources: UNWTO tourism Highlights 2014, Page-02 to 03.

Table 7.2. *Statistical analysis.*

	DirectGDP	TotalGDP	Investment	Totalemployment	Directemployment
Skewness	0.777208	0.81327	0.306947	2.056733	1.974064
Kurtosis	0.465869	0.686831	-1.38993	4.378017	3.97641
ANOVA	109.658	284.8	10.518	18499.34	2781.748
St.Deviation	10.47177	16.87602	3.243147	136.0123	52.74228
F-ratio	1.8	1.4289	3.4826	0.18467	0.46204

Table 7.3. *Descriptive analysis.*

Lag	Autocorrelation	Standard error	Lower bound (95%)	Upper bound (95%)	Partial autocorrelation	Standard error	Lower bound (95%)	Upper bound (95%)
0	1.000	0.000			1.000	0.000		
1	0.388	0.408	-0.800	0.800	0.388	0.408	-0.800	0.800
2	-0.075	0.466	-0.913	0.913	-0.265	0.408	-0.800	0.800
3	-0.343	0.468	-0.917	0.917	-0.258	0.408	-0.800	0.800
4	-0.366	0.508	-0.996	0.996	-0.178	0.408	-0.800	0.800
5	-0.104	0.550	-1.000	1.000	0.047	0.408	-0.800	0.800
6	0.000	0.554	-1.000	1.000	-0.154	0.408	-0.800	0.800

References

[1] Abrate, G., Capriello, A., & Fraquelli, G. (2011). When quality signals talk: Evidence from the Turin hotel industry. Tourism Management, 32, , 912-921.

[2] Ali, M. M., & Parvin, R. (2010). Strategic Management of Tourism sectorin Bangladesh to Rise Gross Domestic Product: an analysis. AIUB Bus Econ Business Paper Series .

[3] ali, P. m., & mohsin, c. s. (2008). Different aspects of tourism marketing straties with special preference to bangladesh: an analysis. Business review, A journal of Business administration.

[4] Ayodele, O. S. (2011). Public –Private Partnership: Will it Fix Infrastructure In Nigeria? Initiative for Public Policy Analysis Policy Paper .

[5] Baisakalova, A. (2009). Economy Diversification: Tourism Cluster Competitiveness and Sustainability. The Second International Conference organized by the Management Forum on "World Financial Crisis and Global Business Challenges" University of Dhaka .

[6] Balaguer, J., & Cantavella-Jorda, M. (2002). Tourism as a long-run economic growth factor: The Spanish case. Applied Economics, 34, , 877-884.

[7] Belloumi, M. (2010). The relationship between tourism receipts, real effective exchange rate and economic growth in Tunisia. International Journal of Tourism Research,12, , 550-560.

[8] Britton, S. (1982). The Political Economy of Tourism in the Third World. ,. Annals of Tourism Research, 9 , 331-358.

[9] Butler, R. (1980). The concept of a tourism area cycle of evolution: Implications fo rmanagement resources. The Canadian Geographer, 24(1), 5–16.

[10] Chowdhury, T., Fahim, S. T., & Dooty, E. N. (2013). Promoting Public Private Partnership for Development of Tourism Sector of Bangladesh: An Exploratory Study. European Journal of Business and Management, ISSN 2222-1905 (Paper) ISSN 2222-2839 (Online) Vol.5, No.32, .

[11] Cohen, B. I., & McKinnon, R. I. (1964). Foreign Exchange Constraints in Economic Development and Efficient Aid Allocation. ECONOMIC JOURNAL, Vol. 74 , 388-409.

[12] Cunill, O., & Forteza, C. M. (2010). The franchise contract in hotel chains: A study of hotel chain growth and market concentrations. Tourism Economics, 16(3), , 493-515.

[13] Davies, B. (1999). Industrial organization – The UK hotel sector. Annals of Tourism .

[14] Deegan, J., Moloney, R., & Tourism, I. W. (2005). Understanding the Economic Contribution of Tourism to Economic Development: The Case of Ireland West. National Centre for Tourism Policy Studies, .

[15] Dritsakis, & Nikolas. (2004). "Tourism as a Long-run Economic Growth Factor: An Empirical Investigation for Greece,". Tourism Economics, 10 (3) , 305-316.

[16] Fayissa, B., Nsiah, C., & Tadasse, B. (2007). The Impact of Tourism on Economic Growth and Development in Africa. Department of Economics and Finance Working Paper Series .

[17] HELPMAN, E., & KRUGMAN, P. R. (1986). Market Structure and Foreign Trade: Increasing Returns, Imperfect Competition, and the International Economy. Journal of Economic Literature, Vol. 24, No. 2 , 713-715.

[18] IOB. (2013). Public-Private Partnerships in developing countries -A systematic literature review. IOB Study, no. 378 .

[19] Karambakuwa, R. T., Shonhiwa, T., Murombo, L., Mauchi, F. N., R.Gopo, N., Denhere, W., et al. (2011). THE IMPACT OF ZIMBABWE TOURISM AUTHORITY INITIATIVES ON TOURIST ARRIVALS IN ZIMBAWE (2008 – 2009). Journal of Sustainable Development in Africa , Volume 13, No.6, .

[20] Katircioglu, S. T. (2009). Revisiting the tourism-led-growth hypothesis for Turkey using the bounds test and Johansen approach for cointegration. Tourism Management, 30, , 17-20.

[21] Khan, D. M., & Ojha, N. K. (2015). A Study of Public Private Partnership (PPP) with Special Reference to Infrastructures. Indian Journal of Applied Research, Managment, Volume : 5 | Issue : 1 .

[22] Khondker, B. H., & Ahsan, T. (2015). BACKGROUND PAPER ON TOURISM SECTOR.

[23] Kim, H. J., Chen, M., & S.Jang. (2006). Tourism expansion and economic development: The case of Taiwan. Tourism Management, 27, , 925-933.

[24] Krueger, A. O. (1980). Trade Policy as an Input to Development. The American Economic Review, Vol. 70, No. 2 , 288-292.

[25] Leea, C.-C., & Changb, C.-P. (2008). Tourism development and economic growth: A closer look at panels. Tourism Management, Volume 29, Issue 1 , Pages 180-192.

[26] Morshed, M. M. (2004). Bangladesh tourism vision 2020. Bangladesh Parjatan Corporation.

[27] Nabi, N., & Zaman, S. (2014). The Sources and Availability of Information for Tourists: A Study on Tourism Sector of Bangladesh. World Journal of Social Sciences Vol. 4. No. 1. , 154 – 166.

[28] Oluwasanmi, O. (2014). Public Private Partnership and Nigerian Economic Growth: Problems and prospects. International Journal of Business and Social Science Vol. 5, No. 11; .

[29] Pan, C. (2005). Market structure and profitability in the international tourist hotel industry. Tourism Management, 26, 845-850.

[30] Parveen, D. J. (2013). Current Status of Tourism Industry In Bangladesh: An Empirical Evaluation. Scientific Research Journal (SCIRJ), Volume 1, Issue 1, .

[31] ProPoorTourism. (n.d.). ProPoorTourism. Retrieved 06 16, 2015, from ProPoorTourism.info: http://www.propoortourism.info/

[32] Public, P. P. (2015). Public Private Partnership Office. Retrieved 06 16, 2015, from pppo.gov.bd: http://www.pppo.gov.bd/projects.php

[33] R.Durbarry. (2004). "Tourism and Economic Growth: The Case of Mauritius,". Tourism Economics, 10, (3) , 389-401.

[34] Sinclair, M. T., & Stabler, M. (1997). The Economics of Tourism. Routledge,.

[35] Song, H., Witt, S. F., & Li, G. (2009). The Advanced Econometrics of Tourism Demand. London: Routledge.

[36] Stabler, M. S. (2002). THE ECONOMICS OF TOURISM. Routledge .

[37] Stabler, M., Papatheodorou, A., & Sinclair, M. (2010). The Economics of Tourism (2nd ed.). Abingdon: Routledge.

[38] Uddin, A. K. (2013). Problem and Prospect of Ecotourism in Bangladesh. CSA Academic Publishing .

[39] UNWTO. (2010). UNWTO Tourism Highlights.

[40] Winckler, Y. M. (2008). The role of the tourism industry in transforming a reinter to a long-term viable economy: The case of Bahrain. Current Issues in Tourism, 11(3), , 237-267.

[41] WTTC, W. T. (2014). Economic Impact of Travel and Tourism. WTTC.

[42] Yilmaz, B. S. (2008). Competitive Advantage Strategies for SMES in Tourism Sector: A Case Study. MIBES .

17

Factors Affecting Information Technology Audit Quality

Yahya Hasas Yeghaneh[1], Mostafa Zangiabadi[2, *], Seyed Mostafa Dehghani Firozabadi[3]

[1]Scientific Group of Accounting, Department of Allameh Tabataba'i University, Tehran, Iran
[2]Faculty of Accounting, Allame Tabatabaee University, Tehran, Iran
[3]Faculty of Accounting, Islamic Azad University, Yazd, Iran

Email address:
Yahya_yeghaneh@yahoo.com (Y. H. Yeghaneh), m.zangiabadi229@gmail.com (M. Zangiabadi), dehghani_firozabadi20@yahoo.com (S. M. D. Firozabadi)

Abstract: Change and the growth of information technology, all aspects of human society have taken in the light of self. Human need, interest in using new technologies emerged as a dominant factor in their organizations and they will force to keep pace with the condition. Since the major factor in advances in information technology in the present world, is the need and necessity. This important, changed the methods and practices and have been transformed of paper-based systems to electronic information systems and software. Accounting and auditing profession, perhaps more than in other areas of financial knowledge have been disposable of Enjoyment and use of the facility is subject to the new environment. New environment recording and reporting of information, has created much effects in the efficiency and effectiveness of the auditing profession And the need to use information technology audit to be felt more than ever. Therefore, in this study, are followed to find the factors affecting on information technology audit quality. In order to, Standard questionnaire was used that test its validity before and also reliability 89% was measured. And results show that from the view of CPAs working in the audit institute and the audit organization, properly accountability of audit team and existence audit framework and process, business criteria and audit scope, auditability, planning and operations, access to resources, relationship with the entity and the business environment, affects IT audit quality.

Keywords: Audit, ITS Audit, Audit Quality

1. Introduction

The spread of information technology and the need for rapid access to detailed, relevant and timely, with minimum cost and maximum efficiency, Interest in using new technologies proposed as a dominant factor organizations and forcing them to keep pace with the condition. Need and necessity is main factor developments and technology in today's world, the need and necessity. This new wave and fast, have changed method of doing things, and the have been change from paper-based systems to electronic information systems and software. Accounting and auditing profession, perhaps more than other areas of financial knowledge, is exposed to enjoy resources of the new environment. New space for recording and reporting of information, many effects in efficiency and effectiveness of this practice has caused [34].

Thus, IT auditing, is one of the aspects of advances in technology in accounting and auditing, can be interpreted in two ways:

1. IT audit, that, The purpose of that , audit accounting information systems and other technologies that are used to collect accounting data as a manifestation of information technology.
2. IT audit, that can know to be used type of Audit software and use computer-based tools for auditing and auditors help. The second is to reduce Iran. Today, efforts to do this important work are in progress. It is hoped that this research addresses this issue, it's important to be able to solve and help this issue.

On the other hand, quality is determinant of audit function is a function of several factors such as: audit capabilities (including knowledge, experience, ability to adapt and technical efficiency) and professional performance (including independence, objectivity, professional care, conflict of interest and judgment). Structure of Audit quality is a multidimensional, but invisible, so it is very difficult to measure the quality, since many factors affect audit quality. The determination framework for identifying audit quality is the important issue [38].

Investigation Effect of audit quality of audit perspective

(supplier of services) is an important issue. In this study examines auditors' views on the impact of factors affecting IT audit quality, factors such as proper accountability audit team, the audit framework and procedures, business criteria and audit scope, auditability, planning and operations, access to resources, relationship with the entity and the business environment, as research independent variables and audit quality IT as a dependent variable to measure the effect of these factors on audit quality. The present study sought to appropriate and scientifically answer to the question, that, whether The factors expressed above, the influence of information technology audit quality or not?

2. The Theoretical Basis and Background of Research

2.1. Information Technology Audit

When auditing the desired computer environments, the overall objectives and scope of audit work does not change, but the audit procedures, the auditor may need to consider the use of computers and information technology, One of the basic definitions of computer audit, is Williamson's definition which according to that, of IT (Computer)audit, the proses of application any system based on of information technology in order to assist auditors in the process of planning, implementation, monitoring, and conducting audit procedures are completed [18]. The use of computer audit has great benefit such as improvement of quality and auditor's judgment, increasing efficiency and reducing cost of auditing and improving in a competitive situation. Given the above, IT audit is the process that Using the same steps and repeat the running time and place, and in the organizations with different workplace and organizational goals are employed [27].

2.2. Important Factors Affecting Audit Quality

Conceptual standpoint, there are three fundamental aspects of audit quality include inputs, outputs and the underlying factors. There is a lot input about audit quality separate from standard. For example, one of the most important personal characteristics auditors is the skill and experience of the auditor, the ethical values and way of thinking. Another important input is the audit process. Audit process refers to such as properly audit procedure, effectiveness of audit tools and convenient access to support technics. All of these cases are involved in audit quality. In addition, the audit outcomes also have a significant impact on audit quality because most stakeholders in their assessment of audit quality outcomes audit report are being addressed [45].

2.3. Audit Quality

Audit quality is defined in different ways. In Applied Literature, audit quality is often defined by the extent of their compliance with auditing standards. In contrast, researchers in accounting and auditing, have been addressed multiple dimensions of audit quality dimensions, this dimensions is often different definitions. Some of the most common definitions of audit quality include: market assessment of the likelihood that the financial statements contain material misstatement, and the auditor shall report the discovery of misstatement [13] likelihood that auditor into the financial statements is likely to contain material misstatement has issued unqualified reports fails Palmerose (1988)[43] defines audit quality in terms of the degree is accredited auditor. Since the purpose of the audit, make sure into financial statements, so, audit quality means financial statements audited being free from material misstatement. In fact, this definition emphasizes the results of the audit, the audited financial statements of reliable, and reflects high quality audit. This definition leads to the following question: "How are users to evaluate the amount of reliable the audited financial statement?" This definition of audit quality is based on the quality of audits conducted, since the reliability level of audited financial statement cannot be determined before play audit. Consequently, the Palmerose definition focuses on real audit quality. Titman and Trueman (1986)[52]. the audit quality is accuracy level of the information that is available to investors have been defined. This definition is similar to the Palmerose definition of audit quality. Davidson and Neu (1993) [15] defines audit quality, auditor's ability to detect and report material misstatement of net income.

2.4. Prior Related Literature

Previous IT audit studies have focused primarily on specific aspects or characteristics of IT audit or assurance tasks. For example, recently authors have explored the IT proficiency of auditors and the importance of IT knowledge for assurance practitioners as one critical component of IT auditing [5, 20, 54, 33, 4, and 10]. Researchers have also used case studies of IT audits to identify potential concerns and improvement opportunities for IT audit [48]. Additionally, researchers have explored the potential impact of group dynamics and group support systems [5, 40, and 41]. Additional research related to IT audit has investigated the impact that IT has on financial audit, internal controls, or other projects. Examples include work that investigates the changing role of IS audit and auditors in US accounting firms [3, 42]; the effect of internal control reliability on IT audit hours and fees [12]; the effect of IT on auditor detection of misstatements [36] and the general implementation of technology for auditing [16, 10, 17].

Recent work by Merhout and Havelka toward developing a theory for the IT audit process utilized group data gathering techniques with IT audit practitioners, internal and external, to create a framework of logical factors related to IT audit quality. They identified a large (over 260) set of attributes (referred to as factors by Merhout and Havelka) that were suggested by practitioners as “critical” to the IT audit process. While they logically categorize the attributes identified, Merhout and Havelka do not provide any empirical evidence to support their framework or to evaluate the importance of the attributes or the categories they suggest [22, 37,24].

There are two primary works which review the literature

and identify measurable attributes:

First, Schroeder, Solomon and Vickrey (1986) surveyed audit committee chairs and audit partners on 15 specific "factors" of audit quality from prior research and identified eight of these as having a strong or very strong impact on audit quality, including executive involvement, planning/conduct field work, communication to management, independence, technical competence, team experience, quality control, and communication to audit committee [47].

Second, the approach of Carcello et al. (1992) extended Schroeder et al. in that they developed a broader survey of audit quality attributes and administered the survey to a combination of external audit, internal audit, and business professionals. Using a factor analysis technique, Carcello et al. identified 12 factors overall, including four primary factors: client experience, industry experience, responsiveness to client needs, and compliance with GAAS [6].

An alternative approach used to identify audit quality factors is through direct solicitation from audit professionals using interviews and group-based approaches. The primary work in this area is by Sutton and Lampe, One of the unique benefits of this approach is the potential detail and rich data set developed. These studies identified 19 specific attributes. Examples of the attributes identified by Sutton and Lampe's studies include audit team expertise, audit timing requirements, audit manager involvement, and prior notes and work papers [50, 51, and 31].

Catanach & walker (1999) introduced a model that illustrates the audit quality is functions of two main audit quality factors related to audit performance. These factors include: the abilities of the auditor (including knowledge, experience, ability to adapt and technical efficiency) and professional (including independence, objectivity, professional care, conflict of interest and judgment). In addition to the performance features, their model includes the effect of economic incentives (such fee, costs, performance, legal claims and consulting services), market structure (including competition, industry concentration and economies in scale) and audit mechanisms, legislation and employment status [8].

On the other hand of 1981 to now, several studies conducted in other countries in the field of audit quality, a fundamental problem in audit quality definition is differentiation between audit quality and auditor quality. Audit quality is simply not possible to measure and the actual quality of audit is invisible and it can only be assessed after performing audits, Palmrrose For example, in 1988, to measure actual quality is used the amount of lawsuits against auditors [21].

Persso & svanstrom (2011) in his thesis entitled Factors affecting audit quality; studies have indicated that the mission of the auditor and the auditor's age, does not matter in audit quality [44].

Zureigat (2011) in a research entitled the impact of ownership structure on audit quality after studies have concluded result show that There is a relation between audit quality and construction companies by institutional ownership or foreign ownership are governed, and ownership concentration have a negatively non-significant relation with audit quality and also institutional and foreign owners are willing to hire high-quality auditors[56].

Makni & et al.(2012) in study entitled the impact of corporate governance mechanisms on audit quality after studies showed that the size of the board, the separation of the chairman of the board, CEO, percentage of the majority owners have a positive impact on the demand for high-quality audit and percentage of the Institutional investors and size of the entity have a negative effect on the demand for audit quality. also existane non-duty members of the board, chairman of the board and the amount owed by the entity has no effect on the selection of quality auditors[35].

Stoel et al.(2012)in study began examines the factors influencing the quality of IT audit, after studies and using questionnaires that distributed among accountants, auditors and IT Audit Creators (accounting software), the factors such as, independed, Having knowledge of accounting and auditing skills, knowledge of business processes, accountability, audit frameworks and procedures, business standards and scope of the audit, auditability, audit experience than the entity's IT awareness and control, planning and operations, access to resources associated with the entity and the business environment as factors affecting audit quality IT identified[49].

Merhout & Havelha (2013) in a study whit titled internal IT audit process quality, were located 26 aspect of internal IT audit quality in 6 Floor, Audit organization, Corporate entity environment, process and procedure, system or objectives process and Audit staff[23] langari (2002) scale of measure the actual quality factor has considered compliance of fifteen audit quality control in audits Audit organization[32].

Mojtahedzade and aghaei (2004) in a thesis entitled "Factors affecting the visual quality independent audit by independent auditors and users", using the auditing literature, accepted auditing standards, statements and terms of environmental, factors affecting Quality audit be identified. The study population consisted of two groups of users of audit services, including management (senior experts) investment companies and executives (senior experts) credit department and independent auditors, including auditing partners, senior managers and technical managers of the audit. The findings of the study indicate that factors such as tenure, industry expertise, complete audit on time budget, employer reputation, audit fee, audit managers and partners to monitor the quality of the audit work performed influence on the independent audit[38].

Jafari (2006) investigated the factors affecting the audit quality auditors paid member of certified public accountants audit. He with gathering questionnaire data and test His hypothesis show that a meaningful relationship among the factors affecting the competence of auditors and auditor independence and audit quality. Secondly investigator with documents, audit reports and 167nomber of stock company financial statements between 2001 till 2003 concluded that formal audits of auditor and report the discovery of a material misstatement of the financial statements is not effectiveness [26].

Zangiabadi (2014) in his dissertation examines the factors influencing the quality of IT audit began after studies and using questionnaires that distributed between CPAs practitioner in audit organization and auditing institute , And results show that from the view of CPAs working in the audit and the audit, independence, knowledge and skills in accounting, auditing, business process knowledge, properly accountability of audit team and the audit process, audit criteria and scope of business, auditability, audit experience to the entity's IT awareness and control, planning and operations, access to resources associated with the entity and the business environment, affects IT audit quality[55].

3. Research Hypotheses

These assumptions of this study According to discussion are provided in previous sections as follows:

First hypothesis: proper accountability audit team members are affected on IT audit quality.

Second hypothesis: the existence of proper framework and audit procedures is affected on IT audit quality.

Third hypothesis: business criteria and audit scope is affected on IT audit quality.

Fourth hypothesis: the auditability of entity is affected on IT audit quality.

Hypothesis V: Planning and implementing effective audit is affected on IT audit quality.

Hypothesis VI: Access to entity resource is affected on IT audit quality.

Hypothesis VII: associated with entity is affected on IT audit quality.

Hypothesis VIII: business environment is affected on IT audit quality.

4. Methodology

This research is applied studies in terms of purpose. Applied research is research that are developed theories, regulation, principles and techniques that in basic research and applies to solve real and executive problems. And this research is causal- descriptive in the nature and content. In other words, this study analyzes the now status and to describe the current situation regularly and systematically and examines the characteristics and attributes and necessary to examines the relationship between the variables. Casual studies are applied studies in terms of purpose and their results usually are used to prevent the recurrence of adverse events, and development of appropriate events [28].

4.1. Data Collection Methods

There are several methods of data collection. In a study may be used of several methods to collect information. In this study are used of literature methods to literature review, in this method was studied literature and sources used in the research of their products. It also examines the views of CPAs are used of standard questionnaire with a Likert five options that have the validity previously been used to test and its reliability is 89 percent. Into analysis obtained data are used of descriptive statistics and inferential statistics. Data analysis After collecting and organizing data, that valuation is based on the Likert scale and tests has been done to determine the T-Student, the data transfer to a PC using, SPSS and Minitab.

4.2. Research Community

The first step in sampling is to define the target population. The participants in the study or in the other hand, statistical community, is CPAs working in the auditing organization and auditing institute, argument of choose CPAs into statistical population is they having a long professional experience, college education, and most importantly, it is possible for auditors to used audit software in audit process.

4.3. Research Sample

In the present study, non-probability purposive sampling method are used to distribute questionnaires and have been trying representative sample of the community. The sample size is calculated from formula kokran as follows [28]:

$$n = \frac{Nz_{\alpha/2}^2 pQ}{Nd^2 + z_{\alpha/2}^2 pQ}$$

In this formula N is the population size and n is the sample size in each sector.

Other components of the formula are as follows:

d: absolute error is equal to 0.1 is considered.

p: ratio of 0.5 is considered to be the maximum size.

q = 1-p: Here's a 0.5.

$z_{\alpha/2}$: Percentile $(1-\alpha/2)*100$ of the standard normal distribution where the 96/1 is the ninety-fifth percentile of the standard normal distribution.

According to the above formula the sample size of 89 patients for auditors which is calculated as follows:

$$n = \frac{1255 \times (1/96)^2 \times 0/25}{1255 \times (0/1)^2 + (1/96)^2 \times 0/25} \approx 89$$

5. Research Findings

First hypothesis: proper accountability of audit team members is affected on IT audit quality.

In follow-up hypotheses testing looking into explaining the effect proper accountability of audit team members on IT audit quality. T-statistics of the hypothesis is equal to -5.708 and a significance level equal to 0.000, which indicates that the null hypothesis i.e. no effect proper accountability of audit team members on IT audit quality rejected and can be adopted against hypotheses That show, proper accountability of audit team members is affecting on IT audit quality.

Table 1. *T - Student For the first hypothesis.*

Mean	Standard deviation	t	Sig
2.000	0.6784	-10.927	0.000

Second hypothesis: existence of proper framework and audit procedures is affected on IT audit quality.

In follow-up hypotheses testing looking into explaining the effect existence of proper framework and audit procedures on IT audit quality. T-statistics of the hypothesis is equal to -14.43 and a significance level equal to 0.000. Which indicates the null hypothesis, i.e. there is no effect existence of proper framework and audit procedures on IT audit quality, rejected and can be adopted against hypotheses that show, existence of proper framework and audit procedures on IT audit quality.

Table 2. *T - Student For the second hypothesis.*

Mean	Standard deviation	t	Sig
1.9	0.4706	-14.43	0.000

Third hypothesis: framework and audit procedure is affected on IT audit quality.

In follow-up hypotheses testing looking into explaining the framework and audit procedure on IT audit quality. T-statistics of the hypothesis is equal to -4.06 and a significance level equal to 0.000, which indicates that the null hypothesis i.e. no effect framework and audit procedure on IT audit quality, rejected and can be adopted against hypotheses That show, framework and audit procedure is affected on IT audit quality.

Table 3. *T - Student For the third hypothesis.*

Mean	Standard deviation	t	Sig
2.6	0.7838	-4.06	0.000

Fourth hypothesis: the auditability of entity is affected on IT audit quality.

In follow-up hypotheses testing looking into explaining the effect the auditability of entity on IT audit quality. T-statistics of the hypothesis is equal to -14.39 and a significance level equal to 0.000, which indicates that the null hypothesis i.e. no effect the auditability of entity on IT audit quality, rejected and can be adopted against hypotheses That show, the auditability of entity is affected on IT audit quality.

Table 4. *T - Student For the fourth hypothesis.*

Mean	Standard deviation	t	Sig
1.768	0.5936	-14.39	0.000

Fifth Hypothesis: Planning and implementing effective audit is affected on IT audit quality.

In follow-up hypotheses testing looking into explaining the Planning and implementing effective audit on IT audit quality. T-statistics of the hypothesis is equal to -14.46 and a significance level equal to 0.000, which indicates that the null hypothesis i.e. no effect Planning and implementing effective audit on IT audit quality, rejected and can be adopted against hypotheses That show, Planning and implementing effective audit is affected on IT audit quality.

Sixth Hypothesis: Access to entity resource is affected on IT audit quality.

In follow-up hypotheses testing looking into explaining the effect Access to entity resource on IT audit quality. T-statistics of the hypothesis is equal to -5.708 and a significance level equal to 0.000, which indicates that the null hypothesis i.e. no effect : Access to entity resource is affected on IT audit quality, rejected and can be adopted against hypotheses That show, Access to entity resource is affected on IT audit quality.

Table 5. *T - Student For the fifth hypothesis.*

Mean	Standard deviation	t	Sig
1.96	0.4188	-14.46	0.000

Table 6. *T - Student For the sixth hypothesis.*

Mean	Standard deviation	t	Sig
2.02	0.6481	-10.95	0.000

Seventh Hypothesis: communication with entity is affected on IT audit quality.

In follow-up hypotheses testing looking into explaining the effect communication with entity on IT audit quality. T-statistics of the hypothesis is equal to -13.68 and a significance level equal to 0.000, which indicates that the null hypothesis i.e. no effect communication with entity on IT audit quality, rejected and can be adopted against hypotheses That show, communication with entity is affected on IT audit quality.

Table 7. *T - Student For the seventh hypothesis.*

Mean	Standard deviation	t	Sig
1.93	.4952	-13.68	0.000

Eighth Hypothesis: business environment is affected on IT audit quality.

In follow-up hypotheses testing looking into explaining the effect business environment on IT audit quality. T-statistics of the hypothesis is equal to -10.74 and a significance level equal to 0.000, which indicates that the null hypothesis i.e. no effect business environment on IT audit quality, rejected and can be adopted against hypotheses That show, business environment is affected on IT audit quality.

Table 8. *T - Student For the eighth hypothesis.*

Mean	Standard deviation	t	Sig
1.9	.48917	-10.74	0.000

6. Discussion and Conclusions

Growth of information technology has taken Beam in all aspects of human society.

Human need, interest in using new technologies emerged as a dominant factor organizations and has forcing them to keep pace with the condition. Because the need and necessity is the main factor in the development of information technology in today's world, this important, techniques and ways of doing things have changed and have been change from paper-based systems to electronic information systems and software. Accounting and auditing profession, perhaps more than other areas of financial knowledge and resources to enjoy the new environment and at risk. New space for recording and reporting of information has created much of the efficiency and effectiveness of this practice. And requires the use of IT audit is felt more than ever. Therefore, in this study, are followed to explore the factors affecting information technology audit quality. According to the first hypothesis, responding to the needs of the entity's audit team and work with it and complete the audit process in management framework, which creates a desire for better auditing. Results this hypothesis with other studies, such as research Carcello et. al 1992; Behn et al 1997, Chen et al 2001; Samelson et al2006; Schroeder et. Al, 1986 and Stoel et al, 2012 are aligned. According to the second hypothesis, methods, procedures, forms and other tools and complete audit can assist auditors in performing quality audit work. The results of this research hypothesis with other studies, such as research, Carcello et. al 1992; Samelson et al, 2006; Behn, et al, 1997; O'Donnell et al 2000; Stoel et al.2012, are aligned. According to the third hypothesis, considering the criteria of any business entity and determine the audit scope properly to carry out helps audit work to performed quality. The results of the research hypothesis with other studies, such as research, Carcello et. al 1992; behn, et al, 1997; Schroeder,& et. Al, 1986 and Stoel et al.2012 are aligned. The fourth hypothesis suggests that, according to the auditability of the audited entity before accepting the job can be done in an audit work quality and be effective. The results of this research hypothesis with other studies, such as research, Carcello et. al 1992; behn, et al, 1997; Schroeder et. Al, 1986 and Stoel et al.2012 are aligned. The fifth hypothesis suggests that to perform any work must have an accurate budgeting and accomplishment audit operating favorably. The results of the research hypothesis with other studies, such as research, Carcello et. al 1992; behn, et al, 1997; Schroeder et. al, 1986 and Stoel et al, 2012 are aligned. The sixth hypothesis suggests that auditors should accept and perform the audit to quality should consider available to entity reliable resources, the results of this hypothesis with other studies, such as research, Carcello et. al 1992; behn, et al, 1997; Schroeder,& et. Al, 1986 and Stoel et al, 2012 are aligned. The seventh hypothesis suggests that have a communication with audited entity case to better recognition auditor into condition and character of that entity and auditors can be detection misstatement in financial statement and enjoyment her performance of high quality. The results of the research hypothesis with other studies, such as research, Carcello et. al 1992; behn, et al, 1997; Schroeder et. al, 1986. Stoel et al.2012; mojtahedzadeh and aghaei, 1383, is aligned. The eighth hypothesis suggests that one of factors affecting on IT audit quality, is business environment, entity activities and risks, which can be to mystification for auditors in condition auditors haven't enough know. But in condition that auditors have sufficient knowledge, it may be help the entity's auditors in order to improvement the quality of audit work. The results of the research hypothesis with other studies, such as research, Carcello et. al 1992; behn, et al, 1997; Schroeder et. Al, 1986 and Stoel et al, 2012 are aligned.

References

[1] Azar. A. & Momeni, M. (1379). Statistics and its Application in Management, Tehran: Publication of the first volume.

[2] Behn B, Carcello J, Hermanson DR, Hermanson RH. The determinants of audit client satisfaction among clients of big 6 firms. AccHoriz 1997; 11:7-24.

[3] Bagranoff N.A, Vendrzy k.VP. "The changing role of IS audit among the big five US-based accounting firms". InfoSyst Cont J 2000; 5.

[4] Brazel J. "A measure of perceived auditor ERP systems expertise". Managerial Aud J2005; 20(6):619–31. acarnaghan C." Discussion of it assurance competencies" .Int J Acc Info Syst2004; 5: 267–273.

[5] Carcello J, Hermanson R, McGrath N." Audit quality attributes: the perceptions of audit partners, preparers, and financial statement Users". Aud J Pract Theory 1992; 11: 1-15.

[6] Carcello J.V. and Nagy A.L (2004),"Audit Firm Tenure and Fraudulent Financial Reporting". Auditing: A Journal of practice & Theory, Vol. 23, Issue 2, pp. 55-69.

[7] Catanach, a.h.jr. and p.l. walker(1999), "the international debate over mandatory auditor rotation: a conceptual research framework", journal of international accounting, auditing & taxation, vol 8, pp 43-66.

[8] Chen CJP, Shome A, Su X. How is audit quality perceived by big 5 and local auditors in China? A preliminary investigation. Int J Aud 2001; 5: 157–75.

[9] Curtis M.B, Jenkins J.G, Bedard J.C, Deis D.R. "Auditors' training and proficiency in information systems: a research synthesis". IntJAccInfoSyst2009; 9: 104–121.

[10] Curtis M.B, Payne E.A. "An examination of contextual factors and individual characteristics affecting technology implementation deci-Sions in auditing" v. IntJ AccInf Syst 2008; 9: 104–21.

[11] Daigle R.J, Kizirian T, Sneathen L.D.J. "Systems controls reliability and assessment effort".IntJ Aud 2005; 9: 79–90.

[12] DeAngelo, L. E. (1981). "Auditor Size and Audit Quality", Journal of Accounting and Economics, Vol. 3, No. 3, 183-199.

[13] DeAngelo, L. (1981). "Auditor independence, "Low Balling," and disclosure regulation". Journal of Accounting & Economics (August), pp. 113-127.

[14] Davidson, R.A. and D. Neu. (1993)"A note on Association between audit Firm size and audit Quality". Contemporary Accounting Research. Vol. 9, pp 479-488.

[15] Dowling C, Leech S. "Audit support systems and decision aids: current practice and opportunities for future research". Int JAcc InfoSyst 2007; 8: 92-116.

[16] Dowling C. "Discussion of "An examination of contextual factors an dindividual characteristic saffecting technology implementation decisions in auditing". IntJAccInfoSyst 2008; 9: 122–126.

[17] For ghandost haghighi, K., (1999), " Computerizing Audit: quality or appearance", Journal auditor, numbers 4 and 5.

[18] Gartner Group. "Gartner says worldwide it spending to grow 5.1 percent in 2011". http://www.gartner.com/it/page.jsp?id=1513614.

[19] Greenstein M, Mckee T.E. "Assurance practitioners and educators' self-perceived it knowledge level: an empirical assessment". IntJAccInfoSyst2004; 5: 213–43.

[20] Hsas yeganeh, Y. (2005), "Philosophy of Auditing", Scientific and Cultural Publications.

[21] Havelka D, Merhout J.A. "Grounded theory of the information technology audit process by external auditor: using group data for Grounded theory development". 1stAnnualPre CISW or kshopon Accounting Information Systems. Phoenix, AZ; 2009.

[22] Havelka, D. Merhout, J. W. (2013), " Internal information technology audit process quality: Theory development using structured group processes", International Journal of Accounting Information Systems, http://dx.doi.org/10.1016/j.accinf.2012.12.001

[23] Havelka D, Merhout J. "Development of an information technology audit process quality framework". AmConferInfoSyst 2007; 13: 1–7.

[24] Hun-Tong T, Kao A. Accountability effects on auditors' performance: the influence of knowledge, problem-solving ability, and task complexity. J Acc Res 1999; 37: 209–23.

[25] Jafari, A. (2006), "Factors influencing the independence and competence of the members of certified public accountants in providing certification services", Ph.D. Dissertation, University of Allameh Tabatabai.

[26] Kearney, B. and Tryfonas T. Security Patterns for Automated Continuous Auditing, Information Security Journal, 2008.

[27] Khalili Shorini, S. (2009), "Research methods in the social sciences", Tehran, Memorial Book, First Edition.

[28] Kinney, W. R. Jr. Z.-V. Palmrose, and S. Scholtz. (2004). Auditor independence, non-audit services, and restatements: Was the U.S. government right? Journal of Accounting Research 42 (3): 561–588.

[29] Knapp M. Factors that audit committee members use as surrogates for audit quality. Aud J Pract Theory 1991; 10: 35–52.

[30] Lampe J.C, Sutton S. G. "Evaluating the work of internal audit:a comparison of standards and empirical evidence". AccBusRes1994; 24: 14.

[31] Langari, M. (2002), "Factors influencing the independence and competence of auditors", Journal of Accounting Research, No. 10, Tehran, 61-69.

[32] Leader B." Discussion of it assurance competencies". IntJAccInfoSyst 2004; 5: 275–9.

[33] Mahdavi, GH. & Mansouri Sh. (2012), "Information Technology and its impact on improving audit quality", auditor, No. 51, 82-89

[34] Makni, L., Kolsi, M.ch. and Affes, h, (2012), "The Impact of Corporate overnance Mechanisms on Audit Quality: Evidence from Tunisia", University of Sfax, Tunisia.

[35] Messier WFJ, Eilifsen A, Austen LA. Auditor detected misstatements and the effect of information technology. Int J Aud 2004; 8: 223–35.

[36] Merhout J, Havelka D. "Information technology auditing: avalue-added it governance partnership between it management and Audit". Comm Assoc InfoSyst 2008; 23: 463–483.

[37] Mojtahedzade, V. and aghaei, P. (2004), "Factors affecting audit quality independent auditors and users perspective", Journal of Accounting and Auditing, Volume 38, Tehran University School of Management.

[38] Momeni, M. (2010) "Data Analysis Using SPSS", Tehran, Frshyvh, Third Edition.

[39] O'Donnell E, Arnold V, Sutton SG. An analysis of the group dynamics surrounding internal control assessment in information systems audit and assurance domains. J Info Syst 2000a; 14: 97.

[40] O'Donnell E, Arnold V, Sutton SG. Reply to discussions of an analysis of the group dynamics surrounding internal control assessment in information systems audit and assurance domains. J Info Syst 2000b; 14: 5.

[41] Omoteso K, Patel A, Scott P. "Information and communications technology and auditng: current implications and future directions". IntJAud2010; 14: 147–62.

[42] Palmerose, Z. (1988)"An Analysis of Auditor litigation and Audit serviceQual ity. The Accounting review.Vol.64, pp. 55-73.

[43] Persso, U. & svanstrom, T., (2011),"factors affecting audit quality", umea school business, spring September 2011.

[44] Rahmani, H. and Godarzi fekri, R. (2012), "Quality Audit", the International Accounting Standards Board to ensure system and (IAASB) of the International Federation of Accountants, (IFAC), Journal of Accounting.

[45] Samelson D, Lowensohn S, Johnson L. The determinants of perceived audit quality and auditee satisfaction in local government. J Public Budg Acc Finan Manage 2006; 18: 139–66.

[46] Schroeder M, Solomon I, Vickrey D. "Audit quality: the perceptions of audit audit-committee chairpersons and audit partners". Aud J Pract Theory 1986; 5: 86–94.

[47] Smith G.I.T. "greatest audit and security risks of 2006". JCorpAccFinan 2007; 18: 43–8.

[48] Stoel, D. & Havelka, D. & Merhout, W.J. (2012)" Ananalysis of attributes that impact information technology audit quality: A study of it and financial aud it pract itioners", International Journal of Accounting Information Systems, 13, 60-79.

[49] Sutton S.G, Lampe J.C."A framework for evaluating process quality for audit engagements" AccBusRes1991; 21: 14.

[50] Sutton S.G. "Toward an understanding of the factors affecting audit quality" DecisSci1993; 24: 18.

[51] Titman, S. and B. Trueman, (1986) "Information Quality and the Valuation of New Issues". Journal of Accounting and Economics. Vol. 8, pp159-172.

[52] Wright S, Wright AM. Information system assurance for enterprise resource planning systems: unique risk considerations. J Info Syst2002:99-115

[53] Wilkinson D. "The CICA's it competency model". IntJAccInfoSyst 2004; 5: 245–250.

[54] Zangiabadi, M. (2014) "Factors affecting audit quality information technology", Master's thesis audit, Allameh Tabatabai University in Tehran.

[55] Zureigat, M.Q., (2011), "The Effect of Ownership Structure on Audit Quality: Evidence from Jordan" International Journal of Business and Social Science Vol. 2 No. 10; June 2011.

18

Conflict Resolution and Management: The Macro Perspective

Moses Onyesom[1,*], Emeke Francis Igbesi[2]

[1]Department of Office Technology and Management, Delta State Polytechnic, Ogwashi-Uku, Delta State, Nigeria
[2]Department of Business Administration, Delta State Polytechnic, Ogwashi-Uku, Delta State, Nigeria

Email address:
chimosaic@gmail.com (M. Onyesom)

Abstract: Conflict is an inevitable phenomenon in this universe as long as humankind exists. This implies that conflict is natural to human nature. However, conflicts usually occur from the pursuit of divergent interests, goals and aspirations by individuals or groups in a defined social or physical environment. Thus, conflict is present when two or more parties perceive that their interests are incompatible, express hostile attitudes, or take, pursue their interests through actions that damage the other parties. Our contemporary world is experiencing varied dimensions of conflicts cutting across religious, tribal, national, racial and socio-cultural inclinations. These macro dimensions of conflicts are open or external expression of dissatisfaction of the aggrieved group which is aimed at injuring other group(s) or reducing if not totally eliminating the existing relationship between the groups. Conflict that has degenerated to macro level becomes difficult and complex for the parties involved to personally resolve their differences alone without the aid of external assistance. Hence, this paper addressed effective styles of conflict resolution and management from the macro perspective.

Keywords: Conflict, Macro, Resolution, Interest, Behaviour

1. Introduction

Conflicts arise from the pursuit of divergent interests, goals and aspirations by individuals or groups in a defined social and physical environment. According to [1], changes in the social environment such as contestable access to new political positions or perceptions of new resources arising from development in the physical environment are fertile grounds for conflicts involving individuals and groups, who are interested in using the new resources to achieve their goals.

The past ten to fifteen years were characterized by the occurrence of some of the most violent conflicts among several ethnic and religious communities in different regions and states of Nigeria. As in [2] hardly was any region spared some of these conflicts, even though the conflicts differed either in prevalence and intensity, or their protracted or non-protracted nature. By definition, it implies that conflict is natural to human nature. That is, all humans or groups of humans have goals and interests which may be different with the goals and interests of other groups. This makes conflict inevitable.

Change is a natural phenomenon that produces the major social forces that shape societies. When these changes occur, especially at the middle and micro levels where their effects are individually or personally experienced, they do not happen quickly but are gradual in altering the ecological order, the system of stratification and the social institutions of an entire society causing societies to undergo industrial, political and urban revolution leaving in its wake social problems such as political and economic exclusion of some groups, injustice, poverty, exploitation, diseases, inequality etc.

These conditions places some people or group at an advantage over others and the inability of the social structures in place to bridge this gap and where possible reduce the disparity can cause frustrations and acts of aggression from the disadvantaged individuals or groups. Where these shows of frustration and aggression are ignored and not nipped at the bud, they most often are excuses to violently play out the hostility towards the exploitative group or groups and may escalate to become larger than the small groups or individuals involved to include an entire ethnic groups or organizations.

2. Overview of Conflict

Conflict is an inevitable phenomenon in this universe. As

long as humankind exists, there must be conflict. Conflict has been variously defined by different authors but it is technically seen as an opposition among social entities directed against each other [3]. Similarly, [4] sees conflict as a political process that generates from diversity of choices and distribution of scarce resources in the society.[5]further adds that the occurrence of cheat and aggressive behavior on the part of individuals or groups that lead to the frustration of others may cause conflict. Also [6] states that conflict is the struggle over values or claims to states, power and scarce resources which the aims of the group or individuals involved are not only to obtain the desired values but are to neutralize, injure or eliminate rivals. Thus, conflict is present when two or more parties perceive that their interests are incompatible, express hostile attitudes, or take, pursue their interests through actions that damage the other parties. These parties may be individuals, small or large groups, and countries.

From the foregone, it can be deduced that opposition is the order of contrast to cooperation. Meaning that wherever and whenever cooperation and understanding is lacking opposition sets in. Therefore, conflict can be explained to be an adversarial relationship involving at least two individuals or collective actors over a range or series of issues such as resources control, power, status, values, goals interest etc.

Conflict is a social situation in which at least two parties are involved who strive for goals, making it goal oriented or directed activity designed to improve the position of one party at the expense of the other. It is a perceived state of incompatibility between two or more people or groups and among values where the achievement of one value can be realized only at the expense of the other values. Conflict is an escalated competition between two or more parties each of which aims to gain advantage of some kind and at least one of the parties believes that the conflict is over a set of mutually incompatible goals. Conflicts may or may not be expressed in behaviours. It is one of the energies of life and thus common, natural and unavoidable but its pattern of expression can make or mar any relationship.

3. Concept of Macro Conflict

When individuals or groups who had previously been latent over their grievances, oppressions, deprivation, injustices etc suddenly or gradually begin to express these feelings through certain obnoxious behaviours in order to call for attention to their situation which escalates to an entire group, ethnic, state or even national and international, macro conflict has occurred. Macro level conflicts are expression of existing adversary's relationships through aggressive behaviours as a result of unresolved incompatible interest in the social structure of the system or organization.

These lapses in the structural functionalism of a society make it difficult for the rules and status that exists to provide social control or social order which is necessary for survival. Macro conflicts are open or external expression of dissatisfaction of the aggrieved group which is aimed at injuring the other party or reducing it if not totally eliminating the existing relationship between both groups. Conflict that has degenerated to macro level becomes difficult and complex for the parties involved to personally resolve their differences alone without the aid of external assistance. Most times the aggrieved parties may not even be able to state the immediate or direct cause of conflict as they usually lose track of the original causes of grievance. Again, conflicts can escalate to its macro level as a result of the presence of indirect or secondary parties to the conflict. These groups of persons or organizations complicate conflict situations and are difficult to identify because their involvements are by proxy through provisions of war aid and weapons, financial support etc. They are known as "shadow" parties in conflict.

Macro conflicts focus on the broader impacts or effects of conflict or its lack thereof. It considers a wider aspect in conflict such as an entire society, age group or age bracket, population groups, countries, economies, social class etc. Macro conflict goes beyond an individual or organization and conflict at the macro level changes social stratification, economic power and diplomatic stance of a society and thereby its future.

3.1. Causes of Macro Conflict

Resources: Conflicts can emerge due to resources. These conflicts arise when two or more groups aspire for the same scarce resources and where the aspiring parties demanding for these resources are more than the available scarce resources. The desire for control of the available scarce resources by a privileged group to the disadvantage of the other aspirants can cause conflicts e.g. the Niger Delta Region crises in Nigeria.

Values: Conflicts may arise due to differences in the value of the people or organization. Values here include philosophy, ideologies, religions etc. The value a group of people or ethnic nationality places on another group may be a constant cause for conflict especially where these values or perceptions are discriminatory and undermines the other group thereby limiting the prospects in certain areas of their lives or hindering their access to certain self actualizing opportunities. Values can bring about oppressive and unequal social structures. e.g Fulani Cattle Herdsmen and some indigent communities in Northern Nigeria, the Igbo cast system.

Oppressive Social Order: Oppressive social order can be a reason for conflicts. Certain social norms are oppressive in nature even though they have always been in existence. This means some people who are by these order placed at advantaged positions can hide behind these orders or norms to do injustice to those at disadvantaged positions and any attempt not to be exploited by the disadvantaged group may cause conflict eruption e.g. violence against women.

Mismanagement of Information: Information is very vital in human and organizational interactions and relationships. Thus any mismanagement of information can generate fatal conflict situations. The average individual's perception of things differs from that of an uninformed individual and also affects their reactions on specific issues at a given time. For example, despite the Nigerian government's perception of the relevance of information and establishment of various information gathering and dissemination agencies (e.g public complaints commission, National Orientation Agency, Ministry of information etc.), there still exist major lapses in the effective management of information in Nigeria leading to escalation of issues and eruption of crisis in Nigeria (e.g. the Ogoni Crisis in Rivers State Nigeria and the Political/Religious Crisis in Northern Nigeria).

3.2. Macro Conflict Management Models/Theories

The Basic Human Need Theory: Human beings have universal and non negotiable basic needs (that is food, safety, shelter, healthcare, employment, freedom etc.) that must be satisfied. So conflict or violence emerges when these needs are not answered [7]. This theory provides a quiet objective basis for understanding the sources of conflict.

The Marxist Theory: Marx argued that society is structured in main classes. The burgoise (who own the means of production and whose source of income is profit), the land owners (whose income is rent) and the proletariat (who own their labour and sell it for a wage). In these classes, struggle constitutes the engine of change. He noticed that conflict is not a deviant behaviour within the society's structure, the structure itself is a derived factor in the struggle of classes, seen as ownership of property given some persons the power to exclude others [8].

Feminist Perspective of Violence Model: Feminists focus on violence against women, perceiving it as a form of social control that limits or undermines women's ability in all aspects of life. As a result, the occurrence of manifest and latent violence against women is a conflictual situation. Hence, it constitutes a central concern in peace studies. They advocate for the use of feminine values towards the radical transformation of an oppressive social order and consider this as an essential principle in the struggle for achieving peace [9]. For example, violence against women can take different form such as physical violence (beating, corporal, torture etc.), psychological violence (psychological torture etc.), sexual violence (rape, sexual assault, sexual harassment etc.), gender based violence (female genital mutilation, rites of female widow), verbal violence (women based stereotypes or insults) and or economic violence (obstruction of economic opportunities for women etc.).

Environmental Perspective Model: The environmentalists condemn the current misuse or over use of environmental resources and the increasing degradation of the environment due to different factors arguing that such situations could have irreversible and dangerous consequences for the earth and human beings [10]. They also point out that the environment may be a source of conflict, underlining that violent conflict may arise from competition for limited or inequitably distributed resources. For instance, the case of the water scarcity and management conflict in the Nile River Region. The Nile River Water area shared among ten countries namely Burundi, Rwanda, Democratic Republic of Congo, Tanzania, Kenya, Uganda, Ethiopia, Eritrea, Sudan and Egypt. The population within the region is increasing and is expected to double in 25 year, adding to the increasing demand for the water generated by growth in industry and agriculture [11].Scarcity, misuse or inequitable distribution of Nile water is the permanent sources of conflicts in these areas.

4. Macro Conflict Resolution and Management

Conflict at the macro level has most often gone beyond the control of the conflicting parties, so even when they see the need for peace, may require the presence and assistance of a third party to initiate the peace move. The third party usually provides neutral ground that are safe enough for peace talk and unbiased opinions for conflicting parties to consider and upon which their decision can be based. Also, warring or conflicting groups may want to enter into peace talks through representative bodies who are expected to, if possible find lasting solution to the existing strives.

Conflict resolution is seen by [10] as a variety of approaches aimed at terminating conflict through the constructive solving of problem while conflict management is defined as the process of reducing the negative and destructive capacity of conflict through a number of measures and by working with and through the parties involved in the conflict. For the purpose of this paper, conflict resolution and management is defined as constructive processes or procedures adopted for solving problems which are aimed at terminating conflicts or reducing its negative and destructive effects by working with and through the conflicting parties.

This means that some conflicts can be permanently resolved when the basic needs of the parties have been met with all necessary satisfiers and their fears allayed and there are non-resolvable conflicts and these can be transformed, regulated or managed e.g. values. Management of conflicts covers the entire handling of conflict positively through its different stages, including efforts made towards prevention by being proactive, conflict limitation, containment and litigation. According to [7], conflict management promotes conditions in which collaborative and values relationships control the behaviour of conflicting parties.

4.1. Macro Conflict Handling Styles

*Alternative Dispute Resolution (ADR):*This looks for and applies non-conventional peaceful methods of settling disputes and resolving conflict situation using the least expensive methods and such ways that satisfy the conflicting parties as well as preserve relationships after a settlement might have been reached. This as an alternative but has special preference for non-violence. The conflict resolution spectrum consists of a range of opinions employable for non-violent management of conflict which are either voluntary processes where the conflict parties have some control over the outcomes of the process and which involves fact finding, in-depth research and case studies, facilitation, negotiation, conciliation, mediation and brokerage or the involuntary processes where the outcomes of the process are outside the control of the conflict parties. Here, the third parties who broker the process hand down outcomes which the parties have to accept either in law or in principle. These involve arbitration, adjudication and law enforcement using the coercive apparatus of state (e.g. warrants & court orders).

Collaboration: The collaboration process is one in which parties work together on their own to resolve problems through constructive dialogue or other activities such as joint projects, shared utilities etc. Collaboration helps to build trust, confidence and mutual respect between groups or nations. When potential or actual conflict parties work together on a number of common issues, projects or themes, it intensifies communication and activities between them. This method is likely to build more mutual respect as well as maintain friendly relations. It is expected that those collaborating are enjoying the relationship and that cooperation in one area can ultimately lead to collaboration in other areas creating a chain of collaborative activities that supports peace building. This method is within the reach of the conflict parties and so, does not involve a third party.

Negotiation: Negotiation is a direct process of structured dialogue and discussion taking place between at least two parties who are faced with a conflict situation [12]. In negotiation, both parties have come to the realization that they have a problem and are aware that by talking to each other can find a solution to the problem. Communication is usually critical to the negotiation process as it can take place only when there is communication between conflict parties and is harder when conflict has escalated and communication is threatened or has altogether stopped. Negotiations are engaged in at the early stages of conflict and are either positional or collaborative in nature. Positional negotiations are aggressive, adversarial and competitive in nature. Parties make inconsiderate demands and perceive themselves to be in competition desiring to win rather than working towards a mutually beneficial outcome. Positional negotiation breaks down easily. Collaborative negotiation are processes where parties educate each other on their needs and concerns and each group seeks for the best ways to solve their problems in ways that the interest and fears of both or all parties are met. The emphasis of collaborative negotiation is on mutual understanding and feeling. All aimed at building a sustainable relationship.

Conciliation: Conciliation is a third party activity which covers intermediary efforts aimed at persuading the parties to a conflict to work towards a peaceful solution. Conciliation involves facilitation. The conciliator communicates separately with the parties and provides the assistance needed from a neutral third party. The aim of conciliation is to reduce tension between parties and in a conflict situation. Conciliation through its many intertwined activities provides a vital background that supports higher activities in conflict resolution and management like mediation [13].

Mediation: Mediation is the process of voluntary intervention undertaken by an external party (third party) that fosters the settlement of differences between parties who retain control over the outcome but which may involve positive and negative inducements. Mediation is usually assisted by a third party where the parties to a conflict admit that they have a problem which they are both committed to solving but in which the mediator manages a negotiation process but does not impose a solution on the parties.

Mediation involves dialogue but requires the presence of a third party. The role of the mediator is to create the enabling environment for the parties to carry out dialogue sessions leading to the resolution of a pending conflict. The mediator helps parties to identify and arrive at common grounds with a view to overcoming their fears and satisfying their real needs. The mediator must have the confidence of the parties to the conflict and refrain from reaching or providing any decisions no matter the weight of the evidence gathered in the mediation process.

Arbitration: Arbitration is the use and assistance of a neutral third party in conflict, who hears the evidence from both parties and thereafter renders a decision which is expected to be binding on both parties called "an award". It is a type of third party intervention for parties to a conflict who select non-violent method of settling dispute. The decisions of the arbitrator are binding but there is a desire to ensure that the outcome in any arbitration process is a fair one.

Adjudication: Adjudication is a non-violent method of conflict management that involves the use of the courts and litigation processes. Parties to disputes may choose to take their case to a court of law before a judge of competent jurisdiction with a legal counsel to represent them. At the end of the adjudication process the court gives a judgment which is legally binding on both parties. The judgment will further be enforced where necessary, by the law enforcement agencies of the state. Adjudication is expected to be a peaceful means of resolving conflicts and disputes. However, its peace is only relative as it tends to destroy trust, love, respect and other forms of confidence between parties but increases suspicion and bitterness of the litigation process for a long time after judgment is given. It usually ends in a win-lose outcomes where the winner takes all leaving the loser with nothing. It is expensive and usually takes long to dispose and is outside the control of the conflicting parties who cannot decide how long they take and cannot choose the nature of the outcomes.

4.2. Crisis Management

A crisis is an extreme situation in conflict which has reached a point where critical decisions have to be taken to avoid the escalation of conflict to a print of extreme violence. Crisis is sometimes a degenerated state of conflict which threatens human security, intense violence characterized by fighting, death, injury, large-scale displacement of populations etc. When crisis occurs, it becomes the responsibility of the government to de-escalate the situation and brings cessation to violence through various means including the use of coercive state apparatus where necessary. Crisis management is usually left to government because when crisis in conflict occurs it threatens and often disrupts communication which can only be restored when normalcy returns. In maintaining crisis situations, many ugly things happen which sometimes consume the state and lead to the collapse of the state as governments are often unable to end the crisis situation resulting in the escalation of violence marked by atrocities and crimes committed against humanity. Also, crisis management can be a statement to the effect that there had been a breakdown of law and order and in which case necessary agencies of law and order are used to contain and where possible restore the situation. These include the police and members of the armed forces. The introduction of the police and other law enforcement agencies may call for the use of extraordinary measures such as force, to restore law and order and may be human rights violations of various descriptions as a result of high-handedness, excess and unprofessional conduct in these exercises. When this happens, the conflicting parties totally lose control of the situation making resolution through non-violent means impossible until normalcy has been restored.

Multi-Track Approach: [11] introduced a multi-track diplomacy systems approach to peace. According to them, there are nine tracks of conceptual and practical framework that assist and work in the peace building sector. This approach emphasizes that there are different parties and stakeholders involved with conflict management and transformation. It goes beyond the traditional believe that the government of a state is the sole machinery of bringing about peace as these governments have most times been unresponsive and are sometimes discovered to be a part of the problem rather than the solution.

Hence, it is important to identify, enlist and provoke the other actors to play their roles in peace building. [11]summarized the nine tracks of peace making activities using the internal level of analysis to include:

(a) *Government:* Government is involved in peace making through formal processes and institutions of government such as in official diplomacy, policy making, peace building activities and crisis management as well as maintenance of law and order.
(b) *Nongovernmental/Professional Conflict Resolution:* This relates to conflict management by professional or non-governmental organizations whose activities are in the areas of analysis, prevention, resolution and management of conflict. This includes the civil society groups.
(c) *Business or Commerce:* Business can make an enormous contribution to peace making in potential and actual forms as it provides economic and commercial opportunities which prevents conflicts. It helps in building both local and international friendship and understanding and opens informal channels of communication and other ways of supporting peace building activities.
(d) *Private Citizen and Personal Involvement:* Individual citizens can be involved in peace building and development activities through citizens' diplomacy exchange programmes, private voluntary organization, non-governmental organization and other peacemaking activities e.g. local "Vigilante" groups.
(e) *Research, Training and Education:* This track covers three areas of research as it connects to educational institutions and specialized institutes, think tanks and special research centers including training programmes in conflict and peace as well as specialized skills of negotiation, mediation and general conflict transformation.
(f) *Activism or Advocacy:* This track covers practices and activities in active non-violence, peace and environmental activism, human rights protection and peace, campaign against proliferation of small arms and light weapons, social and economic justice and protests against governmental policies that threaten peace. For example, "Bring back our girls campaign" in Nigeria
(g) *Religion:* This track deals with beliefs and peace-oriented actions of spiritual and religious communities such as pacifism, humanism, non-violence, brotherliness as preached by dominant religions.
(h) *Funding:* The funding of communities is a silent but important sector in peacemaking activities. Many foundations exist, mostly in the developed countries that provide resources to governmental and private groups that are engaged in peace building activities.
(i) *Communications and the media:* The media and all the channels for the dissemination of information are the aggregate of public opinion and the voice of the people. The media such as print, electronic, video, film etc can promote peace if it chooses to do so and vice-versa.

5. Conclusion

Conflicts are natural phenomenon in human society. Depending on their intensity, conflicts are expressed sometimes in violent or non-violent ways. They are social situations in which at least two parties with incompatible goals strive to achieve these goals at the expense of each other. Conflicts occur at all levels of human interaction. Macro conflicts focus on the broader impacts of conflict on entire groups or social strata. The causes of conflict are varied and includes resources, values, oppressive social order, mismanagement of information etc. and these could be permanently resolved but where this is impossible will be managed through collaboration, alternative dispute desolation (ADR), negotiation, conciliation, mediation, arbitration, adjudication, crisis management and multi-track approach methods. Conflict is an inevitable occurrence in every human existence, at all levels and takes different forms which could be either violent or non-violent ways. At the macro level, conflicts situations affect entire social order and groups or even countries. Conflicts arise as a result of a number of issues and could either be resolved or managed in a number of ways using appropriate methods in consideration of the causes of conflict.

References

[1] O. Otite, Aspects of conflicts in theory and practice in Nigeria. Ibadan: Spectrum Books limited, 2001.

[2] T. V. Best, Philosophical analysis of conflict. Aldershort: Ashgate, 2004.

[3] I. O. Albert, Introduction to third party intervention in community conflicts. Ibadan: John Archers Pubs. Ltd, 2001.

[4] A. Ball, Modern politics and government. London: McMillan Press Ltd, 1983.

[5] R. Stagner, *The psychology of human conflict.* Ibadan: Spectrum Books Ltd, 1995.

[6] A. P. Schmid, Thesaurus and glossary of early warnings and early responses in Introduction to peace studies. National Open University of Nigeria Study Module. Lagos. Canal paper Converters Ltd, 2000.

[7] J. Burton, Conflict resolution and prevention. London: MacMillan, 1993.

[8] R. Runmel, Understanding conflict and war: Conflict in perspectives. Retrieved from www.hawaii.edu/powerkills/CIP.CHAP3.HTM, 1997.

[9] H. Jeongh-Won, Peace and conflict studies: An introduction. Burlington: Ashgate Pub. Ltd, 2000.

[10] C. A. Miller, A glossary of terms and concepts in peace and conflict studies. Geneva: University for peace, 2003.

[11] L. Diamond, and J. MacDonald, Multi track diplomacy: A systems approach to peace. Connecticut: Kumarian Press Inc, 1996.

[12] E. Nnabuife, Organisational behavior and management theories. Nimo: Rex Charles and Patricks Publications, 2009.

[13] V. B. E. Abia, Contemporary issues in international relations. Lagos: Concepts Publishers Ltd, 2000.

Falling Oil Price, Exchange Rate Volatility and Marco-economic Variables in Nigeria

Olure Bank Adeyinka Michael[1], Gbadebo Salako[2], Ajiteru Temilade[2]

[1]Department of Economic, Joseph Ayo Babalola University, Ikeji-Arakeji, Osun State
[2]Department of Economic, Emmanuel Alayande College of Education, Oyo, Oyo State, Nigeria

Email address:
adeyinka67@gmail.com (O. B. A. Michael), gbadebosalako@gmail.com (G. Salako)

Abstract: With the oil price at low level in Nigeria, exchange rate volatility has been manifested at different exchange rate regimes in Nigeria, the study look at the relationship between exchange rate volatility and Macroeconomics variables in Nigeria between 1985-2014. Secondary data were collected from Central Bank Statistical Bulletin, employing Johansen Error Correction Model (ECM) Technique to estimate the collected time-series data and General Conditional Heteroskedasticity (GARCH) to measure volatility. It is therefore observed and recommended that the Nigeria government should employ greater policy sensitivity towards the openness of the economy so that the capital flows that come through foreign direct investment (FDI) will be beneficial to the economy as a whole.

Keywords: Exchange Rate, Foreign Direct Investment, Economic Growth, Marco-economic Variable

1. Introduction

In recent time, one striking feature of the world economy is the growth of Foreign Direct Investment (FDI) and the market for it has become more competitive. Developing countries are becoming increasingly attractive as investment destinations because they can offer investors a range of "created" assets (World Bank 2003). This attractiveness not withstanding investors must also consider the effect of fluctuations in the exchange rate because exchange rate fluctuations hurt producers and investors alike as it affect their planned revenue and costs, including profit margin. Instability in the exchange rate may distort the realisations of such estimates. For example, exchange rate depreciation result in high cost importing raw material and capital goods. The effect of exchange rate volatility on macroeconomics variables performances has continued to generate interest among economists.

FDI is essential for growth and development in Nigeria. In fact, it is argued that low and volatile FDI is part of the challenges to the persistent poverty, high inequality and underdevelopment of Nigeria economic because Nigeria manufacturing sector is highly depending on the importation for it inputs and capital goods. These imported inputs and capital goods are paid for in foreign exchange, which is not stable. Thus, the variations in exchange rates are bound to adversely affect activities in the sector that is dependent on external sources for productive inputs.

The exchange rate situation in Nigeria has been plagued by various problems in the recent time some of which are instability in price of naira, balances of payment, low level of competition due to falling of oil price. The importance of foreign capital inflows to Nigeria is generally perceived as something desirable.

The structural adjustment programme (SAP) which was introduced in july, 1986 led to the adoption of floating exchange rate in Nigeria and devaluation of the Nigeria naira. A cardinal objective of the SAP was the restructuring of the production sectors of with a positive bias for the production of agricultural exports is shown. The foreign exchange reforms that facilitated a cumulative depreciation of the effective exchange rate were expected to increase the domestic prices of agricultural exports and therefore boost domestic production and the regulation of the foreign exchange market aim at improvement of market determined exchange rate, managed floating exchange rate regime. The Central Bank of Nigeria usually intervenes in foreign exchange market through its monetary policy actions and operations in the money market to influence the exchange rate movement in the desired direction such that it ensures the competitiveness of the domestic economy. The introduction of managed floating exchange rate regime tends to increase the uncertainty in exchange rate, thus, increasing the volatility of exchange rate by regime shift. This make the exchange rate to be the most important asset price in the economy. The understanding of exchange rate behaviour is important to the monetary policy (Longmore and Robinson, 2004). Also SAP was aim to develop other export sector of the economy with the goal of diversifying the economy from it dependence on oil Trade, and liberalisation of the economy. However, these policy have analytical support in the counter revolutionary paradigm of Bretton wood school. One of the paradigm propositions is low level of non-oil exports particularly agriculture is caused by exchange rate overvaluation, agricultural taxes, and marketing board profits. Nigeria CBN exchange rate policy has been aimed at preserving the external value of the domestic currency and maintaining a healthy balance of payment position, which, indeed, is a major provision of enabling law. With failure of the Autonomous Foreign Exchange Market (AFEM) in 1995, an Inter-bank Foreign Exchange Market (IFEM) was introduce in 1999 designed as a two way quote system, and intended to diversify the foreign exchange in the economy by encouraging the funding of the inter-bank operations from privately earned foreign exchange. The IFEM is to assist the naira to achieve a realistic exchange rate. The IFEM experienced similar problem and setback as the AFEM, owing to supply side rigidities, the persistent expansionary fiscal policy operations of the government and the attendant problem of persistent excess liquidity in the system.

1.1. Overview of Nigeria Oil Sector

Nigeria is Africa's top oil exporter, and the world's tenth largest oil producing country. It has realized over US$ 600 billion in oil revenues since 1960, a figure greater than the resources used by the Marshall Plan in rebuilding Europe after World War Two and is currently the 8th highest net oil exporter in the world. Nigeria's economy is heavily dependent on natural resources: oil and gas constitutes circa 80 percent or more of government revenues in some years. The 1970's ushered Nigeria into a new era of prosperity, enjoying a bounteous oil windfall due to the increase in global oil prices precipitated by the Arab Israeli crisis. The negative effects of this oil windfall were reflected in exchange rate appreciation, import subsidies, and a decline in vital sectors such as Agriculture and manufacturing in the case of Nigeria, the solid mineral sector also suffered as earlier pointed out. However, the profligacy and waste that accompanied Nigeria's elevation to the status of an oil-rich petro state experienced a hitch at the start of the next decade. The 1980's oil glut forced a sharp drop in oil receipts, and consequently economic growth. Confronted with corruption, capital flight and mounting foreign debt, Nigeria, was left with no option but to undergo structural reforms such as the IMF's Structural Adjustment Programmes (SAP) to address the distortions caused by oil dependence. With the return to democratic rule in 1999, a series of macroeconomic and fiscal reforms have been undertaken, most of them having economic diversification as a core element. It was also able to secure a debt buy back deal from the Paris club in 2006 which reduced the external debt even though her current domestic debt of circa $34 billion is a threshold that is perturbing.

1.2. Significances of the Study

The need to understand the relationship between exchange rate volatility and macroeconomics variables in Nigeria economy is a long time debate. This study is premised on identifying the causes and the consequence of exchange rate volatility on macroeconomics variables with foreign direct investment in Nigeria as is main focus. Foreign direct investment is viewed as major stimulus to economic growth in developing country like Nigeria. It ability to deal with three major problem namely shortages of financial resources, technology and skill labour has made it the centre of attention for the policy maker in low income countries. Despite good performance of FDI, it is characterised by considerable fluctuations over time which phenomenon according to Fucei and boreli (2008) is attributed to exchange rate volatility. Exchange rate volatility is being increasingly recognised as a disincentive to Nigeria as FDI destination (Ogunleye 2008). with all above this study seek to establish how the various exchange rate regime do affects foreign direct investment and other macroeconomics variables in Nigeria.

1.3. Scope and Limitation of Study

The totality of exchange rate volatility and macroeconomics variables in Nigeria are the focus of the study. The study investigates empirically the relationship exchange rate volatility and macroeconomics variables also the variable that effects foreign direct investment in Nigeria. The study use a time series data of 29 years spanning from 1985-2014, collated from secondary sources to include Central Bank of Nigeria (CBN) Statistical Bulletin, Annual report, Statement of Account of various issues.

1.4. Outline of the Study

The study is divided into five part, part one introduce the subject matter of the study, statement of the problem, significances of the study, scope and limitation of the study and outline of the study. Part two, discusses the theoretical and empirical reviews of literature, showing the concept of exchange rate volatility and foreign direct investment in Nigeria. Part three presents theoretical framework, methodology, estimation technique, model specification, and measurement. Part four, have result and discussion of result of findings. While part five talk on summary, conclusion and recommendation.

2. Empirical Review of Literature

Many related empirical studies conducted on some developing countries shows the effect of Exchange Rate Volatility on Foreign Direct Investment (Schuh, 1974;

Ihimodu. 1993; Ogiogio, 1993; Obadan, 1994). In some cases, domestic demand deficiencies are important reasons for a home country to invest in a foreign market. In such situations, the home country's GDP could be negatively related to FDI (Pitelis 1996).

Per capital GDP measures labour productivity and it is expected that high labour productivity encourages FDI. It is also assumed that higher wage rates discourage inward FDI, so the expected sign for the coefficient could either be positive or negative. Thomas and Grosse (2001) reported the negative relationship of GDP and inward FDI to Mexico during the period from 1930-1995 using the general least squares (GLS) method. Brozozowski 2006 studied FDI flows from the European Union (EU) into Mexico for the period from 1994 to 1997. Their results suggest that GDP and real per capita GDP are negative. Pan (2003) studied inward FDI in china during 1984 In 1996 and found a significant but negative relationship. The above literature indicates that inward FDI into a developing country does not hold in the same way as it does for a developed country.

One factor that can adversely impact investor profit is the rate of inflation. Normally, it assumed that the higher the price is for an item the greater the profit will be but a high inflation rate can be viewed as a barrier to FDI. Botric and Skuflic (2006) examined the determinant of FDI in countries in southern Europe from 1996 to 2002 and found that FDI had a positive but insignificant effect on inflation.

In contrast, Trevino et al, 2002 studied FDI flows in Latin America and reported that FDI flows had a negative but insignificant effect on inflation. Cushman (1985,1988).

Unlike the studies reviewed above, the negative impact of exchange rate volatility on FDI was measured by the coefficient of variation of quarterly nominal exchange rate over the past three years, on FDI from developed to developing countries for the 1984-96 period by using annual data. They found that high exchange rate volatility discouraged FDI while the depreciation of local currency promoted FDI from developed countries. Urata and Kawai (2000) included exchange rates and their volatility, which was measured by the coefficient of variation of exchange rate over five-year period, in their study of Japanese firm's decision on the location choice. By analysing a firms level panel data covering 1980-94 for 117 countries from four manufacturing industries in Japan, they also found that high exchange rate volatility discouraged FDI while the depreciation of host country's currency increased Japanese FDI to those countries.

2.1. Theories of Exchange Rate Determination

The exchange rate theories are classified into three which are; Partial, general and disequilibrium models.

Partial Equilibrium Models: include relative purchasing power parity and absolute power parity,which only consider the goods market; and covered interest rate parity(CIRP) and uncovered interest rate parity (UCIRP), which only considers the assets market, and the external equilibrium model, which states that the exchange rate is determined by the balance of payments.

General Equilibrium Models: impact of volatility on FDI has been within a partial equilibrium framework, that is, the only variable that changes in some measure of the variability of exchange rate, and all other factors that influence on the level of FDI are assumed to remain unchanged. However, those developments that are generating the exchange rate movements are likely to affect other aspects of economic environment which will in turn have an effect on FDI flows. Thus it is important to take an account in a general equilibrium framework the interaction of all the major macroeconomic variables to get a more complete picture of the relationship between exchange rate volatility and FDI.Such an analysis has recently been provided by Bacchetta and Van Wincoop (2010). They develop a simple, two country, general equilibrium model where uncertainty arises from monetary, fiscal and technology shocks, and they compare the level of trade and welfare for fixed and floating exchange rate arrangements. They reach two main conclusions. firstly, there is no clear relationship between the level of FDI and the type of exchange rate arrangement, a monetary expansion in the foreign country would depreciate its exchange rate, causing its to reduce its import but the increasing demand generated by the monetary expansion would offset part of the exchange rate effect. Thus, the nature of the stock that causes the exchange rate change can lead to changes in other macroeconomic variables that offset the impact of the movement in the exchange rate.

2.1.1. Concepts and Definition of Exchange Rate Volatility

To stimulate an understanding of exchange rate volatility and Foreign Direct Investment in Nigeria, it is important to define the key concepts that are central to the study. Exchange rate refers to the rate at which one currency exchange for another (Chingan, 2003). Exchange rate is said to depreciate if the amount of domestic currency required to buy a foreign currency increases, while the exchange rate appreciates if the amount of domestic currency required in buying a foreign currency reduces. An appreciation in the real exchange rate may create current account problems because it leads to overvaluation. Overvaluation in turns makes imports artificially cheaper while exports relatively expensive, thus reducing the international competitiveness of the domestic country (Takaendesa, 2006). However exchange rate can be expressed in one of two ways; as unit of domestic currency per unit of foreign currency, as unit of foreign currency per Domestic currency (Charles, 2006). It is a very important price in which the government alikes very active interest (Obadan, 2006). However two concept of exchange rate are commonly distinguished: nominal exchange and real exchange rates. The nominal exchange rate (NER) is a monetary concept which measures the relative prices of two currencies e.g. Naira in relation to US Dollar. But the real exchange rate (RER), as the name implies is a real concept that measures the relative prices of two goods-tradable goods (export and import) in relation to non tradable goods (goods and services produced and consumed locally).

Exchange rate volatility refers to the swings or fluctuations in the exchange rates over a period of time or the deviations from a benchmark or equilibrium exchange rate (Mordi, 1006).

2.1.2. Concepts and Definition of Foreign Direct Investment

Foreign direct investment is that investment which is made to serve the business interest of the investor in a company, which is in a different nation distinct from the investor's country of origin.

According to Kyereboah and Kwame (2008) foreign direct investment is an investment that involves a long term relationship between a foreign investor or parent enterprise or an affiliate enterprise. They further point out that the FDI concept only holds if the investor has a significant degree of influence on the management of the enterprise resident in the other economy. This investment involves both the initial transaction between the two entities and subsequent transactions between them and among foreign affiliates; both incorporated and unincorporated. Economy watch (2008), stresses that the relationship between the resident company and the foreign affiliate qualifies as a FDI if the parent enterprise through its direct investment effort exercises substantial control over the foreign affiliate company. "Control" in this case is the ownership of the greater than or equal to 10% of ordinary shares or access to voting rights in an incorporated firm and an equivalent criterion for an unincorporated firm can be consider. Otherwise, ownership share amounting to less than that 10% is termed as portfolio investment and is not categorised as FDI. Theories that are related to the types of FDI suggests that there are two types of FDI, while some other theories suggests four types of FDI, which include Horizontal (market-seeking), Vertical, In-ward and Out-ward FDI.

2.2. Exchange Rate Vitality and Foreign Direct Investment

There are several arguments concerning the mechanism by which currency exchange rate volatility affect FDI. These arguments relate to the difference types of multinational activities undertaken in a particular location, the destination of the finished goods or service produced and the sources of intermediate inputs. For example, Kiyota and Urata (2004) find that real exchange rates play an influential role for the locational determinants of the FDI of Japanese firms in aggregated and disaggregated industries. Kimino, Saal and Driffield (2007) in their attempt to model Japanese FDI inflows pointed out that the exchange rate differences could have been responsible for the changes in the "marketing seeking" FDI only that they related this argument to FDI flows between developed economies following from Markusen (1998) and Dunning (1993), who suggested that most FDI occurs between high income developed countries where firms are looking to either expand into markets similar to their own or protect their home market from foreign competition. This observation can also extend to FDI flows to low income countries, an example is the current influx of telecommunication companies into Nigeria whose major motivation is mainly "market seeking".

According to Benassy-Quere et al (2001), appreciation of the home currency reduces the cost of capital, enabling firms to invest more easily abroad relative to firms in countries with a depreciated currency. Conversely when MNRs uses the local market as an export platform, then FDI and trade will become compliments.

Froot and Stein (1991) find that depreciation of the host currency leads to larger FDI inflows. They argue that appreciation of the source country currency relative to that of the host currency increases the wealth position of firm reducing the relative cost of capital and allowing them to invest more actively in the foreign market.

Compared with the studies analysing the effects of exchange rate and other variables, there are only few studies that empirically examined the impact of exchange rate volatility on FDI.

2.3. Sources of Real Exchange Movement

In analysing the impacts of real exchange rate volatility on FDI, one should be concerned with the sources of real exchange rate movements. Recent empirical studies suggest that the behaviour of real exchange rate is attributed to the failure of establishing the law of one price (Engel (1993, 1999) and Rogers and Jenkins (1995)). Indeed, these studies found that the distance and the border played important roles in the failure of establishing the law of one price, which in turn becomes part of the source of real exchange rate movements (Engel and Rogers (1996). Engel and Rogers (1996) tested two hypotheses: (1) the volatility of the prices of similar goods between cities should be positively related to the distance between those cities because of the geographical separation of the markets in determining the degree of the failures of law of one price and (2) the volatility should be higher between two cities separated by the national border holding the distance constant. Using the price data of the United States and Canada, their regression analysis confirmed the validity of these two hypotheses: both the distance and the national border were important in explaining the price dispersion between cities when exchange rate is flexible.

3. Model Specification

The model employed in this study takes a lead from the works of Alaba (2003) and Russ (2007) with minor modifications made in Ibrahim and Omoniyi

$$FDI= (GDP, OPN, WOP, EXR, INF, WOP, EXRV) \quad (1)$$

The econometrics representation of the model is:

$$GDP= \beta_0 + \beta iBOP + \beta_2 WOP + \beta_3 FDI + \beta_4 INF + \beta_5 EXRV + n \quad (2)$$

Where:
GDP= Gross Domestic product
BOP = Balance of Payments

WOP = World Oil Price
FDI = Foreign Direct Investment
INF = Inflation rate
EXRV = Exchange Rate Volatility
μ = Stochastic error term
β_0 = Constant term
β_1 - β_s = Estimated parameters
Apriori Expectation

Based on economic theory, the following a-priori relationships are postulated for the estimated results. $B_1>0$ $\beta_2>0$ $\beta_3>0$ $\beta<0$ $\beta_5<0$

3.1. Estimation Techniques

The estimation techniques used to estimate and interpret the econometric and empirical investigation subsisting between endogenous variables using Johansen Error Correction Model (ECM) technique to capture the white noise embedded in the secondary data employed error in the model. The generalised auto-regression conditionally heteroskedastic (GARCH) was used to measure the volatility. The model is later re-specified to get a true picture of the event that taken place between the variables by introducing stationarity-unit root test, co-integration and error correction model. Also, the coefficient of determination is estimated to know the percentage of total variation on the dependent variable explained by the independent variable. The higher the co-efficient of determination the more useful the model will be for policy and predictive purposes. The F - statistics helps to determine whether or not all the partial regression co-efficient is equal to zero. An evaluation of the model equation on these criteria further supports the significance of the explanatory variable. To this end, in order to avoid spurious regression, the study carried out the following additional test:

3.1.1. Unit Root Test

To test the unit root using the DF test, we proceed by estimating the model

$$Y_t + Y_{t-1} = Et \quad (3)$$

Equation (3) is rewritten as

$$Yt = aY_{t-1}\text{-}, \text{-}Y_{t-1}, + Et \quad (4)$$

Equation (4) is rewritten as

$$Yt = (a\text{-}l)\ Y_{t-1} + Et$$

Solving equation (5) where (a-1) = ʚ we have

$$Yt = 0Y_{t-1} + Et$$

If $p < 1$ then $\theta < 1$, then Yt is stationary and it is integrated of order zero i.e. $1_{(0)}$.

Augmented Dickney - Fuller (ADF) Unit root was employed to determine the other of each time series.

3.1.2. Co-integration Technique

Two variables e.g. Ct and Yt are co-integrated if they satisfy the order of integration for the level and the differenced data series.

Then the residuals from the static equation of the variables in their level form are generated. After this, we use ADF Test to determine whether or not the residual Ct is $1_{(0)}$ i.e. are stationary. If the residual are of $1_{(0)}$, then the conclusion is that the equation under scrutiny is co-integrated.

In the event of non-stationary in the series tests, the implication behind this series of tests is that each time series is non-stationary linear combinations of such time series that are stationary might that the long-run movements in these multiple time series are related to each other. Indeed, if there is a long run relationship between two or more non-stationary variables, then the idea of the general concept of co-integration is that deviation from this long-run path are stationary.

3.2. Error Correction Model

The residuals generated from the static regression are called the error correction term. The error correction issue boil down to using the error term so derived to reparameterise the short-run dynamic specification. When this is done, we obtain the error correction model as:

$$Ct = \beta_0 + \beta_1 Yt + \Delta\ \beta_2 et + Vt \quad (5)$$

Here a plays the role of an error correction co-efficient and it should be less than 1. Since adjustment is not fully realised. The starting point of ECM is a test against the null hypothesis that the residuals of the long run (static) model are non-stationary. Here we apply both the ADF and DF tests to the residuals of the static co-integrating regressions. The evidence of the stationary of the residuals indicates that the variable in the models are indeed co-integrated. Adopting Engle - Granger representation is ECM, we employ an error correction dynamic specification dynamic specification of the form:

$$GDP = \beta_0 + \beta_1, L\ (Z) - \beta_2 EC\ t\text{-}_1 + ft \quad (6)$$

Where Z is the vector variable that co-integrate with the gross domestic product L is a general lag operator.

Between the level of inflation and the level of one or more of its determinants are permitted to affect the current change in inflation. Equation (6) can be reduced to a parsimonious equation through the elimination of insignificant terms and the imposition of constraints that hold a reasonable approximation.

Generalised Auto-regression Conditionality Heteroskedastic: it also employed multivariate GARCH model to analyse the exchange rate volatility transmission among the estimated variables. GARCH models, the most popular for time varying estimation, was initially introduced by Engle (1986: 987-1008) and consequently extended by many economist like Bollerslev (1986: 308-326), Bollerslev (1990: 498-505), Bollerslev and Engle (1993: 167-186), Engle (2001: 167-168), Bera and Kim (2002: 171-195). Multivariate GARCH models have also been used to investigate volatility and correlation transmission and spill-over effects in studies of cointagion. It includes both its own conditional variance and covariance.

General Autoregressive Conditional Heteroskedastistic Model (GARCH) differs to the ARCH model in that it incorporates squared conditional variance terms as additional explanatory variables. This allows the conditional variance to follow an ARMA process. If we write the residual as T-statistics and the usual diagnostic tests could also be added to this model. If there was only the one lag on the *h* variable, we could have a GARCH process which is the same as an ARCH process. The main problem with an ARCH model is that it requires a large number of lags to catch the nature of the volatility; this can be problematic as it is difficult to decide how many lags to include and produces a non-parsimonious model where the non-negativity constraint could be failed. The GARCH model is usually much more parsimonious and often a GARCH model is sufficient, this is because the GARCH model incorporates much of the information that a much larger ARCH model with large numbers of lags would contain.

4. Unit Root Test Result

The Augmented Dickey - Fuller (ADF) unit root test shows that inflation rate (INF) and exchange rate volatility (EXRV) are stationary at all level, that is they are integrated of order zero $I_{(0)}$, while foreign direct investment (FDI), degree of trade openness (OPN), exchange rate (EXR), and World oil price (WOP) are stationary at the first difference and this implies that they are integrated of order one $1_{(1)}$, However, the result shows that Gross domestic product (GDP) is stationary at the second difference and this also implies that it is integrated of order two $1_{(2)}$.

4.1. Analysis of ARCH and GARCII (Autoregressive Conditional Heteroskedasticity and Generalised Conditional Heteroskedasticity)

Autoregressive Conditional Heteroskedasticity (ARCH) models are specifically designed to model and forecast conditional variances. The variance of the dependent variable is modelled as a function of past values of the dependent variable and independent or exogenous variables.

Decision Rule:

The decision rule below is based on the rule of the thumb and cited by Yinusa (2004)

If $\alpha + \beta < 1$ No volatility

If $\alpha + \beta \twoheadrightarrow 1$ There is Volatility

If $\alpha + \beta > 1$ This is the case of overshooting, meaning an outrageous level of volatility

Note: α = ARCH term/coefficient, while p = GARCH term/coefficient

From the result of ARCH and GARCH, it revealed ARCH coefficient of 1.227374 and GARCH coefficient of - 0.157777. The summation of the ARCH and GARCH coefficient equals 1.069597. Therefore, since $\alpha + \beta > 1$, i.e. (1.069597 >1), we can conclude that there is a case of overshooting, which implies an outrageous level of volatility, i.e. the variables exhibit element of volatility clustering.

The Short Run Relationship between Exchange Rate Volatility and Foreign Direct Investment, Using Ordinary Least Square (OLS). Substituted coefficients:

$$FDI = - 969294.3 + 3.576131GDP + 35798.71OPN - 8110.553EXR - 762.6544INF + 8156.657WOP + 12531.99EXRV$$

From the regression equation specified above, it revealed a constant value of - 969294.3 and this represent the value of foreign direct investment (FDI) in Nigeria if all the explanatory variables in the model are held constant. The equation further revealed that EXR and INF have a negative relationship with FDI, as a unit increase in EXR and INF will reduce the FDI by 8110.553 and 762.6544 respectively in the short run. However, the result revealed that exchange rate volatility (EXRV) has a positive impact on the FD]. It revealed that a unit increase in the EXRV increases the FDI by 12531.99 within the period under review. Similarly, the result shows that GDP, OPN and WOP have a positive impact on FDI and this implies that a unit increase in them will increase the FDI by 12531.99, 35798.71 and 8156.657 respectively.

The result also revealed an R-square of about 0.879363 and this implies that about 88% of the systematic variations in the FDI is being explained by the variations in the explanatory variables. This shows that the model is a good fit as only about 12% of the variations are not accounted for by the model and this is attributed to the error term.

The result of the Trace test present 5 co integrating equation(s) at the 0.05 level since the trace statistic is greater than critical value at 5%.

The result of the maximum eigen value test indicates two (2) co integrating equations at 5% critical value. However, according to Johansen and Juselius (1996) recommends the use of the trace statistics when there is a conflict between the maximum Eigen value and the trace statistics.

Hence, the long run relationship among the variables will then be determined by the normalised co-integrating coefficient with the highest log likelihood in absolute term. The result Log likelihood is -962.6920

From the result the co integrating equation is specified thus:

$$FDI - 1.045741\ GDP_{t-1} - 98340.37OPN_{t-1} + 18757.31EXR_{t-1} - 19117.08INF_{t-1} - 3\ 8221.19\ WOP_{t-1} + 322177.8\ EXRV_{t-1}$$

The above equation represents the normalised co integrating equation with the highest log likelihood in absolute terms. From the above equation, it revealed that gross domestic product (GDP), exchange rate (EXR) and exchange rate volatility (EXRV) have a long run positive relationship with the foreign direct investment (FDI) and this implies that a unit increase in the GDP, EXR and EXRV will increase the FDI by 1.045741,18757.31 and 322177.8 respectively in the long run. This result conforms to the a-priori expectation earlier stated in the previous chapter of the study as it reveals a positive relationship between gross domestic product (GDP) which is the major indicator of the country's economic performance and the foreign direct investment. This result shows that an increase in the rate of country's domestic economic performance will attract foreign investors in the long run as they will be induced to invest in the economy. However, the result shows that degree of trade openness (OPN), inflation rate (INF) and world oil price (WOP) have a negative long run relationship with foreign direct investment (FDI) in Nigeria throughout the period under review. This implies that a unit increase in the OPN, INF and WOP will reduce the FDI by 98340.37, 19117.08 and 38221.19 respectively in the long run.

The Error Correction Model (ECM) integrates the long-run equilibrium relationship with short run dynamics. The ECM involves two stages. The overparameterized Error Correction Model (ECMi) and the Parsimonious Error Correction Model

R-squared 0.812457

Adjusted R-squared 0.573765

Durbin - Watson stat 2.040760

prob (F- statistic) 0.023842

F - statistic 3.403791

It shows the initial overparametersed ECM] model. All the variables were lagged equally by one period. Since only four variables are significant at 5 percent level significance, there is therefore the need to proceed on the parsimonious Error Model (ECM2).

Parsimonious error correction model (ECM2)

R-squared 0.710950

Adjusted R-squared 0.582483

Durbin-Watson stat 1.966465

F-statistic 5.534117

Prob(F-statistic) 0.00126

The results of the parsimonious Error Correction Model.

The equation of the ECM is therefore specified in line with parsimonious model as follows:

FD1 = 6186.506 - 0.152310FDIt-1+ 0.125527GDPt-1 + 5424.624OPNt-1 -7801.809EXRt -1 - 726.8518INFt-1 +5050J44WOPt.1 +26766.58EXRVt-1, -0.979078ECMt-1

The equation above shows an ECM value of-0.979078 which is otherwise referred to as the speed of adjustment. The speed of adjustment is significant at 5% considering its probability value (0.0001% < 5%) and standard error. Also, the ECM is correctly signed which implies that about 98% of the short-run inconsistencies are being corrected and incorporated rated into the long-run relationship. The implication of this is that the present value of FDI will adjust to changes in GDP,OPN, EXR, INF, WOP and EXRV. The R^2 of about 0.710950 implies that about 72% of the dynamic variation in FDI is being explained by variations in GDP, OPN, EXR, INF, WOP and EXRV. This shows a very good fit of the model as only about 28% variation unaccounted for by the model is r:'-.r.ed to the error term. From the ECMa equation, the present value of FDI has a negative relationship with the previous value of FDJ. This implies that foreign direct investment does not obey the time series property that the past value of a variable should exert positively on the present value of the variable. Also from the equation, it revealed a constant value of 6186.506 which represents the value of the foreign direct investment, if all he explanatory variables in the model are held constant. Also, it revealed that gross domestic product (GDP), degree of trade openness (OPN). World oil price (WOP) and the exchange rate volatility (EXRV) have a positive relationship with the foreign direct investment (FDI) in Nigeria and this implies that a unit increase in GDP, OPN, WOP and EXRV will increase the FDI by 0.125527, 5424.624. 5050.244 and 26766.58 respectively. However, the equation further revealed that exchange rate (EXR) and inflation rate (INF) has a negative relationship with the foreign direct investment (FDI), this implies that a unit increase in EXR and INF will reduce the FDI by 7801.809 and 726.8518 respectively. The analysis of the Durbin-Watson test for autocorrelation reveals that the model is free from first-order serial autocorrelation. This implies that the model is well specified.

4.2. Discussion of Findings

It revealed through the unit root test that gross domestic product (GDP) is stationary at the second difference which implies that GDP can sustain any form of shock passed on it for a long period of time. However, the result of the unit root test further shows that INF and EXRV are integrated of order zero and this also indicates that INF and EXRV cannot sustain any form of shock passed on them. Furthermore, FDI, OPN, EXR and WOP are all integrated of order one and this implies that they can only sustain any form of shock passed on them for a short period of time. Also, the result of the co integration test shows that OPN. \YOP and INF are the only variable having a long run negative relationship with FDI in Nigeria, while GDP, EXR and EXRV contributes positively in the long run to FDI. The equation of the error correction mechanism (ECM) reveals an ECM coefficient which is also the speed of convergence of about, -0.979078 which implies that 98% of the short run inconsistencies are being corrected. While the equation further revealed that EXR. and INF have a negative relationship with foreign direct investment in Nigeria, while all other variables, (GDP, OPN, WOP and EXRV) exerts a positive impact on FDI in Nigeria. Though none of the variables passed the test of significance on FDI except exchange rate (FiXR) which has a positive significant impact on foreign direct investment (FDI) in Nigeria.

5. Summary and Recommendation

From analysis of the empirical results, the result of ARCH and GARCH. the summation of the ARCH and GARCH term is greater than one i.e. (1.069597 >1), it was concluded that there is a case of overshooting, which implies an outrageous level of volatility, i.e. the variables exhibit element of volatility clustering. Also, the result of the co integration test shows that OPN, WOP and INF are the only variable having a long run negative relationship with FDI in Nigeria, while GDP, EXR and EXRV contributes positively in the long run to FDI. The equation of the error correction mechanism (ECM) reveals an ECM coefficient which is also the speed of convergence of about - 0.979078 which implies that 98% of the short run inconsistencies are being corrected. While the equation further revealed that EXR and INF have a negative relationship with foreign direct investment in Nigeria, while all other variables, (GDP, OPN, WOP and EXRV) exerts a positive impact on FDI in Nigeria.

Also, from the result established by the co integration test, we can conclude that gross domestic product, exchange rate and exchange rate volatility are positive determinant of foreign direct investment in Nigeria. This conclusion could be attributed to the role of GDP in the economy as it reveals the performance of an economy, therefore, foreign investors may be attracted to invest in such an economy that witness a persistent increase in her GDP. Likewise the exchange rate volatility, foreign investors will be very conscious about the current fluctuations in price of the local currency of their preferred country at the foreign exchange market. The analysis of the short run relationship in the model revealed an R^2 of about 0.879363 (88%), from this result, it can be concluded that GDP OPN EXR INF WOP and EXRV can explain about 88% of the variations in Nigeria's foreign direct investment.

Recommendations

In the light of the above findings, the following recommendations are made: First, the government should ensure that the profits realised by the Multinational cooperation who supplies Foreign Direct Investment in terms of capital flows should be encouraged to reinvest major parts of their profits into the Nigerian Economy. One way to improve the business environment is by conscious provision of necessary infrastructure which will lower the costs of doing business in Nigeria.

The federal government should ensure that a clean floating rate policy is adopted so as to be able to determine the real status of the Nigerian naira rather than operating a dirty floating exchange rate where the naira exchange is allowed to float between a bound of (+ or -) 5 percent. If the clean floating exchange rate policy is adopted, it will encourage trade liberalisation rather than engaging on devaluation/revaluation of the Nigerian naira to encourage trade liberalisation.

References

[1] Benassy-Quere, A. Fontagne And Lahreche-Revil, A. 2001; *Exchange Rate Strategies In The For Attracting Foreign Direct Investment.* Journal Of The Japanese International Economics, Vol. 15 No 2, Pp 178 - 198.

[2] Obadan, M. I 2004; *" Globalisation And Economic Management In Africa "* Chapter One In: Nigeria Economic Society Paper For The 2003 Annual Conferences (Ibadan Nigeria Economic Society).

[3] Kiyota, K. And Shujiro, U. 2004; *Exchange Rate, Exchange Rate Volatility And Foreign Direct Investment.* The World Economy, Vol, 27 Issue 10, Pp 1501 - 1536.

[4] World Bank 1994; *Nigeria Structured Adjustment Programme. Policies Implementation And Impact.* World Bank Report No: 130534Jni.

[5] World Bank 2003; *Financial Flows And Developing Countries.* A World Bank Business Quarterly Report.

[6] Aseidu, G. 2001; *On The Determinant Of Foreign Direct Investment To Developing Countries. Is African Really Different?* World Development 30(1) Pp 7 – 19.

[7] Cushman, D. O 1998; *Exchange Rate Certainty And Foreign Direct Investment In The United State.* Wethwirtschafilies Archive 124:2 Pp 297 - 308.

[8] Goldberg, Linda And Charles Kolstad. 1993; *Foreign Direct Investment, Exchange Rate Variability And Demand Uncertainty.* International Economic Review. Vol. 36 No 4 Pp 65 - 73.

[9] Ogunleye 2008; *Exchange Rate Volatility And Foreign Direct Investment Inflows In Selected Sub-Saharan African Countries.* Phd Dissertation. University Of Ibadan.

[10] Simeon Oke, O. O. 2005; *Exchange Rate And Industrial Performance In Nigeria.* Journal Of Economics And Social Studies. Vol. 16, 2009.

[11] Takaendesa, P. 2006; *The Behaviour And Fundamental Determinants Of Real Exchange Rate In South Africa.* A Masters Thesis Submitted To Rhodes University, South Africa.

[12] Omoniyi, B. B. And Omobitan, O. A. 2011; *The Impact Of Foreign Direct Investment On Economic Growth In Nigeria.* International Research Journal Of Finance And Economics, London.

[13] FDI Magazine 2003 *http/www.Fdiintlligence.com.*

[14] Johansen, S., 1988. Statistical analysis of cointegration vectors. J. Econ. Dyn. Control, 12: 231-254.

[15] Olayiwola, K. and H. Okodua, 2009. Foreign direct investment, non-oil export and economic growth in Nigeria: A causality analysis. Proceeding for the 14th Annual Conference on Econometric Modelling for Africa, for the African Econometric Society, Abuja 8-10 July.

[16] Chuku, A.C. (2010). Monetary and Fiscal Policy Interactions In Nigeria: An Application of a State Space Model With Markov-Switching. CBN Journal of Applied Statistics, Vol. 1, No. 1, (Dec.).

[17] Anyanwu, J. C. et al. (1997). The Structure of the Nigerian Economy (1960-1997). Onitsha: JOANEE Educational Publishers.

[18] Ekpo, A. H. (2012). Employment, Growth and Poverty Reduction in an Oil Export Economy: Evidence from Nigeria, being paper presented at the 53rd Annual Conference of the Nigerian Economic Society, 27-30 August, Nicon Luxury Hotel, Abuja.

[19] Federal Republic of Nigeria. (2007). Vision 20-2020 Blueprint.

[20] F.Allen and D.Gale, "Competition and financial stability,"Journal of Money, Credit, and Banking pp. 433-480, 2004.

[21] E.Kocenda and J. Valachy, "Exchange rate volatility and regime change: A visegrad comparison" Journal of Comparative Economics, pp. 727-753, 2006.

[22] A.C. Arize, T. Osang, and D.J. Slottje, "Exchange rate volatility and foreign trade: Evidence from thirteen LDCs" Journal of Business and Economics Statistics, pp. 10-17, 2000.

[23] K.L.Wang and C.B. Barrett," Estimating the Effects of Exchange Rate Volatility on Export Volumes" Journal of Agricultural and Resource Economics,pp.225-255,2007.

[24] C.Sauer and A.K.Bohara," Exchange rate volatility and exports: Regional differences between developing and industrialized countries," Review of International Economics, 2001.

[25] G.Corsetti, P.Pesenti, and N.Roubini, "What caused the asian currency and financial crisis?" Japan and the World Economy, pp.305-373, 1999.

[26] A.J. Makin" International economics, finance and trade," The Balance of Payments and the Exchange Rate,vol. I, 2004.

[27] S. Tenreyro," On the trade impact of nominal exchange rate volatility," Journal of Development Economics, pp. 485-508, 2007.

[28] A.R.Ghosh, A.M.Gulde, andH.C.Wolf, Exchange Rate Regimes: Choices and Consequences, The MIT Press, 2003.

[29] H.Duncan," The effect of exchange rate volatility on trade and employment: A brief review of the literature economics" Macroeconomy, Economic Bias andEmployment, vol. 28, no. 3, pp 133 -152, 2001.

Management of Pollutants in Industries

Seyed Ebrahim Vahdat*, Rohollah Askarpour, Pedram Keyhany, Yones Rahimi, Hadi Soflaei

Department of Engineering, Bandar Abbas Branch, Islamic Azad University, Bandar Abbas, Iran

Email address:
e.vahdat@iauamol.ac.ir (S. E. Vahdat), askarpour2002@yahoo.com (R. Askarpour), p.keyhany@gmail.com Pedram Keyhany(P. Keyhany), younesrahimi55@gmail.com (Y. Rahimi), hadi.soflaei@gmail.com (H. Soflaei)

Abstract: In this paper, using fuzzy logic, a model is presented to monitor region wise industrial pollutants in pyrometallurgy industries. The model has been used in a case study that will determine which industry, in which region, producing which and how much pollutants, is ecologically compatible. To assess the ecological compatibility, first, the sets of industries, regions, pollutants and ecology compatibility were defined. Then, to calculate the membership degree of the members of the ecology compatibility set, the membership function of ecology compatibility was defined. By ranking different industries in various regions, producing different pollutants, as continuous figures, the ecological compatibility of these industries was accurately compared. Given the degree of ecological compatibility in a region, the type of pollutant and the related industry, identification of the lowest degree of ecological compatibility was the first priority of this case study. Results of the conducted case study, without considering the region coefficient, show that in December 2005, member C_{241}, with an ecological degree of compatibility equivalent to 0.0559, had the most critical condition in producing carbon dioxide. However, in the same period in 2005, on considering the region coefficient, member C_{121}, with an ecological degree of compatibility equivalent to 0.0655, showed the most critical condition as far the production of carbon dioxide was concerned.

Keywords: Fuzzy Logic, Monitoring, Pyrometallurgy Industries

1. Introduction

In considering capabilities for sustainable development, ecological, economical, and social and industrial concerns have rapidly become the most important challenges in the twenty first century. Due to the existence of many pollutant producers, each producing some kind of pollutants in various regions with different pollution levels, the simultaneous consideration of all the pollutant producers for the purpose of pollution management and control becomes a difficult task. However, through prioritizing them in terms of ecological compatibility as continuous figures, it can be determined that which industry, in which region, producing which and how much pollutants, should be in the priority of investigation. The comparison model of various indices, based on fuzzy logic, shows the relativity of various features, defines a set for each feature, and determines the utility rate of each variable to provide the desired feature by a degree between 0 and 1. This value, as the awarded degree of the desired variable, is measured compared to the mentioned feature. On this basis, desirability degree of 0 would mean that the desired feature is not provided for the desired variable, or the desired variable is not desirable for the desired feature at all. Similarly, desirability degree of 1 means the desired feature is provided for the desired variable or the desired variable is desirable for the desired feature. Following the same reasoning, a desirability degree between 0 and 1 would mean that the desired feature is provided to some degree for the desired variable or the desired variable is to some degree desirable for the desired feature.

Researchers have used fuzzy logic to study the pollutants in the environment. Ref [1] used fuzzy logic in studying the sustainable development of iron and steel industry in the context of ecology in Iran. Ref [2] ranked air pollutants in five regions of Tehran (Iran), however, they did not consider the effect of the pollutants, already existing in the studied regions, in their model. In other words, the effect of produced pollutants is different for less polluted and more polluted regions, which must be considered in any such study. Ref [3] used fuzzy logic to predict the ozone concentration and matched their model with the data obtained from Weather Bureau of Canada. Ref [4] used the fuzzy logic to quantify photochemical model and predict pollutants and matched their model with the data from Weather Bureau of

Hong Kong. Ref [5] applied chemo-metrics, based on fuzzy logic principles, in his environmental studies. Ref [6] used fuzzy logic for the air conditioning system of long tunnels. Ref [7] presented a model based on fuzzy logic to determine the extent of water pollution and then matched it with the data of Water Department of Eber Lake in Turkey.

A consideration of the cited literature shows that a comprehensive model to study the degree of ecological compatibility of various industries, especially taking into account the district effect is yet to be attempted. In this paper, the ecological compatibility feature has been used, so that at a given time, the degree of ecological compatibility of any given industry in any given region in the production of any given pollutant can be monitored, relatively and quantitatively. On the basis of the minimum degree of ecological compatibility, priority in studying and monitoring different industries in various regions, producing different pollutants, can be presented.

In this paper, the fuzzy logic has been used to determine the degree of ecological compatibility of industries in various regions of the world. The set of pollutants can exist in the solid state (such as dust, soot, and lead dust); liquid (such as mercury dissolved in water), gas (such as carbon, carbon dioxide, methane), and also in the form of the sound and wave (such as the radioactive rays). The set of regions in the world is formed from the set of different continents (Asia, Europe, Africa, America and Oceania), and the set of continents from the set of various countries (Russia, China, India, Iran...). Similarly, the set of countries is obtained from the set of different regions (urban, rural, industrial areas, etc.). The set of pollutant producers consist of the set of domestic industries (HVAC systems,...), transportation industries (automobile,...), hydrometallurgy industries (sewage,...), pyrometallurgy industry (iron and steel manufacturing industries, copper, lead, zinc and aluminium, etc.). In the present study, the sizes of data sets have been reduced for the sake of simplification. Accordingly, from the set of pollutants only carbon dioxide has been considered. Similarly, from the set of industries only pyrometallurgy industries, from the set of pyrometallurgy industries only iron, steel, aluminium, lead and zinc, and from the set of regions only one country in each region, namely the Far East, the Middle East, Europe and America, have been considered in this study for calculation and comparison of ecological compatibility degree for each case.

2. Methods

To determine the ecological compatibility, first, the sets of industries, regions, pollutants and ecology compatibility were defined. Then, to calculate the membership degree of the members of the ecology compatibility set, the membership function of ecology compatibility was defined. Figure 1 shows the procedure for implementing the method used in this study.

Definition of the sets

In this study, to assess the ecological compatibility degree of pyrometallurgy industries in various regions using fuzzy logic, three sets have been defined and examined as followings:

Set M: This set includes the industries producing iron and steel, aluminium, copper, lead, zinc, creating pollutants such as carbon dioxide, which are expressed by Eq. (1). Set M can contain m members, and m_i is the ith metallurgy industry being studied:

$$M=\{i\in \mathbb{N},\ i\in [1,..,m],\ m_i\}=\{m_i\} \quad (1)$$

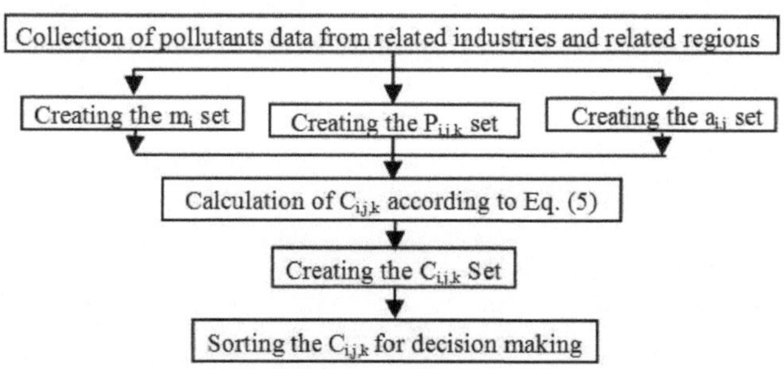

Figure 1. *Fuzzy inference algorithm for determination of the ecological compatibility degree.*

Set A: This set includes the regions in which pollutants are produced, and is defined and evaluated based on Eq. (2). Set A can be the set of regions enclosed in world pyrometallurgy factories such as steel mills in Isfahan (Iran), Hamburg (Germany),..., or the set of Iranian cities such as Ahvaz and Isfahan,..., or the set of world provinces such as Mazandaran (Iran), Florida (USA),..., or the set of world countries such as Iran, Japan,..., or the set of Iranian provinces such as Mazandaran, Gilan,.... It is evident that as the studied regions become broader (worldwide) and the components of set A are more detailed (enclosed regions), the estimates would be more reasonable and acceptable. Set A can have a members and $a_{i,j}$ is the ith industry in the jth region being studied:

$$A=\{j\in \mathbb{N},\ j\in [1,..,a],\ a_{i,j}\}=\{a_{i,j}\} \quad (2)$$

Set P: This set, which is related to the type of pollutants, can contain members such as carbon dioxide, carbon monoxide, sulfur dioxide, lead, nitrogen oxides, volatile organic compounds, cyclic aromatic hydrocarbons, etc., and is defined by Eq. (3). It can include p members, where $p_{i,j,k}$ represents pollutant k produced by the ith industry in the jth region:

$$P=\{k\in \mathbb{N},\ k\in [1,..,p],\ p_{i,j,k}\}=\{p_{i,j,k}\} \quad (3)$$

Care should be taken to normalize the amount of pollutants. Consequently, $p_{i,j,k,normalized}$ would mean the kth pollutant, produced per unit of product in the ith industry in the jth region. To calculate $p_{i,j,k,normalized}$, the following equation can be used:

$$p_{i,j,k,normalized} = (\text{total k pollution in the } a_{i,j})/(\text{total mass production of } a_{i,j}) \quad (4)$$

Set M can include m members, set A can have a members and set P can include p members. Therefore, the number of members in the ecological compatibility set C would maximally be equal to m×a×p .

Determination of the ecological compatibility degree

The aim is to determine the ecological compatibility degree of the ith industry in producing the kth pollutant in the jth region. For this purpose, an ecological compatibility set C is defined, which contains different industries producing various pollutants in different regions. Each member of the set is specified by a membership degree, $C_{i,j,k}$, which indicates a specific industry i, producing a specific pollutant k in a specific region j how much compatible with ecology. Eq. (5) is used to determine the ecological compatibility degree of the members in set C. Eq. (5) is the modified equation used by [8].
with the region factor

$$c_{i,j,k} = \left(\left(\frac{Min\{p_{i,j,k,Normalized}\}}{\{p_{i,j,k,Normalized}\}}\right)\left(\frac{G_{k,Critical}}{G_{k,j}}\right)\right) \quad (5a)$$

Without the region factor

$$c_{i,j,k} = \left(\frac{Min\{p_{i,j,k,Normalized}\}}{\{p_{i,j,k,Normalized}\}}\right) \quad (5b)$$

$$C=\{\ C_{i,j,k}\ \}$$

In the above equation, $G_{k,j}$ is the present value of the kth pollutant in the jth region, which is reported by measuring the pollutant in every region (Air Pollution Control District), and is dependent on the time and location conditions, and $G_{k,critical}$ is the critical value of the same pollutant k in the same region j, which is determined by environmental standards, and is independent on the time and location conditions.

Thus, all industries are ranked uniformly and relatively between 0 and 1, according to the pollutants they produce and the regions they belong to. Therefore, ecological compatibility degree of 0 for $C_{i,j,k}$ member indicates an industry i^{th}, located in the jth region, producing the kth pollutant, which is not at all compatible with ecology. On contrary, ecological compatibility degree of 1 for the same member $C_{i,j,k}$ means that the concerned industry is highly compatible with ecology. Similarly, a ecological compatibility degree between 0 and 1 for $C_{i,j,k}$ member means that the industry is to some extent compatible with ecology.

If the value of the kth pollutant in the jth region, $G_{k,j}$, is greater than the critical value, $G_{k,critical}$, the ecological compatibility degree will become smaller because the region coefficient, $G_{k,critical}/G_{k,j}$, is smaller than one. The lower the ecological compatibility degree; the more difficult it becomes to change conditions to achieve ecological compatibility for the ith industry, which is responsible for the production of kth pollutant in the jth region. On the other hand, when the value of a pollutant in a region is less than its critical value, the region coefficient is larger than one. So, the ecological compatibility degree for some members may be greater than one. Although the membership greater than one has not been defined in fuzzy phenomena, it is meaningful here. The greater the ecological compatibility degree, the easier it becomes to change conditions for ecological compatibility of the desired member.

The most ecological compatible industry is one that has the highest ecological compatibility degree. To determine the most ecological compatible industry, $C_{i,j,k,Environmental}$, the fuzzy maximum rule is used as given below:

$$C_{i,j,k,Environmental} = Max\{C_{i,j,k}\} \quad (6)$$

In a similar manner, the least ecological compatible industry is the industry that has the smallest ecological compatibility degree. To determine the least ecological compatible industry, $C_{i,j,k,critical}$, the fuzzy minimum rule is used as given below:

$$C_{i,j,k,Environmental} = Min\{C_{i,j,k}\} \quad (7)$$

It may seem that monitoring the pollutants in the set of industries can be misleading because for example, an industry which uses advanced production technologies has a high ecological compatibility degree since the normalized value of pollutants is low. However, the total amount of a pollutant in a given time may be very high, so that the industry practically allocates the bulk of production of the pollutant to itself. The significant question is that if the production volume of a product in modern industrial regions with advanced technologies is reduced, what technology will be used to compensate for the deficit caused by the declining production volume? If the intended technology is not an advanced one, the total amount of the pollutant will further increase. The second term in the parenthesis in Eq. (5), $G_{k,critical}/G_{k,j}$, has been included to present the total amount of the variable pollutant over time in a given region.

Determination of the ecological compatibility degree in pyrometallurgy industries: A case study

In this case study, data on four pyrometallurgy industries, namely iron and steel production industry, aluminium production industry, lead production industry, and zinc production industry, published in December 2005, has been used. Accordingly, set M, which represents the industries, contains four members, i.e., m=4. Similarly, for set A, representing the regions in which pollutants are produced, four countries were considered; one in the Middle East, one in the Far East, one in America, and one in Europe. Therefore, set A will have four members, i.e., a=4. In order to avoid prejudice and bias, names of countries studied have not been mentioned. Also, to simplify and integrate the data, only one air pollutant, namely carbon dioxide, has been considered in this study, which means set P, which represents the set of the studied pollutants, has only one member, i.e., p=1. Therefore, the maximum number of members of set C will be equal to 4×4×1=16.

Table 1. *The ecological compatibility degrees for industries in different regions, with and without the region factor.*

ecological compatibility degree with region factor (From Eq. (5a))	CO_2 (measured Value) (ppm) $G_{k,j}$ [13-15]	CO_2 (Critical Value or standard value) (ppm) $G_{k,critical}$ [13-15]	Region Factor $G_{k,critical}/G_{k,j}$	ecological compatibility degree without region factor (From Eq. (5b))	CO_2 (Normal Value) (ppm) (From Eq. (4)) [13-15]	Industry			Description
						i producer	j region	k pollutant	
C_{111} =0.0912	250	300	1.2	0.0760	$P_{1,1,1,normalized}$ = 2.5	1	1	1	Iron and steel industry in the Middle East country
C_{121} =0.0655	280	300	1.07	0.0613	$P_{1,2,1,normalized}$ = 3.1	1	2	1	Iron and steel industry in the Far East country
C_{131}= 0.1056	360	300	1/1.2	0.1267	$P_{1,3,1,normalized}$ = 1.5	1	3	1	Iron and steel industry in the Europe country
C_{231}= 0.0990	360	300	1/1.2	0.1187	$P_{2,3,1,normalized}$ = 1.6	2	3	1	Aluminium industry in a country in Europe
C_{241}= 0.0838	200	300	1.5	0.0559	$P_{2,4,1,normalized}$ = 3.4	2	4	1	Aluminium industry in a country in America
C_{341}= 1.5000	200	300	1.5	1.0000	$P_{3,4,1,normalized}$= 0.19	3	4	1	Zinc industry in a country in America continent
C_{441}= 1.0962	200	300	1.5	0.7308	$P_{4,4,1,normalized}$= 0.26	4	4	1	Lead industry in a country in America continent

Ecological compatibility degree in the iron and steel production industry

Major pollutants in iron and steel production industry are: (i) gaseous pollutants: carbon dioxide, greenhouse gases, carbon monoxide, sulphur dioxide, nitrogen oxides, chloride and fluoride, volatile organic compounds, cyclic aromatic hydrocarbons, dioxins, (ii) solid pollutants: dust, heavy metals such as sponge iron, zinc, cadmium, lead, nickel, mercury, magnesium, and cream, soot, (iii) liquid pollutants: sewage and waste water from the production process, which mainly contain suspended particles, dust and lubricant materials. Sound pollution in the iron and steel production units is due to the handling of steel products and scrap, cooling fans, electric arc melting process in furnace, fuel torches, shaping and cutting tools and transport [1]. To simplify and integrate the data, only one air pollutant, namely carbon dioxide, has been considered, which means k=1.

Ecological compatibility degree in the aluminium production industry

Major pollutants in aluminium production industry area carbon dioxide in the air, hexa fleoromethane, tetra fleoromethane as gas and dust, sulphur dioxide, nitrogen dioxide and mercury [9]. To simplify and integrate the data, only one air pollutant, namely carbon dioxide, has been considered, which means k=1.

Ecological compatibility degree in zinc production industry

Major pollutants in zinc production industry are carbon dioxide in the air, sulphur compounds and nitrogen oxides [10, 11]. To simplify and integrate the data, only one air pollutant, namely carbon dioxide, has been considered, which means k=1.

Ecological compatibility degree in the lead production industry

Major pollutants in zinc production industry are carbon dioxide in the air, lead in air and water, sulphur compounds and nitrogen oxides [12]. To simplify and integrate the data, only one air pollutant, namely carbon dioxide, has been considered, which means k=1.

Calculating the ecological compatibility degree in pyrometallurgy industries

The quantity of carbon dioxide in different regions, $G_{k,j}$, is listed in Table 1. Thus, the region coefficient has different values for different members, $C_{i,j,k}$, in the ecological compatibility set.

$$M=\{i\in \mathbb{N}, i\in [1,2,3,4], m_i\} \rightarrow M=\{\text{Iron and steel production, Aluminium production, Zinc production, Lead production}\}$$

$$A=\{j\in \mathbb{N}, j\in [1,2,3,4], a_{i,j}\} \rightarrow A=\{\text{a country in America, one in Europe, one in the Middle East, one in the Far East}\}$$

$$P=\{k\in \mathbb{N}, k\in [1], P_{i,j,k}\} \rightarrow P=\{CO_2\}$$

3. Results and Discussion

According to Eq. (1) to (5) and data from Table 1, values of the ecological compatibility degree, with and without the region coefficient, have been calculated and are listed in the same Table 1.

According to Eq. (6), considering the region coefficient, the most ecologically compatible member in set C, namely C_{341}, which produces carbon dioxide, with an ecological compatibility degree of 1.5000 (obtained as follows), is the Zinc production industry, in a country in the American continent during the period December 2005:

$$C_{Max}= \{0.0912, 0.0655, 0.1056, 0.0990, 0.0838, 1.5000, 1.0962\} = C_{341} =1.5000$$

According to Eq. (7), including the region coefficient, the least ecologically compatible member in set C, namely C_{121}, which produces carbon dioxide, with an ecological compatibility degree of 0.0655 (obtained as follow), is the steel industry, in a country in the Far East, during the period December 2005:

$$C_{Min}= \{0.0912, 0.0655, 0.1056, 0.0990, 0.0838, 1.5000, 1.0962\} = C_{121}= 0.0655$$

The ecological compatibility degrees, with and without the area effect, for all regions and industries producing carbon dioxide during the period December 2005, have been compared in Fig. 2.

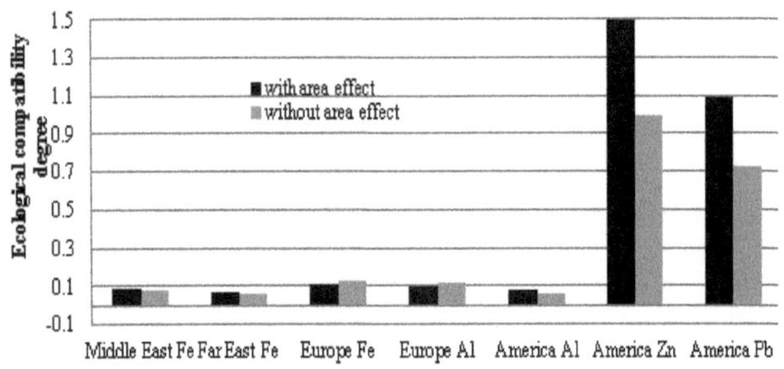

Figure 2. Ecological compatibility degrees, with and without the area effect, for all regions and industries producing carbon dioxide during the period December 2005.

4. Conclusions

In December 2005, in those parts of the world where the amount of carbon dioxide was greater than the maximum allowable limit, i.e., $G_{k,critical}/G_{k,j}$ was greater than 1, emission of even a small quantity of addition carbon dioxide would be dangerous. However, it is practically impossible to stop the production of steel and aluminium because many industries depend on these products for their operation. In addition, for different members, value of $G_{k,critical}/G_{k,j}$ is different in different regions. This means in a region with lower production of carbon dioxide, conditions for the production of these metals is more favourable. Therefore, it is necessary to determine the industry, and the related region, with the least ecological compatibility in the production of carbon dioxide. In other words, it must be determined that which industry, in which region, has more difficulties in changing its manufacturing conditions for attaining higher ecological compatibility degree in the production of carbon dioxide.

In December 2005, in the set of ecological compatibility, $C_{i,j,k}$, member C_{241}, namely the aluminium industry in a country in the American continent, producing carbon dioxide, without taking into account the region coefficient, has an ecological compatibility degree of 0.0559, has the most critical condition in producing air pollutant carbon dioxide. If the region coefficient is taken into consideration, steel industry in a country in the Far East, namely member C_{121}, in the same period of year, with an ecological compatibility degree of 0.0655, has the most critical conditions in producing air pollutant, carbon dioxide.

Therefore, more focus should be put on controlling carbon dioxide emissions in the steel industry in the Far East country. Control methods could include more training for the manpower, the use of new and rehabilitated units, innovation in cleaner technologies, ecological cleanup (such as tree planting); the use of alternative materials to reduce consumption of steel and steel products. By taking into account the region coefficient, and considering the parameters studied, the ecological compatibility degree in other industries in ascending order can be put as the followings:

- Aluminium industry in a country in American continent, C_{241}, with the ecological compatibility degree of 0.0838, is in the second priority for investigation.
- Iron and steel industry in a country in the Middle East, C_{111}, with the ecological compatibility degree of 0.0912, is in the third priority for investigation.
- Aluminium Industry in a country in Europe, C_{231}, with the ecological compatibility degree of 0.0990, is in the fourth priority for investigation.
- Iron and steel industry in a country in Europe, C_{131}, with the ecological compatibility degree of 0.1056, is in the fifth priority for investigation.
- Lead industry in a country in American continent, C_{441}, with the ecological compatibility degree of 1.0962, is in the sixth priority for investigation.
- Zinc industry in a country in American continent, C_{341}, with the ecological compatibility degree of 1.5000, is in the seventh priority for investigation.

Suggestions

1) In this study, for the sake of simplification, only a limited number of industries, regions, and pollutants has been studied. On increasing the number of members of the various sets namely sets of pollutants, industries and regions at different times, a larger range of parameters can be monitored, which will add to the accuracy of the results.
2) Although in this study the proposed model has been used to monitor the pollutants resulting from the operation of metal production industry, the same model can be applied for other industries and pollutants in any other region in the world.

References

[1] S.E. Vahdat and A. Pournaghi, "The Model for Monitoring of Pollutants Located in Different Regions", *Management Science and Practice*, Vol. 1, Iss. 1, PP. 8-13, 2013.

[2] M.H. Sowlat, H. Gharibi, M. Yunesian, M. Tayefeh Mahmoudi and S. Lotfi, "A novel fuzzy-based air quality index (FAQI) for air quality assessment", *Atmospheric Environment*, Vol. 45, pp. 2050-2059, 2011.

[3] R. Mintz, B.R. Young and W.Y. Svrcek, "Fuzzy logic modeling of surface ozone concentrations", *Journal of Computers and Chemical Engineering*, Vol. 29,pp. 2049-2059, 2005.

[4] O.M. Pokrovsky, R.H.F. Kwok and C.N. Ng, "Fuzzy logic approach for description of meteorological impacts on urban air pollution species: a Hong Kong case study", *Computers and Geosciences*, Vol. 28, pp. 119-127, 2002.

[5] A. Astel, "Chemometrics based on Fuzzy logic principles in environmental studies", *Talanta*, Vol. 72, pp. 1-12, 2007.

[6] P.H. Chen, J.-H. Lai and C.-T. Lin., "Application of Fuzzy control to a road tunnel ventilation system", *Fuzzy Sets and Systems*, Vol. 100, pp. 9-28, 1998.

[7] Y. Icaga, "Fuzzy evaluation of water quality classification", *Ecological Indicators*, Vol. 7, pp. 710-718, 2007.

[8] S. E. Vahdat and F.M. Nakhaee, "Air Pollution Monitoring using Fuzzy Logic in Industries", F. Nejadkoorki, Ed. Rijeka, Croatia: *InTech publication*, 2011.

[9] (2005) The Aluminum society website. [Online]. Available: http://www.world-aluminium.org

[10] K. Lamm K., "The CO2 - Story – A Fairy – Tale – (Or a Nightmare?)," *Lead Zinc 2010, MetSoc COM 2010*, A john and Sons Inc., 2010, p. 953.

[11] D. Moradkhani, B. Sedaghat, A. Rashtchi and A. Khodadadi, "Heavy metal pollution potential of zinc leach residues discarded in IZMDC", *Lead Zinc 2010, MetSoc, COM 2010*, A john and Sons Inc., 2010, p. 141.

[12] (2005) The Lead society website. [Online]. Available: http://www.lead.org

[13] Geir O. Braathen, Ed., An overview of the 2005: Antarctic Ozone Hole, WMO Global Ozone Research and Monitoring Project, Word Meteorological Organizationreport no. 49 (WMO TD no. 1312), Maryland, USA, 2005, vol. 49.

[14] (2005) The EPA website. [Online]. Available: http://epa.gov/air/emissions/index.htm

[15] (2005) The SDAPCD website. [Online]. Available: http://www.sdapcd.org.

Local Investments in Nigeria: What Role for Capital Market Operations

Olure-Bank Aadeyinka Michael[1], Omodele Kilanko[1], Gbadebo Salako[2], Ajiteru Temilade[2]

[1]Department of Economics, Faculty of Social Sciences, Joseph Ayo Babalola University, Ikeji-Arakeki, Osun State, Nigeria

[2]Department of Economics, Faculty of Arts and Social Sciences, Emmanuel Alayande College Education, Oyo, Oyo State, Nigeria

Email address:

Adeyinka67@gmail.com (Olure-Bank A. M.), nikeolure@yahoo.co.uk (Olure-Bank A. M.), gbadebosalako@gmail.com (G. Salako)

Abstract: There have been the growing concerns and controversies on the role of the Stock markets on economic growth and development. There have been mixed results; while some are in support of a positive link, some negative link and others do not find any empirical evidence to support such conclusion. In this study. To explored the roles or effectiveness of capital market instruments on Nigerian economic growth. Two models were formulated and data for the period 2004-2014 were collated while the Error Correction and co-integration model were employed for analysis with result of long run equilibrium. This study examines the role of the Nigerian capital market operations on the development of the Nigeria local investment in the manufacturing sector, recommendations were made for active stock market to be developed in the country.

Keywords: Stock Market, Stock Prices, Market Capitalisation, Economy, Nigerian Stock Exchange, Manufacturing, Economic Growth

1. Introduction

Over the years, Economists have been emphasising the need for effective mobilisation of resources as a catalyst for national development in any economy, which can only be achieved through the effectiveness in the mobilisation and allocation of funds to different sectors of the economy, so as to allow them manage their human or material resources which will result in optimal output for a sustainable growth and development in any economy. Basically, the capital market is primarily created to provide avenues for effective mobilisation of idle funds from the surplus economic unit and channel them into the deficit economic unit for long-term investment purpose. It, therefore, serves as a linkage or mechanism between the deficit sector and the surplus sector in any economy. The suppliers of funds are basically individuals and corporate bodies as government rarely supply funds to the market. The users of funds, by contrasts, consist mainly of corporate bodies and government. (Oke, 2011)

The capital market is a highly specialised and organised financial market and indeed essential agent of economic growth because of its ability to facilitate and mobilise saving and investment. To a great extent, the positive relationship between capital accumulation real economic growths has long affirmed in economic theories (--.Anyanwu, 1993).

Success in capital accumulation and mobilisation for development varies among nations, but it is largely dependent on domestic savings and inflows of foreign capital. Therefore, to arrest the menace of the current economic downturn, effort must be geared towards effective resources mobilisation. It is in realisation of this that consideration is given to measure for the development of capital market as an institution for the mobilisation of finance from the surplus sectors to the deficit sectors.

There have been the growing concerns and controversies on the role of the Stock markets on economic growth and development (Oyejide 1994; Levine and Zervos 1996;Demirgue-kunt and Levine 1996;Nyong 1997;Obadan 1998; Sule and Momoh 2009; Ewah,Esang and Bassey 2009).There have been mixed results; while some are in support of a positive link, some negative link and others do not find any empirical evidence to support such conclusion. For instance.

Atje and Jovanovic (1993) found in a cross-country study of stock and economic growth of 40 countries from 1980 to 1988 that there was a significant correlation between the average economic growth and stock market capitalisation.

Levine and Zervos (1996) examined whether there was a strong empirical relationship between stock market development and long-run economic growth. They found a strong correlation between overall stock market development and long-run economic growth.

Demiurgic-Kunt and Levine (1996) using data from 44 countries for the period 1986 to 1993 found that different measures of stock exchange size are strongly correlated to other indicators of activity levels of financial, banking, non-banking institutions as well as to insurance companies and pension funds. They concluded that countries with well-developed stock markets tend to also have well-developed financial intermediaries.

Again, Demiurgic-Kunt and Maksimovic(1998) have shown and re-emphasised the complementary role of the stock market and banks that they were not rival or alternative institutions using 30 countries from 1980 to 1991.

Levine and Zervos (1998) used pooled cross-country time series regression of 47 countries from 1976 to 1993 to evaluate whether stock market liquidity is related to growth, capital accumulation and productivity. They towed the line of Demiurgic-Kunt and Levine (1996) by conglomerating measures such as stock market size, liquidity and integration with world market, into index of stock market development. The rate of Gross Domestic Product (GDP) per capita was regressed on a variety of variables designed to control for initial conditions, political instability, investment in human capital and macro economic condition and then, included the conglomerated index of stock market development. They found empirically that the measures of stock market liquidity were strongly related to growth, capital accumulation and productivity while stock market size does not seems to correlate to economic growth.

Nyong (1997) developed an aggregate index of capital market development and used it to determine its relationship with long-run economic growth in Nigeria. The study employed a time series data from 1970 to 1994. Four measures of capital market development-ratio of market capitalisation to GDP (in %), ratio of total value of transactions on the main stock exchange to GDP (in %), the value of equities transactions relative to GDP and listing were used. The four measures were combined into one overall composite index [p]===]\][\l market development using principal component analysis. The financial market depth was included as control. It was found that the capital market development is negatively and significantly correlated with the long-run growth in Nigeria.

Demiurgic-Kunt and Maksimovic (1998) cited in Henry (2000) found a relationship between economic growth and the stock market activity in the field of transmission of security (secondary market) more than in funds channeling (primary market).

Barlett (2000) demonstrated that a rising stock price raises the wealth of the economy (wealth effect) by encouraging increase in consumers consumption and increase in investment.

Ewan et al. (2009) appraise the roles of the capital market efficiency on the economic growth of Nigeria using time series data from 1961 to 2004.They found that the capital market in Nigeria has the potential of growth inducing but it has not contributed meaningfully to the economic growth of Nigeria because of low market capitalization, low absorptive capitalization, illiquidity, misappropriation of funds among others.

Harris (1997) did not find hard evidence that stock market activity affects the level of economic growth.

1.1. Statement of the Problem

There is abundant evidence that most Nigerian manufacturing businesses have no access to long-term capital. The manufacturing sector has depended mainly on short-term financing such as overdrafts to finance even long-term capital. Based on the maturity matching concept, such financing is risky. All such firms need to raise an appropriate mix of short- and long-term capital.

Most recent literatures on the Nigeria capital market have recognised the tremendous performance the market has recorded in recent times. However, the vital role of the capital market in economic growth and development has been empirically investigated thereby creating a research gap in this area. This study is undertaken to examine the contribution of the capital market in the Nigerian economic growth and development. Aside the social and institutional factors inhibiting the process of economic development in Nigeria, the bottleneck created by the dearth of finance to the economy constitutes a major setback to its development. As a result, it is necessary to examine the Nigerian capital market.

1.2. Objectives of the Study

The main purpose of this study is to examine the activities and roles of Nigerian capital market on local investments. The specific objectives are as follows:

(i) To evaluate the roles of Capital Market on an economy;
(ii) To investigate the performance of the capital market in relation to the local investments in Nigeria economy;
(iii) To examine the operations of the Nigerian capital market.

1.3. Significance of the Study

The study explored the roles or effectiveness of capital market instruments on Nigerian economic growth. Though the scope of the study was limited to the capital market and manufacturing sector of the economy, it is hoped that the exploration of this market will provide a broad view of the operations of the capital market. It will contribute to existing literature on the subject matter by investigating empirically the role, which the capital market plays in the economic growth and development of the country. The main importance of this study is that it will provide policy recommendations to policy-makers on ways to improve operations and activities of the capital market.

1.4. Scope and Delimitation of the Study

The economy is a large component with lot of diverse and sometimes complex parts; this research work only looked at a particular part of the economy (the financial sector). This work did not cover all the facets that make up the financial sector, but focus only on the capital market and its activities as it roles on the Nigerian economic growth. The empirical investigation of the roles of the capital market on the economic growth in Nigeria was restricted to the period between 2004 and 2014. Secondary data was used in this study. The relevant data used were sourced from the publications of the Nigerian Stock Exchange and Central Bank of Nigeria. Some of the publications include; the Nigerian Stock Exchange Fact book, CBN's Statistical Reports, CBN's Annual Reports and Statement of Accounts for the years under review

1.5. Outline of the Study

The study is divided into five (5) chapters and organised as follows: Chapter one form the introduction part, this is where the main theme of the research is given. It comprises of the statement of the problem, objectives of the study, significance of the study, scope and delimitation of the study and outline of the study. Chapter two is the literature review early empirical studies, theoretical and conceptual framework of the roles of capital market on the economic growth of Nigeria. Chapter three forms the research methodology which includes sources of data, method of data analysis and model specification. Chapter four is the data analysis while chapter five includes the summary, conclusion and recommendations.

2. Literature Review

The stock market being a market for dealing in medium to long-term securities provides facilities for stock brokers and traders to trade stock and other securities. It is a market for where long term funds are made available by the surplus unit to the deficit unit.

According to Soyode and Oyedeji (2005), the stock market connotes ideas of surplus and also the savings that result from society income that have not been spent in procuring goods and services.

Al-Faki (2006) stated that the capital market is a network of specialised financial institutions, series of mechanism, processes and infrastructure that in various ways facilitate the bringing together of suppliers and users of medium to long-term fund (capital) for investment in socio-economic developmental projects

Osaze (2009) sees the capital market as a driver of any economy to growth and development because it is essential for long-term growth capital formation. It is crucial in the mobilisation of savings and channeling of such funds i.e. savings to profitable self- liquidating investment. Therefore, the Nigeria stock market provides the necessary lubricant that keeps turning the wheel of the economy.

Okereke (2008) states that the capital market is made up of market and institutions which facilitates the issuance and secondary trading of long-term financial instruments. Unlike the money market which functions basically to provide short term funds, the capital market provides the industries and governments long term funds to meet their long term capital requirement such as financing of fixed investment like buildings, plants, machinery, bridges, e.t.c. Therefore, the capital market plays a very active role in the stimulation of economic growth and development however, in the absence of well functioning capital market, economic growth and development would be hampered, as the money market is not designed to provide such funds. Hence, the stock market is at that core of the capital market development in any country.

2.1. Early Empirical Studies

Several studies have been carried out by different scholars to determine how effective the stock market is, in the growth of the economy (manufacturing sector). In a study carried out by Barlett (2000), he stated that a rising stock prices have two main-effects on the economy; first it raises wealth in the economy. This increase in wealth raises the amount of consumer spending and thereby increases the wealth of the nation. Secondly, rising stock prices can increase investment spending. We see that one way a firm can finance investment spending, is to issue stock. If stock prices rise, it can raise more money per share of the stock issued.

Irving study of 2004 considered the links between stock exchanges and overall socio- economic development to be tenuous, nonexistent or even harmful;. He advised African countries not to devote further scarce resources and efforts to promoting stock exchange, since there are many weightier problems to address in Africa; high poverty level, in adequate social services and undeveloped infrastructure. Even if the resources were available, stock market could expose already fragile developing economies to the stabilising effects of short term, speculative capital inflows.

As shown by Moore et al (2006a), stochastic policy simulations within a flow of funds mode can shed light on the type of financial reforms policies for influencing outcomes for households, companies, banks and government.

As Fleming and Giugale (2000) emphasise, a key advantage of the flow of funds is that it imposes internal consistency on analyses and forecasts, and provide an exposition of the complete financial implications of policy or other changes.

Victor (2009), states that because the financial crisis is characterised by bank fragility, it may impair (through exchange rate and stock price effects) the financial intermediation function of domestic banks in Africa in three main ways;

a. The immediate effect is a reduction in the supply of intermediary capital i.e. a credit squeeze, popularly known as a credit crunch;
b. A collapse of the prices of real assets (e.g. residential houses) and company real assets, leading to a collateral squeeze;
c. Price and other incentives for attracting deposits from household sector fall, leading to a contraction in the supply of savings i.e. a saving squeeze. He also states that the increase in banks competitiveness is matched

by the ability of the banks to extend credit to households and companies.

Ariyo and Adelegan (2005) contend that the liberalisation of capital market led to the growth of the Nigerian capital market, yet its roles at the macro-economy was negligible. Again, the capital market was instrumental to the initial 25banks that were able to meet the minimum capital requirement of N25 billion during the banking sector consolidation in 2005.

Ewan et al (2009) appraise the roles of the stock market efficiency on the economic growth of Nigeria using time series data from 1961 to 2004. They found that the stock market in Nigeria has the potential of growth inducing but it has not contribution meaningfully to the economic growth of Nigeria, because of low market capitalisation, low absorptive capitalisation, illiquidity, misappropriation of funds among others.

A study by Alile in 2002 using Nigerian data provided some dissenting evidence that stock market development statistically had non significant effect on economic growth in Nigeria during the period 1980-2000. He interpreted the result to mean that the Nigerian stock market was unable to make significant contribution to rapid economic growth because of the existence of certain policies that blur the effectiveness of the vehicle or transmission mechanism through which stock market activities influence economic growth.

However, Rajni and Mahendra (2007) employed a time series data for the period 2001-2005 on specific firms and found out that seven (7) out of the sixteen (16) firms listed on Fiji's stock market is volatile. The volatility of stock returns were then regressed against the interest rates and the results showed that the interest rates changes have a significant effect on stock market volatility.

Mohammed and Salahuddin (2008) collated data for the period from 1971 to 2006 for Pakistan and employed a co-integration analysis for testing the long run relationship and ECM for short run dynamics. The findings suggest a positive relationship between efficient stock market and economic growth both in short run and long run.

2.2. Theoretical and Conceptual Framework

Capital market is defined as the market where medium to long terms finance can be raised. The capital market is the market for dealing (that is lending and borrowing) in long term loanable funds. Substantial academic literature and government strategies support the finance-led growth hypothesis, based on an observation first made almost a century ago by Joseph Schumpeter that financial markets significantly boost real economic growth and development.

Schumpeter asserted that finance had a positive roles on economic growth as a result of its effects on productivity growth and technological change. As early as 1989 the World Bank also endorsed the view that financial deepening matters for economic growth "by improving the productivity of investment". (Wikipedia, 2011).

Mbat (2001) described it as a forum through which long term funds are made available by the surplus to deficit economic units. It must however, be noted that although all surplus economic units have access to the capital market, not all the deficit economic units have the same easy access to it. The restriction on the part of the borrowers is meant to enforce the security of the funds provided by the lenders. In order to ensure that lenders are not subjected to undue risks the borrowers in the capital need to satisfy certain basic requirement. It has very profound implication for the socio-economic growth and development of any nation.

Conceptual Framework of Capital Market Operations

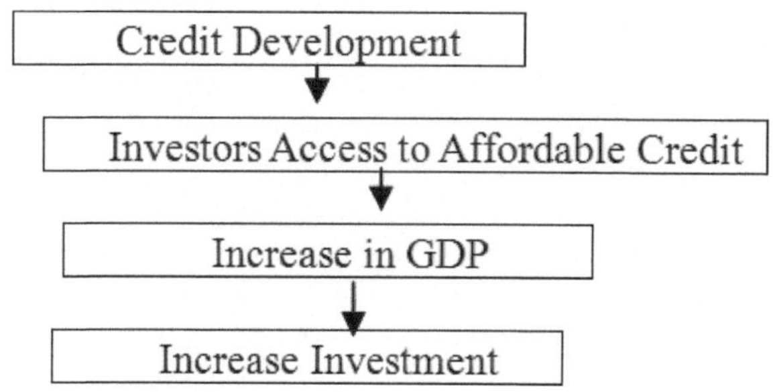

Increase Investment
Source: Author

2.2.1. Capital Market and Economic Growth

In principle, the capital (stock) market is expected to accelerate economic growth, by providing a boost to domestic savings and increasing the quantity and the quality of investment. The market is expected to encourage savings by providing individuals with an additional financial instrument that may better meet their risk preferences and liquidity needs. Better savings mobilisation may increase the saving rate.

The capital market also provides an avenue for growing companies to raise capital at lower cost. In addition, companies in countries with developed stock market are less dependent on bank financing, which can reduce the risk of a credit crunch. The capital market therefore is able to positively influence economic growth through encouraging savings among individuals and providing avenues for firm financing (Charles & Charles, 2007).

Capital market offers access to a variety of financial instruments that enable economic agents to pool, price and exchange. Through assets with attractive yields liquidity and risk characteristics, it encourages savings in financial form.

This is very essential for government and other institutions in need of long term funds and for suppliers of long term funds. Companies can finance their operation by raising funds through issuing equity (ownership) or debenture/bond borrowed as securities. Equity have perpetual life while debenture /bond issues are structured to mature in periods of years varying from the medium to long-term of usually between five and twenty five years.(Mbat, 2001).

Based on the performance of capital market in accelerating economic growth, government of most nations tends to have keen interest in its performance. The concern is for sustained confidence in the market and for a strong investor's protection arrangement. Economic growth is generally agreed to indicate development an economy, because it transforms a country from a five percent saver to a fifteen percent saver. Thus it is argued that for capital market to contribute or roles on the economic growth in Nigeria, it must operate efficiently. Most often, where the market operate efficiently, confidence will be generated in the minds of the public and investors will be willing to part with hard earned funds and invest them in securities with the hope that in future they will recoup their investment.(Ewah et al, 2009)

The theoretical explanation on the nexus between capital market and economic growth is further explicated using Efficient Market Hypothesis (EMH) developed by Fama in 1965. According to EMH, financial markets are efficient or prices on traded assets that have already reflected all known information and therefore are unbiased because they represent the collective beliefs of all investors about future prospects. Previous test of the EMH have relied on long-range dependence of equity returns. It shows that past information has been found to be useful in improving predictive accuracy. This assertion tends to invalidate the EMH in most developing countries. Equity prices would tend to exhibit long memory or long range dependence, because of the narrowness of their market arising from immature regulatory and institutional arrangement. They noted that, where the market is highly and unreasonably speculative, investors will be discouraged from parting with their funds for fear of incurring financial losses. In situations like the one mentioned above, has detrimental effect on economic growth of any country, meaning investors will refuse to invest in financial assets. The implication is that companies cannot raise additional capital for expansion. Thus, it suffices to say that efficiency of the capital market is a necessary condition for growth in Nigeria.(Nyong, 2003).

Ariyo and Adelegan (2005) contend that, the liberalisation of capital market contributes to the growth of the Nigeria capital market, yet its roles at the macro-economy is quite negligible.

In another exposition, Gabriel (2002) as stated by Nyong (2003) lay emphasis on the Romanian capital market and conclude that the market is inefficient and hence it has not contributed to economic growth in Romanian.

Ekundayo (2002) argues that a nation requires a lot of local and foreign investments to attain sustainable economic growth and development. The capital market provides a means through which this is made possible.

Ewah, et al (2009) capital market provide the opportunities for the purchase and sale of existing securities among investors thereby encouraging the populace to invest in securities fostering economic growth.

2.2.2. The Nigerian Security and Exchange Commission

The Nigerian security and exchange commission (NSEC) is the apex institution for the regulation and monitoring of the Nigeria capital market. The commission was established under the security and exchange commission decree 1979, operating retrospectively from 1st April 1978. Prior to the SEC, two bodies had in succession been responsible for the monitoring of capital market activities in Nigeria. The first was capital issues committee, which operated between 1962 and 1972. It could not be seen as the superintendent of the capital market because its functions were more or less advisory without the force of instruction even through its functions included the coordination of capital market activities. The next body was the capital market issues commission (CIC) which came into being in March 1973. The C.I.C, unlike its predecessor, had full powers to determine the price, timing and volume of security to be issued. Despite this wider power, the CIC could not be seen as the apex of capital market because it concerned itself with public companies alone and its activities did not cover the stock exchange and government securities.

The enabling Act of the Securities and Exchange Commission specifies its overriding objectives as investors' protection and development while its functions were divided into two regulatory and development.

The functions of the commission are extensively spelt out in Nigeria Securities and Exchange Commission Decree (Decree No 29) of 1983 and the Nigerian Enterprises Promotion Decree 1990. According to section (6) subsection (9) to (10) the commission is charged with the following duties and functions.

- i Determining the amount of price and time when securities of companies are to be sold to the public whether through offer for sale or subscription.
- ii Registering all securities proposed to be offered for sale to or for subscription by the public.
- iii Maintaining surveillance over the securities market to ensure orderly, fair and equitable dealing in securities.
- iv Protecting the integrity of the security market against any abuses arising from the practice of insider trading.
- v Acting as regulatory apex organisation for the Nigerian capital market including the Nigerian Stock Exchange and its branches to which it would be at liberty to delegate power.
- vi Creating the necessary atmosphere for the orderly growth and development of the capital market.
- vii Reviewing, approving and regulating merger acquisition and all forms of business combination.
- viii Registering Stock Exchange or their branches, registers investment advisers, securities dealers and their agents and controlling and supervising their activities with a view to maintaining proper standards of conduct and professionalism in the securities business.
- ix Undertaking such other activities as are necessary or expedient for giving fall effect to the provisi is decree.

2.2.3. The Nigerian Stock Exchange

As one of the constituencies of the capital market, the exchange is a private, nonprofit making organisation, limited by guarantee. It was incorporated via the inspiration and support of businessmen and the federal government. But owned by about 300 members. The membership includes financial institution, stockbrokers and individual Nigerians of high integrity, who have contributed to the development of the stock market and Nigerian economy.

The Nigerian stock exchange started with the incorporation of the then Lagos stock exchange in 1960. Trading commenced on the exchange in 1961 after the enactment of the Lagos stock exchange Act of 1961, the self regulatory organisation was subsequently reorganised and renamed the Nigerian stock exchange 197, based on the report and recommendation of Pius Okigbo financial system review commission.

The stock exchange is thus an institution of capital market, which provides trading floors where all dealing members operates on every business day. The exchange now has nine (9) branches and all the branches function principally as trading floor.

Functions of Nigerian Stock Exchange

i To provide opportunities for raising new capital.
ii To promote increasing participation by the public in the private sector of the economy.
iii iTo provide appropriate machinery to facilitate further offerings of stocks and shares to the public.
iv To provide a central meeting place for members to buy and sell existing stocks and shares and for granting quotation to new ones.
v To reduce the risk of liquidity by facilitating the purchasing and sale of securities.(Al-faki, 2007).

2.2.4. Economic Growth

Economic growth means an increase in the capacity of an economy to produce goods and services, compared from one period of time to another. Economic growth is a process by which a nation wealth increases over time.

The most widely used measures of economic growth is the rate of growth in a country's total output of goods and services gauged by the gross domestic product (GDP)

Economic growth can also be refers to as the increase of per capita gross domestic product (GDP) or other measures of aggregate income, typically reported as the annual rate of change in the real GDP.

Economic growth is primarily driven by improvement in productivity, which involves producing more goods and services with the same inputs of labour, capital, energy and materials. (Wikipedia).

Economic growth enables improvements or positive changes to take place in various areas of economic activity due to the increased production of goods and services. Economic growth will inevitably lead to economic development provided the following conditions are fulfilled.

Increased production of goods and services is not frustrated by rapid increase in population size.

There is an equitable distribution of the goods and services among individuals and areas.

The increasing level of production does not lead to mass unemployment as a result of using just a few labour-saving devices. as stated by Anyanwuocha (2008).

2.3. The Capital Market and Nigeria'S Economic Development

Obademi O.E and Adeyanju O.D (2010) considering the needed magnitude of growth in real resources and their allocation within an economy, financial markets are germane to the quest for growth not minding the claim that sometimes asset valuation may not adequately reflect the rate of return in investment in productive capacity. The fact is that the capital market cannot be overlooked nor wished away by any nation that is serious about achieving economic growth. The failure of state directed credit to achieve economic growth makes it imperative for the capital market to take the lead.

Also the fact that bank financial investment is often not enough makes the capital market important considering the quantum of funds in dollar conversion of what is needed for development projects after the naira devaluation and the global competitiveness of foreign direct investment quest by developing countries around the world. Moreover, retained profits are no more sufficient for expansion in the face of the present information technology revolution. The situation has been further worsened with the endemic crisis in the banking industry.

The capital market thus among others help in financing the savings-investment gap both domestically and internationally as well as finance other activities that can result in economic growth. Ordinarily the need for long term finance makes the capital market relevant to our development drive. It is common knowledge that in Nigeria in the last few years as a consequence of the liberalisation, privatisation and re-capitalisation policies of the government that has swept across the telecommunication, energy, manufacturing, banking and insurance sub- sector, the capital market has played enviable roles in the attainment of the objectives of the government in pushing up the growth figures and enhanced human welfare coupled with the redistribution of income and benefits within the Nigerian business environment.

Levine et al (1997), in their study on the compatibility of stock market development with financial intermediaries and economic growth posited that stock market development is positively correlated with the development of financial intermediaries and long term economic growth. In Nigeria in recent times, the bank re- capitalisation exercise was facilitated by the capital market.

Sule K.O and Momoh C.O (2009) note that there are a lot of investment opportunities available in the Nigerian Capital Market. The ultimate aim is to create wealth and improve the welfare of the average Nigerian, which automatically translates in the nation"s per capita income. Stock Exchanges play an increasingly important role, not only for channeling resources, but also for promoting reforms to modernise the financial sector legislation as is experienced in Nigeria and other emerging economies.

In a study of, Levien (1991) points out two key arguments on how stock exchanges speed up the economic growth. The first is by making property changes possible in the companies, whilst not affecting their productive process; the second is by offering higher possibilities of portfolio diversification to the agents. Economic growth in a modern economy is hinged on an efficient and effective financial sector that pools domestic savings and mobilises capital for productive projects. Absence of effective capital market could leave most productive projects which carry developmental agenda unexploited. Because capital market connects the monetary sector with the real sector and therefore facilitates growth in the real sector and economic development, thereby improving the quality of lives of the citizenry.

The stakeholders,who also advocated stick and carrot measure as a solution to the growing infraction in the nation's capital market, identified the fundamental channels through which capital market is connected to economic growth and development as follows:

(1) Capital market increases the proportion of long-term savings (pensions, funeral covers, etc) that is channeled to long-term investment. Capital market enables contractual savings industry (pension and provident funds, insurance companies, medical aid schemes, collective investment schemes, etc) to mobilise long-term savings from small individual household and channel them into long-term investments.

(2) Capital market also provides equity capital and infrastructure development capital that has strong socio- economic benefits through development of roads, water and sewer systems, housing, energy, telecommunications, public transport, etc.

(3) Moreover, capital market promotes public-private sector partnerships to encourage participation of private sector in productive investments. The need to shift economic development from public to private sector to enhance economic productivity has become inevitable as resources continue to diminish. It assists the public sector to close resource gap, and complement its effort in financing essential socio-economic development, through raising long-term project based capital.

(4) It also attracts foreign portfolio investors who are critical in supplementing the domestic savings levels. It facilitates inflows of foreign financial resources into the domestic economy.

According to Donwa P. and Odia J.,(2010) in Alile (1984) the capital market has been identified as an institution that contributes to the socio-economic growth and development of emerging and developed economies. This is made possible through some of the vital roles played such as channeling resources, promoting reforms to modernise the financial sectors, financial intermediation capacity to link deficit to the surplus sector of the economy,and a veritable tool in the mobilisation and allocation of savings among competitive uses which are critical to the growth and efficiency of the economy. It helps to channel capital or long-term resources to firms with relatively high and increasing productivity thus enhancing economic expansion and growth (Alile 1997).

Ekundayo (2002) argues that a nation requires a lot of local and foreign investments to attain sustainable economic growth and development and the capital market provides a means through which this is made possible. However, the paucity of long-term capital has posed the greatest predicament to economic development in most African countries including Nigeria.

Osaze (2000) sees the capital market as the driver of any economy to growth and development because it is essential for the long term growth capital formation. It is crucial in the mobilisation of savings and channeling of such savings to profitable self-liquidating investment.

The Nigerian capital market provides the necessary lubricant that keeps turning the wheel of the economy. It not only provides the funds required for investment but also efficiently allocates these funds to projects of best returns to fund owners. This allocative function is critical in determining the overall growth of the economy. The functioning of the capital market affects liquidity, acquisition of information about firms, risk diversification, savings mobilisation and corporate control (Anyanwu 1998).

Therefore, by altering the quality of these services, the functioning of stock markets can alter the rate of economic growth (Equakun 2005).

Okereke-Onyiuke (2000) posits that the cheap source of funds from the capital market remain a critical element in the sustainable development of the economy. She enumerated the advantages of capital market financing to include no short repayment period as funds are held for medium and long term period or in perpetuity, funds to state and local government without pressures and ample time to repay loans.

Again the capital market was instrumental to the initial 25 banks that were able to meet the minimum capital requirement of N25billion during the banking sector consolidation in 2005.The stock market has helped government and corporate entities to raise long term capital for financing new projects,and expanding and modernising industrial / commercial concerns (Nwankwo 1991).

2.4. Roles of the Capital Market

According to Al-Faki (2006), the capital market is a "network of specialised financial institutions, series of mechanisms, processes and infrastructure that, in various ways, facilitate the bringing together of suppliers and users of medium to long term capital for investment in socio-economic developmental projects". The capital market is divided into the primary and the secondary market. The primary market or the new issues market provides the avenue through which government and corporate bodies raise fresh funds through the issuance of securities which is subscribed to by the general public or a selected group of investors. The secondary market provides an avenue for sale and purchase of existing securities.

Sule and Momoh (2009) found that the secondary market activities have impacted more on Nigeria per capita income by tending to grow stock market earnings through wealth than the primary market.

The roles of the capital market in the development of the economy include:

(1) It provides opportunities for companies to borrow funds needed for long-term investment purposes.
(2) It provides avenue for the marketing of shares and other securities in order to raise fresh funds for expansion of operations leading to increase in output/production.
(3) It provides a means of allocating the nations real and financial resources between various industries and companies. Through the capital formation and allocation mechanism the capital market ensures an efficient and effective distribution of the scarce resources for the optimal benefit to the economy.
(4) It reduces the over reliance of the corporate sector on short term financing for long term projects and also provides opportunities for government to finance projects aimed at providing essential amenities for socioeconomic development.
(5) The capital market can aid the government in its privatisation programme by offering her shares in the public enterprises to members of the public through the stock exchange.
(6) The capital market also encourages the inflow of foreign capital when foreign companies or investors invest in domestic securities, provides needed seed money for creative capital development and acts as a reliable medium for broadening the ownership base of family-owned and dominated firms.

2.5. Contribution of the Capital Market to Socio-Economic Development of Nigeria

The capital market is very vital to the growth, development and strength of any country because it supports government and corporate initiatives, finances the exploitation of new ideas and facilitates the management of financial risk. The rate of economic growth has been inexorably linked to the sophistication of the financial market and capital market efficiency. Both markets facilitate the mobilisation and channeling of funds into productive constituents and ensuring that the funds are used for the pursuit of socioeconomic growth and development without being idle (Akinbohungbe1996; Adebiyi 2005)

From 1961, the Nigerian capital market has growth tremendously, particularly during the periods of the indigenisation decrees of 1972 and 1977. The securities increased from 8 in 1961 to about 301 in 2008. Over the years, the Nigerian capital market has witnessed relatively stability and also recorded impressive growth. This has positioned it to positively roles the economy. There is clear evidence that the capital market remained an important source of capital for the nation's economic development in financing infrastructural projects, the privatisation programme of the government and banking sector recapitalisation in Nigeria.

Sule and Momoh (2009) conclude that the recent consolidation exercise of major financial institutions and privatisation exercise of most publicly owned enterprises are key indications of government faith in the capital market to drive growth of the Nigerian economy.

2.6. Capital Market Provides Avenue for FDI for Economic Growth in Nigeria

There is a growing body of empirical literature considering FDI inflows as a catalyst of economic growth. FDI provide host countries with much needed capital, technology; expertise and new managerial skills topped with some access to international export markets.

Chen et al. (1995) report that FDI inflows are positively correlated with post-1978 economic growth in China by contributing to capital formation, export earnings, and bringing about advanced managerial skills.

Blomstrom et al. (1992) finds similar evidence using a panel data from 78 developing countries where technological upgrading and knowledge spillovers are the vehicle through which FDI stimulates growth. Hence the Nigerian capital market provides avenue for FDI in the country for economic growth.

3. Methodology

The secondary data (Bi-annual) and a time series analysis for the period of 2004-2014, which were obtained from sources like the Nigeria stock exchange Annual report, Central Bank of Nigeria Statistical Bulletin. In order to determine the robustness of the independent partial correlation between Nigeria Capital Market operations to the growth of the economy at large, two models were employed, applying co-integration and error correction model to the data obtained. Thus, we use the gross domestic product as a proxy for growth, which is our dependent variable and stock price, market capitalisation number of deals, which are the independent variables.

For the purpose of this study, certain modification is made to model as put forward by Oke (2011). Adopted from Sule and Momoh (2009) who based their model on Demirguc-kunt and Maksimovic (1998) theory of non classical which was modified to measure the roles of stock market on economic growth

$$PCI = \beta 0 + \beta 1 \; mc + \beta 2 \; PER + \beta 3 \; NLS + \mu \qquad (i)$$

Where;
PCI = Per capita income
mc = Market capitalization
NLS = No of listed Securities
PER = Price Earring Ratio, DY-dividend Yields

The basic variables employed for this study are market capitalisation which denotes the size of the market, stock prices, number of deals which are the independent variable and the Gross Domestic Product which is the dependent variable.

Model 1

$$GDP\ (maf) = F\ (MKTCAP, NOD, SKP, \mu) \quad (i)$$

It should be noted that GDP is a proxy for economic growth. For this model, GDP relating to the manufacturing sector will be employed

Where; GDP (maf) = Gross Domestic product,
MKTCAP = Market capitalisation,
SKP = Stock Price,
NOD = Number of Dealings,
μ = Stochastic variable (Error term)

$$GDP\ (maf) = \beta_0 + \beta_1 MCAP + \beta 2NOD + \beta_3 SP + \mu \quad (i)$$

Transforming equation (v) into natural logarithm form, we have

$$logGDP\ (maf) = Log\ \beta_0 + log\beta_1 MCAP + \beta_2 NOD + Log\beta_3 S \quad (ii)$$

Model 2

$$GDP = f\ (MRTCAP, SKP, NOD, \mu) \quad (ii)$$

GDP is a proxy for economic growth
Where GDP = Gross Domestic Product
Econometric Function

$$GDP = \beta_0 + \beta_1 MRTCAP + \beta_2 SKP + \beta_3 NOD + \mu \quad (iii)$$

Transforming equation (iii) into natural logarithm, we have

$$Log\ GDP = log\beta 0 + log\beta 1MRTCAP + log\ \beta 2SKP + log\beta 3NOD + \mu \quad (iv)$$

Where β_0, is constant and it is the intercept of the econometric function. β_1, β_2, β_3, are parameters that show the relationship between the dependent and the independent variable.

4. Result of Finding

The results obtained from the analyses of the two analyses are presented and discussed below

Table I. *Interpretation of OLS Result for Model 1 and 2.*

Dependent variable	Independent variable			
	Constant	SKP	MRTCAP	NOD
$GDP_{(maf)}$	4.693263	0.581171	0.532133	-0.211234
	(1.951916)	(2.65744)	(2.657342)	(-0.945112)
GDP	5.673127	0.351774	0.531779	-0.211606
	(3.134203)	(2.510005)	(3.561249)	(-0.911328)

Note: the t-statistics is given in parenthesis

Table II. *Summary of Results.*

	R	R^2	Adj R^2	Fc	Durbin Watson Stat.
Model 1	0.97	0.9568	0.9266	76.20794	1.368372
Model 2	0.98	0.9767	0.9612	118.2757	1.281065

The tabular presentation of OLS result for model 1 and 2 can also be given in equation form. As it is written below,

Model 1

$$GDP_{maf} = 3.691363 + 0.490071(SKP) + 0.492988(MRTCAP) - 0.199998(NOD)$$

Model 2

$$GDP = 4.524127 + 0.331674(SKP) + 0.5331779(MRTCAP) - 0.168506(NOD)$$

The above result shows that from both models a positive relationship exists between stock price, market capitalisation and GDP (maf) and GDP, while a negative relationship exists between number of deals and GDP (maf) and GDP. The constant parameter also shows a positive relationship to the dependent variables (GDP and GDP maf) in both models. This means that if all the explanatory variables are held constant, GDP (maf) will increase by 3.691363 and GDP will increase by 4.524127. The value of correlation co-efficient (r), in both model with a value of 95% in model 1 and 97% in model 2, shows that a strong positive relationship exist among the variables in both models. The coefficient of determination (r^2) in both model, with a values of 0.9308 in model 1 and 0.9577 in model 2, shows that 93.08% variation or change in GDP (maf) and 95.77% change in GDP can be explained by the explanatory variable (SKP, MRTCAP, NOD) which the remaining 6.92% and 4.23% in both models is being handled by the stochastic error term in both models.

Unit Root Test

Table III. *ADF Unit Root test at level.*

Variable	ADF test stat.	Mackinnon 5% critical values	Order of stationarity	Remark
$GDP_{(maf)}$	-1.694656	-3.1294	1(0)	Not stationary
GDP	-1.844934	-3.1294	1(0)	Not stationary
SKP	-2.597975	-3.1294	1(0)	Not stationary
MRTCAP	-1.891135	-3.1294	1(0)	Not stationary
NOD	-1.669699	-3.1294	1(0)	Not stationary
ECM(Model1)	-3.444869	-3.1294	1(0)	Not stationary
ECM(Mode2)	-3.724015	-3.1294	1(0)	Not stationary

Stationary

The table above shows that the Mackinnon critical values at 5% are all greater than the ADF test, for all the variables in both models. This implies that they are not stationary. The ECM for both model are stationary. Therefore there is need to carry out test at 1st difference to see if the variables will be stationary.

Table IV. ADF Unit Root Test at First Difference.

Variable	ADF test stat.	Mackinnon 5% critical values	Order of stationarity	Remark
$GDP_{(maf)}$	-3.520168	-3.1400	1(1)	stationary
GDP	-3.092087	-3.1400	1(1)	stationary
SKP	-2.943547	-3.1400	1(1)	Not stationary
MRTCAP	-1.729862	-3.1400	1(1)	Not stationary
NOD	-1.659699	-3.1400	1(1)	Not stationary

The above table shows that the dependent variable of model 1 (GDP(maf) and that of model 2 (GDP) are stationary at first difference because their respective ADF statistical value are greater than Mackinnon critical value at 5%. However the independent variables (SKP, MKTCAP, NOD) are not stationary at 1st difference, therefore we proceed to 2nd difference to test their stationary.

Table V. ADF Unit Root Test at Second Difference.

Variable	ADF test stat.	Mackinnon 5% critical values	Order of stationarity	Remark
SKP	-3.772758	-3.0521	1(2)	stationary
MRTCAP	-2.118995	-3.0521	1(2)	Not stationary
NOD	-2.836922	-3.0521	1(2)	Not stationary

The above shows that SKP is stationary at 2nd difference while MRTCAD and NOD are not stationary. The test for stationary is being done at absolute term of the value.

Table VI. Summary of Stationary.

Variables	Order of stationarity
$GDP_{(maf)}$	1(1)
GDP	1(1)
SKP	1(2)
MRTCAP	-
NOD	-
ECM(Model 1)	1(0)
ECM(Model 2)	1(0)

The table above shows that GDP (maf) and GDP are stationary at 1st difference, ECM is stationary at level while SKP is stationary at 2nd difference. However, NOD and MRTCAP are not stationary but will be used because of their importance in explaining the Nigerian Stock Market.

Co-Integration Test

The co-integration test is performed using Johansen likelihood estimation equation, which is done to test whether a long-run relationship exist among the variables. If it shows that at least one co-integrating equation exist among variables under investigation, then a long run equilibrium relationship exist among them. The table below shows the summary of Johansen co integration tests conducted on the two models.

Model 1

Table VII. Result of Johansen Co-integration Test.

Eigen value	Likelihood ratio	5% critical values	1% critical value	Hypothesised no of CE 1st
0.811759	69.48779	47.21	54.46	None**
0.687393	37.75716	29.68	35.65	At most1**
0.534647	15.66379	15.41	20.04	At most 2**
0.057719	1.129577	3.76	6.65	At most 3**

The co-integration equation is specified below

GDP (maf) = 6.499705-0.741436 SKP -1.741329 MRTCAP + 1.997290 NOD

(0.10616) (0.242559) (0.33466)

The above result shows that there exist a long run relationship among the variables in the model as the likelihood ratio of 69.48779 is greater than the 5% critical value of 47.21 at the None hypothesized (None**). The co-integration equations shows that there exist a positive relationship between the constant parameter, NOD and GDP (maf), while a negative relationship exist between SKP, MRTCAP and GDP(maf).

Model 2

Table VIII. Result of Johansen Co-integration Test.

Eigen value	Likelihood ratio	5% critical values	1% critical value	Hypothesised no of CE 1st
0.788262	60.84838	47.21	54.46	None**
0.636259	31.35271	29.68	35.65	At most1*
0.429507	12.13778	15.41	20.04	At most 2
0.074643	12.13778	3.76	6.65	At most 3

The co integration equation is

GDP = 6.185605-0.148026 SKP- 1.948884 MRTCAP + 2.041826 NOD

(0.16114) (0.48690) (0.62841)

This shows that there exist a long-run equilibrium relationship among the variables in the model because the likelihood ratio of 60.84838 is greater than the 5% critical value of 47.21 at none hypothesis (None**). The co integration equation shows that there exist positive relationships between the constant parameter; NOD and GDP while a negative relationship exist between SKP, MRTCAP and GDP.

Error Correction Model

The table below shows the over parameterised and parsimonious ECM for model 1 and 2

Model 1

Table IX. Over-parameterised ECM.

Variables	Co-efficient	Standard Error	T-Stat.	Probability
$D(GDP_{(-1,2)}$	-0.506561	0.137642	-3.680283	0.0042
$D(SKP_{,2})$	0.402089	0.239541	1.678583	0.1242
$D(SKP_{(-1),2})$	0.108638	0.223768	0.485492	0.6378
$D(MRTCAP_{,2})$	0.392128	0.762336	-0.514377	0.6182
$D(MRTCAP_{(-1),2})$	0.258521	0.453328	0.570274	0.5811
$D(NOD_{,2})$	0.388149	0.480070	0.808525	0.4376
$D(NOD_{(-1),2})$	0.205328	0.415713	0.493919	0.6320
ECM(-1)	-1.116356	0.232369	-4.804233	0.0007

$R^2 = 0.865637$

Adjusted R = 0.771582

Durbin Watson stat. = 2.2954

Table X. Parsimonious ECM.

Variables	Co-efficient	Standard Error	T-statistics	Probability
D(SKP,2)	0.062664	0.548688	0.114207	0.9107
D(MRT.CAP(-1),2)	-0.751005	0.930960	-0.806699	0.4333
D(NOD,2)	0.216827	0.453964	0.279376	0.7840
ECM(-1)	0.681760	0.519725	1.311771	0.2107

$R^2 = 0.146389$
Adjusted R = -0.036528
Durbin-Watson stat. = 2.592435

The negativity of the ECM in the over parameterised ECM is in conformity with our a-priori expectation. This implies that the present value of GDP_{maf} adjusts rapidly to changes in SKP, MRTCAP and NOD. The large values of ECM given as 111.6% show a feedback of that value from the previous period disequilibrium of the present level of GDP_{maf} in the determination of the causality between the past level of GDPmaf and the present and past level of SKP, MRTCAP and NOD. The coefficient of determination (R^2) shows that about 86.56% variation in the dependent variable (GDP_{maf}) can be explained by the explanatory variable (SKP, MRTCAD, NOD) while the remaining 13.44% is handled by the stochastic error term.

The coefficient of SKP and NOD in the parsimonious ECM is also in confirmedly with that of the over parameterised ECM as they are positively related to GDP_{maf}. While MRTCAP in the parsimonious model is also conformity with that of the over parameterised model as it is negatively related to GDP_{maf}

Model 2

Table XI. Over-parameterised ECM.

Variables	Co-efficient	Standard Error	T-Stat.	Probability
$D(GDP_{(-1,2)}$	-0.595508	0.162618	-3.662002	0.0044
$D(SKP_{,2)}$	0.182248	0.175562	1,038084	0.3237
$D(SKP_{(-1),2)}$	0.058999	0.143188	0.412039	0.6890
$D(MRTCAP_{,2)}$	0.036420	0.481457	0.075646	0.9412
$D(MRTCAP_{(-1),2)}$	0.156351	0.314060	0.497838	0.6294
$D(NOD_{,2)}$	0.102104	0.316790	0.322308	0.7539
$D(NOD_{(-1),2)}$	0.056150	0.267861	0.209623	0.8382
ECM(-1)	-0.933259	0.297798	-3.133867	0.0106

$R^2 = 0.793857$
Adjusted R = 0.649556
Durbin-Watson stat = 1.852616.

Table XII. Parsimonious ECM.

Variables	Co-efficient	Standard Error	T-statistics	Probability
D(SKP,2)	-0.261087	0.246212	-1.060416	0.3069
D(MRT.CAP(-1),2)	-0.0887867	0.295422	-0.297417	0.7705
D(NOD,2)	-0.081239	0.203139	-0.399919	0.6953
ECM(-1)	0.570433	0.504981	1.129612	0.2776

$R^2 = 0.108645$
Adjusted R = -0.082359
Durbin-Watson stat = 3.059611

The negative sign of ECM in over parameterised ECM is in conformity with our a-priority expectation. This implies that the present value of GDP adjust rapidly to changes in SKP, MRTCAP, NOD. The large value of ECM given as 93.32% shows a feedback of that value from the previous period disequilibrium of the present level from the previous period disequilibrium of the present level of GDP in the determination of the causality between the past level of GDP and the present and past level of SKP, MRTCAP and NOD. The coefficient of determination (R^2) shows that about 79.4% variation in the dependent variable (GDP) can be explained by the explanatory variable (SKP, MRTCAP and NOD) while the remaining 20.6% is left to the stochastic error term to handle.

The coefficient of SKP, MRTCAP and NOD in the parsimonious ECM is negatively related to GDP.

Model 1

Table XIII. Standard error test result.

Variable	Co-efficient	Co-efficient/2	Standard Error	H_0	H_1	Remark
SKP	0.402089	0.2010445	0.239541	Accept	Reject	Insignificant
MRTCAP	-0.392128	-0.196064	0.762336	Accept	Reject	Insignificant
NOD	0.388149	0.1940745	0.480070	Accept	Reject	Insignificant

Model 2

Table XIV. Standard error test result.

Variable	Co-efficient	Co-efficient/2	Standard Error	H_0	H_1	Remark
SKP	-0.261087	-0.1305435	0.246212	Accept	Reject	Insignificant
MRTCAP	-0.087867	-0.0439335	0.295433	Accept	Reject	Insignificant
NOD	-0.081239	-0.0406195	0.203139	Accept	Reject	Insignificant

Decision Rule

If Coefficient > standard Error – Significant (Reject H_0 and Accept H1) 2

If Coefficient < standard Error – Insignificant (Accept H_0 and Reject H1)

The standard error test above shows that the parameters are insignificant in the explanation of the long-run as the standard error statistics are greater than the coefficients of the parameter divided by 2 in both models.

However, the F-test shows that the models are significant in the short and long run as they have F-statistics of 128.2757 in model 1 and 76. 20794 in model 2, which is greater than the f-calculated 3.20

5. Summary of Findings

The study examined the role of capital market on economic development of Nigeria between 2004 to 2014. Having run the OLS and the co integration techniques to test for the short and long-run relationship in both models, it was revealed that the one sector that drives the Nigeria economy in terms of revenue is the manufacturing sector. This was revealed in the short run as an increase in stock prices of manufacturing firms in Nigeria contributes immensely to the share of manufacturing sector to GDP. The long run test revealed that there exists a long run equilibrium relationship among the variable in the models as the counteraction in both model is in deviation from the short run equation but it also justifies the fact that the manufacturing sector contributes majorly to the economic growth of Nigeria.

The short run relationship reveals that stock price and market capitalisation contributes positively to the share of manufacturing to GDP and the GDP as a whole, while the long run equation move in opposite direction that stock price and market capitalisation negatively affect GDP maf and GDP as a whole.

With the regression result confirms that there exists positive relationship between the capital market and economic growth. The relationship is statistically significance. This is in essence means that the roles of the capital market on economic growth is strong and significant.

i) Another major outcome of the study is that a unit increase in total listing of equity and government stock (TLS) result in an increase in GDP. The implication of this is that the economy responds favourable to measures taken to increase TLS in Nigeria Stock Exchange.
ii) The positive result of the total listing of equity and government stock implies that funds raised by the industries and governments in the capital market are spent on productive sector which enhance economic growth.
iii) The result of the value of transaction in the capital market means that the simplicity in buying and selling of securities has potential to influence economic growth positively.

These findings agree with Ewang, et al (2009) who found that capital market in Nigeria has potentials for growth inducing but has not contributed meaningfully to the economic growth of Nigeria due to low market capitalisation etc.

5.1. Conclusion

The study reveals that the capital market roles on economic growth via market capitalisation, value of transaction and total listing of equity and government stock. As it was observed market capitalisation, government stock and value of transaction are important capital market variables that are capable of influencing economic growth. Hence the capital market remain one of the mainstream in every economy that has the power to influence or roles economic growth therefore the organised private sector is to invest in it. The market capitalisation have not roles significantly on the GDP while volume of transaction and total listed equities and Government stock have significant roles on the GDP. The government is therefore advised to put up measures to stem up investors' confidence and activities in the market and more foreign investors should be encouraged to participate in the market for improvement in the declining market capitalisation so that it could contribute significantly to the Nigerian economic growth.

5.2. Policy Recommendations

In order for the Nigeria capital market to be pivotal force in Nigeria economic growth and development, the following suggestion or recommendation are put forward.

i) First improvement in the declining market capitalisation by encouraging more foreign investors to participate in the market, maintain state of the art technology like automated trading and settlement practice, electronic fund clearance and eliminate physical transfer of shares.
ii) There is also need to restore confidence to the market by regulatory authorities through ensuring transparency and fair trading transaction and dealing in the stock exchange. It must also address the reported case of abuse and sharp practices by some companies in the market.
iii) Since the total listing is significant at 1% level of significance but still far cry compare to other exchange like South African and Egypt. Therefore, these should be increase in the total member listed companies to ensure stable macroeconomic environment in order to encourage foreign multinational companies (MNCs) or their subsidiaries to be listed on the Nigerian stock exchange, relax the listing requirements to the first tier market and ensure tax rationalisation in the capital market to encourage quotation and public interest in shareholdings.
iv) Lastly, to boost the value of transactions in the Nigerian capital market, there is need for availability of more investment instruments such as derivatives, convertibles, future, and swaps options in the market.
v) Given the present political dispensation, all the tiers of government should be encourage to fund their realistic developmental programme through the capital market. This will served as a leeway to freeing the resources that may be used in other sphere of the economy.

References

[1] Owolabi A and Ajayi N.O. (2013) Asian Economic and Financial Review, 2013, 3(1):99-110

[2] Atoyebi Kehinde.O. et al (2013) Capital Market and Economic Growth in Nigeria an Empirical Analysis. Journal of Humanities And Social Science, Volume 6, Issue 6 (Jan. - Feb. 2013), PP 60-68

[3] Olawoye (2011) *Roles Of Capital Market On Economic Growth Of Nigeria*

[4] Al–Faki M. (2006). '' *The Nigerian capital market socio-economic development''*. Paper Presented at the 4th distinguished faculty of social science public lecture. University of Benin, 26 July, 9-16.

[5] Alile HI (2002). *''Establishing a stock market – the Nigerian experience''*. Paper presented at the conference on promoting and development capital market in Africa. Abuja No 11-13.

[6] Ariyo and Adelegan O (2005). "*Assessing the roles of Capital Market Reforms in Nigerian; An incremental approach ;* paper presented at the 46th Annual conference of the Nigerian economic society in Lagos in August 2005.

[7] Barlett, B. (2000)". *Opinion Editorial on the effect of stock market on the Economy"*, National Centre for Policy Analysis, Feb 2000.

[8] Beck, T. Demirguc-kunt and Levine (2004). *''Stock Market, Banks and Growth Correlation or Causality?",* Policy research working paper. 2000 Washington DC; World Bank.

[9] Ewang S.E, Esang AE, Bassey JU (2009),'' *Appraisals of Capital Market Efficiency on Economic Growth in Nigeria,"* International journal of business and management, December. 219-225.

[10] Demirguc-Kunt, A and Maksimovic, V (1998), *'' Stock Market Development and Financial Choices of firms",* World Bank Economic Review, (10):341-36

[11] Henry (2001)," *Do stock market liberalisation cause Investment Booms", Journals of Financial economies,* (58):301-334.

[12] Irving, J. (2001)," Africa's *struggling Exchanges-Boost to economic Development of Costly Irrelevance",* Africa Recovery, Abidjan.

[13] Kalu, I.K (2009)," Global *Economic Meltdown" Issues that would reposition the Nigerian Capital market,* http://allafrican.com/stones/2009/06290246.html

[14] Mohammad R and Salahuddin (2008)." *The Determinant of Economic Growth in Pakistan" (1):1-22.*

[15] Moore, Green and Murinde (2006a)," *Financial Reforms and Stochastic policy Simulations: A flow of funds model",* Journal of policy modeling.(28): 319-333.

[16] Okereke Onyiuke Ndi (2008). *''A review of Market Performance in 2008 and outlook for 2009",* the Nigerian stock Exchange. 2008 Edition.

[17] Rajni M and Mahendra R (2007), *''Measuring Stock market volatility in an emerging Economy"*, International Research Journals of finance and Economics, Issue (8):127-133

[18] Soyode A. and Oyedeji (2006*): "The role of Capital Market in Economic development",* Security market journal. 6

[19] Sule and Momoh (2009*), "The roles of Stock Market Earnings on Nigeria per capita Income",* African journal of Accounting, Economics, Finance and Banking Research. (5):77-88.

[20] Victor Murinde (2009),"*Global Financial crisis: Implications for Africa's financial system".*

[21] Adam, J. A. & Sanni, I. (2005). *Stock Market Development and Nigeria's Economic Growth.* Journal of Economics and Allied Fields, 2 (2), 116-132.

[22] Afees, A.S & Kazeem, B.A (2010). *The Stock Market and Economic Growth in Nigeria: An Empirical Investigation,* Journal of Economic Theory, 4,65 – 70.

[23] Osaze B.E. (2009), *''Paradigm Shift Misplaced Concreteness and the Nigerian Financial System'.* Inaugural lecture series.41. University of Benin. 40-41.

22

The Level of Compliance with International Accounting Standard IAS 18 by Listed Firms in Bahrain

Isa Adnan Budaraj[1]**, Adel Mohammed Sarea**[2]

[1]MBA program, Ahlia University of Bahrain, Manama, Kingdom of Bahrain
[2]Accounting and Economics Department, Ahlia University of Bahrain, Manama, Kingdom of Bahrain

Email address:
essabudraj@gmail.com (I. A. Budaraj), Adelsarea@hotmail.com (A. M. Sarea)

Abstract: This Study examines the association between five firm-specific characteristics and the level of compliance with International Accounting Standards (IAS 18) by listed Firms in Bahrain Bourse. A self-constructed compliance checklist was developed and the compliance index was derived to represent the level of compliance among publically traded firms in Bahrain Bourse for the year 2013 to IAS 18 disclosure requirements. The results detected an aggregate mean compliance of 63% to IAS 18 disclosure requirements. A significant positive relationship was found between the level of compliance and a company's size, and auditor type. A significant negative relationship was found between the IAS 18 disclosure level and a company's debt level (leverage). However, a significant relationship between the level of IAS 18 disclosure level and a company's profits or age could not be established in this research. The results of this research can benefit investors and companies as well, as the results will determine what level of compliance to IAS 18 are listed companies in Bahrain Bourse are committed to, and how transparent are the revenues they are reporting in their financials.

Keywords: Corporate Financial Reporting, IAS 18, Disclosure, Bahrain Bourse

1. Introduction

The Kingdom of Bahrain is an oil producing island in the Arabian Gulf, and is a member of the GCC (Gulf Cooperation Council). Bahrain was the first country in the Middle East to discover oil in 1932, and with Bahrain achieving its independence in 1971 a high paced growth started, and Bahrain became the region's leading financial center since the 1980s (Bahrain Economic Yearbook, 2013).

The kingdom of Bahrain is populated by more than 1.2 million, with a composition of expats (54%) and local nationals (56%). Bahrain's GDP (Gross Domestic Product) stood at $31 billion (BD11.5 billion), and a $25 thousand (BD9.3 thousand) GDP per capita. Bahrain's GDP growth rate averaged at 5% between 2000 and 2012, while inflation stood at 2.8% year-over-year in 2012. Inflation in Bahrain fluctuated from 2.0% in 2010 to -0.4% in 2011 and then went up again to 2.8% in 2012, the reason for such fluctuations was the fall in house prices during the period, and the unfortunate public unrest Bahrain had experienced (Bahrain Economic Year Book, 2013).

Rapid globalization of markets internationally has raised demand for a global standard of comparable financial reporting, harmonizing and standardizing of accounting methods and the manner in which financial information is disclosed is one path to promote a more transparent and consistent financial reporting, thus the International Accounting Standards Board (IASB) devised a set of international accounting standards for publically traded entities around the world (Al-Shammari, et al., 2008).

Currently, all publically traded companies in Bahrain are required to prepare and disclose all their financial statements (annual, semi-annual, and quarterly reports) in compliance with the International Financial Reporting Standards (Tait, D. 2005). By the year 1996, International Accounting Standards compliance was imposed on all publically traded companies in Bahrain (Al-Hussaini, et al., 2008). However, it was not formalized until the issuance of The Bahrain Commercial Companies Law (BCCL) in 2001, which necessitated each publically traded entity to prepare and disclose its statement of financial position (balance sheet), profit and loss report (income statement), statement of cash flows, change in owners' equity, and managers' (directors') report for every financial year before three months pass from the end of the financial year, in accordance to IFRS requirements (Tait, D. 2005).

IAS-18 "Revenue" specifies the accounting treatment for when to recognize revenue from the selling of goods, rendering of services, and receiving of interest, dividends, and royalties. The primary issue when accounting for revenues is to determine when to recognize the revenue. The standard was first introduced in 1982 with an effective date of 1984, was revised in 1993, amended in 1998 and 2009, and finally it was decided that IAS 18 will be superseded by IFRS 15 effective from Jan 2017. IAS-18 identifies circumstances when certain criteria, such as the transfer of future economic benefits and the ability to reliably measure those benefits are met and therefore revenue will be recognized (IAS 18).

This research aims to further the findings of other researchers who investigated the level of compliance with IFRS standards in Bahrain and the GCC countries by focusing on one country, Bahrain, and one standard, IAS 18, for the year 2013, and the association between 5 firm specifics, which are size, profitability, leverage, auditor type, and firm age, with the level of compliance. The significance of the study lays in it being in the Kingdom of Bahrain, which is a developing country that has experienced high levels of growth since the discovery of oil, and has a considerable importance both politically and economically. The Kingdom of Bahrain also mandates all publically listed companies to quarterly, semi-annually, and annually, publish their financial statements in compliance with international accounting standards, and that those reports have to be audited by an external independent auditor. This led to a business environment that is highly experienced with international accounting standards reporting.

Though the Kingdom of Bahrain made a public commitment of reaching towards a sole set of high quality international accounting standards through the royal decree no.21 of the commercial companies' law in 2001, evidence that determines the level of compliance to IFRS in Bahrain remains scant. While previous studies have examined the level of compliance in the GCC such as Al-Shammari (2008) and Mazhar (2002), as well as the level of compliance in Bahrain, such as, Al-Mudhaki (2013), Hamdan (2011), and Ramadhan (2002), those studies are scarce, and each of these studies were not as focused as the current study, targeting all listed companies within one country and measuring the level of compliance with one accounting standard.

The Adoption of IFRS has several benefits, to both investors and companies, such as, the significant increase in the quality of the information communicated to investors, which leads to greater transparency in the companies' financial reporting thus increasing the willingness of investors to provide financing to said companies'. Multinational corporations benefit from having to prepare their statements according to one set of standards rather than multiple, with more than 120 countries adopting IFRS (AICPA, 2015).

The level of compliance is an assurance to investors that the information they are receiving is accurate and dependable, thus the objective of this research is to investigate that level of compliance to IAS 18 in the Kingdom of Bahrain and determine whether the company specific characteristics mentioned earlier, have any influence on the level of compliance with IAS 18.

This research aims to measure the level of compliance of all companies listed on BB to IAS 18. Also the relationship between the five firm specific characteristics being investigated by this research and the level of compliance has been be examined. Therefore the research objectives are:

1) To measure listed companies' in BB level of compliance to IAS 18
2) To investigate the relationship between the level of compliance and the company's size.
3) To investigate the relationship between the level of compliance and the company's Age.
4) To investigate the relationship between the level of compliance and the company's Profitability.
5) To investigate the relationship between the level of compliance and the company's Leverage.
6) To investigate the relationship between the level of compliance and the company's Auditor Type.

The results of this research can benefit investors and companies as well, as the results will determine what level of compliance to IAS 18 are listed companies in Bahrain Bourse are committed to, and how transparent are the revenues they are reporting in their financials. The results can help companies' through the assurance of transparent reporting, which helps attract more investors, as well as reassure current investors and lenders regarding the company's revenue. It can also give an indication regarding the state of the market in Bahrain and the level of sophistication it has reached in disclosure of financial information.

2. Literature Review

2.1. Background of IAS 18

Income, as defined by the International Accounting Standards Board, is "an increase in economic benefits during the accounting period in the form of a decrease in liabilities or in the form of an inflow or enhancements of assets that results in an increase in equity". It comprises of both revenues and gains. Revenue is income that is realized through the ordinary activities of the company (sales, fees, royalties,.. etc.), while a gain is the result of a peripheral activity, such as the sale of company equipment for a price higher than the book value, the excess is realized as gains (IAS 18, 2009).

The goal of IAS 18 is to describe the accounting methods related to revenues realized from certain types of events and transactions. The primary issue when accounting for revenues is to determine when to recognize revenue. As prescribed in IAS 18 "revenue is recognized when the future economic benefits are probable to flow into the entity, and the ability to measure those benefits is reliable" (IAS 18, 2009).

Since its introduction in 1982 the standard has been amended several times, until it was finally decided that IAS 18 will be superseded by IFRS 15 effective from Jan 2017 (IASPlus, Deloitte). IAS 18 applies to the accounting for revenue generated from the sale of goods, rendering of services, interest income, royalties, and dividends (IAS 18, 2009).

2.2. The Need of IAS 18

Revenue is usually one of the biggest items in the financial statements. Revenue manipulation was the center of several high profile financial statements fraud in recent years. If financial statements are to fairly and accurately reflect the true economic activities of an entity, a consistent approach to revenue recognition is substantially important (Kelly, 2014).

According to the conceptual framework of financial reporting, financial statements are prepared under the accruals basis of accounting assumption, which matches costs with the revenues they generate. The timing of revenue recognition is crucial to appropriately match costs with revenues in the correct period. The calculation method of revenues is essential to any meaningful understanding of an entity's financial performance. Revenue is generally recognized at the point of sale, because four criteria will have been met at that point, which are:

1. The buyer has been provided with the product or service.
2. The liability to pay the seller for goods and services provided has been recognized by the buyer.
3. The willingness indicated by the buyer to settle the obligation.
4. The establishment of the monetary value of goods and services provided.

Because many investors use the growth in revenues as a key performance indicator, and the direct impact it has on earnings, management may be tempted to manipulate revenues, either overstating them to attract more investors and raise stock price, or understating them to reduce the amount of taxes paid. Either ways, it is the duty of a Certified Public Accountant (CPA) to examine the statements prepared by the public company and confirm that revenues have been prepared in accordance to International Accounting Standards (Kelly, 2014).

Growing firms with ample opportunities generally have fewer established assets, thus they are compelled to exhibit a higher quality of reporting, such as recognizing losses more timely than a firm that is less conservative. Growth opportunities also provide greater discretion to managers on the timing in which to recognize expenses and revenues, thus increasing the potential for earnings management. Further, the increase in the amount of foreign investments will lead to greater separation of ownership and management, a separation like this can result in an agency problem that is also linked to the financial reporting quality (Rosa & Tiras, 2013).

2.3. IFRS Adoption

The development of the international accounting standards began decades ago in an attempt by developed countries to create accounting standards that small developing countries that lack the resources to create their own accounting standards can use. But since then, and with the globalization of the business world, investors, international companies, auditors, and regulators started to realize the increased significance of implementing a common set of accounting standards in all areas of the reporting chain of financial information (AICPA, 2011).

A year after the establishment of the International Accounting Standards Board (IASB) in 2001, European Union members committed to impose a mandatory compliance to IFRS on public corporations in its jurisdiction, with an effective date of 2005 (Rammana & Sletten, 2009).

The IASC set and established minimum disclosure guidelines, which companies, in countries mandating IAS compliance, were required to follow. However, the International Accounting Standards Committee (IASC) as well as the International Federation of Accountants (IFAC) were concerned that many companies were alleging compliance to IAS requirements, while in fact they were not complying with all the IAS's requirements. Prior researches by Street et al., Cairns, and Saleem supported the concerns of the IFAC and the IASC by bringing to light evidence that the level of compliance is very mixed and somewhat selective for companies alleging full compliance to IAS requirements (Joshi & Al-Mudhahki, 2013).

More than one hundred and forty countries, including all European countries, required or permitted the use of International Accounting Standards for financial reporting by 2015. Approximately 85% of those countries mandate the use of IFRS for the preparation of financial reports by local publicly traded companies (SEC, 2008). The United States however, is still using a domestic standard, GAAP (Generally Accepted Accounting Principles), although support for a single set of high quality globally accepted accounting standards is growing, but support for the adoption of IFRS does not exist (IASPlus, 2015)

In 1983 both national and international leading accounting firms in Bahrain were invited by the Ministry of Trade and Agriculture to enter a newly established committee that was tasked with the setting of accounting standards in Bahrain. The decision as to whether International Accounting Standards should be used as Bahrain's national accounting standard was left to the committee. The committee recommended that except for IAS 15 (Information reflecting the effects of changing prices); all International Accounting Standards are to be adopted in Bahrain (Al-Qahtani, 2005).

2.3.1. IFRS Adoption in Developing Countries

Emerging markets can be defined as low income countries that are experiencing rapid growth using economic liberalization as their engine for growth. Those countries are classified as either developing countries in Asia, Latin America, the Middle East, and the African continent, or economies in transition such as China (Broker, 2012).

First we need to identify the reason why developing

countries use IFRS for financial reporting? For some countries, it is due to pressure imposed on them by large international corporations or the World Bank, while for others it is the desire to attract financial resources and promote their development. Cooke and Wallace (1990) found that the level of regulations for financial information disclosure for corporations in several developed nations probably results from internal factors, such as the legal rules of the country, the level of economic development, and the implicit and explicit objectives of society (Albu *et al.,* 2011).

The World Bank, the International Federation of Stock Exchanges (IFSE), the International Organization for Securities Commissions (IOSCO), and the IASC believe that adopting IAS's is appropriate for developing countries, the most mentioned reasons being: reducing the production cost and set up cost of their own accounting standards, improving their level of accounting, and joining the international harmonization drive (Joshi & Al-Mudhahki 2013).

A Study examining the level of compliance in Egypt to IAS 12 "Income Tax" found a low level of compliance, especially for companies audited by local auditing firms (Ebrahim, 2014). Another study in Ghana examined the level of IFRS compliance for companies publically traded on the Ghana Stock Exchange (GSE). An overall mean compliance rate of 85.8% was revealed by the study, with a 62.2% minimum compliance rate and an 85.8% maximum compliance rate (Yiadom & Atsunyo, 2014).

2.3.2. IFRS Adoption in Developed Counties

The first two years of adoption for Europe were difficult, as the transition from local standards to international standards required developing new information and accounting systems, train staff, and deal with managers who were not motivated for the change. However, the transition had a positive impact on earnings, as managers were less motivated to manipulate accounting numbers to increase earnings (Boumediene *et al.,* 2014).

In late 2008 the Securities and Exchange Commission (SEC) released a proposal entitled "Roadmap for the Potential Use of Financial Statements Prepared in Accordance with International Financial Reporting Standards by U.S. Issuers". The proposal was to force publically traded corporates in the U.S. to start implementing IFRS by the end of 2014, 2015, or 2016 (Harper *et al.*, 2012). However, Fitch Ratings stated in a report that the probability of IFRS being fully adopted in the United States in the specified time period is growing less likely due to the IASB and the FASB (Financial Accounting Standards Board) moving further away from full convergence of their standards (Bramwell, J. 2014).

A study conducted in Turkey in the year 2011 examined the level of compliance of companies listed on the Istanbul Stock Exchange, a total of 168 companies, the results showed a level of compliance of 0.79, which is lower than Australia (0.94), Germany (0.81), and the GCC countries (0.82) (Demir & Bahadir, 2014).

2.3.3. IFRS Adoption in Bahrain

Since 1997, the representatives of twenty two Arab countries issued a recommendation during a forum in Dubai to support the use of IAS before 1998. Bahrain never developed its own domestic accounting standards due to the following reasons:

- Bahrain being an international financial center;
- A large number of foreign banks operates in Bahrain, those banks follow international standards as they are considered benchmarks for comparison, and
- Bahrain is a small country with a small population, the required expertise to develop a local standard was limited, or it might have been too expensive to develop a local standard (Joshi & Al-Mudhahki, 2013).

Since 1992 financial year-end, the Central Bank of Bahrain (formerly known as the Bahrain Monetary Agency) required all banks to produce their financial reports in accordance with IAS, and those statements must be audited by an external auditor (Hussain & Isalm, 2002).

Currently, all publically traded companies operating in Bahrain are mandated to prepare their financial reports in compliance with the International Financial Reporting Standards requirements (Tait, 2005). By 1996 all public companies listed on BB were required to follow the requirements of IAS in the preparation of disclosed financials (Al-Hussaini *et al.*, 2008). In 2001 every registered company in Bahrain was mandated to produce an audited Income Statement, Statement of Financial Position, and the directors' report for the previous financial year within the first quarter of the new financial year, in compliance with all IFRS requirements (Tait, 2005).

2.4. Company Characteristics and the Level of Compliance

The level of firm IFRS compliance varies according to several firm specific characteristics. One of those characteristics is firm size, as it is argued that to protect their name and reputation, as well as to avoid government intervention; larger companies will have a higher degree of compliance than smaller ones. The agency theory supports such argument that larger firms are assumed to have a higher level of compliance with accounting standards, as larger firms have higher agency costs due to a more complicated organizational framework, disclosure is used to reduce information asymmetry amidst the company's management (insiders) and equity providers (outsiders) (Demir & Bahadi, 2014).

Another firm specific characteristic supported by the agency theory with the level of accounting standard compliance is auditor type. External auditors are viewed as a mechanism that helps reduce the conflict between shareholders and managers interests. Large audit firms are argued to reduce agency costs by exerting a more monitoring role and limiting managers' opportunistic behavior (Yiadom & Atsunyo, 2014).

Profitability is another firm specific characteristic linked with the level of compliance. As per the signaling theory, it is assumed that managers of more profitable companies wish to signal their strength and success to current and potential investors. Managers in profitable companies also wish to justify their positions and packages, thus are more probable to disclose higher quality of information than companies with lower profits (Demir & Bahadir, 2014).

Agency theory also associated a company's leverage with the level of accounting standard compliance, as companies with high leverage are assumed to disclose more and higher quality information in order to reduce agency cost. High leverage companies, by definition, have lesser equity and are subject to equity risk, therefore, the demand by shareholders for information increases as they need to assess whether the company will be able to meet its financial debt obligations and the risk of future cash flows associated with their investment (Al-Shammari *et al.*, 2008).

The last firm specific characteristic this research will investigate is the age of the company. It is argued that companies who have been operating in the market longer than others disclose more information; this argument is supported by several factors, such as older companies being most likely well established and in possession of professional, well trained, staff in charge of preparing the financial statements. Older firms are also more likely to have a more established accounting system capable of meeting detailed IFRS requirements. It is also argued that while older firms seek to enhance their image and reputation in the market, complying with disclosure requirements is more likely than younger firms who might not disclose full information because disclosing sensitive information to established competitors might be harmful (Demir & Bahadir, 2014). Thus it can be said that the signaling theory is in support of the relationship between the age of the company and the level of disclosure requirement compliance.

2.5. Challenges in Implementing IAS 18

Implementation of IFRS and IAS can have certain challenges, especially in emerging markets, such as resistance to change, the lack of educated and trained professionals, resources, and the reduced power of internal coercive factors (Albu *et al.*, 2011). The movement towards the international harmonization of financial reporting, which would eventually lead to symmetry in accounting standards, can come into struggle with some objectives of financial reports, as well as, more fundamentally, social, economic, and cultural contexts of different accounting systems, and even to some extent, with national sovereignty (Karim, 2001). IAS 18 has been specifically criticized for being vague, leading to inconsistencies when applied in practice. IAS 11, which deals with revenues and costs from construction contracts, has also been criticized as there has been uncertainty about which standard to use, IAS 18 or IAS 11, in some cases. The timing of revenue recognition is a challenge facing the implementation of IAS 18 as some companies lack a clear and comprehensive understanding of IAS 18, this is evident in the case of goods and services, as services are provided over a period of time while goods are sold at a point in time (Kelly, 2014).

2.6. Hypothesis Development

The hypothesis of this study has measured the relationship between the level of compliance with IAS 18 "Revenue" and the 5 firm specific characteristics mentioned earlier, which were chosen based on previous studies.

1) Firm Size: Many researchers, such as Watts and Zimmerman (1978) and Holthausen and Leftwich (1983) found that larger firms have a higher level of compliance with IFRS disclosures due to the reputational risk and their need to attract viable investments. Hossain and Hammami (2009), Juhmani (2012), and Al-Shammari and Al Sultan (2010) found a positive link between the quality of financial information reported by public firms and firms size. However, Demir and Bahadir (2014), and Glaum and Street (2003) failed to find a relationship between firm compliance to IFRS and firm size.
   Hence, based on prior studies, this research hypothesizes:
   H0: There is no significant relationship between firm size and IAS 18 compliance.
   H1: There is a significant relationship between firm size and IAS 18 compliance
2) Firm Age: Literature on firm age and IFRS disclosure show mixed results, Hossain and Hammami (2009) and Al-Shammari (2011) found a positive relationship between IFRS disclosure and firm age based on the argument that older firms are more exposed to the business cycle and have a stronger will to protect their reputation, as well as their ability to hire competent and professional staff who can produce reports in line with IFRS disclosure requirements. However, Glaum and Street (2003), Alsaeed (2006), and Juhmani (2012) found no association between firm age and level of IFRS compliance. Hence this research hypothesizes:
   H0: There is no significant relationship between firm age and IAS 18 compliance.
   H1: There is a significant relationship between firm age and IAS 18 compliance.
3) Profitability: Prior studies such Street and Bryant (2000), Hossain and Hammami (2009) failed to find an association between profitability and the firms level of compliance with IFRS disclosures. Similarly, Al-Saeed (2006), Glaum and Street (2003), and Juhmani (2012) found that profitability is not significantly associated with the level IFRS disclosure compliance. However, there are some, such as Wallace et al (1994) and Agyei-Mensah (2014) who found a positive relationship between profitability and the level of disclosure compliance. Some theories, such as the signaling theory, indicate that profitable firms' management will seek to take advantage of benefits associated with quality reporting to share their success with current and prospective shareholders and

investors. Hence, based on the prior argument, this research hypothesizes:
H0: There is no significant relationship between firm profitability and IAS 18 compliance.
H1: There is a significant relationship between firm profitability and IAS 18 compliance.

4) Leverage: A high leverage ratio may result in difficulty when attracting additional funds from creditors or prospective investors; hence many firms reduce the shareholder-debt holder conflict through providing high quality financial reports by complying with IAS/IFRS requirements (Al-Shammari, 2011). However, Demir and Bahadir (2014) found a negative relationship between the quality of financial report and leverage. Also, Alsaeed (2006), Ali et al (2004), and Juhmani (2012) reported an insignificant relationship between leverage and the level of compliance with IFRS.
To further examine the relation between IFRS compliance and leverage, this research hypothesizes:
H0: There is no significant relationship between firm leverage and IAS 18 compliance.
H1: There is a significant relationship between firm leverage and IAS 18 compliance.
5) Auditor Type: The level of compliance with IFRS has been linked with the type of auditor, for example, Demir and Bahadir (2014) found a positive association between firms audited by one of the big four auditing firms and the level of IFRS disclosure compliance. Even though Hossain et al's (1995) New Zealand study could not find a significant relationship between auditor type and the level of compliance, it is widely accepted that all big four auditing firms value their brand name highly and will not fall under their clients' pressure, while encouraging them to comply with IFRS mandatory disclosure requirements. Based on the previous argument, this research hypothesizes:
H0: There is no significant relationship between firm's auditor type and IAS 18 compliance.
H1: There is a significant relationship between firm's auditor type and IAS 18 compliance.

3. Research Methodology

3.1. Sample Selection

The population of this research consists of the publically listed commercial banks, investment banks, insurance companies, services companies, hotels and tourism companies, industrial companies, and non-Bahraini companies listed on the Bahrain Bourse. The total number of listed companies on the bourse was 47 companies in 2013, which included 2 closed companies and 3 suspended companies which were excluded from the sample. Another 6 companies were excluded from this research as their financials were not available. Excluded companies and the reason for their exclusion can be seen in Table 1. The final sample thus is 36 listed companies from the Bahrain Bourse.

Table 1. *Excluded Companies.*

Company:	Reason
1. Securities and Investment Company	Closed Company
2. United Paper Industries	Closed Company
3. Gulf Monetary Agency	Suspended
4. Taib Bank	Suspended
5. Global Investment House	Suspended
6. United Gulf Investment Corp.	No published audited financial reports
7. Bahrain Car Park Company	No published audited financial reports
8. Bahrain Ship Repairing & Engineering	No published audited financial reports
9. Banader Hotels Company	No published audited financial reports
10. International Investment Group	No published audited financial reports
11. United Finance Company	No published audited financial reports

3.2. Measurement of the Dependent Variable

As mentioned earlier, the dependent variable in this research is the level of IAS 18 disclosure compliance. The level of compliance has been measured through a self-constructed compliance index (CINDEX) similar to prior compliance measurement studies, such as Yiadom & Atsunyo (2014). The compliance index ratio measured what each company presented and disclosed in its end of year audited financials, to what each company is obligated to present and disclose as per IAS 18. The checklist was constructed using paragraphs from the IAS18 standard, when a company is in compliance with the requirements of a paragraph a dummy variable "1" was assigned in the checklist, while non-compliance was assigned a "2", and if the requirement is not applicable for the company, such as exchange of goods or royalties disclosure which is not practiced by all companies, a "3" was assigned on the checklist. The Dichotomous method was used to determine the level of company compliance to IAS18 requirements, where a company is either in compliance with IAS 18 requirements or isn't, if the requirement is not applicable to the company, the company will not be penalized for it. The IAS18 Compliance Index was then computed using SPSS.

3.3. Measurement of the Independent Variables

Five company specific characteristics were examined in order to investigate if those characteristics had any impact on the level of compliance to IAS 18. The five characteristics and their measurements are as follows:

a. Company Size

The natural logarithm of each company's total assets was used to measure the company's size. This method was used in prior studies such as Yiadom & Atsunyo (2014) and Al Shammari (2008)

b. Company Profitability

The company's' profitability was measured by each company's Return on Equity (ROE), which is the company's net profit divided by its total equity. This method was previously used by Demir & Bahadir (2014)

c. Company Leverage

Each Company's leverage ratio was calculated by dividing the total amount of debt by the company's total equity (debt to equity ratio). This measurement was used in previous studies such as Al-Shammari et *al.* (2008).

d. Company Auditor Type

Company's audited by big four audit firms were assigned a dummy variable "1", while company's audited by other auditing firms were assigned a dummy variable of "2". This method was previously used by Yiadom and Atsunyo (2014).

e. Company Age

The number of years since the company was founded.

3.4. Model Development

In order to determine the effect on the level of IAS18 compliance each company characteristic has on the sample companies listed on the Bahrain Bourse the following multiple linear regression model was developed:

$$\text{Cindex} = \beta_1 + \beta_2\text{CSize} + \beta_3\text{CAge} + \beta_4\text{CProfit} + \beta_5\text{CLevrg} + \beta_6\text{CAudit} + \mathcal{E}i.....$$

Where:

Cindex = Compliance Index;

CSize = Log of total assets;

CAge = Company age;

CProfit = Company's return on equity;

CLevrg = Debt to equity ratio;

CAudit = Company's auditor type;

$\mathcal{E}i$ = Random error.

4. Data Analysis and Discussion

4.1. Descriptive Statistics

The mean of the disclosure compliance level with IAS18 for the sample companies was 63% with a maximum of 100% and a minimum of 14% (per IAS18 disclosure requirements). The results are lower than the total IFRS disclosure level in some developed countries such as Australia (0.94, Tower *et al,* 1999), Germany (0.81, Glaum & Street, 2003), Turkey (0.79, Demir & Bahadir, 2014), and Switzerland (0.74, Street & Gray, 2002), however, these results are higher than some neighboring countries such as Saudi Arabia (0.33, Alsaeed, 2006), Jordan (0.63, Naser, 1998), and Bangladesh (0.44, Akhtaruddin, 2005). A study published by Al-Shammari *et al* (2008) measured the total level of IFRS compliance in the GCC, the disclosure mean was 0.82, with the U.A.E being the highest (0.85) and Qatar the lowest (0.71), while Bahrain scored a total compliance mean of 0.82. This would indicate that the disclosure for IAS18 is below average in Bahrain compared to other standards. It is also worth mentioning that the results indicate a level of compliance to one standard (IAS 18) while the comparable results are for an overall level of compliance to all IASs. Companies listed on the Bahrain Bourse ranged in size (total assets) from BD12 billion (Ahli United) to BD6 million (Bahrain Family Leisure Company, with a mean of BD1.5 billion. The size distribution was skewed; the natural logarithm was utilized to mitigate the skewness in the regression analysis, which is consistent with prior studies (Demir & Bahadir, 2014).

Table 2. *Descriptive Statistics.*

	Mean	Median	Max.	Min.	Std. Dev.
Dependent Variable					
IAS18 Compliance	0.63	0.704	1	0.139	0.303
Independent Variables					
Company Size (Ln)	12.422	11.695	16.326	8.691	2.031
Company Age	28.056	31.5	56	3	13.469
Company Profitability (ROE)	0.066	0.071	0.222	-0.192	0.092
Company Leverage	2.136	0.687	10.653	0	2.978
Company Auditor Type	0.833	1	1	0	0.378

Company age had an average of 28 years, and ranged from 56 year old companies, to only 3 year old companies. National Bank of Bahrain is the oldest listed company in Bahrain, and the first national bank to start operations in the Island. While Ithmaar bank is not relatively new to the market, it is considered so due to it merging with its subsidiary (Shamil Bank) in 2010 to form a new Islamic banking entity.

The sample leverage ratio ranged from 0 to 10.65, with an average of 2.13. This would indicate that while some companies had no debt at all, others were heavily leveraged. The high leverage ratio is to be expected as the biggest component of the sample being commercial and investment banks. Auditor type was simply categorized as big four (1) and non-big four (2). The results show that around 83% (30 of the 36 companies in the sample) of the listed companies in

Bahrain are audited by a big four firm.

4.2. Empirical Analysis and Testing of Hypothesis

As previously mentioned in chapter1, these are the hypothesis of this research:

1. H_0: There is no significant relationship between firm size and IAS 18 compliance.
   H_1: There is a significant relationship between firm size and IAS 18 compliance
2. H_0: There is no significant relationship between firm age and IAS 18 compliance.
   H_1: There is a significant relationship between firm age and IAS 18 compliance.
3. H_0: There is no significant relationship between firm profitability and IAS 18 compliance.
   H_1: There is a significant relationship between firm profitability and IAS 18 compliance.
4. H_0: There is no significant relationship between firm leverage and IAS 18 compliance.
   H_1: There is a significant relationship between firm leverage and IAS 18 compliance.
5. H_0: There is no significant relationship between firm's auditor type and IAS 18 compliance.
   H_1: There is a significant relationship between firm's auditor type and IAS 18 compliance.

The aim of these hypotheses is to determine if the independent variables being tested in this research (Company size, age, profitability, leverage, and auditor type) have any effect on the company's IAS18 disclosure level.

As shown below in table 4.4, the resulted R appears to be 22.10% which signifies a weak correlation as per the Cohen (1998) guidelines for the interpretation of correlations. The level of impact the independent variables have on IAS18 compliance (R-square) is around 5% which is also a weak percentage. The resulted p-value is 0.001466 which is less than 0.05, and the F-test value of 4.277 determines that the study model is acceptable.

Table 3. *Testing of Hypothesis.*

Variables	t.test	Sig.
Company Size	2.436	0.006
Company Age	-0.230	0.820
Company Profits	0.557	0.582
Company Leverage	-2.180	0.019
Company Auditor Type	1.978	0.038
R	0.221	
R-Square	0.049	
F-Test	4.278	
p-value (f-statistics)	0.001466	

4.2.1. Company Size

As mentioned previously, the agency theory supports the argument that larger companies are assumed to have a higher level of compliance, as they will act to protect their market standing, reputation, and name. The research results show that there is a positive significant relationship between firm size and level of IAS18 compliance, as Sig. < 0. This is in compliance with previous researches done by Juhmani (2012), Hossain and Hammami (2009), and Al Shammari and Al-Sultan (2010). Thus the alternative hypothesis is chosen

4.2.2. Company Age

This research assumed that due to older firms being well established and having the possession of professional and well trained staff in charge of the preparation of the financial statements, a significant positive relationship should exist. Also, the signaling theory supports the relationship between firm age and level of compliance due to some newer firms choosing not to disclose sensitive information to their older, well established competitors. However, the research results conclude that there is no significant relationship between firm age and level of compliance due to the Sig. > 0.05. The lack of a significant relationship is in compliance with previous research results done by Juhmani (2012), Glaum and Street (2003), and Alsaeed (2006). The null hypothesis is accepted due to the lack of a significant relationship between the level of compliance and firm age.

4.2.3. Company Profits

The hypothesis supporting a significant positive relationship between the level of compliance and the level of profits was supported by this research. The signaling theory also supports the existence of a relationship between the level of compliance and the firm's profits on the basis that as managers in profitable companies wish to disclose accurately their performance to justify their positions and packages. However, this study found no significant relationship between the level of compliance and the firms' profits level, with a Sig. > 0.05. This result is in compliance with prior results of Street and Gray (2001), Street and Bryant (2000) and Hossain and Hammami (2009). The null hypothesis is accepted due to the lack of a significant relationship between the dependent and independent variables.

4.2.4. Company Leverage

This research was in support of a significant positive relationship between a firm's compliance level and leverage ratio. Agency theory also supports the argument that highly leveraged firms' have to disclose more information to satisfy shareholder demands. The access to credit lines also depends on the availability of information regarding the firm so that credit lenders can do proper risk analysis. The results of the research however found a negative significant relationship between the level of compliance and a firm's leverage with a Sig. < 0.05. The negative relationship might be due to highly leveraged firms trying to present a better picture of the firm's performance. This result is in compliance with prior researches such as Demir and Bahadir (2014). The alternative hypothesis is accepted here, regardless of the direction of the relationship, as a significant one does exist between the dependent and independent variables.

4.2.5. Company Auditor Type

A general assumption is that firms audited by one of the big four audit firms is expected to have a higher level of compliance, that being due to the inability of a firm to practice contract pressure on one of the big four audit firms, who value their reputation and firm image more than a single contract from one firm. As expected, the results of the analysis found a significant positive relationship between a firm's level of compliance and the type of auditor responsible for auditing its financials with a Sig. < 0.05. This result is in compliance with prior researches such as Demir and Bahadir (2014). The alternative hypothesis is accepted due to the presence of a significant relationship between the dependent and independent variables.

Table 4. *Hypothesis Results.*

Hypothesis	Expected Results	Actual Results
1. A significant relationship exists between company size and level of IAS 18 compliance	Significant positive relationship	There is a significant positive relationship
2. A significant relationship exists between company age and level of IAS 18 compliance	Significant positive relationship	No significant relationship
3. A significant relationship exists between company profitability and level of IAS 18 compliance	Significant positive relationship	No significant relationship
4. A significant relationship exists between company leverage and level of IAS 18 compliance	Significant positive relationship	There is a significant negative relationship
5. A significant relationship exists between company auditor type and level of IAS 18 compliance	Significant positive relationship	There is a significant positive relationship

5. Conclusion

5.1. Conclusion

This research examined the extent of disclosure compliance with IAS18 by 36 companies listed on the Bahrain Bourse for the year 2013. Five company specific characteristics were measured for the level of influence they had on the company's level of IAS18 disclosure compliance. A compliance index was derived from a self-constructed checklist which represented the average compliance to IAS18 among the selected sample companies. Multiple regression analysis was used, after validating the data gathered in the checklist, to measure the level of relation the level of IAS18 compliance had with the five selected company characteristics. The five company specific characteristics examined in this research were company size, company age, company profitability, company leverage, and company auditor type. The reason behind choosing those characteristics is that they proved to have a significant influence on the level of accounting standard disclosure compliance as per prior studies, such as Al-Shammari (2008) and Yiadom & Atsunyo (2014).

The level of disclosure varied among companies, for there were some companies that settled for a small paragraph no longer than a few sentences to sum up its revenue recognition criteria, whiles others disclosed their treatment of revenues in a much more detailed manner. This caused the level of disclosure compliance among companies to vary, and hence the company characteristics were examined if they had any influence on the level of disclosure. The results show that there is a significant positive relationship between the level of IAS18 disclosure and a company's size, a company's auditor type, as well as a significant negative relationship between a company's leverage level and IAS18 disclosure compliance. However, this research found no significant relationship between the level of disclosure compliance and a company's age or profits. The level of disclosure compliance was 63%, which is low considering that prior studies (Juhmani, 2012) found that the overall disclosure compliance in Bahrain to IFRS requirements was 81%. This would indicate that some standards have a high level of compliance while others have a low level of compliance.

5.2. Implications and Contributions

This level of IAS 18 disclosure compliance among Bahraini listed companies was lower than expected, at 63%, compared to the overall level of compliance to the IAS's and IFRS disclosure requirements, which was measured at 81% by Juhmani (2012). This would indicated that the regulator's nationwide monitoring and enforcement mechanisms need to be improved, as Revenue, as mentioned previously in the research, is usually the biggest item in the financials of a company, and is prone to tampering to reflect an adjusted image of a company's performance.

5.3. Limitations and Future Research

This research had some limitations, as with any research. The biggest limitation of this study was the small sample size which was due to the limited size of the Bahraini economy and the small number of listed companies on the Bahrain Bourse. The already small sample size was reduced further due to some companies being suspended, closed, or do not have any audited published financials. Another major limitation of this study was the absence of a criterion to reflect the level of importance of each disclosure requirement to financial statements users. In this research all IAS18 disclosure requirements were treated equally, which might not give an accurate picture.

Another limitation of the study is the use of certain ratios, such as the leverage ratio (debt to equity) and the return on equity ratio to measure profitability (net income divided by total equity). The results of this research might have varied if different ratios have been used, such as debt to assets ratio to measure leverage, or return on assets to measure profitability. Finally, a limitation to this research was the scarcity of similar researches to compare results with, as most researches done in the region were to measure overall level of compliance and not the level of compliance to a certain standard alone.

As mentioned earlier, one of the major limitations to this research was the small size of its sample, so increasing the sample size by measuring the level of compliance among GCC countries for example is a recommended step. Another suggestion would be to develop a compliance index that takes into consideration the degree of importance each disclosure requirement has, and whether the requirement is a financial one or a non-financial one. Finally, it is also recommended to take into consideration other company specific characteristic which might influence the level of disclosure compliance, such as dual-listing, internationality, and ownership concentration.

Appendix 1. *Disclosure Compliance Checklist for IAS 18.*

	Presentation/Disclosure Requirement
1	The entity disclosed the accounting policies adopted for the recognition of revenue, including the methods adopted to determine the stage of completion of transactions involving the rendering of services.
	The entity disclosed the amount of each significant category of revenue recognized during the period, including revenue arising from:
2	1) Sale of Goods
3	2) Rendering of services
4	3) Interest
5	4) Royalties
6	5) Dividends
7	Disclosure of contingent assets
8	Disclosure of contingent liabilities
9	Revenue is measured at the fair value of the consideration received or receivable
10	Measurement of the fair value of the consideration received or receivable takes into account the amount of any trade discounts and volume rebates allowed by the entity
11	Deferred payment by a customer/client constitues a financing transaction
12	Fair value is determined by discounting all future receipts using an imputed rate of interest for financing transactions
13	The entity did not recognize the exchange of similar goods or services as revenue.
14	The entity recognized the exchange of dissimilar goods or services as revenue
15	The entity measured the revenue generated from the exchange of dissimilar goods or services at the fair value of the goods or services received.
16	Transactions include different separately identifiable components when the entity enters into transactions that comprise more than one component (e.g. delivery of both goods and services, delivery of a number of different goods or services).
	revenue from the sale of goods is recognized when all of the following conditions have been satisfied:
17	a) The entity has transferred to the buyer the significant risks and rewards of ownership of the goods
18	b) The entity retains neither continuing managerial involvement to the degree usually associated with ownership nor effective control over the goods sold
19	c) The amount of revenue can be measured reliably
20	e) It is probable that the economic benefits associated with the transaction will flow to the entity
21	f) The costs incurred or to be incurred in respect of the transaction can be measured reliably
22	The entity did not retain significant risks and rewards of ownership of the goods
23	The entity retained only an insignificant risk of ownership, and the transaction accounted for a sale and revenue has been recognized (Sale of goods).
24	There is no uncertainty regarding the collectability of an amount already included in revenue
25	The potentially uncollectible amount has been recognized as an expense, rather than as an adjustment of the amount of revenue originally recognized
26	Expenses that relate to the revenue transaction can be measured reliably
27	Revenue involving the rendering of services is recognized only when the outcome of the transaction can be estimated reliably
28	Revenue associated with the service transaction is recognized by reference to the stage of completion of the transaction at the end of the reporting period (often referred to as the percentage of completion method)
29	The percentage of completion of the service transactions is determined by using a method that reliably measures the proportion of service actually performed
30	Revenue has been recognized on a straight line basis over the specified period (unless some other method better represents the stage of completion)
31	When the outcome of a service cannot be estimated reliably, revenue will only be recognized to the extent of recognized costs that are recoverable.
32	When the outcome of a service cannot be estimated reliably and it is not probable that the costs incurred will be recovered, revenue is not recognized and the costs incurred are recognized as expenses.
	Revenue in the form of interest, royalties or dividends, recognized only when both of the following conditions are satisfied:
33	It is probable that the economic benefits associated with the transaction will flow to the entity
34	The amount of the revenue can be measured reliably
	Revenue recognized on the following bases:
35	1) Interest: using the effective interest rate method as set out in IAS 39
36	2) Royalties: on an accrual basis in accordance with the substance of the relevant agreement
37	3) Dividends: when the shareholder's right to receive payment is established
38	When entering into agreements for the construction of real estate, the entity will apply IAS 11 rather than IAS 18.

References

[1] A Closer Look at the New Revenue Recognition Standard. (2014). Earnest and Young. (http://www.ey.com/Publication/vwLUAssets/Applying_IFRS:_A_closer_look_at_the_new_revenue_recognition_standard_(June_2014)/$FILE/Applying-Rev-June2014.pdf)

[2] Agyei-Mensah, B.K. (2014). Adoption of International Financial Reporting Standards (IFRS) in Ghana and the Quality of Financial Statement Disclosures. International Journal of Accounting and Financial Reporting, 3(2), 269-282.

[3] Akhtaruddin, M. (2005). Corporate Mandatory Disclosure Practices in Bangladesh. The International Journal of Accounting, 40(4), 399-422.

[4] Albu, N., Nicolae-Albu, C., Bunea, S., Artemisa-Calu, D., and Madalina-Girbina, M. (2011). A Story about IAS/IFRS Implementation in Romania: An Institutional and Structuration theory perspective. Journal of Accounting in Emerging Economies, 1(1), 76-97.

[5] Al Saeed, K. (2006). The Association Between Firm Specific Characteristics and Disclosure: The Case of Saudi Arabia. Managerial Accounting Journal, 21(5), 476-495.

[6] Al-Shammari, B., Brown, P., and Tarca, A. (2008). An Investigation of Compliance with International Account Standards by Listed Companies in the Gulf Co-Operation Council Member States. The International Journal of Accounting, 43(1), 425-447.

[7] Al-Shammari, B. (2011). Factors influencing the extent of mandatory compliance with international financial reporting standards: The case of Kuwaiti listed companies. Journal of International Business and Economics, 11(4), 305-360.

[8] Al-Qahtani, A. (2005). The Development of Accounting Regulation in the GCC. Managerial Auditing Journal, 20(3), 217-226.

[9] Bahrain Economic Indicators, (2013), Central Bank of Bahrain. (http://www.cbb.gov.bh/page-p-economic_indicators.htm)

[10] Ballas, A., Skoutela, D., & Christos, T. (2010). The Relevance of IFRS to an Emerging Market: Evidence from Greece. Managerial Finance, 36(11), 931-948.

[11] Borker, D. (2012). Accounting, Culture, and Emerging Economies: IFRS in the BRIC Countries. Journal of Business and Economics Research, 10(5), 313-322.

[12] Boumediene, E., Boumediene, S., Nafti, O. (2014). Impact of Adopting IAS-IFRS on the Handling of Accounting Data: The Case of France.The Journal of Applied Business Research, 30(4), 1239-1249.

[13] Cairns, D. (1997). IFAC--20 years on. World Accounting Report, 2. Retrieved from http://search.proquest.com/docview/204256361?accountid=44753

[14] Cavalier-Rosa, G., & L. Tiras, S. (2013). Brazil's Adoption of IFRS: Fertile Ground for Examining Earnings Management. Brazilian Business Review, 10(4), 133-146.

[15] Cooke, T. E., & Wallace, R. S. O. (1990). Financial disclosure regulation and its environment: A review and further analysis. Journal of Accounting and Public Policy, 9(2), 79-110.

[16] Demir, V., & Bahadir, O. (2014). An Investigation of Compliance with International Financial Reporting Standards by Listed Companies in Turkey. Accounting and Management Information Systems, 13(1), 4-34.

[17] Desoky, A. M., & Mousa, G. A. (2014). The Value Relevance and Predictability of IFRS Accounting Information: The Case of GCC Stock Markets. International Journal of Accounting and Financial Reporting, 4(2), 215-235.

[18] Ebrahim, A. (2014). IFRS Compliance and Audit Quality in Developing Countries: The Case of Income Tax Accounting in Egypt. Journal of International Business Research, 13(2), 19-37.

[19] Glaum, M., & Street, D.L. (2003). Compliance with Disclosure Requirements of Germany's New Market: IAS versus US GAAP. Journal of International Financial Management and Accounting, 14(1), 64-100.

[20] Hamdan, A. (2011). The Impact of Company Size, Debt Contracts, and Type of Sector on the Level of Accounting Conservatism: An Empirical Study from Bahrain. International Journal of Business and Management, 6(7), 134-146.

[21] Harper, A., Leatherbury, L., Machua, A., & Phillips, J. (2012). The Impact of Switching to International Financial Reporting Standards on United States Businesses. Journal of International Education Research, 8(4), 467-472.

[22] Hla, D. T., Isa, A. H., & Shaikh, J. M. (2013). IFRS Compliance and Nonfinancial Information in Annual Reports of Malaysian Firms. IUP Journal of Accounting Research & Audit Practices, 12(4), 7-24.

[23] Holthausen, R. W. & Leftwich R. W. (1983). The Economic Consequences of Accounting Choice. Journal of Accounting and Economics, 5(1), 77-117.

[24] Hossain, M., & Hammami, H. (2009). Voluntary Disclosure in the Annual Reports of an Emerging Country: The Case of Qatar. Advances in Accounting, Incorporating International Advances in Accounting, 25(2), 225-265.

[25] Hussain, M., Islam, M. M., Gunasekaran, A., & Maskooki, K. (2002). Accounting Standards and Practices of Financial Institutions in GCC countries. Managerial Auditing Journal, 17(7), 350-362.

[26] International Accounting Standard 18: Revenue. (2009). European Commission. (http://ec.europa.eu/internal_market/accounting/docs/consolidated/ias18_en.pdf)

[27] Juhmani, O. (2012). Ownership Structure and Corporate Voluntary Disclosure: Evidence from Bahrain. International Journal of Accounting and Financial Reporting, 3(2), 133-148.

[28] Joshi, P. L., Al-Mudhahki, J. (2013). Empirical Study of Compliance with International Accounting Standards (IAS-1) by Stock Exchange Listed Companies in Bahrain. Journal of Financial Management and Analysis, 26(2), 44-55.

[29] Joshi, P. L., Ramadhan, S. (2002). The adoption of international accounting standards by small and closely held companies: evidence from Bahrain. The International Journal of Accounting, 37(4), 429-440.

[30] Abdel Karim, R. A. (2001). International accounting harmonization, banking regulation, and islamic banks. The International Journal of Accounting, 36(2), 169-193.

[31] Kelly, M. (2014). IAS18 Revenue: Current Accounting Treatment and New Developments. CPA Ireland. (http://www.cpaireland.ie/students/study-support/professional-1/p1-corporate-reporting/p1-corporate-reporting-articles)

[32] Kingdom of Bahrain Economic Year Book 2013, Bahrain Economic Development Board. (http://www.bahrainedb.com/en/EDBDocuments/Bahrain-Economic-Yearbook.pdf)

[33] Mardini, G. H. (2013). Narrative disclosure under IAS 14R and IFRS 8 by Qatar listed companies. GSTF International Journal on Business Review, (2(3), 9-14.

[34] Mande, B. (2014). Emerging nations and financial reporting complex: A case of IFRS adoption in Nigeria. Journal of finance, Accounting, and Management, 5(2), 1-23.

[35] Rahahleh, M. Y., Siam, W. Z. (2009). The importance of applying the International Accounting Standard IAS 32 and its effect on financial statement presentation at Jordanian commercial banks. International Management Review, 5(1), 20-36,105.

[36] Ramanna, K., & Sletten, E. (2010). Why do countries adopt international financial reporting standards?. Rochester: Social Science Research Network. doi:http://dx.doi.org/10.2139/ssrn.1460763

[37] Sarea, A., and Hanefah, H. (2013). The need of accounting standards for Islamic financial institutions. International Management Review, 9(2), 50-59, 95.

[38] Street, D. L., and Bryant, S. M. (2000). Disclosure level and compliance with IASs: A comparison of companies with and without U.S. listings and filings. The International Journal of Accounting, 35(3), 305-329.

[39] Street, D. L., and Gray, S. J. (2001). Observance of international accounting standards: Factors explaining non-compliance by companies referring to the use of IAS. An ACCA Research Monograph, 74.

[40] Sucuahi, W. T. (2013). Firm size as predictor of compliance to International Financial Reporting Standards: IFRS 8. International Journal of Business and Management, 6(1), 45-60.

[41] Tait, D. (2005). Accounting, auditing, and taxation in Bahrain. Doing Business with Bahrain: A Guide to Investment Opportunities and Business Practice, 20(3), 222-229.

[42] Tower, G., Hancock, P., & Taplin, R. H. (1999). A Regional Study of Listed Companies' compliance with International Accounting Standards. Accounting Forum, Vol.23, No.3.

[43] Watts, R., & Zimmerman, J. (1983). Agency problems, auditing and theory of the firm: Some evidence. Journal of Law and Economics, 26(3), 613-633.

[44] Yiadom, E., and Atsunyo, W. (2014). Compliance with International Financial Reporting Standards by Listed Companies in Ghana. International Journal of Business and Management, 9(10), 87-100.

Impact of Macroeconomic Variables on Stock Returns: Evidence from Bombay Stock Exchange (BSE)

Nabila Nisha

Department of Accounting and Finance, North South University, Dhaka, Bangladesh

Email address:
nabilanisha.nsu@gmail.com

Abstract: Numerous empirical studies have examined the relationship between macroeconomic variables and stock returns across different stock markets and time horizons by either outlining the influence of only domestic variables or a few global factors. The aim of this paper is to combine both global and domestic factors and extend this presumed relationship between stock returns and macroeconomic variables to the emerging market of India. Using time-series analysis, this paper employs Vector Autoregression (VAR) to determine the impact of macroeconomic variables on the stock returns of Bombay Stock Exchange (BSE). Findings of this paper indicate that a considerable impact of interest rate, gold price, exchange rate and money supply is observed for the stock returns of BSE. Additionally, a strong influence of the global macroeconomic factor of the world price index is also observed, which implies a gradual integration of BSE towards the global financial markets. Finally, the study highlights the managerial and policy implications, future research directions and limitations from the perspective of India.

Keywords: Stock Returns, Macroeconomic Variables, Vector Autoregression Model, Bombay Stock Exchange, India

1. Introduction

Modern financial theory has increasingly argued that movements in stock prices are highly sensitive to changes in systematic factors and contend upon systematic factors to be sources of risk, such that in the long-run the returns on stocks must reflect the changes in these systematic factors. Since macro changes simultaneously affect many firms' cash flows and may influence the risk-adjusted discount rate, systematic factors are often related to the macroeconomic variables and this implies that a significant relationship can exist between the stock market and the macroeconomic variables of a country.

Numerous empirical studies have investigated this relationship across a number of different stock markets and over a range of different time horizons [1-6]. In fact, studies by [2, 3, 7-9] provided a strong evidence of a linkage between stock prices and macroeconomic activities. The presence of such evidence has made the relationship between stock returns and macroeconomic variables a subject of increasing interest over the last few decades.

Previous studies like [10-12] assumed that the stock market of a country is totally segmented from other stock markets across the world and hence only domestic macroeconomic variables play a deterministic role in the performance of the stock market of an economy. However, since domestic variables can be influenced by external macroeconomic factors like stock price movements in the global economy, international interest rates that govern capital flows, world oil prices and such others, movements in the global variables can have a gradual impact on the stock returns of the domestic economy. As such, various global macroeconomic factors were hypothesized to impact stock returns by some researchers like [13] and [14] under the assumption that, due to the trend of globalization, stock markets of the most developed economies is perfectly integrated.

A different aspect came into view when [15] cited that a more robust approach to such analysis would be to include both domestic and global factors to determine the impact on the stock returns of an economy. Following this evidence, few studies like [16] and [17] have examined the influence of global macroeconomic variables together with domestic factors on the stock returns. Even then, a void in the literature remains as these studies mostly focused on the developed markets and little on the emerging markets of South Asia. Since emerging markets have volatile prices and supernormal yields, they are less static and partially segmented from the global capital markets. This poses a strong potential that both domestic and global macroeconomic variables can impact the stock returns in emerging economies.

This paper thus aims to complement the literature by extending this presumed relationship between stock returns and a set of pre-determined domestic and global macroeconomic variables to the emerging market of India. Evidence for this relationship are drawn in this study through the research methods of Vector Autoregression [VAR] and by applying empirical tests like Johansen cointegration and Vector Error Correction [VEC] estimates. Empirical findings of this research will provide further insights into understanding the underlying macroeconomic factors that can significantly impact the stock returns of a selected Indian stock market. This study can also assist various academicians, researchers, policy makers and particularly the government of the Indian sub-continent to consider the influence of macroeconomic factors when regulating the stock market, its returns and its policies.

2. Literature Review

Studies on the linkage between stock returns and macroeconomic variables are motivated by the use of various asset pricing specifications, based on which a number of empirical research has been conducted in both developed and emerging economies across the world. As such, the current study highlights the notable empirical studies in this regard, followed by the research platform of the study and finally, the theoretical background of the proposed constructs has been discussed to determine the gaps for the study.

2.1. Empirical Studies on Developed Economies

Renowned studies regarding the relationship between stock returns and macroeconomic variables mostly center on the findings of [1-3, 7, and 18].

[1] documented evidence of a strong positive relationship between NYSE stock returns and macroeconomic factors such as capital expenditures, real rate of return on capital and output during the post-1953 period. Findings from this study also reported consistent evidence of a negative relationship between stock returns and inflation rates. Built on this study, [3] found strong positive correlations are found from this study between the NYSE stock returns and industrial production index, changes in risk premium and yield curve, and expected and unanticipated inflation. Empirical evidence by [2, 7 and 18] additionally complemented these studies by confirming the existence of a linkage between stock returns and macroeconomic variables like dividend yield, default spread and term spread.

Some recent studies that complement these notable findings include [4-6, 8, and 19]. [8] observed a long-run linkage between stock returns and local macroeconomic variables like oil price, money supply and GNP for countries like Canada, Germany, Italy, Japan and US; while, [19] found a significant long-run relationship of stock prices to industrial production, consumer price index and foreign stock prices. [4] indicated that domestic macroeconomic variables of inflation and money supply are significantly related to the stock returns of the NYSE-AMEX-NASDAQ. [5], on the other hand, investigated the S&P 500 stock price index and claimed a positive relationship of stock prices to money supply, inflation, industrial production, exchange rate, short-term interest rates and a negative relationship with long-term interest rates. Another study by [6] reported a negative impact of consumer price index and long-term interest rates with US stock returns and of money supply for the Japanese stock returns. However, industrial production index is found to have a significant positive relationship with the stock returns of both the countries in this study.

2.2. Empirical Studies on Emerging Economies

Focus of the researchers then shifted to the stock markets of the emerging economies around the world since substantial liberalization and reforms in the political and economic environments in many regions resulted in massive capital inflows and outflows and high profit potential for the emerging markets.

As such, [12] stated industrial production index to have a positive impact, while consumer price index, crude oil price and Treasury Bills to have a significant negative impact on the stock returns of Malaysia. A cross-sectional study by [20] claimed that global macroeconomic factor of the world market return and domestic macroeconomic variables of exchange rate and interest rate have a significant impact on the stock returns of Turkey. [9] then contributed to these findings by providing evidence of a positive impact of money supply and a negative impact of interest rate, industrial production index, oil price and foreign exchange rate on the Turkish stock returns. Conversely, [21] revealed a negative impact of consumer price index and a positive impact of industrial production index, exchange rate and money supply on the Pakistan stock prices.

Empirical studies conducted on the Indian stock market include the comparable time-series works of [22-25]. [22] observed an impact of industrial production index and inflation, but it reports no association of stock returns with exchange rate, money supply and gold prices. A recent time-series study conducted by [23] examined the impact of macroeconomic variables like industrial production index, exports, foreign direct investment, money supply, interest rate and exchange rate on the Indian stock returns. Their findings support a considerable influence of only interest rates on the stock returns of India. On the other hand, [24] claimed industrial production index to be the only significant macroeconomic variable for the Indian stock prices. [25] also supported the literature by conducting a time-series analysis upon the macroeconomic factors of industrial production, exchange rate and wholesale price index over the period 1995-2009.

2.3. Research Setting of the Study

An interesting strand of literature was conducted by [15-17, 26]. These studies examined the influence of a set of global macroeconomic factors or a combination of both domestic and global macroeconomic variables for the emerging economies. [15] observed the influence of global macroeconomic variables like world stock market return, the return on a foreign exchange index, oil prices, world industrial production and the world inflation rate for 20 emerging economies over 1976-92. However, findings of this study reported these factors to be insufficient to characterize the stock returns of the emerging economies. [16] then studied 20 emerging markets over a period of 1985-97 and their findings suggest that factors like price-to-earnings, dividend yield, real activity, inflation, exchange rate, money supply and world market returns are most significant for the stock returns of majority of these economies.

On the other hand, [17] studied six Asian countries of Indonesia, Korea, Malaysia, Philippines, Singapore and Thailand along with Mexico with regard to the 1997 crisis and reported that global risk factors are more influential in explaining stock returns, although a significant impact of local factors like consumer price index, industrial production, exchange rate and risk-free rate is claimed by their study as well. [26] further examined the four emerging economies of Brazil, Russia, India and China [BRIC] over the period of 1999-2006, but reported no significant association of the stock prices of these emerging countries with exchange rates and oil prices.

Future research directions of many such previous studies claim that there is still scope to examine the impact of macroeconomic variables, particularly the global macroeconomic factors, upon the stock returns. Specifically, the focus needs to be bestowed more upon the emerging economies since the economic environment of these countries are continually changing in recent times.

2.4. Proposed Constructs of the Study

For a comprehensive analysis of the impact of macroeconomic variables on stock returns, selection of the stock markets should be such that it accounts for majority of the stock trading across the country. Hence, the major stock market of Bombay Stock Exchange Limited [BSE] has been selected for analysis in this study. Stock returns of these major stock markets are represented through the general stock price index of these markets, which is why the BSE SENSEX has been selected for India. BSE SENSEX includes the largest and most actively traded stocks of 30 well-established and financially sound companies listed on Bombay Stock Exchange and represents various industrial sectors of the Indian economy.

In order to explain the variations in the stock returns of BSE, macroeconomic variables has been selected for this study in such a way that it complements the interrelationships between the goods market, money market and the capital market on a broad perspective. Hence, the following six domestic macroeconomic variables along with a global macroeconomic factor are selected in light of the literature and availability of data for the purpose of analysis.

2.5. Industrial Production Index

This variable is used as a proxy to measure the sustained domestic industrial growth of India. Since increase in the production of the industrial sector can lead to more profits and high dividends for the industries, its influence on the expected future cash flows can increase stock prices. Hence a positive relationship of the industrial production index with stock prices is expected. As such, the findings of [3, 5-6, 21] support this claim and so this variable is considered to be a significant factor to explain the variations in stock returns in this study.

2.6. Consumer Price Index

This variable measures the average change in prices of domestic goods and services during a specific period and is used in this dissertation as a proxy for the inflation rate of India. Inflation rate is a money market variable and is often related to nominal interest rates and any increase in the nominal interest rates can raise discount rates, which in turn can negatively influence the cash flows and hence stock prices. As such, a negative impact of inflation upon the stock prices is expected. Since [1] and [6] also supports this claim, this variable has been selected for analysis in this study.

2.7. Money Supply

The variable of broad money signifies the domestic money market and is used as a proxy for money supply of India in this study. Broad money includes the currency outside banks, demand deposits, time deposits and the deposits of other financial institutions in the central bank. Money supply has a two-fold impact on stock prices. As supported by [6], an increase in money supply can raise inflation and lower stock prices, thus indicating a negative impact. However, as claimed by [5] and [21], an increase in money supply can increase earnings and cash flows as well, thereby indicating a positive impact. Since this variable provides mixed evidence of their impact upon stock prices, it has been used for analysis in this study.

2.8. Interest Rates

The short-term bank deposit rate represents the domestic money market and is used as a proxy for the interest rate of India. It is paid to the depositor when cash is deposited in the bank and any increase in this rate will increase the opportunity cost of holding money, because the preference to hold money at banks at a high rate will be more favored than investments in stocks. As such, a negative relationship is expected between interest rates and stock prices and since this claim is further supported by [9, 20, and 27], this variable has been selected for analysis.

2.9. Exchange Rates

Exchange rate is the rate at which one currency can be exchanged for another currency and due to the dominance of US dollar in international transactions, exchange rate between India [Rupee] against the US [Dollar] has been used in this study. The impact of exchange rate on stock prices is likely to vary from an export-oriented to an import-oriented country. As evidenced by [27], any depreciation against the US dollar in an import-oriented country results in a negative impact on stock prices since an increase in the volume of imports leads to lower cash flows for the domestic industries and a subsequent fall in stock prices. Alternatively, [5] and [21] claimed that depreciation against the US dollar in an export-oriented country leads to a positive impact on stock prices because an increase in the volume of exports leads to higher cash flows for the domestic industries followed by a rise in stock prices. Since this variable indicates a two-fold impact upon stock prices, it has been selected for this study.

2.10. Gold Price

Gold represents the money market and is considered to be a better and safe investment than stocks, since gold can be used as a hedge against inflation and is often an alternative investment when there is idle money in hold. An increase in gold price can thus reduce the level of investment in stocks and lower stock prices and so a negative relationship is expected between stock prices and gold price. However, no significant relationship between stock prices and gold price is claimed by [9] and [22]. This indicates a scope for further research and hence this variable has been selected for analysis.

2.11. World Price Index

MSCI World Index signifies a value-weighted world price index and is used as a proxy for the global macroeconomic variable in this study. It is a common benchmark index of over 6000 global stocks, representing only the developed economies of the world like Australia, France, Germany, Italy, Japan, New Zealand, Norway, Singapore, Spain, United Kingdom, United States and such others. As such, due to the trend of globalization and consequent integration with the developed economies, a positive impact of the world price index is expected upon the stock prices. Since this claim is further supported by [14-16], this variable has been selected for this study.

3. Methodology and Data

3.1. Research Method

In order to capture the dynamic links between stock returns and macroeconomic variables, an advanced estimation technique of Vector Autoregression [VAR] models has been used in this study. VAR is commonly used for forecasting systems of interrelated time series and for analyzing the dynamic impact of random disturbances on the system of variables. This has become a well-established methodology since it takes into account the long-term relationship between the specified factors and can also help to capture any short-run dynamics that might exist between the variables of the model. The use of VAR models can be found in notable studies like [6, 8, and 19]. As such, this study applies a general VAR model to examine the impact of macroeconomic variables upon the stock returns of BSE.

3.2. Model

Following [3], a pre-specified multi-factor APT model has been developed for this study and the generic model takes the form as given below.

$$SPI_t = \alpha + \beta_1 * IPI_t + \beta_2 * CPI_t + \beta_3 * MS_t + \beta_4 * IR_t + \beta_5 * ER_t + \beta_6 * GP_t + \gamma * WPI_t + \varepsilon_t \quad (1)$$

Table 1. *Model Specifications*

where,	SPI_t = stock price index for month t
	IPI_t = industrial production index for month t
	CPI_t = consumer price index for month t
	MS_t = money supply for month t
	IR_t = interest rate for month t
	ER_t = exchange rate for month t
	GP_t = gold price for month t
	WPI_t = world price index for month t
	ε_t = error term of the regression for month t

Before applying this model to the data sets of India, raw data for the stock price index and the macroeconomic variables are transformed into natural logs. This conversion has been supported in the literature by [3] and in recent times by [20], since the variables converted into natural logs can be interpreted as growth rates on their first difference and as long-term elasticity for their coefficients in the cointegrating vector. As such, the first logarithmic difference of the macroeconomic variables and the stock price index has been used in this model across the same time period to study the case of India in this study.

3.3. Data Sources

To examine the impact of macroeconomic variables upon the stock returns, monthly data series covering a period of 15 years from January 2000 till December 2015 has been analyzed using the statistical package of EViews 8.1 in this study. Data for all the variables is collected from DataStream 5.0, except for money supply and consumer price index, which has been gathered from the database of the Reserve Bank of India [RBI].

4. Data Analysis and Results

4.1. Stationarity Checks

To conduct a time-series analysis, it is important to determine the stationarity of the data series because if a linear combination of the variables is stationary and integrated of the same order, it indicates that a long-term relationship can exist between the variables of a data series. With this expectation, unit root tests are conducted for the data series of this study. The results for the unit root tests of Augmented Dickey-Fuller [ADF] and Ng-Perron [NP] are given below.

Table 2. *Unit Root & Stationarity Tests.*

Variables	Null Hypothesis: variable is non-stationary		Null Hypothesis: variable is non-stationary	
	Augmented Dickey-Fuller [ADF] test statistic		Ng-Perron [NP] test statistic	
	Level	First Difference	Level	First Difference
SPI	-0.19	-10.03***	-0.34	-10.07***
IPI	1.17	-0.75	0.83	-27.95***
CPI	-1.14	-10.74***	-1.14	-10.74***
MS	1.52	-1.88	1.27	-10.32***
IR	-0.99	-5.66***	-1.34	-10.26***
ER	-1.73	-9.08***	-2.10	-9.07***
GP	0.66	-12.64***	0.78	-12.53***
WPI	-1.68	-10.10***	-1.96	-10.21***
1% level	-3.49		-3.49	
5% level	-2.89		-2.89	
10% level	-2.58		-2.58	

***implies significance at 1% level; ** implies significance at 5% level; *implies significance at 10% level

Table 1 indicates that the null hypothesis of non-stationarity for the data series of India cannot be rejected at any significance level under the ADF test. In case of first difference of these variables, the null hypothesis of non-stationarity is rejected by the ADF test at 1% significance level for all the variables, except the industrial production index [IPI] and money supply [MS]. This implies that these two variables has two unit roots and hence to make them integrated of order 1, they are differenced a second time. As such, the variables of industrial production index [IPI] and money supply [MS] will be considered to be lagged by one period for any further analysis of India under this study. For more robust results, NP unit root test was also conducted with an improved finite sample but the results indicate that the null hypothesis of non-stationarity for the data series of India cannot be rejected in level, but all the variables are rejected at 1% significance level in their first difference. NP test results thereby correspond to the ADF test results derived for India in this study.

4.2. Johansen Cointegration Test

To investigate the presence of a long-run equilibrium relationship between the stock price index and the macroeconomic variables, the Johansen cointegration test is used in this study following [28]. This method applies the maximum likelihood technique to a VAR model to determine the presence of cointegrating vectors in a non-stationary time series through two likelihood ratio tests of trace test and maximum eigenvalue test. Thus, if two variables are found cointegrated, it implies some relationship in the long-run and a restricted divergence from the long-run equilibrium path for the variables. For this study, the cointegration test is applied with 3 lags of the variables on the basis of Akaike Information Criteria [AIC] and its general representation has been derived from the VAR model.

Table 3. *Trace Test.*

Null Hypothesis	Trace statistic	5% Critical value	Probability
$r = 0$*	251.84	159.53	0.00*
$r \leq 1$*	168.94	125.62	0.00*
$r \leq 2$*	108.50	95.75	0.01*
$r \leq 3$	67.51	69.82	0.08
$r \leq 4$	30.16	47.86	0.71
$r \leq 5$	16.19	29.80	0.70
$r \leq 6$	5.63	15.49	0.74
$r \leq 7$	0.06	3.84	0.80

*denotes rejection of the hypothesis at the 0.05 level
Trace test indicates 3 cointegrating equations at the 0.05 level

Table 4. *Maximum Eigenvalue Test.*

Null Hypothesis	Max-Eigen statistic	5% Critical value	Probability
$r = 0$*	82.89	52.36	0.00*
$r \leq 1$*	60.44	46.23	0.00*
$r \leq 2$*	40.99	40.08	0.04*
$r \leq 3$*	37.35	33.88	0.02*
$r \leq 4$	13.97	27.58	0.83
$r \leq 5$	10.56	21.13	0.69
$r \leq 6$	5.57	14.26	0.67
$r \leq 7$	0.06	3.84	0.80

*denotes rejection of the hypothesis at the 0.05 level
Max-Eigen value test indicates 4 cointegrating equations at the 0.05 level

Table 2 indicates the rejection of the null hypothesis of no cointegrating vector, at most one cointegrating vector and at most two cointegrating vectors at 5% significance level under the Trace test. Although this implies the presence of three cointegrating relationships among the variables used for India in this study, results of the Maximum Eigenvalue test from Table 3 rejects at most three cointegrating vectors at 5% significance level. In case of conflicting results, the Maximum Eigenvalue test is typically considered and so four cointegrating relationships among the stock price index and the macroeconomic variables will tend to prevail for India.

***Table 5.** Normalized Cointegrating Coefficients.*

Variables	Coefficient	Std. Error	t-statistic	p-value
SPI	1.00	-	-	-
IPI	-0.04	1.05	-0.03	0.531
CPI	-0.06	0.05	-1.15	0.660
MS	-9.01	2.63	-3.43	0.892
IR	0.55	0.09	5.89*	0.032
ER	-1.14	0.39	-2.91	0.583
GP	-1.15	0.07	-17.74	0.990
WPI	-2.11	0.15	-13.74	0.982
Constant	19.96	-	-	-

Critical value at 5% level of significance with 1 degree of freedom for the chi-square distribution: 3.84
*denotes rejection of the hypothesis at the 0.05 level

By using the estimated values of the coefficients in the cointegrating vector from Table 4, the long-run relationship between the stock price index and the macroeconomic variables has been modeled for India as given below.

$$SPI = 19.96 - 0.04 * IPI - 0.06 * CPI - 9.01 * MS + 0.55 * IR - 1.14 * ER - 1.15 * GP - 2.11 * WPI \quad (2)$$

Results indicate that industrial production index [IPI], consumer price index [CPI], money supply [MS], exchange rates [ER], gold price [GP] and the world price index [WPI] in the estimated equation has a negative relationship with the stock price index [SPI] of India in the long-run. However, all these variables exhibit insignificant relationship while only the variable of interest rates [IR] is observed to have a positive and significant impact upon the stock price index [SPI], which means, in the long-run interest rates [IR] will have a considerable influence upon the stock price index [SPI] of India.

4.3. Vector Error Correction [VEC] Estimates

Following the presence of cointegrating relationships between the stock price index and macroeconomic variables, a restricted Vector Autoregression [VAR] in the form of Vector Error Correction [VEC] model is estimated for India. Estimates of the VEC model attempts to capture the long-run causality and the short-run dynamics between the stock returns and its own lags, along with the lags of the macroeconomic variables. It restricts the long-run behavior of the variables to converge to their cointegrating relationships by gradually correcting the deviation of the variables through the error correction term, which is the residual series of the cointegrating vectors normalized under the Johansen cointegration procedure. Following this characteristic, on the basis of Akaike Information Criteria [AIC] the VEC model has been re-parameterized from the VAR process by using 3 lags of the variables and is given below.

***Table 6.** Vector Error Correction Estimates.*

Variables	Coefficient	Std. Error	t-statistic	p-value
Error correction term	-0.17	0.07	-2.58**	0.09
D[SPI[-1]]	0.00	0.12	0.02	0.80
D[SPI[-2]]	0.14	0.11	1.28	0.71
D[SPI[-3]]	0.21	0.09	2.27	0.77
D[IPI[-1]]	0.20	0.17	1.22	0.68
D[IPI[-2]]	0.42	0.24	1.74	0.70
D[IPI[-3]]	0.24	0.15	1.53	0.62
D[CPI[-1]]	0.01	0.05	0.13	0.84
D[CPI[-2]]	-0.01	0.05	-0.15	0.87
D[CPI[-3]]	-0.09	0.05	-1.78	0.69
D[MS[-1]]	-1.46	0.63	-2.32	0.98
D[MS[-2]]	-0.77	0.62	-1.23	0.86
D[MS[-3]]	0.48	0.53	0.90	0.75
D[IR[-1]]	0.05	0.24	0.22	0.72
D[IR[-2]]	-0.49	0.23	-2.07	0.88
D[IR[-3]]	-0.68	0.25	-2.68	0.85
D[ER[-1]]	-0.39	0.47	-0.84	0.59
D[ER[-2]]	-0.17	0.48	-0.35	0.54
D[ER[-3]]	1.19	0.47	2.55	0.93
D[GP[-1]]	0.09	0.16	0.55	0.50
D[GP[-2]]	-0.11	0.16	-0.64	0.61
D[GP[-3]]	-0.06	0.16	-0.38	0.74
D[WPI[-1]]	0.73	0.16	4.43*	0.04
D[WPI[-2]]	-0.15	0.18	-0.79	0.76
D[WPI[-3]]	-0.29	0.17	-1.72	0.84
Constant	0.01	0.01	0.82	0.99
R-squared	0.60			
Adjusted R-squared	0.49			
Residual Sum of Squares	0.39			
F-statistic	5.36			

Critical value at 5% level of significance with 1 degree of freedom for the chi-square distribution: 3.84
*denotes rejection of the hypothesis at the 0.05 level
**denotes rejection of the hypothesis at the 0.1 level

By considering a lag of one period for industrial production index [IPI] and money supply [MS] in order to hold stationarity, estimated coefficients of the macroeconomic variables and the stock price index are used from Table 5 to form the following Vector Error Correction [VEC] model for India.

$$\Delta SPI_t = 0.01 + 0.00\Delta SPI_{t-1} + 0.14\Delta SPI_{t-2} + 0.21\Delta SPI_{t-3} + 0.20\Delta IPI_{t-2} + 0.42\Delta IPI_{t-3} + 0.24\Delta IPI_{t-4} + 0.01\Delta CPI_{t-1} - 0.01\Delta CPI_{t-2} - 0.09\Delta CPI_{t-3} - 1.46\Delta MS_{t-2} - 0.77\Delta MS_{t-3} + 0.48\Delta MS_{t-4} + 0.05\Delta IR_{t-1} - 0.49\Delta IR_{t-2} - 0.68\Delta IR_{t-3} - 0.39\Delta ER_{t-1} - 0.17\Delta ER_{t-2} + 1.19\Delta ER_{t-3} + 0.09\Delta GP_{t-1} - 0.11\Delta GP_{t-2} - 0.06\Delta GP_{t-3} + 0.73\Delta WPI_{t-1} - 0.15\Delta WPI_{t-2} - 0.29\Delta WPI_{t-3} - 0.17\mu_{t-1} + e_t \quad (3)$$

The error correction term [μ_{t-1}] here poses a negative sign as expected but is insignificant in the long-run at 5% significance level, implying that the stock price index [SPI] of India may not adjust to long-run equilibrium and disequilibrium may persist for a long time. That is, there is no evidence of cointegration. However, if the error correction term is analyzed at a less stringent level, then it is found significant at 10% level of significance. This indicates that there is some possibility of cointegration existing for the stock price index [SPI] of India. Results further indicate only a consistent positive relationship of lagged stock price index

[SPI] and industrial production index [IPI] to the stock price index [SPI] of India. While no constant negative relationship is observed, none of the variables exhibit any significant relationship with the stock price index [SPI] of India, except for the first lag of the world price index [WPI]. Partial presence of a long-run causal relationship with the macroeconomic factors thus delays the convergence of the stock price index to the equilibrium. The value of R-squared [R^2] further indicates that the model provides a good fit to the data since the lagged values of the macroeconomic variables explains about 60% of the lags in the stock price index of India. The low value of the minimized residual sum of squares [0.39] and the value of adjusted R-squared [$\bar{R}^2$] [49%] also confirms this result for India.

After the VEC model is estimated, a number of diagnosis tests are conducted to ensure that there are no problems of autocorrelation, heteroskedasticity and the model is well specified. For this purpose, Breusch-Godfrey Serial Correlation LM Test, White Test of Heteroskedasticity and Ramsey's Reset Test has been undertaken in this study. Table 6 provides the results of the diagnosis tests.

***Table** 7. Diagnosis Tests.*

Breusch-Godfrey Serial Correlation LM Test	
F-statistic	0.013
p-value	(0.909)
Durbin-Watson statistic	2.103
(1st order of autocorrelation)	
F-statistic	0.661
p-value	(0.784)
Durbin-Watson statistic	2.116
(12th order of autocorrelation)	
Heteroskedasticity Test: White	
F-statistic	0.502
p-value	(0.806)
Observations*R-squared	3.118
p-value	(0.794)
Durbin-Watson statistic	2.175
p-values are reported in parentheses	
degrees of freedom for F-distribution is (6,172)	
degrees of freedom for chi-square distribution is (6)	
Ramsey's RESET Test	
F-statistic	1.603
p-value	(0.207)
Durbin-Watson statistic	2.090
p-values are reported in parentheses	
degrees of freedom for F-distribution is (6,172)	

*denotes rejection of the hypothesis at the 0.05 level

Durbin-Watson significance table reported a critical lower bound value (1.634) and an upper bound value (1.715) at 5% significance level [29]. The observed test statistic (2.103) is greater than the tabulated lower and upper bounds, which indicates that the null hypothesis cannot be rejected at 5% significance level. Therefore, the 1st order of autocorrelation between residuals is found zero for the estimated VEC model. For further analysis, the 12th order of autocorrelation is also checked for the model. The p-value of F-distribution is greater than 0.05 whereas the observed F-statistic is less than the critical value (1.834) from the F-distribution table [30]. Hence, the null hypothesis cannot be rejected at 5% significance level. Even the Durbin-Watson test statistic (2.116) is greater than the tabulated lower and upper bounds, which indicates that the null hypothesis cannot be rejected at 5% significance level. Therefore, the errors of the estimated VEC model have zero autocorrelation.

The p-value of F-distribution is more than 0.05 whereas the observed F-statistic is less than the critical value (2.175) from F-distribution table [30]. Hence, the null hypothesis cannot be rejected at 5% significance level. Next, p-value of the LM-statistic is more than 0.05 and the value of $n*R^2$ (3.118) is smaller than the critical value (12.59) from chi-square distribution table [30]. Therefore, again the null hypothesis cannot be rejected at 5% significance level. As such, there is no heteroskedasticity in the VEC model which means constant variance exists for the estimates done for this study.

To examine for the general misspecification of the VEC model, the p-value of F-distribution for the Ramsey's RESET test is observed. Following the F-distribution table [30], the observed F-statistic is less than the critical value (2.175) and the p-value is also more than 0.05. Hence, the null hypothesis cannot be rejected at 5% significance level. This means that the VEC model estimated in this study is of correct specification.

5. Findings and Implications

Findings of this study report some consistency with the notable findings of [23]. This partial consistency arises since the two samples share a common period of 8 years between them and some macroeconomic variables as well. Over a sample period of 1995-2007, [23] applied the Johansen cointegration analysis and a number of other empirical tests to examine the impact of industrial production index, exports, foreign direct investment, money supply, interest rate and exchange rate on the stock returns of India. Through cointegration analysis, [23] stated the significance of industrial production index and money supply upon the stock returns, while findings of this study claim only interest rates to have a significant positive impact for India.

Following the VEC model, no long-run causal relationship is observed between the lags of domestic macroeconomic variables and the stock price index of India, implying the absence of short-run dynamic adjustments to the long-run equilibrium of the stock price index. However, the global macroeconomic variable of the world price index exhibits a significant positive relationship with the stock price index of India, indicating a partial presence of a long-run causal relationship with the global macroeconomic factor for BSE. To sum up, the global macroeconomic factor of the world price index plays a deterministic role for the stock returns of India, followed by a considerable impact of the domestic variables of interest rate, gold price, exchange rate and money supply – in the order of influencing strength.

Empirical findings from the time-series and cross-sectional analysis of this study thus imply that a time-variation in the risk exposure arises from the changes in the domestic macroeconomic variables of India and do not conforms timely to the stock prices of BSE. Findings further claim that BSE is gradually moving towards integration with the global capital markets. However, significant time-variation in the risk exposures from the changes in the domestic macroeconomic variables cannot be completely ignored for India.

Results of this study thereby indicate important implications for both researchers and practitioners. From a research point of view, the need to develop a model that can address a gradual integration towards the global financial markets is stressed, particularly for emerging economies like India. From a practical point of view, the revelation of a relationship between macroeconomic factors and stock returns can enable investors of India to adopt better diversification strategies and risk-return trade-offs by considering the influence of external shocks as well as the domestic factors. Policymakers and regulators of India must therefore strictly monitor the dissemination of information and the time-varying risk exposures that can arise from the changes in the domestic macroeconomic factors. Special care must also be taken to monitor the changes in the global macroeconomic factors like the world price index, in order to avoid any unnecessary consequences for the Indian stock market following any adverse changes in the global factors.

6. Limitations and Future Research Directions

The implications of this study, however, are not far-reaching since this study also has some limitations. To begin with, the selection of macroeconomic variables used in this study is arbitrary and the set of variables are not exhaustive. Use of some other domestic and global macroeconomic variables may have given a better insight to the findings of this analysis. Furthermore, the research methodologies used in this study are known to be sensitive to the choice of lags and as a result, findings may be somewhat inconsistent with previous empirical evidences. Finally, unavailability of data and time constraints has deterred the employment of a longer period of data in this study as well as using a different frequency of data like weekly or daily data series for the set of variables. Future research directions can be related to the use of varied global macroeconomic factors like international interest rates, global inflation and world oil prices to examine the influence upon the stock returns of the Indian stock market.

References

[1] Fama, E.F. [1981]. Stock returns, real activity, inflation and money. *The American Economic Review*, *71*, 4, 545-565. Retrieved from http://www.jstor.org/stable/1806180

[2] Fama, E.F. [1990]. Stock returns, expected returns, and real activity. *The Journal of Finance*, *45*, 4, 1089-1108. Retrieved from http://www.jstor.org/stable/2328716

[3] Chen, N., Roll, R. and Ross, S.A. [1986]. Economic forces and the stock market. *The Journal of Business*, *59*, 3, 383-403. Retrieved from http://www.jstor.org/stable/2352710

[4] Flannery, M.J. and Protopapadakis, A.A. [2002]. Macroeconomic factors do influence aggregate stock returns. *The Review of Financial Studies*, *15*, 3, 751-782. Retrieved from http://www.jstor.org/stable/2696720

[5] Ratanapakorn, O. and Sharma, S.C. [2007]. Dynamic analysis between the US stock returns and the macroeconomic variables. *Applied Financial Economics*, *17*, 5, 369-377.

[6] Humpe, A. and Macmillan, P. [2009]. Can macroeconomic variables explain long-term stock market movements? A comparison of the US and Japan. *Applied Financial Economics*, *19*, 2, 111-119.

[7] Schwert, G.W. [1990]. Stock returns and real activity: a century of evidence. *The Journal of Finance*, *45*, 1237–1257.

[8] Cheung, Y. and Ng, L.K. [1998]. International evidence on the stock market and aggregate economic activity. *Journal of Empirical Finance*, *5*, 3, 281-296. Retrieved from http://www.sciencedirect.com/science/article/pii/S092753989700025X

[9] Buyuksalvarci, A. [2010]. The effects of macroeconomics variables on stock returns: Evidence from Turkey. *European Journal of Social Sciences*, *14*, 3, 404-416. Retrieved from http://www.eurojournals.com/ejss_14_3_06.pdf

[10] Kwon, C.S. and Shin, T.S. [1999]. Cointegration and causality between macroeconomic variables and stock market returns. *Global Finance Journal*, *10*, 1, 71-81. Retrieved from http://www.sciencedirect.com/science/article/pii/S104402839900006X

[11] Ibrahim, M.H. and Aziz, H. [2003]. Macroeconomic Variables and the Malaysian equity market: A view through rolling subsamples. *Journal of Economic Studies*, *30*, 1, 6-27.

[12] Tan, B.C., Loh, W.L. and Zainudin, A. [2006]. Dynamics Between Stock Price, Oil Price And Macroeconomic Activities: A VAR And Impulse Response Approach. Proceedings of the 2nd IMT-GT Regional Conference on Mathematics, Statistics and Applications, University of Science Malaysia, pp. 167-179.

[13] Brown, S.J. and Otsuki, T. [1993]. Risk premia in Pacific-Basin capital markets. *Pacific-Basin Finance Journal*, *1*, 3, 235-261. Retrieved from http://www.sciencedirect.com/science/article/pii/0927538X9390025D

[14] Buckberg, E. [1995]. Emerging stock markets and international asset pricing. *The World Bank Economic Review*, *9*, 1, 51–74.

[15] Harvey, C.R. [1995]. Predictable risk and returns in emerging markets. *The Review of Financial Studies*, *8*, 3, 773–816. Retrieved from http://www.jstor.org/stable/2962239

[16] Bilson, C.M., Brailsford, T.J. and Hooper, V.J. [2001]. Selecting macroeconomic variables as explanatory factors of emerging stock market returns. *Pacific-Basin Finance Journal*, *9*, 4, 401-426. Retrieved from http://ssrn.com/abstract=201908

[17] Lint, C.R. [2002]. Risk profiles: how do they change when stock markets collapse?. *Journal of International Financial Markets*, *12*, 1, 59–80. Retrieved from http://www.sciencedirect.com/science/article/pii/S104244310 1000488

[18] Fama, E.F. and French, K.R. [1989]. Business conditions and expected returns on stocks and bonds. *Journal of Financial Economics*, *25*, 1, 23-49. Retrieved from http://www.sciencedirect.com/science/article/pii/0304405X89 900950

[19] Nasseh, A. and Strauss, J. [2000]. Stock prices and domestic and international macroeconomic activity: a cointegration approach. *The Quarterly Review of Economics and Finance*, *40*, 2, 229-245. Retrieved from http://www.sciencedirect.com/science/article/pii/S106297699 900054X

[20] Kandir, S.Y. [2008]. Macroeconomic variables, firm characteristics and stock returns: Evidence from Turkey. *International Research Journal of Finance and Economics*, 16, 35-45. Retrieved from http://www.eurojournals.com/finance.htm

[21] Sohail, N. and Hussain, Z. [2009]. Long-run and short-run relationship between macroeconomic variables and stock prices in Pakistan: The case of Lahore stock exchange. *Pakistan Economic and Social Review*, *47*, 2, 183-198.

[22] Chakravarty, S. [2006]. Stock Market And Macroeconomic Behavior In India. Discussion Paper 106, Institute of Economic Growth, Delhi.

[23] Ahmed, S. [2008]. Aggregate economic variables and stock markets in India. *International Research Journal of Finance and Economics*, 14, 141-163. Retrieved from http://www.eurojournals.com/finance.htm

[24] Agrawalla, R.K. and Tuteja, S.K. [2008]. Share prices and macroeconomic variables in India: An approach to investigate the relationship between stock markets and economic growth. *Journal of Management Research*, *8*, 3, 136-146.

[25] Singh, D. [2010]. Causal relationship between macroeconomic variables and stock market: A case study for India. *Pakistan Journal of Social Sciences [PJSS]*, *30*, 2, 263-274.

[26] Gay, R.D. [2008]. Effect of macroeconomic variables on stock market returns for four emerging economies: Brazil, Russia, India, And China. *International Business & Economics Research Journal*, *7*, 3, 1-8.

[27] Maysami, R.C. and Koh, T.S. [2000]. A vector error correction model of the Singapore stock market. *International Review of Economics and Finance*, *9*, 1, 79-96. Retrieved from http://www.sciencedirect.com/science/article/pii/S105905609 9000428

[28] Johansen, S. and Juselius, K. [1990]. Maximum likelihood estimation and inference on cointegration - with applications to the demand of money. *Oxford Bulletin of Economics and Statistics*, *52*, 2, 169-210.

[29] Durbin, J. and Watson, G.S. [1951]. Testing for serial correlation in least squares regression II. *Biometrika*, 38(1-2), 159-177.

[30] Brooks, C. (2008). *Introductory Econometrics for Finance* (2nd ed.). New York: Cambridge University Press.

Statistical Analysis of the Role of Internal Audit in Promoting Good Governance in Public Institutions in Kenya

Kennedy Sakaya Barasa

Department of Statistics and Actuarial Sciences, Jomo Kenyatta University of Science and Technology, Nairobi, Kenya

Email address:
sakayak33@gmail.com

Abstract: Internal Auditing has increasingly been recognized as an integral part of modern control structures and governance practices in both the private sector and public service. It has also been adding value in organizations across all sectors for many years in order to fight against the global financial crisis and recent cases of corporate frauds that have brought into sharp focus the consequence of the precarious role to be played by the internal auditors in ensuring good corporate governance. The main objective of this study was to find out how the Risk Management, Control Process and Governance Process, which are functions of internal auditing are being recognized today at high level in many organizations, especially in public Sectors, when well structured and given the required mandate to perform, improves performance and serves as valuable contributors in Promoting good governance in its functions which are accountability, transparency, effectiveness & efficiency and responsiveness in the public institutions in Kenya. The research adopted both the descriptive and correlation research designs in order to be successful, where 370 out of 398 respondents, sampled from eighteen (18) public institutions, completed a structured questionnaire. The events were recorded; analyzed, interpreted and described by using SPSS version 20 and the specific tools that were adopted in order to identify the levels of contribution of Internal Audit in Good Governance in the public institutions, respondent responses were determined by their demographic profiles. Parametric statistics were used to derive a meaningful conclusion from the empirical data using tools like descriptive statistics, t-test and Pearson Correlation. The study concluded that there is a strong significant relationship between Internal Audit and Good Governance in Public institutions.

Keywords: Audit, Internal Auditing, Internal Control, Public Sector, Value Addition, Governance, Kenya

1. Introduction

Today globally, internal audit activity has the potential to provide to date unequalled tool to management in the conduct of their duties. This potential has been transformed into a challenge and embodied in the new definition of internal auditing from the institute of internal auditors (IIA, 2008).

In the past, managers in the public sector had a narrower range of expectations for the role of internal audit compared to managers in the private sector. This is why internal audit function in the public sector was dominated by pre-payment audits. Thus, internal auditors devoted most of their time to checking on individual transactions before the payments were made, mainly, to crosscheck the authenticity of the transactions to be paid for. (Asare T. 2008)

Internal auditors are seen more as faultfinders rather than solution providers or witch hunters rather than watchdogs, and partners in the government strive for organizational excellence. However, in recent years internal auditing has developed a strategic dimension to become an essential component of public sector governance and financial management reforms in many developing countries. (Asare T. 2009).

In Kenya, the government established the Office of the Government Chief Internal Auditor (GCIA) based in the Ministry of Finance "as an apex oversight body to co-ordinate, facilitate and provide quality assurance for internal audit activities within Kenya public sector". (PFM, 2011)

An internal audit that performs well is one of the strongest means to monitor and promote good governance system in an organization. Thus, good governance is considered as a tool that is used in order to achieve strategy of an organization (Belay, 2007). As a result, in many countries internal audit has received great attention and has become an important asset of government financial management for improvement of the government performance sector. In connection to this, the researcher targeted public enterprises in Kenya to assess the role of internal audit functions in promoting good public sector governance system.

Thus, to curb corruption and deliver quality service in the public sector, there is a need to promote internal audit for good governance and leadership. In other words, to develop transparency, it is mandatory to install internal audit function (IAF) in government programs and services as part of modern management control system. This in turn needs IAF itself to grow highly qualified human resource in the field.

The above-mentioned problems can be classified into two categories with some overlapping. First, the competency of internal auditor that leads to trivial audit finding, lack of professional development, repetitive audit work, and non-value added internal audit report. Second, structural problem (Weak Governance) in the form of assigned task that impair the auditor independency, and fear of losing promotion, job security , and wrong perception about internal auditors as faultfinders and their task as policing rather than auditing (PFM, 2011).

Above all, weak organizational governance brings: Poorly motivated and frustrated internal audit staff because of limited scope of audit, Lack of independence, and internal auditor can also suffer from low status that leads to inefficient and ineffective internal audit work (PFM, 2011).

The importance of internal audit function to promote good governance within public sectors is well noted by concerned governmental bodies and known scholars. Inadequate auditing and accounting is one of the root causes for corruption and inefficiency in the public sector of Kenya. If such root causes of corruption are not addressed appropriately, the Country's poverty reduction and development programmed will definitely face serious challenges (Belay, 2007)

Moreover, Gansberghe (2005) has also noted that one of the strongest means to monitor ethics and governance in government institutions can be through the audit function. These statements clearly indicate the contribution that internal audit function can have towards to the government's efforts of solving the macro problem, poverty, through effective public sector governance.

Since the independence of Kenya, there has been a critical problem about good governance in public institutions to date. Kenyan government summarized a long term economic development plan called "Vision 2030" with major aspiration to transform Kenya's economy into a middle income country. This will not be achieved unless we transform from a subsistence agriculture economy to a knowledge-based one (Economy), with high levels of savings and private investment led by good governance.

1.1. Statement of the Problem

Internal audit is facing many challenges, some of the challenges identified by the Ministry of Finance , in Internal Audit Manual are: lack of expertise leading to trivial auditing findings, lack of opportunity for professional development, repetitive audit routines which staffed members can predict, being assigned to tasked such as accounting and pre-control of expenditures with the internal auditor subsequently have to audit (conflict of interest) , inability to insist on getting significant information because fears of losing promotion opportunities and job security (lack of independence), wrong perception of the audit function and auditors by the staff of the public body.

1.2. Objectives

1.2.1. General Objective

The overall objective of this research was to establish the role of internal auditing in promoting good governance in public institutions in Kenya.

1.2.2. Specific Objectives

i. To assess the above basic objective, the specific aims of the study focused on answering the following questions.
ii. To assess the quality of internal audit from the perspective of internal audit independence and Public governance.
iii. To examine the internal audit objectivity from the perspective of internal audit independence and corporate governance.
iv. To know the performance of internal audit independence and identify factors that affects the internal audit independence.

1.3. Research Questions

i. What are the factors that stimulate the IAF in the public sector to perform its role in enhancing good governance (if any) and to which level good governance is being applied?
ii. Is there any significant relationship between Internal Audit Function and Good Governance promotion?
iii. Is there any significant relationship between factors that stimulate the IAF in Public Institutions and level of good governance

1.4. Study Hypothesis

The researcher tested the following hypothesis.

H_0: There is no significant relationship between Internal Audit Function and Good Governance promotion.

H_1: There is no significant relationship between factors.

1.5. Definition of Terms

1.5.1. Audit

Referring to Hachette dictionary, "audit" is the operation intending to control the good management and safeguard the financial patrimony of an enterprise and application of correct and sounding decision making. (Pickett, 2010)

1.5.2. Internal Audit

Internal Audit is an independent and objective activity which gives the organization assurance of control on the level of its activities; it contributes advice and improves the value added. (UN, 2005)

1.5.3. Internal Control

It refers to the group or a set of security measures which contribute to the control of an enterprise. It insures the protection and safeguards the patrimony and the quality of the information. On the other hand, it is the application instructions of direction and favoring the improvement of performance. (Barrett, 2002)

1.5.4. Public Sector

The public sector is that portion of society controlled by national, state or provincial, and local governments. The public sector overlaps with the private sector in producing or providing certain goods and services. The extent of this overlap varies from country to country, state to state, province to province, and city to city. This overlap is most often seen in waste management, water management, health care, security services, and shelters for homeless and abused people (IIA, 2006)

1.5.5. Value Added

Internal audit is intended to provide value to the organization by improving opportunities to meet the organizational objectives by identifying operational improvements, and by mitigating risks through objective assurance. Evolving features of internal auditing have brought some modifications to the definition of added value. For example, in a traditional approach, savings from the loss endured in public programs—plugging the hole—was a fundamental goal, compared with the present where delivering services effectively, efficiently, economically, and ethically have emerged as primary goals. (Ball, 2002)

1.5.6. Good Governance

In an organization, it is a tool to achieve organizational strategy. According to the professional guidance of the Institute of Internal Auditors (IIA), public sector governance encompasses the policies and procedures used to direct an organization's activities to provide reasonable assurance that objectives are met and that operations are carried out in an ethical and accountable manner. (IIA, 2007)

2. Methods

2.1. Research Design

This research adopted descriptive and analysis of variance to examine the role of internal audit in promoting good governance in public institutions in Kenya. Giovanis (2011), noted that descriptive and correlation methods are two of the five basic designs of quantitative methods of research. In this study the correlation was intended to investigate the interaction between Internal Auditing and Good Governance by using evidence from public institutions in Kenya.

2.2. Theoretical and Conceptual Framework

2.2.1. Theoretical Framework

There are two variables that were used in this Research:

Independent variable: Internal Audit

Dependent variable: Good Governance

a) Internal Audit

The three main elements of Internal Audit are; Risk Management, According to the United Nation Audit Manual (UN, 2005), The internal audit activity should assist the organization by identifying and evaluating significant exposures to risk and contributing to the improvement of risk management and control systems.

Control, the internal audit activity should assist the organization in maintaining effective controls by evaluating their effectiveness and efficiency and by promoting continuous improvement.

Governance Process, the internal audit activity should assess and make appropriate recommendations for improving the governance process in its accomplishment of the following objectives: Promoting appropriate ethics and values within the organization, Ensuring effective organizational performance management and Accountability, Effectively communicating risk and control information to appropriate areas of the organization, Effectively coordinating the activities of and communicating information among the board, external and internal auditors and management. (IIA, 2006)

b) Good Governance

The United Nations (UN, 2005), in its work on public governance, focused in particular on the principal elements of good governance, namely: Accountability, Government is able and willing to show the extent to which its actions and decisions are consistent with clearly-defined and agreed-upon objectives. Transparency, Government actions, decisions and decision-making processes are open to an appropriate level of scrutiny by others parts of government, civil society and, in some instances, outside institutions and governments.

Efficiency and effectiveness, Government strives to produce quality public outputs, including services delivered to citizens, at the best cost, and ensures that outputs meet the original intentions of policymakers. Responsiveness, Government has the capacity and flexibility to respond rapidly to societal changes, takes into account the expectations of civil society in identifying the general public interest, and is willing to critically re-examine the role of government. (Herbert, 2010)

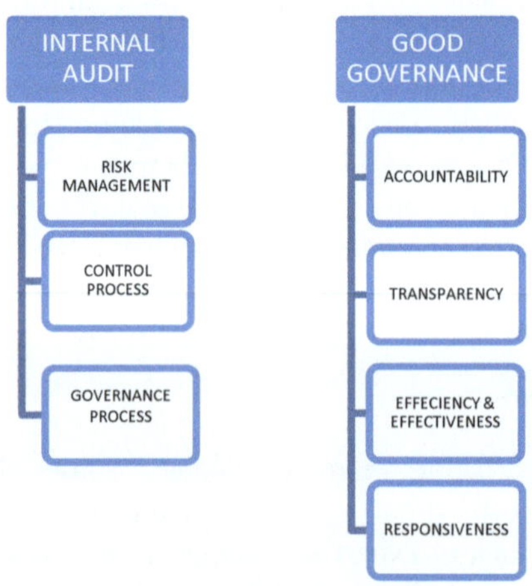

Figure 1. Conceptual Framework.

2.2.2. Conceptual Framework

The theoretical framework was used as a basis for the development of the conceptual framework for this study, with service quality attributes and customer satisfaction as factors upon which the questionnaire for the study was based.

2.3. Target Population and Sampling Techniques

2.3.1. The Population

The government of Kenya is the biggest employer of internal auditors and involves several enterprises divided in many sectors. One of the earliest steps taken by the GOK in the direction of public service reform was the reduction of the number of Ministries and the carrying out of diagnostic studies of management systems.

The intended enterprises of public institutions are categorized in two main categories Ministries, Semi-autonomous entities and Government Business Enterprises, among those enterprises the researcher will investigated on the public institutions that were grouped in 9 sectors which are: Bank, Insurance, Energy and Transport, Industry, Pharmacy, Hotel, Air, Audit organizations and Semi-Autonomous organizations and all are under Ministries, Departments and Agencies (MDAs) by which the researcher selected purposively the employees and different committee members. The people selected have different responsibilities in those public institutions. All those organizations (public enterprises) were grouped in different strata according to their sector and will be randomly selected from those public enterprises in the sectors.

The target population for the current study includes the following:

1. Heads and staff of internal audit departments (IADs) of MDAs.
2. Other ordinary Staff of selected MDAs
3. Internal Audit services users(i.e. managements) of selected public enterprises

A total of about 100,000 people (all public workers) were considered as target population.

2.3.2. Sampling Techniques

The researcher adopted the survey type of research in which a sample of 398 from the target population of about 100,000. The following formula was used:

$$n = \frac{N}{1+N(e)^2} = \frac{100000}{1+100000(0.05^2)} = 398.406 \approx 398$$

Where n is sample size required, N is the size of the target population, e is the margin error which is 0.05. As indicated, the sample size for the population is: 398 and we used a multistage stratified sampling method to select elements.

2.4. Validity, Reliability and Pilot Study of the Questionnaire

The research instruments were tested for reliability. They had to be tested to check if they had the ability to yield the same results consistently when repeated measurements were taken under the same condition. A pilot study was conducted in selected Public Institutions.

The consistency reliability of the research instruments was determined by the use of Cronbach's Coefficient Alpha that is used to test internal consistency. The alpha provided a coefficient to estimate consistency of scores on an instrument when the items were scored as continuous variables (i.e. Disagree to Agree). While the reliability coefficient of 0.7 was acceptable the questionnaire designed by the researcher was sent to 7 experts for content validity and later used to determine the reliability coefficient.

2.5. Development of Research Instruments and Data Gathering Procedures

The study used a questionnaire for data collection .The questionnaire had three parts: the first part examined the profile of respondent and public institutions, the second concerned the internal auditing role in promoting governance, and the third concerned the good governance elements in relationship with internal auditing. Personal contact of the researcher with the respondents gave him the opportunity to explain when necessary to some respondents. Data was collected from the selected public institutions in Kenya between the months of March and May, 2015.

2.6. Statistical Treatment of Data

The data obtained was analyzed using SPSS version 20 and presented in the form of tables. Descriptive statistics such as frequencies, percentages, means, standard deviations, and Pearson product-moment correlation coefficient were used to analyze the data.

3. Findings, Analysis and Interpretation

3.1. Profile of the Respondents

The table below shows aspects that were taken into account with respect to the respondents profile.

Table 1. *Company Distribution (Nature of Entity).*

	Frequency	Percent	Valid Percent	Cumulative Percent
Financial Institution	150	40.5	40.5	40.5
Transportation, Communication and Power	98	26.5	26.5	67.0
Audit Institution	122	33.0	33.0	100.0
TOTAL	370	100.0	100.0	

Table 1 above presents the distribution of the surveyed companies by the natures of Public institutions. They were basically three categories: Financial Institutions (Banks, Insurance, etc); Transportation, Communication and Power; Audit Institution. The distribution shows that 40.5% of respondents work in Financial Institutions and 26.5% work for transportation, communication and power institutions, finally 33.0% work for audit institution.

Table 2 provide the distribution of the respondents

organizations by age brackets whereby 5.9% of the surveyed organizations are aged between 1 and 5 years, 0.5% of the surveyed organizations are aged between 6 and 10 years, 11.1% are aged between 11 and 15 years while 77.0% are aged above 15 years and 5.4% were missing system. This implies that most of the organizations being surveyed are at their maturity ages in operations hence an appropriate choice to survey Internal Audit in Promoting Good Governance issues since most of the current organizations tend to lay more emphasis on public institutions aspects.

Table 2. *Number of Years the Institution Has Been In Operation.*

		Frequency	Percent	Valid Percent	Cumulative Percent
Valid	BETWEEN 1-5 YEARS	22	5.9	6.3	6.3
	BETWEEN 6-10 YEARS	2	.5	.6	6.9
	BETWEEN 11-15 YEARS	41	11.1	11.7	18.6
	ABOVE 15 YEARS	285	77.0	81.4	100.0
	Total	350	94.6	100.0	
Missing	System	20	5.4		
TOTAL		370	100.0	100.0	

Table 3. *Position in the Entity.*

		Frequency	Percent	Valid Percent	Cumulative Percent
Valid	SENIOR MANAGER	18	4.9	5.9	5.9
	MIDDLE MANAGER	40	10.8	13.1	19.0
	OPERATIONAL MANAGER	49	13.2	16.0	35.0
	AUDITOR	128	34.6	41.8	76.8
	EMPLOYEE	71	19.2	23.2	100.0
	Total	306	82.7	100.0	
Missing	System	64	17.3		
TOTAL		370	100.0	100.0	

Table 3 provide the position the respondent in the entity; 4.9% of the respondents were senior managers, 10.8% were middle managers, 13.2% were operational managers, 34.6% were auditors while 19.2% were employees, also there were 17.3% missing system. This proves that the research was done with success because the majority of the respondents were the auditors.

Table 4. *Gender.*

		Frequency	Percent	Valid Percent	Cumulative Percent
Valid	MALE	181	48.9	59.2	59.2
	FEMALE	125	33.8	40.8	100.0
	Total	306	82.7	100.0	
Missing	System	20	5.4		
TOTAL		370	100.0	100.0	

By gender distribution, the study reveals, in this above Table 4, that 48.9% of the respondents are male while 33.8% are female. This distribution is a near evenly distribution for both genders, thus a key indicator on the nature of board composition in organization in terms of gender, additionally the findings have a greater significance on the findings with regard to the role of gender on internal audit and good governance issues.

Table 5. *Work Experience.*

		Frequency	Percent	Valid Percent	Cumulative Percent
Valid	BETWEEN 1-5 YEARS	71	19.2	23.4	23.4
	BETWEEN 6-10 YEARS	112	30.3	36.8	60.2
	BETWEEN 11-15 YEARS	121	32.7	39.8	100.0
	Total	304	82.2	100.0	
Missing	System	66	17.8		
TOTAL		370	100.0	100.0	

The findings of this study indicates that 19.2% of the respondents have been with their respective organizations for a period between 1 and 5 years, 30.3% between 6 and 10 years and 32.7% between 11 and 15 years and 17.8% were missing system. This finding implies that the views of the respondents are reliable and vital given the duration of which they have been members of these organizations. Further, it implies that the respondents at least have some critical knowledge on the internal audit and good governance in these organizations.

3.2. Statistical Analysis of Internal Auditing Role

3.2.1. Risk Management Analysis

Results demonstrated that Risk Management was rated with a cumulative mean of 3.44 (SD= 0.41) concerning the evaluation of the Public Institutions. The highest item is "In preventing Risk in your company, Protection of assets are Audit activities performed by your internal audit function" with a mean of 3.51 and a standard deviation of 0.60. The item "The absence of good internal control increases an agency's risk of producing unreliable accounting data" was rated with a mean of 3.49 and a standard deviation of 0.55. The item "Internal auditing of a system's internal control may decrease an agency's risk in a system" had a mean of 3.46 and a standard deviation of 0.52. The item "The absence of sound internal control increases an agency's risk of non-compliance with laws or regulations" was rated with a mean of 3.41 and a standard deviation of 0.65, the rating of this item was consistent with rating of the similar item "When you assess reliability and good conditions of financial information you prevent risk in your institution" rated with a mean of 3.41 and a standard deviation of 0.60. The following item "The absence of sound internal controls increases an agency's risk of loss from fraud" was rated with a mean of 3.36 and a standard deviation of 0.77. Based on result above, the public institutions of Kenya have the good systems of internal audit to ensure that the public institutions are well managed in terms of risk management.

3.2.2. Control Process Analysis

All the questions were positively confirmed with their means ranging from 3.08 to 3.74. Generally, the study indicates with a mean of 3.50 standard deviation of 0.36 that is a cumulative concerning the control process. The implication of the aggregate score on control process indicates that the respondents perceived the aforementioned to be relatively high and this could influence cultural assimilation, attitude and the workers' behavior. Hence, each item score is analyzed and presented with their respective mean. In the highest item, the respondents tend to agree that "Internal Auditors in service trainings are organized whenever required" with a mean rating of 3.74 (SD= 0.49). They also tend to agree, in the second item level, that "the organization allows internal auditor to identify and monitor risks against the achievement of organization's goal in auditing" at mean of 3.70 (SD= 0.47). They tend to agree that "Internal audit function is strategically positioned to contribute to organizational strategy performance" with mean rating of 3.69 (SD= 0.46) and they also tend to agree that "The internal auditors receive a plan ("planning memorandum") for each performance contract" with a mean rating of 3.66 (SD= 0.61). The item with the lowest mean was with a mean of 3.08 (SD= 0.50), this means that the respondents tend to agree that "The organization's audit department have Staffs who have relevant experience".

3.2.3. Governance Process

Statistical results indicated that all items related to governance process were rated with a cumulative mean of 3.53 and standard deviation of 0.27. The item with the highest mean of 3.79 and a standard deviation of 0.45 was "An internal audit performance verifies that the systems and procedures established" while the lowest item was "Designing and implementing internal control system are some of possible advisory" with a mean of 3.07 and a standard deviation of 0.62. From the highest to the lowest, the following are the analysis and interpretation for other items. "The procedures for setting priorities concern the use of budgetary resources subject to a specific review" was rated with a mean of 3.78 and a standard deviation of 0.47. The findings further indicate with a mean of 3.77 and a standard deviation of 0.47 that Ethical practices & anticorruption programs are some of possible advisory roles of the internal audit to management applicable to your organization. Concerning the item "Sound business process (e.g. reengineering) is one of possible advisory roles of the internal audit to management applicable to your organization" the respondents tend to agree by a mean of 3.39 and a standard deviation of 0.70. The item "The audit covers the relevance of the results assessment criteria established by management" had a mean of 3.36 and a standard deviation of 0.59.

3.2.4. Accountability

Respondents perceived accountability to promote good governance with a cumulative mean of 3.42(SD = 0.40) and other items had their Means ranging from 3.61 to 3.31. The item with the highest Mean was Internal auditor focuses on Project Management while giving their opinion, with a Mean of 3.61 (SD = 0.72). This means that accountability in Public institutions is key elements for considerable in public institutional good governance.

3.2.5. Transparency

The study confirmed that the respondents perceived Transparency to promote good governance with a cumulative mean of 3.50(SD = 0.37) and other items had their Means ranging from 3.77 to 3.06. The item with the highest Mean was "There is utilization of appropriate technology to enhance the provision of internal audit services" with a Mean of 3.77 (SD = 0.51). This means that transparency in Public institutions is one of the key elements for considerable in public institutional good governance. According to IFC (2009), accountability is one of two basic principles of good governance.

3.2.6. Efficiency and Effectiveness

The researcher administered six questions to assess the good governance in public institutions. The results yielded means ranging from 3.23 to 3.50, with an average mean of 3.29 and standard deviation of 0.34. The item with the highest mean was "There are enough internal audit facilities." with a mean of 3.50 (SD= 0.61).

3.2.7. Responsiveness

To evaluate factors good governance in terms of responsiveness six items were tested and positively confirmed with means ranging between 2.91 and 3.21. The aggregate result yielded a mean 3.07 and a standard deviation of 0.43. The item with the highest mean was "Internal auditors regularly review if their recommendations are put in practice." with a mean of 3.21 and a standard deviation of 0.76. The lowest items "The corrective measures are usually taken as a result of weaknesses noted by the internal audit Department" and "The head of internal audit monitors and follows- up action taken by management to recommendations made by the audit function" were rated with a mean of 2.91 and a standard deviation of 0.82.

3.3. Correlation

The study tried to check whether there was a significant relationship between perceptions on the role of internal audit functions on risk management analysis, control process analysis, and governance process and the evaluation rating of good governance promotion in terms of accountability, transparency, efficiency and effectiveness, and responsiveness.

The results in the table 13 represent the significant correlation among all variables by summarizing the values of Pearson's correlation coefficient that shows the correlation coefficient between Internal Audit Functions and Good Governance Functions within public institutions in Kenya; the correlation coefficient between Risk management function and Accountability, Transparency, Effectiveness & Efficiency and Responsiveness showed that is rated between 0.186 and 0.606 with a p-value of 0.000. The result shows that there is significant relationship between Accountability and Risk Management with the Pearson correlation of 0.458, which shows that there is moderate correlation.

The findings indicate that Transparency and Risk Management are related with influences moderation with the coefficient of correlation of 0.606; the findings shows also that there is significant relationship between Effectiveness & Efficiency and Risk Management with the Pearson Correlation of 0.369, this shows that there is moderate correlation, finally it shows that there is significant relationship between Responsiveness and Risk Management with the Pearson correlation of 0.186, which shows that there is weak correlation.

***Table 6.** Correlation Analysis.*

		Accountability	Transparency	Efficiency and Effectiveness	Responsiveness
Risk Management Analysis	Pearson Correlation	.458**	.606**	.369**	.186**
	Sig. (2-tailed)	.000	.000	.000	.001
	N	306	306	306	306
Control Process Analysis	Pearson Correlation	.399**	.681**	.247**	-.150**
	Sig. (2-tailed)	.000	.000	.000	.008
	N	306	306	306	306
Governance Process	Pearson Correlation	.526**	.383**	.284**	-.039
	Sig. (2-tailed)	.000	.000	.000	.500
	N	306	306	306	306

**Correlation is significant at the 0.05 level

On the item of Control Process, the findings reveled that there is significant relationship between Accountability and Control Process with the Pearson Correlation of 0.399; between Transparency and Control Process, there is significant relationship with Pearson Correlation of 0.681, these above to situation shows that there is moderate correlation. between Effectiveness & Efficiency and Control Process is significant with Pearson Correlation of 0.247, this shows that there is weak correlation; and there is significant relationship between Responsiveness and Control Process with the Pearson Correlation of – 0.150 an with P-Value of 0.008 which is less than 0.05, this shows again that there is weak correlation.

On the item of Governance Process, the results shows that there is significant relationship between Accountability and Governance Process with Pearson Correlation of 0.526, between Transparency and Governance Process with Pearson Correlation of 0.383, between Effectiveness & Efficiency and Governance Process with Pearson Correlation of 0.284, between Responsiveness and Governance Process with Pearson Correlation of -0.039 and with P-value of 0.500 which is greater than 0.05, in this case there is no significant relationship.

4. Summary, Conclusions and Recommendations

4.1. Summary of Findings

The research aimed to establish the relationship between this factors such us perceptions on the role of internal audit functions on risk management analysis, control process analysis, and governance process and the evaluation rating of good governance promotion in terms of accountability, transparency, efficiency and effectiveness, and responsiveness. In terms of nature of entity, a big number of 150 Respondents regarding Entity which represent 40.5% are in financial institutions, followed by 122 Respondents regarding Entities represent 33.0% are in Audit Institutions and the lowest number of 98 which represent 26.5% are in Transport, Communication and Power Energy Institutions. This showed that the Government of Kenya has put its effort in investment by using performance contracts and controls by using Monitoring and Evaluation to assess where they in implementing the vision.

In terms of age, a big number of 287 respondents, which represent 77.0%, are in institutions, which are above 15 years, followed by 41 respondents representing 11.1% between 11-15 years old. This showed that the majority of public institutions is older and this aspect is positive for the institutions experiences; With regard to the position of the respondents 128 with 34.6% among them were Auditors and others were senior managers (4.9%), middle managers (10.8%), operational managers (13.2%) and other employees with percentage of 19.2;

Regarding the risk management assessment as one of the internal audit items, the study the study revealed that all respondents tend to agree with the existence of risk management within public institutions by the average mean of 3.50 and on Control Process factor, in public institutions, the results yielded a mean of 3.50. This means that employees in public institutions in Kenya tend to agree with the existence of that item.

Concerning Governance Process, all respondents rated the item with the average mean of 3.53 and this showed that public institutions employees tend to agree with the existence of Governance Process within public institutions in Kenya. Transparency in public institutions, all respondents rated the item with the average mean of 3.50; this showed that they tend to agree with the existence of transparency in Public Institutions in Kenya.

The study found out that, on effectiveness and efficiency, in public institutions, the results of this research showed that all respondents tend to agree, with mean of 3.29 that there is existence of effectiveness and efficiency. The other factor evaluated is Responsiveness, which had been rated with a cumulative mean of 3.07; this rate showed that employees in public institutions also tend to agree to this item.

The correlation coefficient between internal audit functions and good governance functions is between 0.19 and 0.61, on Risk Management and Good Governance Factors, is between -0.15 and 0.68 on Control Process and Good Governance factors and is between -0.04 and 0.53. There was a statistically significant relationship between perceptions on the role of internal audit functions on risk management analysis, control process analysis, and governance process and the evaluation rating of good governance promotion in terms of accountability, transparency, efficiency and effectiveness, and responsiveness within Public Institutions in Kenya.

4.2. Conclusions

With regard to respondent profile, the study revealed that the distribution of the surveyed companies by the natures of Public institutions. The distribution shows that 40.5% of respondents work in Financial Institutions and 26.5% work for transportation, communication and power institutions, finally 33.0% work for audit institution. It was also observed that the distribution of the respondents' organizations by age and it implies that most of the organizations being surveyed are at their maturity ages in operations.

Finally Table 3 provide the position the respondent in the entity; 4.9% of the respondents were senior managers, 10.8% were middle managers, 13.2% were operational managers, 34.6% were auditors while 19.2% were employees, also there were 17.3% missing system. This proves that the research was done with success because the majority of the respondents were the auditors.

4.3. Recommendations

This study focused more on analysis of influence that the identified independent variable, which is Internal Audit, can have on the dependent variable, which is Good Governance, to promote it in the Kenyan Public institutions to enable the Kenyan Government to achieve their Goals summarized in Vision 2030. The study found that internal audit had the greatest effect on good governance within Kenyan Public institutions.

Based on the findings and conclusions, the following were recommended:

i. For the public institution to be effectively mitigate risk they should institute internal auditing in its operation.
ii. The public institutions have to accept internal auditing as a tool for effective internal control so as to realize their objectives set with ease.
iii. in order for the government to be effective in its operation and service delivery they should recognize more contribution of internal auditing,

Acknowledgements

We thank the participants of this study, their suggestions and comments.

Nomenclature

GCIA- Government Chief Internal Auditor
GOK- Government of Kenya
IAD- Internal Audit Department
IAF- Internal Audit Function
IIA- Institute of International Auditors
MDA- Ministries, Departments and Agencies
SPSS- Statistical Package for Social Scientists

References

[1] Asare, T. (2008). A study of the role of internal auditing in the public sector of Ghana: Governance and accountability. Birmingham, United Kingdom: Cornhill

[2] Ball, N. (2002). Enhancing Security Sector Governance: a conceptual framework of UNDP. UNDP

[3] Barrett, P. (2002). Expectation, and Perception, of Better Practice Corporate Governance in the Public Sector from an Audit Perspective. Melbourne: CPA Australia's Government Business Symposium

[4] Belay, Z. (2007). A study on effective implementation of internal audit function to promote good governance in the public sector. addis ababa, ethiopia.

[5] Gansberghe, C. N. (2005). Internal Audit: Finding its Place in Public Financial Management, Public Expenditure and Fiscal Accountability Programme. Washington D.C: World Bank.

[6] Giovanis, G. D. (2011). Evaluation of the Effectiveness of Internal Audit in Greek Hotel Business. International Journal of Economic Sciences and Applied Research , 19-34.

[7] Herbert Robinson, P. C. (2010). Governance & Knoweledge Management For Public-Private Partnerships. southern Gate, Chichester, Weuissex, United Kingdom: John Wiley & Sons, Ltd.

[8] IIA. (2008). International Standards for the Professional Practice of Internal Audit. Altamonte Springs, FL.

[9] INTOSAI . (2004). International Organization of Supreme Audit Institutions. Retrieved June 20, 2015, from http://www.intosai.org/Guidelines for Internal Controls Standards for the Public Sector.

[10] MINECOFIN. (2011). Internal Audit Charter. PP. 1-14.

[11] PFM, S. P. (2011). Guidelines for Chief Budget Managers in Kenya

[12] Pickett, K. H. (2010). The Internal Auditing Handbook, Third Edition. Southern Gate, Chichester, West Sussex, United Kingdom: John Wiley & Sons Ltd.

[13] Sawyer, L. B. (2003). Sawyer's Internal Audit 5th edition/ the Practice of Moderne Internal Auditing. Altamonte Springs, Florida: The Institute of Internal Auditors

[14] United Nations. (2005). The 2005 World Summit. The 2005 World Summit. New York: United Nations. PP.1-2.

Permissions

All chapters in this book were first published in JIM, by Science Publishing Group; hereby published with permission under the Creative Commons Attribution License or equivalent. Every chapter published in this book has been scrutinized by our experts. Their significance has been extensively debated. The topics covered herein carry significant findings which will fuel the growth of the discipline. They may even be implemented as practical applications or may be referred to as a beginning point for another development.

The contributors of this book come from diverse backgrounds, making this book a truly international effort. This book will bring forth new frontiers with its revolutionizing research information and detailed analysis of the nascent developments around the world.

We would like to thank all the contributing authors for lending their expertise to make the book truly unique. They have played a crucial role in the development of this book. Without their invaluable contributions this book wouldn't have been possible. They have made vital efforts to compile up to date information on the varied aspects of this subject to make this book a valuable addition to the collection of many professionals and students.

This book was conceptualized with the vision of imparting up-to-date information and advanced data in this field. To ensure the same, a matchless editorial board was set up. Every individual on the board went through rigorous rounds of assessment to prove their worth. After which they invested a large part of their time researching and compiling the most relevant data for our readers.

The editorial board has been involved in producing this book since its inception. They have spent rigorous hours researching and exploring the diverse topics which have resulted in the successful publishing of this book. They have passed on their knowledge of decades through this book. To expedite this challenging task, the publisher supported the team at every step. A small team of assistant editors was also appointed to further simplify the editing procedure and attain best results for the readers.

Apart from the editorial board, the designing team has also invested a significant amount of their time in understanding the subject and creating the most relevant covers. They scrutinized every image to scout for the most suitable representation of the subject and create an appropriate cover for the book.

The publishing team has been an ardent support to the editorial, designing and production team. Their endless efforts to recruit the best for this project, has resulted in the accomplishment of this book. They are a veteran in the field of academics and their pool of knowledge is as vast as their experience in printing. Their expertise and guidance has proved useful at every step. Their uncompromising quality standards have made this book an exceptional effort. Their encouragement from time to time has been an inspiration for everyone.

The publisher and the editorial board hope that this book will prove to be a valuable piece of knowledge for researchers, students, practitioners and scholars across the globe.

List of Contributors

Khaled Mili
Department of Economics and Quantitative Methods and Computer, Institute of Companies Administration of Gafsa, Gafsa, Tunisia.

Ilhem Elghoul
Department of Computer Science, Mediterranean Institute of Nabeul, Nabeul, Tunisia.

Mostafa Zangiabadi
Faculty of Management and Accounting, Allame Tabatabaei University of Tehran, Tehran, Iran.

Amin Rahimzade
Faculty of Management and Accounting, University of Qom, Qom, Iran.

Mahdie Taboli
Scientific Group of Accounting, Department of Payame Noor University, Zangiabad, Iran.

Martin Muriithi
School of Business Studies, University of Nairobi, Nairobi, Kenya.

Dennis Muriithi
Department of Business Administration, Chuka University, Chuka, Kenya.

Nkogbu Godfrey Oshilim
Human Resource/Administration Department, Odogun Nigeria Limited, Warri, Nigeria.

Offia Patience Akpesiri
Library Department, College of Education, Warri, Delta State, Nigeria.

Richardson Kojo Edeme and Innocent Ifelunini
Department of Economics, Faculty of Social Science, University of Nigeria, Nsukka, Enugu State-Nigeria.

Muhammed Jamshed Alam Patwary
Department of Computer Science and Engineering, International Islamic University Chittagong, Chittagong, Bangladesh.

Mohammad Osiur Rahman, Mohammad Shahadat Hossain
Department of Computer Science and Engineering, University of Chittagong, Chittagong, Bangladesh.

Md Shamimul Hasan and Normah Omar
Accounting Research Institute, Universiti Teknologi MARA, Shah Alam, Malaysia.

Yahiaoui Naima and Megri Zakia
Faculty of Economic, Commercial and Management Sciences, Batna University, Batna, Algeria.

Yousfat Ali
Faculty of Economic, Commercial and Management Sciences, Ahmed Draia University, Adrar, Algeria.

Vesna Micajkova
Integrated Business Faculty, Skopje, Macedonia.

Tulus Tahi Hamonangan Tambunan
Center for Industry, SME and Business Competition Studies, University of Trisakti, Jakarta, Indonesia.

Seyed Behnam Khakbaz
Faculty of Management, University of Tehran, Tehran, Iran.

Maryam Karimi Davijani
College of Farabi, University of Tehran, Qom, Iran.

Burak Omer Saracoglu
Orhantepe Mahallesi, Tekel Caddesi, Geziyolu Sokak, Dragos, Kartal, Istanbul, Turkey.

Bai Yinghui
Xinglin School, Nantong University, Nantong, China.

Xiong Yuanyuan
Bank of Jiangnan, Changzhou, China.

Wang Binru
School of Business, Nantong University, Nantong, China.

Nymatul Jannat Nipa and Jakia Sultana
Department of Management Information Systems, Faculty of Business Administration, University of Dhaka, Dhaka, Bangladesh.

Md.Habibur Rahman
Department of Management Studies, Faculty of Business Administration, University of Dhaka, Dhaka, Bangladesh.

Yahya Hasas Yeghaneh
Scientific Group of Accounting, Department of Allameh Tabataba'i University, Tehran, Iran.

Mostafa Zangiabadi
Faculty of Accounting, Allame Tabatabaee University, Tehran, Iran.

Seyed Mostafa Dehghani Firozabadi
Faculty of Accounting, Islamic Azad University, Yazd, Iran.

Seyed Ebrahim Vahdat, Rohollah Askarpour, Pedram Keyhany, Yones Rahimi and Hadi Soflaei
Department of Engineering, Bandar Abbas Branch, Islamic Azad University, Bandar Abbas, Iran.

Olure-Bank Aadeyinka Michael and Omodele Kilanko
Department of Economics, Faculty of Social Sciences, Joseph Ayo Babalola University, Ikeji-Arakeki, Osun State, Nigeria.

Gbadebo Salako and Ajiteru Temilade
Department of Economics, Faculty of Arts and Social Sciences, Emmanuel Alayande College Education, Oyo, Oyo State, Nigeria.

Isa Adnan Budaraj
MBA program, Ahlia University of Bahrain, Manama, Kingdom of Bahrain.

Adel Mohammed Sarea
Accounting and Economics Department, Ahlia University of Bahrain, Manama, Kingdom of Bahrain.

Nabila Nisha
Department of Accounting and Finance, North South University, Dhaka, Bangladesh.

Kennedy Sakaya Barasa
Department of Statistics and Actuarial Sciences, Jomo Kenyatta University of Science and Technology, Nairobi, Kenya.

Index